OTHER BOOKS BY ROGER HILSMAN

To Move a Nation

The Politics of Policy Making

Strategic Intelligence and National Decisions

INSTITUTE OF WAR AND PEACE STUDIES
School of International Affairs
Columbia University

The Crouching Future: International Politics and U. S. Foreign Policy—A Forecast is one of a series of studies sponsored by the Institute of War and Peace Studies of Columbia University. Among those Institute studies also dealing with prediction and policy making are *The Common Defense* by Samuel P. Huntington; *NATO and the Range of American Choice* by Annette Baker Fox and William T. R. Fox; *To Move a Nation* by Roger Hilsman; *Foreign Policy and Democratic Politics* by Kenneth N. Waltz; *How Nations Behave* by Louis Henkin; *The Politics of Weapons Innovation* by Michael H. Armacost; *The Politics of Policy Making in Defense and Foreign Affairs* by Roger Hilsman; *Planning, Prediction, and Policymaking in Foreign Affairs* by Robert L. Rothstein; *European Security and the Atlantic System* edited by William T. R. Fox and Warner R. Schilling; and *American Arms and a Changing Europe: Dilemmas of Deterrence and Disarmament* by Warner R. Schilling, William T. R. Fox, Catherine M. Kelleher, and Donald J. Puchala.

The Crouching Future

INTERNATIONAL POLITICS AND

U. S. FOREIGN POLICY · A FORECAST

ROGER HILSMAN

DOUBLEDAY & COMPANY, INC.

GARDEN CITY, NEW YORK

1975

To the children, as yet unborn, of
HOYT, AMY, ASHBY, *and* SARAH
since they will no longer think
it all so strange.

Library of Congress Cataloging in Publication Data

Hilsman, Roger.
    The crouching future.

    Sponsored by the Institute of War and Peace Studies of Columbia University.
      1. World politics—1945-   2. Economic history—1945-   3. Twentieth cen-
tury—Forecasts. 4. Twenty-first century—Forecasts.   I. Title.
D843.H54   327′.09′046
ISBN 0-385-06037-8
Library of Congress Catalog Card Number 73-15347

Contents

Forecasting: The Necessity and the Problem

THE GOAL OF this book is to explore the forces shaping the future of international politics and to draw the implications for United States foreign policy. To understand how international politics is changing in turn requires us to look at what is likely to happen inside the countries that are the actors in international politics. Where is the United States headed? What kind of society is it likely to be in the year 2000? The same question has to be asked about the Soviet Union, China, the developed countries of Europe, Japan, and Australia, and the underdeveloped countries of Asia, Africa, the Middle East, and Latin America. And there are other questions. Will the scarcity of resources become the central driving force of international politics? Will pollution become an issue in world politics? Will the weapons of war become even more horrendous? And what about war itself? What role will war play in the international politics of the future?

If we can answer these questions, we will be able to see how

United States foreign policy should be changed right now, the things we *are* doing that we should not be doing, and the things we are *not* doing that we should be doing. The task, certainly, is ambitious. It may be overly ambitious, even presumptuous. How much of the future can really be predicted? Is it possible to say anything at all about the future that is significant enough to make us want to change *today's* foreign policy? What techniques, methods, or tricks of the forecasting trade could be used to make these kinds of predictions? It is to these questions that this preface is addressed.

The Necessity and Problem of Forecasting

Some time in the late 1920s or early 1930s, the people of America made a decision that fundamentally shaped the world we live in today. It determined the style and rhythm of our lives. It determined the pattern of the cities and the suburbs. It changed the landscape of the countryside. It affected even the air we breathe.

But the fact that so momentous a decision had been made appeared in no headlines. The decision was not the subject of debate in Congress. The President did not agonize over it. It was never an issue in an election. What happened was that tens of millions of American families—almost subconsciously—came to accept the notion that the best possible arrangement for the good life was a single-family dwelling on a separate plot of land. If a plot of land and a house near the job or convenient to public transportation seemed out of reach, cheaper land was available within commuting distance on the outskirts, and the mass-produced automobile made the whole dream feasible and within their grasp. At every income level, the American family set about to acquire both a dwelling on a separate plot of land and a private automobile.

Everyone who lived at the time understood in some subliminal way that this mass decision had been made. But no government planner, no journalistic pundit, no academic expert set about systematically to examine its implications for the succeeding generation. No one asked what kind of world this decision would create.[1] But it would have been no great trick to have forecast the consequences; no crystal ball was required or towering genius. A simple extrapolation of trends in population and per capita income would have indicated the number of houses required, the amount of land they would take up, and the number of automobiles on the road. Further simple mathematical calculations would have indicated the roads required and the additional land they would take up. The emissions of an internal-combustion engine were known, and straightforward multiplication would have given an indication of the amount of air pollution. After these estimates were made, further predictions would follow quite obviously, and much of the shape of the future world would have emerged—urban sprawl, the decline of the inner cities, traffic congestion, water and air pollution, and many of the other blights on life today.

Even if someone had taken the trouble to spell out the consequences of this somewhat absent-minded mass decision to build life around a separate dwelling and the private automobile, the decision might still have been the same. Even so, some steps would probably have been taken to blunt the worst consequences, and at the very least we would have been considerably more sensitive to the earlier signs of trouble coming. But the two main lessons of these events still stand: that no one *did* bother to try to forecast the consequences and that if anyone had bothered, the task would not have been all that difficult.

The conviction has grown in the past few years that at least a portion of the future can be foreseen with just as little difficulty, simply by extrapolating current trends and looking for the obvious interconnections. But even if forecasting turns out to be much more difficult than that, no one any longer doubts that we must try. Human society is global now and intricately interconnected. What one particular people do can now affect all the others. We have seen this dramatically illustrated in the ecological sphere. When the farmers of California used DDT on their crops, their

---

[1] As Daniel Bell points out, not only was no attempt made to foresee the consequences of this decision, but even more importantly, no attempt was made to sketch out the alternatives, such as cluster-type suburban developments or concentrated high-rise densities with large open spaces. See his Introduction to Herman Kahn and Anthony J. Wiener, *The Year 2000: A Framework for Speculation on the Next Thirty-three Years* (New York, 1967), p. xxvi.

yields increased spectacularly. When the health officials of Sri Lanka (Ceylon) used DDT to attack malaria-carrying mosquitoes, the drop in the death rate was even more spectacular. But all over the Pacific, people who eat fish began to accumulate alarming levels of DDT in the fatty tissues of their bodies. Similar interconnections are increasingly evident in the social and political affairs of men. Whether mankind finds it difficult or easy, he is going to have to spend more time thinking about the future.

The Problem of Thinking About the Future

How does one go about the job of forecasting, of making predictions? The first thing to be said is probably that most of us spend a lot more time thinking about the future than we realize. We build things for future use, planning a house, a bridge, or a factory. We marry and plan ahead for children, saving for their education. In this sense, we don't so much predict the future as we create it. Two men agree to meet at a future date. Actually, what they agreed to do was to create a future event, their meeting. Society as a whole also makes such agreements that create the future—an example is the constitutional provision that an election for President shall be held every four years. Even so, when a candidate works and plans for a future election he is also doing more than taking note of society's agreement to create a future event. In a sense he is making a prediction that society is stable and will honor its constitution.

In making plans, I also make predictions about the motives of other people and the durability of those motives. If I plan to travel by airplane, I am predicting that the pilot is free of suicidal neuroses. Many of the most simple acts are a combination of these attempts to create the future by working toward a goal on the basis of "predictions" or assumptions. The simple act of striking a match is a "prediction" that fire will result. But for me to be able to make the prediction by striking the match required self-conscious effort to create that future event by the people who made the match, including lumbermen, factory workers, transport workers, and someone with a knowledge of chemistry. The truth is that almost every action of both work and play is directed toward some future goal.

On the other hand, much of the future is unknowable. No man can say with certainty, to give the most obvious example, how long his own life will last. The question is, what distinguishes the knowable from the unknowable?

Predicting Eclipses

One way of getting at this question is to look at different types of predictions that men have successfully made. Consider, for example, predictions of eclipses of the sun and moon, which are among the most consistently successful and precisely accurate of the predictions made by man. Not only can mankind predict within microseconds when and where the next eclipse will occur, but he can predict all the eclipses that will occur thousands of years ahead with equal accuracy. He can even "predict" backward— that is, he can calculate with complete confidence when eclipses occurred so remotely in the past that no men existed to observe them.

This phenomenal success is possible, of course, because mankind has acquired rather full, "scientific" knowledge on the fundamental structure and causal forces of the solar system. A great deal of man's activity is based on this kind of rather full, more or less "scientific" knowledge similar to that used in predicting eclipses. He builds bridges, skyscrapers, railroads, ships, airplanes, rockets, atomic bombs, nuclear power plants, and a great variety of marvelous gadgets, such as television transmitters and receivers, on the basis of this kind of more or less "scientific" knowledge. He has also used similar knowledge to breed new kinds of wheat and rice, and to accomplish other agricultural miracles. He has eradicated some of the ancient diseases that were the scourge of mankind and provided cures for many others.

The Social Sciences

All these examples are from the "hard" sciences—physics, chemistry, and the life sciences. When it comes to the social sciences —economics, psychology, sociology, and the study of politics— mankind's record is considerably less impressive. It is true that he has developed a certain amount of rather reliable knowledge of the workings of different aspects of human society and can use this knowledge to change things and improve man's lot. Psychology has something useful to say about human motivations and emotions; sociology can tell something of the consequences of different kinds of social arrangements; economics can predict certain results from monetary, trade, or other policies; and students of politics can say something useful about, say, voter behavior.

But even if the word "science" is defined rather loosely as an "organized body of knowledge," there is some question whether the social sciences are really "scientific." Our knowledge of social psychology may be good enough to demonstrate the "scientific" validity of the Supreme Court decision that "separate" simply cannot be "equal," but we obviously have not yet learned how to eliminate racial prejudice. We now seem to know enough of the workings of the economy to avoid a major depression like that of the 1930s, but we certainly have not learned enough to eliminate all kinds of economic troubles.

Albert Einstein once explained one of the reasons for this difference between the "hard" and "soft" sciences. When asked why mankind had done so much better with physics than with politics, he said that it was because the subject matter of politics was so much more difficult!

Still other reasons can be found by looking again at our example of eclipses. To be able to predict eclipses mankind must be armed with two analytical models. The first is the Copernican model of the solar system, as modified by Kepler—that is, putting the sun in the center position rather than the earth, and recognizing that the planets travel in ellipses rather than circles. Second, he must be armed with Newtonian physics, particularly Newton's law of gravitation that two bodies are attracted to each other directly in proportion to their mass and inversely in proportion to the square of the distance between them. To predict eclipses, one does not need to know anything about either Einsteinian physics, for example, or the kind of nuclear chemistry that explains why the sun is hot.

Now, the first thing to notice is that the prediction of an eclipse works only so long as the system remains closed—so long as the solar system remains isolated from any outside force strong enough to alter the internal forces determining the orbits of the earth and moon. If a wandering star intrudes into the system in some future aeon, all bets are off.

Second, notice that predicting eclipses requires one to deal with only one operating force, gravity. Making predictions involving the interaction of two or more forces is much, much more complicated.

Thus one of the reasons that the subject matter of politics is more difficult than physics is that in social affairs closed systems are extremely rare. Outside wanderers intruding into the system are the rule rather than the exception. Another reason is that in social affairs a system in which only one force, like gravity, operates is almost unheard of. The norm is systems in which several forces operate simultaneously.

There are also other reasons for the difficulty in acquiring knowledge of political and social affairs for which the example of eclipses offers no help at all. One is the fact that the act of investigating or scrutinizing a phenomena in social affairs can alter it. Economists have discovered to their sorrow that the act of predicting a fall in the stock market can sometimes be self-fulfilling and bring it on. Similarly, the sociologist who interviews activists in a study of student unrest alters their behavior by the nature of the questions he asks. The only consolation for social scientists is that the physicists have at last reached a similar situation in certain of *their* inquiries. As pointed out in the Heisenberg principle of uncertainty, the act of determining the position and velocity of an electron will in fact alter both its position and its velocity.

The ultimate reason that politics is more difficult than physics, of course, is what philosophers have called "free will." In social affairs, there are many different actors, frequently competing. While one actor or group of actors attempts to shape events in one direction, another may be working to shape them in the opposite direction. In the language of systems theory, the social affairs of men are not a zero-sum game, and the outcome is thereby less predictable.

Same Conditions, Same Results

To the eqtent that the social sciences possess analytical models on aspects of economic, social, and political affairs that approach the "scientific" status of the physicists' model of the solar system, they, too, can make accurate predictions with a high degree of confidence. What is remarkable is how many reasonably accurate and undeniably useful predictions can be made with so little complete and "scientific" knowledge.

But perhaps it is not so remarkable when we reflect that accurate and useful predictions have often been made in every field, physics included, with no "scientific" knowledge at all. Primitive man, by simply observing the rhythm of the heavens, was able to predict the summer and winter solstices, as the orientation of numerous very early temples demonstrates, without understanding anything at all about the true nature of the sun, the stars, and the moon. It is even possible, if one interpretation of Stonehenge is correct, that he may have correctly divined the pattern of some eclipses.[2]

Perhaps an even more useful example is primitive man's use of fire. Somehow, probably by accident, he learned to make fire by rubbing dry sticks together—in other words, he could predict the result, fire, of the action of rubbing dry sticks together. His method of prediction was not based on understanding the nature of the process but by assuming that if the same conditions existed, the same results would follow.

Armed with the scientific knowledge that fire is a chemical combination of oxygen and certain other elements under certain conditions of temperature and pressure, modern man can do better in a number of ways. He can predict more accurately when fire will arise spontaneously. He can make gadgets, like matches, that produce fire more quickly and efficiently than rubbing dry sticks together. And he can make fire in places and under conditions that primitive man would find astounding—at the bottom of the sea, for example, with oxyacetylene torches.

But modern man also makes predictions on the same "un-

[2] Gerald S. Hawkins, *Stonehenge Decoded* (New York, 1965).

scientific" basis that primitive man predicted fire, and very useful predictions, too. This is especially true in social affairs, but it is also true in the "hard" sciences. It has been "predicted" with great confidence, for example, that intelligent life exists elsewhere in the universe and even in our own galaxy other than on the planet earth. Man knows in a "scientific" sense that other suns exist similar to ours. He also knows that the probabilities are extremely high that a substantial number of these suns have planets like the planet earth. But mankind does not yet have much understanding of the nature of life, and he is not yet completely certain that the primordial brew of chemicals on a cooling new planet will in fact develop the molecules essential for life. The prediction that life exists elsewhere is in the end of the same order as that of primitive man predicting fire—it is made by assuming that if the same conditions exist, the same results will follow. Conditions on earth produced life; so if those conditions are duplicated on other planets orbiting other suns, life will arise there, too.

Useful predictions, then, can be made in the social and political affairs of men by using more or less "scientific" knowledge when it is available, and also by this method of "same conditions, same results."

Furthermore, even when social scientists must fall back on the "same conditions, same results" approach, they can often enrich it with at least partial knowledge of a more or less "scientific" nature. Population studies are an example. Predictions about the size of future populations in the developing countries are based on the "same conditions, same results" assumption that they will follow the pattern the populations of industrial countries did as those countries developed. But this assumption can be modified by knowledge of the effects of food supply on fertility rates, for example, or the anthropologists' knowledge of different cultures and the deductions they can make about the relative acceptability of contraceptive devices in those different cultures.

Even more important, the model of "same conditions" used in population studies itself represents an enrichment—for it is based on statistical methods that are themselves highly sophisticated. To revert to the analogy of making fire, it is as if at some intermediate stage mankind stumbled on the combination of chemicals used for match tips before he understood the true nature of fire.

Modern man, in sum, is not quite so blind or helpless in the field of social affairs as we sometimes think. A great deal of social "engineering" does in fact take place. Government at the local, state, and national level puts into effect hundreds of thousands of rules, regulations, and pieces of legislation that have the effect they were intended to have.

Even so, for all the reasons discussed above—and particularly the fact that such a multiplicity of forces are operating in social affairs—as the level of prediction goes up, the confidence one can have in its accuracy goes down. It is not too difficult for a traffic engineer to predict accurately the consequences of putting a traffic light on a particular corner in a particular town, but it in fact proved very difficult for a whole battery of engineers and social scientists to predict the full range of social consequences that resulted from the post-World War II decision by the federal government to support a multibillion-dollar interstate highway program. It was not very difficult in the later forties for an economist to predict that the television industry would be a big thing, no matter what, but it in fact proved very difficult for economists as a profession to predict at that same time whether the economy as a whole would or would not go into recession. Economists, as the old joke has it, have predicted eight out of the last three recessions.

Prediction by Trial and Error

But predictions must be made—on big problems as well as little ones. Every action taken in the social and political affairs of men, to repeat, is also a prediction. Every bill passed by Congress, every policy adopted by the Executive, every action by this or any other government rests on some estimate or assumption about the future consequences of the action, on some prediction about where the world is going and how that particular action will affect the probable future. As a result of this tension between the fact that predictions must be made and the fact that the confidence one can have about most predictions must be low, many of the policies adopted by government evolve from a more or less deliberate process of trial and error.

It is an observable fact that most governmental decisions are not made as the result of systematic and comprehensive study of grand alternatives. On the contrary, even major policy changes usually come about through a series of slight modifications of existing policy, with the new policy emerging slowly and haltingly by small and usually tentative steps, a trial-and-error process in which policy zigs and zags, reverses itself, and then moves forward bit by bit. Charles E. Lindblom, in remarking on this phenomenon, argues that it would be physically impossible for a government to give rational consideration to the whole wide range of mankind's goals and the multiplicity of alternative means for achieving them much less to calculate the myriad of consequences and interactions. At the same time it is relatively easy for a government to proceed by means of a series of incremental, tentative, and easily reversible steps.[3] In addition, this tendency for governmental policy to proceed in a series of incremental steps is reinforced by the political nature of the policy-making process.[4] The acquiescence of a key constituency might be given for what could be regarded as a tentative, reversible experiment when it would be withheld for a grand leap.

The fact that governmental policies are arrived at by a series of incremental steps does not negate our conclusion that those policies must rest on a judgment about the future. It has been said that the United States Government did not make a decision to create a welfare state, but only to take each of a series of tentative steps—to alleviate the hardship of unemployment with a few weeks of worker compensation, to lighten the burden of old age for industrial workers with an experimental program of Social Security—and that the initial programs were then gradu-

[3] Charles E. Lindblom, "The Science of 'Muddling Through,'" *Public Administration Review*, XIX (1959); *The Intelligence of Democracy* (New York: The Free Press, 1965); and *The Policy-Making Process* (Englewood Cliffs, New Jersey, 1968).
[4] See my *To Move a Nation* (New York, 1967), especially Chapter 1, "Policy-Making is Politics," and Chapter 35, "Power, Politics, and Policy-Making," and my *The Politics of Policy Making in Defense and Foreign Affairs* (New York, 1971).

ally expanded, covering larger numbers of people and increasing the benefits. The statement is obviously true. But the people making each of these decisions not only had to predict whether or not the particular step under consideration would accomplish its intended result, they also had to consider the precedent set and where a series of such steps would take the society as a whole. And the debates of the time show that they did just that. The fact that they had the power to halt the process if the future that began to emerge was different from their prediction undoubtedly gave them courage to go ahead, but it did not permit them to evade having to make the prediction.

This is not to say, of course, that the predictions made in those debates were necessarily very prescient. Some of the debaters foresaw Social Security measures leading to an authoritarian, "communist" hell. Others saw a heaven on earth. And relatively few predicted anything near to the full range of social consequences that a historian, with the benefit of hindsight, might now ascribe to those decisions.

The lesson for us of the fact that governments tend to proceed in trial-and-error incremental steps, then, is not that judgments do not have to be made about the future, but that we desperately need to find ways of making those judgments better. Obviously, the answer is to improve the quality and to add to the quantity of the "scientific" knowledge available on social and political affairs. But the trouble with that conclusion is that we probably can't wait. Things are clearly happening today that will shape the long-range future. People and governments are probably doing things today that will make the future unpleasant, although they are unaware of these unpleasant consequences. Out of similar ignorance, witlessness, insensitivity, or simply preoccupation with other matters, people and governments are probably failing to do things that would make a better future or head off forces that will make it worse. What we need, in sum, are devices —like the "same conditions, same results" approach—that will permit us to make shrewder guesses about the future even when we lack "scientific" knowledge or when our knowledge is partial or inadequate.

Alexis de Tocqueville

Clues to devices of this kind might be found by studying the methods used by someone who was reasonably successful at the game in the past. What we need is a forecaster writing long enough ago so that conditions today form a test of his predictions. Judged by this criterion, Alexis de Tocqueville is particularly well suited. His *Democracy in America* was written well over a century ago, and it addressed itself specifically to the task of forecasting the future of a whole society.

Tocqueville was a young French aristocrat who was attracted to liberalism and increasingly convinced that democracy was the wave of the future for France and all of Europe. He determined to examine democracy in America first-hand, since America was "the nation, from among those which have undergone it [democracy], in which its development has been the most peaceful and the most complete, in order to discern its natural consequences and to find out, if possible, the means of rendering it profitable to mankind."

This was before the days of foundation grants for research, so Tocqueville and a friend, Gustave de Beaumont, arranged to be sent on a mission by France's Minister of Justice to study the American prison system, since prison reform was then an issue in France. For nine months in the year 1831, they traveled all over the United States, visiting cities, towns, and villages in New England, the Middle Atlantic states, the South, and even pioneer settlements in the western wilderness.

Tocqueville's study was a systematic examination of a whole society, precisely with a view to predicting its future development. His scholarship, furthermore, was for his day and time admirable. He conducted extensive interviews and kept meticulously careful notes.[5] He made copious use of governmental papers, and collected memoranda, local publications, and other documents as he went along.

Tocqueville's analysis of political institutions, of social and

[5] On this and the following points, see Phillips Bradley, "A Historical Essay," Appendix II to the Vintage Book edition of *Democracy in America* (New York: Random House, 1945).

economic conditions, and even of psychological factors was incisive and extraordinarily perceptive. It is probably no exaggeration to say that Tocqueville was the first modern social scientist.

Some of Tocqueville's predictions about the future of America and democracy were truly remarkable; others were just wrong. For our purposes, however, four sets of predictions, some right and some wrong, are particularly useful. These are 1. his prediction about the future power of the United States and Russia; 2. his brief but prescient comments on the then budding Industrial Revolution; 3. his mistaken estimate of the future relationship between the states and the federal government; and 4. his whole set of predictions about racial problems, the place of the blacks in American society, and the possibility of conflict between the North and the South.

The United States and Russia

Tocqueville's most famous prediction was the one about the future power of the United States and Russia. It occurs at the end of Volume 1 of his *Democracy in America:*

> There are at the present time two great nations in the world, which started from different points, but seem to tend towards the same end. I allude to the Russians and the Americans. Both of them have grown up unnoticed; and while the attention of mankind was directed elsewhere, they have suddenly placed themselves in the front rank among the nations, and the world learned their existence and their greatness at almost the same time. . . .
>
> All other nations seem to have nearly reached their natural limits, and they have only to maintain their power; but these are still in the act of growth. . . . The Anglo-American relies upon personal interest to accomplish his ends and gives free scope to the unguided strength and common sense of the people; the Russian centers all the authority of society in a single arm. The principal instrument of the former is freedom; of the latter, servitude. Their starting point is different and their courses are not the same; yet each of them seems marked

out by the will of Heaven to sway the destinies of half the globe.

The Industrial Revolution

Analyzing this prediction alone should be instructive for our purposes, but the others are equally promising. On the Industrial Revolution, which was in his time only in its beginnings, Tocqueville predicted, in a chapter entitled "What Causes Almost All Americans to Follow Industrial Callings," both the victory of the Industrial Revolution and the decline of agriculture. And in the next chapter, entitled "How an Aristocracy May Be Created by Manufactures," he anticipated not only the writings of Karl Marx but some of the economic and social conditions that aroused Marx—by ten years in the case of the *Communist Manifesto* and by twenty-five years in the case of *Das Kapital.*[6]

Federal vs. State Power

The third set of predictions concerned the relationship between the states and the federal government. Tocqueville was convinced that the power of the states would increase, and that the states would come to dominate. In another facet of the same mistake, he also saw a continuing major strength for America in the New England town meeting form of democracy—failing to see that it would decline under urbanization.

The Civil War and Race Relations

Tocqueville's fourth set of predictions—those about the place of the black in American society, the possibility of conflict between the North and the South, and the future of race relations in America—are mixed. Some have turned out to be correct and some incorrect. But they are particularly interesting and instructive in light of recent American experience, when the place of the black in American society came more violently to the fore than at any other time since the Civil War.

On the question of the condition of the black in America in his own day, Tocqueville's analysis was remarkably clear and

[6] On this point, see Bradley, p. 474.

free from either bias or self-delusion. He wrote of racism and the oppression of the blacks in searing language, blunter and more direct than any modern Kerner report has done. "If we reason from what passes in the world," he wrote, "we should almost say that the European is to the other races of mankind what man himself is to the lower animals: he makes them subservient to his use, and when he cannot subdue he destroys them. Oppression has, at one stroke, deprived the descendants of the Africans of almost all the privileges of humanity."[7]

And Tocqueville spoke with great psychological insight of how slavery debases and degrades a man:

> Am I to call it a proof of God's mercy, or a visitation of His wrath, that man, in certain states, appears to be insensible to his extreme wretchedness and almost obtains a depraved taste for the cause of his misfortunes? The Negro, plunged into this abyss of evils, scarcely feels his own calamitous situation. Violence made him a slave, and the habit of servitude gives him the thoughts and desires of a slave; he admires his tyrants more than he hates them, and finds his joy and pride in the servile imitation of those who oppress him. His understanding is degraded to the level of his soul.
>
> The Negro enters upon slavery as soon as he is born; nay, he may have been purchased in the womb, and have begun his slavery before he began his existence. Equally devoid of wants and of enjoyment, and useless to himself, he learns with his first notions of existence that he is the property of another, who has an interest in preserving his life, and that the care of it does not devolve upon himself; even the power of thought appears to him a useless gift of Providence, and he quietly enjoys all the privileges of his debasement.
>
> If he becomes free, independence is often felt by him to be a heavier burden than slavery; for, having learned in the course of his life to submit to everything except reason, he is too unacquainted with her dictates to obey them. A thousand new desires beset him, and he has not the knowledge and energy necessary to resist them: these are masters which it is neces-

[7] Vol. 1, p. 344.

sary to contend with, and he has learned only to submit and obey. In short, he is sunk to such a depth of wretchedness that while servitude brutalizes him, liberty destroys him.[8]

On the possibility of conflict between the North and the South, Tocqueville concluded, first, that the odds were extremely high that the South would secede and the federal union be dissolved. Indeed, he thought that "the continuance of the Federal government can be only a fortunate accident."[9] He believed that the most likely way for a dissolution of the Union to come about would be as a result of the tension between the North and the South. Impressively, his analysis of the causes of the tension agrees with that of the most respected of today's Civil War historians who work with all the advantages of hindsight. The issue of slavery, Tocqueville realized, was only a part of it, operating indirectly rather than directly. "Slavery has not created interests in the South contrary to those of the North," he wrote, "but it has modified the character and changed the habits of the natives of the South."[10] The more important cause, he believed, would be the steady decline in the relative power and political influence of the South. "The inhabitants of the Southern states are, of all Americans, those who are most interested in the maintenance of the Union; they would assuredly suffer most from being left to themselves; and yet they are the only ones who threaten to break the tie of confederation. It is easy to perceive that the South . . . which is peopled with ardent and irascible men [which Tocqueville saw as one of the effects of slavery on the masters], is becoming more irritated and alarmed."[11]

But Tocqueville decided that on balance the secession of the South would not be followed by civil war. Secession would not jeopardize the security of the North, he argued, since it was the potential naval power of the North that was the main deterrent to outside threats. Indeed, at one point he argued that the North might actually be stronger if it were free of the South and its debilitating problems. Neither would secession affect the economic and commercial interests of the North. The South would

[8] Ibid., p. 345.
[9] Ibid., p. 414.
[10] Ibid., p. 410.
[11] Ibid., p. 418.

still be economically dependent on the North, no matter how hard it tried to cultivate trade with England. Finally, Tocqueville was convinced that the institution of slavery had affected the masters in the South as profoundly as the slaves, that it had determined what Tocqueville called the "manners" of the region—not only creating the "ardent and irascible men" mentioned above, but the whole personality structure and lifestyle in social terms. Thus the differences between the South and the rest of the country were greater than between any other of the different regions. Tocqueville concluded from this that the country would be less reluctant to see the South secede than any other group of the states.

Race Relations

Whether or not the Union was dissolved, Tocqueville considered the problem of tension between the black and white races as central to the long-run future of the United States. "The most formidable of all the ills that threaten the future of the Union arises from the presence of a black population upon its territory; and in contemplating the cause of the present embarrassments, or the future dangers of the United States, the observer is led to this as a primary fact."[12] He was convinced the South would seek to perpetuate slavery. "When I contemplate the condition of the South, I can discover only two modes of action for the white inhabitants of those states: namely, either to emancipate the Negroes and to intermingle with them, or, remaining isolated from them, to keep them in slavery as long as possible. All intermediate steps seem to me likely to terminate, and that shortly, in the most horrible of civil wars and perhaps in the extirpation of one or the other of the two races. Such is the view that Americans of the South take of the question, and they act consistently with it. As they are determined not to mingle with the Negroes, they refuse to emancipate them."[13]

Yet Tocqueville was equally convinced that slavery would inevitably be abolished. "Whatever the efforts of the Americans of the South to maintain slavery, they will not always succeed.

[12] Ibid., p. 370.
[13] Ibid., p. 394.

Slavery, now confined to a single tract of the civilized earth, attacked by Christianity as unjust and by political economy as prejudicial, and now contrasted with democratic liberty and the intelligence of our age, cannot survive. By the act of the master, or by the will of the slave, it will cease; and in either case great calamities may be expected to ensue."[14]

The only possibility of avoiding these calamities and the only true bond of union between the two races, Tocqueville felt, was for them to intermix. When no man of a country is either entirely black or entirely white, "the two races may really be said to be combined, or, rather, to have been absorbed in a third race, which is connected to both without being identical with either."[15] But he was skeptical that it would ever happen. He recalled that his own country, France, had been full of inequalities that had been created by law. Nothing could be more fictitious, he argued, than a purely legal inferiority, yet these fictitious divisions were perpetuated for ages in France. They still existed in many places and left vestiges in others. "If it be so difficult to root out an inequality that originates solely in the law," he asks, "how are those distinctions to be destroyed which seem to be based upon the immutable laws of nature herself?" Remembering the extreme difficulty with which aristocratic forms were erased and the great effort made to preserve the boundaries of caste inviolate, Tocqueville said that the possibility of "seeing an aristocracy disappear which is founded upon visible and indelible signs" left him in despair. "Those who hope that the Europeans will ever be amalgamated with the Negroes appear to me to delude themselves."[16]

What is more, Tocqueville argued that the very form of government in America—democracy—would make amalgamation even more unlikely. "I do not believe that the white and black races will ever live in any country upon an equal footing. But I believe the difficulty to be still greater in the United States than elsewhere. An isolated individual may surmount the prejudices of religion, of his country, or of his race; and if this individual is a

14 Ibid., p. 397.
15 Ibid., p. 389.
16 Ibid., pp. 372–73.

king, he may effect surprising changes in society; but a whole people cannot rise, as it were, above itself. A despot who should subject the Americans and their former slaves to the same yoke might perhaps succeed in commingling their races; but as long as the American democracy remains at the head of affairs, no one will undertake so difficult a task; and it may be foreseen that the freer the white population of the United States becomes, the more isolated will it remain."

Not only would the two races not amalgamate, in Tocqueville's opinion, but neither could they coexist in equality. In a tightly reasoned and fantastically perceptive analysis, he argued not only that the abolition of slavery would not solve the tension between the races in America, but that after abolition, racism and prejudice would actually increase. "If I were called upon to predict the future," he wrote, "I should say that the abolition of slavery in the South will, in the common course of things, increase the repugnance of the white population for the blacks."[17]

Tocqueville's Reasoning

To support this conclusion, Tocqueville offered two sets of arguments, one analytical and deductive and the other empirical —what a modern social scientist would call a "research finding." Briefly the analytical argument runs as follows. There is a "natural prejudice that prompts men to despise whoever has been their inferior long after he has become an equal."[18] This was demonstrated in ancient times, principally in Rome, when slaves were the same race as the masters and often superior in education. Second, there is the prejudice of race. Tocqueville reserves his particular execration for those European Christians of the sixteenth century who after a thousand years of freedom not only re-established slavery but restricted it to only one of the races of mankind. And the language he uses to describe the racism of his fellow Europeans is unsparing: "You may set the Negro free, but you cannot make him otherwise than an alien to the European.

17 Ibid., p. 390.
18 Ibid., p. 371.

Nor is this all; we scarcely acknowledge the common features of humanity in this stranger whom slavery has brought among us. His physiognomy is to our eyes hideous, his understanding weak, his tastes low; and we are almost inclined to look upon him as being intermediate between man and the brutes."[19] Finally, there is the prejudice of color: "No African has ever voluntarily emigrated to the shores of the New World, whence it follows that all blacks who are now found there are either slaves or freedmen. Thus the Negro transmits the eternal mark of his ignominy to all his descendants; and although the law may abolish slavery, God alone can obliterate the traces of its existence."[20] And Tocqueville saw with perfect clarity the vicious circle that has endured for a century and a half: "To induce the whites to abandon the opinion they have conceived of the moral and intellectual inferiority of their former slaves, the Negroes must change; but as long as this opinion persists, they cannot change."[21]

The "research finding" that led Tocqueville to feel that prejudice would actually increase after abolition, came from his study of what had happened in those northern states that had abolished slavery. "Whoever has inhabited the United States must have perceived that in those parts of the Union in which the Negroes are no longer slaves they have in no wise drawn nearer to the whites. On the contrary, the prejudice of race appears to be stronger in the states that have abolished slavery than in those where it still exists; and nowhere is it so intolerant as in those states where servitude has never been known."[22] Ohio, for example, prohibited slavery, but it also forbade free blacks to enter the state or to hold property in it.

With abolition, then, Tocqueville predicted, would come an increase in racism and prejudice and a denial of the blacks' civil rights. Eventually, however, Tocqueville believed, the black would acquire both the means and the will to do something about his condition. "The Negroes may long remain slaves without complaining; but if they are once raised to the level of free-

[19] Ibid., p. 372.
[20] Ibid.
[21] Ibid., p. 372, fn. 32.
[22] Ibid., p. 373.

men, they will soon revolt at being deprived of almost all their civil rights; and as they cannot become the equals of whites, they will speedily show themselves as enemies."[23] And once again, Tocqueville's reasoning is remarkably perceptive:

> As long as the Negro remains a slave, he may be kept in a condition not far removed from that of the brutes; but with his liberty he cannot but acquire a degree of instruction that will enable him to appreciate his misfortunes and to discern a remedy for them. Moreover, there exists a singular principle of relative justice which is firmly implanted in the human heart. Men are much more forcibly struck by those inequalities which exist within the same class than by those which may be noted between different classes. One can understand slavery, but how allow several millions of citizens to exist under a load of eternal infamy and hereditary wretchedness? In the North the population of freed Negroes feels these hardships and indignities, but its numbers and its powers are small, while in the South it would be numerous and strong.[24]

Thus Tocqueville predicts a black rebellion *after* the abolition of slavery brought on by an increase in racial prejudice and the continued denial of civil rights.

Since the black is in America to stay, since it is "impossible to foresee a time at which the whites and the blacks will be so intermingled as to derive the same benefits from society," and since it must therefore be inferred that "the blacks and the whites will, sooner or later, come to open strife," what, Tocqueville asks, will the issue of the struggle be likely to be?

Facing so awesome a question, even a Tocqueville hesitates. At such a point, he says, "it will be readily understood that we are here left to vague conjectures." He then continues: "The human mind may succeed in tracing a wide circle, as it were, which includes the future; but within that circle chance rules, and eludes all our foresight. In every picture of the future there

[23] Ibid., p. 394.
[24] Ibid., p. 388.

is a dim spot which the eye of the understanding cannot penetrate."[25] But he does, finally, screw up the courage to essay an
answer, even though he clothes his prediction with qualification.

Two assumptions—both explicit—influenced his final judgment.
One turned out to be correct, and the other quite wrong. The correct assumption was about the trend in the relative size of the
white and black populations. "The white population," Tocqueville
observed, "grows by its natural increase and at the same time by
the immense influx of immigrants; while the black population receives no immigrants and is upon the decline."[26] Tocqueville
knew that the percentage of blacks had dropped from 19.3 per
cent in the census of 1790 to 18.1 per cent in the census of 1830.
He cites statistics from Philadelphia to show that the death rate
of blacks was higher than that of whites to suggest that the rate
of decline would proceed even more rapidly in the future.

The second assumption was that the black population would
continue to be concentrated in the South, as it was in Tocqueville's day. He believed that this situation would continue not
only because of the inertia of population concentrations but because most of the laws abolishing slavery in the North worked to
effect a further movement of blacks to the South. Most of the
laws did not free existing slaves, which would have created an
argument for expensive compensation to the owners, but declared that the future children of existing slaves would be free,
thus driving northern slaveholders to transport their slaves to the
South to protect their investment by ensuring that any children
would also be slaves. What Tocqueville did not foresee was the
migration of blacks to northern cities, which began during the
labor shortages of the first World War.

Tocqueville really offers two alternative answers to his question
on the outcome of the struggle between the blacks and whites,
one if the Union is dissolved and the other if it survives. If the
Union is already dissolved when the struggle begins, Tocqueville
felt that the black population accumulated along the coast of the

25 Ibid., pp. 390–91.
26 Ibid., p. 383.

Gulf of Mexico would eventually emerge victorious. He suggested the following scenario:

> The Federal tie once broken, the people of the South could not rely upon any lasting succor from their Northern country-men. . . . Yet at whatever period the strife may break out, the whites of the South, even if they are abandoned to their own resources, will enter the lists with an immense superiority of knowledge and the means of warfare; but the blacks will have numerical strength and the energy of despair upon their side, and these are powerful resources to men who have taken up arms. The fate of the white population of the Southern states will perhaps be similar to that of the Moors in Spain. After having occupied the land for centuries, it will perhaps retire by degrees to the country whence its ancestors came and abandon to the Negroes the possession of a territory which Providence seems to have destined for them, since they can subsist and labor in it more easily than the whites.[27]

27 Ibid., p. 391. In this last clause, expressing the notion that blacks can subsist and labor in hot climates more easily than whites, Tocqueville uncritically accepts a bit of the racist mythology of his day—racist either in thinking that blacks are inferior to whites because of their ability to survive and work in "inferior" tropical climates or racist in thinking they are *superior* to whites because of being tougher! However, the source of the myth did have empirical roots. In the early days of the plantations in the Caribbean, where it all began, black slaves and white indentured servants came in about equal numbers. But the whites died off very rapidly, and the plantation owners rather quickly came to prefer blacks—especially what they called "seasoned" blacks—people who had lived in the New World for several years and survived and later those who were born and raised there. But the reasons for the differing death rates can be found in epidemiology, not race. Each of the races brought with him diseases native to the region of his origin. The black brought strains of malaria and yellow fever, both of which were endemic along the west coast of Africa. Their virulence is attested to by the fact that the death rate of whites stationed in the string of coastal forts where the slaves were assembled for the sea passage was over six hundred per 1,000 per year! The white, for his part, brought the killer respiratory diseases, like tuberculosis. Each also brought a certain immunity to his own diseases, and this gave the black a two to one advantage over the white. The whites died off very rapidly. The poor Carib Indians had no immunities except for native diseases, which were apparently not nearly so deadly, and they were totally wiped out in a very few years. An interesting and instructive statistic is the comparative death rates in the slave ships in the dread Middle Passage. The slaves between decks were highly valuable cargo. This meant that the master and the crew had a great economic incentive to pack in as many as possible, which made for deplorable conditions. But the same economic incentive also worked to make the master and crew do everything they could to ensure the survival of as many as possible, consistent with the crowded conditions and fear of rebellion. However, according to the available statistics, at least some of which are very good, the death rate was still 145 per 1,000. The sta-

If the Union was not dissolved when the struggle between the races begins, on the other hand, Tocqueville saw the struggle— at least within the United States—going the other way. The difficulties of foreseeing every detail of the future are great, he repeats, and "dim spots" appear in every picture of it. He then continues:

> it appears, however, extremely probable that in the West Indies islands the white race is destined to be subdued, and upon the continent the blacks.
>
> In the West Indies the white planters are isolated amid an immense black population; on the continent the blacks are placed between the ocean and an innumerable people, who already extend above them, in a compact mass, from the icy confines of Canada to the frontiers of Virginia, and from the banks of the Missouri to the shores of the Atlantic. If the white citizens of North America remain united, it is difficult to believe that the Negroes will escape the destruction which menaces them; they must be subdued by want or by the sword.[28]

After almost a century and a half, it is still too soon for the final answer on whether Tocqueville will eventually be right or wrong in his prediction on the fate of blacks in America. But Tocqueville certainly could claim to have predicted not only the black rebellion of the post-World War II decades but its central cause—the continued denial of civil rights. The only surprise for Tocqueville would be that it took so long in coming. Although he recognized more clearly than most the powerful means for oppression available to the whites and the disadvantages burdening the blacks, he underestimated just what powerful forces they were for delaying the ultimate rebellion.

Tocqueville's Mental Processes

Let us try to reconstruct the mental processes that Tocqueville must have had to go through to reach each of these four pre-

---

tistics on the death rate of the white crews clears up much of the mystery. It was over 200 per 1,000. See Philip D. Curtin, "Epidemiology and the Slave Trade," *Political Science Quarterly*, Vol. 83, No. 2 (June 1968), pp. 190–216.
[28] Vol. 1, p. 391.

dictions. For the prediction that Russia and the United States would become the dominant world powers, he started with a more or less explicit and more or less "scientific" set of propositions about the sources of national power. Population, territory, and natural resources were among the prime considerations. By these criteria, he quite explicitly eliminated a number of the great powers of his day, such as France and Italy. None of these countries, he pointed out, had enough territory to support the kind of population that would develop in Russia and the United States, and the effort to acquire additional territory from their neighbors would meet with exhausting resistance. Japan, if Tocqueville considered it at all, would have been ruled out for the same reason. Germany would also have been eliminated on the grounds of lack of territory, even if Tocqueville assumed that the problem of unifying the then petty principalities could be solved. For England, Tocqueville seems to have made an additional judgment—that even though extensive colonies might add to economic wealth, colonial troops were not the same as one's own, and a large colonial population would not enhance a nation's military power to the same degree as a very large population of one's own.

There still remain China and India. Both had territory and both had large populations. From what Tocqueville could have known of China in 1830, it is likely that he would have decided that it was not a contender for great power status in the coming century on the basis of two other factors—about which he is less explicit than he is about territory and population, but which are at least implicitly included among his set of factors contributing to national power. The first is the central importance of political cohesion and unity, and the second is the necessity for technological knowledge and skills. China lacked both in 1830, and it would need much time both to solve its political problems and to acquire the necessary technological knowledge and skills. India would also have been eliminated as a contender for great power status for the same reasons, even without the additional handicap of having first to throw off a colonial yoke.

Now, consider this set of propositions about the sources of national power—population, territory, resources, political cohesion, technological knowledge, and skills—with which Tocqueville was more or less explicitly armed. The first thing that strikes today's reader is that although the contemporary social scientist may have more refined and sophisticated sets of propositions, they are not essentially different in *kind*. The contemporary social scientist, for example, might have some additional concepts that Tocqueville didn't—such as the concept of per capita gross national product as a measure of economic strength. (Parenthetically, we might also note that the contemporary social scientist also has more reliable and precise techniques, by way of statistical analysis and polling, for acquiring some kinds of data than Tocqueville's rather haphazard method of traveling and chatting with people he met.) The contemporary social scientist might also have more refined notions about some of the same factors that Tocqueville used. He might explicitly recognize, for example in the case of China, that a very large population may actually be a handicap, since it is the relation of population to total production (i.e., the "disposable" population over minimum production) that is most significant for national power. But the fact remains that Tocqueville was not without more or less "scientific" knowledge of causality—he was not without some degree of the same kind of knowledge that is used to predict eclipses and the behavior of the solar system. For even after conceding all the handicaps of dealing with social affairs, the fact remains that both Tocqueville's set of propositions and the contemporary social scientist's are the same type of knowledge as that used in making predictions about the solar system, even though it may be considerably less full than would be desirable and considerably less precise.

A second observation about Tocqueville's process of thought, of course, is that he also used the "same conditions, same results" technique. Tocqueville notes, to give only one example, that slave owners in ancient times were prejudiced against former slaves, and although he offers no psychological explanation for the phenomenon, he expects the same prejudice to appear after the abolition of slavery in the United States.

The Analysis of Trends

Still another technique on which Tocqueville relies heavily is the analysis of trends. Neither Russia nor the United States had exceptionally large populations in 1830—the United States, in fact, had a population at that time of less than 13 million. And the United States also still lacked the territory to support a very large population. For the solution of both these problems of prediction, Tocqueville relied on the analysis of trends. Russia already had the necessary territory, and Tocqueville noted simply that the population of Russia had increased more rapidly than that of any other country of Europe and that there was no discernible reason that it would not continue to increase. For the United States, however, the problem was more difficult. There were the past trends—a steady western movement in the case of territory and a natural increase in population augmented by a large flow of immigrants from Europe. Before assuming that both trends would continue, however, Tocqueville very carefully analyzed forces that might halt or reverse them.

On the trend of western movement and steadily expanding territory, he analyzed the possibility of effective resistance from the American Indian and dismissed it. He also analyzed the possibility that Mexico might be an effective obstacle, and dismissed that, too—predicting, on the contrary, that the Americans would soon take from Mexico the province of Texas. Finding nothing that might halt or reverse the trend, he accepted it— quoting a calculation that the movement west had advanced every year a mean distance of 17 miles along the whole vast boundary as evidence of how unrelenting the movement was. The western movement, he said, was a "deluge of men rising unabatedly, and daily driven onwards by the hand of God."[29]

On the question of population increase, he did the same, noting that the population of the United States had doubled every twenty-two years, all during colonial times as well as after independence, and—a point he found particularly convincing—that this increase had continued unabated even during the long, bitter war for independence. Noting that North America covered an area equal to three fourths of Europe and that the population of Europe was 205 million, Tocqueville concluded that the population of North America would reach 150 million before the middle of the following century. As we have seen, his argument

[29] Ibid., p. 414.

was based both on "trend analysis" and on the "same conditions, same results" approach. In other words, Tocqueville not only looked for trends, but systematically looked for forces that seemed likely, in the light of historical experience, to alter or reverse those trends.

Any attempt at more or less general prediction must inevitably rely on the analysis and extrapolation of trends of one kind or another. One type is a simple straight-line projection, either up or down. Population and GNP are the most obvious examples, but there are many others. Another type of trend is the cyclical—long-range weather predictions, business activity predictions, and so on, all rely to some extent on the analysis and extrapolation of cyclical trends. Still another type of "trend" is the continuation of the status quo. In the absence of forces making for a change, one may extrapolate the continuation of the present situation. In the absence of other forces, for example, Tocqueville could safely assume that the future world would be made up mainly of sovereign states.

Technological Skills and Political Cohesion

So far, Tocqueville's prediction that Russia and the United States would each "sway the destinies of half the globe" seems fairly easy. But if he had to make a judgment about technological skills and political cohesion for China and India, he certainly had to do the same for Russia and the United States—and here he eventually ran into very serious problems.

The question of technological skills apparently presented no great difficulty. The American population was largely European, sharing its knowledge, and immigrants continually added to the pool. For Russia, the problem looked simpler to Tocqueville in the 1830s than it would have looked to an observer later on in the nineteenth century. Peter the Great had started the westernization of Russia, and in Tocqueville's day Russia was not so far behind the others as to be remarkable. In any case, in spite of Czarism, industrialization had made considerable progress by the time of the Communist revolution, with a truly tremendous spurt coming in the decade of the 1890s. Industrialization could have bogged down in either country, but even hindsight does not suggest that either country enjoyed a particular advantage or suffered a particular handicap, at least in terms of technological skills.

It was on the question of political cohesion that the difficulty arose, especially in the case of the United States. Tocqueville did not offer the extensive analysis for his predictions on Russia that he did for those on America, and one can only assume that the question of political cohesion was solved for him by nationalism.[30] He would also have to have predicted that Russia would somehow get past the inefficiencies of Czarism, but it would not have been too difficult to conclude that there were no really significant forces tending to break the nation to pieces.

For the United States, on the other hand, Tocqueville could not fall back on an established nationalism, and his final judgment required a lengthy and sophisticated analysis. He saw a number of powerful forces for continued unity. By remaining united, the Americans remained strong against foreign foes. Second, there were no conflicting economic interests among the different regions that worked to separate them. On the contrary, there were many reciprocal and common interests. Although divided into states, the Americans constituted one people—in terms of both political and religious opinions and moral and philosophic principles.

On the other side of the issue, as we saw, Tocqueville did finally conclude that the South would secede. But he also concluded that the rest of the country might well be stronger for it. In the first place, without the South the country would be even more politically cohesive and unified. In the second, without the South the rest of the country would have even greater incentives to build the only kind of military forces that would make them a global power:

> Reason and experience prove that no commercial prosperity can be durable if it cannot be united, in case of need, to naval force. This truth is as well understood in the United States as

---

[30] Tocqueville's prediction that Russia and the United States would be dominant logically requires that he examine and reject the possibility of some new conglomerate, say, a United States of Europe. Although there is no evidence that he thought such an analysis necessary, from what he has to say about European nationalisms, however, we can safely assume that he would have regarded a European union as highly unlikely at any time in the following century.

anywhere else: the Americans are already able to make their flag respected; in a few years they will make it feared. I am convinced that the dismemberment of the Union would not have the effect of diminishing the naval power of the Americans but would powerfully increase it. . . . When I contemplate the ardor with which the Anglo-Americans prosecute commerce, the advantages which aid them and the success of their undertakings, I cannot help believing that they will one day become the foremost maritime power of the globe. They are born to rule the seas, as the Romans were to conquer the world.[31]

Also on the other side of the issue is Tocqueville's prediction that the power of the federal government would decline and that of the states increase. The end of that trend could well be complete dismemberment of the Union. He was able to accept this possibility, but he could not believe that it would completely negate his prediction. He thought the general cohesiveness— common interests, common religion, common moral and philosophic principles—would still prevail. At this point, he talks of "North America" including Canada, rather than the United States, and of the "British race" rather than the "Americans." "It must not, then, be imagined that the impulse of the British race in the New World can be arrested. The dismemberment of the Union and the hostilities that might ensue, the abolition of republican institutions and the tyrannical government that might succeed, may retard this impulse, but they cannot prevent the people from ultimately fulfilling their destinies."[32] In effect, Tocqueville is hedging by arguing that even though the Union may be dissolved, the similarities in background, in belief, and in character will prevent the inhabitants of the different regions, even though politically separated, from "becoming aliens to one another."

In the end, Tocqueville decides that one way or another there will be sufficient cohesion and political unity for the Americans

[31] Tocqueville, op. cit., pp. 446–47.
[32] Ibid., p. 450.

to fulfill their destinies. If they stay united, there is no doubt. If the South breaks off, the rest of the country will alone be sufficiently powerful. And if the dismemberment goes even further, there will still be sufficient similarity in the different parts in terms of common political philosophy and purpose to ensure that they will exert a large influence in the world even though they quarrel among themselves.

The Level of Generalization

One instructive point here is that much depends on *the level of generalization* of the prediction. Tocqueville was uneasy about the political cohesion of the Union, yet he had high confidence in everything else: the growing size and prosperity of the Americans and the common direction of their influence. There is something here of the deliberately cryptic vagueness that has been the trick of all prophets and seers back through history to the oracle at Delphi.

Similarly, and perhaps with less justification, when Tocqueville says that Russia and America will each "sway the destinies of half the globe," he has adopted a very high and vague level of generalization indeed. He did not say, and probably did not believe that each would actually *conquer* half the globe, but he certainly did believe that both would loom larger than any other of the powers in the coming century and that each would exert an influence on events appropriate to its power. By leaving the prediction in such vague language as "sway the destinies of half the globe," Tocqueville not only covered both contingencies but left all sorts of escape routes through the many possible interpretations of the word "influence." All this has much in it of the trickiness of the Delphic priestesses, as we say, but it still results in a legitimate and useful prediction.

Another, related point is worth noting. In making predictions about the future power of states, the factors that have to be considered are only those that are sources of power or that affect power. One needs to consider trends in population to make a prediction about the power of a nation in the future, but not about trends in its fashions. But even in considering factors that do affect power, one can neglect those that are not likely to have *differential* effects. Scientific knowledge, for example, could have an enormous effect on relative national power. But between the present-day Soviet Union and the United States, one can safely assume that there will be no differential effects worth noting. One can assume that neither will draw ahead of the other in scientific knowledge in any significant way for any significant period of time, and that this particular source of national power, scientific knowledge, can be ignored in a prediction made today about the future strength of the two.

The Effect of World Wars I and II

Events—war, pestilence, and famine—can shape history. But many events can also be ignored, even some events that are cataclysmic. For example, although Tocqueville did not specifically predict World Wars I and II, he did predict that wars in general would be fought by Russia and the United States and that they would win some and lose some. But he argued that neither war nor its outcome would affect the basic forces working to make Russia and the United States the dominant powers of the twentieth century. "Europe," he wrote in what is only one example, "divided as it is between so many nations and torn as it has been by incessant wars growing out of the barbarous manners of the Middle Ages, has yet attained a population of 410 inhabitants to the square league. What cause can prevent the United States from having as numerous a population in time?"[33]

And, generally speaking, he was correct in assuming that war could not do any more than slow the trends on which his prediction was based. It seems very clear, for example, that the Treaty of Versailles had little effect on the trends that Tocqueville was concerned with. The Kaiser was not so different from Lloyd George, Clemenceau, and Woodrow Wilson, and one can presume that the treaty he would have dictated would simply have been the mirror image of Versailles.

A German victory, certainly, would not have fundamentally altered the trends in the United States. As for Russia, the major effect would have been to deprive her of the Ukraine, as laid down in the Treaty of Brest-Litovsk, as well as Finland, Latvia, Estonia, Lithuania, and the Russian part of Poland. The Ukraine today

[33] Ibid., p. 451.

contains 18 per cent of the Soviet population, and comprises 3 per cent of the territory of the Soviet Union. It contains important proportions of industry, agriculture, and mining, and did so at the time. In the short run, certainly, the loss of the Ukraine would have spelled economic disaster. But in the longer run, it seems probable that Russia would have been able to make up for its loss in power terms. The main effect would probably have been that Soviet development of both industry and agriculture would have taken place elsewhere.

But the truth is that it is very doubtful that the Ukraine could have maintained its separate existence for more than a generation. Even a victorious Germany could not have stopped the shifting balance of power in the world, and the Soviet Union would have seized its opportunity the first time that Germany's back was turned. The fate of the Ukraine would seem more likely to have ultimately been that of Latvia, Lithuania, and Estonia than even Finland, i.e., it would have been reincorporated into the Soviet Union.

On balance, it does seem fair to say that World War I was simply irrelevant to Tocqueville's prediction—that Russia and the United States would have turned out the same no matter who had won that war. It is not so clear, however, that World War II was so irrelevant. As it turned out, World War II hastened the developments that Tocqueville predicted. If the war had gone the other way, on the other hand, and Hitler had succeeded in conquering Russia, at least the possibility exists that Tocqueville's prediction would not have looked so prescient. It does seem doubtful that Nazism could have succeeded in either subjugating the nationalisms of Europe or in winning them over to loyalty to a German-dominated Nazi empire. But Hitler was capable of genocide.

"Turning Points"

And here is another point that seems instructive to the problem of prediction when scientific knowledge is not fully adequate. If Hitler had won World War II and had succeeded in vastly reducing the population of Russia through a policy of genocide, it would have constituted what historians call a "turning point"—

an event or series of events that radically alters the direction of subsequent history; a reversal, in effect, of a whole set of trends. European colonialism, for example, clearly had this decisive effect in Africa. The many different peoples and tribes that make up a country like Nigeria, for example, have no common historical past except the fact of British colonial rule. The borders of most of the present-day countries of Africa are not divisions along ethnic, tribal, or cultural lines, but are the result either of the accident of the European scramble for colonies or the convenience of colonial administration. And all other aspects of social and political life in Africa have been just as profoundly shaped by the colonial experience.

Colonialism in Asia was a turning point in some countries but not in others. In the Philippines, it was very clearly a turning point, and it probably was in the subcontinent of India and Pakistan. But colonialism was probably not a turning point anywhere in Southeast Asia. Burma, for example, existed as a historical entity before the British came, and its present borders, though including many non-Burmese peoples, owe as much to the distant past as to the British period. Burmese culture—in all its aspects including religion, language, literature, and so on—was thick and deep before the British came, and the British period left only superficial marks. British colonialism swept away the kingship and other governmental institutions of feudal Burma, but they would have disappeared or been transformed into forms of a constitutional monarchy in any case. The important point is that the present-day Burmese institutions owe much more to Burmese history than British, and the present-day governmental forms resemble the old kingship system more than British parliamentary democracy. The only marks left by the British period are on portions of the bureaucracy, on some aspects of the judicial system, and perhaps on higher education. But little more.

The Mistaken Prediction on the Power of the States

This concept of "turning points" helps explain why Tocqueville went wrong in his assessment of the future power of the states and the federal government. He correctly assessed both the situation of his own day and the trend existing at that time. The federal government was very weak in the 1830s, and the trend was for it to get weaker. Tocqueville also catalogued and assessed the forces working against the trend—the forces making for additional power at the center—and correctly concluded that they were not sufficient in themselves to bring about a reversal. It seems to have been only the intervention of a "turning point" event, in other words—the Civil War—that caused the change. Tocqueville felt, to repeat, that the Civil War was not likely, that the South would secede but that the North would not fight. Now the fact of the matter is that there was nothing inevitable in the North's decision to fight, no overwhelming force pushing in that direction, and the decision could very easily have gone in either direction. Once the fighting began, however, the decision inevitably hardened. As casualties mounted, more and more of the northern population became emotionally involved, and the northern leaders developed a heavier and heavier stake in the decisions already made. The commitment increased to the level of full-scale war. And once the North became fully engaged in large-scale war, it was necessary and inevitable that it would develop a stronger central government. Just how the decision to fight would go, in other words, was chancy, precisely because of the trend to weakness that Tocqueville recognized. But the decision itself created a "turning point" situation that reversed the trend.

Turning Points and Alternative Futures

The obvious lesson to be drawn from all this is to be sensitive to possible "turning points." Faced with one, the only device the forecaster has to fall back on is that of "alternative futures"— If the North decides *not* to fight when the South secedes, the trend of the states growing more powerful while the federal government grows weaker will continue. But if the decision goes the other way, the trend will be reversed.

The Problem of the Few vs. the Many

But there may be still another lesson here—a lesson in the fact that Tocqueville was successful in predicting the growth of Russian and American power and less successful in predicting what the North would do in response to secession. What Tocqueville's experience seems to suggest is that it may be easier to predict a future that is determined by the behavior of a great many people and more difficult to predict a future that is determined by the behavior of only a few people.

One cannot, of course, think of future history as already written—an electronic tape, say, preprinted and rolled up inside a cosmic computer. There are choices to be made at every juncture, and very human men and women ultimately make those choices.

Now, it is certainly possible to predict how a particular individual might behave in making these choices. If he is motivated by enlightened self-interest, if he is rational, and if he proceeds logically, prediction is feasible provided one has sufficient information on the person's values and mode of analysis. One makes the same logical calculations of enlightened self-interest that the subject will have to make and predicts that he will behave accordingly.

In certain circumstances, one would be able to predict an individual's behavior even if the latter were not rational. If the individual is mad, for example, and his madness is compulsive, patterned, and identifiable, prediction might well be possible. Winston Churchill called World War II the "unnecessary war," presumably because he felt that enough was known about Hitler and his mania to be certain he was bent on war, and that if he remained in power, war was inevitable. If so, World War II was one historical situation in which preventive war—say, in 1936 when Hitler occupied the Rhineland—was fully justified.

One difficulty in predicting individual behavior is that whether or not the individual is motivated by enlightened self-interest, much less whether or not he is mad, may be known only to his psychiatrist. His motives may be less than mad but still too erratic for prediction. He may act out of whimsy or sheer cussedness. He may also be responding to a misconception of the situation that the outside observer has no way of knowing about. He may even be responding to private and personal pressures rather than the situation and the social forces generated. More than one historian has wondered whether a Napoleon on some historical occasion was responding to some necessity of grand strategy in his decision or a quarrel with Josephine. And even if the forecaster is correct in his judgments on how the individual will behave, the prediction is dependent on the personal fate of the individual—whether he lives or dies and whether he continues to hold the power to make the decision in question.

If one is dealing with the many, the situation is different in a number of ways. First of all, private and personal pressures tend to cancel out. The behavior to be predicted is the response to pervasive, long-term conditions and social forces and pressures. At an elemental level, examples would be climate, the availability of resources, the basic human drives of survival, and striving for material gain. On a more complicated level, examples would be population pressures, the workings of an industrial economy, and international rivalries. It is the fact that these pressures operate on everyone in a society, and over a long period of time that makes prediction more feasible.

The second difference in attempting to predict the behavior of the many rather than the few is that the effect of the odd individual who behaves erratically also tends to be canceled out. If the social pressures require choices to be made not by one or two individuals but by many, the chances are greater that the final result will be determined by reactions to the pressures in accordance with logical calculations of enlightened self-interest. The situation is reminiscent of the scientist using Boyle's Law on the behavior of gases. Boyle's Law does not make it possible to tell how any particular molecule will respond to change in pressure and temperature—the movement of any particular molecule might be entirely erratic. But it does make it possible to tell how the collectivity of molecules, the total volume of the gas, will respond.

If in a particular situation a number of these conditions and social pressures are all working in the same direction, if there are also a large number of individuals whose choices are pertinent to the outcome of the situation by whom these pressures are felt, and if the likelihood is high that the pressures will continue for a substantial period of time, a prediction can be made with some confidence. In the case of Tocqueville's prediction on the abolition of slavery, for example, the pressures he catalogued were all in the same direction. Slavery no longer made economic sense; Christianity and the rising philosophies of democracy were both against it; and the South was the last place in the civilized world that continued to cling to the institution of slavery and thus was isolated. Sooner or later, "by the act of the master or the will of the slave," Tocqueville could predict with great confidence, "It will cease."

The fewer the number of individuals whose choices are determining, the more difficult is the prediction. Tocqueville was making the same point, in effect, when he predicted that prejudice would increase after the abolition of slavery and argued that this was even more certain because the United States was a democracy—that an "isolated individual may surmount the prejudices of his religion, of his country, or of his race; and if this individual is a king, he may effect surprising changes in society; but a whole people cannot rise, as it were, above itself." And the trouble is that many of the decisions of governments, and especially those of war and peace, are made by the few rather than the many.

There are circumstances, of course, when one might very confidently predict a particular war. War between the early Mohammedans and the Christians, for example, would undoubtedly have been predictable—principally because in addition to the other forces making for a clash, both sides were motivated by fanatical religious hatreds and both sides had doctrinaire commitments to the use of force, the Christians to the crusading martial spirit of "chivalry" and the Mohammedans to proselytizing by the sword. If Nazism had been less dependent on the particular personality of Hitler, the same might be said of it.

The rivalry between the Soviet Union and the United States, however, is more typical. An analysis of the pressures and tensions between the two at the end of World War II would certainly have permitted predicting the Cold War—as many observers and analysts did. But if at that time one attempted to predict whether the Cold War would at some point turn into a hot war, the problem became impossible. In the first place, although there were formidable pressures toward rivalry and hence a very high risk of war, there was nothing in the ideology of either the Communist world or the West that emphasized war as an instrument of policy for its own sake. Second, the pressures did not run all in the same direction, but were mixed. The closer the rivalry got to war, in fact, the more counterpressures developed. Finally, on both sides the decision for war or peace would not be made by the many over a long period of time, but by relatively few over a short period of time. Each one of these considerations made a prediction more difficult—whether predicting that the Cold War would turn into a hot war or that it would not.

The Purposes of Prediction and the Self-defeating Prophecy

But this, in turn, raises the question of the purposes of prediction. If the purpose of attempting prediction in the social affairs of men is to permit wiser and better-informed choices and policies, then being able to predict how the forces and pressures operate to create a situation such as the Cold War, which perpetuates a high risk of actual war, is still highly useful. Predicting the Cold War in fact induced an effort on both sides to develop policies designed to reduce the risks of war and to deter those on the opposite side who might be inclined in the direction of war. Whether or not the actual policies adopted in this particular case were the wisest ones may be something else again, but at least the purpose of prediction was served. A forecast of disaster that is self-*defeating* because it triggers preventive action can be the most useful prediction of all. Its only possible rival is a prediction of alternative futures cast so that we may by our actions in the present create the future we prefer.

Heuristic Devices

To recapitulate the argument up to this point, we have identified three basic modes of prediction: predictions based on a more or less "scientific" knowledge of causality; predictions based on the "same conditions, same results" approach; and predictions based on trends, extrapolations of no-change, steady-state, straight-line, whether up or down, and cyclical. We have also examined various techniques for using these different modes, and especially how one decides whether a trend will be altered or reversed—including the use of the concept of historical "turning points" and the device of "alternative futures." And we have examined some of the conditions in which predictions are more or less feasible, as, for example, whether the social and political pressures involved operate on a large or small number of individuals making choices, or over a long period of time or a short one.

So far, we have examined in some detail two of the four of Tocqueville's predictions that we picked for analysis: his prediction about the future power of Russia and the United States and his prediction about the relative power of the states and the federal government. And we looked at some aspects of his prediction about race relations and the possibilities of civil war. What about the remaining prediction, in which he anticipated Marx in foreseeing not only that industrialization would sweep all before it but that it would bring much injustice in its wake?

What Tocqueville did here is reminiscent of the achievements of the great discoverers in science, for it seems to be related to the role of implied assumption in obscuring insight. Newton took a large step forward when he suddenly realized that the pull of gravity might work in both directions, rather than just one, as everyone had assumed—that the earth and the apple pulled on each other. Einstein was led to the theory of relativity when he recognized that Newtonian physics was based on the implied assumptions that time and space were uniform and began to search for a theory that would hold if they were not. Freud, to take an example from the social sciences, recognized that the psychology of his day was based on the implied assumption that human behavior was conscious and deliberate, and turned to dreams in his search for a theory that would hold if it was not. The problem is that it is easy enough to say that major discoveries are often made by identifying implied assumptions, but if an assumption is only implied, it is quite a trick of insight to identify it—frequently, it seems, requiring genius!

Both the genius and more ordinary mortals attempting systematic prediction presumably keep asking themselves what the implied assumptions might be, what hidden forces might be operating, or what unrecognized relationships might be at work—all of which would presumably add to the knowledge of causality and hence to the ability to predict. The mechanics of insight that the genius brings to the making of prediction remain obscure. But in applying existing knowledge to speculation about the future, both the genius and the more ordinary investigator have used a variety of heuristic devices—devices that aid in discovery, that stimulate thinking, or that sensitize the investigator to unrecognized relationships or hidden social and political forces, such as a potential "turning point." Some of these heuristic devices have been little more than analogies, so false as to be more dangerous than useful. For example, in social affairs many an analyst has been tempted by the analogy of the life cycle—birth, childhood, adolescence, adulthood, and old age. Civilizations, societies, or nation-states are seen as going through a dependent, vulnerable childhood; an aggressive adolescence; a peaceful, stable maturity; and the decay and degeneration of old age. Now it may be that on one occasion or another a useful hypothesis came out of using this kind of false analogy, but if so, it was simply happenstance. Nations are not organisms. They have neither nervous systems nor life of their own beyond those of the men and women who make them up, and using analogies to organisms, which do have nervous systems and life, seems bound in the end to confuse more than it can possibly enlighten.

Checklists

Of the legitimate heuristic devices, the simplest and most common is probably the checklist, simply a catalogue of all the factors, conditions, or pressures that brought about the current situation and those that are necessary to maintain it. The investigator can then examine each factor in turn in an effort to find out how it might change and thus work to affect the total situation.[34] Tocqueville's long list of factors—climate, topography, the political and judicial systems, the institution of slavery, and the structure of the economy—was just such a checklist. Systematically he examined how each factor, condition, or pressure had worked

[34] This is the device explicitly described by Edmund Leach as the method he used in his *Futuribles* study, "The Political Future of Burma," *Futuribles: Studies in Conjecture*, ed. Bertrand de Jouvenel (Geneva: Droz, 1963).

to create the present, how it might change in the future, and what the effect would be on the total system. The utility of the checklist device is not great, but it does have its place. Although Tocqueville would probably have found it impossible to overlook the institution of slavery, for example, such a checklist would ensure that he would have to consider it, estimate the probability that it would come to an end, and be sensitive to the very substantial changes that would ensue as a consequence. A checklist like this would force an investigator in the 1930s, for example, to consider colonialism even if he accepted it as a God-given part of world society. It would then be hard for him to escape seeing the high probability that it would soon end, and the enormous changes that could be predicted as a consequence.

A second utility of this particular form of checklist, one that thinks of the future as the progression of a set of separate factors working through time, is that it encourages the analyst to weave back and forth from past to present to future in a search for causal relationships and thus gives him both perspective and a better chance for discovering new factors and unknown causalities.

The "Overriding Problem"

Another heuristic device is what Daniel Bell has called the "overriding problem."[35] As one example, Bell cites a study of the breakdown of the Weimar Republic that puts the government's inability to solve the unemployment problem in this overriding, central position. For another example, he cites a study of the political future of Pakistan (before the secession of Bangladesh) that puts in the overriding position the problem of finding a national identity in a state that is divided territorially, ethnically, and linguistically, and whose only unifying element is a common religion.[36] It could be argued that in his analysis of the South, Tocqueville treated slavery as an "overriding problem" that would determine the future of the region. As to the utility of the concept, it is undoubtedly true that in some societies at certain

[35] "Twelve Modes of Prediction," *Daedalus* (Summer 1964).
[36] Karl D. Bracher, *Die Auflösung der Weimar Republik* (Stuttgart, 1957); and Leicester Webb, "Pakistan's Political Future," *Futuribles* op. cit.

periods, the future of the society has hung upon the solution of one central, overriding problem and that predicting the future of that society meant giving that problem its central position. But the circumstances would seem to be too rare for this particular heuristic device to have very extensive utility.

Scenarios

Although researchers at "think tanks" such as RAND and the Hudson Institute frequently use the word scenario interchangeably with "alternative futures," which were described above, the "scenario" does seem logically distinguishable as a separate heuristic technique. A scenario is an attempt to postulate and construct a series of plausible events, one leading to another, that will eventuate in a markedly different future situation than indicated by current trends. Herman Kahn, for example, uses a scenario to show both the possibility of a world in which the majority of larger powers have nuclear weapons and something of the nature of such a world by describing a plausible series of events by which Japan is led to acquire nuclear weapons, followed by West Germany, Italy, Sweden, Switzerland, and India.[37] Interestingly enough, it was a scenariolike device that Tocqueville used in his speculation, already described, about the possibility of a black nation emerging along the Gulf of Mexico. He postulated, to repeat, first a break between the South and the federal government that would destroy the possibility of aid from the North; second, a black rebellion; and finally, the whites gradually retiring, as the Moors did from Spain.

If the utility of the checklist approach is that it makes the investigator look at past trends in order to get at future ones, the "scenario" approach serves two slightly different purposes. One is to stimulate the imagination to encompass a future possibility that is strange or unwelcome, such as an all-nuclear world. The second is to help in weighing the probabilities of the alternative future envisaged. If a series of plausible events cannot be imagined that would bring about the alternative world, the probability of such a world coming to pass will presumably be small.

[37] Kahn and Wiener, *The Year 2000*, pp. 242–47.

Tocqueville's "Preponderant Fact"

It was a heuristic device, one of his own making, that led Tocqueville to his prediction that industrialization would sweep all before it. He used the device very explicitly, and he put it central to his whole method of forecasting. Superficially it seems similar to the "overriding problem" device, but it is actually quite different. "Upon close inspection," he wrote, "it will be seen that there is in every age some peculiar and preponderant fact with which all others are connected; this fact almost always gives birth to some pregnant idea or some ruling passion, which attracts to itself and bears away in its course all the feelings and opinions of the time; it is like a great stream towards which each of the neighboring rivulets seem to flow."[38]

In Tocqueville's analysis of American society this "preponderant fact" was what he called "equality of condition." To him, it was central. The opening words of *Democracy in America* deal with it:

> Among the novel objects that attracted my attention during my stay in the United States, nothing struck me more forcibly than the general equality of condition among the people. I readily discovered the prodigious influence that this primary fact exercises on the whole course of society; it gives a peculiar direction to public opinion and a peculiar tenor to the laws; it imparts new maxims to the governing authorities and peculiar habits to the governed.
>
> I soon perceived that the influence of this fact extends far beyond the political character and the laws of the country, and that it has no less effect on civil society than on the government; it creates opinions, gives birth to new sentiments, founds novel customs, and modifies whatever it does not produce. The more I advanced in the study of American society, the more I perceived that this equality of condition is the fundamental fact from which all others seem to be derived and

[38] *Democracy in America*, Vol. 2, p. 100.

the central point at which all my observations constantly ter-
minated.[39]

Equality of Condition and the Industrialization Prediction

What Tocqueville meant by "equality of condition" was essentially the democratic ideal—not so much the fact of equality as
the aspiration for equality, equality in all aspects of life. Tocqueville became convinced through his personal observations that
this ideal, this aspiration, was universally held in America, by
all men in all strata of society. Second, it was equally clear that
the facts of social life fell far short of the ideal. And here was
what Tocqueville perceived would be the central dynamic of
American society for ages to come—the tension between the universally held ideal of equality and its imperfect realization.

This notion of "equality of condition" and its dynamics led
Tocqueville to see the democratic revolution as the *cause* of the
Industrial Revolution rather than its effect. "As the conditions of
men constituting the nation become more and more equal, the
demand for manufactured commodities becomes more general
and extensive . . ."[40] He also saw a reciprocating dynamic in
the process. In an aristocracy, one's position in society was fixed,
and ambition had no point. In a society in which equality is the
universal aspiration and is to some small extent approximated in
reality, the opposite is true. The effect, Tocqueville argued, is to
drive more and more people into commerce and manufacturing,
which in turn creates a greater demand for manufactured goods:

> Suppose an active, enlightened, and free man, enjoying a
> competency, but full of desires; he is too poor to live in idleness,
> he is rich enough to feel himself protected from the immediate
> fear of want, and he thinks how he can better his condition.
> This man has conceived a taste for physical gratifactions,
> which thousands of his fellow men around him indulge in; he
> has himself begun to enjoy these pleasures, and he is eager to
> increase his means of satisfying these tastes more completely.
> But life is slipping away, time is urgent; to what is he to turn?

[39] Vol. 1, p. 3.
[40] Vol. 2, pp. 169–70.

The cultivation of the ground promises an almost certain result to his exertions, but a slow one; men are not enriched by it without patience and toil. Agriculture is therefore only suited to those who already have great superfluous wealth or to those whose penury bids them seek only a bare subsistence. The choice of such a man as we have supposed is soon made; he sells his plot of ground, leaves his dwelling, and embarks on some hazardous but lucrative calling.

Democratic communities abound in men of this kind; and in proportion as the equality of conditions becomes greater, their multitude increases. Thus, democracy not only swells the number of working-men, but leads men to prefer one kind of labor to another; and while it diverts them from agriculture, it encourages their tastes for commerce and manufactures.[41]

And as Tocqueville pondered these developments, he also foresaw that industrialization would lead to exploitation and degradation of the workers and the possibility, on which he warned the "friends of democracy" to keep their eyes anxiously fixed, that industrialization would permit the rise of a new "manufacturing aristocracy." Industrialization, Tocqueville reasoned, depended on specialization of function. But specialization and division of labor was also an evil. "When a workman is unceasingly and exclusively engaged in the fabrication of one thing, he ultimately does his work with singular dexterity; but at the same time he loses the general faculty of applying his mind to the direction of the work. He every day becomes more adroit and less industrious; so that it may be said of him that in proportion as the workman improves, the man is degraded. What can be expected of a man who has spent twenty years of his life in making heads for pins?"[42] At the same time, as more and more men go into industry and can afford to buy manufactured goods, Tocqueville argued, and as a greater and greater variety of goods are mass-produced rather than hand-crafted and become cheap enough to be within the range of more and more people, the opportunity for capital and entrepreneurs is also vastly increased. "Hence

[41] Ibid., pp. 163–64.
[42] Ibid., p. 168.

there are every day more men of great opulence and education who devote their wealth and knowledge to manufactures and who seek, by opening large establishments and by a strict division of labor, to meet the fresh demands which are made on all sides. Thus, in proportion as the mass of the nation turns to democracy, that particular class which is engaged in manufacture becomes more aristocratic."

Tocqueville's final judgment on this latter point, the possible rise of a "manufacturing aristocracy," was a warning, essentially a policy recommendation:

> I am of the opinion, on the whole, that the manufacturing aristocracy which is growing up under our eyes is one of the harshest that ever existed in the world; but at the same time it is one of the most confined and least dangerous. Nevertheless . . . if ever a permanent inequality of conditions and aristocracy again penetrates into the world, it may be predicted that this is the gate by which they will enter.[43]

Race Relations

In the case of Tocqueville's predictions about relations between blacks and whites, "equality of condition" also played a central role, although other concepts were also crucial. In his forecast that racism would increase after the abolition of slavery, for example, he relied more on his knowledge of how prejudice had worked in history, on his personal experience with prejudice among the European aristocracy, as well as on his first-hand observations in America. Where "equality of condition" was key was in his very specific prediction that the black would "revolt at being deprived of his civil rights," which Tocqueville was convinced would happen following abolition, even if the black did not successfully revolt under slavery. "Men are more forcibly struck," to repeat the words quoted earlier, "by those inequalities which exist within the same class than those which may be noted between different classes. One can understand slavery, but how allow several millions of citizens to exist under a load of

[43] Ibid., pp. 170–71.

eternal infamy and hereditary wretchedness?" Notice also that Tocqueville not only predicted that the blacks would revolt, but that much of their political leverage would come from the guilt felt by the whites, who also believed in the "equality of condition."

Thus it was also the notion of "equality of condition" that led him to his final judgment: "If ever America undergoes great revolutions, they will be brought about by the presence of the black race on the soil of the United States; that is to say, they will owe their origin not to the equality, but to the inequality of condition."[44]

Tocqueville's Qualifications on the Concept

Thus Tocqueville uses the notion of "equality of condition" to predict many different and unlikely aspects of future American society, and with considerable success. Even so, he explicitly denies that he held to a monistic, single-cause theory. "Because I attribute so many different effects to the principle of equality, it might be inferred that I consider this principle as the only cause of everything that takes place in our day. This would be attributing to me a very narrow view of things."[45] And he goes on to argue that the nature of the country, the origin of its people, their religion, and their acquired knowledge all exercise an immense influence on American modes of thought and feeling quite independent of the "equality of condition." And in fairness, throughout his book, as we have seen, his analysis draws on many different causalities.

Tocqueville's Ideas and Predictions Today

What can be said of the utility of Tocqueville's ideas for the problem of making predictions in our own day? To make a judgment it is necessary first to distinguish between the notion, of "equality of condition" and Tocqueville's idea that there is "in every age some preponderant fact with which all others are connected." The notion of "equality of condition" is a causality. It

44 Ibid., p. 270.
45 Ibid., p. v.

possesses a dynamism working toward change—the tension between the universally held belief in equality in all things and the reality of inequality. The idea of a "preponderant fact" is a heuristic device. Tocqueville is saying that all societies are integrated around some central notion that can explain the interrelationships of all the other institutions and manifestations of the society. "Find the central fact and you will understand the society," is what he is saying. If he is right, the notion of a "preponderant fact" is an almost classic example of a heuristic device.

Tocqueville and Myrdal: A Comparison

Considering "equality of condition" first, it seems clear that Tocqueville hit upon at least a crude form of one of the more important factors shaping American society. On this point, it is useful to consider for comparison Gunnar Myrdal's monumental study of racial relations in America, *An American Dilemma.*[46]

"Every social study," Myrdal writes, "must have its center in an investigation of people's conflicting valuations and their opportune beliefs."[47] And at the absolute center of Myrdal's analysis is the contention that such a set of values and attitudes exists in the United States that is not only widely shared in the society, but incorporated into basic law and custom. Myrdal calls it the "American Creed."

Every society has some such set of values and attitudes, but in America, Myrdal argues, it is particularly prominent. America, he says, "compared to every other country in Western civilization, large or small, has the *most explicitly expressed* system of

[46] Myrdal, incidentally, confirms in a more "scientific" way our more impressionistic conclusions not only that Tocqueville's predictions were in several important instances correct, but that the dynamism was what he perceived it to be. One example is the rise of racial prejudice following abolition, and another is the effect of slavery and racism on what Tocqueville called the "manners" of the South, i.e., personality structure and lifestyle in social terms. It is also interesting that Myrdal also made some predictions of his own that are now, some thirty years later, clearly turning out to have been correct. The most important of these was very similar to Tocqueville's prediction that the black would revolt against the deprivation of civil rights following abolition—that *"not since Reconstruction has there been more reason to anticipate fundamental changes in American race relations, changes which will involve a development toward the American ideals."* See Gunnar Myrdal, *An American Dilemma: The Negro Problem and Modern Democracy* (New York, 1944), p. xix, for the quotation (Myrdal's emphasis), and Chapters 2, 4, 20, and 21 for confirmation of Tocqueville's predictions.
[47] Ibid., p. l.

general ideas in reference to human interrelations."[48] In America, too, the commitment to the set of values and attitudes, in emotional and moral terms, is deeper. The most striking thing about America, Myrdal points out, is its heterogeneity, its dissimilarities and chaotic unrest. "Still," he goes on to argue, "there is evidently a strong unity in this nation and a basic homogeneity and stability in its valuations. Americans of all national origins, classes, regions, creeds, and colors, have something in common: a social *ethos*, a political creed. It is difficult to avoid the judgment that this 'American Creed' is the cement in the structure of this great and disparate nation."[49]

What makes this concept of the "American Creed" so useful to Myrdal in analyzing the position of the black in American society and in making predictions about him is not only the fact that it is central to the society but that it involves a causal dynamic. The creed sets extraordinarily high goals, yet the emotional commitment is so deep that failure to meet them sets up feelings of guilt, psychological vulnerability, and leads progressively to social unrest and so ultimately to a society in which change is built-in. Relating all this to the position of the black, Myrdal writes:

The American Negro problem is a problem in the heart of the American. It is there that the interracial tension has its focus. It is there that the decisive struggle goes on. This is the central viewpoint of this treatise. Though our study includes economic, social, and political race relations, at bottom our problem is the moral dilemma of the American—the conflict between his moral valuations on various levels of consciousness and generality. The "American Dilemma," referred to in the title of this book, is the ever-raging conflict between, on the one hand, the valuations preserved on the general plane which we shall call the "American Creed," where the American thinks, talks, and acts under the influence of high national and Christian precepts, and, on the other hand, the valuations on specific planes of individual and group living, where personal and local interests; economic, social, and sexual jealousies; con-

48 Ibid., p. 3.
49 Ibid.

siderations of community prestige and conformity; group prejudice against particular persons or types of people; and all
sorts of miscellaneous wants, impulses, and habits dominate
his outlook.[50]

The *mechanism* of this dynamic, Myrdal believes, works
through the great institutional structures like the church, the
school, the university, the foundation, the trade union, and the
state itself. These institutions accommodate to local interests and
prejudices, but at the same time they manifest a pertinacity in
adhering to the ideals of the creed and a reluctance to deny
them in a formal, collective way through the institution. Thus individuals acting through the school, the church, and the legislature end up slightly above the prejudice median of the individuals acting as individuals. "When the man in the street acts
through his orderly collective bodies," Myrdal writes, "he acts
more as an American, as a Christian, and as a humanitarian than
if he were acting independently. He thus shapes social controls
which are going to condition even himself."[51]

Myrdal describes the content of the "American Creed" in
terms of the personality it produces. The American is moralistic,
and "moral-conscious." He is the opposite of a cynic. Although
rationalistic and pragmatic, he is a true believer—a sort of practical idealist. He believes in the dignity of the individual and the
perfectibility of mankind. Myrdal develops the content of the
"Creed" in considerable detail, examining in the process both the
historical and philosophical roots of the "Creed," but for our
purposes here, the point to note is that "equality" is the central
concept. "For practical purposes," Myrdal writes, "the main
norms of the American Creed as usually pronounced are centered
in the belief of equality and in the right to liberty."[52] And of the
two, equality is first:

Liberty, in a sense, was easiest to reach. It is a vague ideal:
everything turns around *whose* liberty is preserved, to *what*

[50] Ibid., p. xlvii.
[51] Ibid., p. 80.
[52] Ibid., p. 8.

extent and *in what direction.* In society liberty for one may mean the suppression of liberty for others. The result of competition will be determined by who got a head start and who is handicapped. In America as everywhere else—and sometimes, perhaps, on the average, a little more ruthlessly—liberty often provided an opportunity for the stronger to rob the weaker. Against this, the equalitarianism in the Creed has been persistently revolting. The struggle is far from ended. The reason why American liberty was not more dangerous to equality was, of course, the open frontier and the free land. When opportunity became bounded in the last generation, the inherent conflict between equality and liberty flared up. Equality is slowly winning.[53]

It is clear, in sum, that in "equality of condition" Tocqueville hit upon a cruder version of Myrdal's concept of the "American Creed," and that Tocqueville sensed some of the dynamism that Myrdal makes more explicit. And Myrdal would agree with Tocqueville that the dynamic here applies to democracies in general.[54]

With his notion of "equality of condition," Tocqueville, very much ahead of his time, sensed a causality that anticipated the work of Freud, Max Weber, and a long line of those that have followed them. With *his* concept of the "American Creed," Myrdal was applying, as well as contributing to, this body of knowledge stemming from both Freud and Weber to the effect that value and attitude systems, which form the reference frame in the integration of personality, are a central causality in the social affairs of men.

So much, then, for "equality of condition" as a causality. What of the more general heuristic device, of which Tocqueville thought that "equality of condition" was simply one example? In terms of the way that Tocqueville stated it—that there is "in every age some peculiar and preponderant fact with which all others are connected"—the notion seems to be obvious nonsense. A particular society may on some occasion find itself dominated by one single, preponderant fact, but it would be rare. And the

[53] Ibid., p. 9. Myrdal's emphases.
[54] Ibid., p. 25.

truth is that although "equality of condition" was certainly central to Tocqueville's analysis, he quite successfully used concepts and ideas that were totally unrelated to "equality of condition." But if we ignore Tocqueville's formulation of the heuristic device he used and concentrate on the essential characteristics that made "equality of condition" such a useful analytical concept, we might still find something instructive.

First of all, "equality of condition" had a built-in dynamic. As we have seen, it was in tension with society as society existed. Since the ideal was so distant from the reality, a commitment to the notion of equality would require movement in the society—indeed, revolutionary movement. "Equality of condition" was a continual pushing impetus for change in society. What is more, the mechanism for change also existed. Technology and industrialization had reached a stage so that the individual had an option other than agriculture and the traditional crafts through which he could better himself. And the democratic form of government and the other institutions of society in the United States provided the other mechanisms through which change could be wrought, however slowly, as suggested in Myrdal's analysis of the more narrow question of racial prejudice. Thus any heuristic technique ought to focus particularly on looking for forces with this kind of built-in dynamic, for forces that are in tension with certain aspects of things as they are and that have at hand mechanisms through which the forces of change can work.

Moreover, the need for a heuristic technique of some kind lies in the fact that such a dynamic is more often hidden and unrecognized—a "subversive causality," so to speak, working beneath the surface, inexorable and deep, like an undertow.[55] An example is the beginnings of modern science. "Louis XIV dazzles Europe," writes Daniel Halevy, "but alongside him, out of his sight and grasp, [are] the forces which will determine the future: the event of the 17th century is not the grandeur of Versailles, it is the beginnings of a knowledge which will change the world."[56]

But notice that there is one outstanding characteristic of

[55] The phrase "subversive causality" is Michel Massenet's. See his "Methods of Forecasting in the Social Sciences," Commission on the Year 2000, American Academy of Arts and Sciences.
[56] As quoted by Massenet, ibid.

"equality of condition" and the implied heuristic device that Tocqueville was using—a characteristic that makes prediction really possible and feasible. The characteristic is that the "subversive force" or undertow that one is looking for already exists. It is established and operating even though its importance or even its existence may not yet be generally recognized or fully comprehended. To make predictions on the basis of "equality of condition" did not require Tocqueville to anticipate something that had yet to appear on earth. What it required him to do—or permitted him to do, once he had recognized its importance—was to extrapolate the further consequences of a dynamic that had not yet run its course or wrought its full effects. Take the example of atomic energy. The heuristic notion here does not help a forecaster to predict the advent of the scientific knowledge needed to harness atomic energy. What it does is to call on him to recognize that a new social dynamic has begun to operate the minute that fission is achieved in the laboratory and to set him to work exploring the further consequences. Or, to take an example from social affairs, this heuristic notion does not help a Tocqueville visiting Jerusalem in the first century B.C. to predict the birth of Christ or the advent of Christianity. But it does call upon a Tocqueville visiting Rome in the third century A.D., and certainly in the fourth when the Emperor Constantine himself turned to the new religion, to recognize that Christianity was a social dynamic with fateful consequences for the Roman Empire and the whole of Western civilization.

"Equality of condition," to repeat, already existed as a force in that it was a central part of a value and attitude system that was widely accepted in the society. What made it so useful in predicting was the fact that it had not yet fulfilled its dynamic or produced its full effects. It was a causality in process.

And this, of course, is what made prediction feasible and also what made it seem so profound and prescient. The heuristic device was to search for and be sensitive to these in-process, existing but unfulfilled causalities. What made prediction so impressive was the fact that the forces were an undertow, by and large unperceived in any conscious or deliberate way by contemporaries or accepted without anyone bothering to ask about their ultimate consequences, like the failure to ask about the consequences of the mass decision of the 1930s to seek a separate dwelling and a private automobile. What made prediction successful was the dynamic, the fact that the causality had yet to work its full effects. Nothing really had to be predicted that did not already exist in embryonic form—what one looked for, in Michel Massenet's suggestive phrase, is the "future crouching in the present."

The task of prediction, then, is not completely impossible, even though full "scientific" knowledge in social affairs is limited. Much of the future will remain unknowable. But enough can be usefully done to divine the future to make the task worth doing. One can apply what "scientific" knowledge of causality that we have available. One can extrapolate trends, and one can hopefully make shrewd guesses as to which trends will change and how. One can apply experience and the principle of "same conditions, same results" and make the guesses somewhat shrewder. One can look for "turning points" and, when necessary, fall back on the device of offering "alternative futures." One can weight the forces at work in various ways, such as by determining whether they operate on a large or small number of individuals making choices or over long or short periods of time. And finally, one can quite deliberately search for in-process, unfulfilled dynamics—for the "future crouching in the present." And from all this, perhaps enough of the outline of the future world can be discerned to make our own actions today, our posture and our policy, at least a modicum more intelligent.

ROGER HILSMAN

Hamburg Cove
Lyme, Connecticut

Morningside Heights
New York City, New York

Part I

THE UNITED STATES: TRAJECTORY TO
TOMORROW

CHAPTER 1

The Superindustrial Society

THE KEY TO social forecasting is to find the "future crouching in the present," a central dynamic that is established and operating but has not yet run its course or wrought its full effects.[1] The trick is recognizing the presence of such a dynamic, for it is most likely to be unobtrusive and unnoticed—a subversive causality. An example is modern science. "Louis XIV dazzles Europe," writes Daniel Halevy, "but alongside him, out of his sight and grasp, the forces which will determine the future: the event of the 17th century is not the grandeur of Versailles, it is the beginnings of a knowledge which will change the world." It would be unreasonable to ask a forecaster visiting Jerusalem in the first century B.C. to predict the birth of Christ, but it is not unreasonable to ask a forecaster visiting Rome in the fourth century A.D., after the Emperor Constantine himself turned to the new religion, to recognize that Christianity was a social dynamic with fateful

[1] This notion of the "future crouching in the present" is more fully developed in the Preface.

consequences not only for the Roman Empire but for the whole of Western civilization.

For the modern, industrialized world, the central dynamic is hardly anonymous. It is not really an undertow beneath the surface but is obtrusive, even insistent. The future is not so much crouching in the present of the industrialized societies as pushing and shoving, hustling them along. What drives the industrialized societies are the fantastic achievements of technology, the fact that technology never goes backward but cumulates, and the ever-increasing affluence that it makes inevitable.

Consider what has been happening in the United States, the unhappy prototype of the industrialized countries and the guinea pig for the experimenting future. The United States is the first country in the history of the world to become a "service economy"—an economy in which more than half of those who work are engaged in something other than the production of food, housing, clothing, tools, or other tangible goods.[2] "In 1947, employment stood at approximately 58 million. Now it is about 73 million. Virtually all of this increase occurred in industries that provide services, e.g. banks, hospitals, retail stores, schools, government, and such. The number employed in the production of goods has been relatively stable: modest increases in manufacturing and construction have been offset by declines in agriculture and mining."[3]

One reason for this shift to service industries is rising income. A man can eat only so much. There is also a limit on the number of cars, houses, and other tangible goods he can effectively use.

Another reason is that productivity has grown more rapidly in the production of goods than in services, with few exceptions. A TV performer can entertain millions at one time, and even more millions by putting his performance on tape. But most people employed in services have not benefited very much from recent advances in technology. Despite some improvements in productivity, the doctor, the dentist, the retail clerk, and the repairman

[2] If domestic servants are counted, underdeveloped countries would also show a high service component. But when an industrialized country becomes a "service economy" domestic servants are a tiny part of those engaged in services.
[3] Victor R. Fuchs, "The First Service Economy," *The Public Interest*, No. 2 (Winter 1966).

can still serve only one person at a time. The increase in productivity brought about by the mechanization of the farm and automation in industry has not been matched in the service industries.

The Changing Nature of Work

Another change that has been happening before our eyes in the United States, one that is in part a consequence of the first, is in the kind of work that most people do. In the first place, in the United States, the heavy, brutalizing, mind-killing work that has always been the lot of some workers in every society that ever existed has been or shortly will be abolished. Machinery has taken over the heavy work. And things have gone much farther than that. For well over a decade now, white-collar workers have outnumbered blue-collar workers. Automation is taking over the operation of machinery.

Automation and computers, furthermore, are changing the nature of the work that both white- and blue-collar workers do. More and more of the dull, repetitive, routine work—tending a machine in the factory and such tasks as collating or addressing envelopes in the office—is being done electronically. In both the factory and the office, work has more of a personal character than before. The trend is toward providing opportunities to deal more with people, to develop personal skills, and to solve problems rather than follow standard routines.

Another aspect of the shift to a service economy and the changing nature of work is the disruption of the trend toward large organizations. For example, between 1962 and 1971 the number of people working for organizations of over 500 employees actually dropped from 26.4 per cent of the work force to 26.1 per cent.[4]

Base of Communications

A third change in the United States is in the ease of communications and the availability of information. In 1965, there were 478 telephones for every 1,000 Americans; in 1970 there were

[4] Bureau of the Census, County Survey (1962 and 1971), Table 1c.

583. By 1969, 95 per cent of American households had a TV set. Radios are now so numerous and cheap that they are no longer specialty items worth counting or even possible to count. An estimate, however, is that each household in America has at least 5. In 1970, well over 80 billion pieces of mail were delivered—411 for each person. Only newspaper circulation is dropping, a reflection of increased reliance on TV and radio for news. Newspaper circulation has dropped from 1.12 per family to .99.[5]

The Library of Congress keeps only about 1 out of every 5 books or other items that are published in the United States, yet it has over 16 million books and 72 million "pieces" on its shelves. It has been estimated that the total number of published titles has doubled every 20 years since the invention of movable type in 1450.[6] It has also been calculated that by the midsixties very nearly 1,000 new titles were being published in the world every day.[7] By 1950, the number of scientific periodicals being published each year was *alone* about 100,000.

Computers will have an impact even greater than the printing press. In 1950, only 10 to 15 computers were in use. By 1968, there were 40,000 in the United States, 15,000 in Western Europe, and 3,000 in Japan.[8] By 1975, there could be 100,000 computers at work worldwide. Digital communication between computers over land lines already exceeds human conversation in the United States; shortly, it is expected to exceed conversation across the Atlantic.[9] Performance figures are even more impressive. Taking as a measure of capacity the ratio of memory size and speed of processing, one authority asserts that, "beginning with the machines of 1940, there has been a thousandfold increase every 10 years. In 1950 capacity had increased by a factor of 1000 over 1940 levels; in 1960 by a factor of a million; and by 1970 it is expected to increase by a factor of a billion."[10]

Beginning in the 1960s, the Bank of America in California of-

[5] All figures are from *Statistical Abstract of the United States, 1971* (Washington, D.C.: U. S. Bureau of the Census, 1971).
[6] C. E. Black, *The Dynamics of Modernization* (New York, 1966), p. 12.
[7] Alvin Toffler, *Future Shock* (New York: Bantam Books, 1970), pp. 30–31.
[8] Charles R. DeCarlo, "Computer Technology," *Toward the Year 2018,* eds. Foreign Policy Association (New York, 1968).
[9] Zbigniew Brzezinski, *Between Two Ages: America's Role in the Technetronic Era* (New York, 1970), p. 32.
[10] DeCarlo, op. cit., p. 99.

fered a service to doctors and dentists that suggests the future for all business.[11] The doctor or dentist phones in charges and payments at the end of each day. The bank's computer then takes over, preparing monthly statements for each patient, mailing the bills, and sending final accounting reports to the doctor. It is clear that the banking industry will eventually be sufficiently computerized to make it possible to eliminate checks entirely, and to reduce money itself to a rather quaint convenience for use in purchasing odd items from small sellers or cranks who don't have a computer terminal on their premises. Each store could have a computer terminal to its bank and thence to the clearing house and the customer's bank. The amount of the sale could be transferred from the customer's to the store's account by the act of ringing up the sale on the computerized cash register. What is more, much shopping would not even require a visit to the store. Goods could be inspected by TV without leaving home.

It is well within the realm of possibility to transfer all the information in the books, periodicals, and other materials in the Library of Congress to computers (and the information could then be stored in the room now containing the card catalogue). Any office, school, or home could have a terminal linked to the central computer, and all of its information would be instantly available. Any of the material could be reproduced on the terminal screen or by means of a high-speed printout. Bibliographic service by computer could give annotated comments, or the computer could search for and reproduce relevant material from books touching only peripherally on the topic being researched. The computer could even test certain kinds of hypotheses against the information stored in the library, eliminating one of the traditional bread-and-butter jobs of graduate students.

Increased Rate of Change

The fourth change is in the rate of change itself and the fact that change is now sought deliberately, planned for, and cre-

[11] Paul Armer, "Computer Aspects of Technological Change, Automation, and Economic Progress," in Appendix, Vol. 1, *The Outlook for Technological Change and Employment* to National Commission on Technology, Automation, and Economic Progress, *Technology and the American Economy* (Washington, D.C.: U. S. Government Printing Office, 1966).

ated. Modern man—Homo sapiens—has been around for about 40,000 years. Most of that time his "means of production" was hunting and gathering. Eight thousand years ago came the first agricultural economy; 150 years ago the first industrial economy; and 10 years ago the first service economy. In energy, man depended on his own musclepower for most of the 40,000 years. Animal muscle began to be used 8,000 years ago. Coal first came into use in China 4,000 years ago, and the Greeks and biblical peoples also used it. But it did not come into general use as a source of energy until about 150 years ago. Oil became important only about 100 years ago, and the first nuclear reactor used as a source of power went into operation in England in 1956. In the field of transportation, man traveled on foot at about 3 to 5 miles an hour most of those first 40,000 years; 8,000 years ago he started riding on horses and camels at speeds of about 10 miles an hour for long distances; 5,000 years ago he invented sailing ships, which got him up to 12 to 14 miles an hour; 150 years ago came the railroad, which eventually reached average speeds of 100 miles an hour; and 75 years ago came the automobile, with average speeds of about 75 miles an hour, except in traffic jams and during periods of fuel shortage! Propeller aircraft for passenger traffic came into general use just over 30 years ago with speeds of about 300 miles per hour, and jet aircraft, with speeds of 600 miles per hour, came into general use just over 15 years ago. The first moon rocket was in 1969, and it had a speed of 18,000 miles per hour.

Most of these changes came about as the result of accident or inspired tinkering. More recently, change has come as the result of deliberate planning and a massive effort at research and development. The most vivid example is the development of the atomic bomb through the 2-billion-dollar Manhattan Project. Increasingly, new discoveries and new inventions will come not through happy accidents—serendipity—but as the result of such planned, deliberate efforts.

Rising Per Capita Income

The final point concerns income. The per capita national income of the United States in 1970 was about $4,600 in 1970 dollars and

about $3,600 in constant, 1965 dollars. We are all terribly con-
scious today of the misery of the poor in the ghettos, in backward, rural areas, and among the Chicanos and the Indians. Yet
an official government report estimates that it would take transfer
payments of only $10 billion more than current programs, such as
Social Security and welfare, to eliminate poverty as it is officially
defined—about a third of what was spent in Vietnam every year
from 1965 to 1970.[12]

This, then, is where the United States is today. But it seems
likely that these trends will continue or even accelerate. If so, it
is entirely possible that in the United States, national income
will be as much as $12,000 per person in 1965 dollars by the year
2000 and as much as $25,000 per person 25 years later. Everyone,
in effect, could live at a level available today only to a millionaire.

Changes in Attitudes and Values

Anyone who reflects on these figures begins to wonder: May
not such dramatic changes themselves produce still further
changes—in values, in attitudes, and in the very structure of society? The past, certainly, suggests that the consequences may
be far-reaching. In the traditional agricultural society about 85
per cent of the work force were farmers. In a highly industrialized society like the United States, fewer than 5 per cent are. In
an agricultural society, the pattern of life is rural, while in an industrial society it is urban. But the most dramatic changes are
not so much these as those in values, attitudes, and the structure
of society.

In the transformation from agricultural to industrial society,
the most obvious change in attitudes was that toward time. In an
agricultural society the rhythm of work is determined by the
rhythm of nature. At the time of planting and the time of harvest,
work is intense and continuous. In other seasons the animals
have to be fed and the cows milked, but otherwise the days
could be filled with idleness or not, depending on the individual's preference. In a basically agricultural society, the same pat-

12 *Toward Balanced Growth: Quantity with Quality, Report of the National
Goals Research Staff* (Washington, D.C., 1970), p. 153.

tern prevailed in other kinds of work, including such manufacturing as there was. Cloth workers in England before the Industrial
Revolution, for example, were especially notorious for alternating
spells of frenzied work with bouts of drinking and long periods of
idleness.[13] Letters, documents, and publications of the early
years of industrialization in England are filled with complaints
about the difficulties of getting workers to come to work on time
and regularly. Even a primitive factory requires a team of workers, and the lack of punctuality and regularity not only made for
inefficiency but something close to chaos. It was not until the
1840s that these complaints began to drop off and an "increasing
regularity and reliability" was noticeable in workers.

All societies making the transition from the agricultural to the
industrial mode have the same problem. A classic description of
the problem in a Communist context is given in Arthur Koestler's
Darkness at Noon in a scene about the preparations for the 1938
purge trials. An NKVD interrogator, a man named Gletkin, is trying to persuade Rubashov, an Old Guard Bolshevik, to confess
to "industrial sabotage." If it isn't sabotage, Gletkin asks, what
does account for the sad state of Soviet industries?

> "Too low piece-work tariffs, slave-driving and barbaric dis-
> ciplinary measures," said Rubashov. "I know of several cases in
> my Trust in which workers were shot as *saboteurs* because of
> some trifling negligence caused by over-tiredness. If a man is
> two minutes late at clocking-in, he is fired, and a stamp is put
> in his identity-papers which makes it impossible for him to find
> work elsewhere."
>
> Gletkin looked at Rubashov with his usual expressionless
> gaze, and asked him, in his usual expressionless voice:
>
> "Were you given a watch as a boy?"
>
> Rubashov looked at him in astonishment. The most con-
> spicuous trait of the Neanderthal character was its absolute
> humorlessness or, more exactly, its lack of frivolity.
>
> "Don't you want to answer my question?" asked Gletkin.

[13] J. B. Schneewind, "Technology, ways of living, and values in 19th-century
England," *Values and the Future*, eds. Kurt Baier and Nicholas Rescher (New
York: The Free Press, 1969), pp. 128–29.

Certainly [I was given a watch]," said Rubashov, more and more astonished.

"How old were you when the watch was given you?"

"I don't quite know," said Rubashov; "eight or nine probably."

"I," said Gletkin in his usual correct voice, "was sixteen years old when I learnt that the hour was divided into minutes. In my village, when the peasants had to travel to town, they would go to the railway station at sunrise and lie down to sleep in the waiting-room until the train came, which was usually about midday; sometimes it only came in the evening or the next morning. These are the peasants who now work in our factories. For example, in my village is now the biggest steel-rail factory in the world. In the first year, the foremen would lie down to sleep between two emptyings of the blast furnace, until they were shot. In all other countries, the peasants had one or two hundred years to develop the habit of industrial precision and of the handling of machines. Here they only had ten years. If we did not sack them and shoot them for every trifle, the whole country would lie down to sleep in the factory yards until grass grew out of the chimneys and everything became as it was before."[14]

Koestler is wrong in thinking that peasants in the other developed countries had one or two hundred years to develop modern attitudes, and he is also wrong in thinking that the Soviet Union did the job in only ten. In spite of the draconian measures of the Stalinist period, the process of industrialization in the Soviet Union took about forty years—just about the same as in other countries, such as Japan. "Thus history's verdict on Russian Communism in its Stalinist form," writes one economic historian, "is not that all its outrages were too wicked to be borne; it is simply that they were unnecessary."[15] This may be, although it might also be argued that the miseries suffered by the workers in the early years of capitalism were no less onerous than those suffered by the workers under Stalin. The important point, however, is

[14] New York, 1941, pp. 224–25.
[15] John Strachey, "The Strangled Cry," *Encounter*, XV, No. 5 (November 1960), p. 7.

that attitudes and values did have to change, and fundamentally.

Changes in Motivation

Changes in attitudes toward time, regularity, and factory discipline in England in the early years of industrialization were accompanied by changes in motivation. In agricultural societies, workers are supposed to be content with their station in life, and as a result they were not responsive to wage incentives beyond subsistence. An incident illustrating this phenomenon was the trigger that launched Max Weber on his massive study of the great religions of the world and their effects on social life, the study that culminated in his thesis on the Protestant ethic and the rise of capitalism. He knew the owner of a small button factory in a remote village of Bavaria. To increase production, the owner instituted piecework wages, but, paradoxically, the peasant Catholic women who were the workers simply worked until they had earned the wage to which they had been accustomed and to which their needs had become adjusted and then went home.

Eventually, materialistic values became more important, and money did become a greater incentive. But it took time.

Also, social mobility became a reality. A man could hope to change, if not his own station in life, at least that of his children and his children's children. The rigid structure of feudal society began to disintegrate.

Rise of the Nuclear Family

Another consequence of the shift from agricultural to industrial society was on the family, its role, and its structure. In an agricultural society, the extended family tends to be the rule. In an industrial society, work is separated from family life, and the family becomes less dominant as the source of status and the determinant of values. "As the possibilities of geographic and social mobility, and the pressures toward it, increased, it became less and less likely that one would live, work, and raise a family where one's family had always done so; less likely therefore that one would form part of a continuous family group; and less likely that family skills, customs, trades or beliefs would be maintained."[16]

The extended family system declined, and the so-called nuclear family—man, wife, and children, with perhaps the grandparents at most—became the rule, and this had crucial consequences for the psychology of the individual and the integration of personality. For example, the Oedipus complex, which is presumed to be a normal and natural stage in the development of personality in societies based on the nuclear family, is apparently very rare in societies based on the extended family system.[17]

The Rise of Class Consciousness

Nor did the changes stop with the family. It is clear not only that industrialization was principally responsible for the disintegration of feudal forms and strata but that from it also flowed the development and spread of class consciousness in its modern form. In feudal times, the bourgeoisie were tiny in numbers and confined to the few larger towns and cities. The proletariat were virtually nonexistent. Society consisted of royalty, the aristocracy and landed gentry, priests and monks, and the peasant masses. It was a stratified society, to be sure, but the strata are better described by the word *orders*, in the feudal sense of ranks in the community, than by the word *classes*. Classes, in the modern sense of the word, arose with industrialization.

If all these changes in values, attitudes, and the structure of society came about as the secondary consequence of the transition from agricultural to industrial society, the uneasy expectation seems justified that the tide of technology and the ever-increasing level and spread of affluence will bring equally fundamental and far-reaching changes. What will mass affluence do to the traditional American values like freedom, equality, and justice? What will it do to the production-oriented and achievement-oriented values of the "industrial ethic"? As long ago as 1930, John Maynard Keynes glimpsed the possibility and voiced the concern. Pointing out that the economic problem, the struggle for subsistence, has always been the primary, most pressing prob-

[16] Schneewind, op. cit., p. 128.
[17] Margaret Mead, *Coming of Age in Samoa* (New York, 1939), p. 213.

lem for the human race, Keynes argued that if the economic problem is solved, then mankind would be deprived of its traditional purpose. "Will this be a benefit? If one believes at all in the real values of life, the prospect at least opens up the possibility of benefit. Yet I think with dread of the readjustment of the habits and instincts of the ordinary man, bred into him for countless generations, which he may be asked to discard within a few decades. . . . Thus for the first time since his creation man will be faced with his real, his permanent problem—how to use his freedom from pressing economic cares, how to occupy the leisure, which science and compound interest will have won for him, to live wisely and agreeably and well."[18]

Some of those who have begun to worry about what is happening to the developed world have called what seems to be emerging the "postindustrial" society, others have called it the "superindustrial" society, and one has even coined a new word for it, the "technetronic" society.[19] However, the thought—the awesome thought—is the same for all: at some point, industrialization, mechanization, and automation begin to be so complete as to constitute a society that is as fundamentally different from the industrial society we have known as that society was from the agricultural society that preceded it.

Black Militancy, Women's Liberation, and Student Unrest

Affluence, then, brought about by the cumulative effect of technology, is the dynamic, the future crouching in the present, to which we should pay most attention in searching for clues to the future shape of society in the developed world. What will it do to traditional values? Junk them, modify them, or transform them completely? What new values will affluence bring? At least some clues to what is happening to traditional values and attitudes, and hints of the nature of those still to emerge are inherent in three recent movements—all of which, I would argue, arise as a result of recent gains in affluence and in anticipation of those to

[18] "Economic Possibilities for Our Grandchildren (1930)," reprinted in Keynes' *Essays in Persuasion* (New York, 1963), pp. 366–67.
[19] Daniel Bell, "Notes on the Post-Industrial Society (I) and (II)," *The Public Interest*, No. 6 (Winter 1967) and No. 7 (Spring 1967); Brzezinski, op. cit.

come. What I have in mind are the new militancy of the blacks, especially, but also of the Chicanos and the Indians as well, the women's liberation movement, and the turmoil on the college campuses during the late 1960s and early 1970s.

CHAPTER 2

Clues to Value Changes: Black Militancy, Women's Liberation, and Student Unrest

WHY, AFTER ALL these years of second-class citizenship since the abolition of slavery, have blacks suddenly become militant? It seems obvious that greater prosperity—growing affluence—is the answer. When a minority group, held down by an array of different instruments of oppression, is barely subsisting, subsistence is about all they can worry about. But when most of a minority gets to the stage where minimum food, clothing, and housing are reasonably secure, civil rights become more and more important. At the same time, affluence also works on the majority. The ideals of America have always included prosperity for all and equality for all. But when there isn't enough to go around anyway, achieving the ideals is threatening to the jobs and security of part of the populace and patently hopeless to the rest. Inequality is accepted even by those who deplore it. Now for the first time the society has the economic means to achieve its ideals, and needs only the will to overcome its inertia. As the society comes closer and closer to solving the economic problem, various minority groups step forward to demand both their economic and their civil rights. The blacks have been the leaders, but the Indians, the Puerto Ricans, and the Mexican-Americans are close behind.

The major point here is that this demand on the part of blacks and other minorities does not represent a change in traditional American values but their reaffirmation. The research on attitudes among blacks overwhelmingly demonstrates that what the vast majority of blacks want is *"in"—in* to middle-class American values, *in* to middle-class American education, *in* to middle-class American prosperity, and *in* to middle-class American way of life.[1] Out of frustration and bitterness, some blacks develop desperate views and programs, such as certain factions of the Black Panthers have done. But in general the black community understands the reasons that some take such positions, but does not adopt them for its own.

None of this, of course, means that the black community would necessarily choose to blend inconspicuously into the white middle class if the black community ever is offered that opportunity. Many recognize the profound psychological insight expressed by Stokely Carmichael and Charles Hamilton in their book *Black Power*.[2] Their thesis is that before the black community can accept integration—indeed, before integration could possibly work —the blacks must attain equality as blacks, as a black community. It was on the basis of their blackness that they were oppressed, and it is on the basis of their blackness that they must achieve equality. Both blacks and whites must come to recognize

---

[1] In a vast literature, see especially the following: Edward Franklin Frazier, *Black Bourgoisie* (New York, 1952); Stokely Carmichael and Charles V. Hamilton, *Black Power: The Politics of Liberation in America* (New York, 1967); Oswald G. Villard, "The Objects of the National Association for the Advancement of Colored People," *The Black Man and the American Dream*, ed. June Sochen (Chicago, 1971); Richard F. America, Jr., "What Do You People Want?" *Harvard Business Review* (March–April 1969); Nathan Hare, Jr., " 'Black Power': Its Goals and Methods," *Black Viewpoints*, eds. Arthur C. Littleton and Mary W. Burger (New York, 1971); Bayard Rustin, "Toward Integration as a Goal," also in *Black Viewpoints;* Eli Ginzburg and Associates, *The Middle Class Negro in the White Man's World* (New York, 1967); Whitney M. Young, Jr., *To Be Equal* (New York, 1966); and Philip S. Foner, ed., *The Black Panthers Speak* (New York, 1970).

[2] Already cited above.

the achievements of blacks, that "black is beautiful," as an essential first step.

Tocqueville believed, as described in the Preface, that the white race would simply not be capable of overcoming their racial prejudice, ever. We can reject such total pessimism, but the consequences may be almost as bad if the white race is simply too slow in overcoming their prejudice—a possibility that experience over the century since emancipation indicates is possible. Great strides have been made in civil rights *legislation* in the past decade, but discrimination of a more subtle but very effective kind obviously continues. Since it is very, very obvious that black insistence on their rights will not diminish, but increase in the years ahead, what is the likely outcome?

An Independent Black Nation?

If white prejudice and discrimination is very slow to change, it is not inconceivable that another of Tocqueville's predictions may yet come true—the emergence of a separate and independent black nation from among the southern United States. The possible scenario begins with the population statistics of Mississippi, South Carolina, Louisiana, Alabama, and Georgia and voter registration. The 1970 census showed that 36.8 per cent of the population of Mississippi was black; 30.5 per cent of the population of South Carolina; 29.9 per cent of Louisiana; 26.4 per cent of Alabama; and 25.9 per cent of Georgia. As demonstrated by the experience of Charles Evers running as a black candidate for governor of Mississippi in 1971 and earlier experiences, such as the voter registration drive in Lowndes County, Alabama, described by Carmichael and Hamilton, registering black voters in the South and getting them to vote is not easy in the face of economic retaliation by white landowners and employers and the terror tactics of beatings, arson, bombings, and murder. But in time the blacks of these five states will be registered and will vote for black candidates if white candidates do not change their attitudes on race. If white prejudice declines, the South will see black officials elected partly with white votes, as Carl Stokes was elected mayor of Cleveland with a combination of black and white votes. If this happens, a long stride will have been taken toward building a society free of prejudice. But if white prejudice does not decline or declines too slowly, the tension between the races will increase and the future scenario will be bleak. It seems obvious that the blacks will not submit, but will grow increasingly militant in demanding their civil and other rights. The blacks in the South will in time become thoroughly politicized. They will register and they will vote. First, they will gain political control in small towns and counties where blacks are the majority, such as Lowndes County, which is 85 per cent black.

To continue the scenario, suppose that the blacks, having gained control in those counties, set about to develop them economically with the aid of capital from the North. Jobs will become available and opportunities increase in an environment favorable to blacks. Suppose a movement is then organized to encourage migration of blacks from the North. At the same time, if white prejudice remains undiminished, extremist black organizations can be expected to arise and to follow the examples they have learned from the whites on how to use terror. If the whites in the inner cities of the North have migrated to the suburbs to escape the black tide and in fear of "crime in the streets," there is no reason to believe that they would not also begin to drift away from a strife-torn, racially tense Southland. Black inmigration and white outmigration would combine to bring a shift in the population. Blacks would eventually achieve a majority, and this would in turn hasten the process.

It seems highly unlikely that prejudice among whites will be so hard and unbending as to bring about these developments, but if it is—and experience certainly gives little encouragement for optimism—then Tocqueville's prediction described in our Preface, about a separate and independent black nation arising in the South could conceivably come to pass. Blacks move south to escape white prejudice and to enjoy living in a land controlled by blacks; whites, like the Moors in Spain, retire by degrees to the North; blacks, finally come to control not only the political structure of whole states in the South, but increasingly the economic structure as well. Once control is achieved, harmony with the North might be established, and black-controlled states and white-controlled states could exist side by side. But if racial tension continued in the North, the black-controlled bloc of southern states would inevitably begin to think of secession. And if they did secede, it seems ever more likely that where Tocqueville was wrong before, he would on this occasion be right. Before the Civil War, Tocqueville predicted that if the South seceded, the North would not fight. As it turned out in 1861, the North did fight, but the next time it probably would not. For after what would then be a century and a half of racial turmoil and dissension, who in the North, among either the integrationists or the segregationists, would wish to preserve so mismatched a union?[3]

My own, admittedly personal instincts reject this scenario as being almost unthinkable, but such optimism may be little more than wishful thinking. It was always hoped that the essential goodness in men, their sense of justice and moral right, would eventually eliminate prejudice, especially as education came increasingly to all elements of society. Clearly these factors have worked to lessen prejudice among the more privileged and enlightened, but the results are still profoundly discouraging. If change is this slow, our scenario may turn out to be terrifyingly accurate.

The Dynamics of Affluence

When one searches for some new factor, some cause, social force, or dynamic that will hasten the process of eliminating prejudice, one finds only—again—affluence. In the past, in both the South and in northern cities, economic pressures have very clearly reinforced prejudice. In the South, Jim Crow legislation sought to exclude blacks from the more desirable jobs. In the North, union rules and more subtle devices accomplished many of the same results. Fear of falling property values also reinforced prejudice in the attempts to keep blacks from buying houses in white neighborhoods. Increasing affluence will at least remove this kind of economic reinforcement of prejudice. But this is only slight comfort: Economic pressures are only secondary factors in

[3] Another factor working in this same direction is the probable future attitudes toward the nation-state, which will be explored in succeeding chapters.

prejudice, and their removal can be the basis for only a modest degree of optimism.

Of one thing, however, we can be certain: the blacks and other minorities will achieve equality. If white prejudice diminishes rapidly, the differences between whites and blacks will someday go as unnoticed as the differences between blondes and brunettes, the tall and the short. To the extent that some blacks, Chicanos, or Indians do maintain a separate identity in a society that is finally free of racial prejudice, the motives will be their own desire to preserve the essential elements of their particular culture. The result will be neighborhoods of blacks, or other minorities, regarded in no way differently from Italian, German, or Irish neighborhoods today. In time intermarriage will erase them all, and all will merge into a new amalgam, a "race" that can only be described as American. On the other hand, if white prejudice proves resistant to sufficiently rapid change, tension, turmoil, and, increasingly, bloodshed will be the fate of all Americans. One or the other of Tocqueville's "alternative futures" will inevitably be the outcome. "If ever America undergoes great revolutions, they will be brought about by the presence of the black race on the soil of the United States; . . . they will owe their origin not to the equality but to the inequality of condition." In the face of this vision of racial civil war, the other alternative, far from being almost unthinkable, will seem a blessing to all: a separate and independent nation in the South, ruled by and for blacks.

But the one thing certain, to repeat, is that the blacks will achieve equality, one way or another. One may hope that equality will come sooner and peacefully rather than later and violently. But in this we can echo Tocqueville: Equality will prevail, hopefully by the act of the oppressor, but if not, by the will of the oppressed.

Women's Liberation

The second of the three recent movements sparked by increasiny affluence—but one whose final implications are more obscure—is the women's liberation movement.[4] Some of the leaders of the

[4] The literature of women's lib is becoming substantial, but the following are particularly noteworthy: Simone de Beauvoir, *The Second Sex* (New York: Knopf,

movement may have acted like termagants, and they may have exaggerated the exploitation women are subjected to, the degree of women's resentment and hatred of men, and the extent to which differences between the behavior of men and women are purely cultural. But at least three facts remain beyond challenge. The first is that women have indeed been exploited throughout history and women are exploited today. The second is that just as it is becoming feasible to eliminate poverty, it is also becoming feasible to rectify the exploitation of women, at least to the extent that economic factors are involved. And the third fact is that there are social forces working for a change in women's status and role quite apart from the activity emanating from the various organizations of "women's liberation."

As far as the facts of exploitation are concerned, there is no need to give details here on what is so well known. Women today in many industries are still paid less for the same kind and amount of work as men. There are obstacles to their being hired for the higher jobs in the hierarchy of most organizations or being promoted into them.

Other Factors Working to Free Women

The feasibility of eliminating the exploitation of women rests on more than simple affluence. In an industrial society, machines replace musclepower, human and animal, and the natural advantage men have in their greater physical strength is lessened. Today machines are being automated, and strength is even less necessary. Increasingly, women will be able to do any job that men can do. Second, the wife of the future will not necessarily have to stay home to care for the children. Day-care centers will not only do the job, but will probably give most children a richer experience and help them to better-developed personalities than most mothers could do working alone in their own homes. Indeed, a number of psychologists argue that "the monogamous

1953); Betty Friedan, *The Feminine Mystique* (New York: Norton, 1963); Kate Millet, *Sexual Politics* (Garden City, New York: Doubleday, 1970); Germaine Greer, *The Female Eunuch* (New York: McGraw-Hill, 1971); and Carolyn G. Heilbron, *Toward a Recognition of Androgyny* (New York: Knopf, 1973).

family . . . permanently scars the child by involving him in the intense, emotionally debilitating relationship between the parents."[5] As of 1970, there were more than 11.6 million working mothers in the United States, and more than 4 million of these had children under 6 years of age. Only 640,000 of these children were in day-care centers; the rest of the children had private arrangements with relatives, friends, or professional baby-sitters. But the trend is clear. Women increasingly want to work, and many have no alternative to day-care centers or prefer them.[6] An official Department of Labor estimate is that by 1985, the labor force will be 107.1 million and 39.4 million of these will be women.[7] This compares with 30 million out of 84 million in 1969, and 23 million out of 72 million in 1960. In fact, the trend may well accelerate.

Women, to sum up, will be able to do the work in physical terms, and day-care centers will give them the time to do it. Will they continue to want to? Certainly forces are operating that will lead them in this direction—that is, forces are operating that will make it necessary for them to find something to do, whether they call it a vacation or an avocation, other than care for the home and children.

Future Life Patterns for Women

The forces are as simple as they are powerful. The means to limit family size are already at hand—the pill, the loop, and the diaphragm—and they will improve rapidly in effectiveness. Increasingly, too, social pressure, especially in the developed countries, will mount to limit family size to two children. Indeed, the pressure may eventually take the form of legal restraints. Fears of the effects of explosive population growth may lead to legislation requiring prospective parents to obtain a license before they have a child. Day-care centers and preschool training will

[5] Myron Orleans and Florence Wolfson, "The Future of the Family," *The Futurist* (April 1970). See also Barrington Moore, Jr., *Reflections on the Causes of Human Misery and Upon Certain Proposals to Eliminate Them* (Boston: Beacon Press, 1972); and Bruno Bettelheim, *The Children of the Dream, Communal Child-Rearing and American Education* (New York: Macmillan, 1969).

[6] New York *Times* (November 30, 1970).

[7] U. S. Department of Labor, GPO 1970 *United States Manpower in the Nineteen Seventies.* See also New York *Times* (November 11, 1970).

reduce the time that a mother needs to be available to a child full-time to 2 years or less. Her whole family may thus take up no more than 5 years, full-time, of a typical woman's working life. At the same time, her working life will be much longer. Life expectancy in the United States increased from 49.2 years in 1900 to 70.1 years in 1970. The increase in working life was even more dramatic. Until the middle of the nineteenth century, life expectancy everywhere was 35 years or less, and working life was about 20 years. By 1900, working life was up to very close to 30 years in the United States; today, even with people going to work later, it has risen to about 45 years. In the immediate future better health care and clearly achievable advances in medicine will lengthen it even more. Also, it is easily possible that new discoveries in the process of aging may lead to fantastic extension of the normal life span—to life expectancies of, say, 120 years as the norm. But even without the fantastic, at the very minimum, women—and men— will be able to count on working lives of 50 to 60 years. If child care takes up only 5 of these years, what will a woman do with the rest of her life? It seems perfectly obvious that most women will do exactly what the men will do. Most will want more education, to make both their work and their leisure more meaningful. Most will want some kind of work career, to give them psychological satisfaction, higher income, and more independence. And most will want to develop avocations to enrich their leisure.

Implication

The major implication of these trends is that the cultural differences between men and women, between their roles and status, and between their lifestyles will tend to disappear. We see the signs of this today not only in the "women's liberation" movements and the increased numbers of women entering the labor market and the professions, but also in the enormously greater sexual freedom today as compared with not just a generation ago, but a mere decade ago.

The Future of the Nuclear Family

Does all this mean the end of the "nuclear family" as the basic unit of society? Certainly the incentives for marriage and raising a family will be fewer in number. In agricultural societies there was a strong economic incentive to have children. The more hands on the farm, the better off everyone was. Even in the early stages of industrial society, children provided a form of old-age insurance. All that has changed. To the extent that the economic factor is relevant at all, it provides a disincentive to having children.

The ego gratification of having the family line continued and the name perpetuated has been an incentive for having children in the past, but that, too, has weakened if the fact that fewer sons have their father's first name is valid evidence. Most of the trends—child-care centers, "women's liberation," greater sexual freedom, and greater security in society—seem to point to still further weakening of ego gratification as a motive for marrying and having children.

What is left? Children are necessary for the perpetuation of the species, but this means only that if the incentive for marriage and children becomes so low as to threaten the continued existence of society, society will have to find ways for the function to be performed other than through the nuclear family. "Test-tube babies" and government-run crèches are only two of a number of possibilities.

Two other possible incentives remain. One is that having children and performing the role of the parent are necessary for full psychological development and maturation. But this is questionable. We see around us and in history too many emotionally mature, creative, happy people who have neither married nor had children, to believe that the psychological function that marriage and having children perform cannot be provided for in other ways. The second, and unchallengeable, motive is that children—most of the time—are fun to have around.

Speculation about the future of the "nuclear family" has ranged widely. Some contend it will survive, even that the blurring of distinctions between men and women—the emergence of "unisex"—will actually strengthen the nuclear family. Others foresee both men and women living bachelor lives, with essentially casual encounters for sex never lasting longer than a weekend or so. Still others see men and women living together for much longer periods but still in temporary arrangements—polygamy seriatim, Hollywood style. Still others see group marriages—two or three males living connubially with two or three females.[8]

Contemporary evidence can be mustered to support any one of these different speculations. An impressive number of highly sophisticated, relatively "free" men and women seem to find monogamy psychically satisfying. What is remarkable today is not so much the high divorce rate, but how many couples stay married to each other in spite of the ease with which they could obtain a divorce. At the same time, examples abound of people who find each of the possible arrangements satisfactory. The Hollywood tradition of polygamy seriatim has already been mentioned. We all know people who prefer the bachelor life. The suburban phenomenon of spouse-swapping parties—"swinging"—could be interpreted as an experiment in group marriage, but even if it is not, group marriage is in fact practiced today in the United States on a scale that is rather surprising. Failure is apparently high, but some group marriages seem to have been rather successful.[9]

Only two things seem possible to say with any confidence about the future of the family. The first is that for the next two or three generations, the nuclear family will undoubtedly be the predominant form. Sheer social inertia will see to that. The second is that society will probably be increasingly tolerant of deviations from that norm in arrangements between men and women and that those arrangements will be increasingly diverse. Here again, affluence seems to lead society to feel that it can afford greater diversity in economic terms and this in turn leads to less rigid insistence on adhering to traditional mores. The greater sexual freedom that clearly exists today, the greater tolerance for deviant behavior, as demonstrated by the now open movement among homosexuals to bring about changes in legislation directed against them—all seem to be linked, although admittedly in complex ways, to greater affluence. And there seems to be no reason to suspect that the trend will be any different in the future.

[8] The prophet of this particular arrangement is Robert H. Rimmer. See his novel *The Harrad Experiment* (Los Angeles: Sherbourne Press, 1966) and his *The Harrad Letters to Robert H. Rimmer*, which is partly autobiographical and partly selections from letters received about his novel.
[9] See Herbert A. Otto, ed., *The Family in Search of a Future* (New York, 1970).

Personality Development in a Liberated Society

An even more significant consequence of the liberation of women than a new family structure may be in personality development—for both sexes, for it seems possible that the emancipation of women and a change in the basic relationship between men and women might result in greater emotional maturity for both. In her book *Sexual Politics*, Kate Millet argues that the relations between men and women are political. All societies at present are patriarchies. "The fact is evident at once if one recalls that the military, industry, technology, universities, science, political office, and finance—in short every avenue of power within the society, including the coercive force of the police, is entirely in male hands."[10] In simple terms, males rule females. "Through this system a most ingenious form of 'interior colonization' has been achieved. It is one which tends moreover to be sturdier than any form of segregation, and more rigorous than class stratification, more uniform, certainly more enduring. However muted its present appearance may be, sexual dominion obtains nevertheless as perhaps the most pervasive ideology of our culture and provides its most fundamental concept of power."[11] Giving examples of sexual descriptions from literature, she points out the "large part which notions of ascendancy and power played within them." In a patriarchy, even the act of love between an individual man and woman, she argues, is part of the domination of women. "Coitus can scarcely be said to take place in a vacuum; although of itself it appears a biological and physical activity, it is set so deeply within the larger context of human affairs that it serves as a charged microcosm of the variety of attitudes and values to which culture subscribes. Among other things, it may serve as a model of sexual politics on an individual or personal plane."[12] Millet's point is that the personality traits and behavior of women—what we think of as feminine, as opposed to female; as gender, as opposed to sex—

[10] Millet, op. cit., p. 25.
[11] Ibid.
[12] Ibid., p. 23.

are culturally determined. A woman is socialized to behave like a woman; her feminine traits are not biological. The implication is that the woman in a patriarchal society is less than a whole person. "The limited role allotted the female tends to arrest her at the level of biological experience. Therefore, nearly all that can be described as distinctly human rather than animal activity (in their own way animals also give birth and care for their young) is largely reserved for the male."[13]

But if the female in a patriarchal society is less than a whole person, a warped rather than a fully mature, autonomous person, what about the male? Betty Friedan, one of the foremost pioneers of the women's liberation movement, thinks it affects him, too. She rejects the antimale stance of the extremists and sees the movement as a "two-sex revolution." "Many people think men are the enemy. . . . Man is not the enemy. He is the fellow victim."[14] The implication is that the personality of a man in a patriarchal society may also be warped—that a man as well as a woman may be less than a whole person in such a society; that he, too, may be less than fully mature emotionally. If so, full equality might bring not only fuller maturity to both men and women but healthier, fuller love between individual men and women. Speaking of Betty Friedan, one of her colleagues made the point to an interviewer in the following way: "She found that love between unequals can never succeed and she has undertaken the immense job of bringing up the status of women so that love can succeed."[15]

The truth is that this all makes good psychological sense, and quite a few psychologists—male psychologists—would agree. One is Erik Erikson, who is no favorite of the women's liberation movement and one of the targets in Kate Millet's *Sexual Politics.* Speaking in criticism of Gandhi's account of his relationship with his wife, Erikson writes: ". . . not once, in all of your writings, do you grant that a sexual relationship could be characterized by what we [psychiatrists] call 'mutuality.' This is by no means a capacity easily developed or sustained without self-

13 Ibid., p. 26.
14 As quoted by Paul Wilkes, "Mother Superior to Women's Lib," New York *Times Magazine* (November 29, 1970), p. 28.
15 Ibid., p. 150.

control and sacrifice, but as an approximation and a goal, it describes the only kind of sexual relationship in which the other person does not become a mere object either of sexual or aggressive desire. . . . The point is that mutual consent and artful interplay truly disarm what debasement and what violence there is in merely taking sexual possession of one another."[16] If true sexual fulfillment for the male is mutuality rather than dominance, then man is indeed the "fellow victim."

The comment that might turn out to be relevant when we come to speculate about how these changes in values and attitudes might affect international politics is a very simple and perhaps rather optimistic one. The usual tone of writing on the future of values and especially of those writings that contemplate an erosion of the nuclear family is pessimistic and gloomy, as if any change in the current relationship between men and women can only be bad.[17] But the evidence can just as easily be used to support the opposite case. Without burdening the reader with a review of the psychological and sociological literature, let me say only that in terms of that literature the argument is rather persuasive that the behavioral characteristics of men and women are more the result of socialization and culture than of biology. The argument is also persuasive that the gender roles imposed on both men and women in a patriarchal society warp the personality and prevent the development of emotionally mature, whole persons. A major element in the development of personality is the relation of men and women, and an even earlier and more fundamental element is the connection between these relations and the emotional environment of the growing child. If there is tension in that relationship, either because it is "unnatural" or no longer appropriate to the economic-social-cultural situation, personality would inevitably be affected. Patriarchal society may have arisen to provide for specialization in hunting-gathering or in early agricultural cultures, or it may have arisen

16 Erik H. Erikson, *Gandhi's Truth, On the Origins of Militant Nonviolence* (New York: Norton, 1969). See also Margaret Mead, *Male and Female: A Study of the Sexes in a Changing World* (New York: Dell, 1967).
17 For example, Herman Kahn and Anthony J. Wiener, *The Year 2000: A Framework for Speculation on the Next Thirty-three Years* (New York, 1967), passim.

in early religion and superstition; the realization of the male role in procreation, for example, may have brought a shift from the mother-fertility goddess to the phallus and thence to patriarchy—or it may have arisen though a combination of these and other factors. But it does not matter how patriarchy arose or the function it performed in earlier times. What does matter is that patriarchy is not necessarily appropriate to modern man and his condition and that it may be damaging. It is possible, in sum—not predictable, but possible—that the trend toward further liberation of women and a change in the role and status of both men and women may not only permit love between men and women to be fuller, richer, and less inhibited and guilt-ridden, but it might also permit the development of more mature, autonomous personalities among both men and women. The implication is that a society composed of more mature, autonomous personalities will be less interested in prestige and power goals, more skeptical of the rationale for international adventuring offered by ambitious or vainglorious leaders, and less likely to permit themselves to be manipulated into either war or other kinds of group action whose purpose is the aggrandizement of either leaders or special interests.

Student Unrest

The casual reader of American newspapers might think that student unrest was an expression solely of students' dislike of the Vietnam War and the slow progress in civil rights. Both were connected with student unrest—and not just in America— but an end to the war and dramatic progress in civil rights at any particular point in time would not have ended the matter. Unrest on the campuses was a genuinely new phenomenon in America, and it was neither ephemeral nor accidental. The campuses have never been a focus for political agitation in the United States. Yet there have been issues before Vietnam that were deeply troubling to the youth of the day. In the Great Depression, for example, American society was in a situation that could be more accurately described as prerevolutionary than the situation in the late 1960s or early 1970s. By and large, it is the cities that were troubled in the latter period; the small towns and rural areas prospered. During the Depression, cities, small towns, and rural areas were all equally desperate. Yet in the Great Depression, youth and campuses were hardly in the march at all, much less in the vanguard. Any analysis of student unrest must account for why the campuses should suddenly become the focal point for political activism when the tradition in America has always been the other way.

An analysis of student unrest must also explain two other puzzles of the phenomenon. The first is why student unrest erupted in the particular countries it did. Excepting Latin America, where student activism is a tradition that sets it apart, unrest occurred in the United States, Japan, Western Germany, France, Italy, and to a lesser extent in Great Britain.[18] Why these particular countries rather than a dozen others that come to mind? The second puzzle is that within these countries, the trouble occurred not so much at less-privileged colleges or those whose student population contained a high percentage of minorities or the disadvantaged, but more often at the richest and most prestigeful universities of them all. In the United States the hardest hit were among the very best of both the private and state universities—Harvard, Columbia, and Chicago on the one hand, and Berkeley and Wisconsin on the other. In Germany it was Berlin; in France, the Sorbonne. In Japan it was not the provincial colleges that suffered the greatest troubles, but the most prestigious university in the land—Tokyo—where merely to matriculate means an assured position in business or government. What is it about these particular countries and these particular universities that gives rise to student upheavals?

The Generation Gap

A popular but very serious explanation attributes student unrest to the conflict between generations and sees the root cause in Freudian terms as an Oedipal rebellion against parents. The foremost proponent of this view, Lewis S. Feuer, argues that all

[18] Students played a big role in the upheavals of the Cultural Revolution in China, as described below, but since the "Red Guard" movement was inspired by Mao and was in fact his instrument, it hardly qualifies as a student rebellion.

student movements throughout history are rooted in the conflict of generations, which is in turn founded on the "most
primordial facts of human nature."[19] Student movements are
triggered by the older generation's loss of authority in the eyes
of the young, but then deeper, unconscious forces come to the
fore—death wishes toward the father and guilt and self-hatred
for having harbored such wishes. Thus student movements, Feuer
says, all share overtones of "regicide, parricide, and suicide."

The objections to this theory are many. One is that at least in
the United States the evidence is overwhelming that many of
the most radical, activist students are not really rebelling against
their parents and their values, but pursuing them. Many come
from extremely liberal, often radical families and often have the
sympathetic encouragement of their parents. The mother of one
of the leaders of the upheaval at Columbia in 1968, for example,
referred proudly to him as "my son, the revolutionary." Bettina
Aptheker, one of the leaders of the Berkeley riots, is the daughter
of a long-time member of the Communist party and himself a
famous radical, Herbert Aptheker.

Another objection is that although the Oedipal explanation
"uses psychoanalytic terms, it is bad psychoanalysis."[20] The real
psychoanalytic account is that the Oedipus complex is universal in
all normally developing children. "To point to this complex in
explaining student rebellion is, therefore, like pointing to the fact
that all children learn to walk. Since both characteristics are
said to be universal, neither helps us understand why, at some
historical moments, students are restive and rebellious, while
at others they are not."

Margaret Mead and the Generation Gap Theory

Margaret Mead comes closer when she speaks of a "generation
gap"—since she defines it in a very special way. Most cultures
from time immemorial have changed very slowly. The continuity
of the culture rested on the living presence of three generations.

[19] Lewis S. Feuer, *The Conflict of Generations: The Character and Significance
of Student Movements* (New York, 1969).
[20] Kenneth Keniston, "You Have to Grow Up in Scarsdale to Know How Bad Things
Really Are," New York *Times Magazine* (April 27, 1969), which is also the source
of the quotation that follows.

The children looked upon the grandparents and saw what they would become. The grandparents looked upon the children and could not "conceive of any other future for the children than their own past lives."[21] Change was slow, and if there was any conflict between generations—as there often was—it was not the result of a "gap," but part of the particular culture. Sons might quarrel with their fathers and go West to make their fortunes, but the father had done so, too, and it was expected. A generation gap occurs when the entire situation changes so radically that the experience of the older generation is irrelevant to the younger. "When the young are the first native-born generation of a group of immigrants, the first birthright members of a new religious cult, or the first generation to be reared by a group of successful revolutionaries, their progenitors can provide them with no living models suitable for their age."[22] The pioneer to the United States, Canada, or Australia, for example, had no precedents in their own lives to guide the children. How far they should be allowed to wander from home was only the most obvious difference. Something similar to this, Mead feels, is what has happened simultaneously all over the world. "Today, suddenly, because all the peoples of the world are part of one electronically based, intercommunicating network, young people everywhere share a kind of experience that none of the elders ever have had or will have."[23] No part of the world and no culture have escaped. "Suddenly, so that no matter where they were before, whether they were in the Stone Age or Paris—they were all born into a different world."[24] The result is a generation gap—and one that is worldwide. "Even very recently, the elders could say, 'You know, I have been young and *you* have never been old.' But today's young people can reply: 'You never have been young in the world I am young in, and you never can be.'"[25]

For Margaret Mead, then, the explanation of student unrest is

[21] *Culture and Commitment: A Study of the Generation Gap* (Garden City, New York: Natural History Press/Doubleday, 1970), p. 1.
[22] Ibid., p. 37.
[23] Ibid., p. 64.
[24] Margaret Mead, Arthur Clarke, and Alvin Toffler, "A Panel Discussion on the Future of Man," *University Review*, No. 12 (1970).
[25] *Culture and Commitment*, p. 63.

not so much a rebellion of the students against their parents and a rejection of their values as an entirely different situation bringing different life experience and ultimately a different value structure.

Objections to Mead's Argument

Mead's argument is persuasive, and it at least attempts to explain why students as different as Japanese and Americans are affected. But Mead's explanation, first, fails to answer the question why the United States, Japan, Western Germany, France, and the others should have student upheavals, and not India, Pakistan, Australia, or the countries of Africa, Southeast Asia, and the Middle East. A second puzzle emerges when the United States and Japan—both of whom have had student upheavals—are compared. The great change in the experience of different generations for Japan came at the end of World War II. Except for city-dwellers, most Japanese born before World War II had little experience with such items of modern technology as automobiles and radios, much less the range of electronic and technological wonders that the postwar generation takes in its stride. But in the United States, the different experiences between the generation born after World War II and their parents were not as great as the differences between the generation of their parents and their grandparents. The grandparents, born just before and after 1900, spent their childhood in an era when the horse was still the most common form of transportation for short distances, and in which radios, movies, the automobile, and the airplane were great curiosities. The parents, born in the period following World War I, took all these things for granted—things that created a technological environment more similar to the electronic age of their children, the post-World War II generation, than to the pre-World War I situation of their parents.

Another puzzle that Mead's generation gap theory fails to account for is that research on values among student activists— at least in the United States, where so much more has been done—shows that traditional American values remain central to their concern. It is because they are so deeply committed to the traditional American value of equality, for example, that the student activists have been in the forefront of protest about civil rights. It is because of their commitment to the traditional values of democracy, anticolonialism, and anti-imperialism—and perhaps to traditional American sympathy for the underdog—that they regarded the Vietnam War as immoral and reprehensible. Speaking of young American radicals, on whom he has done considerable research, and their commitment to traditional American values, Kenneth Keniston argues that much of the militancy comes not from new values but because old values are taken *seriously*. Instead of taking traditional American values as pious platitudes or utopian aspirations, student activists are taking them "as the basis for political action and social change."[26]

The "Luddite" Explanation

Where Mead sees the source of student unrest in developments that have already taken place—the technological innovations that have created a worldwide communications network—others see it as an anticipation of events to come. They see the source in an unconscious but nevertheless real uneasiness about the coming superindustrial society and fear by the students that they will have no place in that society. Zbigniew Brzezinski, for example, makes a distinction between this unrest and true revolutions, which are those with a program and content related to the future that made them historically relevant. "This was the case," he writes, "with the French Revolution, with the 1848 Spring of Nations, and the Bolshevik Revolution."[27] Most revolutionary outbreaks are not true revolutions, so defined, but are spasms of the past, with neither content nor program. They are really counterrevolutions. His examples are most peasant uprisings, anarchist revolutions, and most especially the Luddites —who smashed machines in a vain attempt to stem the tide of the Industrial Revolution. The source of the recent upheavals is, in Brzezinski's view, the same. The leaders of the upheavals

[26] Keniston, op. cit. For further evidence on the commitment of student radicals to traditional American values, see also his *Young Radicals: Notes on Committed Youth* (New York: Harcourt, Brace, 1968).
[27] "Revolution and Counterrevolution (But Not Necessarily About Columbia!)," *The New Republic* (June 1, 1968).

are "people who increasingly will have no role to play in the new technetronic society. Their reaction reflects both a conscious and, even more important, an unconscious realization that they are themselves becoming historically obsolete. . . . Thus, rather than representing a true revolution, some recent outbursts are in fact a counterrevolution. Its violence and revolutionary slogans are merely—and sadly—the death rattle of the historical irrelevants."

Objections to the "Luddite" Theory

My own work with students at Columbia University, both graduate and undergraduate, and in conversations-interviews with very nearly a thousand students at approximately fifty colleges and universities across the country leads me to the conclusion that Brzezinski is right in making a connection between student unrest and the foreshadowing of the superindustrial society, but wrong in his analysis of the nature of the connection. Specifically, I believe that student unrest is indeed related to the emerging superindustrial society but that the reaction is not at all comparable to the Luddites' reaction.

One of the reasons for the difficulty in pinpointing the cause of student unrest is that although they do try to analyze their feelings and articulate them, the students are still not very clear in their own minds about exactly what is bothering them. It is clear that part of what they find troubling is the gap between the aspirations and goals of their society and the reality. When American students compare the ideal of equality without regard to race, creed, or color to the reality of the condition of the black, the Indian, or the Spanish-American, their reaction ranges from disturbing doubts about the society to flaming moral outrage. The Japanese student has a similar reaction to the gap between the goal of a democratic society and the reality of power in Japan's economic and political life.

But another part of what is bothering students—which is the part that Brzezinski is probing toward—is more elusive. One Columbia University student who attempted to give it words is worth quoting. In the fall of 1967, before the upheaval that came the following spring, I had remarked to a Columbia student on what seemed to me to be a difference in attitude and mood between the young men at Columbia and the young women at its sister institution just across Broadway at Barnard. "It's true," he said. And then he added, somewhat archly, "That thirty yards across Broadway is almost as big a gap as the thirty years between your generation and mine." His parents' generation (to which I belonged), he went on to say, had been dominated by the Great Depression or the memory of it. None of that generation could be entirely certain there would be enough jobs to go around, and the possibility always existed that we might not all be able to have careers, a family, and a decent life. In such circumstances we had had to work hard in college to compete and certainly could not afford to raise probing and embarrassing questions. The girls at Barnard, of course, were different from their mothers in many ways. Most of them wanted marriage and families like their mothers did. But they wanted much more. They wanted careers and a professional life. He knew of two who had already set their sights on being the first woman appointed to the U. S. Supreme Court. But, like the men of the Depression generation, they were not at all sure there would be places for them all in professional life. So they, too, had to work hard to compete, and many of them were also a little hesitant about raising embarrassing questions.

On the boys' side of the street, however, it was quite different. In this affluent age, there was simply no doubt at all that a man with a Columbia University degree could have a career if he wanted one. The point was that for the first time in the history of mankind, a whole generation—or at least those from the best institutions—could afford to ask those embarrassing questions. They could afford to spend some time considering whether they really wanted that career, whether the "rat race" was really worth it. More and more, they had at least the option of choosing a career that might not earn quite so much money but would be more meaningful. "We're not saying, 'Stop the world, we want to get off,'" he said. "What we are saying is, 'Slow it down a little, so we can be sure it's heading in the right direction.'"

In terms reminiscent of Erik Erikson's observation that young adults frequently need a "psychocultural moratorium" at a certain stage in their development, this student went on to say that sometimes he and his friends were gripped with a sense of "near-panic." "This society has to have highly trained people to make it function. The training takes a long time, and everyone understands you have to start early. But this puts us, the kids, on an escalator before we're old enough to know what's happening to us. You just get carried along. All of a sudden, you wake up and realize that in a year or two you are going to be spewed out the other end, thrust into an office in some big corporation, probably married to some girl and installed in a house in suburbia, and spend the rest of your life commuting—all this, without ever once having had a chance to ask whether that is what you really want. It's frightening."

An Alternative Explanation

Thus my own work with American students indicates that Brzezinski is right in sensing that student unrest is related to affluence and is a form of anticipation of the emerging super-industrial society. But I would say that it is not a Luddite reaction. A very small percentage do feel powerless to change existing society or are so alienated that they don't see the point of even trying. These drop out—frequently to a hippie life pattern. Many of the hippies and street people live the life for only a year or two—dropping out is simply their form of "psycho-cultural moratorium." But those who are truly alienated may stay that way, or lead a hermitlike existence on a farm in Vermont or a small ranch out West. A proportion of the very radical, very activist students also come to a feeling of powerlessness and frustration. Some of these become even more radical and even more oriented toward violence. This tends to isolate them still further from the bulk of the students, and they become anarchist-extremists, Weathermen, or go into exile in Cuba, perhaps, or Algeria. But the vast majority of students who share the feelings of uneasiness and are properly a part of "student unrest" are neither so alienated as to drop out nor so outraged as to resort to bombs and guerrilla warfare. These do not feel powerless. On the contrary, they feel they are special, the elite of their generation. At times, indeed, their habit of referring to themselves as "the best of our generation" becomes annoying. They know they will rise to leadership. They intend to do so. And they are determined to change society as soon as they achieve power.

An alternative hypothesis to Brzezinski's, in other words, is that the source of student unrest is a vague but real sensing among college youth that the emerging superindustrial society opens new vistas for mankind that demand to be explored. They understand that the new affluence permits the achievement of old goals: equality and the end of poverty. If they believe that society has failed to implement these goals now that it has acquired the means to do so out of laxity rather than evil, they are impatient. If they feel that society has failed deliberately —out of racism or greed—they are morally outraged and angry. They also sense that the even greater affluence of the future will permit different lifestyles from the old rut of compulsive work, suburbia, and routine. They sense that the emerging super-industrial society will free mankind and permit people to lead more meaningful lives. At the same time, they also sense some of the dangers of the superindustrial society: bigness, impersonality, pollution, a mass society rushing hither and yon in a churning business in which the individual is totally submerged. "I am a human being," one of the placards at the Berkeley riots read, "Do not bend, fold, staple, or mutilate."

If this hypothesis is correct, it would explain the three puzzles with which we began: Why unrest at this time? Why in these particular countries? Why at the most prestigeful colleges and universities? The time is now because this is the first time that man has achieved enough affluence to implement goals that have been really out of reach, and because this is the first time in the history of mankind that he can see ahead to a time in which he will be relieved of the age-old struggle for mere subsistence and free to pursue a more meaningful life—if only he can discover what a meaningful life is. Student unrest has erupted in the United States, Japan, Western Germany, France, and the others because these are both the most highly industrialized countries in the world, the ones that are in fact approaching a superindustrial stage, and because these countries are all relatively open societies in which dissent, protest, and student activism can be expressed more easily and with lighter punishment than in less open societies. The fact of the matter is that there are signs of student unrest in the Eastern European countries and the Soviet Union, which suggests that similar eruptions would occur there, too, if controls were somewhat less strict. Finally, the unrest occurs at the most prestigeful colleges and universities precisely because it is students at those institutions who are most assured of significant places in the emerging society and who are in the best position to sense both the opportunities and the problems that the future holds.

Kenneth Keniston's Evidence

This hypothesis has been most fully developed and researched among American students by Kenneth Keniston.[28] Briefly, Keniston's argument is that the sources of student unrest lie in two revolutions, not one. The first revolution is a "continuation of the old and familiar revolution of the industrial society, the liberal-democratic-egalitarian revolution that started in America and France at the turn of the 18th century and spread to virtually every nation in the world." Thus the United States is now approaching the completion of this first revolution and has developed the capacity to complete it for all segments of its society. In these circumstances, the youth see these values not as goals, but as *rights*. Poverty, for example, is no longer an unpleasant fact of life, but an unnecessary leftover from an outmoded age and hence an outrage. For the educated, privileged, affluent, upper-middle-class youth who has "never experienced poverty,

[28] In addition to his article "You Have to Grow Up in Scarsdale to Know How Bad Things Really Are" and his book *Young Radicals*, both of which have already been cited, see also his book *The Uncommitted: Alienated Youth in American Society* (New York, 1960); his article "Social Change and Youth," *The Challenge of Youth*, ed. Erik H. Erikson (New York, 1961); his article "The Sources of Student Dissent," *The Journal of Social Issues* (1967); his article "Alienation in American Youth," an address to the Division of Personality and Social Psychology, American Psychological Association (New York, September 1966; the latter two are reprinted as appendices in *Young Radicals*); and his collected articles, *Youth and Dissent* (New York, 1971).

discrimination, exploitation or oppression, even to *witness* the existence of these evils in the lives of others suddenly becomes intolerable." The young people at the center of campus unrest, to repeat, come from upper-middle-class families who are affluent and tend to be liberal. The students are not so much rebelling against the values of their parents as taking them seriously. The second revolution is our hypothesis: that a major source of student unrest is a vague, inchoate, but nevertheless real sensing that the emerging superindustrial society opens both new vistas for mankind that demand to be explored and new dangers to be avoided. There is no program in this sensing, no ideology, and no firm or widespread convictions about what the new values should be. The "second revolution" is an uneasiness, a vague feeling of discontent, the discovery that affluence is not the whole answer and that we ought to look hard before we leap into a superindustrial age. For Keniston, the feeling is summed up in the statement of a young student that Keniston made the title of one of his articles: "You have to grow up in Scarsdale to know how bad things really are." As Keniston says, that comment would sound arrogant to a poor black, but to the student it meant something. "He meant that even in the Scarsdales of America, with their affluence, their upper-middle-class security and abundance, their well-fed, well-heeled children and their excellent schools, something is wrong."

In addition, Keniston has one further highly perceptive and important point to make about student unrest. Keniston argues that in terms of the opportunity of young people for continuing intellectual, ethical, and emotional development and in terms of the relationship of young people to the institutions of society (whether or not the young are engaged in those institutions)— that in terms of these two factors, the present situation in the advanced countries is without precedent in history. Keniston points out that the separate stage of childhood was not recognized until the end of the Middle Ages. Infancy ended at six or seven years, and the child was then integrated into adult life and treated as a small man or woman. Adolescence was not recognized as a stage of life until the nineteenth or twentieth centuries. Partly this was because higher productivity meant that society could afford to defer the beginning of working life and partly because these advanced societies required higher levels of training and psychological development. "Today," Keniston writes, "in more developed nations, we are beginning to witness the recognition of still another stage of life. Like childhood and adolescence, it was initially granted to only a small minority, but is now being rapidly extended to an ever-larger group."[29] Keniston calls this stage "youth"—a period in which the person continues his disengagement from the institutions of society, a period of psychological development that intervenes between adolescence and adulthood.

Let me support and illustrate Keniston's point with an anecdote about one of my own students. The student in question was extraordinarily intelligent and personable. Politically he was left of center, but moderate—years before as a freshman he had joined the Students for a Democratic Society, but found their ideological bickering so simplistic and unreal that he soon quit. He and two other graduate students were working as teaching assistants, conducting discussion groups and grading examinations. Although likable and charming, this particular student had throughout the semester behaved like an irresponsible adolescent. He was invariably late for meetings and even for some of the classes he was instructing. He almost never had finished his preparations. Finally came a meeting in which his role was crucial. He had forgotten it, and it took forty-five minutes to find him—and we then discovered he had neglected to prepare the contribution that was so crucial. My patience was exhausted, and I upbraided him in terms I had not used since I was an Army lieutenant in World War II. My tirade of barracks oaths reminded me that during the war I had been just about his age, so I asked him just how old he was. Yes, he was twenty-six. "At twenty-six," I said haughtily, intending what he would call a "put-down"—"at twenty-six I commanded a whole battalion. I was responsible for the lives of almost five hundred men."

"But it was different in your generation," he said very earnestly, striving hard to make me understand. "I am not supposed to be

29 Keniston, "You Have to Grow Up in Scarsdale to Know How Bad Things Really Are," op. cit., pp. 122–24.

grown up like you were. I'm not ready for responsibility. I'm still maturing."

Most of the parents of the post-World War II generation find it difficult to understand a response like that, much less to think it or the behavior behind it as something to be applauded or encouraged. Keniston recognizes that student revolts stem in part from this extension of youth. The higher education and longer opportunity to develop "encourages the individual to elaborate a more personal, less purely conventional sense of ethics" —even though it also creates the often infuriating moral self-righteousness of the concerned student. In this sense, the colleges have not failed, but have been hugely successful. The colleges are accused of cranking out "machinelike robots" who provide skilled manpower for the economy. But they are also producing highly critical citizens—"young men and women who have the opportunity, the leisure, the affluence and educational resources to continue their development beyond the point where most people in the past were required to stop it." What the advanced nations have done, Keniston writes, "is to create their own critics on a mass basis—that is, to create an ever-larger group of young people who take the highest values of their societies as their own, who internalize these values and identify them with their own best selves, and who are willing to struggle to implement them." Freed from the requirements of work, gainful employment, and even marriage, the students can criticize their society from a protected position of disengagement.

On balance, Keniston feels that the extended youth is a good thing for the student. "Put in an oversimplified phrase, it tends to free him—to free him from swallowing the unexamined assumptions of the past, to free him from the superstitions of his childhood, to free him to express his feelings more openly and to free him from irrational bondage to authority.

Implications for the Future

The question is: Does all this give us any worthwhile clues as to how values and attitudes might be changing under the impact of affluence and the emerging superindustrial state? Student unrest does seem, clearly, to be rooted in a vague awareness that affluence and the superindustrial society are working changes in the world, and an uneasiness among the youth about where it might all end up. But is their sensing of the direction of the change perceptive enough to give us clues as to the nature of the future society?

It is important to stress that the "youth" under scrutiny here are the middle range of students at the mainly large, mainly prestigious colleges and universities most affected by student unrest. Thus we have not focused on vast numbers of college students attending the somewhat less prominent institutions and the smaller colleges. These have clearly been affected by the same forces and show the same symptoms, but to a much less marked degree. Also, we have completely ignored both the permanently alienated dropouts and the violently militant activists, like the Weathermen. Neither are representative of the mass of their fellow students. Although they exercised considerable influence in the middle sixties, even this has steadily dwindled. A number of factors have contributed to this, but the most important is probably their increased emphasis on the use of violence. To the middle students, physical violence, senseless violence, was an anathema, the negation of what they felt was the true meaning of the student movement.[30]

Of these middle-range students, it should also be emphasized that they have not worked out any clear-cut, internally consistent value system, ideology, or program to which any significant number can give their loyalties. Which is not to say that some claims to see a new, fully developed value structure have not been made—claims that are usually sentimental and romanticized, sometimes even a little mystical, and occasionally downright pandering for student approval.

Charles A. Reich and the Greening of America

Of the claims to have identified a new and complete value structure in the student movement, the one that has attracted the most attention is probably Charles A. Reich with his book, *The Greening of America* (the title is meant to suggest re-

[30] On this point, see Kenneth Keniston, "The Agony of the Counter-Culture," *Yale Alumni Magazine* (October 1971).

birth, as in the green of spring).[31] Reich sees the youth of America as having a "new consciousness" that has "emerged from the machine-made environment of the corporate state, like flowers pushing up through a concrete pavement." He calls this new consciousness, "Consciousness III" as opposed to "Consciousness I," which represents the values of rural and small-town America of the nineteenth century, and "Consciousness II," which is the outlook of the industrial age and of the technologically and institutionally oriented "American corporate state." "In Consciousness III," Reich writes, "we can see not a superficial moralistic improvement but a growth of understanding, sensibility, and the capacity for love that, for the first time, offers hope that man will be able to control and turn to good uses the machines he has built." The new consciousness is expressed in many ways, including the clothes, the jeans and jackets, beads, and all the rest. "The clothes are earthy and sensual. They express an affinity with nature. . . . These clothes express freedom . . . they are extremely expressive of the human body inside them, and each body is different and unique." The new music, Reich contends, is also an important manifestation. "Indeed, the new music has achieved a degree of integration of art in everyday life that is probably unique in modern societies. . . . Like a medieval cathedral or the carvings in a tribal village, the art of rock is constantly present as a part of everyday life. . . ."

Persistent Themes in Student Unrest

Reich's rather breathless arguments can be dismissed as sentimental romanticism, but it may still be true that the uneasy probing of the students does suggest, however vaguely and tentatively, at least the direction of the changes in values and attitudes that the superindustrial society will bring; for everyone who has studied unrest on the campuses has identified the same recurring themes, which are few in number, but persistent.[32]

[31] New York, 1970.
[32] In addition to those authors already mentioned—Keniston, Mead, Brzezinski, Bell, and Reich—see also Richard Flacks, "The Liberated Generation: An Exploration of the Roots of Student Protest," *Journal of Social Issues*, Vol. XXIII, No. 3 (1967).

One theme—directly related to affluence and the anticipation of the emerging superindustrial society—is that the old stress on materialism, and on the Calvinist virtues related to it, no longer seem appropriate. In an automated, superindustrial, affluent age, no purpose seems to be served by revering the so-called "industrial ethic," whether Protestant, socialist, or communist, that stresses "self-discipline, delay of gratification, achievement orientation, and a strong emphasis on economic success and productivity."[33] The whole industrial ethic is in question, and along with this questioning is a tendency to reject notions of quantity in preference to notions of quality.

Another theme is doubt about the sincerity of the commitment to traditional American values, such as equality, freedom, and justice. The word that recurs in this context is "hypocritical"—the suggestion that society is hypocritical. The society talks egalitarianism, for example, and civil rights, but tolerates power elites who run things for their own benefits, the continuation of poverty, and the continuation of racial prejudice and oppression. Another aspect of this theme is an insistence on moral purity, even moral self-righteousness. The implication is that "to assume conventional adult roles usually leads to increasing self-interestedness, hence selling-out, or 'phoniness.' "[34] Keniston pushes the point even further. Doubting the continuing validity of the "industrial ethic" and the moral imperative behind production, acquisition, and materialism, the students, Keniston says, begin to question the moral authority, the "credibility" of society itself. Hence the frequency with which requests by college presidents and other representatives of authority for restraint or conformity are seen as repression or an attempt to manipulate students into joining the establishment. Hence, also, the vague feeling among students that they are being oppressed.

Another theme is fear of the trend toward the institutionalization of society, the increasing bigness of those institutions, and their impersonal nature—all of which seem to be making the individual merely a number for the convenience of computers. The

[33] "You Have to Grow Up in Scarsdale to Know How Bad Things Really Are," p. 126.
[34] Richard Flacks, "The Liberated Generation: An Exploration of the Roots of Student Protest, op. cit., p. 57.

other side of this coin is a stress on human values and individuality—a "revolt against uniformity." Long hair and bizarre dress are obvious illustrations, even though they sometimes become uniforms in themselves. Less obvious is the demand, in Keniston's words, "that individuals be appreciated, not because of their similarities or despite their differences, but because they *are* different, diverse, unique, and noninterchangeable."

A related theme is that of community and "togetherness." It was this almost mystical feeling of being at one with each other that was so prized at the mass rock music festivals at Woodstock and even at the Powder Ridge, Connecticut, festival where there wasn't even any music, because of a legal injunction. Another aspect is the search for "meaningful human relationships" in which people "relate" to each other without pretense or masks of any kind.

Still another theme, which is also related to the fear of institutional bigness and impersonality, is a search for ways for the individual to become involved in the decisions that affect his life. This is what is meant by "participatory democracy," but it connotes much more than just the consent of the governed or the freedom to make one's voice heard if one can. It extends to every aspect of society, and it sometimes implies almost an obligation to participate, to express oneself.

The final theme also carries with it the implication of obligation. This is the quest for self-realization. One observer sees it as romanticism—often expressed "in terms of leading a 'free' life— i.e., one not bound by conventional restraints on feeling, experience, communication, expression."[35] It is this theme that is behind the suspicion of "institutionalized careers" and of society's "escalator," thrusting one into a career, marriage, suburbia, and a lifetime of commuting. It also accounts for the curiosity about drug-related "expansion of consciousness." The reason is that "this is the first generation in which a substantial number of youth have both the impulse to free themselves from conventional status concerns *and can afford to do so.* In this sense they are a 'liberated' generation; affluence has freed them, at least for a period of time, from some of the anxieties and preoccupations

[35] Flacks, "The Liberated Generation," op. cit.

which have been the defining features of American middle class social character."[36] In Keniston's terms there seems to be an imperative for youth to seek "imagination, self-actualization, individuality, openness and relevance." The question of the meaning of life in an age of affluence cannot wait; it must be answered now.

Hints and Implications

What hints are contained in these several themes beyond what they say expressly? The most obvious—and in some ways startling—is the renewed emphasis on such traditional American values as equality, freedom, and justice. Student, women's, black, Chicano, Indian, and other minority movements all stress these same basic goals. What seems to be happening is that equality, freedom, and justice come even more strongly to the fore precisely because they need no longer be unattainable dreams. Affluence can make them realities.

A second hint concerns the potential for personality development. Among students an awareness has grown that affluence makes possible a quest for self-realization. In the past, individuals might be in a position to embark on such a quest, but for the first time in history a whole segment of society can afford it and soon a whole people may. The black movement argues on sound psychological grounds that neither blacks nor whites can develop whole, healthy personalities in a segregated, racist society or in one containing even the remnants of racism. The women's liberation movement argues on sound psychological grounds that neither women nor men can develop whole, healthy personalities in a patriarchal, sexist society or one containing even remnants of sexual discrimination. Among the restless students few have articulated their uneasiness with much success or groped beyond the vaguest hint of the shape of the values yet to come, yet the evidence is persuasive that they—the generation that is to be the first to live in the superindustrial society—has at least sensed the need for re-examining the old values and working out some new relation between man and society. Affluence will at least give

[36] Ibid., p. 61.

them the time, in the extension of youth, and the opportunity—whether or not they use it well—for intellectual and psychological development appropriate to those new values. Thus all three movements contain the promise of a future in which people have been able to achieve a fuller development and integration of personality than ever before, people who are emotionally more stable and mature, who are more nearly autonomous, and who have developed a value system that is both satisfying in human terms and appropriate to the new, superindustrial age.

CHAPTER 3

Values and the Industrial Ethic

THE STRIKING difference between the student movement, on the one hand, and black and women's lib movements, on the other, is the fact that the students seem instinctively to realize, as the others do not, that affluence is going to do much more than just make it possible finally to achieve equality, freedom, and justice. Stated flatly, the point here is one we have already made, that affluence not only re-emphasizes the traditional values of equality, freedom, and justice, but that it will inevitably destroy the production-oriented and achievement-oriented values associated with the "industrial ethic." Inexorably and inevitably, these values will become obsolete and anachronistic. They will no longer perform a social function. In fact, in the jargon of social scientists, they may actually become dysfunctional—that is, if they are not changed they may actually undermine the new superindustrial society rather than sustain it or merely be irrelevant to it. What the student movement seems to sense is the emotional crisis that mankind will have in finding something to put in the place of these outmoded values. What the crisis will bring, in fact, is an almost tragic irony for those who are now struggling for equality. A large element of the equality that blacks and women demand is equality in work opportunity. Yet the affluence that is making equality possible is also going to destroy work opportunity— and do it at just about the time that equality is finally achieved. What the student movement seems to sense and the others do not is that the equality they will achieve will be equality in the agony that Keynes foresaw of having to face mankind's "real, his permanent problem." The truth of the matter is that there will be very little work to do, not nearly enough for everyone for very much of their time.

The Specter of Unemployment

Already, the work week is getting shorter. A number of industries have already adopted a three-day, thirty-to-thirty-six-hour work week, and they report both enthusiastic response from workers and higher productivity.[1] The United States, in sum, has already reached a stage at which for the first time in history not only can poverty be abolished but it can be done while everyone can have more time than he must spend either in working or in the necessary business of sleeping, eating, and caring for himself. We spoke before of national income as high as twelve thousand dollars per person in 1965 dollars by the year 2000 and as much as twenty-five thousand dollars per person twenty-five years later. At the same time, the total hours of work per year could easily go from the present two thousand to one thousand. And the one thousand could be arranged in various ways—as a work year of fifty two-day weeks of twenty hours each with a two-week holiday or as twenty-five five-day weeks of forty hours with a twenty-seven-week holiday.

The trend toward mechanizing and automating will certainly continue. It is technically feasible to put the mail system, for example, on an electronic and computer basis. A great deal can be done immediately to make garbage and rubbish collection more

[1] New York *Times* (January 4, 1970 and June 4, 1971).

mechanized than it is. In the office, an example is the clerical task of sending out bills, paying them by check, the clearinghouse work, and the banker's chore of keeping accounts, which we have already mentioned. All these actions could be taken by computers without any flow of paper at all. Any routine, repetitive task can be done by automated machinery. Increasingly the only work left for humans will be problem-solving, diagnosing and repairing breakdowns, maintenance, and the work of the service industries. The largest occupational group will be the service trades, and within industry the work to be done will be professional-technical rather than either blue-collar or the clerical grades of white-collar.

With increasingly little work to be done, how will the problem of allocating job opportunities be solved? Clearly, it will be a problem of formidable implications. "Let us remember," Norbert Wiener writes, "that the automatic machine, whatever we think of any feelings it may have or not have, is the precise economic equivalent of slave labor. Any labor which competes with slave labor must accept the economic conditions of slave labor. It is perfectly clear that this will produce an unemployment situation, in comparison with which . . . even the depression of the thirties will seem a pleasant joke."[2]

How will the limited number of jobs available be distributed? The industrial age would let competition and economic incentive do the allocating. Geniuses and near-geniuses would then presumably compete for the interesting jobs, which would offer security but would not be very well paid. The really unpleasant, dirty, boring jobs that could not be automated might be very highly paid. Then about all that would be left for the rest of us would be some form of welfare.

The Distribution of Available Jobs

This puzzle of what to do about the allocation of work and income has been central to everyone who has speculated about the future in advanced societies. Aldous Huxley in *Brave New World* solved the problem with an ingenious combination of bi-

[2] *The Human Use of Human Beings* (Boston, 1950), p. 189.

ology, technology, and drugs. All birth was a test-tube process whose standardized procedures produced the perfect caste system—intelligent Alphas for the brainwork, stupid Epsilons for the sewage work, and appropriate gradations for all kinds of work intermediate between the two. Scientific experiments determined that 7½ hours of work gave the best balance, and scientific and technological development was halted at the appropriate level. The drug (soma), sex, and a further development of the cinema ("feelies") kept everyone happy and obedient.

Dennis Gabor: Inventing the Future

Huxley had satirical points to make, but people who have no thought of being satirical sometimes offer rather similar proposals in utter seriousness. Dennis Gabor, for example, in his book *Inventing the Future*, argues that in the future only the top 5 per cent of the population in terms of intelligence and ability will be needed to perform the work of the world. He assumes that socially relevant work is a source of psychological satisfaction that fills an important human need—hence the dilemma. One alternative for society is to perpetuate a fraud. It could go on having such routine jobs as delivering the mail done by hand. Another alternative is a tricky feat of social engineering, changing the attitudes of the bulk of the population toward both work and technology without interfering with the attitudes of the most gifted. In the end, Gabor adopts a compromise. He suggests that society halt its technological development at a level that would require 6 hours of work 5 days a week. There would be no reason actually to lie to the people. Just as a person accepts the doctor's advice about taking more exercise than suits his "natural laziness," the common man could accept the idea that a certain amount of work is necessary to "keep him mentally alert and give him the feeling that he is useful and even creative."[3] Or he could be persuaded to take work in the same spirit as he does sports—just as a high jumper or a runner eschews machinery, so could the mailman stop short of electronics and regard delivering mail as he would a craft. In Gabor's scheme, the top 5 per cent would also need some

[3] *Inventing the Future* (New York: Knopf, 1964), p. 139.

psychological conditioning. "The leading minority must forget that the majority is objectively useless because they could be replaced by machines. It must find its reward in the happiness of the common man, in a paternal feeling which must never show itself in paternalism."[4]

The problem of attitudes toward work and income, however, is probably quite different from the way that Gabor and others operating on elitist and Calvinist assumptions see it. It seems very doubtful that such sharp differences in ability and intellect would exist in a society affluent enough to provide ample education for all. And it seems even more doubtful that work provides any psychological satisfactions that could not be equally well filled by an avocation, whether it is writing poetry or simply gardening.

We can predict with great confidence that the problem of allocating work and income in the superindustrial society will be absolutely central. We can also predict that the problem will agitate the developed societies long before a truly superindustrial society actually emerges. It is upon us now. We can also predict that many different schemes for solving the problem will be tried and found wanting before a more or less satisfactory solution is found. In such circumstances to try to predict this final solution seems the height of foolishness. Yet it seems both simple and obvious what that final solution will be. It will be to break the ancient tie between work and the distribution of income.

The Birthright Income

What makes this notion so heretical and what will make society try so many other schemes before it settles on this simplest and most obvious solution is the fact that the tie between work and income is so tightly tied to our puritanical notions that only those who work should eat. To break this tie seems, in fact, to sin, to fly in the face of nature and of God.

But difficult though this particular change in values and attitudes may seem, change seems inevitable. Automated machines will very quickly bring into question all the basic premises behind

[4] Ibid., p. 140.

economic institutions and living standards, and an entirely new ethical standard is bound to result. In moral terms, when work is done by automated machines and not human labor, the right to a share in the output is divorced from the labor input. As John McHale puts the point, "From this time forward, man may potentially produce in abundance all his material life-sustaining requirements without the need to exact human labor in equable return. In effect, since science and technology are directly based on the availability of all recorded human knowledge, all human equity is already invested in the whole process. The invention of the zero is as important as that of the transistor. It is therefore a realistic, rather than merely philosophical, premise that the only universal credit card for access to the fruits of the whole enterprise is membership in the human race."[5]

The Calvinist abhorrence of idleness and leisure—or at least *unearned* leisure—is firmly entrenched, but it will become increasingly inappropriate in a superindustrial society. Even today, proposals attempting to deal with the problems brought by advanced industrialization find unlikely allies. Clare Boothe Luce, for example, toward the end of a lifetime of conservative, "bigbusiness" Republicanism, became an advocate of the guaranteed annual wage. When confronted with the Calvinist objection that some would make no attempt to find work and revel in idleness, Luce's response was that a certain segment of society already did —some of whom were recipients of inherited wealth, but mainly divorcees and the widows of the upper-middle-class overachievers who had worked themselves to an early death. In terms of the ethical question, she said that if there had to be idlers in society it made no difference whether they were lazy men of the working class or middle-aged women of the middle class.

Once the puritanical obstacle is passed, some very simple basis for distributing income is likely to be the one chosen. Various welfare schemes to bring about transfer payments and lessen the inequities worked by the industrial economy have already been tried and found wanting. Others—like the guaranteed annual wage—may be given a trial in the interim. But it seems most likely that what is eventually adopted will be a much simpler proposal

[5] *The Future of the Future* (New York, 1969), pp. 277–78.

—for example, to give each American citizen a flat monthly allowance as a birthright beginning the day he is born. In the year 2000, as suggested earlier, the per capita national income in the United States can easily reach $12,000 reckoned in the purchasing power of a 1965 dollar. If every person were given an allowance of, say, $300 a month, or $3,600 a year, a family of 4 would have the equivalent in today's purchasing power of $14,400, even if no one in the family worked.

Some such scheme might be adopted sooner than anyone thinks. If world events permit a sharp downturn in defense expenditures, an allowance of some lesser amount might become a reality as soon as the 1980s. But no matter what, some such proposal is bound to become a political issue soon. Indeed, it could be argued that the beginning was George S. McGovern's "$1,000" proposal in the election of 1972. The more difficult question is: What further changes in values and attitudes will the fact of having such a birthright allowance bring about?

The Birthright Income and Value Changes

Affluence alone will have profound effects on the social life of man, but affluence without work will have even more. Most of the literature on the future is concerned with technological trends; among those few who have attempted to analyze trends for clues to value and attitude change is Nicholas Rescher, with the help of Olaf Helmer and his colleagues at the RAND Corporation.[6] The method used was the so-called "Delphi" technique—which is a fancy name for using the informed guesses of experts. A detailed questionnaire was prepared under four categories: 1. current "folklore" about American values; 2. specific values (e.g., one's own pleasure, self-respect, success, power, devotion to family, law and order, patriotism, internationalism, and some thirty others); 3. trends in various categories of values (e.g., self-regarding values, such as prudence and self-advancement, as opposed to other-regarding values, such as service to others and tolerance); and 4. whether values would be affected by certain probable scientific, technological, demographic, or socioeconomic

[6] Nicholas Rescher, "A Questionnaire Study of American Values by 2000 A.D.," in Kurt Baier and Rescher, *Values and the Future* (New York, 1969).

changes. This questionnaire was sent to 75 high-level scientists and science administrators. Rescher cautions that his sample was minute and that it was biased in the direction of the "hard" scientists, but even though the results were more suggestive than conclusive, he believes them useful.

On Question 1—concerning the current "folklore" regarding American values—there was a high degree of consensus that Americans continue to be committed to the old values. The exceptions were less commitment to religious values and more to righting social injustice. The respondents foresaw no cataclysmic changes, such as losing our attachment to the values that reflect genuine human needs (health, friendship, freedom, etc.). They also foresaw a boom in aesthetic values—rejecting any idea that our taste is being debased by television, pulp magazines, similar mass-culture products.

For Question 2—changes in specific values—the consensus was that people would have higher standards regarding "pleasure," "comfort," "convenience," "security," and "leisure." Since less work would be required to meet these standards, less emphasis on values such as "self-reliance" and "conscientiousness" will be needed, while more emphasis could be laid on "beauty," "culture," "self-fulfillment," and "service to others." At the same time, the respondents foresaw a decline in patriotism and a strengthening of mankind-oriented values, such as peace, social justice, and internationalism.

The answers to Question 3, dealing with trends in different categories of values, were consistent with the answers to Question 2—"strengthening of materialism; broadening of value horizons from local to international perspectives; greater emphasis on social values; a strengthening of intellectual, cultural, and aesthetic values."

Question 4 dealt with whether values would be affected by different specific developments of a scientific, technological, demographic, or socioeconomic nature. Almost all of the possible political-economic-social developments listed in the questionnaire (such as population explosion, urban sprawl, proliferation of atomic weapons, a collapse of the UN) were felt to have significant implications for value change, and so were possible developments in education and "psychotechnics" and "biotechnics" having to do with aging and reproduction. What was surprising to the author, however, was that of a whole range of possible economic-technological developments, such as weather control, the respondents saw only two affecting values—automation in commerce and industry, and the discovery of remote intelligent life. Since the respondents were men with especially well-equipped imaginations, the author can account for this reaction only by concluding that the respondents were convinced that "the scheme of American values has already discounted for the foreseeable developments in this essentially technico-technological area." The only other conclusion of note is that in their answers to all four categories of questions, the respondents were basically optimistic—that is, they welcomed the value changes that they foresaw.

Kahn and Wiener on Value Changes

The only other major attempt to look at personal values in a systematic way seems to be that of Herman Kahn and Anthony J. Wiener. Like Rescher's respondents, Kahn and Wiener foresee a weakening commitment to work-oriented values, including those related to advancement and achievement. Kahn and Wiener argue that in the superindustrial society many who now look on work as an occupation or a career will come to regard work as an interruption and a source of short-term additional income, and that many of the lower classes will shift to regarding work as an occupation or career. And they think that people who have a missionary zeal for work will be looked upon as unfortunate or even harmful. Kahn and Wiener hedge by pointing out that professionals in the service sector will be so busy and so well rewarded that they may be slow to change and that many workers will also be slow to change because of desires for some of the still-expensive luxury items such as vacation homes in exotic places and sporty personal vehicles for road, water, snow, and air. But their general conclusion is that the satisfaction and psychological benefits now derived from work would be met in other ways.

However, Kahn and Wiener argue that the effects of affluence would be different on different segments of society. The relatively poor would be heavily subsidized, and the stigma of accepting welfare is likely to be less. In Kahn and Wiener's words, the feeling that the world owes them a living would go largely unquestioned.

In the superindustrial society almost anyone could be paid today's equivalent of twenty thousand dollars a year or more, while enjoying a greatly reduced work week. A worker could do even better by moonlighting or by having his wife work as well as working himself. Their problem of what to do with their leisure, Kahn and Wiener feel, might be solved with traditional hobbies—golf, bowling, fishing, hunting, motorboating, drag racing, and all the rest.

Kahn and Wiener think the upper middle class would tend to emulate the lifestyle of the landed gentry of the nineteenth century—travel, education, country homes, and the pursuit of cultural values. Kahn and Wiener see the possibility of unstable marriages, alienated children, and an interest in strange and exotic political ideologies.

Youth, they feel, could be especially self-indulgent or alienated. "Indifference to moral and ethical values and irresponsibility of personal behavior would be combined with feelings of outrage about the vast discrepancies between the wealth of the rich nations and the poor. . . ."[7]

Thus even though Kahn and Wiener appear on the surface to agree with Rescher's respondents, basically the disagreement is profound. Kahn and Wiener on the one hand, and Rescher on the other, agree on lessened commitment to work-oriented values. Rescher's respondents see in their place an intellectual, cultural, and aesthetic rebirth. Kahn and Wiener see some segments of society moving in this direction, but they also see other segments of society moving in much less pleasant directions. Basically, Rescher's respondents are optimistic; Kahn and Wiener are pessimistic.

Their disagreement is even greater when it comes to the question of public vs. private values. Where Rescher's respondents

[7] *The Year 2000: A Framework for Speculation on the Next Thirty-three Years* (New York, 1967), p. 207.

foresee a greater commitment to social and public values and less emphasis on private and individual values, Kahn and Wiener see the trend as being exactly opposite. First, Kahn and Wiener argue that an affluent society will undoubtedly see a decrease in the constraints imposed by the harsher reality of today. At the same time, an affluent society may appear to be one that has solved all its problems. Kahn and Wiener point out that the well-known finding that suicide rates drop sharply during wars and economic depressions may suggest that external and public challenges "can serve crucial integrative or compensatory functions for some personalities, and, perhaps, less dramatically, for many others."[8] Although stopping short of predicting that alienation will be the most prevalent reaction to the lack of restraint and the absence of challenge for society as a whole, Kahn and Wiener conclude that the superindustrial society will be a fertile ground for the growth of alienation. "Thus, whatever the economic system, the politics (and even the culture) of plenty could become one not of contentment but of cynicism, emotional distance, and hostility. More and more of the good life would be defined in Epicurean or materialistic, rather than Stoic, or bourgeois terms."[9]

Kahn and Wiener also argue that other aspects of cultural change than those related to affluence may also contribute to increased alienation. In effect, they ask whether some of the malaise of our own times are trends that will continue into the superindustrial society. Kahn and Wiener admit that the causes of alienation today are debatable and that speculation about the future is even more uncertain. "In any case," they write, "it seems plausible that the 'end of ideology' and an inevitable disenchantment with the ideals and expectations of American democracy and free enterprise, coupled with a continued decline in the influence of traditional religion and the absence of any acceptable mass ideologies, have and will continue to contribute to a common spiritual and political rootlessness."[10] Perhaps the most important influence, Kahn and Wiener feel, will be simply the ab-

[8] Ibid., p. 199.
[9] Ibid., p. 200.
[10] Ibid., p. 211.

sence of the traditional challenge of work, community approval, and national needs. Thus for some, Kahn and Wiener see work-oriented values being replaced by "humanist" values. "Indeed, unless there is a surprising interruption in the exponential progress of prosperity, sensate-humanist and epicurean values almost surely will come to dominate older bourgeois virtues. . . ."[11] But for many other people, they see work-oriented values replaced by alienation, emotional distance, cynicism, and hostility. They also feel that the new value structure may also produce irrational and self-indulgent behavior. Many will be alienated from society, in other words, and many more will act like the proverbial "spoiled child."

To sum up, Kahn and Wiener see the superindustrial society as leisure-oriented, epicurean, sensate-humanist, and, in significant part, alienated. But they also think that such a society might be very stable, with an emphasis among some people on the ideal of the "gentleman," as mentioned above, that will require putting a great deal of effort into self-development. Thus there might be a great emphasis on sports, music, art, languages, travel, and on the study of science and philosophy. They point to the fact that today, in spite of the permissiveness of middle-class America toward their children, "when it comes to socially important achievements in school, dancing, music, athletics, and so on they tend to be startlingly demanding."[12] Kahn and Wiener argue that this trend will continue, that in the long run the superindustrial society will develop strong social pressures for self-improvement toward the ideal of the "gentleman." "The crucial point here is that a large majority of the population may feel it important to develop skills, activities, arts and knowledge to meet very high minimum absolute standards, and a large minority more or less compete to be an elite of elites."[13]

Rescher's repondents, to repeat, are optimistic about the consequences on society of changes in values in the superindustrial society. Kahn and Wiener are optimistic about some of the consequences on some segments of society and gloomy about others.

11 Ibid., p. 215.
12 Ibid., p. 218.
13 Ibid., p. 217.

One final view will complete the possible range—the very pessimistic views of Roderick Seidenberg.[14] In the not-too-distant future, Seidenberg argues, mankind will reach a plateau in terms of his knowledge of the world around him and his ability to manipulate it and in terms of the technical and economic development of society. At that stage, in Seidenberg's words, man "will remain encased in an endless routine and sequence of events, not unlike that of the ants, the bees and the termites." Since man will experience no stress, his emotions will atrophy and even his consciousness will wither away.

Conclusions: Value Changes in the Superindustrial Society

Given this wide range from optimism to extreme pessimism on the question of values associated with work in the future, what judgments can be made? First, it seems obvious that we can reject the implication in Keynes' remarks that changes in the values and attitudes of the ordinary man, "bred into him for countless generations," is necessarily something to be regarded with "dread," that there is any biological determinism involved, or that the change will necessarily be all that slow. As we have seen, the oldest industrial society has existed for only slightly more than a century, and although the changes in attitudes and values were profound in every society in which the changeover has taken place, they took not "countless generations" but usually forty years, regardless of whether the political context was authoritarian or laissez-faire.

Attitudes, then, will change, and probably very rapidly. We can probably agree with all the other commentators that one change will be a weakening of the so-called "industrial ethic"— not only in terms of the puritanical values of the virtue of delaying gratification to save, but also in terms of the achievement orientation and measuring success in economic and materialistic terms. If material reward is not so directly linked with labor, the incentive behind the industrial ethic is weakened, and so is the incentive of parents to inculcate such values in their children.

[14] Roderick Seidenberg, *Post-Historic Man* (Chapel Hill, North Carolina: University of North Carolina Press, 1950).

And where is the distinction of economic success if anyone can achieve it?

On the other hand, my own inclination is to reject both the implication in the predictions offered by Rescher's respondents that changes in attitudes and values will tend to be uniform over the whole society, and the specific conclusion reached by Kahn and Wiener that value and attitude changes will not only follow class lines but sharpen them. I would also be skeptical both of the prediction by Rescher's respondents that social values will dominate the future, and the prediction by Kahn and Wiener that private values will dominate.

The most prudent assumption seems to be that the changes in attitudes and values will vary widely and that the over-all pattern will *not* be one of uniformity. No one set of values seems likely to prevail. If so, the most descriptive word for this aspect of the superindustrial society will probably be diversity.

In the past, of all the forces making for uniformity, social pressure has undoubtedly been the strongest, with authority, both political and religious, a close second. As Erik Erikson says, "there are always islands of self-sufficient order—on farms and in castles, in homes, studies, and cloisters—where sensible people manage to live relatively lusty and decent lives: as moral as they must be, as free as they may be, and as masterly as they can be." But social, political, and religious pressures prevail for most people most of the time and force even the free souls to give the appearance of conformity. In the past these pressures have been reinforced by the economic problem, the struggle for subsistence, and sometimes by the security problem of defending the group against outside enemies. Natural intolerance of deviant values and attitudes was reinforced by the very practical consideration that society could not really afford deviant attitudes. Affluence removes this pressure. A certain amount of natural intolerance continues to operate and will continue to operate. But we have also seen an increased commitment to the opposite value: freedom for the individual. On balance, it seems likely that in the absence of the pressures of necessity, the commitment to freedom is likely to prevail.

If this argument that in the absence of pressure or necessity the commitment to freedom for the individual will prevail and produce a diversity of value structures is not sufficiently persuasive, the case can also be put in Marxist terms. The Marxist argument is that values follow the "modes of production"—that the modes of production in an agricultural society produce a feudal value structure and that the modes of production in an industrial society produce capitalist values, the so-called industrial ethic. If machines are to do most of the work, a machine-slave economy is the mode of production, which leaves the individual free or at least does not dictate his behavior and hence his values. The individual is freed from the bonds of the mode of production and can follow preferences and values that are peculiarly his own, or at the very least, values that are not dictated by *economic* imperatives.

A Diversity of Subcultures

The result is likely to be a diversity of subcultures, with different attitudes toward work and work-associated values. The pattern is already beginning to take shape. We have already mentioned the trend toward prolonged youth among college students and the increasing use of this time for self-realization. We have also already mentioned the increasing demand that work be meaningful and relevant, and the willingness to sacrifice higher pay for greater work satisfaction. But even more diverse reactions are also becoming apparent. One is the commune phenomenon. No official count has been made, but an inquiry by the New York *Times* turned up nearly two thousand communes in thirty-four states.[15] "It is now becoming clear," the *Times* concluded from the evidence their correspondents gathered, "that the commune phenomenon, which began most recently in the later nineteen-sixties with the hippie movement, is growing to such proportions that it may become a major social factor in the nineteen-seventies." The average size of the communal groups ranges from five to fifteen persons, frequently in their late teens or early twenties but sometimes all over thirty. The groups share space, finance, the chores of cooking and cleaning, and some-

[15] December 17, 1970, p. 1.

times work and goals. Although the popular myth is that free sex is the principal motivation behind the commune movement, monogamy appears to be the most common arrangement.

Others will use the opportunity given by a birthright allowance or its equivalent to "drop out" of society not in groups but as individuals or traditional families. Again, the phenomenon is already here. A study by reporters of *The Wall Street Journal* of who are availing themselves of various welfare programs and the food stamp program turned up the fact that a certain number of the 13 million people on the welfare rolls in the fall of 1970, although small in percentage terms, were so-called "dropouts" who had learned to use welfare and the food stamp program to finance their way of life.[16] Some are in the cities, sometimes in the traditional places like Greenwich Village, but more frequently in the neighborhood of universities such as Harvard, Columbia, and the Berkeley campus of the University of California, where they could take advantage of libraries, lectures, and other cultural events. Others imitate Thoreau in Vermont, Maine, Arizona, and California. An example cited by the *Journal* is a 35-year-old former science writer with degrees from both Harvard and Columbia. He is building a wooden house on 25 very remote acres in the Redwood country some 200 miles north of San Francisco, which he shares with his friend, Carol, and their baby son. No jobs are available in that remote region, and as a consequence the family qualifies for $168 a month in aid to dependent children. Thirty dollars of this buys $84 worth of food stamps, and $50 goes to the mortgage on the land. The remainder goes for other necessities, seed for the garden, feed for 30 chickens, 2 goats, and a cow, and for materials for building the house. Another example is suggested by the effects of welfare on certain American Indians. A number of anthropologists have remarked that federal welfare programs, though never intended to accomplish that purpose, are the major factor in permitting the Navaho culture to survive. In much the same way, the welfare programs may be permitting new subcultures to be born.

In the future those who drop out, whether as individuals or in

16 January 5, 1971, p. 1.

communes, will probably not be the majority. A substantial proportion will probably continue to work in spite of receiving a birthright allowance, even though many may take no great pleasure in their work. For some the motive will be hedonistic— simply to lead a better life in material terms, to be able to afford the superluxuries available in a superindustrial society, and to be able to fill the long vacations with travel, with a second home in an exotic place, and all the rest.

Others will continue to work a certain minimum in order to afford particular hobbies, the enthusiasts of which will themselves constitute subcultures. Here again we need only look at present trends. Subcultures already exist around surfing, sky diving, motorbiking, snowmobiling, scuba diving, sailing, fishing, hunting, and a host of other hobbies and avocations.

At the same time, if the trend toward machines taking over the routine and repetitive tasks, leaving mainly problem-solving tasks to be done by humans continues, the work that needs to be done in a superindustrial state will be more interesting. A lot of work might not be so absorbing and challenging as to lead to total commitment, but it might be fun for a few hours a day— like solving a puzzle is diverting fun, even though one would not want to make puzzle-solving a life work.

For many other people—those whose work is challenging in terms of intellect, skills, or artistry—work will continue to be the center of their lives. They will continue, as they have in the past, to be devoted to their work as the major source of psychological satisfaction and well-being. We have all known too many individuals like this to doubt that this love of work is likely to be frequent among scientists, doctors, engineers, and others among the professions.[17] But the same motivations will also apply to a number of craftsmen of all types.

Still others may continue to work to fill other kinds of satisfactions. A small shop, for example, is a center of gossip, companionship, and social life, especially in small towns. A shop-

[17] If any further evidence is needed, see James A. Wilson, "Motivations Underlying the Brain Drain," *Values and the Future*, eds. Baier and Rescher, p. 431. Wilson found that the major motivation for the brain drain among scientists and engineers was neither money nor dissatisfaction with life in the homeland, but the superior opportunities to pursue a particular scientific specialty.

keeper may well prefer the life in such a shop to either idleness or devoting himself to a hobby. And for still others there is also satisfaction in the performance of routine tasks.

A Golden Age of Art and Literature

One final possibility also exists: that a birthright allowance will produce not only a proliferation of subcultures but also a great burst of creativity, a golden age of literature and art. Most of the arts require a long apprenticeship and period of growth in which there is normally little or no income. Few people have enough energy left over to be creative after working at a normal job eight hours a day, although there are exceptions. One thinks of Wallace Stevens, who was both a noted poet and a successful insurance company executive. Usually, however, the aspiring artist had to live freezing and starving in a garret, enjoy inherited wealth, or have the luck to acquire a rich patron. Some forms of art require an even greater subsidy. Consider only one example, Eugene O'Neill. To become the great playwright that he was, O'Neill needed an education. He also needed a period of knocking around the world to learn about life. During this period, he did not need a subsidy. But for the next several years, he did—to give him the time to write, tear up, and write again. A playwright also needs one further subsidy: actors and a stage, so he can see the plays and learn why they should be torn up and rewritten. O'Neill was lucky. His father was one of the most successful actors of his day, especially in financial terms. He supplied O'Neill's direct support. The actors were friends, who were either themselves being supported or acted for O'Neill during periods when they were "at liberty." The stage was the Provincetown playhouse—an old fishing pier converted into a summer theater by O'Neill and his friends.[18]

No one can say with certainty that a birthright allowance will produce a golden age of creativity; but one can say that the potential is there. If in the past a potential O'Neill, Shakespeare, Beethoven, or Picasso remained unknown because of lack of opportunity, he will not remain unknown for that reason in the

[18] For the facts on O'Neill's life, see Arthur and Barbara Gelb, *O'Neill* (New Jersey, 1962).

future. At the very least, one of the subcultures of the future is bound to be one devoted to excellence in literature and the arts. Kahn and Wiener's vision of an upper class committed to the concept of the life of the "gentleman" seems questionable principally because the increased commitment to egalitarianism combined with great affluence seems destined to blur class divisions. But it does seem likely that one of the subcultures of the superindustrial society will be something along these lines—a subgroup committed to a life of excellence, culture, and taste.

Summation

To sum up what we can say about values and attitudes in a superindustrial society, then, it seems safe to say that equality, freedom, and justice will be values increasingly shared by all and increasingly realized. Some among the racial and ethnic minorities will find equality in integration, and others will find it in maintaining their separate identity for a time, at least, along the lines, say, of the Amish in Pennsylvania. At the same time, the increasing equality of women will have its effects on conceptions of femininity and masculinity and on the concept and role of the family. The nuclear family will probably survive for quite some time, but society will be increasingly tolerant of individual arrangements radically different from the norm.

Affluence with less work will bring a change in how we conceive the relation of work to income. As a result, each person will be given a birthright allowance—or something similar will come to pass that will give people great freedom in how much they work, when they work, or whether they work at all.

The judgment here is that this will bring about fundamental changes in values and attitudes, and it will do so rather quickly. One of these changes will almost certainly be a weakening of the so-called "industrial ethic"—both the puritanical attitudes, such as that toward savings, and the achievement attitudes that measure success and self-esteem in economic and materialistic terms.

Beyond this, the result seems likely to be not uniformity in values and attitudes, but diversity, with a great variety of subcultures having different attitudes toward work, toward achievement and excellence, toward pleasure and the good life, and toward public and private values.

On the issue of public values vs. private values, if there is to be a rich variety of subcultures with differing mixes of values and attitudes toward work, then it seems likely, as suggested above, that both Rescher's respondents and Kahn and Wiener are wrong. Some of the subcultures described above are clearly oriented almost exclusively to private values. The commune movement is the most obvious example. But others have a high potential for being oriented toward public values. Many of those who continue to be dedicated to their work are automatically committed to public values by the nature of their work. Other subgroups may not be inherently committed to public values but will follow the national leadership if it goes in that direction. The search for a meaningful and relevant life seems likely to continue among at least a proportion of the highly educated young, and some of these will find it in service to others. Moreover, they will not lack in opportunities. In their own countries, the elimination of the vestiges of poverty, prejudice, inequality, and injustice will not come easily, as Tocqueville foresaw long ago. Much work will need to be done in bringing about the change in attitudes. And abroad, in the underdeveloped countries, the opportunity for public service will remain for several generations, at least.

What does seem highly likely is that public values that require across-the-board, wholesale commitment of the entire society will only rarely command support. A diversity of subcultures is not conducive to that kind of commitment by the whole society. What is more, all the various trends—from the trend in personality development to the trend toward diversity of subcultures— seem to work to erode support for what might be called chauvinist goals, such as national power and prestige, quasi-imperialist notions of managing events abroad, or interventionist attitudes. If some future leadership is bent on the pursuit of power and prestige goals, they would probably be successful in winning public support only if they could point to a threat to national security and survival. Even in these circumstances, a society made up of a diversity of subcultures will be highly skeptical, and support for such goals would be forthcoming only if the threat were very obvious and clear-cut.

It may be, of course, that power may be so concentrated at the top in the emerging superindustrial society that the leadership may be able to direct the society's effort to any goals they see fit, with or without public support. President Johnson and the top leaders of his Administration had the power to decide on escalation in Vietnam and to make Vietnam an American war without obtaining advance approval from either the Congress or the public. President Kennedy and his top advisers had the power to blockade Cuba and force the Soviet Union to withdraw its missiles also without obtaining any advance approval. One might regard those decisions as either wise or foolish, but many of those who disagree as to the wisdom of one or the other decision would share an uneasiness about the fact that so much power was so concentrated at the top, an uneasiness that the Presidents and their top advisers were so free to pursue their own goals and values. Thus even though the society as a whole seems unlikely to be interested in power and prestige goals, the leadership may have the power to pursue such goals without regard to the wishes of the wider public. It is to this question of the social structure of superindustrial society and the locus of power within it that we now turn.

CHAPTER 4

Social Structure and the Locus of Power

BESIDES THE SPREAD of egalitarianism, freedom, justice, and the diversity of subcultures, what can be foreseen about the social structure of the superindustrial society? What about Social Security, health, education, crime, and—most important of all for our purposes—the locus of political power?

For most of these, the trends are obvious. For those who choose to work, unemployment compensation, retirement, and survivors' benefits will probably continue as supplements to the birthright allowance for as long as necessary, so that the individual can continue the lifestyle he has chosen in spite of the ups and downs of employment, sickness, and old age. The present-day medical care financed by the government also sets a trend. Sooner or later free medical care from cradle to grave is bound to come.

A similar trend is apparent in higher education. The notion of democracy on which the American republic was founded seemed to require a literate citizenry. It followed in the thinking of the Founding Fathers that education for the responsibilities of citizenship must be free, financed by the society as a whole. Indeed, it also followed that the individual did not have the right *not* to acquire the necessities for citizenship in a democracy; education to that level must also be compulsory. Most of the work to be done in a superindustrial society will require very high levels of education and training, and since the society will be dependent on a steady flow of such highly trained people, it seems inevitable that society will not long continue to depend on the willingness of parents, rich alumni, and foundations to guarantee that flow. The costs of college education will be paid by the society as a whole, and students will be supported by the government. And in terms of the level of income, being a student will be little different from being a working graduate. Indeed, it is likely that people will frequently go back to school in midcareer, for refresher courses to catch up on new knowledge in their field.

But even though it seems likely that in the superindustrial society anyone who desires it and is willing to do the work can have a higher education, it seems doubtful that higher education would be compulsory. Since the work of society could be done by a fraction of the population, the needs are likely to be filled by those who are willing to volunteer.

Crime in the Superindustrial Society

What will happen about crime in the superindustrial society is less obvious. One would suppose that crimes of passion would continue about as before, with perhaps a little lessening if the trend toward fuller personality integration continues. Equality, education, more freedom, a longer period for maturing—all these would seem to mean a higher proportion of emotionally stable, mature people, and this may mean a significant lowering of such crimes statistically. But even so, it seems likely that a certain number of husbands, wives, and lovers will continue to drive each other to murder, as they have throughout the history of mankind. A certain number of barroom quarrels also seem likely to end up in a shooting or a broken skull. Rape is also likely to continue to be familiar. A higher percentage of more mature people and greater sexual freedom will lower the statistics. But enough rapists and potential rapists will still be around to make it necessary for mothers to warn their daughters.

One is less sure about the future of organized crime. Presumably even the great affluence of the superindustrial society would not lessen the incentive for criminals who saw opportunities for stakes that were grand enough. On the other hand, the kind of organized crime that requires large numbers of underlings whose take is relatively small (such as in the numbers racket) seems likely to decline. With a birthright income, the incentive would be very small.

The type of crime that seems most likely of all to decline is what so alarms most people today—muggings, holdups, and burglaries. In a superaffluent society with money for all, the incentive for this type of crime would be low indeed. Even the drug addict—in the unlikely event that the problem survives—could probably find easier ways to finance his habit.

Suicide may actually increase, and so may a very special kind of crime springing from similar causes as suicide—the kind of senseless killing typified by the murder of movie actress Sharon Tate by members of the Charles Manson "family," and the 1970 murder of the California eye surgeon, Dr. Victor M. Ohta, his wife, and children, by a mystic who "signed" the crime "Knight of the Pentacles" and "Knight of the Wands," the names of two of the cards in the tarot system of fortune telling.[1] The imperative to find a goal to substitute for the struggle for survival, the need to find meaning and relevance to life without work, seems likely to bring some personality types to a crisis. This charge on the individual to find his own meaning, plus social boredom—the absence of goals imposed by society, such as war or depression—may well lead some people to despair and suicide. Others might be led to strike out at the imagined causes of their discontent. The murderer of Dr. Ohta and his family apparently saw them as the symbol of a hated materialism. Still other personality types may be led into subcultures with bizarre political and social theories that bring them to commit the crime as a group. The Manson

[1] New York *Times* (October 22, 1970).

"family," for example, had developed a theory of a coming race war that only they would survive, and they murdered Sharon Tate and her friends in order to trigger the events they believed were inevitable.

Locus of Power in a Superindustrial Society

More pertinent to our interests here and these aspects of future society is what is likely to happen to the locus of power. Of those who have attempted to discern the shape of the superindustrial society, only a very few have addressed themselves directly to this particular point. Of these, three will suffice to give us the range of the thinking that has been done—Zbigniew Brzezinski, John Kenneth Galbraith, and Daniel Bell.[2]

Brzezinski's Position

Brzezinski sees a number of changes in the locus of power. First, he sees the university becoming the center of activity. In the *industrial* society, he argues, the university "is an aloof ivory tower, the repository of irrelevant, even if respected wisdom, and for a brief time the fountainhead for budding members of the established social elite."[3] But in the superindustrial society—or "technetronic" society, as he calls it—the university becomes an involved, activist "think tank," a source of political planning and social innovation.

But he also sees other changes in political power in the "technetronic" age, which he contrasts with both the industrial and the agricultural ages. In the shift from agricultural society to industrial society, social leadership passes from the traditional rural aristocracy to an urban-plutocratic elite. In the technetronic age, Brzezinski feels, this plutocratic leadership will be challenged by a political leadership heavily laced with people possessing special skills and intellectual talents. "Knowledge becomes a tool of

[2] Kahn and Wiener, for example, in spite of having written a massive book about the future, do not argue the subject, but seem to assume that the power structure of the superindustrial society will be much the same as that of the present day, with the university playing a slightly more significant role than it does today.

[3] Zbigniew Brzezinski, *Between Two Ages: America's Role in the Technetronic Era* (New York, 1970), p. 12.

power and the effective mobilization of talent an important way to acquire power."[4] He does not say that the universities will become centers of power, but he does imply that people of a type likely to come from the universities will be wherever the center of power is.

Brzezinski believes that ideologies will play a less important role in the superindustrial society. Ideologies thrive in an industrial society, he argues, because the industrial society is dependent on reading and writing for communication, which leads to "static interrelated conceptual thinking, congenial to ideological systems." But in the technetronic age, audiovisual communications will lead to more changeable, disparate views of reality. At the same time, the increasing ability to reduce social conflicts to quantifiable terms, he believes, will reinforce the trend to more pragmatic approaches to social problems.

The role of the masses in a technetronic society, Brzezinski feels, will be a problem. In agricultural societies, the masses are passive. In an industrial society, they become active, and there are political conflicts over such matters as the right to vote. In the technetronic age, the question will be one of ensuring real participation in decisions that seem too complex and too far removed from the average citizen. Political alienation becomes a problem. But so does equal rights for all segments of society—such as women. Since strength is even less necessary in automated plants, women will demand still greater equality.

The masses are organized in industrial societies through trade unions and political parties, unified by rather simple ideological programs. Political attitudes are influenced by appeals to nationalist sentiments through newspapers using the national language. In the technetronic society, the trend, Brzezinski believes, is toward aggregating the individual support of millions of unorganized citizens by attractive personalities who exploit the potentials of electronic means of communication. Television, with its emphasis on imagery rather than language, creates "a somewhat more cosmopolitan, though highly impressionistic, involvement in global affairs."

Economic power, in Brzezinski's view, will also change. In the

[4] Ibid.

early stages of an industrial society, economic power is associated with personalities—like Henry Ford in the United States or bureaucratic officials like Kaganovich in the Soviet Union. The next stage shows a tendency to "depersonalize" economic power stimulated by the appearance of a highly complex interdependence between governmental institutions (including the military), scientific organizations, and industrial organizations. "As economic power becomes inseparably linked with political power, it becomes more invisible and the sense of individual futility increases."[5]

Galbraith's View

Galbraith in his analysis uses the factors of production to illustrate the locus of power in the past and how it is changing today.[6] In an agricultural era, land was the decisive factor of production, and the owners of land were the power holders. With the Industrial Revolution, power shifted to the owners of capital. Recently, Galbraith points out, power has been shifting again, away from capital. The actual *owners* of the big corporations are losing power. It is rare, to give just one of his examples, that stockholders can control a large corporation in any way—even in firing the management, much less in influencing particular policies. "Power," he writes, "has passed to what anyone in search of novelty might be forgiven for characterizing as a new factor of production. This is the structure of organization which combines and includes the technical knowledge, talent, and experience that modern industrial technology and planning require. . . . It embraces engineers, scientists, sales and advertising specialists, other technical and specialized talent—as well as the conventional leadership of the industrial enterprise."[7]

The market, Galbraith argues, no longer determines demand, price, or cost of inputs for a particular product, much less the

[5] Ibid., p. 13.
[6] Galbraith addresses himself specifically to the possible locus of power in the future in "The Shift of Power, Technology, Planning, and Organization," *Values and the Future*, eds. Baier and Rescher. The basic theme, however, is more fully elaborated in his *The New Industrial State* (Boston, 1967) and his *Economics and the Public Purpose* (Boston, 1973).
[7] "The Shift of Power, Technology, Planning, and Organization," pp. 359–60.

over-all allocation of resources for the whole of the society. All are planned and manipulated. Advertising and sales personnel *create* demand. Both price and cost are determined by explicit and implicit negotiation with competitors, government, and union leaders combined with a certain amount of arbitrariness.

Power is gravitating not so much to the management of the big corporations, in Galbraith's view, as to the individuals who possess the knowledge. For an example Galbraith contrasts General Leslie Groves, who commanded the whole Manhattan Project, with Enrico Fermi, who rode a bicycle to his work at Los Alamos. "It was Fermi and his colleagues, and not General Groves in his grandeur, who made the decisions of importance." These men who possess the knowledge are already laying claim to the "eminence and influence" that results from this shift. "The President or Board Chairman, who had as his principal qualification his close liaison with the financial community, is probably an anachronism. Capital is no longer that important. He is being replaced by men whose skills are relation to organization, recruitment, information systems and the other requisites of effective group action."[8]

Galbraith also suggests that the academic will have a greater voice as a consequence of the shift of power to the technocrat in the large corporations, but he then stops short. The new recipients of power, he says, unequivocally, are not individuals—"the new locus of power is collegial or corporate." The implication seems to be that in the future, power will come only through institutions, that a man may wield power only in the name of an organization and as the result of a long climb up the institutional ladder.

Galbraith's major purpose was to analyze the present and anticipate the immediate next stage, not to adumbrate the farther future. Also, he confines himself to economic power, and does not extend the analysis to political power. Even so, the thrust of his analysis is consistent with the conclusions reached by Brzezinski —a highly complex interdependence among governmental organizations, scientific organizations, and industrial organizations and a political leadership "heavily laced" with people possessing special skills and intellectual talents.

[8] Ibid., p. 366.

Bell's Position

It is Daniel Bell who has been most specific in his thinking about the locus of power in the superindustrial, or as he terms it, the postindustrial society. For Bell what is decisive in determining the nature of the postindustrial society is the "new centrality of *theoretical* knowledge, the primacy of theory over empiricism, and the codification of knowledge into abstract systems of symbols that can be translated into many different and varied circumstances. Every society now lives by innovation and growth; and it is theoretical knowledge that has become the matrix of innovation."[9] In the nineteenth and early twentieth centuries the great inventions and the industries that came from them—steel, electric light, telephone, and automobile—were the work of "inspired tinkerers" who often had no idea of the theoretical knowledge lying behind their inventions. Today and in the future, technological advances come from the systematic application of theoretical and scientific knowledge to achieve the planned production of new things. A similar close connection between theory and action appears in the larger decisions affecting the economy and society.

One consequence of this decisive centrality of theoretical knowledge, Bell concludes, is that the university—since it is the place where theoretical knowledge is systematically sought—will become the primary institution of the new society. "Perhaps it is not too much to say that if the business firm was the key institution of the past hundred years, because of its role in organizing production for the mass creation of products, the university will become the central institution of the next hundred years because of its role as the new source of innovation and knowledge."[10]

The technocratic mode has become established because it is the mode of efficiency, of production. "Things," Bell says, "ride men." In the Western world, furthermore, every industrialized

[9] Daniel Bell, *The Coming of Post-Industrial Society: A Venture in Social Forecasting* (New York, 1973), p. 212 ff.; see also his "Notes on the Post-Industrial Society (I)," pp. 28–29.
[10] Bell, "Notes on the Post-Industrial Society (I)," p. 30; *The Reforming of the General Education* (New York, 1966), Chap. 3; and *The Coming of Post-Industrial Society*, pp. 245–46, 344.

society has come to be mobilized—the major resources of the society are concentrated on a relatively few specific objects defined by the government. But in every case, the mobilizer has been military preparedness. "Soldiers," Bell continues, "ride things."

The implication seems to be that Bell is agreeing with Brzezinski and Galbraith—that in the superindustrial age, power will shift to technologists, in the university and in the military. But Bell goes on to argue quite differently. He believes that on the contrary, the political arena will become more decisive "in the United States"—for three reasons. First, the United States is now a *national* society, in the sense that "crucial decisions, affecting all parts of the society simultaneously (from foreign affairs to fiscal policy) are made by the government, rather than through the market. . . ." Second, the United States has become a *communal* society—in the sense that many more groups—farmers, workers, blacks, and the poor—seek to make their claims on society through the political arena as groups rather than as individuals. And finally, the increasing *future orientation* of the society will mean that government will necessarily have to do more and more planning. "But since all of these involve policy decision, it cannot be the technocrat alone, but the political figures who can make them. And necessarily, the two roles are distinct, even though they come into complicated interplay with each other."[11]

In the postindustrial society all these trends will intensify. The needs of the public sector and of public services will mean that government decisions take over even more social and economic decisions from the market. Still more planning will be required, and the more planning there is, the more open group conflicts there will be. For planning "provides a specific locus of decision, and thus becomes a visible point at which pressures can be applied."[12] The nature of many of the issues will make it impossible to decide them on technical grounds. Shall we accept the noise of jets in communities near airports or force a reduction in weight and payloads, for which the industry and traveler must pay?

[11] Bell, "Notes on the Post-Industrial Society (I)," p. 35, and *The Coming of Post-Industrial Society*, p. 360.
[12] Bell, *The Coming of Post-Industrial Society*, p. 364.

Such decisions, Bell argues, involve not technical, but value and political choices.

But when Bell looks at what has happened in the political and governmental arena in the United States and what is likely to happen all over the world, he sees a shift of power and the locus of decision from the politicians in the legislatures to the presidents, prime ministers, and their technologists in the executive branches—the implication being that this shift will leave the general citizenry with even less voice in these choices than ever. Bell cites V. O. Key, David Truman, and others on the nature of the political process in the United States—to the effect that the animating forces of politics are group interests. He quotes Key on nature of the process:

"At bottom, group interests are the animating forces in the political process. . . . The chief vehicles for the expression of group interests are political parties and pressure groups. Through these formal mechanisms groups of people with like interests make themselves felt in the balancing of political forces."

And again on the role of the politician:

"The problem of the politician or the statesman in a democracy is to maintain a working balance between the demands of competing interests and values. . . . The politician in a democracy . . . must be able to hold together enough of these special interests to retain power; he must yield here, stand firm there, delay at the next point, and again act vigorously in a confusing complex of competing forces and interests. . . . The politician . . . must play the part of arbitrator and mediator, subject to the criticism of all."[13]

Bell then argues that Key's description of the political process has been rendered "astonishingly out of date" by three decisive "shaping elements" of national policy today: the influence of foreign policy, the "future orientation" of society, and the increasing role of technical decision-making. Foreign policy, Bell points out, is not formed in reaction to the needs and pressures of domestic interest groups but in response with great-power and ideological interests. In consequence, under conditions of the Cold

13 Both of the quotes Bell chose are from V. O. Key, *Politics, Parties and Pressure Groups* (New York, 1942), pp. 23–24.

War following World War II, the United States became a mobilized society, centralizing decisions about the allocation of an enormous proportion of the resources of the nation. The future orientation—that is, the commitment to economic growth and the rapid social change it brings—has the same effect. Rapid social change has greater impact on larger sections of society. The need to anticipate change and direct it puts even greater emphasis on planning, "on the need to become more conscious of national goals and with the 'alternative futures' which a society with a steady increase in productivity . . . can provide."[14] The combination of these two creates the third, the increasing role of technical decision-making. "The shaping of conscious policy, be it in foreign policy, defense, or economics, calls to the fore the men with the skills necessary to outline the constraints ahead, to work out in detail the management and policy procedures, and to assess the consequences of choices."[15] The most important political consequence of this, in Bell's view, is that legislative and parliamentary bodies will lose power. It will pass to a new kind of executive, what Bertrand de Jouvenal calls a Principate—a chief executive and a body of technologists closely associated with him. The example is the American presidency—the President, and the staff grouped around him in the White House proper and in the Executive Office of the President, including the Bureau of the Budget, the Council of Economic Advisers, and the Office of the Science Adviser. It is here, in the Principate, that the interplay takes place between the politician and the technologist, and not in the Congress or Parliament.

Bell's over-all conclusion is that the "decisive social change taking place in our time . . . is the subordination of the economic function to the political order. . . . The autonomy of the economic order (and the power of the men who run it) is coming to an end, and new and varied, but different, control systems are emerging. In sum, the control of society is no longer primarily economic but political."[16] One of the consequences of this is that more persons are involved, and it takes more time, and cost, to reach decisions. More claimants push into the decision-making

[14] Bell, *The Coming of Post-Industrial Society*, p. 311.
[15] Ibid.
[16] Ibid., p. 373.

process, and interests multiply.[17] Having denigrated V. O. Key's and David Truman's analyses of the interest group basis of politics as "astonishingly out of date," Bell blithely goes on to say that this "politicization of decision-making—in the economy and in the culture—invites more and more group conflict."[18] Indeed, he goes even farther. "Often one hears the statement that individuals or groups feel 'powerless' to affect affairs. But there is probably more participation today than ever before in political life, at all levels of government, and that very increase in participation leads to the multiplication of groups that 'check' each other, and thus to the sense of impasse. Thus increased participation paradoxically leads, more often than not, to increased frustration."[19] If all this is not an "interest group basis of politics," one is hard put to imagine just *what* is!

A Different View

What judgments can be made on this question of the probable locus of power in a superindustrial society? My own view is that Bell has much the best of the argument over Brzezinski and Galbraith, but that in the end he draws the wrong conclusions from his analysis. Putting it another way, it seems to me that Bell is right in saying that the major decisions of the superindustrial society will be made in the political arena and that it is therefore in this arena that power will lie, rather than with technocrats in the big corporations or even in a "complex interdependence" of technocrats in industry, scientific organizations, and government, combined with political leadership "heavily laced" with people possessing technical skills and special intellectual talents. It is true, as Bell says, that the political arena will be central in the future because the United States is now a national society in the sense that crucial decisions affecting the whole of society are made by the government rather than through the market. Another way of putting the point is to say that modern, fully industrialized societies are *articulated* societies—different regions, different strata, and different occupations are intimately interconnected,

[17] Ibid., p. 469.
[18] Ibid., p. 482.
[19] Ibid., p. 469.

and what happens in one region, stratum, or occupation affects the others. In the economic sphere, this articulation is the consequence of specialization of function. In other spheres—cultural life, the realm of ideas, civil liberties, the realm of politics, and the rest—it is a function of communications, of egalitarianism, and of what has been happening to political power. It is also true, as Bell says, that the political arena will be central because the United States is now a communal society, in the sense that more and more interest groups seek to make their claims on society. In the past, workers endured hardship and unfair treatment for an unbelievably long time before they organized. So did blacks and women. But the lesson has been learned, even by such unlikely special interests as homosexuals, whose Gay Liberation Front is busy in the legislative lobbies at the local, state, and federal levels. It is also true, as Bell says, that the increasing "future orientation" of society will require more planning and that this, too, will throw decisions more and more into the political arena. But there is another, still more fundamental reason that more and more of the crucial decisions of society in the future will be political. We have said that modern, fully industrialized societies are articulated societies. This trend will continue and accentuate. This means that what happens in one segment of society will more often affect other segments of society. The potential for conflict inevitably increases. Earlier we also concluded that the long-term trend toward egalitarianism in American society would also continue and accentuate. Simultaneously, better and more extensive education will increase self-awareness and sensitivity to how these interactions affect one's own group and one's own individual position. These consequences will be enormously heightened by increasingly fantastic means of rapid, mass communication. In the past, segments of society such as workers, blacks, and women were slow to recognize that they were exploited, slow to organize, and slow to develop and exercise the political power that could right their wrongs. It is inconceivable that groups with a grievance or even a potential grievance will be so slow in an egalitarian, educated, self-aware society armed with modern means of communication, and it is equally inconceivable that a highly articulated, interconnected mass society will be able to allocate resources, plan for the future, or even function on a day-to-day basis without producing grievances or at least without raising questions of potential grievances and other issues that can be resolved only through processes that in essence are political. Not only will the political arena be central in the superindustrial society, it will also be lively!

But even though Bell is right in thinking that the crucial decisions in the future will be made in the political arena, I would argue that he is wrong in thinking that the university will be the key institution in the superindustrial society and wrong in thinking that power will pass away from the legislature and other places it resides today and become concentrated in a principate of the chief executive and his aides.

The Politics of Policy Making Today

To explain this disagreement and lay the groundwork for a projection of what seems a more likely future locus of political power require a foray into the subject of the politics of policy making in a modern, mass society, and more specifically into the contemporary Washington scene. This is a subject on which many have written at greater length than would be appropriate here. What follows is an attempt to summarize the argument to permit us to see how the locus of power might change in the future.[20]

The Contemporary Washington Scene

What strikes the observer of the Washington scene today is the fact that all the participants in the policy-making process seem to feel relatively powerless—even Presidents. Some anecdotes will illustrate. Following the election of 1952, President Truman, contemplating the prospect of turning over the presidency to General Eisenhower, used to say, tapping his desk, "He'll sit here, and he'll say, 'Do this! Do that!' *And nothing will happen.* Poor Ike—it won't be a bit like the Army. He'll find it very frustrat-

[20] The literature is vast. What follows is an adaptation of my own work on the subject, principally from *To Move a Nation* (1967) and *The Politics of Policy Making in Defense and Foreign Affairs* (1971). Anyone interested in pursuing the subject further should consult the works of Neustadt, Lindblom, Huntington, Schilling, Allison, and the others cited below.

ing."[21] President Kennedy, on more than one occasion when friends made policy suggestions or offered criticisms, used to say, "Well, I agree with you, but I'm not sure the government will." Once at a press conference some weeks after he became President, he surprised his aides by answering a question about Allied trade with Cuba with a promise to put into effect certain measures that were still under discussion among the different departments. "Well," he said afterward with some exasperation, "today I finally made a little policy!"

As Richard E. Neustadt once put it, "Underneath our images of Presidents-in-boots, astride decisions, are the half-observed realities of Presidents-in-sneakers, stirrups in hand, trying to induce particular department heads, or congressmen, or senators to climb aboard."[22]

Since Presidents can very rarely command, they persuade, maneuver, and pressure, using all the levers, powers, and influences they can muster to get the people concerned to come around. Often they succeed, but sometimes they do not. Then they must either pay the political costs of public disunity or make some concession to achieve the unity of compromise. On some occasions, the President clearly makes the decision, even if he cannot make it exactly as he might wish. On other occasions, the decision is just as clearly made by Congress. But in action after action, responsibility for decision is as fluid and restless as quicksilver, and there seems to be neither a person nor an organization on whom it can be fixed. At times the point of decision seems to have escaped into the labyrinth of governmental machinery, beyond layers and layers of bureaucracy. At other times it seems never to have reached the government, but to have remained in either the wider domain of a public opinion stimulated by the press or in the narrower domain dominated by the maneuverings of special interests.

The Multiplicity of Participants

And there is a multiplicity of participants. The President, his personal staff, the secretaries, undersecretaries, and assistant sec-

[21] Richard E. Neustadt, *Presidential Power: The Politics of Leadership* (New York: Wiley, 1960), p. 9. Emphasis in original.
[22] "White House and Whitehall," *The Public Interest*, 2 (Winter 1966).

retaries and their aides who make up an administration are only the beginning. There are a host of subagencies, bureaus, and offices within the various departments that may have interests of their own at variance with the interests of the departments to which they belong. There is the Congress, with rival committees and committee staffs. There are the courts—which by their decisions add to the law as well as interpret it. And there are a lot more people involved than just those who hold official positions. It is no accident that the press is called the "fourth branch of government." It plays a role in the process of governance and performs necessary functions. There are the lobbies and formal interest groups, of which we have already spoken. The academic world plays a role, and there are the quasigovernmental research groups, such as RAND and the Hudson Institute. Both contribute to policy, and have some power to influence it. There are the political parties—and they play a role in policy making as well as in getting people elected. There are the "attentive publics"—audiences who are not formally organized but who are knowledgeable on particular issues and who follow them closely. And there is the mass electorate, which also plays a role.

Of all this multiplicity of participants in the policy-making process, the one whose influence is probably most difficult to determine in any precise way is that of the attentive publics and the mass electorate. But the impression, at least, is that their influence is quite substantial, even though it is subtle and indirect. An examination of presidential policies and public statements over the past twenty years certainly demonstrates that all the Presidents of the postwar period spent an extraordinary amount of time and energy attempting to build public support for their policies and to counter opposing views. Although a purist might argue that this is hardly democracy, the motive behind this presidential effort is fear of retaliation at election time, and even though its influence is indirect, the mass does have influence. The complexity is that what is influential is what the President and other officials *think* the public wants, or even more accurately what influences policy is the President's *estimate* of the results of the policies and how well these results will fulfill what he *thinks* are the policy preferences of the mass public. The process is two-way—that is, the President influences what the attentive public wants if he can, and he adapts his policies to those preferences of the mass public if he can't. But the fact remains that the preferences of the mass public do affect policy.

An example of this complex interplay is President Nixon's Vietnamization policy. From his past statements and personal political history, the outside observer would assume that when Nixon became President, he would prefer a victory in Vietnam and would resist making any sort of a "deal" with the Communist side. On the other hand, the opposition to the Vietnam War was so great by the beginning of his Administration that a decision by Nixon to continue President Johnson's policies would have been politically disastrous. So Nixon tailored his policy to maximize his personal policy preferences and minimize the strength of the opposition. The result was Vietnamization—withdrawing American troops while building up the number, quality, and equipment of the Republic of Vietnam's troops, combined with negotiations leading to the withdrawal of American troops rather than a final settlement of the war. The attentive publics opposing the war did not get what they wanted by far, but they did influence policy in the direction they wanted. President Nixon, in turn, did not succeed in persuading everyone in his direction, but he did persuade enough people with influence to reduce the power of the opposition quite significantly, at least for a time.

The Intermediate Structure

Between the mass publics and the President are not just interest groups, as Bell's quote from Key implies, but what David B. Truman calls the "intermediate structure" of government. "This structure—which in simplest terms includes at least the great array of interest or pressure groups, corporations, trade unions, churches, and professional societies, the major media of communication, the political parties, and, in a sense, the principal state and local governments—this pluralistic structure is a central fact of the distribution of power in the society. It is a structure that is intervening between government at the national level and the rank and file of the population, intervening rather than subordinate or dominating."[23]

On the input side of policy making, the function of this intermediate structure is the "articulation of interests."[24] It is through the intermediate structure that people define their interests, and work out the implications of various policy proposals, laws, and so on, for the interests identified. The intermediate structure articulates interests, identifies these interests to individuals, and identifies people sharing an interest to each other and to those with the power to do something about satisfying the interest. And the structure also facilitates movement in the opposite direction: the transmission downward to the membership of information, interpretation, and potential conflict with other values and interests and with other, rival or opposition interest groups.

All large societies have some device to perform this function of interest articulation. In both Hitler's Germany and Stalin's Soviet Union, for example, there were various mass organizations performing this "transmission belt" function both upward and downward, even though in both cases membership was mandatory and the instrument was often more a tool of government for its purposes than a tool of the membership for its purposes. In non-Western societies, we see the same function performed through quite different instrumentalities. Instead of labor unions and granges articulating the interests of workers and farmers, for example, in certain Asian countries the function is performed by the extended family system, and in at least one country—Vietnam—at a certain period in history partly by a series of secret societies or sects.

At the output side of policy making, the Washington end, there is struggle and conflict. At the same time, there is a "strain toward agreement,"[25] an effort to build a consensus, a push for accommodation, for compromise, for some sort of agreement on

---

[23] This particular quote is from one of Truman's articles, "The American System in Crisis," *Political Science Quarterly*, 74 (December 1959), but the full analysis is contained in his book *The Governmental Process: Political Interest and Public Opinion* (New York, 1951).

[24] See Gabriel A. Almond and G. B. Powell, Jr., *Comparative Politics* (Boston, 1966).

[25] The phrase is Warner R. Schilling's. See his "The Politics of National Defense: Fiscal 1950," *Strategy, Politics, and Defense Budgets*, eds. Warner R. Schilling, Paul Y. Hammond, and Glenn H. Snyder (New York, 1962), p. 23.

the policy decision. There are independent participants in the process who may be able to block a policy, or sabotage it, or at least to snipe away at it from the sidelines. There may be other men whose active, imaginative support and dedicated efforts are required if the policy is to succeed, and it may take concessions aimed directly at them and their interests to enlist this kind of willing cooperation. Finally, there is in all participants an intuitive realization that prolonged intransigence, stalemate, and indecision on urgent or fundamental issues might become so intolerable as to threaten the very form and structure of the system of governance.

The Concentric Circles of Policy Making

Viewed from Washington, the process presents itself as a series of concentric circles. The innermost circle, of course, is the President and the men in the different departments and agencies who must carry out the decisions—staff men in the White House, the secretaries of the great departments and agencies, the director of the CIA, and the assistant secretaries of State, Defense, and so on, who bear responsibility for whatever the particular problem may be. Some matters never go beyond this circle, but even here the process is political. The various factions may be represented at the very table—during the long struggles over Vietnam policy, for example, most of the time both "doves" and "hawks" were present at this inner circle. But even when they are not, their presence is felt.

Beyond this innermost circle lie other departments of the Executive Branch and other layers within the agencies and departments already involved, including presidential commissions, scientific advisory panels, and so on. Even though the debate might still remain secret from the press, the Congress, and the public, the struggle can still be fierce. And if the interests affected are fundamental, the debate will not long remain within this closed circle. One illustration will suffice. In 1957, President Eisenhower set up the so-called Gaither Committee to study civil defense in terms of nuclear war. The study soon took up the "New Look" decision to concentrate on air power, and the whole of the Eisenhower administration's defense policy. Several hundred people worked that whole summer, and the debate between the two factions was fierce. But there was no leak—mainly because both sides still hoped to persuade the President to their view. Toward the end of the summer, however, when it became clear both that the report would recommend far-reaching changes in the Administration's defense policy and that the President would probably not accept those recommendations, a crucial battle took place. The battle was not on the substance of policy, but on the issue of whether there would be two hundred Top Secret copies of the report or only two. Everyone knew without saying so that if the President did not accept the Gaither Committee's recommendations, it might be possible to keep the report from leaking to the press and Congress if there were only two copies, but never if there were two hundred. The committee won the battle, and two hundred Top Secret copies were distributed within the Executive Branch. The President did not accept the recommendations, and, sure enough, within a few days Chalmers Roberts of the Washington *Post* was able to write a story, covering almost two newspaper pages, that contained an accurate and comprehensive account of both the Top Secret report and its recommendations.

The final arena, of course, is the public one, involving Congress, the press, interest groups, and attentive publics. If the issue requires legislation, the power of all these to influence policy is obvious. But if the issue is important enough to sustain attention, and if it lasts long enough for the different factions to muster support, all these many participants can eventually exercise their influence. The most dramatic example, of course, is the reversal of President Johnson's policy on Vietnam, his decision to stop the bombing of North Vietnam, to negotiate in Paris, and to withdraw from the presidential race of 1968. No votes were taken, but the steadily growing opposition to his policy of escalating the war—among students, in the wider publics, in the press, in Congress, and within his own Administration—eventually convinced Johnson that he had no other choice. The alternative would have been an obstructive and paralyzed Congress and a polarized society.

The Sources of Power

Now, if the above analysis of the politics of policy making is correct, what can be said about the locus of power and about its *sources?* It is beyond dispute that power is a factor in any political process. Everyone recognizes the obvious fact that some people have more power than others in every society in the world, and all the great social thinkers have devoted their attention to the nature of power. As Robert A. Dahl has pointed out, the existence of so much comment arouses two suspicions.[26] The first is that where there is so much smoke there must be fire, and some "Thing" that can be called power must exist. The second suspicion is that "a Thing to which people attach many labels with subtly or grossly different meanings in many different cultures and times is probably not a Thing at all but many Things. . . ."

At certain times and in certain places, military power, for example, may be starkly central in domestic affairs; civil war is the obvious example. But to the extent that military strength is a *source* of power on the domestic scene, the mechanism is not so crude. In the making of foreign policy there has been a policy view and position emanating from what President Eisenhower called the "military-industrial complex" on some issues, such as arms control and Vietnam, both of which involved a large military stake. In such cases power has clearly been exerted in support of that view and position. But as a force, the military-industrial complex has been loosely organized, amorphous, more potential than structured—nothing, certainly, that resembles in the slightest the "power elites" described in Marxist and neo-Marxist literature.

On the domestic scene, clearly, power has more varied and subtle sources than in either force and violence or wealth and class. Power grows not only "out of the barrel of a gun," as Mao Tse-tung would have it, but also in legitimacy, in legal authority, in expertise, and in special interest that is recognized as legitimate, such as the interest of the farmer in agricultural policy or the banker in monetary policy. It is so varied and subtle in its sources, indeed, that one wonders whether "power" is the most useful word.

[26] "The Concept of Power," *Behavorial Science* (July 1957).

Power can be the negative power that Congress has of making life difficult for the President if one of its treasured views is ignored. It can be the legal and constitutional right to decide in a formal sense—which is more the right of Congress in domestic affairs and more the right of the President in foreign affairs, but in both is sometimes the reverse. It can be influence, in the sense of having the ear of the President or the respect of the leaders of Congress without holding any office at all. It can be the ability to have one's views at least taken into account because one represents a special interest group like the farmers, as we said, whose legitimacy is recognized. It can also be the ability to have one's views taken into account simply because one has convinced the world that one speaks for a wider public and that there will be political consequences if one is ignored. An example is Ralph Nader, who picked up the issue of safety in automobiles as a private citizen and raised enough hell to become so recognized as a spokesman for consumers that he made some of the giant corporations tremble. It can also be the ability to have one's views taken into account because of one's personal expertise. When George Kennan speaks about policy toward the Soviet Union, for example, the government listens even when it abhors the advice offered and refuses to take it. Power can also come simply because one has a "platform" that gives one the opportunity of enlisting a particular constituency. An Adlai Stevenson or a Chester Bowles out of office could influence policy by his ability to command a hearing before "liberals" and the possibility that he might swing the whole constituency with his persuasiveness. A scientist who is completely unknown outside the scientific community might develop such leverage, for example, and if the subject matter concerned a scientific question, his leverage might be overwhelming. No President would lightly go against the consensus of scientists on a matter in the area of their specialty.

In some circumstances, power can be a position from which simply to *interpret* events. This is the real power of the press. It is not just the columnists, whose writings are clearly labeled as interpretation, but in the news stories. Which facts are selected for reporting and the way those facts are arranged can be more effective interpretation, even though only implied, than the persuasiveness of a Walter Lippmann, a James Reston, or an Eric Sevareid. Again, Vietnam provides a dramatic example. The press played the news of the Tet offensive in the spring of 1968 very dramatically, suggesting that the Viet Cong could strike anywhere in Vietnam almost at will, that the defenses against them were weak, and that the optimism that had come from the American Embassy, the military headquarters, and Washington had been exposed as false. The Johnson administration, on the other hand, interpreted the offensive as a "desperate last gasp" of a defeated enemy, as a total failure resulting in prohibitive casualties for the Communist side and as a prelude to an imminent collapse of the enemy effort. It was vitally important to the Johnson administration which interpretation was to win the struggle for general acceptance. If the enemy was virtually defeated and victory a matter of only a few more months of cleaning up, public and congressional support for the war effort could undoubtedly be sustained. But if the Viet Cong were stronger than ever, as suggested by the press interpretation, and the war would have to go on for a long time at even higher levels of violence and sacrifice, then public and congressional support would almost immediately collapse. With the benefit of hindsight it can be argued that both interpretations were oversimplifications, but the fact is that in the end it was the interpretation offered by the press that generally prevailed, and not that offered by the President and other members of the Administration. Because of this, the opposition in the Congress, the public, and even within the Administration was immeasurably strengthened, and Johnson felt impelled to reverse his whole policy—and, to make the change credible, also to withdraw as a candidate for re-election.

Within the Executive Branch, some bureaucrats are able to build enormous personal power—at least over the area of their responsibility—that is quite independent of everyone, including the President. J. Edgar Hoover is the classic example. For forty years he headed the FBI, cultivating its natural constituency among the state and local police forces, within the Congress, and by a skillful manipulation of the press, magazines, and movies. By the time of President Roosevelt's death he was beyond the

power of any President to fire him or even to arrange for his retirement!

But where some within the Executive Branch have power independent of the President, many have the power precisely because they are close to him and enjoy his confidence. Power also
comes from using a "job platform" so that it fills a larger need,
which can bring still wider responsibility and more power. The
position and title—the "platform"—that McGeorge Bundy occupied in the Kennedy administration existed in Eisenhower's day,
but it was Bundy who made it powerful. Power comes from expertise, from representing a particular constituency, whether
within or outside the government, from institutional backing,
and from statutory or designated authority and responsibility.
The mere title of Secretary of State gives a man authority, in addition to what he acquires through statute and custom.

The richness of the sources of power goes back to the nature of
the political process of conflict and consensus-building by which
policy is made. Within the government and outside it, to repeat,
there are different constituencies with a stake in the outcome.
The State Department may have jurisdiction over the general
problem, for example, while the Pentagon must implement one
aspect of it and the Agency for International Development another. Even if the President's prestige and position are not involved, his approval may be a legal or a political necessity. This
may be true of Congress, also. If so, the outside constituencies
are likely to be drawn in—interest groups, newspapermen, academic commentators, and the still wider constituency of the particular attentive public.

On a major issue the advocate of a particular policy, even if
there is neither a rival advocate nor a rival policy, must build a
consensus to support his policy in the different constituencies
within the government and frequently outside as well. He needs
the active cooperation and support of some, the formal or informal
approval of others, and at least the acquiescence of still others.
He may prevail over the active opposition of one or another constituency, but rarely if it is from within the government and the
enterprise is large, for even passive opposition can bring a large
and complicated enterprise to failure, not by sabotage, but sim-

ply by lack of enthusiasm. When there are rival advocates or rival policies, on the other hand, there is not only debate before the different constituencies, but competition for their support. Alliances are formed, and all the techniques of consensus-building appear: persuasion, accommodation, and bargaining.

Over some of this at certain times the President may merely preside, if it is a matter of slight interest to him and has little impact on his position. But if *he* is an advocate or if the outcome affects *his* position and power, then the President, too, must engage in the politics of policy making. In the field of foreign affairs, the President's power in recent years has been immense. His has been the monopoly of dealing with other states. But he, too, must build a consensus for his policy if it is to succeed. He must bring along enough of the different factions in Congress to forestall revolt, and he must contend for the support of wider constituencies, the press, interest groups, and the attentive publics. Even within the Executive Branch itself, his policy will not succeed merely at his command, and he must build cooperation and support, obtain approval from some, acquiescence from others, and enthusiasm from enough to carry it to completion. This is the truth that Vice President Dawes was alluding to when he said that cabinet ministers are a President's natural enemies. It is the truth that so amused President Truman when he said that Eisenhower would find that the presidency was "[not] a bit like the Army." It is the truth that President Kennedy had in mind when he said that although *he* agreed, the government might not. And it is the "half-observed realities" that Neustadt saw of "Presidents-in-sneakers, stirrups in hand," trying to persuade all the barons of Washington to go along.

A Power Elite in America?

One final question that bears most directly on the question of the locus of power in American society is whether there is any truth to the charge that policy in the United States is determined by a "power elite." The most famous and most often quoted of these charges are those of C. Wright Mills.[27] Mills argues that

[27] The following is drawn from Mills' article "The Structure of Power in American Society," *British Journal of Sociology* (March 1958), where the argument is more succinctly stated than in his book *The Power Elite* (New York, 1956).

power in the United States is monopolized by three elites: military, economic, and political. "The power to make decisions of national and international consequence is now so clearly seated in political, military, and economic institutions that other areas of society seem off to the side and, on occasion, readily subordinated to these." Each of these three elites, Mills asserts, has become increasingly interlocked with the others. The result, Mills argues, has been the development of one over-all power elite whose parts act together for their mutual interest—that in effect they conspire. "For as each of these domains has coincided with the others, as decisions in each have become broader, the leading men of each—the high military, the corporation executives, the political directorate—have tended to come together to form the power elite of America."

Although Mills denied that he believed the coordination among the three is the result of a deliberate plot, he said that the three are so unified and single-minded that the result is the same as if it were conscious and deliberate. This unity, he argues, comes from several sources. One is a similar social background. Another is what he calls "interchangeability of positions," by which he apparently means mainly that retired military men take positions in industry dealing with defense. And finally, he sees all three as having a common self-interest: "the development of a permanent-war establishment, alongside a privately incorporated economy, inside a virtual political vacuum."

His over-all judgment on American society and his basic conclusion is expressed in a single paragraph:

> The top of modern American society is increasingly unified, and often seems wilfully coordinated: at the top there has emerged an elite whose power probably exceeds that of any small group of men in world history. The middle levels are often a drifting set of stalemated forces: the middle does not link the bottom with the top. The bottom of this society is politically fragmented, and even as a passive fact, increasingly powerless; at the bottom there is emerging a mass society.

Mills has been heavily criticized for his cavalier treatment of scientific method, rigor, and objectivity and for what sometimes seems a deliberate disregard for facts. Talcott Parsons, for example, points out that "Mills' close identification of the very rich (i.e., the holders of 'great fortunes') with the 'corporate rich' (the primary holders of executive power in business organizations) as a single class cannot be accepted in any useful sense." With a few exceptions, Parsons says, control has passed from families "to professional career executives, who have not reached their positions through the exercise of *property* rights but through some sort of process of appointment and promotion."

Another ground for criticism is Mills' assertion that the power elite stem from similar social origins, while the examples he himself uses show a very wide diversity. One general mentioned by Mills, for example, is not from an upper social class, as he suggests, but is actually the adopted son of an Irish coal miner. Even the five Presidents since World War II illustrate a social diversity that is difficult to reconcile with Mills' assertion. Truman was the son of a middle western farmer. Eisenhower also came from the Middle West, but from a small-town background rather than from farming. Neither had wealth. Kennedy was the son of a man who was very, very rich, but whose family was immigrant Irish and never fully accepted in aristocratic Boston. Johnson was the son of a Texas rancher, whose ranch was in the impoverished piedmont rather than the rich cattle lands. Nixon, finally, was the son of a grocery store owner in a small town in California. The only one who comes near Mills' description is Kennedy, and even he lacked the social connections implied in some of Mills' assertions. To find a President who had the social connections as well as wealth, one would have to go back to Franklin D. Roosevelt, who came from a moderately wealthy, aristocratic New York family with old Dutch antecedents.

C. Wright Mills can be dismissed rather easily, but the question of whether there is a "power elite" does deserve serious attention. Robert A. Dahl, partly in criticism of Mills and others, laid down the requirements to demonstrate the existence of a power elite.[28] First of all, Dahl rejects "quasimetaphysical" theories. The following would be an example: If it turns out that the overt

[28] "A Critique of the Ruling Elite Model," *The American Political Science Review* (June 1958), p. 463.

leaders of a community are not a ruling elite, the theory can be saved by arguing that behind the overt group there is a set of covert leaders. If the evidence shows that the covert group does not constitute a ruling elite, the theory again can be saved by arguing that behind the first covert group lies another—and so on.

Dahl also rejects a number of "bad tests." One of these is confusing a ruling elite with a group that has a very high *potential for control*. Mills' triumvirate certainly has such a potential. But a potential for control is not the same thing as actual control, or even significant influence. "The actual *political effectiveness* of a group," Dahl writes, "is a function of its potential for control *and* its potential for unity. Thus a group with a relatively low potential for control but a high potential for unity may be more politically effective than a group with a high potential for control but a low potential for unity."

The second improper test is to confuse a ruling elite with a group of individuals who have more influence than others. Obviously, the President, the Secretary of State, and the Secretary of Defense have more influence over foreign policy than the rest of us, but that does not make them a ruling elite.

The third improper test is "to generalize from a single scope of influence." Bankers, for example, have more influence than the rest of us on fiscal policy. Oilmen have more influence on oil policy. Grange officials have more influence on agricultural policy. This is natural in the working of attentive publics, congressional constituencies, and so on. If bankers and oilmen are part of a ruling elite they must be shown to have more influence over, say, agricultural policy than grange officials do.

Dahl's conclusion is that the hypothesis of the existence of a ruling elite can be strictly tested only if:

1. The hypothetical ruling elite is a well-defined group.
2. There is a fair sample of cases involving key political decisions in which the preferences of the hypothetical ruling elite run counter to those of any other likely group that might be suggested.
3. In such cases, the preferences of the elite regularly prevail.

If this threefold test is used, the United States has no ruling elite in any meaningful sense. The people who make policy are certainly not a well-defined group. On the contrary, a wide variety of people are involved—the President, the members of the Cabinet, other members of an administration, civilian and military officials in all the many departments and agencies, ambassadors and their staffs overseas, members of the Congress and their staffs, the press, interest groups and lobbies, specialists and experts in the universities and research organizations, attentive publics, and, on occasion, the mass electorate.

And any examination of particular cases of either foreign or domestic policy certainly shows little unity, even among the people most intimately involved. On every major issue of both domestic and foreign policy, there has been disagreement, and frequently the disagreements have cut across institutional lines. Even on Vietnam, for example, there have been military "doves" as well as military "hawks."

When faced with such evidence, some proponents of the ruling-elite theory will concede that those involved in making policy do not constitute a well-defined group and that there is no evidence that any ruling elite, overt or covert, is behind the scenes giving them orders—i.e., that there is no evidence that the big corporations, for example, have any direct voice on, say, Vietnam policy. But, they argue, all those involved in policy making share an American "capitalist-imperialist" outlook, and they make their foreign-policy decisions in the interests of the big corporations or Mills' military-economic-political power elite without being told to do so. Now, this is very close to one of the "quasimetaphysical" theories that Dahl describes, but it also cannot be denied that the people who make policy are Americans and that Americans do share certain attitudes. The trouble is that the attitudes that foreign observers agree Americans share are too general to be guides to specific policies of any kind, much less "capitalist-imperialist." Most foreign observers agree, for example, that Americans are pragmatic, activist, and egalitarian, but none of these qualities necessarily suggests that American foreign policy in the Middle East, for example, will be conducted to serve the interests of the oil companies.

In addition, the general assertion that the people involved in the making of American policy have an ingrained "capitalist-imperialist" outlook that leads them to act in the interest of the big corporations ignores a number of attitudes that are hostile to those interests. There is a populist tradition in America, strongly held by a number of powerful congressmen, for example, that regards the big corporations and the eastern seaboard financial interests as greater enemies than either communism or fascism. There is also an isolationist sentiment that runs equally strong.

The assertion that United States foreign policy is conducted to serve the interests of the big corporations also ignores United States foreign policy. It is obvious, for example, that United States foreign policy in the Middle East, where oil reigns supreme, has been more responsive to the pressures from the American Jewish community and their natural desire to support Israel than it has to American oil interests.

No one can deny there is evil in American society and that some governmental policies have resulted in evil. The proponents of a ruling-elite theory believe that this evil is the result of a concentration of power, but in fact the opposite is more nearly the case. Consider two examples: H. L. Hunt and the National Rifle Association (NRA). H. L. Hunt, the Texas oil multimillionaire, is purported to be the richest man in the United States, if not in the entire world. He is, clearly, an outstanding candidate for a place in a ruling elite. His views on social questions, his policy preferences, can best be described as right-wing extremist. He is opposed to recent civil rights legislation, to Social Security, to Medicare, and so on. He has spent a great deal of money to further his policy preferences, but in his own view as well as that of others, he has had remarkably little impact. The members of the National Rifle Association, on the other hand, in general do not qualify for membership in a ruling elite. They are mainly lower-middle-class, from rural and small-town backgrounds. But on one issue, gun control legislation, they have prevailed against all comers. For over thirty years, public-opinion polls have shown that more than 60 per cent of Americans favor gun-control legislation. In addition, a formidable array of people who should be part of any ruling elite, if one exists, have worked hard to get an effective gun control law—including Nelson A. Rockefeller, as governor of New York, and Edward M. Kennedy, as senator from Massachusetts. But the NRA, with a membership of only 825,000, has prevailed. One half of 1 per cent has blocked 60 per cent. In a society where power is diffused, a minority that feels intensely can often have its way on a narrow policy issue over a majority that feels differently but not so strongly.

Some decisions on United States policy are made by a very few men, most often in foreign affairs. The decision to bomb North Vietnam and to send American combat forces to the war is an example. That decision was made by President Johnson and not more than a dozen others. When such a decision results in evil, it can be fairly attributed to a concentration of power. But most of the evils in American society—the long oppression of the blacks, the decline of the cities and the crime that is thereby generated, the poverty, the pollution of water and air—stem not from the concentration of power, but at least in part from its diffusion. The very profusion of so many centers of power makes building the kind of consensus necessary for positive measures a formidable task.

Role of the Universities in the Future

Against this background on the political arena of today, the disagreement with Bell and Brzezinski about how it will look in the future becomes clear. The universities, to take their first point, are not likely to become power centers. It may well be true that the holders of high office will have greater need to be learned and well-trained, and the university will presumably continue to have a hand in their training. But that does not mean that the university as such will have either more or less power than it has had in the past. Individuals who are knowledgeable and articulate will also be able to develop personal influence in the future, as Ralph Nader and others have done in the past. But, again, even though the universities will probably continue to have a hand in the training of these men, it is not likely that the university will be their platform either more or less often than it has been their platform in the past.

If, as Bell and Brzezinski assume, the university does in fact continue to be a center of research and the production of new knowledge, it will have some power. It will have a very powerful voice in setting priorities for future research and over the allocation of monies for research. But just because they produce new knowledge in foreign affairs or economic affairs, say, does not mean that the universities as institutions will have power over foreign policy or economic policy. Experts have had power in the past and will in the future, but they will exercise that power *indirectly* so long as they remain in the university—through the persuasion of their writing, as teachers of practitioners, as witnesses at hearings, and as advisers to participants in the policy-making process. The only way they will exercise power *directly* will be as ex-academics turned participants.

And the fact of the matter is that it is not certain that the universities will be the source of new knowledge and theory, as Bell and Brzezinski assume. Since World War II, a substantial amount of research in the physical and biological sciences has been done in laboratories run by big corporations. In the social sciences and in the fields of foreign and defense policy, especially, a new kind of research institution has also appeared—the independent, nonprofit "think tank" run on government contract, such as RAND, the Hudson Institute, and the Institute of Defense Analysis. Government contracts with the universities, which financed a huge proportion of the research done in universities in the fifties and early sixties, have declined drastically, and student unrest may cause them to decline even more. Increasingly, the universities may be concentrating on teaching rather than research. If so, the universities will exercise power only over their narrow concern, as other specialized industries do—as a constituency for policy dealing with teaching subsidies for students and such, just as farmers are a constituency for agricultural policy and crop subsidies.

The Presidency and a Principate of Power?

On the broader question of the locus of power in the future, it seems very doubtful indeed that the new mode will be a principate of the Chief Executive and his immediate cohorts. The situation that has developed since World War II is not a further concentration of power in the hands of the Executive, but a diffusion of power, or more accurately a proliferation of additional power centers. Congress has, it is true, lost some power, but not so much to the Executive as to a whole variety of groups and subgroups within the "intermediate structure." The pattern is clear across the whole range of domestic affairs. Blacks, Spanish-Americans, and Indians are all organizing and demanding a voice in their own affairs. Teachers, policemen, sanitation workers, and even welfare *recipients* are both better organized and more determined to be heard. Local communities are demanding a bigger voice in school policies. Even the federal government's poverty program failed on the issue of lack of local participation and control. In domestic affairs, the President is still the first, but he is the first among many. He is hardly a principate.

It is only in foreign affairs that the President has resembled a principate in this period since World War II—and here he has, indeed, reigned supreme. President Truman had to have congressional approval for the Marshall Plan and the Atlantic treaty, but it is doubtful that anyone could have successfully said him nay. And for the Truman Doctrine and his decision to enter the Korean War, he needed no formal approval at all. Neither did Eisenhower for the Lebanon landings, Kennedy for either his decision to neutralize Laos or for his action in the Cuban missile crisis, or Johnson for his decision to intervene in the Dominican Republic or the more momentous decision to bomb North Vietnam, send American combat troops, and make the Vietnamese war an American war.

But the very fact of these decisions, and especially the Vietnam decisions, may already be working a change. The fact that Presidents have such awesome power and that they exercise it in such an awesome era, dominated as it is by nuclear weapons and intercontinental missiles, has troubled people at every level of society for some time. But President Johnson's stubborn and insistent policy on Vietnam turned the doubts of a number of people in a position to do something about it into a determination. President Nixon's continuation of the war for four years and his imperious decisions to mine Haiphong Harbor, to invade Cambodia, and to launch a massive bombing campaign on North Vietnam in December 1972, reinforced this determination. The mood is not confined to liberals. Senator John Stennis, one of the most powerful conservatives in the Senate, said that the most important lesson of the Vietnam War was that in the future no President should be allowed to send American troops abroad without a declaration of war by the Congress.[29]

Even with the help of men like Stennis, the Congress found the problem of curbing the President's power in foreign affairs slippery. The point, however, is that the effort has been and is being made. The curb on the war powers of the President passed by the Congress in the autumn of 1973 will undoubtedly turn out to be only the first of what will be many proposals. How far the Congress can go in curtailing the power of the President in foreign affairs will depend on events. If the international environment is not particularly threatening in the next decade, they are likely to go very far indeed. But merely making the effort will have some effects in that direction. For the next decade, at least, Presidents will be extraordinarily reluctant to take action that will be seen as adventuring likely to lead to another disaster like Vietnam, and the Congress and the press will be extraordinarily vigilant and aggressive in probing to see if any action can be seen in that light. Even without legislation, this sensitivity alone will curb the President's power in foreign affairs to some extent.

A Diffusion of Power

What Brzezinski foresees, to repeat, and Galbraith seems to support, is that power in the future will be wielded in a highly complex interdependence by highly trained people in government, scientific organizations, and industrial organizations combined with a political leadership "heavily laced" with people possessing special skills and intellectual talents. Although I am not entirely certain exactly what is meant by this statement, in one aspect it seems consistent with the trends we have been examining, and in another aspect, inconsistent. If the statement

[29] As quoted in the Washington *Post* (January 12, 1971), p. A2.

means that the political leadership will change from the kind of ward-heeler/wheeler-dealer/interest-group-broker kind of politician who made public office a career for personal livelihood and hopefully personal fortune to a more public-spirited, issue-oriented, intelligent, and highly educated type—if this is what is meant, there can be no quarrel. This change began when Franklin D. Roosevelt's New Deal took welfare out of the hands of the city bosses and their political machines—but the point is more succinctly put in Edwin O'Connor's novel *The Last Hurrah* than in any political science treatise. And in spite of the fact that his first two successors were more in the traditional mold of politicians, the trend was given an additional push by John F. Kennedy.

On the other hand, there seems to be a hint in both Brzezinski's and Galbraith's formulation that the technologists of government, industry, and scientific organizations, combined with the political leadership, will form something similar to a nineteenth-century elite. If this is what they really do foresee or if there is any implication even of concert between the various power centers out of mutual self-interest, much less collusion or conspiracy, then I have doubts. If this is not what is intended, if Brzezinski and Galbraith mean only that people in all these different institutions and at all these different levels of society will be involved and have a voice in decisions in the area of their particular responsibilities— if they mean this, then again there can be no quarrel. It seems to me that all these different trends we have discussed—egalitarianism, higher education for more people, affluence and hence time and freedom, fuller and more rapid communications, greater interdependence of the economy and other aspects of life—that all these trends combine into an over-all political trend toward more participants in the policy-making process with more nearly equal power. It is undoubtedly true that lone individuals will have difficulty exercising influence. Only those with high expertise, prestige, and gifts of persuasion in speaking and writing will be able to exercise individual influence. The rest will exercise their power and influence through organizations. But there will be more of these, expressing a greater variety of interests and exercising greater, yet more nearly equal power. The political arena, in other words, will be marked by a further diffusion of power, or more accurately a further proliferation of power centers. The intermediate structure, to pick up the social science jargon, will contain more power centers with bigger voices.

Psychological Consequences of a Diffusion of Power

One final question remains to be asked: what the psychological consequences are likely to be of this diffusion of power and the effects on social cohesion. We have seen the fears of present-day youth of bigness and of the impersonality of institutions, their desire to be treated as unique individuals, their search for meaning and relevance, and their hopes for a governmental process in which the individual can participate in the decisions that affect him and for "participatory democracy." And it is not only the youth who share these concerns. Brzezinski, for example, worries over the question of "ensuring real participation in decisions that seem too complex and too far removed from the average citizen" and the political alienation that may result. He sees economic power becoming invisible in a merger with political power and is concerned that the result may be an increasing "sense of futility." How will all these fears and aspirations be affected by a society in which power is diffused?

It seems obvious that anyone whose satisfaction depends upon feeling that he and he alone is responsible for a particular decision or policy is doomed to frustration and alienation in such a society. Today, when power is only partly diffused, even Presidents, as we have seen, are familiar with the feeling of frustration.

It also seems obvious that the frustrated and alienated will also include most of those whose satisfaction depends upon being involved with the entire range of public issues and with equal personal impact. In a society in which power is diffused, it will take long, hard effort to acquire power in even one or two problem areas. Only Presidents, congressional majority leaders, and a very few commentators—the new Walter Lippmanns—will have any feeling of being involved and influential across a range of problem areas.

Those who are unwilling to devote time, energy, and a great

deal of hard work will also be among the frustrated and alienated —or, to put it with greater precision, in this case among the apathetic. When power is spread in roughly equal amounts among a large number of rather large institutions forming power centers, it will take a lot of work to achieve an influential position in any particular power center, and even more work to build a consensus around your view among enough of the other power centers, to prevail.

On the other hand, people who are willing to do the necessary work, who want to see change accomplished in a particular problem area more than to feel that they are solely responsible for the change—such people are likely to find a society in which power is diffused rather to their liking. Certainly there will be a wide variety of ways to get into the policy-making act. In addition to elective and appointive office, there will be a host of interest groups and other power centers in the intermediate structure, the press, television, radio, and the possibility of exercising influence through one's own research and writing. Again, the example of Ralph Nader comes to mind, but perhaps a better example is the 1954 U. S. Supreme Court decision that "separate" could not be "equal." The lawyers and justices directly involved in that decision deserve much credit and can take much personal satisfaction. But probably an even greater share of the credit really belongs to a vast army of social science researchers, teachers, publicists, and civil rights workers who demonstrated over several generations that separate could not be equal in psychological and cultural terms, who made people aware of the injustice of segregation, and who laid the groundwork that made the Supreme Court decision possible.

In psychological terms, in sum, it seems to me that a society in which power is diffused offers enough avenues for the individual to work for change to accommodate most people. A much more real worry in such a society seems likely to be whether the society is capable of any really rapid and fundamental change at all. We have said that some of the evil in American society comes from the diffusion of power—that the fact of so many centers of power makes building a consensus for positive change a formidable task. What happens in a society in which power is even more diffuse?

A Society of Permanent Revolution?

It seems likely that change on some very specific and relatively narrow subject could be most quickly accomplished in a society in which power is concentrated. In an absolute monarchy or a dictatorship, a gun-control law, for example, could be instituted by the decision of just one man, if that man was the monarch or dictator. But paradoxically, change may be broader and more continuous in a society in which power is diffused—such a society, in fact, may be in a state of more nearly continuous, "permanent revolution."

The argument, which has been stated most forcefully by Charles E. Lindblom, is as follows.[30] It is an observable fact that policy in the United States is not made on the basis of systematic and comprehensive study of all the implications of a wide range of alternatives, nor could it do so. The United States did not decide to inaugurate the nuclear age, but only to try to build an atomic weapon before its enemy did; it did not make a formal decision to become a welfare state, but only to take each of a series of steps; to experiment with an income tax at some safely innocuous level like 3 per cent; to alleviate the hardship of men who lost their jobs in a depression with a few weeks of unemployment compensation; or to lighten the old age of industrial workers with a tentative program of Social Security benefits. Rather than through grand decisions on grand alternatives, policy changes seem to come through a series of slight modifications of existing policy, with the new policy emerging slowly and haltingly by small and usually tentative moves, a process of trial and error in which policy zigs and zags, reverses itself, and then moves forward in a series of incremental steps. The reason for this incrementalism, as Charles E. Lindblom has pointed out, is the sheer physical impossibility of giving rational consideration to the whole wide range of goals and the multiplicity of alternative means for

30 See Lindblom, *The Policy-Making Process* (Englewood Cliffs, New Jersey: Prentice-Hall, 1968), fn., p. 41, and Chap. 4, passim.

achieving them and calculating the myriad of consequences and interactions.[31] Policy, as Lindblom says, tends to proceed in a series of incremental steps, tentative and easily reversible. It seems clear that this is true, not only because of the impossibility of analyzing the grand alternatives rationally, but also because of the political process of consensus-building among a number of power centers by which policy is made. The acquiescence of a key constituency might be given for what could be regarded as a tentative, reversible experiment when it would be withheld for a grand leap. Now, a policy-making process in this incrementalist style is conservative in the sense that it avoids upsetting the basic social and political framework. But in certain circumstances a series of incremental changes can proceed very rapidly. Society adjusts to one incremental step and is ready for another, and in this way a very drastic change can be wrought in the matter of only a decade or two. An example is the shift in power to the labor unions, begun in the latter years of the nineteenth century and completed in the 1940s. Another is the creation of a "welfare state," which was begun under Roosevelt's New Deal, and was at least firmly established in principle by the passage of the Medicare legislation under Lyndon B. Johnson. In many societies such drastic changes would have required a revolution, and successful revolutions are rare.

Anticipating the argument that the position of blacks might be cited as evidence of the slowness of change through a policy-making process tending toward incrementalism, Lindblom argues that after the rather drastic changes in policy toward blacks at the time of the Civil War, a long period followed in which policy proceeded incrementally but in the *other direction*, i.e., to take away some of the gains that blacks had made. For many decades thereafter, no changes in policy toward blacks were made at all. No significant group in the policy-making process took the initiative for change. It was only when blacks began to organize after World War II and white liberals began to take up the cause of civil rights that a new series of incremental steps, this time toward gains for blacks, was begun.

[31] Lindblom, *The Intelligence of Democracy* (New York, 1965) and his "The Science of 'Muddling Through,'" *Public Administration Review* 19 (1959).

For my own part, I think Lindblom's view is too optimistic, or at the least that it is necessary to make distinctions between different kinds of change. It seems to me, first, that in a society in which a large number of different power centers hold more or less equal power, it will be extraordinarily difficult to take established rights away from any group that shares in that power. In South Africa, for example, the so-called Cape coloureds, people of mixed ancestry, had a limited form of representation for generations, but when the Afrikaners' Nationalist party came to office, they succeeded in taking it away from them. It seems clear that something like this simply could not happen in a society in which power is diffused. At the same time, any change that is predicated on fundamental changes in deeply held attitudes by the great mass of the people seems likely to be slow in a society in which power is widely spread. As Tocqueville said of prejudice, whether racial, class, or national, it is difficult for a people to rise above themselves.

However, it seems clear that when a society in which power is dispersed does institute such change, it will be both successful and stable; for achieving the consensus necessary to institute the change would require changing the fundamental attitudes of a significant proportion of the population.

Over-all Conclusion

Our over-all conclusion, then, is that power in the superindustrialized United States, at least, will be diffused among a larger number of power centers of almost nearly equal strength. Thus we can answer the question with which we began this chapter on the locus of political power by saying that it is unlikely that the top leadership of the superindustrial society will hold such concentrated power that they could direct the efforts of the society toward their own personal goals, including national power goals, without seeking or needing public support. Earlier we concluded that the superindustrial society is unlikely to be easily aroused by nation-oriented public values, such as national power and prestige, but that it would be made up of a variety of subcultures, each stressing a different mix of mainly private values and attitudes and more internationalist than nationalist public attitudes. To that conclusion we can now add a second, that the locus and distribution of power is likely to be such that the leadership will not be able to act without public support, and that the essentially private and internationalist goals of the society are also likely to be the goals of the state.

Part II

THE SOVIET UNION: TOWARD A
SUPERSOCIALIST SOCIETY

CHAPTER 5

The Soviet Union

If SPECULATING about the future in general is risky, speculating about the future of the Soviet Union borders on the foolhardy. But in spite of this, "sovietologists," both professional and amateur, are fascinated by the subject and return to it again and again. There is no lack at all of expert opinion on the future of the Soviet Union. The difficulty lies elsewhere—in the fact that the experts are in a high state of disagreement, splitting into at least three quite distinct schools of thought.

The Pessimists' View

One school of thought is typified by Bertram D. Wolfe.[1] Wolfe sees the Soviet Union as the epitome of the modern totalitarian state. Totalitarianism, he says, puts the state above all else.

[1] Wolfe is best known for his *Three Who Made a Revolution* (Boston, 1957). The thesis described here is most fully propounded in his *Six Keys to the Soviet System* (Boston, 1956) and his *Communist Totalitarianism: Keys to the Soviet System*, 2nd edition (Boston, 1961).

"There can be *nothing* beyond its control. There can be no institutions with the right to remain independent, to have an autonomy and a validity of their own. There can be no room, no scope for the individual, his judgment, his conscience, his private purposes, hopes and dreams, his love for those who are close to him, his personal dignity."[2] The totalitarian state, as Wolfe sees it, is compelled to "wage constant and unending war against its own people."

The result is a sort of modern version of oriental despotism. The difference is that the modern version is infinitely more effective and infinitely more tenacious and long-lived, because of the fact that modern technology gives the state so many more effective instruments of force, of communication, indoctrination, and control. "In fact they [modern totalitarianisms] could only exist in an era of advanced technology where the state can reach with loudspeaker, newspaper, telephone, police wagon, tank, and plane all the far corners and most secret places of its domain."[3]

The Soviet Union's institutional structure is, for Wolfe, enduring and fundamental and contains a dynamic that perpetuates totalitarianism, dictatorship, the use of terror, and all the other instruments associated with totalitarianism. Briefly, the structure is "an atomized society; a centralized monolithic, monopolistic party; a single-party state; a regime of absolute force supplemented by persuasion or by continuous psychological warfare upon its people; a managerial bureaucracy accustomed to take orders and execute them . . . ; a centrally managed, totally state owned and state regulated economy . . . a monopoly of the means of expression and communication; an infallible doctrine stemming from infallible authorities, interpreted and applied by an infallible party led by an infallible leader. . . ."[4] In such a system, when the dictator dies a "collective leadership" may arise and continue for a time, but the thrust is inevitably toward the emergence of a new dictator. "The important point to remember," Wolfe writes, "is that triumvirates, duumvirates, directories, are notoriously transitional in the succession to a despot where there is no legitimacy to provide a successor, and where there are no

[2] *Six Keys to the Soviet System*, p. 245.
[3] Ibid.
[4] *Communist Totalitarianism*, pp. 280–81.

socially organized checks, below and outside the central power, to restrain the flow of power to the top."[5]

Once the dictator comes out on top, he may play hard or soft, as he sees fit for particular occasions. But he never really compromises on issues of power, since to do so would be to risk destruction. Terror is inevitable. Organizations and institutions are necessary for the system to function, and inevitably circumstances arise in which the leader of one or the other begins to gain power. This the dictator cannot tolerate. He uses whatever methods are at hand to bring the potential rival down. Inevitably there will be times when only terror will be effective, and when needed, it will be used. Thus any periods of relaxation in the totalitarian state, any moves toward liberalization, are simply lulls, when all potential rivals have been temporarily eliminated, or they are out-and-out shams. The totalitarian state cannot change; it either continues unchanged or it is destroyed in war or civil war.

In foreign affairs as in domestic, the drive of the totalitarian state is for power and domination. Such theorists as Wolfe, two critics write, "hold that Soviet policy is undeviatingly committed to the destruction of the free world, and that it is premised on this destruction being ultimately effected by force of arms. All treaties, agreements, arrangements and understandings are purely tactical manoeuvres to gain time or other advantage. The Soviet word cannot be trusted, the very idea of good intentions is alien to them, and negotiation with them can have no other useful purpose than to demonstrate *our* gullibility or our good intentions."[6]

The "Convergence" Theories

The rosiest view of the development of Soviet society is probably that of Isaac Deutscher, who sees Soviet society gradually but inevitably becoming both liberal and democratic.[7] The more typical view of this particular school, however, sees the Soviet

[5] Ibid., p. 282. Wolfe's emphasis.
[6] Alex Inkeles and Raymond A. Bauer, *The Soviet Citizen: Daily Life in a Totalitarian Society* (Cambridge, 1959), p. 378. The emphasis is that of the authors.
[7] The theme is most fully developed in Deutscher's *The Unfinished Revolution: Russia 1917–1967* (New York, 1967).

and American societies "converging"—moving toward each other. Thus in this view the "capitalist" countries are not only becoming more socialist, but also more authoritarian; and the Soviet Union is not only becoming more democratic, but also more capitalistic.[8]

The basic assumption in this view is on the nature of the dynamism—the notion that industrialization will create similar attitudes and values, similar social institutions, and similar political forms in all countries that industrialize, regardless of cultural and national differences at the beginning. Although most analysts will surround the dynamism they describe with an array of qualifications, at bottom it is a sophisticated, qualified economic determinism descended directly from Marx. And the concept in one variation or another is, incidentally, shared widely by Western social scientists, even among those who explicitly reject "convergence" theories—including men of widely differing views, such as John Kenneth Galbraith, Walt W. Rostow, Gunnar Myrdal, Allen Kassof, Clark Kerr, A. F. K. Organsky, and many others.[9] A wide variety of examples of similarities between the two systems are cited, ranging from attitudes resulting in a nuclear family to materialistic attitudes and an achievement orientation toward work. Numerous scholars, as the author of a survey of "convergence" theories points out, go even farther. "The European Communist countries and the societies of Western Europe and North America, they point out, share many of the problems of urban living, from delinquency, alcoholism, and generational conflict to water and air pollution and the rapid exhaustion of natural resources by reckless entrepreneurship. Indeed, it could easily be argued that in both systems the demands of entrepreneurship dominate and even cause such problems as urban sprawl and inadequate city planning, to name only two."[10] However, it was a sophisticated and urbane Eastern European Communist

---

[8] For a survey of the literature on "convergence," see Alfred G. Meyer, "Theories of Convergence," *Change in Communist Systems,* ed. Chalmers Johnson (Sanford, 1970). It should be noted that the theorists of "convergence" are not only Westerners. One is the noted Soviet physicist, Andrei D. Sakharov. See his *Progress, Coexistence, and Intellectual Freedom* (New York, 1968).

[9] Meyer, "Theories of Convergence," pp. 322–33.

[10] Ibid., p. 317.

who offered the ultimate example of convergence. "It says something about the similarity of the two systems, about their thrust toward the lowest common denominator and mediocrity," he remarked in 1968, "that the United States finds itself with Nixon and Agnew and the Soviet Union with Brezhnev and Kosygin."[11]

The Crisis View

A radically different view of the future of the Soviet Union is foreseen by Zbigniew Brzezinski—a crisis, in fact, that will force the Communist party to face a choice between watching the political system degenerate and become unstable or transforming it into a "more pluralistic and institutionalized" political system.[12]

Brzezinski's argument is keyed more to a political than to an economic dynamism. Under Stalin, Brzezinski argues, the political system was increasingly institutionalized bureaucratically, and the exercise of power "involved a subtle balancing of the principal institutions of the political system: the secret police, the party, the state, and the army (roughly in that order of importance)."[13] Even the Politburo itself was split into minor groups, and Stalin personally performed the function of integration. When Khrushchev came to power, he, too, performed the function of political integration. None of the top posts in the Soviet Union have been institutionalized sufficiently to endow its occupant with the "special prestige and aura" that the President of the United States gains on assuming office, but the same need exists. Stalin tried and eventually succeeded in transferring from the party to himself a sort of "routinized charisma," which accomplished the same purpose. But Khrushchev did not inherit this peculiar charisma of Stalin's, and in trying to cope with the problem, he replaced Stalin's colleagues with a younger generation of bureaucratic leaders. The eventual result was a bureaucratic dictatorship. "By the time he was removed," Brzezinski writes, "Khrushchev had

[11] Personal communication.
[12] Brzezinski, "The Soviet Political System: Transformation or Degeneration," *Dilemmas of Change in Soviet Politics,* ed. Brzezinski (New York: Columbia University Press, 1969). Brzezinski's article and the others in that book were first published in *Problems of Communism* in the years 1966–68.
[13] "The Soviet Political System," p. 4.

become an anachronism in the new political context he himself had helped to create."[14]

For Brzezinski, this raises the question whether the Soviet system will be able to continue to supply the kind of leadership that will be effective. A highly bureaucratized political setting encourages conformity and caution. Citing Margaret Mead, Brzezinski points out that social evolution "depends not only on the availability of creative individuals, but also on the existence of clusters of creators who collectively promote social innovation."[15] How can a bureaucratic dictatorship provide such clusters of creativity? "It is doubtful that any organization can long remain vital if it is so structured that in its personnel policy it becomes, almost unknowingly, inimical to talent and hostile to political innovation. Decay is bound to set in, while the stability of the political system may be endangered, if other social institutions succeed in attracting the society's talent and begin to chafe under the restraints imposed by the ruling but increasingly mediocre *apparatchiki*."[16]

At the same time, the political and ideological issues facing the leadership of the Soviet Union have become much less grand. Khrushchev's "homilies on the merits of corn" or even his virgin lands campaign do not compare with Stalin's dilemma about collectivizing 100 million peasants. One result is that the struggle has "become less a matter of life or death, and more one in which the price of defeat is simply retirement and some personal disgrace." Another result, stemming both from the lessened importance of the issues and the development of a bureaucratic dictatorship, is the creation of "a ready-made situation for group pressures and institutional clashes." What is happening, then, is a trend toward greatly increased political participation, the play of group interests operating through a variety of bureaucratic institutions.

It is here that Brzezinski sees the crisis. Citing Samuel Huntington's argument that stable political growth requires a balance between political "institutionalization" and political "participation,"

[14] Ibid., p. 7.
[15] Ibid., p. 10.
[16] Ibid.

Brzezinski argues that if this increased political participation is not accompanied by political institutionalization, the result will be decay.[17] As with Stalin and Khrushchev, the major function of the party has been that of integration between different group and class interests—preferring to deal with each group bilaterally so as to maintain the "unity of political direction as well as the political supremacy of the ruling party." A bureaucratic dictatorship encourages mediocre leadership that is less able to perform the integrative function, and at the same time greater participation in the political process means more group interests that must be resolved. Yet if the party weakens in performing this function, as seems likely, the result will be anarchy.

However, degeneration, Brzezinski believes, is not inevitable. It depends on how the Soviet elite react to the crisis. If they follow a path of retrenchment, increasing dogmatism, and violence, the result could be a situation of tension in which the "possibility of revolutionary outbreaks could not be discounted entirely." On the other hand, the threat of degeneration could be lessened by a set of adaptations designed to institutionalize the political system. First, if outstanding scientists, economists, and others were brought into the Presidium, the transformation of the leadership into a regime of clerks could be averted and the alienation of other groups halted. Second, the office of the chief executive would have to be institutionalized and endowed with legitimacy and stability. Third, if tension, conflict, and "even anarchy" are to be avoided, there must be created an "institutionalized arena for the mediation of group interests." In effect, what Brzezinski proposes is transforming the Central Committee into something like a true parliament, with a much more representative membership and the "predominance of the party bureaucrats watered down."

Brzezinski recognizes that implementing these proposals will profoundly transform the whole Soviet system. But he argues that it is the absence of such fundamental change that is creating the crisis, and that perhaps the "ultimate contribution" the party can make is to adjust to its own withering away. "In the mean-

17 The citation is to Huntington's article "Political Development and Political Decay," World Politics (April 1965).

time," he then goes on to say, "the progressive transformation of the bureaucratic Communist dictatorship into a more pluralistic and institutionalized political system—even though still a system of one-party rule—seems essential if its degeneration is to be averted."[18]

The "Evolving but Different" View

A fourth and final view of the future of the Soviet Union is that the Soviet regime is in no danger of collapse, that it is adaptable and evolving, but that its evolution is along lines that are peculiarly its own. The version of this view expounded by Alex Inkeles and Raymond A. Bauer is particularly interesting, because it rests on a massive effort at interviewing Soviet refugees conducted by the Russian Research Center at Harvard.[19]

A number of findings emerged from the interviews. First, throughout Soviet society there is a deep and long-lasting impression that the arbitrary and despotic methods of the Stalinist regime were a "terrible aberration." A general determination runs throughout Soviet society that it must not happen again. Second, the economic hardship associated with collectivization of the farms and forced-draft industrialization was a source of resentment second only to the terror. Only a convincing external threat would make the people accept such hardship again.

Nevertheless, the social change that Stalin set in motion with collectivization and industrialization has permanently altered the attitudes and value structure of the Soviet people. The values of the peasant are a thing of the past. The new Soviet man is an industrial man. Achievement, success, security, happiness for one's children, financial comfort—these have taken the place of the traditional peasant family goals rooted in the local community and religion.

In spite of the resentment engendered by the terror and forced-draft industrialization, the system as a whole is accepted. Criti-

[18] "The Soviet Political System," p. 34.
[19] "The Future of Soviet Society," *The Soviet Citizen: Daily Life in a Totalitarian Society.* Other versions of essentially the same view can be found in Merle Fainsod, "Roads to the Future," *Dilemmas of Change in Soviet Politics,* already cited; and Allen Kassof, "The Future of Soviet Society," *Prospects for Soviet Society,* ed. Allen Kassof (New York, 1968).

cism is of particular organizations—the secret police, for example
—or, most often, of the way that policies have been carried out.
No one questions the concept of government ownership and operation of industry or of a government-run welfare state controlling
jobs, health care, and retirement. The opportunity for social mobility that the system provides is appreciated. There is pride in
the nation's achievements.

Finally, thoughout Soviet society, it seems, there was "not only
little understanding, but relatively little need felt for the *strictly
constitutional* apparatus of guarantees, rights and safeguards
which characterize the democracy of Western Europe."[20] The
people want good rulers, rulers who care for the people's welfare.
But they seemed little interested in the forms of parliamentary
democracy.

Following the death of Stalin, the Soviet leaders moved in-
telligently and forcefully to eliminate or reduce the sources of
resentment Stalinism had aroused—demonstrated that the Soviet
system has considerable capacity for change and adjustment
and thus possesses considerable stability, at least in the short
run. But, Inkeles and Bauer argue, this says little about either the
system's capacity for long-run stability or what long-run stability
will be like if is achieved. To find the answer, they believe, one
must address the basic question: "In what degree are the distinctive features of Soviet totalitarianism compatible with the
rest of the social structure we associate with large-scale industrial
society?"[21]

By "Soviet totalitarianism" the authors mean "a system of absolute, autocratic and essentially unconstitutional 'above the law'
rule, exercised by a single party holding a monopoly of power and
organized on the principles of an army under the leadership of
an all-wise supreme commander assisted by a general staff largely
of his own selection."[22] They are armed with an eschatological
ideology preaching the necessity of violence in destroying the
evil of the old system, and their principal instrument is the
state. No associations or organizations that might compete with
the party and the state for loyalty are permitted. Consensus is

[20] Inkeles and Bauer, op. cit., p. 381. Their emphasis.
[21] Ibid., p. 384.
[22] Ibid.

manufactured, and thought is controlled through manipulating not only the means of mass communications but art and literature as well. When necessary, force and police terror are used. "An effort is made in this way to secure the total mobilization of all resources, and above all personal human resources, in the assault on the goals set for the society by its ruling elite. It is this absence of pluralism, and the denial of the validity of a private sphere of life as against the complete or *total* subordination of the individual and institutions to the purpose of the state, which lends its special name to totalitarianism."[23]

The Nature of Industrialism

The authors find it more difficult to define the second element in their basic quesion: the nature of the modern industrial social order. But the central feature, in their view, is the "superfirm"— "one integrated, coordinated and highly ramified organization which controls a very large portion of the production of a crucial section of the economy." The American automobile, steel, or chemical industries are examples. In this pattern, management becomes divorced from ownership and increasingly develops into a specialized profession. The superfirms tend to become elaborate bureaucracies, with special patterns of recruitment, in-service training, and so on. Long-range planning and centralized funding are pervasive. Since capital is less scarce than labor, fringe benefits and other special efforts are made to maximize the yield from labor. There is an emphasis on rationalized production, on scientific research for the development of new products and processes, and on shaping and assuring the market in various ways.[24]

The authors enter a more controversial area when they attempt to assess the social consequences of these characteristics of the industrial state. They disagree, for example, with the widely held idea that the citizen of the industrial society is "atomized." The vast urban conglomerates that characterize industrial societies do, they feel, lead to the attenuation of all sorts of extended primary group ties—the village community, the clan, the tribe,

---

[23] Ibid., p. 385. Authors' emphasis.
[24] On this point, see also John Kenneth Galbraith's *The New Industrial State* (Boston, 1967).

and the extended family all atrophy. They believe that the result is to reduce the differentiation of subgroups in the population. (This conclusion, incidentally, is diametrically opposed to the conclusion we reached about postindustrial societies, which we believed would be marked by a great variety of subgroups with distinctive attitudes, values, goals, and lifestyles.) In their view, the industrial society is characterized by "an extensive homogenization of values and life styles" resulting from the common experience as employees of superfirms, reinforced by uniform schooling, uniform exposure to communications from the mass media, physical mobility from the highly developed transportation system, and the fact that other agencies will be taking over the inculcation of values from the primary groups.

Comparing totalitarianism and the modern industrial society, so defined, Inkeles and Bauer see no clash of any consequence. As they say, the principle of the superfirm is very strong in the Soviet Union: Management is divorced from ownership, the emphasis is on long-range planning, the market is assured. "If anything," they write, "the Soviet formula has carried the industrial society to its most exaggerated manifestation."

The most crucial argument against their view, the other authors feel, is that the emphasis on rationality in an industrial society, its dependence on science and research, its larger and larger corps of educated engineers, professionals, and managers will create a new class, which will find totalitarianism unacceptable. Inkeles and Bauer reply that the argument is based more on faith than on substance. Hitler's Germany, for example, was a country with one of the best-educated populations in the world. Further, their evidence from interviews is that "the underlying principles of Soviet political control over the *ends* of economic and administrative behavior are accepted by most Soviet engineers and managers, indeed are willingly supported by them. They accept these as 'political' decisions to be decided by political specialists. They are, in other words, largely withdrawn from politics, 'organization men' similar to their counterparts in the United States."[25]

The over-all conclusion that Inkeles and Bauer reach is that

[25] *The Soviet Citizen*, p. 389. Authors' emphasis.

"there is no necessary, or even compelling force in the modern industrial social order which clearly makes it incompatible with totalitarianism. On the other hand, we do not mean to suggest that there is an inherent tendency in the modern industrial social order which drives it *toward* totalitarianism. Our position is rather that the modern industrial order appears to be compatible with either democratic or totalitarian political and social forms."[26]

Inkeles and Bauer also consider the possibility that the problem of the succession crisis will never be solved in the Soviet Union and that eventually one of the struggles for power will break into an open conflict that will destroy the regime. They conclude, however, that even in the unlikely event that such a struggle did develop into open conflict, the most likely course the victor would follow would be to reimpose the same totalitarian system.

They also consider the possibility that some future breakup of the Soviet "satellite empire," along the lines of the revolt in Hungary, might trigger repercussions within the Soviet Union serious enough to bring about fundamental changes. Here again, they feel the response within the Soviet Union would be increased totalitarianism—although they fail to consider the potentialities of non-Russian nationalisms.

Change, however—and fundamental change—does seem inevitable to Inkeles and Bauer. They see this change as coming out of "the industrial maturation of Soviet Russia" and the "mellowing of its social structure." What they foresee is an evolution of the Soviet Union along the lines on which it has already clearly embarked. "In our opinion the formidable challenge which faces the world rises not from the unchanging character of the Soviet Union, but precisely from the fact that its present leaders have been able to make the adjustments in the structure which have adapted it to take account of the earlier development of the society."[27] And the crucial point is that they have done so without sacrificing any of the basic features of the system. Another supporter of this view, Allen Kassof, describes the future Soviet system as "a more or less benevolent authoritarianism of great

[26] Ibid., p. 390. Authors' emphasis.
[27] Ibid., p. 396.

vitality and long-range durability."[28] Still another, Merle Fainsod, describes the future Soviet system as "a looser, more pragmatic, and pluralistically-based party in which the differentiated interests of an industrial society find freer expression and where the party leadership acts as the manager of their inter-relationships and as the custodian of the national interests of the Soviet state."[29]

Counterarguments

Faced with such a wide range of differing views, what can be said? First, from the vantage point of the decade of the 1970s, it seems clear that Wolfe's view of the Soviet Union is too extreme. Wolfe and his supporters, of course, would cite the fact that recently dissident activities that are not forbidden by law are being punished by dismissing the offender from his job or by putting him in an insane asylum and argue that this is proof that the liberalization of the past few years is only superficial. And they would cite the invasion of Czechoslovakia in 1968 as proof that on the fundamental issues of power and domination in foreign affairs, Soviet attitudes are equally unchanged. But the ordinary Soviet citizen, as opposed to those who are either active dissidents or at the dangerous pinnacle of power, clearly has a sense of security and stability today that is fundamentally different from Stalin's era. He would think Wolfe completely mad to call the changes only superficial. And perhaps even more important is the persuasive evidence that Inkeles and Bauer amassed indicating the widespread resentment of both the terror and the hardship associated with collectivization and forced-draft industrialization and that all segments and levels of Soviet society are determined that it shall not happen again. Another extensive and careful study specifically on political terror in Communist systems by Alexander Dallin and George Breslauer powerfully supports that conclusion. They not only find that the incidence of political terror sharply declines as Communist systems pass beyond the

[28] Kassof, *Prospects for Soviet Society,* p. 506.
[29] "Roads to the Future," in Brzezinski, ed., *Dilemmas of Change in Soviet Politics,* op. cit. (p. 235 above), p. 134.

mobilization stage, but that the dynamics of the developing political system tend to go against its use.[30] The very top of the political structure, where the struggle for power may continue without the development of any settled system for legitimizing changes, may continue to look Byzantine. Arbitrary measures may also continue to be used against those who transgress the limits of what the government—and society—regard as acceptable behavior. But it seems clear that the great bulk of the activities of the great bulk of the Soviet people will be governed by law. Yet it is central to Wolfe's argument that terror—widespread terror —is inevitable in totalitarian systems. Similarly, Wolfe sees an aggressive foreign policy and a thrust toward world domination as an essential feature of Soviet communism. Yet over the broad sweep of history the rule has been that movements based on revolutionary ideology or religion continue as institutions, and as institutions, they continue to trumpet the rhetoric of world domination long after their proselytizing has ceased as a practical matter. It may well be that the Soviet Union will continue to be authoritarian and that it will continue to pursue an aggressive foreign policy, but for our purposes Wolfe's particular description of the nature of Soviet society and the direction it will take in the future are more misleading than helpful.

Objections to the "Convergence" Theories

Neither do the convergence theories seem to be very useful for our purposes. On the non-Communist side of the equation, the developed countries may well become more "socialist." Clearly the welfare state, if that is a characteristic of socialism, is well established. Clearly, also, ownership of industry has long since been divorced from management—if that is a characteristic of socialism. And if our analysis of the superindustrial society is correct, income will increasingly be divorced from work—if that is a characteristic of socialism, which at least the present-day Soviet spokesmen would deny.

On the other hand, we have seen no evidence of social forces leading a superindustrialized society toward authoritarianism.

[30] Dallin and Breslauer, *Political Terror in Communist Systems* (Stanford, California: Stanford University Press, 1970).

The evidence we examined, in fact, was that those forces were working in the opposite direction, toward a further diffusion of power.

On the Communist side of the equation, it would be little short of silly to argue that recent moves toward creating more economic incentives in the Soviet Union constituted a trend toward "capitalism." The Soviet and American economies may end up looking very much alike, but it will clearly not be because the Soviet economy has become capitalist.

The real, and more difficult question is whether there are social forces, either inherent in the Soviet system or inherent in humanity, working toward democracy. As for the Soviet system, the only candidate is the modern industrial society, and, here again, it seems to me that Inkeles and Bauer have made a persuasive case that such a society is compatible with a wide range of political forms. Certain obvious patterns of individual lifestyle and family and social attitudes are bound to be similar in different societies that are all industrial, as we have said. It also seems likely that modern industrial society requires a certain measure of predictability in social relations and that this does seem to work toward the establishment of a rule of law. But nothing in the modern industrial society seems to be working toward any particular *political* form.

The Nature of "Democracy"

The difficulty arises over the question of whether there is something inherent in humanity itself that leads toward democracy. To deal with the question, however, requires a digression to be sure we are clear about the nature of democracy.

It is a mistake, first of all, to assume that democracy is either identical with or a prerequisite for *individual* freedom. It is also a mistake, second, to assume that democracy is a form of government in which the people decide on issues of public policy. Democracy is neither of these things, but what complicates the situation is that democracy does have some relationship to both. For the practical purposes of analysis, the most satisfactory definition of democracy is that of Joseph A. Schumpeter. The key assumption in the classical definition of democracy, which had the people deciding on issues, was the notion of the "common good," which was to be the beacon light of policy. The notion of the "common good" implies that any rational man can see it—i.e., that it takes no special knowledge or training to be able to identify the common good. The notion of the common good also implies that it contains the answer to all policy questions; every measure is either good or bad. In the ideal democracy, then, it is both plausible and feasible for the people to decide on issues, for the people to determine policy. In a very large community, however, the affairs of government take up so much time that some compromise with this ideal becomes necessary. The people therefore should decide only the most important of the issues, by referendum or as an integral part of elections (i.e., by choosing between parties offering alternative policies), and through elections appoint a committee (a representative legislature) to determine policy on lesser issues. In the case of parliamentary democracies, this committee in turn appoints a smaller committee (the Cabinet or Executive) and a chairman (Prime Minister) to execute the policies determined. In the case of a congressional democracy, the chairman is separately elected and appoints his executive committee with the advice and consent of the policy-determining committee.

The question that Schumpeter poses, with considerable scorn, is: Whose is the common good? It is precisely the struggle of politics to determine whose good shall be the common good. The common good furthermore not only means different things to different people, but it means different things to the same people.

Not even compromise necessarily reflects the majority will. "The chances for this to happen," Schumpeter writes, "are greatest with those issues which are quantitative in nature or admit of gradation, such as the question how much is to be spent on unemployment relief provided everybody favors some expenditure for that purpose."[31] But in the case of qualitative issues, such as whether to persecute heretics or to enter upon a war, a compromise may be equally distasteful to everyone. Schumpeter argues in fact that in such circumstances a decision imposed by a

---

[31] *Capitalism, Socialism, and Democracy,* 2nd ed., (New York: Harper, 1942, 1947), p. 255.

nondemocratic agency will often prove more acceptable than a compromise. He gives as an example Napoleon's action on the Church issue when he was First Consul and the head of a military dictatorship. Napoleon imposed a settlement that gave a certain amount of religious freedom while strongly upholding the authority of the state. Any "democratic" attempt at solution, Schumpeter argues, would have been a disaster: "Deadlock or interminable struggle, engendering increasing irritation, would have been the most probable outcome of any attempt to settle the question democratically. But Napoleon was able to settle it reasonably, precisely because all those groups which could not yield their points of their own accord were at the same time able and willing to accept the arrangement if imposed."[32]

Having rejected the classical theory of democracy with its assumption of a common will and goal of having the people actually decide on particular issues, Schumpeter offers an alternative definition. Democracy, according to his definition, is government in which there is competition for political leadership, and the role of the people is not to decide on issues but to produce a government. Democracy, he writes, "is that institutional arrangement for arriving at political decisions in which individuals acquire the power to decide by means of a competitive struggle for the people's vote."[33]

Schumpeter argues that his definition has a number of advantages over the classical definition. First, it provides a practical test, one that can be used in the real world. Second, it leaves room for the role of leadership, noticeably lacking in the classical theory. Third, insofar as a groupwide "good" or "will" exists—say, minority groups, or labor, or the unemployed—Schumpeter's theory leaves ample room for the group to act in terms of their collective good—i.e., a minority group can vote for leadership on the basis of the leadership's policy stand on the issue affecting the particular group. Thus the theory provides for competition, but as in economic life, the competition is not perfect.

Schumpeter's theory, too, allows for the electorate to influence policy—it explains the form of indirect control that the electorate

[32] Ibid., pp. 255–56.
[33] Ibid., p. 269.

can exercise on occasion. The role of the people is primarily to make a government, and this implies the function of evicting it. So the electorate does not control policy decisions while the government is in power, but only evicts it on stated occasions and circumstances if it is displeased with the *results* that the government achieves. Hence the influence of the electorate on policy during the term of the government is the threat of throwing the government out if it does badly, leaving the government to find out, if it can, not so much whether the electorate approves of given policies, but the further step of whether the final *results* of given policies will or will not please the electorate. It does not really matter, for example, if the majority of the people at the time thought that bombing North Vietnam in 1965 was a good policy. The important thing is that the majority of the people came to be dissatisfied with the result, the fact that the bombing did not bring the war to a successful conclusion, that women and children were killed, and that the results of the action were evil.

Schumpeter, finally, argues that his theory also explains more satisfactorily than the classic theory some of the consequences of democratic society, especially the relationship between democracy and individual freedom. He points out that no society tolerates absolute freedom and no society reduces freedom to zero. Democracy, he argues, does not necessarily grant more individual freedom than other political systems. It may, in fact, grant less. If the vast majority sees certain kinds of behavior as morally repugnant, the chances are that it will be very repressive indeed—probably more so than a monarchy or dictatorship, especially if the monarchy or dictatorship lacks a puritanical streak. The same denial of freedom can happen to a minority if the majority is racist or prejudiced, as the American black can testify. The relation between democracy and freedom is that if in principle at least everyone is free to compete for political leadership, then in most cases this will mean a considerable freedom of discussion for all and will normally mean a considerable amount of freedom for the press.

If democracy is seen in this way, the difficulty is cleared up. Certainly humanity has no inherent drive toward such a particularized arrangement for acquiring the power to decide on issues. In truth, any inherent drive that humanity has toward freedom is not necessarily toward the particular freedoms that democracy seems to enhance. If there is such a drive, it is toward a rather wide range of freedoms, and it can clearly be satisfied by a government that is responsive to a range of human needs while being restrictive over the freedom to choose leadership, the freedom to discuss certain kinds of political issues, and the freedom of the press to discuss those issues. History has produced so few democracies that one suspects that those that have emerged are the result of historical accident rather than any deep drive. The Soviet Union, clearly, is responsive to a wide range of the needs and aspirations of its people, including certain kinds of freedoms, and there seems little reason to believe that there is any deep, unsatisfied drive toward the political forms of democracy as it is known in the Western countries. Soviet society is obviously changing, and one of the changes may be toward an enlargement of certain kinds of freedom. But like Wolfe's view, the convergence theories' particular description of these changes seems for our purposes to be more misleading than helpful.

Objections to the Brzezinski "Crisis" Theory

Turning to Brzezinski, it seems to me that his analysis is intellectually sound and in its theoretical insights often brilliant. But his over-all conclusions of "degeneration" and "decay," with more than a hint of a possible collapse, are not persuasive.

The great contribution of Brzezinski's analysis is the emphasis it gives to political factors, turning us away from the trap laid by an oversimplified, neo-Marxian stress on the economic. He is clearly right about the routinization and bureaucratization of the Soviet political system, and he may well be right that one consequence of this is to discourage men of talent from taking up political careers and to encourage and foster the rise of mediocrities. But from this point on, it becomes more difficult to agree with what Brzezinski has to say.

The problem may be partly semantic. If the words "degeneration" and "decay" mean nothing more than a possibly temporary slowdown in the pace of social change, a marking time, then there would be no quarrel. What I have in mind is the Soviet equivalent of what happened in the United States during the

Eisenhower administration—a sort of pause in the struggle with the social problems facing the society. The Eisenhower period of ignoring such things as the continued oppression of the blacks, the deterioration of the inner cities, urban sprawl, and the looming crises in transportation and pollution may have aggravated the problems and made the task of dealing with them more difficult, but the aggravation was not nearly dramatic enough to justify saying that the whole society was degenerating or decaying. The pause was noticeable enough to give John F. Kennedy a winning slogan in the election of 1960—the need to "get America moving again"—but not sufficiently noticeable to qualify as a crisis. But Brzezinski seems to mean something a good deal more than just a period of marking time. As he sees it, the degeneration is so serious as to require measures of reform that are nothing less than draconian.

One reason for the disagreement about the long-run stability of the Soviet system seems to be that Brzezinski puts less weight on the momentum or inertia of a social system and more on the influence of political leadership; in my view, he underestimates the inertia of a social system and overestimates the capacity of leadership to control the direction of a social system. Another reason for the disagreement—and one for which the evidence can be more easily mustered—is a slightly different assessment of the evidence that what might be called an "interest group" structure has developed in the Soviet Union. The case for this view will be described below, but for the moment, let us say only that Brzezinski cites this evidence and explicitly applauds the trend among political thinkers to look at the Soviet political system in terms of a "group conflict" model that "suggests the kind of alliances, group competition, and political courtship that probably prevail."[34] But it seems to me that he does not push this analysis far enough or attempt to draw the implications from it that bear on this question of the stability of the Soviet system.

An Alternative View

From what we have already said in criticism of the other views of the future of the Soviet system, it is clear that, on balance, our

[34] "The Soviet Political System," p. 23.

own analysis is more in line with the Inkeles and Bauer view that the Soviet political system is functioning adequately; that however insecure any one set of men at the top may feel, the political system itself is stable; and that although the system will undoubtedly change, the changes will be evolutionary and along lines that are peculiarly Russian and Soviet. However, our analysis attempts a line of reasoning beyond where Inkeles and Bauer were prepared to go and may therefore lead to somewhat different implications for the future of Soviet society.

Basically, we have no disagreement with the over-all conclusions Inkeles and Bauer reach. The insight into the attitudes of ordinary Soviet citizens that the interviews enable Inkeles and Bauer to make are invaluable. Their findings clearly destroy the assumption that Soviet society is "atomized" or lacks social structure. What they have discovered about attitudes among the ordinary Soviet citizen jibe with and tend to support our speculation that whatever urge toward "freedom" that is inherent in humanity is not a thrust toward "democracy" as such or necessarily toward the particular set of freedoms that democracy tends to provide for. And Inkeles and Bauer's argument that the modern industrial order is compatible with either democratic or totalitarian political and social forms seems overwhelmingly persuasive— although we did, and will again in more detail later, disagree with their conclusion that industrial society leads to homogenization of values and attitudes and the blurring of subgroups.

Basically, however, this conclusion that the industrial order is compatible with either system only argues against the possibility of change in the direction of democracy. It does not directly support the conclusion that Soviet society is stable, with nothing on the horizon but evolutionary change consistent with past development. In fact, the only argument that Inkeles and Bauer offer in direct support of that conclusion is the fact that the leadership has been able to make adjustments in the structure to meet various contingencies, such as the changes made to reduce or eliminate the resentments engendered under Stalin. What I would argue is that an analysis along the lines implied by the suggestions made by Brzezinski, Fainsod, and others that the Soviet Union is developing an interest-group or conflict-consensus group structure will show very positive reasons to expect the Soviet political system to be stable. And such an analysis should also suggest a number of other characteristics the evolving Soviet system will tend to develop.

CHAPTER 6

A Conflict and Consensus-Building Model of the Soviet Political System

THE NOTION to be explored, then, is the possibility that the Soviet political system has developed into something that is not adequately described by traditional, essentially normative concepts like "democracy" or "authoritarianism." Although neither Merle Fainsod nor Zbigniew Brzezinski has attempted to develop a full analysis along these lines, both have suggested at least the outlines of one. Fainsod speaks of an "interest group structure" emerging as Soviet society has become more professionalized and differentiated. "The armed forces," Fainsod writes, "the police, the managers of industry and agriculture, the scientific community, and the cultural intelligentsia—all have their specialized interests to defend, and since they cannot be promoted outside the party, the party has itself become an arena in which these competing interests must be adjusted and reconciled. One of the results has been to introduce a strong adaptive ingredient into the party leadership's mobilizing and coordinating role."[1] Brzezinski, for his part, saw something similar even in Stalin's day—he describes Stalin's power as "institutionalized bureaucratically" and argues that "its exercise involved a subtle balancing of the principal institutions of the political system: the secret police, the party, the state, and the army (roughly in that order of importance)."[2] Developments since Stalin's time—principally increased difficulties in the way of achieving personal dictatorship and the kind of relaxation typified by the fact that defeat in the political struggle can now result in comfortable retirement rather than execution or exile—have created a "ready-made situation for group pressures and institutional clashes." Thus Khrushchev, in exercising power, "was preoccupied with mediating the demands of key institutions, such as the army, or with overcoming the opposition of others, such as the objections of the administrators to economic decentralization or of the heavy industrial managers to nonindustrial priorities."[3] One consequence is that participation in policy decisions is now much wider. "In the past, the key groups that had to be considered as potential political participants were relatively few. Today, in addition to the vastly more entrenched institutional interests, such as the police, the military, and the state bureaucracy, the youth could become a source of ferment, the consumers could become more restless, the collective farmers more recalcitrant, the scientists more outspoken, the non-Russian nationalities more demanding."[4] The suggestion that Brzezinski seems to be presenting, in sum, is what he calls a "group conflict" model of policy making in which the Communist party mediates and integrates conflict among different interests, groups, and institutions.

A Conflict and Consensus-Building Model

Sketchy though these descriptions are, what is striking is how suggestive they are of the conflict and consensus-building model

[1] Fainsod, "Roads to the Future," *Dilemmas of Change in Soviet Politics,* ed. Zbigniew Brzezinski (New York: Columbia University Press, 1969), pp. 131–32.
[2] Brzezinski, "The Soviet Political System: Transformation or Degeneration," *Dilemmas of Change in Soviet Politics,* ed. Brzezinski (New York: Columbia University Press, 1969), p. 4.
[3] Ibid., p. 18.
[4] Ibid., p. 20.

of policy making developed in our analysis of the political process of policy making in the United States. To recap that analysis, we saw a mass public with needs and interests, but with few structured views on particular policy choices. Between this mass public and the proximate actors in the policy-making process are what we called the "intermediate structure"—the great array not only of interest groups and lobby groups, corporations, trade unions, and the like, but also churches, professional societies, the media of communication, political parties, and, most important, state and local governments. The intermediate structure performs the function—necessary in all mass societies—of articulating and aggregating interests upward and transmitting downward not only information and interpretation but potential costs, the nature of opposition, and potential penalties if interests are pushed too far.

The proximate actors in the policy-making process are individuals working in institutions—individuals of unequal power as well as varying ability and skill, and institutions with different legitimacy over different issues. The actors are in conflict. They argue, persuade, bargain, and manipulate. Sometimes their battles are to get their institution to take a stand, exercise its power, fight for its interests and position. At other times, their battles are within a broader framework, trying to make the view of their institution prevail against individuals representing other institutions. There is conflict and accommodation, attempts at building a consensus. Deals are made to gain allies. And there is also bargaining among opponents. Concessions are exchanged; compromises are struck.

Out of this most subtle and complex of all games comes policy. Both the fact that the procedure is noisy and undignified and the fact that the policy produced is often internally inconsistent, inappropriate to the problem at hand, or satisfies completely no one of the factions doing battle, are traceable to the nature of the process, the fact that it is political.

As an analytical tool, this "policy making is politics" model has a number of advantages in trying to understand both the substance of governmental policy in the United States and the Washington scene. It accounts, as we have said, for the noise and lack of dignity, on the one hand, and for the frequency that policy is internally inconsistent, inappropriate, and unsatisfactory to its major architects, on the other. The model also has other advantages. Many analysts of international politics work with concepts based on assumptions that all states pursue the same goals, because they are states, and that they pursue them rationally. They assume that the goal of all states is power and prestige, and that states strive to adopt policies that are rational means toward maximizing these goals. The advantage of the "policy making is politics" model is that it provides a place for power and a role for power but without assuming that power is the sole motivating force or even necessarily the most prevalent one. Indeed, the politics model has the advantage of being able to accommodate the possibility that a number of different participants can be pursuing different or even mixed goals—some can be motivated by power, some by economic gain, some by a conviction on policy, and some by a combination of all three.

The point is that if the Soviet Union is indeed developing a political process of policy making, even though the context in which it operates is peculiarly Soviet with authoritarian traditions and socialist forms, if it is at all similar to this system as we see it in the United States, it will tell us something about the Soviet future we might otherwise miss. In looking at the United States, this politics model is a useful device not just because it helps one understand why people behave the way they do in Washington and why policy takes the form it does. It also helps explain the *stability* of the social structure in the United States. A procedure is provided by the political process of policy making for identifying the interests of various power centers in society, for reconciling the clash of interests among different power centers, and for approximately satisfying these interests through the policy adopted as a result of the political bargaining and maneuvering. Since the power of different segments of society is unequal, the results are not necessarily just. But the possibility is held out to any particular group in society that by organizing, publicizing, winning allies, and other political maneuverings, it can build sufficient power to make its demands felt and force favorable responses in terms of policy outputs. Thus, however halting and inefficient it is or however unjustly it operates in the short run, a procedure is provided for approximately satisfying demands of existing power centers in the society and for continuous social change and the creation of new power centers. The result is both a certain responsiveness and a certain stability. As we say, if the Soviet process of policy making is similarly political, providing for ways to identify, reconcile, and satisfy the interests of different groups in the society and for ways for bringing about continuous change and the creation of new power centers, then we would expect, among other things, that the Soviet society would exhibit a very high level of stability.

The Cuban Missile Crisis as a Case Study

Also, if the Soviet Union is indeed developing a political process of policy making, it might help us understand, as it did for the United States, why people behave the way they do in Moscow and why policy takes the peculiar form it sometimes does. Consider an example of a Soviet policy decision of the highest moment that puzzled the top leaders of the United States at the time and continues to puzzle scholars: the Soviet decision in 1962 to put missiles in Cuba.

The Soviet Union sent its first arms to Castro in the summer of 1960. In November, the Eisenhower administration announced that at least twelve Soviet ships had delivered arms, ammunition, tanks, artillery, and similar equipment and that the total so far had amounted to some twenty-eight thousand tons. Shipments continued intermittently until early 1962, when there was a lull. Then, some time in May and June of 1962, the Soviet Union reached a decision to send not only conventional arms and ammunition for the use of the Cubans, but long-range missiles, manned by Soviet troops and armed with nuclear warheads.

As we later learned, the Soviet plan was in two phases. In the first phase, Cuba was to be ringed with defenses: twenty-four batteries of surface-to-air anti-aircraft missiles with a slant range of twenty-five miles; over one hundred MIG fighters; short-range (thirty-five to thirty miles) harbor defense missiles; and coastal patrol boats armed with ship-to-ship missiles. The second phase was to bring in the offensive weapons, the IL-28 light bombers and the ballistic missiles. These would be accompanied by four battle groups of special ground troops armed with tactical nuclear weapons to give the missiles close-in protection—a formidable force of Soviet infantrymen that could, in fact, have defeated the whole Cuban Army in very short order.

There were to be four ballistic missile complexes: Two would have three battalions each of one-thousand-mile Medium-Range Ballistic Missiles (MRBMs), and two would have two battalions each of the two-thousand-mile Intermediate Range Ballistic Missiles (IRBMs). Thus two of the sites would have twelve launching pads and two would have eight—a total of forty pads.

The logistics problem was immense. Each of the 24 anti-aircraft sites had twenty-four missiles 30 feet long, and a variety of special trailers, fueling trucks, and radar vans. Each of the ten IRBM and MRBM missile battalions was to have eight missiles 60 feet long, and dozens of special vehicles per battalion: missile trailers, fueling trucks, radar vans, missile erectors, and personnel carriers. The grand total came to several thousand vehicles and over twenty thousand men. It needed a sealift of more than one hundred shiploads.

The fact that in political terms the decision to send nuclear missiles to Cuba was momentous is obvious. It precipitated the world's first nuclear crisis. What is perhaps not so obvious is that in military terms the decision was not like pressing a button to start automatic procedures but one that required many weeks of long and sustained effort by the top echelons of the Soviet military. Sending missiles to Cuba was a major military deployment, in some ways as complicated to plan and carry out as a landing on a hostile shore.

When the men in Washington learned that the Soviet Union was installing long-range nuclear missiles in Cuba, it was vital for them to know the motive. What did the Soviets hope to accomplish by putting missiles in Cuba? Was it the prelude to war? How had this decision been made? By whom? Did it mean that the politicians were no longer in charge in the Kremlin and the military had taken over? Or had Khrushchev made the decision with some grand political deal in mind—the missiles in Cuba, say, in exchange for West Berlin?

The Official U.S. View of Soviet Motives

In their accounts of the Kennedy administration, both Arthur M. Schlesinger, Jr., and Theodore C. Sorenson have detailed the different theories of why the Soviets put missiles in Cuba developed by the men at the top in Washington at the time—men who included not only generalists in foreign affairs like the President and the Secretary of State, but also men who had spent their lives becoming specialists on the Soviet Union, like Llewellyn Thompson.[5] Both agree that the explanation given widest credence among the top levels of the American leaders was that the move was a Soviet probe of the American will and intentions —"the *supreme* probe of American intentions."[6] Khrushchev believed, the argument runs, that the risks were low because the American people were too timid and "liberal" to face the possibility of nuclear war, and would do no more than protest. If the Americans failed the test, as he expected, then Khrushchev could move in more important places. The vision in the minds of the people in Washington was that Khrushchev had a well-developed plan in which he would appear at the UN in November, say, following the American elections, reveal the missiles poised in Cuba, and dictate his terms on West Berlin.

Other motives—lesser and not necessarily competing with the theory of a supreme probe—were also advanced. One was that the move was intended primarily to redress the military imbalance, without any particular political purpose in mind but the general expectation that the political as well as the military balance of the world would be altered in the Soviet's favor. Another theory was that the purpose was to entice the United States into an invasion, which would divide the Western world and permit the Soviets to move on West Berlin without fear of concerted Allied action. Still another was that a Soviet satellite in Latin America was so valuable to Khrushchev that either a U.S. invasion or a Cuban collapse had to be avoided at all costs—although this par-

[5] Arthur M. Schlesinger, Jr., *A Thousand Days: John F. Kennedy in the White House* (Boston, 1965), pp. 795–97; and Theodore C. Sorenson, *Kennedy* (New York, 1965), pp. 676–78.
[6] Schlesinger, *A Thousand Days*, p. 796. My emphasis.

ticular theory had difficulty explaining why these purposes could not be served better with military aid in conventional arms rather than nuclear forces manned by Soviets.

Sorenson reports that Kennedy accepted the theory of the supreme probe, although Kennedy thought it probable that redressing the missile imbalance and protecting Cuba were likely secondary motives.

Perhaps the most important point about these theories of why the Soviets decided to put missiles in Cuba is that they share the assumption that the decision-making process in the Soviet Union is unitary and rationalized rather than multiple and political. The assumptions are that the Soviet leadership acts as one man; that its goals are national—power, prestige, strategic balance—rather than a mixture of national, organizational, and personal; and that the means to achieve these goals are chosen because they are rationally related to the goals—i.e., they can be expected to achieve the desired goals most directly and economically.

Applying a "Policy Making Is Politics" Model

In contrast, let us consider the kind of hypotheses that would flow from applying a "policy making is politics" model.[7] The basic assumption, to repeat, is that different segments of the Soviet leadership will see particular advantages and disadvantages to any particular decision according to their own parochial interests and responsibilities—some military, some economic, some political in terms of the worldwide Communist movement, some political in terms of the relations among governments.

With this basic assumption in mind, consider the view from Moscow in January 1961, eighteen months before the deployment of the missiles in Cuba. Inside the Soviet Union, the domestic situation seemed good. Work was proceeding on the party program and on the twenty-year plan for increasing domestic pro-

[7] The analysis that follows of the Soviet motives in the Cuban missile crisis is adapted from my *To Move a Nation*, and reflects the analysis made at the time of these events in the Bureau of Intelligence and Research of the State Department, of which I was director. For a more recent attempt to reconstruct the Cuban missile crisis in terms of the "policy making is politics" model, see Graham T. Allison, *Essence of Decision: Explaining the Cuban Missile Crisis* (Boston, 1971), especially pp. 230–44.

duction. The struggle for power among the top leaders, if not finally settled, was at least quiescent.

The world situation was also good. First and foremost, the Soviets were still basking in the afterglow of the Sputnik success, and the world generally assumed that the military and strategic balance had significantly shifted in the Soviets' favor. In the United States, a new, young, and presumably inexperienced President had just taken over the reins of government after an extremely close election, and he seemed to have few prospects except continued deadlock in the political arena and recession in the economy. The Atlantic community had made little progress toward unity. The underdeveloped world was in ferment, offering exciting prospects for the Soviets: Africa, Latin America, and Southeast Asia all seemed full of opportunities. Finally, and most important, the Sino-Soviet dispute, although still disturbing, appeared to be contained for the moment. The eighty-one Communist parties had just met, and a *modus vivendi* with the Chinese still seemed possible.

Khrushchev expressed his satisfaction with all these favorable prospects in his speech of January 6, 1961. Confidently, he laid out an ambitious and aggressive program to extend Communist influence throughout the world—from Berlin, where he revived threats of an ultimatum, to the underdeveloped world, which he invited to embark on new and better "wars of national liberation."

But by the spring of 1962, things looked quite different from Moscow. President Kennedy and the West had stood firm on Berlin. There had been movement in the Atlantic community toward unity. The difficulties of dealing with the underdeveloped world had begun to sink in—the expense of foreign aid, the political instability of the emerging nations, their touchiness, their extreme nationalism, their inexperience, and also their instinctive skill in playing the great powers off against each other rather than being dominated by one of them.

And the Sino-Soviet dispute had gotten out of hand. In one sense, communism is a doctrine of acquiring and using power. The trouble was that the Chinese were behaving like Communists, and the dispute had come to have a dynamism of its own.

Domestically, the Soviet leaders found that the demands they had themselves created with "de-Stalinization" and promises of consumers' goods had become a tiger that they were finding it difficult to ride. There were just not enough resources to meet the whole long list of demands: a better life for consumers; the needs of the space program, prestigious though it was; the foreign aid required to play an active, worldwide role; and, above all, the effort to achieve military supremacy.

Thus many of the different segments of the leadership had reason to be unhappy: those concerned with the operation of the economy and the allocation of resources, those concerned with the space program, those concerned with consumer goods and with the morale of the general public, those concerned with foreign aid and relations with the underdeveloped world, those concerned with foreign relations in general, and those concerned with relations with the fraternal parties and the effect of the Sino-Soviet dispute. And probably most unhappy of all were those responsible for defense.

For the military situation, too, had changed—radically. When the Soviets completed their first experiments with rockets and began to lay out their longer-run program, they apparently decided on a bold move. They elected to skip the logical next step—rockets of about 350,000 pounds' thrust, like the American Atlas—and to leap to giants of about 800,000 pounds' thrust. The successful result was the behemoth that gave the Soviets Sputnik and the lift for their many other space achievements. But this rocket was also intended to serve as the workhorse of the Soviet ICBM force, and American intelligence was rightly impressed. As the intelligence community looked at the evidence in 1958, 1959, and 1960, and even through the first half of 1961, they saw a missile gap developing that would come to a peak in about 1963. Both the intelligence community and the Air Force made a major effort to win approval for a crash program through orthodox channels, but failed to change the Eisenhower administration's policies. Inevitably, the more convinced among the Air Force and intelligence people then tried an end run through leaks to senators and newspaper columnists who were favorably disposed. Reluctantly, the Eisenhower administration upped the American program. When Kennedy came in, he upped it again. But it was apparently neither of these decisions that erased the missile gap, but something that happened inside the Soviet Union itself.

In the meantime, the Soviets had begun to deploy their giant rocket as an ICBM near Plesetsk in the north. And this was apparently the fatal blow to any hopes they may have had of achieving a decisive advantage. For they discovered, one must assume, that this behemoth was just too big, too bulky to serve as a practical weapon. A newer, smaller, more streamlined missile had to be designed instead, and the Soviet ICBM program must have been set back many months.

The Soviets, of course, knew that their hopes of catching up with the United States had been set back, but so long as the Americans did not know the true situation, the Soviets still enjoyed the immediate benefits of seeming to be about to catch up with the United States or even of having just surpassed it. What is more, so long as the United States did not know the true situation, any pressure from the Soviet military for a crash ICBM program could be rather easily turned aside. When the Kennedy administration took office in 1961, the evidence on the Soviet missile deployment was still inconclusive. The U-2 flights had been discontinued after Francis Gary Powers had been shot down on May 1, 1960, and even before that, there was great difficulty obtaining pictures of the deployment because of the almost constant cloud cover over the northern areas of the Soviet Union, where the big missiles were being emplaced. Secretary of Defense McNamara became impatient with the wide spread between the high and low estimates when he saw them, and pressed hard for better intelligence. But even as late as June 1961 the evidence was contradictory and the intelligence community continued to be split, with some Air Force estimates still going as high as three hundred Soviet missiles deployed and some Navy estimates as low as ten. It was not until the summer and fall of 1961 that the Americans launched a series of successful reconnaissance satellites and discovered the true situation.

After considerable agonizing, the Kennedy administration decided to tell the Soviets that they now knew not only that the United States was not behind in the missile race but that it was way ahead—principally to deter the Soviets from the drastic action on Berlin that Khrushchev had been threatening.

For the Soviets, the implications of the message were horrendous. It was not so much the fact that the Americans had military superiority—that was not news to the Soviets. What was bound to frighten them most was that the Americans *knew* that they had military superiority; for the Soviets must have quickly realized that to have reached this conclusion the Americans must have made an intelligence breakthrough and found a way to pinpoint the location of the Soviet missiles that had been deployed as well as to calculate the total numbers. A "soft" ICBM system with somewhat cumbersome launching techniques, which is what the Soviets had at this time, is an effective weapon for both a first strike, a surprise attack such as at Pearl Harbor, and a second, retaliatory strike so long as the location of the launching pads can be kept secret. However, if the enemy has a map with all the pads plotted, the system will retain some of its utility as a first-strike weapon, but almost none at all as a second-strike weapon. The whole Soviet ICBM system was suddenly obsolescent.

While the Soviet leaders fretted over these intractable problems, Castro clamored more and more insistently for military protection, magnifying the threat of an American invasion—perhaps even raising the question of nuclear missiles himself, although Khrushchev has taken credit for the original idea.[8] In any case, among the Soviet leadership, all these problems, fears, and demands somehow converged on the thesis that at least a temporary and expedient solution to their several problems would be to install some of their older, more plentiful medium- and intermediate-range missiles in Cuba. It would give them a cheap and immediate substitute for the newer, more expensive ICBMs and let them stretch out the ICBM program to ease the pressure on resources. And it would meet Castro's demands and protect what had become, since Castro's self-proclaimed membership in the Communist bloc, not just another "war of national liberation" but the first opportunity to project Soviet power into the Western Hemisphere.

[8] See *Khrushchev Remembers: With an Introduction, Commentary, and Notes by Edward Crankshaw*, trans. and ed. Strobe Talbot (Boston, 1970), p. 493.

A Different View of Soviet Motives

Thus the Soviets did not put missiles in Cuba with the intent of using them any more than the United States put Minuteman ICBMs in Montana with the intent of using them. The motive for the decision was strategic, but only in a very broad sense that a general improvement in the Soviet military position would affect the entire political context, strengthening their hand for dealing with the whole range of problems facing them—and unanticipated problems as well. But even though the motive was general and multiple rather than some specific security or foreign policy goal, once the decision was made, it also offered enticing prospects for foreign affairs gains as ancillary benefits. If the move in Cuba were successful and the over-all Soviet position strengthened, their leverage on Berlin would indeed be improved. NATO would surely be shaken, and the chances of the United States successfully creating a multilateral nuclear force would be reduced. In Latin America, other potential "Castros" would be encouraged. American power would be less impressive and American protection less desirable, and some of the Latin American states would move in the Soviet direction even if their governments were not overthrown.

Then, too, a successful move in Cuba would cut the ground from under the Chinese Communists and go far toward convincing Communists everywhere that the Soviet leadership was strong and Soviet methods in dealing with the "imperialists" effective.

Thus the hypothesis is that each segment of the Soviet leadership, each power center of Soviet society, supported the decision to put missiles in Cuba, or acquiesced in it, because they came to believe the move would meet their over-all policy preferences in terms of ideology, philosophy, or simply expectations about the nature of international politics or because it served some parochial personal or organizational interest. Thus "hard liners" saw the decision as appropriate to their view of the world. Doctrinaire ideologists saw it as foiling the "imperialists" who would inevitably and ruthlessly exploit the strategic situation. The military found in the decision a way to redress the immediate imbalance until a buildup of ICBMs could take place. Those concerned with the economy and the allocation of resources saw a way of stretching out rearmament and thus reducing the pressure. Advocates of continuing the space effort or foreign aid saw an opportunity to avoid too-drastic cuts in their programs. Those wrestling with the Sino-Soviet dispute and Communist party relations felt it would restore Soviet prestige and spike the Chinese political guns. The officials dealing with foreign relations in general, and especially with the Western powers, must have thought of the leverage the new strategic balance would bring, especially on the problem of Berlin and Germany. And there were undoubtedly those who were intrigued by the enticing prospects that would open up throughout Latin America.

Supporting Evidence for the "Interest Group" Model

What evidence can we adduce that the Soviet Union has developed a decision-making process that can be best understood by this "interest group" or "policy making is politics" model? It could be argued that one is the practical test of results. As the Cuban events unfolded, no evidence came forth that indicated the Soviets had any clear idea in mind of a specific purpose the missiles would serve, as several alternative analyses of Soviet motives would require. There was no evidence of preparations to present an ultimatum on Berlin at the UN, for example, or to make any sort of grand deal. One would expect that if such a plan did exist, a variant of it would have been presented as the basis for negotiations. Similarly, the "politics" model would lead one to expect the leadership to experience relatively little trouble in weathering the aftermath of the crisis, while the other ways of looking at the Soviet decision-making process all imply considerable trouble. There seems to be no doubt that Khrushchev himself lost prestige and was blamed by a number of his colleagues for the Cuban gamble and its failure.[9] However, this seems to have contributed only slightly to Khrushchev's fall two years later, and at the time the "collectivity" of the leadership was

[9] For the evidence, see Michel Tatu, *Power in the Kremlin: From Khrushchev to Kosygin* (New York, 1969), pp. 273–83.

publicly stressed. From the way people in Moscow behaved—
the lack of evidence that any particular power center was willing
to use the failure of the decision to enhance its own position—indicates that all the major power centers with a legitimate interest
in the decision had a voice in it.

The contention that the Soviet process of decision-making can
best be understood as an interest-group structure gets some support from Khrushchev himself, to the extent that one can accept
the testimony of his memoirs.[10]

On this point—whether one can accept the testimony of
Khrushchev's memoirs—the opinion of the experts is, first, that
Khrushchev undoubtedly did dictate the basic material onto
tape. He was working from memory rather than documents, and
his memory did not always serve him well, as numerous small errors testify. In another sense, however, his memory served him
only too well—in that it was highly selective, remembering best
those events and interpretation of events that make Khrushchev
himself look good. Also, Khrushchev obviously quite deliberately
doctors the record—obscuring his mistakes and his role in some of
the more evil episodes, such as Stalin's purges, and exaggerating
his role in other events. Still another self-serving hand also appears: the person or persons who leaked the transcripts to the
Western world, who selected which transcripts were to be leaked,
and who prepared them for leaking, including at least some doc-
toring. One motive behind this unknown hand or hands was
clearly anti-Stalinism—i.e., one motive was to discredit those
among the present leadership who are opposed to further de-
Stalinization. But with these various caveats, the memoirs can be
taken as genuine, and for purposes such as ours they are very,
very useful indeed.

Among the various reasons for sending missiles to Cuba,
Khrushchev's personal interests require him to protect Cuba from
an invasion by the "imperialist" United States first and foremost,
which he does. By doing so, he can then point to the fact that

---

[10] *Khrushchev Remembers*, according to the publisher, is made up of "material
emanating from various sources at various times and in various circumstances."
Much of it, however, was apparently dictated by Khrushchev, and transcripts
were circulated in privileged circles in Moscow.

part of the deal by which the Soviet missiles were withdrawn was a public announcement by the United States renouncing any intention of invasion, and so claim that *his* purpose was served and that he in fact achieved a victory rather than suffered a defeat. But having done so, he also makes several other points, some explicitly and some by implication. What he obviously considers most important is a point he makes very explicitly indeed: redressing the strategic balance. "In addition to protecting Cuba," Khrushchev writes, "our missiles would have equalized what the West likes to call 'the balance of power.'"[11] Second, also explicitly, he speaks of Soviet ambitions in the rest of Latin America and the importance of Cuba as a base. He says that the Americans "feared, *as much as we hoped,* that a Socialist Cuba might become a magnet that would attract other Latin American countries to Socialism."[12] Hammering away on the invasion theme, he argues that the loss of Cuba as a socialist state would be a terrible blow to Marxism-Leninism worldwide. Soviet prestige and stature would be "gravely diminished."

Khrushchev does not explicitly link the Cuban decision with groups whose interests would be served by putting missiles in Cuba, but he does describe a process of consensus-building. He stresses that the decisions were "collective," that there were many discussions inside the government. President Kennedy, as the central figure in a political process of policy making, often spoke of the crucial importance of keeping the government together, of keeping various individuals representing different power centers "on board," and on occasion he jokingly would say that he agreed with a particular view but was not at all sure that the United States Government would. In Khrushchev's memoirs in one passage describing the decision-making process during the Cuban missile crisis, it could have been Kennedy speaking about Washington rather than Khrushchev about Moscow, with changes only in the jargon:

It wasn't until after two or three lengthy discussions of the matter that we had decided it was worth the risk to install

---

[11] *Khrushchev Remembers,* p. 494.
[12] Ibid., p. 492. My emphasis.

missiles in Cuba in the first place. It had been my feeling that the initial, as well as the subsequent, decisions should not be forced down anyone's throat. I had made sure to give the collective leadership time for the problem to crystallize in everyone's mind. I had wanted my comrades to accept and support the decision with a clear conscience and a full understanding of what the consequences of putting the missiles in Cuba might be—namely, war with the United States. Every step we had taken had been carefully considered by the collective.[13]

Obviously, it is in Khrushchev's interest to stress that he had not acted arbitrarily or irresponsibly on his own, but even discounting this, at least the outlines appear of an interest-group structure at work during the crisis, involving as a minimum the interest of the Soviet armed forces in equalizing the balance, and those segments of the political leadership with an interest in foreign affairs and most especially with extending Soviet influence in Latin America.

Soviet behavior following the crisis is also consistent with the "policy making is politics" model. Our hypothesis is that the Soviet decision to put missiles in Cuba was an attempt to solve a set of problems that affected the interests of various elements of Soviet society: a strategic imbalance in nuclear missiles; the exigencies of the Sino-Soviet dispute; the impossible combination of demands on their limited resources made by defense, their space program, and their people's appetite for consumers' goods; and the drain of foreign aid needed to support their foreign policy. The hypothesis further is that the various segments of the Soviet leadership representing these elements of Soviet society participated in the decision or acquiesced in it. When the crisis was over and the missiles withdrawn, the same set of problems remained. If one assumes that the decision-making process in the Soviet Union is unitary, that the Soviet leadership acts as one man, and that it is rationalized, that the policies are designed to achieve economically and efficiently such national goals as power and prestige, one would expect the Soviets to adopt a crash ICBM program to redress the strategic imbalance, while

[13] Ibid., p. 499.

continuing with both the space program and foreign aid. One could assume that they would not be deterred by the fact that this would mean austerity at home, a return to the coldest kind of Cold War abroad, and in party relations an immediate healing of the Sino-Soviet dispute on Chinese terms.

If one assumes an "interest group" structure, on the other hand, these costs to segments of Soviet society not primarily concerned with national goals would matter very much. If the "policy making is politics" model is used, one would expect the Soviets to search for a policy that spread the costs and that served the interests of all the different segments of society as much as possible. And this is what actually happened. The policy adopted was one of easing the tensions of the Cold War, with the limited test-ban treaty negotiated in 1963 as the first concrete step. With international tensions eased, the ICBM program could safely be stretched out over several years. The burdens of competing so aggressively in the underdeveloped world could be safely lightened. The demand for consumers goods could be at least partially met. There were even advantages in the competition with the Chinese among the fraternal Communist parties. In 1956, Khrushchev had revised Lenin's thesis about the inevitability of war during the final stages of "imperialism"—arguing among other things that the advent of nuclear weapons had created a new situation. In a sense, what Khrushchev was saying was that the ends no longer justify the means if the means entail a high risk of nuclear war. Thus even though easing international tensions inevitably led to a sharpening of the Sino-Soviet rift, the Soviet Union could use the 1956 revision and the tension of the Cuban missile crisis to its advantage. The Soviet Union could paint itself as the champion of world peace and the Chinese as wreckers, adventurers, warmongers, and nuclear madmen.

The evidence that the Soviet Union has developed an "interest group," "policy making is politics" system of decision-making is suggestive, perhaps even persuasive, but it is far from being conclusive. For our purposes, however, the risks in taking it as our working model of the Soviet policy-making system are acceptable. The model jibes with the evidence available more than any of the other analyses offered, even though that evidence is insufficient to make a final judgment. Put another way, this method of looking at the Soviet Union gives a positive explanation of what has been not only the observations of the most persuasive school of experts but also the historical fact that the Soviet Union continues as a viable system. The Soviet Union has survived for half a century, in spite of unbelievable tests: collectivization; forced-draft industrialization; the terror and the purges of the thirties; the massive devastation of World War II; the power struggles among the leadership; the endless troubles with Communist allies, including Yugoslavia, China, Poland, Hungary, and most recently Czechoslovakia; and crises in international affairs, from Berlin to the missiles in Cuba. A system that can survive such strains obviously has means for resolving tensions and reconciling internal conflict.

Adapting the "Interest Group" Model to the U.S.S.R.

Of course, to be useful for the purpose of looking at the Soviet Union, an analytical model developed with the United States primarily in mind needs certain modifications. Some are really little more than a change in emphasis—although the effect on the lives of individual citizens may be enormous. For example, the Soviet system obviously has an "intermediate structure" that performs similar functions to the "intermediate structure" in the United States. It identifies and articulates interests in the mass publics, and it transmits information downward about potential opposition and costs that may lead to a scaling-down of aspirations or even a change in interests. But since the masses lack the ultimate sanction of the ballot as a means of expressing their interests and since such institutions as the secret police have great authority, the downward function of the intermediate structure in shaping interests and manipulating mass attitudes and demands obviously gets greater emphasis in the Soviet system than in the American.

The number of power centers is also likely to be different, at least up to the present. Brzezinski, speaking of Stalin's day, named four: the secret police, the party, the state, and the Army. Fainsod spoke of the armed forces, the police, the managers of industry and agriculture, the scientific community, and the cultural intelligentsia. One would expect a number more than these, but one would also expect the total at the present time to be considerably fewer than the array that participates on the Washington scene.

Up until recently, at least, the penalties for those on the losing side in a struggle over policy that had any power overtones were also greater in the Soviet Union. The penalties in the United States can be great—as some of Senator Joseph McCarthy's victims can testify. But they are not so severe as what happened to Stalin's opponents in the forced labor camps or in the basement of Lubyanka Prison.

The role of the press is also obviously different. As Schumpeter pointed out, one characteristic of democracy is a tendency toward a free press. Consequently, the press becomes a vehicle in the attempt to gain allies and build a consensus. The contending policy advocates strive for publicity, and this contributes to the noise level in a capital like Washington as well as to some of the more ridiculous antics of politicians in a democracy. It also accounts for the prevalence of leaks. If a group inside the government is defeated on an issue, the temptation is strong to leak information to the press to gain allies in the Congress and the wider public. Top Secret facts and figures on Soviet missile strength, for example, almost invariably appear in the American press when the annual appropriation for the armed services is taken up by the Congress. In the Soviet Union the press is much less of a vehicle in the competition for allies. Leaks do occur in the Soviet Union, but they are carried by the Moscow rumor mill rather than appearing in the press. To the extent that the press is used as a vehicle, its use is masked—hence the skill that Soviet citizens—and foreign observers of the Soviet scene—develop in reading between the lines, and the great importance attached to such clues as the position the different leaders occupy in the lineup on a reviewing stand.

Conclusion

Our conclusion, then, is not only to agree with Inkeles, Bauer, Fainsod, Kassof, and the others who see the Soviet system as both stable and unique, but to go further, adopting the position that the Soviet system is indeed developing an "interest group" structure, as various people have speculated, and that a "policy making is politics" model is already the most useful way of looking at the Soviet political system. Thus we would agree with Inkeles and the others that the notion should be rejected that the Soviet Union is either about to collapse or to become a Western-style democracy. We agree that industrialism is consistent with either democratic or totalitarian forms. We agree that the Soviet system is flexible and adaptable, that it is evolving, but along lines that are peculiarly its own. We agree with Kassof that the direction of this evolution is toward "benevolent authoritarianism of great vitality and long-range durability." And we agree with Fainsod that the result will be a "looser, more pragmatic, and pluralistically-based party in which the differentiated interests of an industrial society find freer expression and where the party leadership acts as the manager of their inter-relationships and as the custodian of the national interests of the Soviet state." But pushing the same line of analysis farther and arguing that the Soviet system can best be understood in terms of a "policy making is politics" model leads us to describe the top levels of Soviet society as a number of organized power centers with particular, parochial interests. Examples are the police; the armed forces; the managers and executives of industry and agriculture; the scientific and academic community; the cultural and literary community; and various regional interests, such as the Ukraine or the Leningrad area. We see particular segments of the top leadership of the Communist party and the Soviet state as representing these particular power centers and drawing their own individual power from them. We see the party as providing the arena for a process of conflict and consensus-building by which these various interests are reconciled and policies are adopted, with the top leadership serving as the political brokers as well as power centers with particular interests themselves. Between this top structure and the mass of the people, we see an intermediate structure that serves the function of transmitting policy and interpretation to the masses, molding opinion, and mobilizing the masses, but also passing upward information on attitudes, values, and interests among the mass of the population.

Thus the mass of the population, although denied the kind of ballot that could change leadership as an expression of discontent with policy, does in fact have some influence on policy through the expression of attitudes, values, and interests by the vehicle of the intermediate structure. Partly this is because the cooperation of the mass is required on so many policies, and partly it is because the intermediate structure, which is tied in with the power centers at the top, derives its power and influence from its role as spokesman of the mass. The top levels of any particular power center have a stake in representing and serving the interests of the intermediate structure associated with them. The intermediate structure in turn has a stake in representing and serving the interests of the masses with whom they are connected. Thus people at all levels have some stake in seeing that particular interests are served at least sufficiently to blunt discontent and to enlist loyalty.

We have said that the Soviet Union is evolving along lines that are peculiarly its own out of its own political form of authoritarianism, and that the United States is evolving along lines that are peculiarly its own out of its own political form of democracy. We have also said that the fact that both are highly industrialized states will not alter this conclusion—that both authoritarianism and democracy are compatible with industrialization—although industrialization will make the Soviet Union and the United States similar in a number of other, very important respects. Similarly, we can say that the fact that both the United States and the Soviet Union are developing policy-making systems along the lines of an "interest group," "policy making is politics" structure will not alter the conclusion either. Both authoritarianism and democracy are as compatible with an "interest group" structure as they are with industrialization.

The ordinary Soviet citizen will increasingly live his life under the rule of law, with a wider range of civil liberties guaranteed. The Soviet Government will continue to be essentially authoritarian and socialist, with the state being the owner of industry and the principal employer. The policy-making process will increasingly be political—with policy decisions being the outcome of the clash of interest groups and the party playing the central political role of broker. Political power will thus continue to be the monopoly of the party, and shifts of power or the succession of power will take place within its structure. All sorts of freedoms will eventually be ensured—excepting only the political freedom to challenge the party's monopoly of power and its central function of political brokerage.

CHAPTER 7

Implications: The Future of the Soviet System

IF OUR ANALYSIS of the Soviet system is correct, what are the implications? The first has already been mentioned: A society with an "interest group" structure tends to be fairly stable. The Soviet system, like others whose policy is made in a political process, provides ways in which the different centers of power within the society may articulate their interests, needs, attitudes, and aspirations; ways for reconciling the clash of interests between the different power centers; and ways for approximately satisfying those interests though the policy adopted as a result of political bargaining and maneuvering. As it develops further, a political process of policy making also tends to develop procedures for shifts in power, the emergence of new power centers, and the fading away of outmoded ones. Thus such a system is resilient and flexible, with sufficient capacity for change and adjustment to avoid discontent and opposition from becoming so widespread as to threaten the existence of the regime itself. Nothing in this is incompatible with authoritarianism, however, and we see the Soviet Union continuing its basically authoritarian political form. However, because of the developing "interest group" structure, we also see the Soviet Union being more and more responsive to the interests and aspirations of the mass population—increasingly so now that a high level of industrialization and national power has been achieved.

Power and Prestige Goals

In an "interest group" structure, any particular set of goals must compete with others for resources and national effort. This is as true of national goals of power and prestige as others. Because of this and because of the fact that once an "interest group" structure becomes established, it tends to encourage the formation of still other groups to articulate still other competing interests, we would expect it to be difficult for some future group of Soviet leaders to turn the society to the pursuit of national goals of power and prestige exclusively or fanatically. To put it more precisely, we would expect national goals to remain strong competitors in the policy struggle over priorities for Soviet goals and the allocation of resources, but we think the odds are against them becoming so dominant that the Soviet Union would embark on a course of national aggrandizement in the sense that Germany did under Hitler or Japan did under the militarists of the 1930s.

Ideological Goals

For many of the same reasons, we would also expect it to be equally difficult for some future group of Soviet leaders to turn their society to the pursuit of ideological goals. This expectation is powerfully reinforced by a look at the fate of all revolutionary movements of the past, whether ideological or religious. Inevitably, they have been routinized. Even though the verbiage of the movement may remain incendiary or become even more incendiary, action slows down and finally ceases.

It is also worth noting that the conclusion that this process of routinization is already well along in the case of Marxism-Lenin-

ism is shared by a number of students of communism and the
ideological history of Marxism-Leninism. The most carefully reasoned case for this view has been offered by Robert C. Tucker.[1]
Tucker argues that Marxism-Leninism has never been static, but
that in the post-Stalin era, change was both rapid and profound.
The year 1956 was the watershed. At the twentieth party congress in 1956, Khrushchev not only denounced Stalinism, but also
enunciated several major changes in Communist doctrine. The
most important was his revision of Lenin's thesis of the inevitability of war in the final stages of "imperialism." Khrushchev proclaimed that since worldwide "forces for peace" were now so
strong, wars, though still possible, were no longer inevitable. In
elaborating the argument, Soviet leaders argued that nuclear
weapons were so awesomely destructive that the more sober elements among the leadership of the "imperialist" powers would
avoid policies that ran a high risk of nuclear war. The Communist
and non-Communist worlds could not only successfully coexist,
but they could co-operate in keeping world peace. Competition
between the two systems would continue, but it could be economic. Communism would still be the wave of the future, but it
would spread by the attractiveness of its example. Revolution
was no longer the only path by which power could be taken from
the hands of the capitalists; the parliamentary route was now also
possible.

Western observers, Tucker points out, tend to view these ideological innovations as essentially tactical adjustments to the
necessities of the nuclear age. The Maoist faction of the Chinese
party, on the other hand, calls them "revisionist," and they see
these ideological changes as fundamental, symptoms of degeneration, a turning away from revolutionary Marxism-Leninism, the
beginning of the routinization of communism similar to the routinization of other revolutionary movements in the past. In Tucker's view, it is the Chinese who are right.

Tucker calls the phenomenon "deradicalization." "Deradicalization signifies a subtle change in the movement's relation to the

[1] "The Deradicalization of Marxist Movements," *The American Political Science
Review* (June 1967). The article is also reprinted as Chapter 6, "The Deradical-
ization of Marxist Movements," in Tucker's *The Marxian Revolutionary Idea* (New
York, 1969).

social milieu. Essentially, it settles down and adjusts itself to existence within the very order that it officially desires to overthrow and transform. This is not to say that the movement turns into a conservative social force opposed to social change. Rather, it becomes 'reformist' in the sense that it accepts the established system and its institutionalized procedures as the framework for further efforts in the direction of social change."[2]

"Deradicalization," Tucker argues, "is caused mainly by changes in leadership and by worldly success, and it seems always to be the fate of radical movements that survive and flourish without remaking the entire world." Examining the history of the Soviet Union, Tucker concludes that the process is well along. Thus the Chinese view that the Soviets are changing is essentially correct. Westerners, Tucker goes on to say, sometimes think the Sino-Soviet dispute is a "mere smokescreen" for clashing national ambitions and rivalries. "To ignore the national, imperial, and personal factors in the conflict would be wrong," he writes. "But it would be no less an error, and perhaps a greater one, to fail to perceive that ideological and political fundamentals of communism really are at stake in this dispute."[3]

Thus we see the Soviet political system, to repeat, as attempting to serve the interests of a number of different segments of society, each with power in its own right, and hence unlikely to concentrate its efforts as a society exclusively on either national or ideological goals.

All this is rather encouraging. The Soviet political system is stable. Although likely to continue to be authoritarian, it is increasingly responsive to the interests and aspirations of the mass of the people. The goals and purposes of the society are pluralistic. Neither the goals of national power and prestige nor those of ideology are likely to become so central that the Soviet Union will become a threat to the outside world in military terms. But what does continue to bother the non-Soviet observer—and in all likelihood a number of Soviet observers as well—is the lack of convincing evidence that the Soviet Union will be able to solve the problem of the succession of leadership and the transfer of

[2] *The Marxian Revolutionary Idea*, p. 185.
[3] Ibid., p. 212.

power. The lack of well-established and widely accepted constitutional procedures for replacing one leader or set of leaders with another means a behind-the-scenes struggle for power that on one occasion or another could conceivably have fateful consequences for the entire world. For the moment, however, the question is what is likely to happen to the Soviet Union, its people, and their values when they, too—as they surely will—become a superindustrial society. Will any of the conclusions and predictions we have made so far have to be changed?

Values in a Superindustrial U.S.S.R.

As the United States moves into a superindustrial age, to recapitulate, we foresaw a range of consequences. The first, which we are already seeing, is a renewal of old values. The new affluence permits the realization of old, long-postponed goals, and impatience will mount at any delay in achieving them now that achievement is possible. Not only will there be an end to poverty and economic insecurity, but inequalities of every kind will be eliminated—including those between men and women, as well as those between minorities and the majority. Relieved of the economic burden of survival, man will have endless opportunities for education and the fullest cultivation of his talents and interests. All these changes will in turn bring at least the opportunity for fuller self-realization and the development of more mature, autonomous personalities among both men and women.

Affluence will also bring a change in how people conceive the relation between work and income. It seems likely that society will come to give each person a birthright income or something similar that will give individuals great freedom in when they work, how much they work, and on what they work. Fundamental changes in the whole range of human values are likely to result. One change that will clearly come is a weakening of the so-called industrial ethic—both in the puritanical attitudes associated with work, savings, and the rest, and in the achievement attitudes that measure success and self-esteem in economic and materialistic terms.

We foresaw greater tolerance about values, and thus a move away from the conformity of traditional society toward great diversity, with an array of subcultures having different values and different attitudes toward work, toward achievement and excellence, toward pleasure and the good life, and toward public values. We felt that it was unlikely that public values that require across-the-board commitment of the entire society—such as national prestige values—would be able to gain the support of sufficient of these varied subcultures ever again to dominate.

In terms of social structure and the locus of power in a super-industrial United States, we concluded that these various trends —egalitarianism, higher education for more people, affluence and hence time and freedom, fuller and more rapid communications, greater interdependence of the economy and other aspects of life —combined into an over-all political trend toward more participants in the policy-making process with more nearly equal power. We saw the political arena marked by a diffusion of power in the sense that there will be more power centers in the intermediate structure with bigger voices.

The question now is: How much if any of this will apply to the Soviet Union?

There seems to be no question, first, that the Soviet Union will become a superindustrial society. In 1970, the per capita income for the United States was $3,910 in 1965 dollars; and for the Soviet Union, $1,678. The growth rate for the United States since about 1870 has been 1.8 per cent per year; for Russia, about 2.8 per cent per year. At that rate, the Soviet Union will achieve the American 1970 per capita national income within the next thirty years, and move rather rapidly from that position into superindustrial status. Actually, there is reason to believe that the rates for both countries will be considerably higher, with both moving into superindustrial status that much sooner.[4] What is more important, however, is that the thrust of Soviet society is toward a higher and higher state of industrialization. Ideological values are strongly in that direction and so are social values. The institutions of the society are geared to implement these values, including the organization of the economy by central planning. Even if there were evidence of a change in either the values or the organ-

4 Herman Kahn and Anthony I. Wiener, *The Year 2000: A Framework for Speculation on the Next Thirty-three Years* (New York, 1967), p. 119.

ization of the economy—which there is not—the Soviet Union would probably arrive at a superindustrial condition before sufficient change in those values and institutions could be brought about to halt the trend.

If this is correct, and the Soviet Union is heading toward a superindustrial condition, what will be the consequences?

The only attempt among specialists on the Soviet Union to speculate directly about the possible impact of superindustrial affluence on the Soviet Union is in Brzezinski and Huntington's *Political Power: USA/USSR*. Brzezinski and Huntington agree that some universal traits inherent in modern industrial and urban order affect the style and values of mass culture. Thus, Soviet citizens are more similar to Americans and Western Europeans in dress, social behavior, and some of their personal aspirations than they were twenty-five years ago. But the authors argue against any notion that the consequences of having similar economic structures necessarily go any deeper than this—so far, say, as to dictate the political superstructure of a society. They stress the importance of looking at both the character of the political system and the character of the economic growth. "If, in the Soviet and American cases, both the political systems and the character of economic growth are different, it is reasonable to conclude that the influence of economics on politics, and vice versa, is also likely to be quite different in the two societies."[5] In the Soviet Union, an underdeveloped, relatively backward society was modernized and industrialized through "total social mobilization effected by terroristic means wielded by a highly disciplined and motivated political elite."[6] The very nature of the process was inimical to the emergence of political pluralism. In the United States, the revolution freed the society from a restraining aristocratic order. "The diversity, the pluralism, the fear of central control which characterized the early settlers, living in isolation not only from the world but also from one another, expressed itself in a political and social system designed to protect that diversity."[7] The modern American society, Brzezinski and Huntington argue,

[5] *Political Power: USA/USSR*, p. 421.
[6] Ibid., p. 421.
[7] Ibid., p. 422.

whose hallmarks are industrial dynamism and corporate efficiency, is governed by an anachronistic political system designed
for early nineteenth-century America. In the Soviet Union, on
the other hand, the political system came before the society—a
power-motivated political elite set about to destroy the old social
order and to construct a new one. "Thus if it can be said that
American politics can best be understood in terms of American
society, Soviet society can best be understood in terms of Soviet
politics. In the latter, political power preceded economic power;
in the former, economic power preceded political."[8] Because of
this, ideology and professional political bureaucracy play more
important roles in the Soviet Union than in the United States,
and, conversely, factors such as economic change and the activities of interest groups play more important roles in the United
States than in the Soviet Union. "Thus, changes in Soviet economic management and methods of planning and allocation
need not challenge the ideological and power monopoly of the
ruling Party." Citing Peter Wiles, the authors point out that the
computer, linear programming, and other modern techniques
make it easier for the Soviets to pursue economic development
while retaining their ideological-political structure.[9] A large,
complex economy can be centrally controlled and also be made
efficient, something that could not be done in Stalin's day.

All the evidence, Brzezinski and Huntington argue, indicates
that the party leaders intend to protect the ideological-political
structure and to retain the party's monopoly of the political function of integration. The two authors maintain that a "multiplicity
of expertises"—by which they seem to mean what we have referred to as an "interest group" structure—is not the same thing
as "social-political pluralism based on group automomy"—by
which they seem to mean the peculiar diffusion of power characteristic of the United States. Their conclusion, similar to our own,
is that the Soviet and American societies will not "converge," but
will each develop along its own lines. In the case of the Soviet
Union, this means along the lines of authoritarianism, with the

[8] Ibid., p. 423.
[9] The citation is to Peter Wiles, "Will Capitalism and Communism Spontaneously
Converge?," *Encounter* (June 1963).

party retaining the monopoly of political power even though the policy-making process provides ways in which the interests of various groups in the society can be served, and thus those groups have power in particular policy areas.

Beyond this, Brzezinski and Huntington argue that the consequences of affluence depend on how affluence is obtained. "Affluence achieved by a mixed economic process, involving both the political system and independent individual and group activity, consolidates social diversity and creates new loci of social and political power." They cite the rise of the trade unions and their achievement of both economic and political power as a case in point. Furthermore, when affluence came to the United States, it came to a society that had been not just poor but free. In the Soviet Union, affluence is being brought about by means of political control wielded by a political elite. When affluence does come it will have come to a society that has always been poor and *unfree*. In addition, the Soviet Union will remain relatively less affluent than the United States and a number of other countries for quite some time, and so the feeling of being less well off will persist. For all these reasons, Brzezinski and Huntington feel that the pressures for political moderation inherent in general well-being will be weak in the Soviet Union. Thus they see no reason to believe that affluence will change the authoritarian form of Soviet society, and much reason to believe that it might actually reinforce it.

The two authors do believe that affluence will diminish the tendency in the Soviet Union toward excessively high goals and impossible demands on the society. Greater rationality will be possible in both planning and social mobilization.

Since American affluence has come from the interaction between "segmented corporate productive wealth and individual purchasing power," consumption patterns have tended to be individualistic. It is this and the absence of an over-all political perspective that many critics see as the cause of poverty, discrimination, and other evils in American society. The evidence is that Soviet leaders are concerned to prevent their affluence from assuming such an individualistic character. They speak of communal living, communal rest homes, free mass transportation

rather than individual automobiles, free social services—of "affluent collectivism" as their goal. "Should this come to pass," Brzezinski and Huntington write, "it is unlikely that such forms of affluence will impede the relationship of control and mobilization
between the political system and the society. The political system
will be characterized by greater rationality, less coercion, increased reliance on social self-control. The society will suffer less
from the tensions originating in the lack of resources and, initially, from the absence of social consent for the new political-so-
cial system. A system combining self-sustaining popular control
over social behavior, based on a highly collectivist affluence, with
centralized managerial direction from above, will differ profoundly from the earlier Stalinist model, but also from the existing Western affluent societies."[10]

Conclusions

Nothing in our own analysis would lead us to disagree with
these conclusions, either as to how the Soviet system is presently
evolving or the probable impact of affluence on that system.
Brzezinski and Huntington would probably agree that, using our
terms, the Soviet system is evolving an "interest group" structure,
a political process of policy making, within authoritarian forms—
i.e., with the political function of broker and the power associated
with it reserved to the leaders of the Communist party and with
recruitment to leadership confined to the membership of the
party. At the same time, we would agree that affluence could be
adapted to a collectivist, rather than individualist form.

Looking at the Soviet Union in terms of the conclusions we
reached about the United States, this is merely to say that where
affluence is permitting the United States to give renewed emphasis to its old values of equality, an end to poverty, and freedom, in the Soviet Union affluence will permit them to give renewed emphasis to *their* old goals of equality, an end to poverty,
and collectivism. Similarly, a fuller realization of these goals,
combined with the opportunity for education and fuller cultivation of one's talents, are just as likely to lead to fuller self-realiza-

[10] *Political Power: USA/USSR*, p. 427.

tion and the development of more mature, autonomous personalities in the Soviet Union as in the United States. The spectrum of man's nature is broad, and both individual freedom and a "collectivist" need for relationship with others are part of it. The probability that more mature, autonomous personalities will come from the fuller development of the one part of the spectrum is just as high as it is that they will come from the fuller development of the other.

Depending on their decisions about the growth rate of the economy and about population controls and family size, the United States by the year 2000 could have a per capita national income as low as $5,000 in today's terms or as high as $12,000. If it is halfway between these two it would mean that a worker's family of four would have an annual income of $34,000 in today's terms. At some point between now and then, we estimated, the United States will institute some form of birthright income largely divorced from work. The U.S.S.R., depending on their decisions about growth rate and population controls, by the year 2000 could have a per capita national income as low as $2,000 or as high as $8,000. Thus if their economic growth rate is high and their population growth is low, the Soviet Union would be in a position to institute a birthright income by the year 2000, and even if the rates are adverse, it should be able to do so twenty-five years later. The first question is: Will they? I would argue that they will. As we said of the United States, the superindustrial economy is a slave economy, even though the "slaves" are machines. It will bring many problems. But it seems highly unlikely that either the American or the Soviet society will tolerate a fraud by which development is arrested for the sole purpose of avoiding the problems that divorcing work from income will bring. It may come later in the Soviet Union, but the Soviets, too, will want to let machines do the work if they can. Sooner or later, machines will be doing all the work that machines can do, and at that time the Soviets, too, will come to something like a birthright income divorced from work. What do the masters do in a slave economy? Soviet man will have to face the question just as his Western counterpart will.

The trends are already noticeable, and noticeable to the Soviets as well as to outside observers. Dr. Pyotr L. Kapitsa, a noted Soviet physicist, for example, writing in *Voprosy Filosofii* (*Questions of Philosophy*) noting that the technological revolution already has produced signs of social decay among youth in highly developed capitalist countries, then suggests that the Soviet Union will not be immune to similar problems.[11] (It might be noted that publication of such an article in the Soviet Union is unusual in that the more orthodox line is that the problems confronting capitalist countries as they move toward further development are unique to capitalism.) Kapitsa, at least by implication, also sees affluence as the fundamental cause. "Young people," he writes, "not having to fear for tomorrow, lack the necessity to fight for their existence and this gives rise to a situation in which they face no problems that required their strength and will. All this, taken together, deprives the life of young people of any permanent inner substance." It turns out, he goes on to say, that society is still not prepared to make profitable use of the material wealth and leisure time with which it has been endowed by the scientific-technological revolution. Stirrings of a women's liberation movement have also become increasingly apparent in the Soviet Union as well.[12]

Clearly, in the Soviet Union commitment to the so-called industrial ethic will weaken, just as we expect it to weaken in the United States. But one hesitates to assume that Soviet society will parallel American society in the next step. With such a strong emphasis in Soviet society on "collectivism," with a leadership and party committed to "collective" values and with the power they have to influence the direction of Soviet society, it seems doubtful that tolerance about values will develop in the same degree or that Soviet society will move so far from the conformity of traditional society toward great diversity and an array of subcultures. What seems more likely is that Soviet society will use its affluence to continue to experiment with "collectivist" forms of human fulfillment and self-realization. Soviet society in a super-

[11] As reported in the New York *Times* (August 2, 1971).
[12] Reports on women's lib in the Soviet Union appear in *The Wall Street Journal* (January 6, 1971); the New York *Times* (January 25, 1971); and the New York *Times* (November 1, 1971).

industrial age will be vastly different from what it is today, but it will also be different from Western societies.

There is some pressure in the Soviet Union today, mainly from the "literary intelligentsia"—writers and artists like Solzhenitsyn—for greater freedom of expression for writers and greater freedom to read whatever they like by the public at large. In the future, more freedom may well be granted. But whether it is or not will be a function of increased feeling of security on the part of the leadership and confidence in the appeals of the Soviet system than of affluence. There is even deeper and broader demand in Soviet society, extending to the leadership itself, for justice, for a rule of law as opposed to the arbitrariness of the Stalin days, and for more responsiveness by the ruling leadership to the mass of the people. The rule of law, like freedom, is less dependent on affluence than it is on a sense of security; but the demand is so broad in Soviet society that it seems clearly destined to prevail. More responsiveness to the mass of the people is more dependent on affluence, and this demand, too, seems likely to be fulfilled.

The array of subcultures that we predicted for Western societies in the superindustrial age seemed to reinforce the tendency of an "interest group" structure to resist public values that require across-the-board commitment of the entire society—such as national prestige values. It is not so readily apparent that "collectivist" forms would be equally resistant to such public values, but neither is it apparent that they would lend themselves to such values. Soviet ideology is not like Hitlerism or militarism in Japan, both of which had inherent philosophical dynamisms toward national aggrandizement. One would expect affluence to bring fundamental changes in values, but in the same direction the society is already moving, not in such radically different directions.

Similarly, on the question of social structure and the locus of power, affluence is likely to bring change, but along the lines the society is already moving, rather than in a radically different direction. The United States is already moving toward a pluralism that diffuses power. The Soviet Union, on the other hand, seems to be moving toward an "interest group" structure, a political process of policy making, that is similar in some ways but retains authoritarian forms. Various segments of society will increasingly have a large voice in policy areas of direct concern to them, but there seems to be nothing in affluence per se that works toward a diminution of the monopoly held by the party leadership of the role of broker and of the political power associated with that role. Neither is there any evidence that affluence will necessarily affect the fact that it is the party that is the sole organization for the training and recruitment of the leadership. In this, as in so many other things, it seems likely that the major difference between a socialist country today and a socialist country in the superindustrial age is that in the superindustrial age it will be a *rich* socialist country.

Part III

WESTERN EUROPE, EASTERN EUROPE, AND
THE POLITICAL ORGANIZATION OF THE
DEVELOPED WORLD

CHAPTER 8

The Future of Nationalism and the Nation-State

MUCH OF WHAT we have said about the United States will probably be equally true of Western Europe, Japan, and Australia. Somewhat less of what we have said of the Soviet Union will probably be true of Eastern Europe.

Certainly there can be no doubt that affluence will come to the other democratic, developed nations. The per capita national income of Great Britain in 1965 was $1,800; France, $1,900; Western Germany, $1,900; Japan, $857; and Australia, $2,000. Great Britain in the year 2000 could have a national income of $8,400, and by the year 2020, $20,300. In 2000 France could have $9,000, and in 2020, $22,100. In 2000 Western Germany could have $10,400, and in 2020, $27,400. Similarly, the figures for Japan are $10,000 and $35,900; and for Australia, $6,000 and $16,000. Although they will arrive at the superindustrial stage later than the United States, there can be no doubt that they will arrive.

Will the consequences be similar? One looks in vain for any

force working in the opposite direction. The motives for higher standards of living, higher levels of technological development, and the creation of a machine-slave economy are strong, and nothing is on the horizon that indicates their weakening. Sooner or later all these nations will also come to the position in which they can divorce income from work, through some such device as the birthright income, and there is no plausible reason to expect that they will not.

When their economies, too, become "machine-slave" economies, the industrial ethic and all its associated values will also weaken. These countries, too, will then have the resources to achieve the old values of freedom, equality, and justice, and they will undoubtedly bring about a renewed emphasis on achieving them completely and without delay. Equal stress will be given to providing full opportunity for education and personal fulfillment. All this—the new equality and the dignity it brings, the education, and the opportunity for fulfillment—should, as in the United States and the U.S.S.R., make for better-integrated, more mature personalities for most people. At the same time, facing the problem of finding a meaningful life and purpose when the economic problem has been solved will be more than some people can stand. While the majority are likely to be more mature, better-integrated people, some, as in the United States and the U.S.S.R., will fail. In the first stages of the superindustrial society, at least, the suicide rate may be higher, as well as the rate of neurotic breakdowns. In Western Europe and the other countries, as in the United States, the final result seems likely to be not uniformity in values, but diversity. Here, too, one can foresee a great variety of subcultures each with a different attitude toward work, toward achievement and excellence, toward pleasure and the good life, and toward public and private values.

To the extent that public values are in the fore, among these nations, as in the United States, the likelihood seems to be for a turning away from such national goals as power and prestige and toward essentially internationalist or globalist goals. It should be easier to get public support for projects tending to unite the world or dealing with issues affecting the whole of mankind than for goals that benefit only the particular nation.

It also seems likely that among these developed nations the locus of power in the future will also follow the pattern we have seen in the United States. The same forces seem to be at work in all these countries, leading to a proliferation of power centers—more participants in the policy-making process with more nearly equal power. Here again, policy making will probably be political. Thus we would also expect that since power will be widely distributed, the leadership would need wide public support before it could commit the nation, and that the result will be that the essentially private, internationalist, and globalist goals of the society are also likely to be the goals of the state.

Our conclusion, then, is that the developed nations of Western Europe, Japan, and Australia are likely to follow the pattern we foresee in the transition of the United States to a superindustrial society. But nothing in this conclusion is meant to imply that the national identity of each of these states will be submerged in some grand superindustrial identity. If a characteristic of the superindustrial society is the prospering of a variety of subcultures, it also seems probable that a superindustrial France will include many subcultures that retain the cultural values and attitudes that we think of as peculiarly French. And so it is likely to be for all the rest.

Eastern Europe

For Eastern Europe, the more developed Communist countries, the judgment is more difficult. Affluence, certainly, will eventually come. The per capita national income of Czechoslovakia is $1,100; for Poland it is $780; for Hungary it is $2,068; for Romania it is $720, and for Yugoslavia it is $530. This means that all these countries have much, much farther to go than their Western European neighbors, but again, there is no force working, so far as we can see, against the trend toward greater affluence.

Thus the Eastern European countries, like the Soviet Union, will also someday see a birthright income, even though the day is still quite distant. They, too, will undergo a weakening of the values and attitudes associated with the industrial ethic. Also like the Soviet Union, the Eastern European countries are developing an "interest group" structure for the making of national policies, and this trend, too, seems likely to continue. What is much less certain is how strong their commitment is to the authoritarian form of government and to the various "collectivist" ideals and values. The suspicion is that Yugoslavia may be the model for at least some of the other Eastern European countries rather than the Soviet Union. In Yugoslavia it is already clear that the notion of collectivist forms in social and economic life is virtually dead. Perhaps even more significant is the fact that the Communist party of Yugoslavia is also experimenting with sharing power or at least playing a role other than that of monopolizing the function of broker and the political power associated with that function. Throughout Eastern Europe similar tendencies are manifest, although in greatly varying strength. What is more difficult to perceive is the dynamic behind these tendencies. The cultural pull of Western Europe may have some effect. So, too, may the need in Eastern Europe for technological help and for trade and the conviction that the Soviet Union cannot possibly fill the entire need. But a more likely candidate as the dynamic here is probably nationalism.

Nationalism is strong in all the Eastern European countries. But at the same time, none of these countries is large and powerful enough to be able to afford to make an enemy of the Soviet Union. On the contrary, in dangerous times—in a time, say, when some new Hitler was on the rampage—they would need Soviet protection. But submitting too completely to the Soviet embrace and patterning themselves too thoroughly on the Soviet model would smother nationalism. Thus the tendencies to diverge from the Soviet pattern in matters that do not imply a risk to security but that will preserve an independent identity are probably due to nationalism.

Nationalism as the Key Dynamism

Nationalism, in fact, may well be the key to understanding much of the future of the developed world, especially of its political organization. It is the only conceivable force that could possibly break up some of the large states, such as the Soviet Union. Second, it is also the single most formidable obstacle to the hopes of combining the established nation-states of the developed world into some larger entity, such as a United States of Europe.

Most men throughout most of history have had few political loyalties beyond their immediate community. Throughout most of history, the peasants of Europe, Asia, Africa, and the Western Hemisphere identified with and loved a village or locality and were unaware or indifferent to any larger government that may have ruled over them. When men have given political loyalty to entities larger than the local community it has been to a great variety—at different times to the tribe, to the clan, to the city-state, to feudal lord, to the Church, to the King, and to the Emperor. Sometimes the forces generating larger political loyalties have been economic, sometimes religious, sometimes ideological. But the one that has been that most potent force of all in the history of the states of Europe, Eastern and Western, is nationalism. It has made big states out of small ones. Germany and Italy, for example, were only geographic expressions like Asia, Europe, and the Americas, until nationalism swept away the feudal principalities and forged nation-states where none had existed before. And it has made small states out of a big one. The territory of what was the one state of Austria-Hungary, for example, is now divided among six. *All* of the early candidates for superindustrial status, in fact, are nation-states. Clearly, any prediction about the political organization of the world in the future—whether the highly industrialized states will survive in their present form, be broken up into smaller units, or merge into larger ones—must begin with an examination of the nature of nationalism, the functions it has performed, and subsequently make a judgment on whether or not it has run its course.

Nationalism in History

The most striking thing about nationalism is how very recent a phenomenon it is. We think it old. But if a careful and precise distinction is made between a sense of identity and the true phenomenon of nationalism, no shred of evidence can be found of nationalism anywhere in the world earlier than two centuries ago, and some nationalisms are no older than two or three decades. The Chinese, the French, Japanese, and many others had a sense of common identity going back many centuries and in some cases perhaps even millennia. But their common sense of identity had no more operational significance, as indicated earlier, than the common sense of identity today among Europeans, Asians, or Africans. We think nationalism old partly because of the need of nationalism and hence of nationalists to foster myths about the nation. "We imagine the past," L. B. Namier once said, "and remember the future."[1] For nationalism and nationalists, the first part of the aphorism, at least, is supremely true. It suited De Gaulle's purpose to evoke Joan of Arc as a French patriot, but the truth is, as Charles Seignobos, a leading French historian, testifies, Joan herself was loyal not to France, but to the king of the Armagnac party, which was at war with the Burgundian party, allies of the English.[2] Seignobos maintains that the Hundred Years' War had no effect on the development of the French nation. "This war," he writes, "carried on by adventurers with no national character, was a war between two royal families rather than between two nations." The hostility toward the English, he argues, came from local patriotism, not national. To give a more recent example, it suited Nkrumah's purpose to change the name of the newly independent Gold Coast to Ghana, but the truth is that the medieval empire that was Ghana probably embraced no territory at all controlled by the present state.

In his monumental study of the origins of nationalism, Hans Kohn found in the history of France and England nothing at all, whether in song, poetry, or historical documents, suggesting the modern concept of nationalism before the middle of the eighteenth century. In America, the colonists had no sense of America, but only of the individual colony. In 1760, for example, the father of Gouverneur Morris provided in his will that his son never be sent to Connecticut so as to avoid the danger of his being infected with "that low craft and cunning so incident to the

[1] *Conflicts: Studies in Contemporary History* (London, 1942), p. 70.
[2] *The Evolution of the French People*, trans. Catherine Alison Phillips (New York, 1932), p. 153.

people of that country." Both the historians of nationalism and the historians of the American revolution agree that nationalism had little role in the American struggle for independence.[3] In Asia, nationalism did not appear until the twentieth century, with the one exception of Japan, and it made only modest headway until World War II. In most of Africa it began to arrive only in the 1950s.

Nationalism as we know it, then, began in the latter half of the eighteenth century in Western Europe. As good a date as any is 1789.

The Nature of Nationalism

Louis L. Snyder, in the Introduction to his *The Dynamics of Nationalism,* defines nationalism as "a condition of mind, feeling or sentiment of a group of people in a well-defined geographic area, speaking a common language, possessing a literature in which the aspirations of the nation have been expressed, being attached to common traditions, and, in some cases, having a common religion"—although he hastens to add that there are exceptions to every part of his definition.[4] Carlton J. H. Hayes speaks of cultural and historical forces, in which he includes language, historical traditions including religious past, territorial past, political past, and economic and industrial past.[5] Rupert Emerson speaks of an "ideal model" of a nation—"a single people, traditionally fixed on a well-defined territory, speaking the same language and preferably a language all its own, possessing a distinctive culture, and shaped to a common mold by many generations of shared historical experience."[6] Pointing out that no such nation ever existed in total purity, he goes on to identify four elements "which insistently recur as essential to the creation of a sense of common destiny": territory, language, a common historical tradition, and "the intricate interconnections of state and na-

[3] Kohn, *The Idea of Nationalism: A Study of Its Origins and Background* (New York, 1948); and C. H. Van Tyne, *The War of Independence: American Phase* (Boston, 1929), p. 271.
[4] Princeton, 1964, p. 2.
[5] *Nationalism: A Religion* (New York, 1960), pp. 3-4.
[6] *From Empire to Nation: The Rise and Self-Assertion of Asian and African Peoples* (Boston, 1960), p. 103.

tion." Elements that have appeared with "less regularity and whose relevance for this purpose is more dubious are race, religion, and a common economic system."

Common language, history, and the others are not, as Dankwart A. Rustow has pointed out, "among the defining characteristics of a nation," but they are "likely to promote feelings of nationality."[7] As such—i.e., as conditions likely to promote feelings of nationality—they might be illuminating in assessing the future of nationalism. Specifically, let us look at four: language and literature; religion; shared history, culture, and traditions; and territory and statehood.

Language and Literature

The birth of nationalism in Western Europe, certainly, was vastly aided by the existence of a common language and literature. This was true in those cases in which a state already existed —such as France, the Netherlands, Spain, Portugal, and Great Britain (where English had already replaced both Scottish and Welsh as a practical matter)—and also in those cases in which a single state did not yet exist, such as Poland, Germany, and Italy. It was aided even more if the language was spoken *only* in the particular area and nowhere else, providing dramatic evidence of a people's similarities to each other and differences with their neighbors, which was true in all these cases. But distinct nationalisms have also developed in neighboring states sharing the same language and literature—notably in Latin America. And, of course, nationalism has also triumphed where there was no common language. In Switzerland, four different languages are spoken—French, German, Italian, and Rhaeto-Romansh—each in different cantons, and yet a nationalism arose that was peculiarly Swiss. The same is true of Belgium. In one or two cases, nationalism can be said to have facilitated the spread of a language rather than the other way around. In Ireland, the revival of Irish was motivated solely by Irish nationalism and the hatred of the English. Kohn also cites the case of Norway and Denmark, whose people were of "common racial stock" and spoke almost the same

[7] *A World of Nations: Problems of Political Modernization* (Washington, D.C., 1967), p. 23.

language. "Nevertheless," as Kohn says, "they consider them-selves as two nationalities, and the Norwegians set up their own language only as the result of having become a nationality."[8]

Religion

Although not nearly so influential as language, religion has clearly played a role in the development of nationalism and con-tinues to do so. Hans Kohn credits religion as being one of the major factors in giving the Catholic Croats and the Orthodox Serbs a different sense of national identity and also in the sepa-rate development of the Netherlands and Belgium.

Ireland and Israel are other examples where religion played a major role. It might also be noted that the sole reason for the for-mation of Pakistan as a state was a common adherence to Islam and fear of Hindu domination. It is too early to speak of Pakistani nationalism, even in the western remnant surviving the secession of Bangladesh, but if nationalism does develop, religion will have played a central role.

Shared History, Culture, and Traditions

A shared history, culture, and traditions in some measure also facilitate the growth of nationalism. In a number of countries—such as Japan, Hungary, Thailand, and Ireland—a sense of com-mon identity existed long before modern times and long before what we think of as nationalism arose in those countries. A shared history, culture, and traditions were important factors in creating the sense of identity. Usually, a distinct language was also present, but not always—as mentioned above, Irish was re-vived in Ireland as a *result* of nationalism.

But none of these three factors seems to be particularly power-ful. First, in many countries, the mass of the people had no identification with history until nationalism gave it to them. To the extent that Prussians and Bavarians or Bretons and Bur-gundians considered that they shared a history with anyone it was with Prussians, Bavarians, Bretons, and Burgundians, not with fellow Germans and fellow Frenchmen. Boyd C. Shafer

[8] *The Idea of Nationalism,* p. 14.

contends that for most contemporary European peoples a common group history is almost wholly fictional if it is pressed back much beyond the nineteenth century. "The belief is real," he writes, "the actuality never existed."[9]

Second, as we have seen, a proportion of the shared history as a nationality is manufactured, a myth created by nationalism consciously or unconsciously, precisely to further nationalism. An even more dramatic example than those given before is Turkey. Kemal Ataturk offered a theory that the Turks were a white, Aryan people, originating in Central Asia, and that they migrated to various parts of Asia carrying civilization with them. "Chinese, Indian, and Middle Eastern civilization had been founded in this way, the pioneers in the last named being the Sumerians and Hittites, who were both Turkic peoples. Anatolia had thus been a Turkish land since antiquity. This mixture of truth, half-truth, and error was proclaimed as official doctrine, and teams of researchers set to work to 'prove' its various propositions."[10] Ataturk also solved the dilemma posed by the need to adopt foreign words so that Turkish would have the necessary technical vocabulary and the countervailing need to extol all things Turkish. His method was to advance the theory that Turkish was in fact the mother of all languages, so any foreign term, properly "re-Turkified," was merely returning to its own.[11]

Territory and Statehood

"The nation is not only a community of brethren imbued with a sense of common destiny," writes Rupert Emerson, "it is also a community which, in contrast to others such as a family, caste, or religious body, is characteristically associated with a particular territory to which it lays claim as the traditional homeland."[12] The Jewish people before the establishment of the state of Israel is often cited as an example of a nation without a territory, but Emerson also attacks this as an example. "Whatever the propriety of regarding the Jews as a nation at all times in their history

[9] *Nationalism: Myth and Reality* (New York, 1955), p. 54.
[10] Bernard Lewis, *The Emergence of Modern Turkey* (London, 1961), p. 353.
[11] Emerson, op. cit., p. 138.
[12] Ibid., p. 105.

rather than as a religious community," he writes, "they stand out as a people for their devoted attachment to the land of their fathers. Throughout the centuries of the Diaspora the Jews through their religious ceremonies and by other means fervently maintained the symbolism of identification with the country from which they had been driven in the far-off past; and no other corner of the earth's surface could meet the need they, or at least many among them, felt to return to their own."[13]

It seems entirely natural that a human being would develop an affection for his immediate surroundings, the village and locality where he was born and grew up, whose people, hills, valleys, streams, fields, and woods he knows well. But even with modern methods of transportation, most citizens of a country will never get to know very much of the terrain of the whole country so intimately, much less the people. At the time that nationalism arose in Europe, the masses had little awareness of any ties with anyone beyond their immediate locality—whether of language, culture, or blood. Indeed, there were fewer similarities before nationalism than after, for nationalism was the most powerful force of all in blurring the differences in dialect and in spreading a single, national culture. Like all the other characteristics of nationalism, territory is both an element contributing to feelings of group identity and something which nationalists use in trying to promote those feelings.

Statehood is much the same. Some states, like Austria-Hungary, have succumbed to disparate nationalisms within them. But in others a major factor in developing nationalism seems to have been the fact of the state. In Latin America the independence movement occurred before the rise of nationalism. States were formed around the old colonial administrative units—presidencies, *audiencias*, and captaincies. Thus to the extent that nationalism has developed, it seems to be the fact of the state that has been most influential of all. Much the same can be said of the Arab states, whose boundaries, except in Palestine, generally follow the lines of the partition of the Ottoman Empire between 1830 and 1920.[14] To the extent that a Czechoslovak nationalism

13 Ibid., p. 106.
14 On this point, see Rustow, op. cit., p. 67.

as opposed to a Czech nationalism has developed or to the extent that a Yugoslav nationalism has developed as opposed to the five separate nationalisms of the constituent peoples of Yugoslavia, it is again the fact of the state that seems to have had the dominant influence.

To sum up, all these elements—language and literature; religion; shared history, culture, and traditions; and territory and statehood—all can and do contribute to feelings of nationalism and facilitate its growth. But nationalism can also grow in the absence of any one of them. We have said that fundamentally nationalism is the notion that there is such a thing as a group of people who are "one nation" and that such a "nation" has a natural right to be a state. "Nationality," says Kohn, "is therefore not only a group held together and animated by common consciousness; but it is also a group seeking to find its expression in what it regards as the highest form of organized activity, a sovereign state."[15] Self-determination, in which Woodrow Wilson at the Versailles Peace Conference put so much faith, is offered as the answer to the question, Who will be a state? "On the surface," Sir Ivor Jennings once remarked, "it seemed reasonable: let the people decide. It was in fact ridiculous because the people cannot decide until somebody decides who are the people."[16] The fact is that no one has come up with a definition of nationalism that will hold water except that it is a state of mind. Ernest Renan called it a "daily plebiscite."[17]

Prerequisites for Nationalism

Of course, the seeds of a national consciousness existed in Europe, notably in France and England, before 1789. In both countries, the monarchy, based on what Karl W. Deutsch calls "core areas," such as the Île de France, had broken the power of the feudal lords and created a larger political unit that could be the vehicle of nationalism.[18] Religion had, in Hans Kohn's

[15] Kohn, op. cit., p. 19.
[16] Jennings, *The Approach to Self-Government* (Cambridge, 1956), p. 56.
[17] Renan, *Qu'est-ce qu'une nation?* (Paris, 1882), trans. Ida Mae Snyder in Snyder, *The Dynamics of Nationalism,* op. cit.
[18] Deutsch, *Nationalism and Social Communication: An Inquiry into the Foundations of Nationality* (New York, 1953).

words, been "depolitized and deterritorialized" in the Reformation and the wars of religion. The printing press had a big role. Knowledge and learning were carried by the universalist language, Latin, known only to a tiny elite. But as more than one observer has remarked, when the printing press made it possible to reach the masses it was easier for the learned men to write in the vernacular than for the masses to learn Latin. This, and the translation of the Bible into the vernacular—done for purely religious reasons—tended to erase regional and local differences in language and to make everyone aware of a wider kinship than just their own village and locality. Finally, nationalism, as Hans Kohn observed, is inconceivable without the ideas of popular sovereignty preceding it. "The traditionalism of economic life had to be broken by the rise of the third estate, which was to turn attention away from the royal courts and their civilization to the life, language, and arts of the people. This new class found itself less bound by tradition than the nobility or clergy. . . . In its rise, it claimed to represent not only a new class and its interests, but the whole people. Where the third estate became powerful in the eighteenth century—as in Great Britain, in France, and in the United States—nationalism found its expression predominantly, but never exclusively, in political and economic changes. Where, on the other hand, the third estate was still weak and only in a budding stage at the beginning of the nineteenth century, as in Germany, Italy, and among the Slavonic peoples, nationalism found its expression predominantly in the cultural field. Among these peoples, at the beginning it was not so much the nation-state as the *Volksgeist* and its manifestations in literature and folklore, in the mother tongue, and in history, which became the center of the attention of nationalism."[19]

Nationalism's Links with Egalitarianism and Modernization

All the historians and other students of nationalism have remarked upon its links with both modernization and with egalitarianism. The term "modernization" describes a process in which men gain control over nature by co-operating with each other in

[19] Kohn, op. cit., pp. 3–4.

a division of labor, a process that also transforms society and the values of individual men and their attitudes, especially their attitudes toward nature, toward time, and toward each other. The beginnings of modernization came in the Renaissance, and nationalism only in the eighteenth century. But then they proceeded hand in hand. "Since then, in Latin America, Asia, and Africa, nationhood and modernity have appeared as two facets of a single transformation—a dual revolution loudly proclaimed and often ardently desired but never accomplished quickly or with ease."[20]

Egalitarianism also had earlier beginnings—and these, too, were linked with modernization. As implied in the quotation from Hans Kohn above, the traditionalism of economic life had to be broken, and to do so—to pave the way for an economic division of labor—the feudal notions of inequality also had to be broken. Nationalism implied equality; membership in the nation was the important thing, not one's class or position. Thus nationalism served the purposes of modernization, and modernization served the purposes of nationalism.

It was the French revolution that launched the modern idea of nationalism. Even though it is linked to modernization and egalitarianism, nationalism is fundamentally the idea that there is such a thing as a group of people who are "one nation" and that such a "nation" should by natural right be a state—that it is the "nation," and only the "nation," indeed, that legitimizes the state.

"The French Revolution presented the challenge . . ." in Rupert Emerson's words, "of a state which was no longer the king but the people, and thrust across the face of Europe the power of a nation in arms."[21] Even when Napoleon became the sovereign, Emerson goes on to say, he headed not the France of Louis XIV, but the French nation.

Nationalsim did not sweep all before it following the French revolution, but grew only slowly against the active resistance of many of the aristocratic elites, who recognized its links with egalitarianism and hence with democracy, which they feared.

[20] Rustow, op. cit., p. 2. See also Rustow on modernization, op. cit., p. 3.
[21] Emerson, op. cit., p. 190.

As late as 1862, Lord Acton could say, "A state may in course of time produce a nationality; but that a nationality should constitute a state is contrary to the nature of modern civilization."[22] But nevertheless the notion spread and grew stronger, unifying Germany and Italy in 1871 and achieving full recognition in the rest of Europe at the end of World War I in the Treaty of Versailles.

In Asia, Japan saw the beginnings of nationalism in the Meiji restoration in 1868, which was motivated in part as a deliberate defense against the encroachment of the West. In China, its beginnings were in Sun Yat-sen's revolution of 1911. Everywhere else in Asia, nationalism found its beginnings in the anticolonial movements starting mainly in the 1920s and 1930s and achieving independence in the wake of World War II, even though nationalism had not yet fully developed in some Asian countries and has not yet done so. And in Africa, as mentioned earlier, even the beginnings did not come until a decade after the war had ended.

Karl W. Deutsch and the Theory of Nationalism as Social Communication

The nature of nationalism is obviously a puzzle. But much of the confusion—and mystery—surrounding nationalism has been cleared up by the work of Karl W. Deutsch, who studied the rise of nationalism as a communications process, and, later, with several colleagues, the amalgamation and breakup of various states in the North Atlantic area.[23] Deutsch starts with the premise that nationalism is a process of social learning and habit forming, resulting from a marked increase in social communication. Typically, the increase came from changes in the pattern of life associated with the beginnings of modernization. In Europe, the process began around a "core area"—the Île de France, Prussia, Prague, or Piedmont. The core area developed both needs and capabilities, economic and administrative, that were of benefit

[22] "Nationality," *The History of Freedom and Other Essays* (London, 1909), p. 292.
[23] Deutsch, *Nationalism and Social Communication*, op. cit., and Deutsch et al., *Political Community and the North Atlantic Area: International Organization in the Light of Historical Experience* (Princeton, 1957).

to the hinterlands. Communication developed along natural lines —valleys, rivers, and in the case of Switzerland, around the passes.[24]

Language developed and culture and common customs spread along with increased social communication. Consider the development of the Czech language and Czech nationalism in Bohemia, which Deutsch used as one of his case studies. Deutsch speaks of the proportion of a population that is at any given time *mobilized* for increased communication by economic, social, and technological changes, which can be identified by various yardsticks—engaged in occupations other than agriculture and forestry, living in towns, literacy rates, and so on. At the beginning of the nineteenth century, somewhat less than a third of the population of Bohemia was "mobilized" for intense communication, and of these, half spoke German—the language of the rulers—including not only ethnic Germans but ethnic Czechs. Of the underlying population, which took no significant part in intensive communication, considerably more than two thirds were Czech. In the following century, industrialization and social mobilization were extensive. By 1900, the proportion of Czech speakers among the mobilized population was proportional to the number of ethnic Czechs in the whole population. National conflict was intense. Some Germans, principally those living in the Sudetenland, were never assimilated and after World War II were expelled. But a considerable proportion of Germans were assimilated and became Czech, including not only city dwellers but many who were originally in the underlying population living in wholly German villages.

"In the political and social struggles of the modern age," Deutsch writes, "*nationality*, then, means an alignment of large numbers of individuals from the middle and lower classes linked to regional centers and leading social groups by channels of social communication and economic intercourse, both indirectly

---

24 "The rise of Switzerland from the thirteenth century on," Deutsch writes, "was related to the changes in the technology of transport and bridge building which made the St. Gotthard Pass crucial in world trade and furnished the economic basis for an independent 'pass state' in that region." *Nationalism and Social Communication*, p. 16.

from link to link and directly with the center."[25] As Deutsch points out, when the phenomenon of nationalism is approached in this way it becomes clear "why all the usual descriptions of a people in terms of a community of languages, or character, or memories, or past history, are open to exception. For what counts is not the presence or absence of any single factor, but merely the presence of sufficient communication facilities with enough complementarity to produce the overall result."[26] Although the Swiss speak four different languages, they are still one nation, Deutsch argues, because "each of them has enough learned habits, preferences, symbols, memories, patterns of land-holding and social stratification, events in history, and personal associations, all of which together permit him to communicate more effectively with other Swiss than with the speakers of his own language who belong to other peoples." To illustrate the point, Deutsch quotes the editor of a prominent German-Swiss newspaper. "I found that my German was more closely akin to the French of my [French-Swiss] friend than to the likewise German (Ebenfallsdeutsch) of the foreigner. The French-Swiss and I were using different words for the same concepts, but we understood each other. The man from Vienna and I were using the same words for different concepts, and thus we did not understand each other in the least."[27]

The link between nationalism on the one hand and language and literature; religion; shared history, culture, and traditions; and territory, and statehood on the other is simply that they facilitate increased social communication and thus the process of social learning and habit forming. Nationalism in turn blurred the differences among dialects of language, or elbowed out competing languages, gave a sense of identity with events in the past, spread culture, and thrust toward statehood. The link between nationalism and modernization was similarly reciprocal: The modernization increased social communication. Increased social technological and social changes that marked the beginnings of communication led to nationalism, which permitted still greater social communication. The link between egalitarianism and na-

[25] *Nationalism and Social Communication*, p. 75.
[26] Ibid., p. 71.
[27] Ibid.

tionalism was also reciprocal. The middle and lower classes—the masses—derived the greatest benefits from modernization and were in the forefront in spreading the idea of nationalism. Nationalism implies that all the members of the nation are equal, and the carriers of the idea of nationalism were those who benefited most from egalitarianism.

All these were the functions that nationalism performed in bringing about the nation-state. Once established, the nation-state takes over still other functions, especially in the modern, social-service state. Deutsch and his associates found "that the increase in the responsibilities of national government for such matters as social welfare and the regulation of economic life has greatly increased the importance of the nation in the lives of its members."[28] Thus nationalism has become both more popular than ever before and more intractable.

Nationalism and Personality Integration

One further aspect of nationalism remains to be explained. "The nation is today," writes Rupert Emerson, "the largest community which, when the chips are down, effectively commands men's loyalties, overriding the claims both of the lesser communities within it and those which cut across it or potentially enfold it within a still greater society, reaching ultimately to mankind as a whole. In this sense the nation can be called a 'terminal community' with the implication that it is for present purposes the end point of working solidarity between men."[29] All those who write on the subject of nationalism speak in much the same way, of the emotion that nationalism evokes, of the passion, of the command that nationalism has over men's loyalties, of the fact that men die in the name of nationalism and that they seem to do so in modern times more willingly than for Church, ideology, class, or any other claimant to their loyalty. What remains to be explained, then, is the emotion.

In exploring possible tests for nationalism, Deutsch speaks of a nationality as a community of people in which there is *pre-*

---

[28] Deutsch et al., *Political Community and the North Atlantic Area*, p. 23.
[29] Emerson, op. cit., p. 96.

dictability from introspection. "We try to predict other people's behavior by 'putting ourselves into their place,' by comparing it with the results of our own introspection. We try to predict their overall performance by comparing it with our own. To the extent that we succeed, we say we understand them. Here is one of the most important bases for the notion of a people, for that 'consciousness of kind,' of familiarity and trust, which we have for people whom we understand. . . ."[30] Such prediction from introspection, Deutsch warns, should not be confused with *prediction from familiarity.* "Prediction from introspection is based on analogy of structured habits, prediction from familiarity on remembered outside observations from the past. A white Southerner may think that he can predict what another white Southerner will probably think or do in a certain situation, because he is a man of 'his own kind.' The same white Southerner may also believe that he can predict what a Negro will think or do in a certain situation, because, he thinks, he 'knows Negroes.' Both types of prediction are very much subject to error, but the second type is merely based on outside familiarity with overt behavior, usually only in a very limited range of situations, even if these limited situations, perhaps such as those between master and servant, may have occurred for many years."[31]

Deutsch points out that the experience of "foreignness" as being unpredictability is related to the feeling of strangeness so often described by the historians of nationalism, and suggests that both are related to the psychological process of identification and to the concept of "basic personality structure." Put another way, it could be argued that the emotional content of nationalism is related to the source of the referents around which personality is integrated. The integration of personality—the development of "identity"—is a complex process of interaction among the individual, his parents, family, peer group, school, and community. Many of the referents—the values, attitudes, ways of looking at things—come from a very broad culture. Some of the values and attitudes around which both the Frenchman's and the American's personality is integrated, for example, may be

[30] Deutsch, *Nationalism and Social Communication*, p. 85.
[31] Ibid., p. 86.

the same, deriving from Western culture broadly conceived. But beginning with the latter part of the eighteenth century, the principal value and attitudinal framework for personality integration has been increasingly supplied by nationalism. Hence the emotion. Nationality becomes part of the self, part of the individual identity. It is the larger identity that permits him to relate to other human beings effectively. A Welsh nationalist —it is typical that he was a secondary school teacher of his nation's literature—commenting on the steady submersion of things Welsh into the larger British culture and nation, put it most poignantly of all. "Soon," he said, "there will be no fellow human left who loves the things I love, or even hears sounds the way I hear them or sees the earth and sky the way I see them. As a Welshman, death will be more final for me."

CHAPTER 9

A Supranational State?

AGAINST THIS background, what can be said of the future of nationalism in the developed world and of the possibility of organizing the world by means of some entity larger than the nation-state? Obviously, the first place to look for signs of some new kind of "future crouching in the present" is Europe. Even if the prospects for the emergence of a superstate in North America were better than they appear, it would, given the overwhelming size of the United States, look like the result of an annexation rather than a merger. Elsewhere, only Japan, and, perhaps, Australia would qualify as highly developed, and the possibility of a merger between these two seems even more unlikely.

In Europe, nationalism is no longer a force for changing the status quo; it *is* the status quo. Deutsch argues that a more or less scientific test for nationalism is feasible and can be developed if enough time and effort are put into the task—too much time and effort to be justified for the limited purposes we have

in mind here. On the other hand, almost all observers agree
that since nationalsim is a matter of degree, as a practical matter
it is not difficult for people using their own rules of thumb to
reach substantial agreement that one particular state is a nation
and another is not. In making this same point, Dankwart A.
Rustow says, for example, that "it is fairly easy to agree, by a
series of intuitive judgments, that Malaysia today is less of a
nation-state than Algeria, Algeria less than Turkey, Turkey less
than Belgium, Belgium less than Sweden. . . ."[1] In Western
Europe, there is no question about Norway, Sweden, Finland,
Denmark, the Netherlands, France, Spain, Portugal, Italy, Austria,
Greece, Iceland, and Ireland. All are nation-states. So are Great
Britain and Switzerland. Northern Ireland presents a problem,
due more to Irish irredentism than to Northern Irish nationalism,
but as mentioned earlier, the Welsh, the Scottish, and the English
have long since melded into a single nationalism. So have the
cantons of Switzerland. Belgium, too, as we have seen, is a single
nation, although the tensions between the Flemings and the Walloons might make Belgium as a whole more receptive to, say, a
United States of Europe than others among the European peoples. There remains in Western Europe only Germany—which is
a special case, a nation divided by the accidents of history and
the Cold War into two states.

Nation-States in Eastern Europe

In Eastern Europe, Poland, Hungary, Romania, Bulgaria, and
Albania all have established nationalisms. All are nation-states.
Czechoslovakia, Yugoslavia, and the Soviet Union require more
difficult judgments. Czech nationalism developed in the context
of the pan-Slav movement, but came to be distinct. But attempts
in the nineteenth century to create a national consciousness
among Hungarian Slovaks separate from Austrian Czechs did not
entirely succeed, principally because too many Protestant Slovaks
felt the affinity with the Czechs too deeply.[2] Thus in spite of the

[1] *A World of Nations: Problems of Political Modernization* (Washington, D.C.,
1967), p. 25.
[2] Hans Kohn, *The Idea of Nationalism: A Study of Its Origins and Background*
(New York, 1948), p. 721.

fact that Czechoslovakia is 65 per cent Czech and 30 per cent Slovak, it seems more nearly correct to call it a nation-state than a multinational state.

In Yugoslavia, the population includes five national groups: Serbs, 42 per cent; Croats, 23 per cent; Slovenes, 9 per cent; Macedonians, 5 per cent; and Montenegrins, 3 per cent. All but the Macedonians are closely related in linguistic and ethnic terms and developed in the context of the Pan-Slav movement. But the situation is different from that in Czechoslovakia. Czechoslovakia is composed, as we said, of one group that developed a distinct nationalism and another that retained much of the Pan-Slav orientation—some Czech nationalists, for example, were Slovaks. But of the groups in Yugoslavia, the Serbs and the Croats, at least, and perhaps the Slovenes as well, can be said to have developed distinct nationalisms. Because of this, the word "multinational" may seem more appropriate for Yugoslavia than "national." And this judgment is supported by the federal structure of the government, which recognizes six constituent republics —Serbia, Croatia, Slovenia, Bosnia-Herzegovena, Macedonia, and Montenegro—and permits them a substantial measure of self-government. On the other hand, interviews with members of the leadership strata of Yugoslavia indicate that the incentives for promoting nationalism are strong.[3] Since many of the factors facilitating nationalism are also present, the final judgment would have to be mixed. Yugoslavia is not a nation-state, and Croat nationalism, at least, does imply the threat of secession. Both the student riots in the early 1970s and Tito's troubles with the Croatian Communist party testify to that possibility. Yet the very smallness of the nation-states that might be formed out of the present state of Yugoslavia gives even the most ardent Croat nationalist pause. The cost of independence for such a tiny entity in terms of security and of economic viability would be high.

Nationalism in the Soviet Union

In the Soviet Union, Great Russians constitute 55 per cent of the population. The remaining 45 per cent is composed of

[3] Conducted by the author in 1966.

Ukrainians, 18 per cent; Byelorussians, 4 per cent; Uzbeks, 3 per cent; Armenians, 1.5 per cent; Georgians, 1.5 per cent; and over one hundred other nationalities, including Latvians, Estonians, and Lithuanians, of even smaller percentages. Some of these national groups, even though tiny, have a very distinct nationalism. Thus it might be argued that the Soviet Union could be called a "national empire"—a Russian nation-state ruling over subject peoples no different from any other imperialism. However, as one authority on nationalism in Russia points out, the peculiar history of nationalism in Russia and the way that it arose makes the term inappropriate.[4] The European imperialists carving out colonies in Africa or Asia or the Japanese imperialists carving out a colony in Korea had no doubt about their separate identity. In Russia, however, the Great Russians developed a national consciousness at the same time that they had to deal with national movements directed against themselves. The absence of sharp natural or long-established frontiers kept them from being "fully conscious of being strangers in their vast and amorphous land." Russian settlers moved "steadily outwards, engulfing or bypassing other ethnic groups, often without realizing that they were engaged in an imperial venture." Thus the Russians never developed either an imperial mentality or an imperial constitution. "They created and ruled an empire as if they were creating and ruling a national state."[5]

For some observers, the fact that 45 per cent of the population of the Soviet Union is not Russian casts doubt on the judgment that the Soviet Union can be thought of as a nation-state in the same way that Sweden can be. On the other hand, a number of other facts cast even greater doubt on the idea that nationalism will lead to the breakup of the Soviet Union or transform it into something very different from other large nation-states. One of these is the fact that only one nationality—the Ukrainian—of the well over one hundred non-Russian nationalities that make up the Soviet Union constitutes more than 4 per cent of the total population. Another is the fact that many of these nationalities

[4] Richard Pipes, " 'Solving' the Nationality Problem," *Problems of Communism* (September/October 1967). Special issue: *Nationalities and Nationalism in the USSR*, Vol. XVI, No. 5.
[5] Ibid., p. 126.

live in regions with a mixed population, including a high percentage of Great Russians. All this leads to the general conclusion that the Soviet Union is going to have problems with its constituent nationalities, but that none is likely to succeed in breaking off and establishing a separate nation-state, with one possible exception: the Ukraine.

Actually, one might expect assimilation to be easier in the case of the Ukrainians than other of the Soviet minorities. The Russian and Ukrainian languages are similar and so is much of the culture, including religious practices. Russia and the Ukraine shared much of the beginnings of their history, and for many centuries they were ruled by a common government. However, by World War II resentment of Stalin's policy of Russification and of the commune program, which hit the Ukraine particularly hard, had grown so rapidly that a substantial segment of the Ukrainian population actually welcomed the invading German troops. The situation was saved by the fact that the Nazis made little attempt to take advantage of this sentiment or to encourage it. They continued the commune system, which they regarded as an efficient way of extracting grain from the peasants, and they treated the Ukrainians as a subject people rather than an independent nation.

After Stalin's death, Khruschchev, who had been party boss in the Ukraine for many years, abandoned the Russification policy and adopted one of "partnership." This implied that the Ukrainians, being fellow Slavs and sharing so much of Russian history, were coleaders of the Soviet Union and different from other minority peoples. Such a policy, bringing with it a large role in Soviet affairs for Ukrainian leaders, goes far to quiet Ukrainian discontent.

Still another factor in muting Ukrainian nationalism is also at work, and in the long run it may prove to be even more important than conciliatory policies from Moscow. Ukrainian culture patterns are essentially rural; the Russian, urban. What happens to Ukrainians who move to the city is difficult to measure, but the evidence suggests that eventually they become Russian, through the same mechanisms by which the Slavic Wendish peoples of Germany became German, the Swedes living in Finland became Finns, and the German villagers living in Bohemia became Czechs. The census of 1926 showed that nearly a quarter of urban Ukrainians had come to regard Russian as their first language.[6] In the meantime, urbanization of the Ukraine has gone on at an increasingly rapid rate. In 1926, less than 20 per cent of the population was urban; by 1965, it was over half.

On balance, then, the earlier judgment stands. The Ukrainians, too, will give the central government trouble in the years ahead, but they are not likely to succeed in breaking off and establishing a separate state.

The argument so far, to sum up, is that in Europe, Eastern and Western, nationalism is no longer a force for changing the status quo, but that nationalism is the status quo. It can be said that in most of the countries of Europe, nationalism has virtually completed its functions of modernizing, equalizing, setting up and legitimizing states, and unifying the people within the resulting state, blurring regional and local differences. The modern, social welfare state is the decision channel for so much of life—economic activity, health, job and old-age security, the environment—that possible change in the nation-state implies a threat to almost every other aspect of life. But this is not really a function of nationalism. The one, true ongoing function of nationalism is providing an over-all frame of referents for personality integration. Thus change away from the nation-state can be a threat to psychological identification, as we have seen—a threat to the very self. For all these reasons, we can assume that any force that has the capacity for bringing about a fundamental change in the present system of nation-states in Europe—either to break them up or to combine them into larger entities—will have to be both pervasive and powerful. It may be a "future crouching in the present," but it should not be easy to overlook.

Forces Tending to Break Up Nation-States

When one looks for disintegrative forces, forces at work in Western Europe that might break up one or another of the exist-

---

[6] Robert S. Sullivant, "The Ukrainians," *Problems of Communism* (September/ October 1967), Special issue: *Nationalities and Nationalism in the USSR*, Vol. XVI, No. 5, pp. 46–54.

ing nation-states, evidence is very hard to find. No economic forces work in this direction. Religion, with only minor exceptions, has been depoliticized. The only possible candidate, again, is nationalism. Yugoslavia and the Soviet Union have already been discussed. It is possible that Yugoslavia could break up into its constituent nationalisms, but not probable. Of the many nationalisms in the U.S.S.R., only Ukrainian would have the potential of viability, but our judgment is that on balance, Ukrainian nationalism is waning rather than waxing. Irish nationalism—or, more properly, irredentism—may someday detach Northern Ireland from the United Kingdom. But the other minority nationalisms in Great Britain and in the rest of Europe seem to be working toward something more complicated than the breakup of existing nation-states, as we shall see below. Even in Belgium, where tensions between the Flemings and the Walloons is so high, the costs of a breakup are clearly too much for most Belgians to contemplate.

Forces Making for Even Larger Entities

When it comes to forces working *toward* integration or the amalgamation into larger entities, on the other hand, some evidence clearly *can* be found. Public-opinion polls, for example, were taken in France and West Germany over a period of years since 1945 on the question of joining a Western European federation in which final authority would lie with a central government rather than member governments. The responses show a high percentage consistently in favor. In 1964, in France, for example, 46 per cent of the total population was in favor and over 65 per cent of the higher-educated, professional and executive strata were. In West Germany in the same year the figures were 57 per cent of the total population and over 85 per cent of the higher-educated, professional, and executive strata.

Other evidence also exists. Using the communications-process approach and the allied concepts developed in his study of the origins and growth of nationalism, Karl W. Deutsch and a number of associates studied ten cases of both successful and unsuccessful "integration" of two or more states. To begin, Deutsch distinguishes two types of integration. One type is the amalgamation of two or more states into a single state, as the thirteen colonies became the United States. The second type is a much looser association—a "pluralistic security community," such as the relationship between the United States and Canada since the 1870s. In a "pluralistic security community," enough sense of community, similar institutions, and similar practices exists to ensure a dependable expectation that any change will be peaceful and that any problems that arise will be resolved without resort to war.[7] In other words, what Deutsch calls an "amalgamated security community" is a single new superstate made up of what were states in their own right. The example is the United States, a new superstate made up of the established colonies. What he calls a "pluralistic security community" is a relationship between two or more states involving numerous contacts of all kinds coupled with the expectation that war between members of the community is unthinkable—a "no-war community." The example is the relationship between the United States and Canada since the 1870s and among the United States, Canada, and Mexico since the 1930s.

Deutsch's findings, first of all, cast doubt on several widespread beliefs about political integration. "The first of these beliefs is that modern life, with rapid transportation, mass communications, and literacy, tends to be more international than life in past decades or centuries, and hence more conducive to the growth of international or supranational institutions."[8] The case studies cast doubt on this idea, and so does other evidence. Most countries, for example, devote a larger percentage of their resources to the domestic economy and less to foreign trade than they did fifty years ago. Peaceful and voluntary migration across national boundaries has largely come to an end. Even the flow of international mail, Deutsch contends, is down. There is no evidence, in sum, of any "automatic trend toward internationalism."

A second popular notion upset by Deutsch's findings is that the

[7] Deutsch et al., *Political Community and the North Atlantic Area: International Organization in the Light of Historical Experience* (Princeton, 1957), pp. 5–6.
[8] Ibid., p. 22.

growth of states resembles a snowballing process or has a band-wagon effect—that a successful growth in the past accelerates the rate of growth in the future. On the contrary, "our findings suggest that greater political capabilities, and in particular greater political responsiveness, cannot be expected to emerge as an automatic by-product of historical evolution, or of earlier stages of the amalgamative process. Rather, these may have to be striven for as distinct and specific political and administrative aims if political integration is to be attained."[9]

A final notion upset by the findings is that a motive for political integration was either fear of anarchy, on the one hand, or, on the other, fear of war among the integrating states, i.e., that war seemed both probable and unattractive. If fear of anarchy were a motive, one would expect newly formed states very quickly to establish strong laws, courts, and police forces. If fear of war among the integrating states were a motive, one would expect the new superstate quickly to build a strong army reporting directly to the central government and looking to it for pay and support. But the evidence is the other way. The United States Army, for example, remained at seven hundred men, fewer men than the militia of most of the states for many years, and the Navy was not established at all until 1798. Deutsch could also have added that a national police force was not established until after World War I.

In general, the Deutsch group found that both superstates and no-war communities of several states are practicable pathways toward political integration, but that the no-war community, not surprisingly, is easier to attain and maintain. They also found that integration was not an all-or-nothing process analogous to crossing a threshold. "Somewhat contrary to our expectations, however, some of our cases taught us that integration may involve a fairly broad zone of transition rather than a narrow threshold; that states might cross and recross this threshold or zone of transition several times in their relations with each other; and that they might spend decades or generations wavering uncertainly within it."[10]

[9] Ibid., p. 25.
[10] Ibid., p. 33.

Enough of a "sense of community, institutions, and practices" to assure a dependable expectation that change would be peaceful was part of the original hypothesis, but the group found that the sense of community was more complicated than verbal attachment to the same set of values, at least for the creation of a new superstate. "The kind of sense of community that is relevant for integration, and therefore for our study, turned out to be rather a matter of mutual sympathy and loyalties; of 'we-feeling,' trust, and mutual consideration; of partial identification in terms of self-images and interests; of mutually successful predictions of behavior, and of cooperative action in accordance with it—in short, a matter of perpetual dynamic process of mutual attention, communication, perception of needs, and responsiveness in the process of decision-making. 'Peaceful change' could not be assured without this kind of relationship."[11]

Again, as with the growth of nationalism, the role of "core areas"—their capabilities and responsiveness to the loads placed on them—was crucial. England was thus the core area for the amalgamation of England, Wales, Scotland, and Ireland. It had capabilities—power, economic strength, administrative efficiency —to meet needs in the peripheral areas. Its political decision-makers also had the ability "to redirect and control their own attention and behavior so as to enable rulers to receive communications from other political units which were to be their prospective partners" and to give them "adequate weight in the making of their own decisions, to perceive the needs of the populations and elites of these other units, and to respond to them quickly and adequately in terms of political or economic action."[12] The most notable failure in this was when the British Parliament failed to respond quickly and adequately to the Irish famine of 1846—a failure not caused by lack of resources but one of "attention, perception, and decision-making." And it was this failure, more than any other one thing, that caused the Irish to break away from the union.

For the development of a superstate some background conditions were helpful but not essential. Among these were previous

[11] Ibid., p. 36.
[12] Ibid., p. 40.

administrative and/or dynastic union, ethnic or linguistic assimilation, strong economic ties, and foreign military threats. In
cases of military threats, the effects were particularly transitory.

However, some nine background conditions were found to be
essential for the development of a superstate. Of these, the most
important was shared values. In all cases studied, there was a
"compatibility of the main values held by the politically relevant
strata of all participating units." Sometimes this was supplemented by a tacit agreement to "depoliticize" any incompatible
values—as the "depoliticization" of the difference between Catholic and Protestant religious values was an essential precondition
for the amalgamation of both Switzerland and Germany.

It was also essential that these values be incorporated into
political institutions and habits of political behavior that permitted the values to be acted upon and thus to strengthen
people's attachment to them. This interconnection the Deutsch
group called "way of life," and all cases of successful amalgamation were accompanied by such a distinctive way of life—"that
is, a set of socially accepted values and of institutional means
for their pursuit and attainment, and a set of established or
emerging habits of behavior corresponding to them."[13]

Other essential conditions were widespread expectations of
joint economic rewards for the participating units as a result of
amalgamation; a marked increase in political and administrative
capabilities and in economic growth in at least some of the
participating units; unbroken links of social communication both
between different territorial regions and between different social
strata; a broadening of the political elite; mobility of persons
among the politically relevant strata; and finally, a multiplicity
of ranges of communication and transaction.

All the above refers to the amalgamation of a number of different political units into one superstate. For no-war communities
such as the loose association between the United States and
Canada, all the conditions discussed above are helpful in bringing
about the community, but only two seemed to be essential. These
were the compatibility of major values relevant to political decision-making, and the "capacity of the participating political

[13] Ibid., p. 48.

units or governments to respond to each other's needs, messages, and actions quickly, adequately and without resort to violence."[14]

The outstanding issue leading to a no-war community was "the increasing unattractiveness and improbability of war among the political units concerned." In some cases, war became unattractive because it promised to be both devastating and indecisive. The example given is the United States and Canada. American land power could devastate Canada, while British sea power could devastate American seaports and shipping. But American land power could not destroy the sources of British sea power, nor could British sea power destroy the sources of American land power. In other cases, war became unattractive because of the danger of international complications. The example here is Sweden's decision not to fight to prevent Norway's secession because of fear that Germany, Russia, or Great Britain might then intervene. In still other cases, it was the domestic unpopularity of the particular war. The example here is the unpopularity of a war with Mexico among the American public in the 1920s and 1930s in spite of the dispute over American oil properties.

One final point is that once a no-war community is established, it is remarkably stable and long-lasting. The Deutsch group identified and studied some thirteen no-war communities, and only one deteriorated to a point where war between the participating countries seemed a serious possibility. This was Austria-Germany in 1933—brought about by the threat of forcible amalgamation of Austria into Nazi Germany, which was accomplished in 1938.

Deutsch and his group applied their tests to the North Atlantic area, including the United States and Canada, rather than to either Western Europe or to Europe as a whole. Of the fourteen conditions they considered either essential or merely helpful, they found that eight were high. Of the six conditions that were low, one—responsiveness—they felt to be essential for establishing either a no-war community or a superstate. Their conclusion was therefore that not even a no-war community existed in the North Atlantic area at present.

[14] Ibid., p. 66.

What would be the conclusion if the tests developed by the Deutsch group were applied to the most likely candidate of all, not Europe as a whole, but the nations that are members of the European Economic Community—France, West Germany, Italy, Belgium, the Netherlands, Denmark, Ireland, Norway, Luxembourg, and, more recently, Great Britain?

Values

If democracy, including constitutionalism or the rule of law, and non-Communist economics, which the Deutsch group concluded were the "main" values for the North Atlantic community, are indeed central, then it can surely be said that compatibility is high.

Mutual Responsiveness

Certainly the formation of the European Economic Community, Euratom, and other regional institutions are evidence of responsiveness in the economic area, although a fuller test would come with a major recession or some other economic crisis. At the same time, a large number of political issues have divided the members of the EEC, and there seems to be no reason to believe that this will not continue to be the case. The rating would have to be neither high nor low, but intermediate.

Distinctive Way of Life

In 1957, the Deutsch group, looking at attitudes toward war, national income, and other such factors, concluded that the nations of the North Atlantic area did share a distinctive way of life, with the exception of Spain and Portugal, with Italy in a somewhat doubtful position. A decade and a half later, it seems clear that Italy is no longer doubtful. What is more, the whole of Western Europe is moving steadily toward a superindustrial society, and as we have seen, this will accentuate the trend toward a way of life that is, indeed, distinctive when compared with industrial and preindustrial times.

Core Area, Superior Economic Growth, Expectation of Joint Economic Reward, Wide Range of Mutual Transactions, Mobility of Persons

All these conditions are high. France and Germany fulfill the function of core area alone, and the addition of Great Britain to the EEC will enhance the capability. There has been superior economic growth. Expectations of gain accompanied the formation of the EEC, and these are substantially being fulfilled. The formation of the EEC itself brought about an increase from 2 in 1946 to 230 in 1965 of regional nongovernmental organizations—interest groups and others formed to express regionwide interests and to influence the decisions of such intergovernmental agencies as the EEC itself, Euratom, and so on. Mobility of persons is also high, as indicated by the movement of labor from Italy, where there has been a surplus, to France and Germany. Tourism is another indication. The time is not far distant when many people will as a matter of course spend their working lives in the core industrial areas of Germany, France, or Britain, and their vacations along the Mediterranean, to which they will eventually also retire.

Broadening of Elites and Links of Social Communication

At the time that Deutsch was working on his study of the North Atlantic community—1955–56—he felt that information was most scarce on these two conditions—the broadening of elites and links of social communication. In the meantime, however, considerable change has taken place, and much additional research has been done.[15] One of the men doing this research,

[15] See the following: U. W. Kitzinger, *The Politics and Economics of European Integration* (New York, 1963); Ernest B. Haas, *The Uniting of Europe* (Stanford, California: Stanford University Press, 1958); Amatai Etzioni, *Political Unification* (New York, 1965); Leon N. Lindberg, *The Political Dynamics of European Economic Integration* (Stanford, California: Stanford University Press, 1963); Bruce M. Basset, *Trends in World Politics* (New York, 1965); Leon N. Lindberg and Stuart A. Scheingold, *Europe's Would-be Polity: Patterns of Chance in the European Community* (Englewood Cliffs, New Jersey: Prentice Hall, 1970); Donald J. Puchala, "The Pattern of Contemporary Regional Integration," *International Studies Quarterly*, Vol. XII, No. 1 (March 1968) and "Western European Integration: Progress and Prospects," Ph.D. dissertation, Yale University (1966), in addi-

Donald J. Puchala, points to the large number of interest and lobbying groups that arose when supranational institutions were given regulatory powers.[16] Their purpose was to exert influence on the men making decisions affecting the entire region. This in turn stimulated the growth of a "transnational polity" in Western Europe. Within this polity, finally, "messages" about European unity, supranationality, the Common Market, and federation began to reach an ever-increasing number of people through their contacts with the transnational organizations. The result was more support for the notion of European unity and political federation. Puchala's findings, he writes, "strongly suggest that a transnational elite did emerge in Western Europe during the 1950's."[17]

Judged by the Deutsch tests, then, Western Europe of the EEC by 1970 had become a no-war community, and the question becomes whether it will proceed in the future to become a superstate—a United States of Europe.

Most of those who have worked more recently on the question of European integration would agree that the EEC community is, indeed, a no-war community. Even more dramatic than the establishment of the Common Market and the other regional agencies is the fact that for the first time in history not one of these nations is making any preparations for war with any of the others. There are no Maginot lines under construction, much less any Schlieffen plans being concocted. War among any of them is now unthinkable.[18]

---

tion to his two works cited below; and the various publications of the Program on International Integration, University of California, Berkeley, and especially Ernst B. Haas, "The Study of Regional Integration: Reflections on the Joy and Anguish of Pretheorizing," *International Organization*, University of Wisconsin, Vol. 24, No. 4, 1970.

[16] "Patterns in West European Integration," paper presented at the 1970 annual meeting of the American Political Science Association, Los Angeles, California.

[17] "National Distinctiveness and Transnationality in West European Public Opinion, 1954–1962," a paper presented at the Eighth Congress of the International Political Science Association, Munich, August 31–September 5, 1970.

[18] The conclusion that the whole set of attitudes now held by the European elite rejects war and accepts further steps toward European integration is supported by 147 interviews of elite members in France and 173 interviews in West Germany conducted in 1964. See Karl W. Deutsch, Lewis J. Edinger, Roy C. Macridis, and Richard L. Merritt, *France, Germany, and the Western Alliance: A Study of Elite Attitudes on European Integration and World Politics* (New York, 1967). My own interviews conducted in 1966–67 are overwhelming on this point.

But in the process of research on the integration of Western Europe some rather curious things have turned up. Perhaps the most curious of all is that as all forms of regionalism have grown in Western Europe and integration dramatically increased, nationalism appears *not* to have weakened and may have grown stronger. Integration has proceeded in Western Europe. It has had very specific and palpable consequences for the lives of people in economic terms, in institutional terms, and in terms of the patterns of individual lives. But it has not meant the submergence of nationality in some transnational identity.[19]

International Integration and Nationalism

The significance of this may be very great; it may be that international integration can take place side by side with nationalism without either affecting nationalism or being affected by it. In Donald Puchala's words: "European integration has included the international merger of governing institutions and policy-making processes. It has involved a good deal of transnational cooperation among governmental and non-governmental leaders, agencies, organizations, and interest groups. It has produced regional economic policies, externally directed commercial policies and even some coordination of foreign policies. But . . . Western European integration has meant neither the disappearance nor the dilution of nationality as the important determinant of political opinion in the different countries. As far as the distribution of political attitude was concerned, the Western European population was not a transnational society before institutional steps toward regional integration were taken. Nor is there evidence to show that this regional population was becoming a transnational society after, or as a result of, institutional merger."[20]

The possibility exists, then, that when nationalism has accomplished the functions of achieving and legitimizing statehood, and when it has substantially accomplished the function of modernization, it may under certain conditions not impede

[19] Puchala, "National Distinctiveness and Transnationality in West European Public Opinion, 1954–1962," p. 23.
[20] Ibid.

certain kinds of international integration. What we might end up with, in other words, is neither a superstate nor a no-war community. What we might end up with is a combination of both—a pluralistic, no-war community in which the nation-states continue as individual entities for certain purposes, especially those related to culture and personality integration, but transfer decision-making in a wide number of specified fields to international regional agencies.

Conclusions

Is this "curious creature" a part of the future? Deutsch and the others have given us a list of the conditions essential to integration in the past, and we can expect these same conditions generally to continue to be essential in the future. But beyond this, about the only guide to the future is to ask what *functions* would be served by this kind of integration, what functions would be performed by the "curious creature" we have postulated. If the functions performed seemed necessary, beneficial, and unlikely to be well served by any alternative, then the incentives to form and maintain the "curious creature" would be strong and we could safely assume that it will indeed arise.

The answer seems to be a definite yes—that our "curious creature" combining formal regional organization and the nation-state can serve essential functions that cannot be effectively served in any easier way. In the economic sphere, the case is overwhelming. A common market gives all the economies of scale. Large markets permit mass production, more and better goods, and better wages. There is a larger capital market. Labor is more mobile. Better transportation is possible. The opportunities for a wider, richer life are enhanced. Integration would not have served these functions in a preindustrial society. Even in an industrial age, it is only at the more advanced stages that a larger-size economy becomes so crucial. But then it *is* crucial, and it is obviously even more crucial as these societies move toward a superindustrial stage. Advanced technologies and the advanced and continuous research they require cannot be sustained without large-scale enterprises. Even some individual satisfactions may depend on the existence of such large-scale enterprises. The so-called brain drain from Europe to the United States, for example, resulted more from the opportunity to work on interesting problems in these large-scale research efforts than from differences in salary levels.

Our "curious creature" also serves other functions. It *could* serve a defense function against outside threat. But in the case of the European Economic Community, integration has taken place, first, under a wider umbrella provided by NATO and the alliance with the United States, and, second, at a time when the sense of being threatened from the outside, notably from the Soviet Union, was diminishing. On the other hand, the maintenance of a no-war community among the members themselves is itself an important function.

In certain circumstances the pooling of power made possible by such a community may also be significant. Although not exactly pertinent to today's circumstances, if the world were sharply bipolar, the promise of obtaining a greater voice in world affairs by integrating might well be an important incentive.

The interlocking of the economy, greater mobility of persons, and increased communications would also tend to serve a political function of putting pressure on the individual governments to even out social and welfare legislation. Conceivably this might prove to be an incentive to segments of particular populations. On the other hand, it does not seem likely that this will be so highly visible and prized a function that the possibility of achieving it would mobilize any significant support for the establishment of our "curious creature."

Still other functions that could be served by this "curious creature" combining regional authority with the nation-state are also possible. Increasingly, as any newspaper reader has seen, advanced technologies are bringing ecological and environmental problems. In meeting these problems, regions, such as Europe, will have to be treated as entities—in fact, for some ecological and environmental problems the entity will have to be the entire globe. Increasingly, too, the measures to meet ecological problems will require uneven sacrifices, and hence increasingly they will become the subject of political struggle. If so, regional policy and decision-making agencies will come to be indispensable.

One other function may also be served by this "curious creature." As we have seen, values and fundamental attitudes toward life are undergoing rapid change, and the likelihood is for even more rapid change in the future. A part of this is a feeling of helplessness, of impotency, a feeling of being a nonentity, nothing more than a number on an IBM card, of being pushed and pulled about by the impersonal machine of big government. In reaction to this, there seems to be a need for ways of organizing government and its programs that would permit fuller participation by those affected by policies and decisions. The failure of the Washington-run poverty program, for example, seems to lie here. This same frustrated feeling of having no control over government policies and programs that affect their lives seems to lie at the heart of many other controversies all over the United States and even the world—from the Ocean Hill-Brownsville school controversy in New York City to New Delhi's troubles with Kerala. The point is that at least a need is felt and is likely to be increasingly felt for some sort of synthesis that will permit the benefits of bigness without sacrificing either a sense of participation or a sense of uniqueness on the part of members of smaller communities.

All these functions we have so far discussed are ones that could be effectively served by the larger entity, by the device of transferring decision-making power to regional, international authority. If the nation is also retained, as it would be in our "curious creature," the functions it would perform are less tangible, but probably no less important. One is another facet of the decentralization we have just discussed. Nothing would do more to preserve a sense of uniqueness on the part of members of the smaller communities in a larger whole than preserving the nationality of those communities. Preserving the nation in a larger combination of regional authority would mean that the nation would serve cultural functions, and, most particularly, the functions of providing the fundamental referents for the integration of personality.

The evidence, then, is that the members of the European Economic Community are proceeding at a fairly steady pace toward a form of political organization that is new in the world —a "curious creature" that combines international organization and authority with the nation-state. Will something like this also be the future of Eastern Europe? As yet, of course, nothing similar to the EEC has been set up in Eastern Europe. The Comecon—the Communist economic community organization— is dominated by the Soviet Union, and this alone seems to preclude its development along lines similar to the EEC. The fact of the matter is that Western Europe exerts a strong pull— culturally and economically, at least—on a number of the Eastern European states. As mentioned before, there are ancient cultural ties, and the East Europeans also feel they need technological help and trade that the U.S.S.R. cannot supply by itself. It may well be that as the tensions of the Cold War lessen and disappear, some of the Eastern European states will be drawn closer and closer to the European Economic Community, and some may even eventually become full members. Others of the Eastern European countries may find themselves drawn into a much closer association with the Soviet Union.

The question of whether this "curious creature" has a future in the underdeveloped countries of Asia, Africa, and Latin America must wait for our more detailed scrutiny in later chapters. But our "curious creature" may also have a bigger future among the developed countries of the world than just the EEC. We have suggested that many of the internal troubles of the developed countries stem from a frustrated feeling of impotence in the face of big government and that the need in the future may be for a synthesis, permitting both bigness and individuality. We saw that the possibility of nationalism breaking up established states in Europe seemed to be slim, even in the case of multinational states like Yugoslavia. Yet, paradoxically, nationalism has not weakened, but may actually be growing stronger.

Consider one example—nationalism in Wales—and how it may be working for something quite different than the older goal of establishing a separate and independent nation-state. Plaid Cymru, the Welsh nationalist party, was founded in 1925. It fought its first election in 1929 in one district and received only 1.6 per cent of the vote. In 1966, however, it won a seat in Parliament, although later it lost it again. In 1970, Plaid Cymru contested all thirty-six Welsh seats for the first time, and took 11.5 per cent of the total vote. In the nineteen districts that it had also fought in 1964 and 1966, its average was 16 per cent of the total, nearly double the best it had ever done before. Plaid Cymru is clearly making headway, but what is most significant for our purposes is the program on which this nationalist appeal is based. The slogan is "freedom but not independence." The party rejects home rule, as in Northern Ireland, and it also rejects a federal system. What it wants is self-government within a true British commonwealth or common market, in which the different states are co-equal and there is no central government—a model very much like our "curious creature" with regional agencies making decisions and policies on many matters but nation-states retaining their identity and their authority over everything else.

Thus our "curious creature" may well have an important part of the future. This seems to be most likely in the case of existing nation-states grouping themselves together, as in the example of the European Economic Community. But it may also be true in the case of some of the existing larger states, although a judgment on this possibility will have to wait upon an analysis of a number of other questions. Not only may it turn out to be no exaggeration to say that there is a future for loose regional associations performing some of the functions of a superstate while the constituent nation-states continue to operate, but it may also be true that in this "curious creature" we have an example of the "future crouching in the present." It may turn out that organizational syntheses of this kind is a dynamic that is just making its appearance in the world but that has only just begun to work the transformation for which it is destined.

Part IV

THE UNDERDEVELOPED WORLD

CHAPTER 10

Nationalism, Industrialization, and Modernization

OF ALL THE forces shaping the future in the underdeveloped world of Asia, the Middle East, Africa, and Latin America, the most fateful are those contesting for and against industrialization, modernization, and nationalism. It is in the interaction of these forces that we are most likely to find the "future crouching in the present," the dynamic that has yet to run its course.

Nationalism does not spring forth spontaneously. It is created —created because it serves practical social, political, and economic functions. Nationalism results from a process of communications in which political, economic, and social centers grow up that can serve various needs in the hinterlands, which can in turn benefit the centers. Both the leadership and the mass benefit; both share a stake in taking the process further.

In Europe in the nineteenth century, the leadership strata most central in fostering nationalism was the emerging middle class. The instruments for encouraging the spread of nationalism were varied: newspapers, literature, schools, commerce, transport, and to some extent legislation and government action. In more recent times, the leadership strata fostering nationalism is more likely to control the government. Increasingly, they also have not only stronger motives for fostering nationalism, but stronger and more effective means for doing so. Laws can be passed concerning language, for example. Schools can be established and rules laid down about what is taught in them—the language taught and the historical myths. Roads, transport, communications, the regulation of commerce—all can be manipulated to further the development of nationalism.

So long as the center effectively supplies the benefits and services desired, the local leadership in particular localities of the hinterlands and the masses they represent have an incentive to co-operate in the development of nationalism and the strengthening of unity—or at least they have an incentive to acquiesce in these. Whether or not their incentive is strong enough to overcome rival identifications of language, culture, and local traditions and institutions depends on many things—not only on language, culture, and local traditions but on how much power the center can exercise and its willingness to exercise it, on how sensitively the center perceives the needs and problems of outlying localities, and how effectively it deals with them. If the center fails, whether through lack of capability or through indifference, the process can be reversed. The localities may revolt and strive for their own, rival nationalism. We saw this take place in Ireland. In the early part of the nineteenth century the process of integrating Ireland into a wider British nationality was almost as well along as it was in Scotland and Wales, in spite of resentments engendered by anti-Catholic laws, absentee landlordism, and the rest. Then came the potato famine, and the failure, largely through indifference, of the central government in London to take effective measures to deal with it.[1] The Irish independence movement was given powerful impetus, and its leadership proceeded with deliberate measures, such as reviving the Irish language, to create an Irish nationalism.

[1] Cecil Woodham-Smith, *The Great Hunger: Ireland 1845–1849* (New York, 1962).

We have seen the modern counterpart of the potato famine in the great cyclone that struck East Pakistan in 1970 and killed perhaps as many as five hundred thousand people. The fact that the central government, dominated by West Pakistanis, failed to give adequate warning of the coming of the cyclone or to take effective measures to ease the hardships and famine that followed marked the beginning of a rapid end of the Pakistani union. After the disaster, Sheik Mujibur Rahman, the East Pakistan political leader, denounced the "bureaucrats, the capitalists, and the feudal interests" of West Pakistan and threatened secession if demands for elections leading to autonomy were not met. "If the elections are aborted," he warned, "the people will owe it to the million who have died in the cyclone to make the supreme sacrifice of another million lives, if need be, so that we can live as a free people."[2] The elections were held, and Sheik Mujibur won. But the central government refused autonomy, and sent troops instead. The troops were brutal in their repression. Thousands, perhaps hundreds of thousands were massacred. Some ten million fled to India. Out of all this—a sense of being neglected, of being exploited, and, finally, horror and hatred at being butchered—most East Pakistanis found their sense of being Bengali overwhelming any sense they still had of being Pakistani. Left to itself, this incipient nationalism would have had to overcome many obstacles before it could achieve the goal of statehood. But with the intervention of India, events were telescoped, and Bangladesh was established as a state in 1971–72.

Nationalism, Modernization, and Industrialization

It is here, in this process of reciprocal benefits and social communication, that the link is found between nationalism and the industrialization and modernization process. Historically, as we have seen, nationalism has gone hand in hand with the two. Its function has been to give precommercial, preindustrial, peasant peoples a larger identity and to mobilize them for the tasks of industrialization. An incentive toward nationalism will become

[2] New York *Times* (December 4, 1970).

an incentive toward industrialization and modernization. The egaltarianism implicit in nationalism will lead the nationalist to want to see the masses lifted from their poverty; the pride in the nation will lead him to want to see it strong and powerful. The nationalist will know—or he will soon learn—that only industrialization can both give the nation strength and lift the people from poverty. In similar ways, an incentive toward industrialization will transform itself into an incentive toward nationalism. The industrializer and modernizer will know—or soon learn—that nationalism is a powerful instrument for mobilizing the populace, and that neither industrialization nor modernization is possible unless the populace is mobilized. The industrializer is likely to become a nationalist, even if he is not one to begin with.

We have seen something of the incentives for industrialization and the development of nationalism at its start in Western Europe. Elsewhere, the incentives at the beginnings of nationalism and development were related. In Japan, the leadership decided on a course of industrialization, modernization, and fostering nationalism in 1868, as we mentioned before, at the time of the Meiji restoration. The decision was conscious and deliberate, and it came from one element of the leadership strata, from the samurai in the lower ranks of the old aristocracy. The incentive was fear of Western imperialism. The leadership strata that came into power with the Meiji restoration saw the spread of colonialism in Asia and quickly came to the conclusion that the only way to avoid a similar fate for Japan was to acquire the foreigner's weapons. They understood that acquiring such weapons would necessitate industrialization and the modernization of Japanese society, that the people would have to be mobilized, and that nationalism would be the most effective instrument both for mobilizing the people and for unifying them. In Rupert Emerson's words, "the Japanese people were deliberately aroused to a passionate devotion to their national heritage and to a sense of their all-embracing duty to the nation. . . . In the new Japan the nation, with the Emperor restored as its supreme symbol, was raised to exalted place, but the transformation was enforced from above and the management of national affairs was reserved to

274 The Underdeveloped World

the few at the top."[3] The results, of course, were remarkable, even though they were highly uneven, with some segments of Japanese society modernized and others relatively untouched until the period following World War II.

Elsewhere in Asia, and in the Middle East and Africa, the beginnings of industrialization and nationalism were also related to Western imperialism and colonialism, but in a different way. The humiliation of colonialism, its racism, its oppression —all these gave an incentive for unity that was unique and powerful. They gave a sense of identity even where none otherwise existed. The disguised colonialism of gunboat diplomacy, as in China and the Caribbean, had the same effect, even though it permitted nominal independence to continue. The shared resentment of a prenationalistic people or otherwise unrelated peoples subjected to colonialism gave them an incentive to unity and identity, and the long and sometimes bloody struggle to achieve independence created bonds that tended to continue after the colonial power was ousted.

Fear of "Neocolonialism"

Except for the blacks of South Africa and Rhodesia and a few islands and other bits and pieces, classic colonialism is dead. Even Angola and Mozambique are nearing independence. But the incentive that colonialism created for the leadership of developing nations to foster nationalism continues in the fear of what many of these leaders, especially among the radicals but not just among them, call "neocolonialism."[4] They suspect the

[3] From Empire to Nation: The Rise to Self-Assertion of Asian and African Peoples (Boston, 1960), p. 257. See also E. Herbert Norman, Japan's Emergence as a Modern State (New York, 1940); A. F. K. Organski, The Stages of Political Development (New York, 1965); and William Lockwood, The Economic Development of Japan (Princeton, 1954).
[4] What follows not only on attitudes among the leadership of developing states toward neocolonialism but also on their attitudes toward the other subjects discussed in these chapters on the developing world, is based on three sources. The first is secondary literature, as cited in the footnotes. The second is the result of a survey of speeches, parliamentary debates, newspaper editorials, and similar material. In general these will be cited only when actual quotes are used or when the finding is unexpected. The third source is from interviews conducted by the author in various countries in Asia, Africa, and the Middle East during 1966 and 1967.

old enslavement in a new guise. In the wake of World War II and through the 1960s, when so many African colonies became independent, the fear was that independence would be some kind of trick. Since the "imperialists'" goal is to continue the old order, the reasoning went, their intention is to give only nominal freedom—"the practice," as Kwame Nkrumah, then President of Ghana, said, "of granting a sort of independence by the metropolitan power with the concealed intention of making the liberated country a client-state and controlling it effectively by means other than political ones."

Some of the leaders who wave a bloody shirt of neocolonialism are more or less deliberately creating a myth precisely to foster nationalism, which they had decided to encourage on quite other grounds than fear of neocolonialism. Frequently the utility of struggle in achieving their aims is quite explicitly recognized. President Sukarno of Indonesia, for example—one of the most flamboyant of all the radical leaders—in his speeches endlessly repeated the theme of the necessity for struggle. "If, for example, at this moment," he said in a typical speech, "an angel were to descend from the heavens and say to me: . . . 'I shall grant you a miracle, to give the Indonesian people a just and prosperous society as a gift, as a present,' then I would reply: 'I don't want to be granted such a miracle, I want the just and prosperous society to be the result of the struggle of the Indonesian people.'" Ahmed Ben Bella, to give another example, is reported to have argued that Britain consciously and deliberately betrayed Nigeria by giving it independence on easy terms, knowing that this would preserve Nigeria's Englishness.[5]

But in part the fear of neocolonialism is completely genuine, even when it is less than completely rational—a fear that in some mysterious, convoluted, inscrutable *Western* way, Wall Street, the CIA, the Pentagon, or the "military-industrial complex" will succeed in replacing the direct controls of colonialism with indirect controls.

[5] Russell Warren Howe, "Would-Be Leader of the 'Third World,'" *The New Republic* (June 19, 1965).

Impact of the Developed Countries

But the developed countries impact on the underdeveloped ones no matter what. Oil and mining interests come on their search for raw materials, and if oil and minerals are found, they set about on arrangements to bring in machinery, technicians, and all the rest. Other companies are looking for tea, or copra, or rubber, or a host of other agricultural products, and the time comes when they want to introduce modern technology and farming techniques. Tourists come. Airports are needed and luxury hotels and local transportation. In a myriad of ways, the developed countries intrude on the undeveloped—usually by a search for raw materials, investment opportunities, trade, markets, and tourism, but sometimes by less commonplace needs, such as the need for a military base, a weather station, or a scientific expedition or observation post. These intrusions bring stimuli or require responses—by the government of the underdeveloped country and by individuals and groups of individuals among the people. Some governments have gone to extraordinary lengths to try to isolate their countries from the influences of the outside world, but their success has never been more than partial. Communist China tried it for a time, but abandoned the policy under pressure from what the leaders regarded as the imperatives in maintaining their security and their desire to play a role in the world appropriate to China's size and ancient civilization. Burma under Ne Win has been even more persistent in isolating itself from the outside world, but a certain seepage of outside influences is inevitable, and one wonders how long any country can maintain an effective isolation.

The "Demonstration Effect"

Perhaps the strongest incentive to industrialization and modernization is the most simple: people wanting to acquire the material benefits that others in the industrialized countries are seen to be enjoying. For the leadership strata the motive takes the form of wanting to relieve their people of the misery of poverty, of hunger, of disease, and of squalor. For the poor masses, it is the yearning of those who have nothing. There may have been a time when the masses of the undeveloped countries had no knowledge of the material products of industrialization and no hope of ever acquiring those they did know about; but this is changing so fast that the process has been dignified with its own piece of jargon: the "demonstration effect." Improved transportation systems are bringing more and more manufactured goods to more remote areas, and the movies, the transistor radio, and, increasingly, television, are opening visions of even more.

"Take a walk through any African city, visit its markets," reads the opening sentence in the report of a survey of Africa by correspondents of the New York *Times.* "In an hour you will learn more about why there is such a strong urge for development in Africa than from any long study of the latest five-year plans."[6] The focus of excited attention in the markets are the modern articles and gadgets—ball-point pens, watches, transistor radios, brassieres, shoes, "and almost anything that will fulfill African desires to move into the modern world." Throughout most of the African continent, the correspondents report, the ordinary African has been bitten by the "bug" of modernity. "The new fever started with the promises of a better life after independence, and it has grown with Africans' increased awareness of the outside world. It has not penetrated everywhere, but it is spreading."

Much the same attitude can be observed in Asia, the Middle East, and still in many places in Latin America. The mass desire is growing. It is bound to grow even more, and the political leadership will almost always respond with some sort of effort toward economic development. If it does not or is ineffective, a rival leadership is likely to come to the fore who make the promise of a thrust toward development the basis for their bid for power.

Nationalism as a Force for Mobilizing the Populace

Usually, the utility of nationalism as an instrument for mobilizing the populace in the thrust toward modernization is clearly understood. Even those individuals among the leadership strata who are not students of the history of nationalism understand the

[6] Brendan Jones, "Africa: Ferment for Better Life," "Survey of Africa's Economy," New York *Times* (January 29, 1971).

function instinctively—or come to learn it. Sukarno, for example, in his autobiography speaks of the task of the leaders of the independence movement as one of *creating* nationalism, and he brags of beating the drums of nationalism under the noses of the Japanese occupation in speeches delivered supposedly on behalf of collaborating with them. He says that he learned as a boy that his people had fought colonialism for generations, but had failed because they fought in isolated bands and were not united under a larger identity.[7] Sukarno came to understand that only nationalism could unite the people of Indonesia and give them that larger identity. Only nationalism could arouse them. It seems inevitable that when the task is no longer achieving independence, but an effort at economic development that requires the same unity and the same commitment, the utility of nationalism will become equally apparent.

Although it is more difficult to document, an incentive for nationalism also seems present in many of the underdeveloped countries quite independent of its functions as the handmaiden of industrialization and modernization. What I have in mind is a sort of emotional need for a larger identity. Many of these peoples have long had a sense of a larger identity, based on ethnic background, language, culture, shared history, and sometimes the existence of an established state. The Vietnamese are a particularly good example of a people in which the sense of identity was strong, since the bonds of common language, culture, religion, and an established state were reinforced by the sharp difference between the Vietnamese and neighboring people and by the memory of repulsing Chinese invasions. But even in Vietnam the sense of identity was different from nationalism. Familism and regionalism were overriding.[8] The sense of identity, in other words, was vague—stronger, certainly, than one feels today about being a European, an Asian, or an African, but not too much more than that. In Asia, the mass of the people were turned inward on themselves in a village culture. In Africa, it has been more tribal, and in Latin America the masses tended to be isolated in castes and semifeudal subcultures. In the few decades

[7] *Sukarno: An Autobiography, as Told to Cindy Adams* (New York, 1965), p. 41.
[8] David Joel Steinberg, ed., *In Search of Southeast Asia* (New York, 1971), pp. 68–72, 123–33.

since World War II, however, there seems to be a reaching out for a larger identity; a need, inflamed by contact with the developed world, to escape the localism of village and even tribe. And nationalism is there, readily at hand.

In addition to this emotional need for a larger identity, the leadership strata in an underdeveloped country have a very practical incentive toward nationalism. One of the fundamental problems for the leadership of an underdeveloped country is to overcome the localism, the isolation of the different regions and provinces, the inward focus of the villages, the differences among tribes and regions. The leadership is constantly confronted with the need to find ways of concentrating sufficient power at the center to permit them to make and carry out decisions applicable to the whole country.[9] Again, nationalism is there, readily at hand. It will do the job better than any visible alternative; there are practical and obvious ways that the leadership can contribute to its growth; and the fact that an emotional need for a larger identity is already present eases the process. Local leaders—like the East Pakistani leader mentioned above—sometimes have an incentive to encourage a sense of the differences between their people and others in the state, an incentive to encourage what is essentially a rival nationalism. But for those leaders who occupy the central seats of power, the incentive will be toward encouraging an over-all nationalism that will give everyone encompassed by the state a common identity and loyalty.

Nationalism as an Expression of Pride

The most powerful independent incentive for nationalism of all, however, especially for the leadership, but to some extent for the masses as well, is the combination of pride and resentment that has resulted from the confrontation of developed and underdeveloped societies, quite apart from colonialism. Many of the underdeveloped countries spring from ancient cultures, rich in literature, in religion, in philosophy, in art, and in the whole range of human accomplishment. Even those who do not think of

[9] On this point, see W. Howard Wriggins, "Political Development: Varieties of Political Change and U.S. Policy," *Foreign Policy in the Sixties*, eds. Roger Hilsman and Robert C. Good (Baltimore, 1965).

themselves as either ancient or rich in culture see their society as something unique and precious. There is pride here, pride that their people can accomplish as much as any other. Coupled with this is resentment, resentment of the arrogance of the developed nations, resentment of having been relegated to second-class status. Mao Tse-tung does not speak for Asians outside of China, but he once said something about his own country that the leaders of most Asian countries would like to say about their own. "China," he said, "has stood up." The image is of a downtrodden country, struggling to its feet to look other nations, the Soviet Union as well as the United States, level in the eye. It is a goal that most members of the leadership of an underdeveloped country will set whenever it has the potential. Through industrialization, they hope to see their people fed, clothed, decently housed, cured of disease, and freed of the indignities and misery of poverty. But they also want their countries to have the things that make a state strong—steel mills and transportation systems and jet aircraft and, often, modern weapons. It was hardly wise, but it is no accident that one of the first things Nkrumah did when Ghana got its independence was to search for the foreign aid to build a steel mill. It was hardly wise, but no accident that one of the first things Sukarno did was to ask the Soviets to give Indonesia a cruiser. The overarching goal of most of the leaders of most of the underdeveloped countries is for their country to stand tall in the world. These peoples are fiercely determined to be masters of their own fate, to make their own decisions about what happens to their own country. And they are equally determined to take their proper place at the decision-making councils in their own region and in the world. They want to make their own decisions about themselves in their own way, and they want a voice in the affairs of the world—a hand on the steering wheel of the planet.

In general, then, the incentives to move toward industrialization, modernization, and nationalism are strong for those who occupy positions in the central government. Local leaders, on the other hand, may have an incentive not so much to oppose industrialization and modernization as to demand a full or even more than full share for their own region and, if the makings of a local nationalism are there, to encourage that local nationalism in competition with that of the state as a whole. This tendency makes for explosive situations, but it is still a thrust toward nationalism, even though it is in competition with the nationalism sponsored by the center.

Resistance to Nationalism

If these are the incentives toward industrialization, modernization, and nationalism, where is the resistance? One would expect resistance to be strongest among the religious and aristocratic elites. In Asia, one would expect most resistance from the Buddhist hierarchy, the bonzes and village priests in mainland Southeast Asia, among the intensely devout Muslims, called *santri*, in Indonesia, and in the strongholds of religion and caste in India. One thinks also of the aristocratic and princely families, who usually combine wealth, prestige, and political influence. In the Middle East, one would again expect resistance to be centered in the religious and aristocratic strata. In Africa, one would expect it to be tribal councils and chieftaincies, and in Latin America among the old oligarchic families and class. One would expect that all these groups would sense the egalitarianism implicit in nationalism and have no doubt of its consequences to them and their privileged positions. One would also expect these strata to resist industrialization and modernization because of the obvious threat they pose to the whole range of traditional values to which the old religious and aristocratic strata would be committed to uphold.

But it is not entirely true of any of these strata that they are inevitably and unalterably opposed to industrialization, modernization, and nationalism in all their forms. In Thailand, for example, the *Social Science Review* received a large number of letters from Buddhist monks associating themselves with the "modern, assertive Thai culture which that journal advocates."[10] In the Philippines, the Jesuits have been a vital support to the modernization effort, including education for birth control. The fact is that evidence of some degree of support for modernization can be

[10] Steinberg, op. cit., Chapter 35, "Cultural Reconstruction and Postwar Nationalism."

found within religious and aristocratic strata in every single country of Asia, Africa, the Middle East, and Latin America. Occasionally, in fact, those who are leading the march to development come principally from these strata. In Iran, it was the Shah himself who was in the forefront. In Cambodia, from independence in 1954 until the *coup d'état* in 1970, the leader was Sihanouk, the hereditary King who abdicated to base himself upon the peasantry. And in Thailand, the leadership in modernizing has not been a single individual, but virtually the entire stratum of the traditional aristocracy.

As a general rule, the traditionalist strata of the leadership who do follow their natural inclination to react to the threats that modernization poses to traditional patterns are less inclined to oppose nationalism than industrialization and modernization. But even so, they rarely oppose even industrialization and modernization in principle and across the board. They tend to resist particular changes or to protect particular practices. An example is the agitation in India about medical training. The aim was not to oppose training in Western medicine but to provide schools devoted to the traditional ayurvedic medicine alongside those devoted to training in Western medicine. Speaking of the traditionalist Hindu parties in India, Myron Wiener makes a comment that is generally valid for traditionalist strata throughout the underdeveloped world: "What weakens the Hindu parties in their political efforts is their failure to have a clear-cut political program for returning to the old order; theirs is to a large extent a kind of rear-guard action, aiming to prevent the passage of government legislation affecting the Hindu social structure, to minimize the use of English in the educational system, and more positively, to fight for the passage of legislation banning cow slaughter."[11]

In most of these countries the mass of the populace is unresponsive and apathetic, turned inward on itself, and insulated by the traditional pattern of life in which they are caught from either appeals or incentives to industrialization, modernization,

[11] "Some Hypotheses on the Politics of Modernization in India," *Leadership and Political Institutions in India*, eds. Richard L. Park and Irene Tinker (Princeton, New Jersey, 1959), p. 21.

and nationalism. But among the leadership stratum, to sum up, it seems clear that the incentives are both ubiquitous and powerful, and that the forces working among the leadership stratum to resist, although prevalent and far from weak, seem in the long run to be no match. The incentives are not uniform, the surges toward development will be intermittent, the opposition significant, and the effort spotty. But it still seems clear that in all the underdeveloped countries of all the regions—Asia, the Middle East, Africa, and Latin America—sooner or later one or another stratum of leadership will pick up the banner of development and nationalism. Whether or not they will be successful and how long it will take them is another matter. But the effort toward development clearly will be made.

Conclusion

Our conclusion, then, is that in each of the underdeveloped countries of the world, with only anachronistic exceptions, sooner or later one or another leadership elite will attempt to launch the country on a course of industrialization and modernization. In some cases nationalism will be a major incentive for the effort, but where it is not, the leadership will sooner or later turn to nationalism as the handiest instrument available for mobilizing the populace for the industrialization effort. In some countries the traditional elites will be the ones to lead this march. Where they do not, they will be overthrown—by a middle class, by a Communist revolution, or by a nationalist faction of the military, as Nasser led the revolution in Egypt against King Farouk. But no matter where the leadership comes from, it will feel the incentives for a drive to industrialization. The leaders will need industrialization to give their country the strength to take the place in the world that pride demands and to vindicate the humiliation of colonialism or of simply being left behind. They will need it to centralize sufficient power to make and carry out decisions in the name of the whole state. They will need it because the masses have seen or sensed the possibility of an end to poverty, sickness, degradation, and misery, and demand the industrialization and modernization that bring these dazzling gains, even though they do not understand the effort required. And where nationalism is not already virile and thriving, these leaders will inevitably be driven to create it. For nationalism—to repeat once again—is the instrument for accomplishing all the rest.

CHAPTER 11

The Process of Development

SOONER OR LATER each of the underdeveloped countries will decide that it must develop. But what is needed for a country to develop? Just what is the so-called process of development? When the United States first embarked on programs to aid the underdeveloped countries, many of its efforts were dictated by the imperatives of the Cold War—defense took priority over development. Of those programs that did aim principally at development, it must be said that they were all too frequently based on the blithe assumption that capital, technical knowledge, and a few specially trained people were all that was needed. The notion was that if these three ingredients were made available and directed toward building up a few key sectors of the economy of an underdeveloped country, then development would more or less automatically follow. What these programs produced—fertilizer plants in Korea, the Volta Dam in Ghana, roads in Thailand, and the like—did add to the economies of the countries, but they did not trigger a spiral of self-sustaining growth.

Strategic Sectors of the Economy

Certain sectors of the economy of an underdeveloped country are obviously of strategic importance. John Kenneth Galbraith illustrates the point with an example from the history of American development.[1] In the American colonies, food was not plentiful. The space between the mountains and the sea was limited, and not everywhere was it fertile. Food often had to be imported from Europe. A development plan along modern lines, Galbraith notes, would have emphasized agricultural colleges, extension services, storage facilities, and the like. Transport would have undoubtedly been mentioned, but it might well have gotten lost among all the rest. What actually happened was that a major effort was put on a key strategic sector, although the choice may have been more luck than prescience. In 1825, New York State built a canal that linked the "black lands of the west with the centers of population," and the food shortage came to an end. Successful economic development, quite obviously, will indeed require capital, technical knowledge, and specially trained people aimed at strategic sectors. But a great deal more is also needed.

Many of the requirements for successful development are obvious and elementary. The first prerequisite is good government. Economic development is impossible with a government so weak that it cannot keep peace, so corrupt that taxes are diverted to the ministers' numbered bank accounts in Switzerland, or so incompetent that major programs collapse in a morass of inefficiency.

A second prerequisite is education. Studies by Theodore Schultz and others have shown that outlays for education bring large returns in the form of increased production.[2] But even without the evidence in such studies, common sense would tell us that both the mechanic who can read a manual and the farmer who

[1] *Economic Development in Perspective* (Cambridge, 1962).
[2] Schultz, "Investment in Human Capital," *The American Economic Review* (March 1961) and "Capital Formation by Education," *Journal of Political Economy* (December 1960).

can read an agricultural bulletin will do better than mechanics and farmers who cannot.

A third prerequisite is a set of social arrangements that create incentives for improvement among all segments of the population. Economic development is hardly likely under social conditions in which a tiny elite has the monopoly of wealth and power and the masses are denied both rights and opportunity. As Galbraith says, "Even the most eloquent agricultural extension expert cannot explain the advantage of growing two grains of wheat where but one flourished before if the peasant knows full well that both will go inevitably to the landlord."[3]

All this helps us understand some of the necessities of the process of economic development, but it does not help very much in the task of predicting whether a particular effort at development will be successful. As Galbraith puts the problem, "In these early stages, also, development encounters the appalling problems of the closed circle. How does a country without effective organs of public administration develop them, since bad government is not self-correcting but self-perpetuating? How does a country without an educated elite create one, since to extend education takes educated people? How bring about social reform when the class structure places political power in the hands of those who are likely to resist it?"[4]

Walt W. Rostow and The Stages of Economic Growth

Of the several attempts to answer these questions in the recent past, the one that has created the most controversy is undoubtedly Walt W. Rostow's *The Stages of Economic Growth: A Non-Communist Manifesto.*[5] Rostow sees the process of economic development proceeding through five stages: first, the stage of traditional society; second, the stage of preconditions for "take-off" into self-sustaining growth; third, the "take-off" itself; fourth,

[3] Galbraith, op. cit., p. 9.
[4] Ibid., p. 15.
[5] Cambridge, 1962. The notion of stages of economic growth has a long history—at least two hundred years. For a discussion of the history of the idea see Bert F. Hoselitz, "Theories of Stages of Economic Growth" in Hoselitz et al., *Theories of Economic Growth* (Chicago: The Free Press of Glencoe, 1960).

the "drive to maturity"; and fifth, the stage of high mass consumption.

The traditional society Rostow describes as one "whose structure is developed within limited production functions, based on pre-Newtonian science and technology, and on pre-Newtonian attitudes toward the physical world." The traditional society could and did change. Populations waxed and waned; trade flourished and declined; empires rose and fell. Various innovations permitted increases in economic output—such as irrigation canals or the introduction of a new crop. But the central fact was that a ceiling existed on the level of output per person that was attainable—a ceiling resulting "from the fact that the potentialities which flow from modern science and technology were either not available or not regularly and systematically applied."[6] The limitation on productivity generally means that the major effort of the society is in agriculture. Flowing from this, the social structure tends to be hierarchical, with little room for vertical mobility. Family and clan play a large role. The value structure tends to "long-run fatalism"—the assumption that the "range of possibilities open to one's grandchildren would be just about what it had been for one's grandparents." Finally, the center of gravity of political power generally lies not at the center, but in the various regions, in the hands of those who own or control the land.

The second stage is one of transition, when the society is developing the preconditions for "take-off." Here, Rostow distinguishes two different types. In the more general case—embracing most of Europe and the greater part of Asia, the Middle East, and Africa—creating the preconditions for "take-off" requires fundamental social, political, and attitudinal changes in a well-established traditional society. The other case covers the small group of nations—the United States, Australia, and Canada principally—created out of a Britain that was already well along in the transitional process, usually by nonconformist groups, and usually in a physical setting of abundant land and natural resources. For these countries the process of development was mainly economic and technical.

[6] *The Stages of Economic Growth*, p. 4.

In the more general case, creating the preconditions for "take-off" means shifting the bulk of the working force from agriculture to industry and commerce; changing the attitude toward having large families; shifting the income above consumption from those who spend it on mansions and servants to those who will spend it on roads, railways, schools, and factories; changing attitudes so that men are valued not for their family or clan but for their skills; and, "above all, the concept must be spread that man need not regard his physical environment as virtually a factor given by nature and providence, but as an ordered world which, if rationally understood, can be manipulated in ways which yield productive change and, in one dimension at least, progress."[7]

Rostow believes that in the general case an essential condition in the transition period is that investment be increased and the so far unexploited technological innovations be brought to bear on agriculture and the extractive industries, where quick results are possible. Food will be needed for the likely rise in population, and increased agricultural production and production from extractive industries will help in holding down the drain of foreign exchange and, especially in the case of extractive industries, may even earn it.

The Rise of a New Elite

Outside the sphere of economics, Rostow believes the single most important prerequisite is the emergence of a new elite. Historically, Rostow argues, the new, modernizing elites have been coalitions—the Junkers and the Western men of commerce in Germany, the samurai and the grain merchants in Japan, and "in post-1861 Russia, the commercial middle class and the more enterprising civil servants and soldiers." Profit was among the motives activating them, but it was rarely central. "Men holding effective authority or influence have been willing to uproot traditional societies not, primarily, to make more money but because the traditional society failed—or threatened to fail—to protect them from humiliation by foreigners."[8]

[7] Ibid., p. 19.
[8] Ibid., pp. 26–27.

"Take-off"

At a certain stage, a society "takes off" into development. "Take-off" to Rostow is that "decisive interval in the history of a society when growth becomes its normal condition."[9] He also speaks of it as the time when a "truly self-reinforcing growth process gets under way." The beginning of "take-off," Rostow contends, can usually be traced to a particular sharp stimulus. It may take the form of a political revolution that affects the balance of social power, the character of economic institutions, and such things as the distribution of income. This was the case, he feels, with the German revolution of 1848 and the Meiji restoration in 1868 in Japan. A technological innovation that sets in motion a chain of secondary expansion might do it. So might a new favorable international environment. Here he gives as an example the opening of British and French markets to Swedish timber in the 1860s.

The leading sectors in "take-off" have historically been varied. For Britain, it was cotton textiles. For the United States, France, Germany, Canada, and Russia, it was the railroad. The railroad lowered transport costs and brought new areas into the economy. It permitted new and enlarged exports. And, most important, it stimulated the development of coal, iron, and engineering industries. Modern processing techniques applied to raw materials and foodstuffs can also serve as the leading sector. This was the case with Sweden's timber and pulp industries, and with Denmark's shift to meat and dairy products. Even the manufacture of consumption goods as a substitute for imports can be the leading sector, Rostow argues, as was the case in Australia.

Rostow points out that some "take-offs" have occurred with very little capital imports—as in the case of Britain and Japan. Others—the United States, Russia, and Canada—utilized a great deal of imported foreign capital. But some countries have imported a great deal of capital without triggering "take-off." Rostow's examples are Argentina before 1914, Venezuela until recently, and most recently, Zaïre (formerly the Belgian Congo). In short, whatever role capital imports play, the ability to mo-

[9] Ibid., p. 36.

bilize domestic savings will be essential, in Rostow's view, for "take-off."

With appropriate caveats and qualifications, Rostow identifies the "take-off" date for Britain as 1783–1802; for France, 1830–60; for the United States, 1843–60; for Germany, 1850–73; for Sweden, 1868–90; for Japan, 1878–1900; Russia, 1890–1914; and for Canada, 1896–1914.

The "Drive to Maturity"

The next stage is the "drive to maturity," which Rostow defines as the period when a society effectively applies the range of modern technology known at the time to the bulk of its resources.

In the "drive to maturity," new leading sectors supplant the original ones. As Rostow describes it, countries that took off with railroads as the leading sector, in which coal, iron, and engineering were at the center of the growth process, then moved on to steel, the new ships, chemicals, electricity, and the products of the machine tool industry. In Sweden it was the evolution from timber to wood pulp and paper, on the one hand, and, on the other, from extracting ore to manufacturing high-grade steel and finely machined metal products.

Rostow estimates that Britain had achieved maturity by 1850; France, by 1910; the United States, by 1900; Germany, by 1910; Sweden, by 1930; Japan, by 1940; the Soviet Union, by 1950; and Canada, by 1950.

The Age of High Mass Consumption

The society in the stage following maturity has a choice. One path is the national pursuit of external power and influence—by allocating increased resources to military strength and to the purposes of foreign policy. Presumably Rostow would say that this is the path that Germany followed after achieving maturity in 1910.

A second path is to use the resources of the "mature" economy to construct a welfare state. The power of the state can be used to achieve social objectives that the free-market process does not—to redistribute income, shorten the working day, provide income in periods of unemployment, and equalize opportunities for med-

ical care and enjoying a comfortable old age. Presumably it is
Sweden after 1930 that Rostow has in mind as an example.

The third possibility is to expand consumption levels beyond
food, shelter, and clothing to include the range of durable consumers goods and services. The example, of course, is the United
States. "The United States took to wheels . . . truly the age of
the mass automobile. With the automobile the United States began a vast inner migration into newly constructed single-family
houses in the suburbs; and these new houses were filled increasingly with radios, refrigerators, and the other household gadgetry
of a society whose social mobility and productivity had all but
wiped out personal services."[10]

This, then, is Rostow's theory of the stages of economic
growth: traditional society; the stage of building preconditions
for "take-off"; the "take-off" itself; the "drive to maturity"; and,
finally, the stage of high mass consumption leading to the pursuit
of national power and prestige, to the welfare state, or to mass
consumption of durable consumers' goods and services. Much of
the historical material from which Rostow constructs his theory
is, of course, already familiar to us from our examination of the
rise of nationalism. What is different is the dynamism it suggests,
and the question is how useful this theory of dynamism is to us in
our attempt to discern the future of the underdeveloped world.

Criticisms of Rostow's Theory

Rostow's theory stirred up an impressive amount of controversy and academic debate. At one level, much of the criticism
seemed a storm in a teacup. As Rostow himself remarked at an international conference of economists held to discuss his theory of
the stages of economic growth, "the introduction of a new concept—especially a new term ["take-off"]—is an act of aggression
against respected colleagues and friends."[11] Others are more serious. There is a question among economists, for example,
whether the concept of stages possesses analytical content. The

[10] Ibid., p. 77.
[11] W. W. Rostow, ed., *The Economics of Take-off into Sustained Growth; Proceedings of a Conference Held by the International Economic Association* (New
York, 1965), pp. xiii–xiv.

definition of a particular stage, in the words of one friendly critic, "might mean something purely descriptive, for example that we lived in the automobile age because there were now lots of motor-cars which clearly did not exist in the past."[12] This same critic said that he occasionally felt that "take-off" in any particular country occurred when Professor Rostow felt that it occurred, a procedure that was somewhat lacking in precision.

The Rostovian Dynamic

But for our purposes the question, as we said, is the notion in Rostow's theory that a stage is reached at which growth is self-sustained, the notion that the process of economic growth contains a dynamic. At several points in his book, Rostow hedges and qualifies this notion. At others, however, he is explicit in speaking of a dynamic: "These stages are not merely descriptive. They are not merely a way of generalizing certain factual observations about the sequence of development of modern societies. They have an inner logic and continuity. They have an analytic bone-structure, rooted in a dynamic theory of production."[13] It is fair to say that there is also throughout the book the strong suggestion that once the preconditions for "take-off" have been acquired, an effective "trigger" will sooner or later more or less inevitably appear, a "trigger" that will thrust the society into "take-off," and that from then on the process is more or less automatic. Acquiring the preconditions for "take-off" has been accidental for some societies. For others, the preconditions were created by the intrusion of a developed country, through colonialism or trade and foreign investment. For still others the preconditions were planned to at least some degree. Then came the "trigger"—which can be so many different things that one seems bound to appear, even if it is not actually planned and provided for, which is also possible. Then—away we go in a rush for development. No massive effort seems to be necessary, no particular striving—the dynamic takes over.

This description of the impression Rostow gives is, of course, an

---

[12] Professor Robert Solow, *The Economics of Take-off into Sustained Growth*, p. 469.
[13] *The Stages of Economic Growth*, pp. 12–13.

exaggeration. But it is not very much of an exaggeration. Although Rostow would clearly concede that a particular country laboring under adverse circumstances might fail to "take off" even when the preconditions were right and a seemingly appropriate "trigger" applied, he would also quite clearly regard such a failure as a rarity.

Almost ten years after the publication of *The Stages of Economic Growth,* Rostow wrote another book—a book intended to enlarge on the earlier book so as to include politics in his theory of development as well as economics. In this later book, Rostow sharpens his qualifications in deference to the criticism of his theory of stages, but does not give up the core notion of self-sustained growth.[14] Once traditional society is fractured, he argues, "certain forces operate more or less steadily to move the society toward modernization." Widened contact with more modern societies are one of these forces; so is the rise of trade and the growth of cities; so is the emergence of new generations less wedded to the old ways. All these are mutually reinforcing and gradually begin to shift the whole society. "There is, to a degree, then," he writes, "a kind of automatic slide in the direction of modernization set up by the nature of the forces which have fractured the traditional society."[15]

Rostow is more willing to concede in this later book that there is "nothing automatic and easy about the inner mechanics—the logistics, as it were—of sustained growth." But he hastens to assert that the process really *is* inevitable even so, that it can go only one way, that is toward development, because of deeper forces propelling it toward growth. After making his concession to the difficulties, he then writes: "In a larger sense, however, the experience of take-off appears, on present evidence, to be a definitive transition, like the loss of innocence. . . . Phases of difficulty and even relative stagnation after the take-off may, of course, occur; and they may be protracted. Men in societies must continue to struggle to keep growth moving forward. But it appears to be the case that the larger psychological, social, technological, and institutional changes required for a take-off are such as to

[14] *Politics and the Stages of Growth* (Cambridge, 1971).
[15] Ibid., p. 61.

make it unlikely that there will be a true lapsing back. The deeper fundamentals required for an effective take-off appear sufficiently powerful to make growth an ongoing process. . . ."[16] Rostow obviously is quite sincerely convinced that a dynamic does exist.

Thus it is essential for our purposes here to reach a judgment on Rostow's theory—not for one reason but two. The first is that if Rostow is right, we can with great confidence predict what the underdeveloped world will look like in the future. We have already concluded that since the social forces at work in the underdeveloped countries push the leadership toward making the attempt to develop, sooner or later a particular leadership will succumb to the pressures and take up the banner of modernization, industrialization, and nationalism or it will be replaced by one that will. If Rostow is right, the attempt will in due time succeed. Indeed, Rostow makes precisely this prediction. In 1960, he wrote that "it is as sure as anything can be that, barring global catastrophe, the societies of the underdeveloped areas will move through the transitional processes and establish the preconditions for take-off into economic growth and modernization. And they will then continue the process of sustained growth and move on to maturity; that is, to the stage when their societies are so structured that they can bring to bear on their resources the full capabilities of modern technology."[17] And in 1962, he went even farther: "For the central fact about the future of world power is the acceleration of the preconditions or the beginnings of take-off in the southern half of the world: Southeast Asia, the Middle East, Africa, and Latin America. . . . Put more precisely, the take-offs of China and India have begun. Pakistan, Egypt, Iraq, Indonesia and other states are likely to be less than a decade behind."[18]

The second reason it is essential that we reach a judgment here on Rostow's theory is that his theory has been accepted by many people high in the governments of many of both the underdeveloped countries of the world and of the developed countries that

[16] Ibid., p. 100.
[17] *The United States in the World Arena* (New York, 1960), p. 412.
[18] *The Stages of Economic Growth*, p. 126.

might be expected to help in the process of development. Because Rostow's theory is so widely accepted, in other words, it is actually one of the factors bearing on the future! His theory is affecting the behavior of at least some of those who will be leading the march to development, and anyone attempting to think about the future of the underdeveloped world must take that fact into account.

Myrdal's Critique

Rostow's harshest critic—in terms of the part of his theories that most concerns us, the dynamic of growth—has been Gunnar Myrdal. Myrdal concedes that the concept of stages may provide useful insights even if the theory does not accord very well with reality. He gives Karl Marx as an example. Marx's theories assumed a progression of stages—feudalism, capitalism, socialism—and Marx's theories did not turn out to accord very well with reality. But they still provided some useful insights and aided greatly in developing economic theories that did correspond more closely with reality. But Myrdal will not be so generous to Rostow's theories for several reasons.

Myrdal's first objection to Rostow's theory is that his approach is based on the fundamental preconception of the *"Similarity of evolution* in different countries at different historical periods." This, of course, is why theories can be and are used for prediction. "But," Myrdal argues, "similarity depends on the level of abstraction and the choice of features compared. Such comparisons can be refuted only by demonstrating that other principles of selection and comparison are equally possible—and, of course, *ex post* that the predictions do not come true."[19]

Second, Myrdal argues that Rostow's approach is teleological—"one in which a purpose, which is not explicitly intended by anyone, is fulfilled while the process of fulfillment is presented as an inevitable sequence of events."[20] This means that it can never be either proved or disproved. "This selection of strategic factors and of assumptions about their role remains *a priori*, however much illustrative material is amassed. It never is—and, in this

[19] *Asian Drama* (New York, 1968), p. 1,847. Myrdal's emphasis.
[20] Ibid.

teleological approach it never can be—empirically verified or refuted."[21] This leads to logical confusion and circular reasoning. It also leads to what in Myrdal's view is an even greater crime—a tendency to play down the importance of policies. Policies are often regarded as being caused by or emerging from development as "mere elements in a historical process." Actually, policies are and should be regarded as the result of deliberate, conscious choice.

Finally, Myrdal charges, the Rostow approach is both specious and tautological. "Thus tautologies take such forms as the proposition that countries grow because they have propensities to grow, where the test of the presence of the propensity is actual growth; or that civilizations flower because a suitable challenge meets with a proper response, where the test of suitability of the challenge is the flowering of the civilization; or that it is the changing sequence of leading sectors that characterizes the stages of growth, where leading sectors are simply those that happen to be ahead of the others."[22] What infuriates Myrdal especially is the thought that these very flaws seem to help the theory survive: "The tautology lends it an air of scientific truth, the speciousness an impression of significance."

Myrdal's Alternative Theory

In rejecting Rostow's theory of stages of economic growth, Myrdal offers a rival theory to replace it—a theory that is "purged of teleology and formulated in such a way that the valuations are brought out as explicit value premises." The value premises Myrdal makes explicit are what he calls the "modernization ideals"—such specifics as economic development, rise in productivity and levels of living, social and economic equalization, rationality in public debate, improved institutions and attitudes, and national consolidation and independence. He does not suggest that the masses of the people in the underdeveloped countries take these "modernization ideals" as their value premises, but he does assume that the elites do, since these ideals are the official goals of the governments.

[21] Ibid.
[22] Ibid., pp. 1,855–56.

Second, Myrdal conceives of a number of social conditions as being causally interrelated, so that a change in one will cause changes in the others. A social system, in Myrdal's view, is simply this set of causally interrelated conditions.

Myrdal classifies these conditions in six broad categories: outputs and incomes; conditions of production; levels of living; attitudes toward life and work; institutions; and, finally, policies.

Myrdal thinks of the first three conditions as "economic," while attitudes and institutions are "noneconomic." The last one, policies, is a mixture. In a social system, Myrdal says, there is "no up and down, no primary and secondary, and economic conditions do not have precedence over the others." However, Myrdal simply assumes that for South Asia, the object of his study, the various conditions are undesirable because a "one-way change" in them is necessary for engineering and sustaining development, in accordance with his explicit value premises.

Myrdal elaborates and explains his six conditions with South Asia in mind. In terms of the first category, output and incomes, South Asia is, of course, low. Myrdal also argues that although not a definition of underdevelopment, labor productivity and per capita income are useful if imperfect *indexes* of the level of development.

By the term "conditions of production" Myrdal means the structure of the economy. In South Asia, the industrial sector is small. In all other sectors, especially agriculture, the techniques of production are primitive, and capital intensity is low. The savings/income ratio is low, and so is the savings per head. The overhead capital in the form of roads, railways, ports, power plants, and other items of infrastructure is inadequate.

By "levels of living" Myrdal means food intake; housing conditions; availability of public and private hygiene and medical care; facilities for vocational and professional instruction and training; and educational and cultural facilities of all sorts.

By "attitudes toward life and work" he means all those related to modernization. In South Asia, Myrdal specifically means "low levels of work discipline, punctuality, and orderliness; superstitious beliefs and irrational outlook; lack of alertness, adaptability, ambition, and general readiness for change and experiment; contempt for manual work; submissiveness to authority and exploitation; low aptitude for cooperation; low standards of personal hygiene, and so on." To these attitudes Myrdal adds an "unreadiness for deliberate and sustained birth control. The steep and accelerating rise in population in these countries is a principal cause of poverty, and birth control is the only means of checking this trend since we cannot wish to increase mortality or even check its continuing decline."[23]

By "institutions" Myrdal means social institutions. In South Asia the land tenure system is detrimental to development in agriculture. The institutions for enterprise, employment, trade, and credit are undeveloped. Government agencies lack authority, standards of efficiency and integrity in public administration are low. There is a weak infrastructure of voluntary organizations. And at the root of everything is a rigid, inegalitarian social stratification.

By "policies," of course, Myrdal means acts by the government to bring about change in the first five conditions. Planning would then be the co-ordination of policies to bring about development.

All these conditions are causally interrelated in a "unidirectional" way, both within a particular category and among the different categories. Thus within the second category, conditions of production, the low savings ratio tends to keep down the formation of capital, while primitive production techniques are partly the result of low capital intensity. The same is true of the maldistribution of the labor force: too many workers in sectors requiring little or no capital, too few in those that require capital and that would raise output. Low labor input and low labor efficiency are in part the result of the primitive techniques used and the lack of capital.

Between categories the same causal interrelationship also pertains. All the low conditions of production cause low productivity of workers and low per capita income and are in turn caused by them. Low incomes keep down total savings and perpetuate the situation of low capital intensity, poor techniques, and low labor productivity. Low levels of income in turn cause low levels of living, while low levels of living cause low labor input and low

23 Ibid., p. 1,862.

labor efficiency. Similarly, attitudes are both a result of all the above and a cause. Institutions, in turn, are the principal support of the prevailing attitudes. Through their effects, the various categories "—conditions of production, levels of living, and attitudes toward life and work—this whole set of unfavorable institutional conditions shares responsibility for the low levels of productivity and low incomes and thus also, indirectly, for the low levels of living. At the same time the low incomes and the low levels of living and, in particular, the low levels of literacy and education perpetuate the deficiencies in communal institutions."[24]

This, then, is Myrdal's theory—six broad categories of conditions and "circular causation" among them. "If these conditions for a country were to be completely listed and specified so as to serve ideally the purpose of intensive analysis," he writes, "and if all the causal interrelationships were assessed correctly, we could give a full explanation in terms of causes and effects, why things are as they are at a particular point in time and why they change as they do, or why they do not change."[25]

Myrdal's Theory in Operation

Rostow's theory not only makes change inevitable, but it permits change in only one direction: toward development. Myrdal's, on the other hand, permits a steady state, that is, stagnation; it permits development; and it also permits retrogression. The steady state is a vicious circle. The example Myrdal uses is from Ragnar Nurkse: "For example, a poor man may be weak; being physically weak, his working capacity may be low which means that he is poor, which in turn means that he will not have enough to eat; and so on. A situation of this sort, relating to a country as a whole, can be summed up in the trite proposition: 'a country is poor because it is poor.' "[26]

Retrogression, a cumulative downward movement, can also occur. If the man gets less than the critical amount of food to maintain health, through, say, an accident, he will be unable

[24] Ibid., p. 1,863.
[25] Ibid., p. 1,870.
[26] Ibid., p. 1,844, quoted from Nurkse, Problems of Capital Formation in Underdeveloped Countries (Oxford, 1953), p. 4.

to maintain his former level of production and will get even less food. Instead of stagnation and a vicious circle, the result is retrogression in a downward spiral. A historical example that Mrydal cites is what happened in Java. The island was over-populated and poor. As the population grew further, squatters took over more of the forest reserves. The capacity of the soil to hold water was reduced, and some soil washed away. Less land was available suitable for growing food, so the pressure to take over more of the forest increased.[27]

Similarly, the process could go the other way and become a benevolent spiral. If the poor man is given more to eat, his health and strength improve. He can work harder and more pro-ductively, and thus get still more to eat. There is, in Myrdal's phrase, a cumulative upward movement.

So Myrdal, like Rostow, also has a dynamic! And although it is neither unidirectional nor inevitable, Myrdal's dynamic seems to make development almost as easy as Rostow's. Since causation is circular among all six categories of conditions, it should be possible to break the circle at any point and start the cumulative process going. If attitudes cannot be changed immediately, then an infusion of capital from outside in the form of foreign aid could get things going. In time, due to circular causation, atti-tudes *would* change, and that change would induce secondary changes all around the circle once more. With approval, Myrdal again quotes Nurkse: "The circular constellation of the stationary system is real enough, but fortunately the circle is not unbreak-able. And once it is broken at any point, the very fact that the relation is circular tends to make for cumulative advance. We should perhaps hesitate to call the circle vicious; it can become beneficent."[28] In the end, "cumulative advance" does not seem very different from "self-sustained growth"—if this isn't "take-off," it is certainly close to it.

But Myrdal is not optimistic about the possibilities for the underdeveloped countries, but pessimistic. It is because Rostow

[27] *Asian Drama*, p. 1,845, as quoted from Nathan Keyfitz, "The Interlocking of Social and Economic Factors in Asian Development," *Canadian Journal of Economics and Political Science* XXV, No. 1 (February 1959).
[28] *Asian Drama*, p. 1,847, from Nurkse's *Problems of Capital Formation in Under-developed Countries*, p. 11.

makes it all sound so easy that Myrdal is impatient with him. The fact is that Myrdal is only too well aware that things have not worked out the way his theory tells him it should. Historically, in country after country, a major investment—the introduction of railways, creating a textile industry, or the transformation of agriculture—has induced only minor secondary effects in other parts of the economy and society. Instead of a cumulative gain and self-sustained growth, the result may be stagnation at a slightly higher level. Or one segment of the society is better off while the rest continues at its previous low level. And this development of "dual economies" can happen on a grand scale. The South of the United States remained backward long after the rest of the country was developed. In Japan, economists spoke of a "dual economy" until after World War II. In Italy, money spent in the South to bring it out of backwardness for a long time merely "leaked," in terms of secondary effects, to stimulate the industrialized North or even other countries.

Myrdal's Modifications to His Theory

Mrydal puts the trouble between what his theory predicts and the observable reality in the following way. First, he points out that although it is conceivable that the various conditions could attain precisely such levels as to represent a balance between the forces, but only by a rare chance. "Secondly," Myrdal then writes, "the balance, if established, would be broken as soon as some outside event or some policy intervention at home moved one or several of the conditions up or down. Any such change in some conditions would tend to cause other conditions to move in the same direction, and these secondary changes would, in their turn, result in tertiary changes all around the system, and so on in a circular fashion."[29] One would therefore expect that the normal condition would be movement, up or down. All social systems, if the theory is correct, would be highly unstable.

Yet the facts are that throughout history most social systems have been astonishingly stable. "Balance," Myrdal goes on to say, "far from being the fortuitous result of an unusual and ob-

[29] *Asian Drama*, p. 1,871.

viously unstable combination of forces, seems to be the rule, not the rare exception. The great bulk of historical, anthropological, and sociological evidence and thought suggests that social stability and equilibrium is the norm and that all societies, and underdeveloped societies in particular, possess institutions of a strongly stabilizing character."[30]

To rehabilitate his theory and reconcile it with the observed fact that societies are highly stable and resistant to change, Myrdal introduces three additional notions: the concept of "thresholds" created by time and inertia; the concept of independent counteracting changes; and the concept of counteracting changes released by development itself.

Although he continues to hold to the concept of circular causation, Myrdal points out that relatively long periods of time may be necessary for the process to take place. More food, for example, will have some beneficial short-run effects on labor productivity, but the main effect may have to wait until a whole new generation of workers, people who have eaten better since childhood, enters the labor force.

The second element in the first notion is inertia, by which Myrdal means principally the inertia of attitudes and institutions. In effect, about all Myrdal is saying at this point is that attitudes and institutions are so resistant to change that they and the time factor build up a "threshold." Rising production, incomes, and levels of living, including education, for example, should result in changes in community institutions and attitudes. "But all the existing community institutions, like the attitudes that are fostered within them and at the same time uphold them, are part of the wider cultural setting, and the results of gradual advances in these other respects may be insignificant for a long time. Even in the very long run, attitudes and community institutions may stay much the same, in spite of all efforts to raise educational levels, if the inegalitarian social stratification remains rigid. . . ."[31]

Time and inertia combine to create a "threshold," and a primary change has to be large to get the whole system over this "thresh-

[30] Ibid.
[31] Ibid., p. 1,873.

old" and into a cumulative process. "The general reason why this factor of inertia may prevent a development process from becoming self-sustained or, at least, delay this event," Myrdal goes on to say, "is that circular causation will give rise to a cumulative movement only when, by the interaction of all conditions in the social system, a change in one of the conditions will ultimately be followed by a feed-back of secondary impulses to a further change of that particular condition big enough not only to sustain the primary change, but to push it further."[32]

Inertia of attitudes and institutions and the buildup of "thresholds" would seem to be enough to account for the difficulties of breaking out of the vicious circle of a traditional social system, but Myrdal still has the two counteracting changes as well. The first is independently acting change, and of these the most important is clearly the population explosion. A high and rising rate of population growth simply nullifies all the other gains. In an underdeveloped country in which the population continues to rise at these high rates, a few may prosper, but the mass will sink to even lower levels.

The second set of counteracting changes are those resulting from development itself. Irrigation, for example, can destroy the land if proper attention is not given to drainage. Without proper drainage, salination and waterlogging set in. Developing new lands can lead to deforestation. Even education can have a negative economic effect if the attitude develops that an educated person is too good to soil his hands with work.

All these factors account, to Myrdal's satisfaction, for the stability of social systems throughout history and for the difficulty the underdeveloped countries have so obviously encountered in attaining self-sustained growth. But Myrdal's final conclusions are that circular causation is a fact and that it does mostly have unidirectional, cumulative effects.[33]

The obstacles to development that Myrdal sees lead him to believe that development will take a determined, conscious, deliberate effort, that planners would be well advised to begin development with a "big push" to get the society over the

[32] Ibid., p. 1,875.
[33] Ibid., p. 1,978.

"threshold," and that it is crucially important for a developing country to adopt "deliberate policy measures directed specifically at improving the attitudes and reforming the institutions" of the society. But if all these things are done and done properly, Myrdal believes the society will enter a period in which growth will indeed be self-sustaining. "At the start, big efforts are needed to set the process in motion. Thereafter, the planners can relax or they can harvest proportionately ever larger and quicker yields from sustained efforts."[34]

Objections to Myrdal's Theory

Although Myrdal's theory, as finally qualified, is not likely to lead to overly optimistic predictions about the future of the underdeveloped countries, my own view is that it needs still further qualification and refinement. The dynamism contained in the notion of circular causation is still the problem. The trouble is that the obstacles to development can also be circular. Everyone who has been involved with the effort at development in a particular country, with foreign aid programs and the like, has his own favorite anecdote of nonrational or at least uneconomic responses to economic incentives. The classic example is the worker or peasant who responds to higher wages or higher farm prices by working less—the familiar backward-sloping supply curve. My own favorite concerns a peasant farmer—the best and most progressive in his remote Laotian village—who was persuaded to plant the new "miracle" rice. "Miracle" rice, he was told, had a yield five times that of his old seed. He was persuaded that the new seed would indeed yield five times as much as the old, and he eagerly agreed to be the pioneer in his village. So convinced was he that the new seed would do what it was supposed to, indeed, that he planted one fifth his usual acreage!

The interesting point, however, was that his reasons were not the familiar one of "survival" or subsistence attitude that caused the worker and peasant to work less in the classic examples. When asked why he had planted only one fifth his usual acreage, this particular peasant's answer was that there was no one to

[34] Ibid., p. 1,899.

buy his rice, no place to store it, no road to get it to a town
where it could be sold, and nothing in the village market to buy
even if he could sell it or trade it. And the truth of the matter is
that to break this kind of vicious circle more was needed than
the things that were so obvious to the peasant—buyers, storage,
a road, and things to buy in the market. A more efficient government would be needed with better methods of tax collection
before it could build the road. Investment would also be needed
in some sort of light industry in the town to attract workers
from subsistence farming, to give them the income to buy the
rice and the facilities to produce the goods—sewing machines,
clothes, transistor radios—that the peasant wanted to buy. And
we haven't spoken of education, power plants, and ways of earn-
ing foreign exchange.

This particular kind of vicious circle of obstacles to change can
be found in as many different sectors of life as the circles of
causation. The drugs used to treat a disease that is estimated to
infect 80 per cent of the population of northeastern Thailand, to
give another example, are effective only if protein intake is adequate. Yet the main source of protein for people in northeastern
Thailand is paste made from raw fish—which reinfects them.

Myrdal's dynamic of circular causation assumes that a change
in any one of his conditions—output and incomes, conditions of
production, levels of living, attitudes, and institutions—will set
off changes in each of the others, and that each of these secondary changes will in turn set off tertiary changes. But the suspicion arises that change in the social system does *not* occur
unless change in several, if not all, of the conditions can be
brought about simultaneously and in the same direction. Certainly that has been the lesson that officials in the American
foreign aid effort feel they have learned over the past twenty-
five years. A country clearly benefits from an effort at improving
agriculture—investing in irrigation, fertilizer and pesticide manufacturing plants, new seeds, and training programs. It will also
benefit from an effort in developing a suitable industry—processing plants for its raw materials, factories for consumer goods
or for goods for export. Subsidiary benefits can also be traced
from educational programs, reform of various institutions, and

efforts to change attitudes. Each type of effort also clearly has some spread effects into other conditions. But when an effort is made in only one or only two or three sectors, the usual result is an improvement in those sectors and sometimes those sectors alone. Most of the time there is some spread effect to other sectors of the economy, but usually it is slight and is followed by a quick leveling off. Only very rarely do the secondary effects seem to spread back to stimulate the two or three sectors where the original effort was made. In recent times, the only countries in which the effort at development has succeeded in establishing and sustaining a high rate of growth for any significant period of time are those countries—like Taiwan—in which the development effort was not only large but right across the board—industry, agriculture, governmental effectiveness, living conditions, attitudes, and institutions, and including such mundane things as administrative procedures in banking and the postal system.

In terms of theory, this experience raises a doubt about the whole notion of the dynamic of circular causation, but not about the notion of the vicious circle of obstacles. A vicious circle of obstacles does not preclude the notion that a primary change can on occasion cause changes in other conditions. For example, if peasants are driven from the land by the introduction of sheep and eventually find employment in industry that is emerging in the cities, their attitudes toward punctuality and regularity will eventually change. But the notion of circular causation goes much farther than this. For there to be circular causation, the secondary change must feed back and change the primary condition still more. The workers' new attitudes toward punctuality and regularity must bring about a change in the structure of industry.

Obviously, examples of circular causation can be found. An investment results in higher productivity and higher incomes. Higher incomes result in higher savings, and the higher savings feed back into higher investment—i.e., the change in the secondary condition in turn caused a change in the primary condition. A well-documented, indisputable case of circular causation that came as a total surprise to everyone concerned occurred in

Thailand in the 1960s. An investment was made through American foreign aid in a road, Friendship Highway, from Saraburi to Korat. The reasons for building the road were mainly military and administrative, but quite spontaneously, without encouragement much less any effort to change their attitudes, large numbers of peasants abandoned their traditional villages and cleared and occupied land along the highway as squatters. What is even more remarkable is that along with their usual subsistence crops, they also planted two crops with which they were not familiar that were in demand on the world markets, maize and kenaf (a fiber used for burlap-type bags). The road gave them access to markets and to a port to the outside world, and the result for Thailand was an increase in foreign exchange that could be used for further investment.[35]

An Alternative View

But such examples are almost invariably concerned with purely economic factors, and even with purely economic factors, circular causation does not appear to be automatic and guaranteed. High incomes *permit* higher savings, but they don't guarantee them. The increased income can go into high living. Similarly, the foreign exchange earned by exporting maize and kenaf could be used to purchase limousines for corrupt officials, or simply go into a numbered bank account in Switzerland.

Furthermore, when it comes to noneconomic conditions—attitudes and institutions—the evidence seems to be against the notion of circular causation. In the first place, the historical evidence of attitudes changing in response to changed conditions is plentiful, while the evidence of changes in attitudes bringing about changes in other conditions is scarce.[36] In general, attitudes and institutions are *adapted* to changes in other conditions, but with as little modification as possible.[37] It frequently

[35] Dr. Puey Ungphakorn, "Thailand," *Asian Economic Development,* ed. Cranley Onslow (New York, 1965), p. 172.
[36] For a look at how attitudes and values change from several different points of view and for a partial guide to the literature, see Kurt Baier and Nicholas Rescher, eds., *Values and the Future* (New York, 1969).
[37] Albert O. Hirschman, citing experimental work in psychology done on "cognitive dissonance" theory, argues that value changes may follow changes in behavior rather than precede them. The implication is that if you can bring men to change

does happen that a change in attitudes makes it easier to bring about a further change in other conditions, but evidence that an attitude change *caused* a further change in other conditions or was the impetus to a further change is rare. Far from inducing further change, the effect of an attitude change that is really an adaptation is to blanket, damp down, and blunt the effects of the primary change to which the attitudes are being adapted.

Myrdal vs. Myrdal

The most effective way to make this point is to use Myrdal against Myrdal. In his monumental study of the place of the black in America, *An American Dilemma,* published in 1944, Myrdal argues that the economic backwardness of the South can be explained only by its history and by the attitudes of its people. "This pattern of common exploitation—where everyone is the oppressor of the one under him, where the Negroes are at the bottom and where big landlords, merchants, and Northern capital are at the top—is obviously the extension into the present of a modified slavery system."[38] As Myrdal says, after a few half-hearted attempts at a wage system the South adopted share-cropping as the pattern into which the blacks and later the poor whites were pressed. Even the plantation system was revived. Although many poor whites were sharecroppers on small hold-ings, as late as World War II the sharecroppers on plantations were largely black. During slavery, the police and courts were used to pursue and punish runaway or troublesome slaves; afterward, they were used to recruit black sharecroppers. Harsh vagrancy and lien laws were passed, and landlords could get black tenants by paying their fines and debts. It is no accident

---

their behavior to ways that speed growth, then the values and attitudes will change later. If, for example, you can persuade intellectuals in an underdevel-oped country with a mandarin tradition to do manual work because of some spe-cial condition or reason—say, patriotism in time of war—then, gradually, the man-darin attitude that educated men should not work with their hands will itself change. My own response would be that changing behavior presents many of the same problems as changing values, that is, that the evidence is that men change their behavior so as to *adapt* to change in the other conditions, and the effect is still the same as that described below. See Hirschman, "Obstacles to Development: A Classification and a Quasi-Vanishing Act," *Economic Development and Cultural Change* (July 1965).
[38] P. 221.

that, as Myrdal says, the South built up "a labor organization as similar as possible to slavery"—the institution to which it was accustomed.

Evidence of this kind is so plentiful that the conclusion seems inescapable that although attitudes do change in response to changes in other conditions, the change is to adapt, and the effect of this is to damp down the primary change rather than induce still further change. If so, then we must be skeptical of the concept of circular causation, at least insofar as noneconomic factors and conditions are concerned. The truth of the matter seems to be that Myrdal's dynamic is just as questionable as Rostow's. From the evidence, in fact, we must reluctantly conclude—reluctantly because the implications are so profound—that the whole notion of self-sustaining growth is nothing more than a myth.[39]

If self-sustained growth is a myth, a significant rate of growth can be achieved and maintained in only one way. The leaders of an underdeveloped country that wants to modernize and industrialize will have to be determined, strong-minded, and able men, who have themselves the necessary expertise or can obtain it, who are willing to work long and hard and to make their people do so, too, and who will force change all across the board, in agriculture, industry, governmental efficiency, administrative procedures, living conditions, and attitudes and social institutions. Development and modernization is not riding an escalator but trudging up a long, rough hill.

[39] For support for this view, at least in terms of economic development, see Simon Kuznets, "Notes on the Take-Off," in Walt W. Rostow, ed., *The Economics of Take-Off into Sustained Growth*, p. 40; and Cranley Onslow, "Asian Economic Development: A Comparative Analysis," *Asian Economic Development*, op. cit., p. 222.

CHAPTER 12

The Resources for Development

IF A determination to develop will in time inevitably seize each of the underdeveloped countries and if self-sustaining growth is a myth, the world may be heading for a time of great troubles. What are the prospects for development? Are the underdeveloped countries well or poorly endowed for the task?

National Income

Statistics from the underdeveloped countries are neither precise nor reliable. At best they are rather crude estimates. They also fail to take into account price differences and style of life. The Indonesian peasant, for example, pays much less in his village market for a sack of rice or a pound of vegetables than the American shopping at his supermarket, and the Indonesian can often pick fruit in his own backyard. Very little of the peasant's income goes for transportation, while an American worker's automobile might cost him more in a month than the Indonesian's yearly income. The peasant's heating bill is minute in the tropical climate—fuel is charcoal for cooking. A bamboo hut is adequate housing. But even though the statistics available fail to reflect differences in lifestyles such as these and even though the statistics are imprecise and unreliable, they do illustrate the crude magnitude of the differences between the developed and underdeveloped worlds.

The per capita national income in the United States at the beginning of the 1970s was approximately $3,600 per year. For Sweden it was approximately $2,700; for France, $1,800; for Japan, $1,200.

In Asia, among the underdeveloped countries only Singapore, Malaysia, and Taiwan had annual per capita incomes of over $200. Cambodia, Sri Lanka (Ceylon), South and North Korea, the Philippines, South and North Vietnam, and China had per capita incomes varying between $100 and $200 per year. All the rest—which includes India, Pakistan, and Indonesia, the countries with some of the largest populations—had per capita annual incomes of less than $100.

In the African continent south of the Sahara, Equatorial Guinea, Gabon, Ghana, the Ivory Coast, Rhodesia, and Zambia had per capita incomes ranging between $200 and $300. Only one country exceeded the latter level—South Africa, with an annual per capita income of slightly over $500. Cameroon, the People's Republic of the Congo, Kenya, Liberia, Mauritania, Senegal, Sierra Leone, and Swaziland ranged between $100 and $200. The per capita income in all the remaining nineteen states was less than $100. In Nigeria, the most populous of all the African countries, it was $63.

In the Middle East, Israel must be counted as a developed country. Its per capita income was $1,016. Of all the rest, only Kuwait rivals the developed countries. With a population of 700,000 and nearly one fifth of the world's total oil reserves, Kuwait had a per capita national income of $3,200. The next highest was way behind—Libya, with an annual income of about $800. Lebanon, Saudi Arabia, and Turkey had incomes varying between $300 and $400. Algeria, Iran, Iraq, Jordan, Syria, and Tunisia all had annual per capita incomes between $200 and

$300. The remaining countries ranged from $100 to $200, with the exception of Afghanistan and Yemen, whose incomes fell below the $100 mark.

In Latin America, no country's per capita income exceeded $1,000; however, only one, Haiti, fell below $100. Argentina, Mexico, Trinidad and Tobago, Uruguay, and Venezuela headed the list with per capita incomes of between $500 and $900. Brazil, Chile, Costa Rica, Cuba, Jamaica, and Panama were over $300 but less than $500. All the rest were between $150 and $300.

Stark though the picture is that these statistics paint, the irony is that the figures tend to make the economic plight of most people in most of these countries look much better than it actually is. The fact that the distribution of income in the United States is grossly unequal is familiar to most Americans. It is well understood that some segments of American society, particularly in the ghettos and remote, rural areas remain outside the industrialized, affluent economy that people in other countries think of as typical of the United States. Yet the range of inequality in the distribution of income is much less in the United States than it is in most underdeveloped countries. In the latter, the rich tend to be very, very rich and the poor tend to be very, very poor. The enormous wealth of the select few raises the statistical average and distorts the picture the national income statistics suggest.[1] In India, for example, according to a survey conducted in 1955-56, 50 per cent of the population was living on $0.10 a day, or $36.50 a year. One authority estimated that only 10 or 11 per cent of the Indian population could actually spend as much as or more than $0.20 a day, or $73 a year, which was the average per capita national income.[2]

Natural Resources

One might hope that the natural resources and endowment of the underdeveloped world would provide a quick and easy

[1] See Irving B. Kravis, "International Differences in the Distribution of Income," *Review of Economics and Statistics*, XLII, No. 4 (November 1960). Gunnar Myrdal has a discussion of inequality of income in *Asian Drama* (New York, 1968), pp. 563 ff.
[2] P. C. Mahalanobis, "Science and National Planning," *Sankhya: The Indian Journal of Statistics*, Vol. 20, Parts 1 and 2 (September 1958), pp. 74-75.

solution to the problem. But with very few exceptions—such as oil-rich, underpopulated Kuwait—the underdeveloped world is not all that fortunate in its natural resources.

It is, of course, possible to industrialize in spite of being poorly endowed with natural resources. Denmark has no resources "except the sites to put the factories on."[3] Japan is not much better endowed than Denmark. The fact that both countries were able to develop a highly skilled labor force prevented the burden of having to import raw materials from becoming more of an obstacle to industrialization than it was. With a highly skilled labor force, manufactured goods were still economic in spite of the costs of importing raw materials. As labor became even more highly skilled, capital could be substituted for labor, which further increased the productivity of labor and made the need to import raw materials still less of a burden. As Gunnar Myrdal points out, resources become much more significant as either an asset or obstacle when labor is not skilled, when work discipline and efficiency are low, and when capital is scarce. Resources can become a source of foreign exchange and capital if they are plentiful, on the one hand, and, on the other hand, a drain on foreign exchange and capital if they have to be imported.

In Asia, the natural endowment of most countries is poor. Only India and Korea have the coal, iron, and other raw materials to sustain a high degree of industrialization, and both of them are handicapped by lack of oil. Taiwan has coal, sulphur, natural gas, and some timber. The Philippines have iron ore, copper, gold, manganese, chromium, and a few other minerals, as well as valuable timber. Pakistan has oil, chromite, and natural gas, but only inferior coal and iron ore. Most of the countries of South and Southeast Asia have only one or two major minerals. Burma has tin, tungsten, copper, lead, and zinc deposits. Sri Lanka has graphite. Indonesia, Malaysia, and Thailand all have tin deposits. Indonesia leads in petroleum deposits, although they represent only 1.6 per cent of the world's proven reserves. Most of the countries have important forest reserves—with the notable exceptions of Korea, India, and Pakistan.

[3] The phrase is Gunnar Myrdal's.

Speaking of South Asia, Gunnar Myrdal concludes that India alone possesses enough of the required resources to concentrate on heavy industry in its strategy of industrialization. "For the most part," he writes, "the industrial resources of the other countries do not appear adequate to support large-scale, indigenous manufacturing activity." It is possible that future discoveries will be made, he goes on to say, but present information suggests that South Asia has not been generously endowed. "Nor do any of the countries, except India, have an appropriate combination of resources for industrial development. Each country has one or several types of natural resource, but a favorable combination of them is conspicuous by its absence."[4] The same conclusion applies to the whole of non-Communist Asia, with Korea being the only possible exception.

The potential for agriculture in Asia also appears to be limited. Myrdal points out that land resources are generally poor— "either because they were so to begin with or because they have been damaged by overcrowding and the climate."[5] The great river valleys of Burma, Thailand, and Vietnam are rice bowls and have been traditionally net exporters of rice. But war and population changes have been reducing the surplus available for sale abroad. Ceylon has excellent land for the cultivation of tea, coconuts, and rubber, although it is limited in extent. Malaysia and Indonesia have considerable land suitable for rubber. Malaysia, Thailand, Burma, Sri Lanka, and the Philippines— as mentioned above—also have large areas of forest that have not yet been fully utilized. Finally, adequate surveys have yet to be made in most of Asia. Nevertheless, Myrdal concludes, "it seems improbable that most of the countries [of Asia] will ever equal the average Western country in raw materials."[6]

The Middle East

With the notable exception of oil, the countries of the Middle East and North Africa are if anything even worse off than those of Asia. The oil supplies of the Middle East, of course, are

[4] *Asian Drama*, p. 516.
[5] Ibid., p. 677.
[6] Ibid.

fantastic. The Middle East contains two thirds of the world's total oil reserves and accounts for a third of the world's total production of oil.[7] For North Africa, production is about one fifth of the Middle East's and the known reserves are considerably less, although ultimately more reserves may be discovered.[8]

Other mineral resources in the Middle East and North Africa cannot compare with oil. Phosphates, however, do occur in abundance. Morocco supplies 20 per cent of the world's total production. More modest supplies are found of iron, salt, coal, lead, chrome, potash, manganese, sulphur, and cobalt.

The potential for agriculture in the Middle East is also discouraging. From Morocco to Iran between one half and four fifths of the population are engaged in agriculture on about one fifth of the land area. The problem is lack of water. The cultivable land is fertile, but without sufficient supplies of water, production is low. The climate also prevents full utilization of the available soil. Torrential rains wash away topsoil and erode the land during the rainy season, and the sun bakes the soil hard during the dry season. Forests have been denuded, and everywhere the land has been overgrazed. The quality of the land in consequence is low.[9] The southern regions of the area are so arid that in the past they could support only nomads, following their flocks of camels, goats, and sheep in a yearly migration.

The key to any agricultural development in the Middle East and North Africa is irrigation. In ancient times, irrigation was practiced on a large scale, and it could be done again. Five river systems—the Tigris, the Euphrates, the Litani, the Jordan, and the Nile—if properly harnessed could increase arable land by eight million acres, and much of the increase could be three-crop land. The implications of developing and extending irrigation networks are great indeed in countries with poorly nourished populations dependent on grain imports. Israel's experience with modern irrigation techniques is suggestive. In 1967, 40

[7] A. J. Meyer, "Economic Modernization," *The Middle East: Yesterday and Today*, eds. David W. Miller and Clark D. Moore (New York, 1970), p. 281.
[8] John H. Lichtblau, "Oil in the North African Economy," *State and Society in Independent North Africa*, ed. Leon Carl Brown (Washington, D.C.: The Middle East Institute, 1966), p. 270.
[9] Arthur Mills, "Present-Day Economic and Social Conditions," *The Middle East: Yesterday and Today*, p. 285.

per cent of Israel's arable land was irrigated. In that same year Israel's agricultural exports reached $140 million, as compared with less than $20 million in 1948. Other modern agricultural techniques, such as increased use of fertilizers, mechanization, and reforestation, have also helped increase production.[10]

Tropical Africa

Iron ore is mined in Mauritania, Guinea, Sierra Leone, Liberia, Angola, and Rhodesia.[11] Since coal is close by only in Rhodesia, the ores of most of these countries are exported. Other minerals include copper, lead, zinc, columbite, cadmium, lithium ores, bauxite, cobalt, and industrial diamonds. So far, mineral wealth is concentrated—three countries account for three quarters of present production in tropical Africa, and fewer than ten countries have production of any significance. Further exploration, however, may well reveal even greater deposits than those now known.

In terms of energy resources, the picture is better. There is little petroleum or coal of the better grades. But there is a wealth of water power and the raw materials of nuclear power.

The fact that Africa is a "plateau" continent is significant for transportation as well as agriculture. Behind narrow coastal plains are scarp zones that form a barrier and also make the rivers less suitable for navigation than they are on most other continents. The rivers not only have rapids but also a high seasonal variation in the rate of flow.

The soils of Africa are generally poor. Badly structured and leached latosols cover most of the savanna and rainforest areas. The soils of the semi-arid regions are also poor in quality if compared with those of similar regions in other continents. Overall, the conclusion is that African soil and climate are not well suited for efficient agricultural production. One authority puts it as follows: "The soils of Africa form a patchwork of very varied quality, but on the whole they are inferior to those in tropical

[10] Economic Resource Service, U. S. Department of Agriculture, *Israel's Agricultural Economy in Brief* (Washington, D.C., February 1969), p. 1.
[11] The authoritative work on African economic development is William A. Hance, *African Economic Development*, rev. ed. (New York, 1967). The following section draws on it heavily.

South America. They are worse than those of Southeast Asia but better than South India and the eroded hills of southern China."[12] The pronounced rainy and dry seasons take a toll from the land as well. The heavy, driving rains wash away topsoil. The dry season often brings harsh, hot winds, such as the harmattan off the Sahara, which parch the land and make cultivation difficult.

Three fifths of Africa as a whole and two fifths of tropical Africa are steppe or desert with inadequate supplies of water. One third of the tropical portion is savanna with enough rain but great variation in the different seasons, which makes production undependable. Water control and irrigation projects offer some hope. If ways could be found to desalt water economically and pump it to the dry areas, the results would be stupendous.

Latin America

Latin America's phenomenal diversity, ranging from the arid deserts in northern Mexico to the glacier-carved, snow-capped peaks of Tierra del Fuego, precludes simple generalizations. Some countries, such as Panama, possess little more than a favorable geographic location. Others, such as Brazil, comprise vast regions containing numerous valuable minerals. Brazil has one of the last great frontiers on earth—the 2.3 million square miles of the Amazon River basin—a territory equal in size to all of Europe from the Atlantic to the Dnieper. Although the Amazon basin covers more than half of Brazil's total area, the "green hell" of the rain forest contains only 8 per cent of the population and produces only 4 per cent of the national income. However, untapped riches lie underneath the steaming jungles. In 1967, geologists located what are believed to be the world's largest iron ore reserves. Bauxite and manganese deposits are also being mined. Brazil ranks with the Soviet Union and India as a leading producer of manganese, one of the world's great deposits of which is located in southwestern Mato Grosso.[13]

12 René Dumont, *False Start in Africa*, trans. Phyllis Nauts Ott (New York, 1966), pp. 28–29.
13 "Conquest of the Amazon: How High a Price?," *Newsweek*, LXXX (July 3, 1972), pp. 24–30.

Other portions of the South American continent are also well endowed with valuable minerals. Extensive, high-grade iron ore deposits have been discovered close to the surface, and cheap, open-pit mining is feasible. Chile and Peru own vast copper ores. Only the great copper mines in North America and Central Africa compare with the enormous Chilean deposits. Total tin resources in the Bolivian Andes are estimated to rank third in the world, behind Southeast Asia and Equatorial Africa. South America also has considerable bauxite, which is especially plentiful in the Guianas and northern Brazil; silver in Peru and Bolivia; platinum in Columbia; and nitrates in Chile.

Central America's mineral resources are relatively modest. Some gold, silver, zinc, lead, copper, and small amounts of nonmetallic minerals are produced. No commercial deposits of mineral fuels are known.

On the other hand, South America is well endowed with petroleum. Roughly one fourth of the area contains sedimentary basins that might have oil-bearing strata. Venezuela has by far the largest petroleum resources, and ranks second in the Western Hemisphere and seventh in the world. Argentina, Colombia, Peru, and Bolivia also have large proven petroleum reserves.

Unlike North America, however, South America has almost no coal. Only three countries—Colombia, Chile, and Brazil—have even a modest production. Hydroelectric power is a little more extensive. By the mid-1960s less than 10 per cent of the Andes' estimated hydroelectric power potential had been harnessed. On the eastern half of the continent, the Amazon River systems have more than eight hundred miles of navigable waterways; but there are few possibilities for power development because the slopes are too gentle.

More than most of continents of the underdeveloped world, Latin America is favorably endowed for agriculture—even though the region is subject to wide variations in climate and only a small percentage of potential agricultural land is under cultivation. One third of Latin America lies in the temperate zone; the rest is in the tropics. Wide climatic variations exist, sometimes within thirty miles of each other. Some 3.7 billion acres of land in Latin America are under cultivation, including forestry. Although 20 per cent of all Latin American land is potentially arable, only 8 per cent is so far used. Much of the forested land is inaccessible, and the rest has been scarcely touched.[14] In some areas, conditions are so favorable as to be exceptional. Part of the Argentine pampas rivals the American corn belt, and "with the exception of California, middle Chile is probably the best farming country anywhere. . . ."[15]

In the temperate zones, the land suitable for agriculture is settled, and agriculture is well developed. Increases in production will depend on the use of fertilizer and modern techniques and a favorable government policy. For the tropical areas, increases in production can be brought about by developing the vast areas that remain untouched.

Structure of the Economies: Asia

The structure of the economies in Asian countries, shaped mainly by colonialism, is frequently inappropriate to rapid industrialization. The industrial sector is small. What is more, an unusually large proportion of manufacturing is in consumer goods, with production concentrated mainly in cottage industry. Manufacturing also lacks diversity. The infrastructure of ports, transportation systems, and the rest is rarely adequate. Agriculture is the major element in the production of national income. Where plantations are an important element in agriculture, the output is highest. Intensive use of land can support large populations, as in the river valleys, where wet paddy cultivation is practiced. When the ratio of people to land is high and agriculture is extensive, as in India and Pakistan, income is lowest and nutrition is poorest.

Structure of the Economies: Middle East

The structure of the economies of Middle Eastern countries is similar to those of Asia, except when oil is present. The modern

[14] Montague Yudelman and Frederic Howard, *Agricultural Development and Economic Integration in Latin America* (Inter-American Development Bank, April 1969), pp. 1–5.
[15] Theodore W. Schultz, *Economic Growth and Agriculture* (New York, 1968), p. 176.

sector of most economies is small, including food processing, leather and textile production, ceramics, mineral processing, and glass and cement making. The traditional sector comprises handicrafts, such as carpet weaving, and some small-scale food processing, such as milling and oil pressing. As in most developing countries, large numbers of people flock to the cities looking for factory jobs and fail to find any. Rapid urbanization is combined with wretched poverty.

The economic infrastructure in the Middle East is more encouraging. Parts of the area were important in the transit trade and developed good communication and transportation systems. The roads and railroads of Morocco are an example. For the rest, it is somewhat better than in many other underdeveloped regions.

The man-to-land ratios constitute another favorable element, with the exception of such countries as Lebanon and Israel. Where the man-to-land ratio is good and oil is plentiful, the future seems very bright indeed. Iraq, which also has a good water supply, is a case in point.

Structure of the Economies: North Africa

In parts of North Africa a modern agricultural system exists side by side with a traditional one. The modern farms are mechanized, irrigated, and use selected seeds and plants and modern marketing techniques.[16] The produce is geared toward European markets, and absentee ownership is frequent. In the traditional sector, the wooden plow and other rudimentary tools are still prevalent. Irrigation is nonexistent. Small holdings predominate, and portions of the output are bartered for essentials that cannot be produced on the farm. The modern farms, as would be expected, take up the best land, yielding three to four times as much as the poorer. The problems that result from all this are sometimes nothing short of ludicrous. Algeria, to give a rather special example, produces half a billion gallons of wine a year. The Muslim religion prohibits drinking any form of alcohol, and most of the Europeans emigrated at the time of independence. So

[16] Charles F. Gallagher, *The United States and North Africa: Morocco, Algeria, Tunisia* (Cambridge, 1963), p. 148.

virtually the entire wine crop must be exported, mainly to France, which doesn't really need it. As one author sums it up: "two thousand hectares of Algerian land is devoted to a product which cannot be consumed in the country, is unneeded abroad and is occupying land which might be used for food production in a country that must import food."[17]

Structure of the Economies: Tropical Africa

The structure of the economies of the countries of tropical Africa is even more of an obstacle to development than in most of the other underdeveloped areas of the world. In general, tropical Africa is in transition from a subsistence to an exchange economy. Manufacturing and industry are a tiny part of the gross national product. Most manufacturing involves the primary processing of export products, which do not require large work forces and add little to domestic economic development. Around the cities, the new industry is concentrated in textiles, food processing, and other consumption articles. The picture is one of islands of economic activity surrounded by vast undeveloped areas lacking in transportation, communication, or exchange facilities, with the people scratching out a bare subsistence. Large numbers have flocked to the islands of activity—the cities—undeterred by the lack of jobs, the lack of housing, the lack of all forms of necessities, even water.

In agriculture, traditional methods are still practiced in many areas. This so-called shifting cultivation is essentially the slash/burn technique of Southeast Asia. The ground cover is burned, the ashes serving as fertilizer, and the land is cultivated until it is exhausted. The whole tribe or community then picks up and moves on to repeat the process elsewhere.

Population pressure and governmental prodding have replaced the traditional method in most countries of Africa with slightly more modern techniques. The farmers stay in one place, cultivate specific areas, and have rights to holdings that extend to the area in bush fallow.[18] The sizes of the farms vary greatly, with

17 Ibid., pp. 149–50.
18 John C. de Wilde et al., *Experience with Agricultural Development in Tropical Africa*, International Bank for Reconstruction and Development (Baltimore, Maryland: The Johns Hopkins University Press, 1967), p. 19.

some almost as large as a plantation. The individual farmer usually has some land producing cash crops, such as groundnuts, coffee, cacao, or cotton, and the rest is used for subsistence. But the lack of a modern market economy and modern transportation and communication systems retards specialization—70 per cent of the land and 60 per cent of the labor force are devoted to subsistence.

Structure of the Economies: Latin America

The structure of the economies of the Latin American countries is considerably more complex than those of most of the underdeveloped countries, partly stemming from their history and partly from the fact that Latin America is generally farther along on the path to development.

The history of economic development in Latin America explains a portion of their present difficulty. First, from common Spanish and Portuguese colonial backgrounds came similar systems of land ownership with high concentrations of wealth in the hands of a very small percentage of the population. These early large land appropriations to the conquistadors were duplicated by later concessions to large plantation and mining interests.

Second, much of the extractive and agricultural primary sector of the Latin American economies is owned by foreigners. For instance, the United Fruit Company holds enormous plantations in six different Latin American countries, and three different private foreign companies formerly controlled copper mining in Chile. Thus where demand for primary products increased—as in copper, tin, lead, petroleum, and silver—much of the revenue leaked out of the Latin American countries into foreign coffers. Similarly, foreign-owned plantations siphoned off domestic revenues. Even domestic producers of such products as cotton, sugar, bananas, coffee, and cacao, who have increased production significantly, have not benefited the majority of the population, due to the lopsided land ownership.

In the manufacturing sector, growth began during the Great Depression and World War II as imports became more difficult to obtain. Much of this growth occurred in textiles, food, and other small consumer goods, which were formerly supplied by a handi-craft type of manufacturing. This was labor-intensive, and as the more capital-intensive, modern techniques have replaced the tra-ditional methods, unemployment has risen.

The increased use of technology in farming, the natural in-crease in population, and the manufacturing expansion have led to a rapid influx of people to the urban centers and a proliferation of the "shanty towns" that are a common feature of the cities and large towns of Latin America.

In agriculture, it is the pattern of ownership that is the great-est obstacle to further development. The large farms, or *lati-fundios*, owned by 10 per cent of the farmers, take up 90 per cent of the land in most countries and 100 per cent of the *best* land.[19] Although the internal organization of the *latifundios* var-ies somewhat, generally speaking they have a monopolistic structure, very low income for the workers, deplorable social conditions, and absentee ownership. In many cases, the so-called *colono* system of labor prevails. This permits temporary or tradi-tional use of a parcel of land and other privileges in lieu of cash payment, combined, in most cases, with tenancy or share-crop-ping.

In the other 90 per cent of the farms—the *minifundios*—the holdings are usually too small even to support one family ade-quately. Fragmentation, shifting cultivation, rapid population growth, exhausted land, and no contact with the market economy exacerbates the trouble. A measure of the problem can be seen in the high proportion of small farms in so many countries. In Ecuador and Peru, 90 per cent of the farms are too small to pro-vide a reasonable living for a family. In Colombia the figure is 67 per cent. In Guatemala and Brazil it is almost as bad. Even in Argentina and Chile, about 40 per cent of the farms are too small for a single family.

The Terms of Trade

One final set of observations about the structure of the econo-mies and agriculture should be made that applies to all of the un-

[19] Thomas F. Carroll, "The Land Reform Issue in Latin America," *Latin America: Issues, Essays, and Comments,* ed. Albert O. Hirschman (New York: Twentieth Century Fund, 1961), p. 164.

derdeveloped countries. It concerns their trade, balance of payments, and prospect for obtaining foreign capital needed for development. The trading pattern of the underdeveloped countries is usually not regional, but with the developed countries, which are mostly distant. A second characteristic of the trading pattern is that most of the underdeveloped countries are dependent on one or two products for export, which makes their balance of payments peculiarly vulnerable. A third characteristic is that these products tend to be raw materials. Consequently, the demand from the developed countries is relatively inelastic, and their imports of these products do not increase proportionately with economic growth. A study of the prospects to 1980 for exports from South Asia, for example, concludes that the "outlook is positively gloomy for such commodities as tea, sugar, cotton, and jute."[20] In general, the same thing can be said for most of the products exported by the underdeveloped world, with the notable exceptions of petroleum and liquefied natural gas. For most of the underdeveloped countries, the prospects for acquiring capital for development through trade are not bright.

Over-all Prospects

On purely economic grounds, to sum up, the prospects for development are discouraging. In Asia, only India has enough of the required resources to concentrate on heavy industry in its strategy of industrialization. The potential for agriculture is not good. The Middle East has oil but little else. What potential for agriculture that exists requires extensive irrigation systems. Africa has a potential in water power and uranium for nuclear power, and a variety of minerals are produced in a few African countries. But it cannot be said that Africa is rich in resources, nor is the potential for agriculture encouraging. Of all the developing world, Latin America is best endowed with minerals of all kinds, the only exception being coal. The prospects for agriculture are also better than in the other underdeveloped regions.

In terms of the structure of their economies, every one of the underdeveloped regions suffers from imbalance, feeble industrial

[20] *UN Economic Bulletin for Asia and the Far East* (December 1963), p.15.

sectors, ownership and land tenure problems, generally unbalanced and unfavorable trade balances, and lack of capital and foreign exchange.

On purely economic grounds, to repeat, the prospects for development are discouraging. Kuwait, with its fantastic oil production and tiny population, can say that economic factors are highly favorable for its development. Iraq, too, is in a good position. But the number of other underdeveloped countries that can be optimistic are pitifully few.

CHAPTER 13

Obstacles to Development: Government, Attitudes, Education, Health, and Population

IF ECONOMIC RESOURCES are a hindrance rather than a help to development, even more formidable are other obstacles: the quality of government and other institutions, social attitudes and customs, education, health, and the threat of an ever-increasing population.

Some of these obstacles to modernization and development have already been discussed in the chapter on the process of development and can be summed up here in very general terms. One of these is the quality of government. What we said before needs little elaboration. Economic development is impossible with a government so weak that it cannot keep peace, so corrupt that taxes are diverted to the officials' numbered bank accounts in Switzerland, or so incompetent that major programs collapse in a morass of inefficiency.

The need for other institutions of quality is equally obvious.

A modernized, developed country could hardly exist without universities, for example. Banks and a banking system are needed, whether governmental or private; postal and communications networks; transportation systems; health facilities; and on down through a long list.

Social Attitudes and Customs

Social attitudes and customs as obstacles to development and modernization have also already been discussed. Superstition, primitive notions of time, and indifference to punctuality are all examples of attitudes that form obstacles to modernization. So are religious or philosophical beliefs that see mankind in strata ordained by God or nature. To be ambitious in such a belief system is to be blasphemous.

Max Weber suggested that modernization and industrialization were related to the "Protestant ethic," that man earned his salvation in heaven through his hard work on earth. Actually, it seems more likely that the work ethic develops gradually with industrialization, but there is no doubt that the lack of the set of attitudes lumped under the notion of the "work" or "industrial" ethic is an enormous handicap to a country at the beginning of industrialization and modernization.

Many social institutions work the same way to impede modernization. The land tenure system is the most common example, but there are others. Marriage customs can work to form an obstacle, as can the customs or laws of inheritance. The extended family system, again, is another example. An individual is expected to care for the members of his extended family when good fortune comes his way rather than advance his own interests. As a consequence, the small entrepreneur often has difficulty separating family and business interests, especially when he is expected to utilize company funds to help family members. Tribal ties often foster similar relationships. Traditionally, there has been little difference in the tribal members' individual economic status, since resources have been exploited in common for the group's rather than the individual's benefit.

Whatever their cause, the fact is that the prevailing attitudes and patterns of individual behavior in the developing countries are contrary to those needed for development. There are, in Gunnar Myrdal's words, "low levels of work discipline, punctuality, and orderliness; superstitious beliefs and irrational outlook; lack of alertness, adaptability, ambition, and general readiness for change and experiment; contempt for manual work; submissiveness to authority and exploitation; low aptitude for cooperation; low standards of personal hygiene. . . ."[1] And to all this, as we shall see, is an "unreadiness for deliberate and sustained birth control," which has consequences that are nothing less than profound.

Education

Education is as much an accumulation of capital as roads, dams, and industrial plants. The simplest and most obvious example of how important education is to development is literacy: A peasant farmer will be more productive if he can read instructions for planting, fertilizing, and caring for his crop. A worker must be able to read the manuals on the care and operation of his machine. The very first steps of economic development become impossible if a population is not functionally literate—if farmers and workers are not able to read instructions and do the simple mathematical calculations that permit them to operate effectively at their jobs. At each stage of development, more and more people with higher and higher levels of education are needed. Functionally literate peasants and workers, along with at least a few planners and managers, are essential at the earliest stage. At subsequent stages, engineers will be key, engineers to design and build roads, railroads, canals, dams, power plants, factories, and all the rest. Still later, in the final stages, it will be research scientists to create new technology to keep pace and sustain growth, and managers, computer operators, and the other personnel necessary for large-scale, complex enterprises.

If the common-sense view that education is vital to development is not persuasive, economists have supplied support from their research. A number of economists have weighted the in-

[1] *Asian Drama* (New York, 1968), p. 1,862.

crease of gross national product attributable to inputs of capital and labor and concluded that the "residual" increase, which is substantial, must be the result of improvements in the quality of labor—in other words, to improvements in education and skills.[2]

Paul G. Hoffman, managing director of the United Nations Special Fund, has pointed out that the underdeveloped countries need high-level manpower just as urgently as they need capital. "Indeed," he goes on to say, "unless these countries are able to develop the required strategic human resources they cannot effectively absorb capital."[3]

What is more, in countries composed of a variety of tribes, cultures, and languages, education can be a necessary precondition for national unity. Without it, as one authority points out, communication between one citizen and another or between the government and the citizenry as a whole is almost impossible and so, therefore, is the order and control that are vital to economic growth.[4]

Education is vital for economic development of the country as a whole in terms of productivity. It is equally vital for the individual in raising his personal standard of living. But education contributes more than this. It contributes to increased mobility, to adaptability to changing conditions, as Harbison and Myers point out, and to willingness to apply technology. Education, in fact, is probably the major factor in changing the traditional atti-

[2] Theodore W. Schultz is prominent in this work. See his "Investment in Human Capital," *The American Economic Review* (March 1961); "Education and Economic Growth," *Social Forces Influencing American Education, 1961,* the Sixtieth Yearbook of the National Society for the Study of Education, Part 2, ed. Nelson B. Henry (Chicago: University of Chicago Press, 1961); "Capital Formation by Education," *Journal of Political Economy* (December 1960). See also the following: Simon Kuznets, *Six Lectures on Economic Growth* (New York: The Free Press of Glencoe, 1959); Robert M. Solow, "Technical Change and the Aggregate Production Function," *Review of Economics and Statistics* (August 1957) and his "Technical Progress, Capital Formation, and Economic Growth," *Papers and Proceedings of the Seventy-fourth Annual Meeting of the American Economic Association, December 1961;* Edward F. Denison, "Education, Economic Growth, and Gaps in Information, *Journal of Political Economy, Supplement, October 1962;* Frederick Harbison and Charles A. Myers, *Education, Manpower, and Economic Growth* (New York, 1964).
[3] *One Hundred Countries and One and One Quarter Billion People: How to Speed Their Economic Growth and Ours—in the 1960's* (Washington, D.C.: Committee for Economic Development, 1960).
[4] Adam Curle, *Educational Problems of Developing Societies* (New York, 1969), p. 7.

tudes and customs that are such a formidable barrier to development.

And even this is not the end. Education is itself a goal of modernization. More than the material progress and wealth to which it contributes, education is part of the end goal of dignity for the individual, of self-fulfillment, of the enrichment of personal life. "The goals of modern societies . . ." as Harbison and Myers put the point, "are political, cultural, and social as well as economic. Human resource development is a necessary condition for achieving all of them. A country needs educated political leaders, lawyers and judges, trained engineers, doctors, managers, artists, writers, craftsmen, and journalists to spur its development. In an advanced economy the capacities of man are extensively developed; in a primitive country they are for the most part undeveloped. If a country is unable to develop its human resources, it cannot develop much else, whether it be a modern political and social structure, a sense of national unity, or higher standards of material welfare."[5]

If it is agreed, then, that education is a vital need for development, what is the status of the underdeveloped world in terms of education?

Illiteracy

Look first at illiteracy. To provide a standard, note that illiteracy in the Soviet Union, the United States, and Japan stands at about 2 per cent, while in Sweden it is virtually zero.

In Asia, illiteracy runs from 80 to 90 per cent in Pakistan, Nepal, Laos, and Afghanistan. In mainland China, India, Indonesia, and Malaysia it is from 50 to 80 per cent. In North and South Korea, Sri Lanka, and Mongolia it is low, between 10 and 20 per cent. In all the other countries of Asia illiteracy stands around 30 to 40 per cent.

In Latin America, Haiti has an illiteracy rate of 90 per cent, but most of Latin America is better off. Illiteracy is between 50 and 70 per cent in Bolivia, Guatemala, Honduras, and Nicaragua. It runs from 30 to 50 per cent in Brazil, Colombia, Ecuador, and

[5] *Education, Manpower, and Economic Growth*, p. 13.

Peru. It is between 20 and 30 per cent in Chile, Cuba, Mexico, Panama, Paraguay, and Venezuela. And it is less than 10 per cent in Argentina and Uruguay.

Among Middle Eastern countries, illiteracy is between 80 and 90 per cent in Algeria, Iran, Iraq, Morocco, Saudi Arabia, Southern Yemen, and Yemen. Egypt, Turkey, Tunisia, Syria, Libya, Kuwait, and Jordan have between 50 and 70 per cent illiteracy. Only Lebanon and Israel, which is not an underdeveloped country, have less than 20 per cent.

In Africa, the situation is worst of all. Of the larger countries, only three have illiteracy rates of less than 80 to 90 per cent: Nigeria and Ghana, with 75 per cent, and Zaïre, with 42 per cent. The many smaller countries—about twenty—almost invariably have rates of 80 to 95 per cent, excepting only Malagasy, Equatorial Guinea, and Mauritius.

Enrollment in Primary, Secondary, and Higher Schools

If illiteracy is a measure of the educational status of the different countries, a measure of their immediate prospects is enrollment in primary and secondary schools and enrollment in institutions of higher learning. However, it must immediately be said that enrollment figures constitute an even cruder measure than illiteracy. First, the composition of a population in terms of age levels can vastly affect the figures, and second, enrollment says nothing at all about the quality of education the students are getting. Still, it is a measure.

Again, Japan, Sweden, the United States, and the Soviet Union can provide a standard. In Japan, 18 per cent of the population are enrolled in primary and secondary schools and 1.3 per cent are students at institutions of higher learning. In Sweden, it is 15 per cent and 1.5 per cent. In the Soviet Union, 24 per cent of the population are primary or secondary school students, and 2 per cent are students at higher institutions. In the United States it is 23 per cent and 3.6 per cent.

In Asia, among the larger countries, the highest percentages for primary and secondary school enrollment are Indonesia, with 14 per cent; North Korea and Thailand, with 15 per cent; and South Korea, with 20 per cent. Burma, China, and North and

South Vietnam all range between 10 and 13 per cent. Pakistan is 7 per cent, and India is about 1 per cent.

In higher education, only North Korea rivals the more highly developed countries, with 2.4 per cent, although China does not do badly, with 1 per cent. The others range from .01 per cent for Burma and .02 per cent for Thailand to .5 per cent for Indonesia.

Among the Latin American countries, Haiti is again the worst off—6 per cent of the population is enrolled in primary or secondary schools and .03 per cent of the population in institutions of higher learning. For most of the Latin American countries, however, the enrollment in primary and secondary schools compares favorably with Sweden, Japan, the Soviet Union, and the United States. For Argentina, Brazil, Colombia, Mexico, Venezuela, Bolivia, and Chile, to pick only the larger countries, enrollment ranges from 15 per cent for Bolivia, Colombia, and Venezuela up to a high of 20 per cent for Chile.

In terms of enrollment in institutions of higher learning, Latin America does not fare so well. It is 1 per cent for Argentina and between .2 and .4 per cent for Brazil, Colombia, Mexico, Venezuela, Bolivia, and Chile.

In the Middle East, taking only the larger countries, Morocco has 8 per cent of its population enrolled in primary or secondary schools; Algeria has 10 per cent; Iran, 11 per cent; Iraq, 12 per cent; Egypt, 13 per cent; and Turkey, 16 per cent.

For students enrolled in institutions of higher learning, Egypt leads with .6 per cent; Iraq is next, with .4 per cent; Turkey is next, with .3 per cent; Iran is next, with .2 per cent; Algeria is next, with .1 per cent; and Morocco is again last, with .04 per cent.

Africa, as one would expect, is very badly off indeed. Taking only the seven countries with the largest populations, Ghana leads in enrollment in primary and secondary schools with 15 per cent of the population; Zaïre is second, with 13 per cent; Kenya is third, with 10 per cent; Tanzania is fourth, with 6 per cent; Nigeria is fifth, with 5 per cent; Sudan is next, with 3 per cent; and Ethiopia is last, with 2 per cent.

The order changes when it comes to enrollment in institutions of higher learning, although the figures are still very, very low.

Nigeria is first, with .07 per cent; Ghana is next, with .06 per cent; Kenya, Zaïre, and Sudan follow with .05 per cent, .03 per cent, and .02 per cent, respectively; and Tanzania and Ethiopia are last, with .01 per cent.

Dropout Rate

These statistics, as we said, give only a crude measure of the educational problems of the underdeveloped countries. In fact, they are actually misleading. The dropout rate, for example, is extraordinarily high. Frequently, according to one authority, less than 20 per cent complete the first five or six years of primary school, and in some areas between half and two thirds of the expenditure on primary education is fruitless. "In Ghana, in fact," he goes on to say, "it was once calculated that it took 26 school years to produce one primary school graduate. This is appallingly wasteful. It is wasteful of human potential, and it is wasteful economically in that only one graduate has been produced for an outlay that could have produced as many as five."[6]

Myrdal points out that in Pakistan only 15 per cent of those beginning primary school actually finish it, and only 40 per cent in Indonesia. In India, the distribution of children among the different grades in primary and secondary schools vividly illustrates the point. Instead of being divided evenly among grades 1 through 12, enrollment declines precipitously: Twenty-nine per cent of the boys and 36 per cent of the girls are enrolled in the first grade, while only 16.5 per cent of the boys and 18.7 per cent of the girls are enrolled in the second grade; by the sixth grade, it is 6.2 per cent of the boys and 4.6 per cent of the girls; by the eleventh and twelfth grades, it is 1.3 per cent of the boys and 0.7 per cent of the girls.[7]

The reasons for the high dropout rate are varied. One is the school environment. If school is conducted in a building rather than under a tree, it is hot in summer and cold in winter. Even more important is the usual level of teaching. Many of the teachers have less than ten years of schooling themselves. The meth-

[6] Curle, op. cit., p. 48.
[7] Myrdal, op. cit., p. 1,795.

ods are frequently recitation by rote, accompanied by threats, beatings, kicks, cuffs, and pinching. The teachers are likely to regard able students as a personal threat. "It is hardly surprising," Curle writes, "that for most primary age children schooling is an experience at once tedious, frightening, and pointless. Naturally the younger they are, the more they suffer from it. In fact there can be little doubt that the major cause of dropouts throughout primary education, and particularly during the first year, is the abysmally low standard of education, and the misery which this involves for the student."[8]

Frequently, and especially at the university level, teachers are part-time, "meeting crowded classes during the morning or evening and holding down other jobs in government or in a profession. . . ." It has been estimated that in Mexico the proportion of part-time professors in colleges and universities is as high as 70 per cent.[9]

Another cause of the high dropout rate is the fact that in many underdeveloped countries, the incentive for education is low. Children are more useful working in the fields or with the animals than in school, and school contributes almost nothing to their capacity to do that kind of work. The so-called "hunger for knowledge," as Myrdal argues, is largely a myth. "The masses of people in countries like those in South Asia do not calculate rationally in terms of costs, returns, and maximum profit; often, indeed, they are not interested in raising their living levels. This fact, which is well brought out in Kusum Nair's important book, *Blossoms in the Dust,* and confirmed by anthropological studies all over the world, means that education, even when directed toward practical problems of development, does not provoke an immediate response among the people, least of all in the village."[10]

Even when people in the underdeveloped countries do calculate rationally, the incentive for education may be low. As Curle points out, school enrollments in the underdeveloped countries have normally expanded more rapidly than the economy, so that

[8] Curle, op. cit., pp. 52–53.
[9] Harbison and Myers, op. cit., p. 124.
[10] Myrdal, op. cit., p. 1,692.

there are not enough jobs in the modern sector to go around among the graduates who are qualified to perform them.[11]

One of the greatest of the many ironies concerning education in the developing countries is that a principal cause of both the high dropout rate and low literacy is the shortage of materials for either writing or reading. "One of the main reasons why minimum literacy is often not transformed into functional literacy and why the barely literate lapse into illiteracy is that people have nothing to read and no paper on which to write."[12]

Miseducation

One of the most disturbing aspects of education in the underdeveloped countries is that it is frequently *miseducation*. Myrdal puts the point as follows: "The South Asian peoples are not merely being insufficiently educated; they are being miseducated on a huge scale. And there are important vested interests, embedded in the whole attitudinal and institutional system, that resist or warp policies intended to overcome both deficiencies."[13] One of the attitudes at fault, as we have already mentioned, is that education is valued because it is a way of *escaping* manual labor, yet skilled manual labor is what is most necessary for development. In Sri Lanka (formerly Ceylon), for example, children are tested at age 14 to separate the able from the less able. The able go to academic secondary schools. Only the less able will follow "practical" subjects and enter industry at the bottom to work their way up. As a result, "Ceylon will fail to produce enough of that type of man on whom industry is peculiarly dependent—the shop foreman. He is the man who, in Western industrialized societies, entered the works at the bottom, worked at the bench and in the foundry, and made his way upward through native ability. As foreman he stands as a link between practice and theory."[14]

As Harbison and Myers point out, in most underdeveloped

[11] Curle, op. cit., p. 15.
[12] Myrdal, op. cit., p. 1,696.
[13] Ibid., p. 1,649.
[14] T. L. Green, "Ceylon: Case Study of Educational Evaluation and Social Progress," *The Year Book of Education*, 1954 (New York: Teachers College, Columbia University, 1954), p. 616, as cited ibid., p. 1,762.

countries, the high-prestige occupations are not usually the most critically needed for development. Landlords, lawyers, government officials, owners of large family enterprises, and military leaders enjoy both high status and political power, while the status of professional engineers and scientists is usually low. "A social structure of this kind obviously is an obstacle to growth along modern lines; and it must be drastically changed if the newly articulated goals of the partially developed countries are to be achieved."[15]

The tendency to miseducation derives first from the individual and his incentives. Who wants to be a mere technician or agriculturist if he is bright enough and his family well enough off to permit him to go to a university and become a top leader in government, commerce, or industry?

But the government is equally at fault in most countries. Harbison and Myers, for example, call attention to the unpublished report of the federal government of Nigeria stating that in 1962 each of four new universities was opening faculties of law, despite the fact that there were 1,213 lawyers in Nigeria, half of whom were underemployed.[16]

This pattern of investing in the wrong kind of education for education is widespread. "Both Egypt and India, for example, produce more secondary school and university graduates than their countries can employ. In both cases there are large numbers of unemployed law, arts, and humanities graduates. And both are exporters of educated or high-talent manpower."[17]

Some exceptions do exist. China has taken draconian measures to downgrade the classics, law, the humanities, and the arts and to expand university and subuniversity work concentrating on industrial specialties. Radical reform in education has apparently been a keystone in China's forced-draft industrialization.

The governments of most underdeveloped countries, in other words, have given first priority to primary education and to university education. The emphasis is understandable although paradoxical. There are strong political pressures for the high

[15] *Education, Manpower, and Economic Growth*, p. 92.
[16] Ibid., p. 85.
[17] Ibid., p. 183.

priority for primary education, and universities are symbols of national prestige and grandeur. Irrationally, the secondary schools, which are most relevant to economic development, are neglected. Indeed, secondary schools in the developing countries are commonly private, fee-charging institutions. The secondary school bottleneck, as Harbison and Myers contend, is probably the greatest obstacle in the path of economic and social progress.

There is also great imbalance within the secondary school system itself. Academic secondary schools prepare for entry into the university, and these attract the most students and the best students. The technical schools, which prepare for lower positions in commerce, industry, and government, attract fewer students and less able students. The teacher-training or normal schools attract the fewest and least able of all. In Latin America, for example, the majority of secondary students are in academic schools; 10 per cent are in normal or commercial schools; 5 per cent are in industrial schools; and the fewest of all are in agricultural schools. This is true even in China, which as we have seen has done rather well in directing its educational system toward the necessities of development. In 1957, 4,196,000 students were enrolled in general secondary schools; 273,000 were enrolled in vocational schools, including industrial, commercial, and agricultural schools; and 337,000 were enrolled in normal schools.[18]

Education is essential for development, and education in the underdeveloped countries of the world is deplorable. If development is to proceed, something drastic will have to be done. Doing something drastic will be costly, but just how costly, no one really knows. It has been estimated that developing countries as a whole spend around 10 billion dollars annually on education—roughly 4 per cent of their GNP—although one tenth of the 10 billion dollars comes from external sources.[19] Several plans have also been drawn up by international conferences for expanding education in the developing countries under the sponsorship of UNESCO. The Karachi Plan, which aimed at expanding primary education in fifteen Asian countries, set a

18 Ibid., p. 81.
19 Philip H. Coombs, *The World Educational Crisis* (New York: Oxford University Press, 1968), p. 150.

goal of increasing expenditure on primary education from 1.2 billion U.S. dollars in 1961 to 2.8 billion dollars in 1980—for primary education only. The Addis Ababa Plan, aimed at increasing education at all levels throughout Africa, set a goal of increasing expenditure from 584 million U.S. dollars in 1961 to 2.6 billion U.S. dollars in 1980. The Santiago Plan, concerned with all levels of education throughout Latin America, set a goal of increasing expenditure from about 8 billion U.S. dollars in 1961 to 34 billion dollars in 1980. The total amounts to a fourfold increase in a period of 20 years. Yet the fact of the matter is that the figure represents a much more modest gain than it appears if population increases are taken into consideration, even though some gain in gross national product can also be anticipated.

Taking the developing countries as a whole, it seems highly likely that education will improve only very slowly over the next generation—until the year 2000—except in rare instances. And even in those countries where education does improve substantially, the gain will probably be the consequence of a near-miracle of effort both by the country itself and some outside friends who make significant contributions.

Health

As with education, health is as much a goal of modernization and development as a means to it.

That modernization and development cannot be achieved without better health is obvious. How can people work productively and efficiently when they are sick or weakened by chronic, debilitating disease? It has been estimated, for example, that three quarters of the people in northeastern Thailand are infected with liver fluke, a painful and debilitating parasite. An extraordinarily high percentage of the peasants in both Egypt and China are infected with a similar parasite, schistosomiasis. In South Asia, before DDT came into widespread use, malaria attacks ranged from one attack per person per year to one attack per person in three years. It is reasonable to suppose, Gunnar Myrdal concludes, that virtually everyone in South Asia was suffering from malaria. Although malaria has a very low case-fatality ratio, in some countries of Asia, malaria accounted for 20 per cent of all deaths.[20] "In one area of the Philippines, "according to one authority," daily absenteeism in the labor force due to malaria was 35 per cent; after initiation of an antimalaria program, absenteeism was reduced to less than 4 per cent and 20 to 25 per cent fewer workers were required for any given task than was previously the case. In Haiti it was estimated that a yaws eradication campaign returned 100,000 incapacitated workers to their jobs.[21]

But even if good health were not an essential means to modernization and development, it would still be a principal goal. The very purpose of modernization and development is to eliminate human misery and attain human fulfillment. Bad health and high early death rates are a principal source of human misery and an obstacle to human fulfillment. Bad health means pain for much of one's life. Bad health means seeing children suffering and dying, often not just one child but most of the children of a large family.

Some of the misery of humanity is caused by overpopulation, as we shall see, and another essential means to modernization and development is control of population. But bad health can never be accepted as a means for controlling population, even though better health will undoubtedly lower death rates and in the absence of other steps cause still further rises in population growth. As we say, good health is one of the primary goals of modernization and development, and that means good health for all the people in all the world.

But the magnitude of the problem is formidable. The United States is one of the most highly developed countries in the world. Yet it is estimated that twelve million Americans are inadequately fed, and the presumption is that as many as three or four times that many receive inadequate medical care.[22] In the many underdeveloped countries the situation is unimaginably worse. It has been estimated that one half of the world's popula-

[20] *Asian Drama*, p. 1,569.
[21] John Bryant, *Health and the Developing World* (Ithaca, New York: Cornell University Press, 1969), pp. 98–99.
[22] New York *Times* (May 7, 1973), from a study by the staff of the Senate Select Committee on Nutrition and Human Needs, "Hunger—1973."

tion receives no medical care at all and that for a majority of the rest, the care they do receive is grossly inadequate and usually inappropriate to the diseases from which they suffer.[23]

Encouraging Progress

Yet in spite of these dismal facts, great strides have been made in the period since World War II, much of it due to DDT. Sri Lanka (Ceylon) launched the first efficient antimalaria campaign in the underdeveloped world in 1946 and extended it to cover the whole island in 1949. The results were astounding. In the period 1937–45, about half the population suffered from malaria, and 112 per 100,000 died from it each year. By 1960 only 5 per 100,000 suffered from the disease, and the death rate from it was negligible.

DDT probably also accounted for the fact that plague also became a minor problem during the same period. The efforts to control cholera have also been good, although not nearly so impressive as with malaria and plague.

Great strides have also been made in controlling tuberculosis. In 1950, tuberculosis accounted for 20 per cent of all deaths in the cities of India and the Philippines, 10 per cent in Malaya, and 5 per cent in Sri Lanka. Sri Lanka was again the pioneer, and through the use of X-rays, BCG vaccination, and chemotherapy, the number of new cases of tuberculosis dropped from the 2,200 per 100,000 in 1948 to about 100 per 100,000 in 1960–62. Other countries have had less dramatic success, but where programs have been instituted the results are impressive.

Smallpox is another encouraging story. Vaccination has brought it under control almost everywhere, although the problem is still rather serious in India, Pakistan, Indonesia, Burma, and in Africa, especially among small children.

Incidence of Disease

But these success stories are inconsequential when compared with the over-all picture in the underdeveloped world. The

[23] Bryant, op. cit., pp. ix and 53. In the section that follows, I have relied heavily on Bryant, on Myrdal's *Asian Drama*, and on the various UN and World Health Organization publications.

facts are so overwhelming that all we can do here is present a few, more or less at random, that illustrate rather than exhaust. The most vivid statistics concern children. In rural Senegal, the infant mortality rate is five times that of France. Among children one to four years old, the rates are 15 to 40 times higher in Senegal.[24] In Guatemala and Colombia during the first six months of life, the mortality rate is six times that in the United States. During the next four years it is almost thirty times. The causes are diarrhea, influenza, pneumonia, and malnutrition, principally, with tetanus, measles, malaria, tuberculosis, dysentery, and whooping cough close behind. In one typical village in Nigeria, the infant mortality rate was 295 per 1,000—12 per cent from diarrhea; 12 per cent from pneumonia; 12 per cent from malnutrition and marasmus; 8 per cent from malaria; 8 per cent from measles; 8 per cent from pertussis (whooping cough); 5 per cent each from tuberculosis and smallpox, and 35 per cent from all the rest. In *any* village of West Africa of 2,000 people in *any* given year, Bryant estimates, ten old people will die, eight people in their working years; one or two mothers, and forty children under five.

In India, 2 million people are estimated to have leprosy, and the proportion is probably similar throughout the underdeveloped world. The incidence of trachoma is probably higher still. The lack of a safe water supply and adequate sewerage coupled with the low level of personal hygiene means a high level of water-borne diseases—cholera, typhoid fever, dysentery, diarrhea, and diseases of intestinal parasites. Mosquito-borne diseases—malaria and filariasis (elephantiasis)—are also linked with water and drainage.

In Sri Lanka, which is better off than most, a survey of 71,000 children showed 80 per cent with health problems of some sort —hookworms, malnutrition, anemia, and tooth defects being the most common. A similar survey of 592 children between the ages of 10 and 14 in Bangkok showed 1,863 diseases—3.1 per child. Trachoma (67 per cent), skin disease (25 per cent), bowlegs (22 per cent), and goiter (20 per cent) led the list.

Statistics on diseases in the underdeveloped countries are rare

[24] Bryant, op. cit., p. 35.

for obvious reasons, but two reports are indicative. The first is a report by the Indian Health Survey and Planning Committee. According to the report, almost everyone in India suffered at one time or another from intestinal infections like typhoid, dysentery, diarrhea, and helminthic disorders. Diphtheria, whooping cough, pneumonia, and meningitis were common. Rabies and filariasis were endemic in some areas. Nutritional disorders and deficiency diseases were very common. Leprosy afflicted 100 in 100,000. Five to 8 per cent of the population probably had a venereal disease. In some states 15 per cent of the people had yaws. Trachoma afflicted 35 to 78 per cent of the population in the northern areas, and in India as a whole 120 persons out of 100,000 were blind. A total of 2.5 per cent of the population had tuberculosis. Ten per cent had malaria. Ten to 40 cases of smallpox and cholera were reported annually per 100,000 of the population.

The other report is the result of a questionnaire sent by the World Health Organization to 147 governments asking about their health problems. The answers are highly instructive. The European countries, Australia, New Zealand, Japan, the United States, and Canada reported their major problems were venereal disease, environmental deficiencies, infectious hepatitis, accidents, cancer, and chronic degenerative disease and mental disorders. The underdeveloped countries reported all of these, but less acute by far than malaria, tuberculosis, leprosy, helminthiasis, bilharziasis, diarrhea and dysentery, filariasis, malnutrition, smallpox, cholera, meningitis, yaws, enteric fevers, and trachoma.

Accompanying this grisly array of disease is a pitiful lack of facilities, of doctors and nurses, and of money available to be spent on improving health. A brief look at health statistics gives some notion of the situation. In the United States, there are 120 inhabitants per hospital bed and 670 inhabitants per doctor. In the Soviet Union, there are 100 people per hospital bed and 400 per doctor. In Sweden, there are 62 people per bed and 890 per doctor.

In Asia, among the larger countries, India has 1,700 people per bed and 4,800 per doctor. Indonesia has 1,200 people per bed and 23,000 per doctor. Thailand has 1,100 people per bed and 8,500 per doctor.

In Africa, Nigeria, with about one quarter of the population of all of Africa, has about 1,800 people per bed and 36,500 per doctor. A few African countries are slightly better off, but many are much worse off—with figures like 1 doctor to over 75,000 people.

. In the Middle East, things are slightly better. Egypt has 470 people per bed and 2,300 per doctor. Iran has 900 people per bed and 5,000 per doctor.

Latin America, not unexpectedly, is best off of all the underdeveloped regions, although some of the statistics are surprising. Argentina has 160 people per hospital bed but 530 per doctor. Brazil has about 300 per bed and 1,800 per doctor. Mexico has 530 per bed and also 1,800 per doctor. Some of the smaller countries, as might be expected, are worse off. Ecuador, for example, has 400 per bed and 3,000 per doctor. Bolivia has 220 per bed and 3,500 per doctor.

These bare statistics, moreover, are highly misleading. What is a hospital bed? "It may be a rope stretched between the sides of a wooden frame, or it may be canvas with no sheets or blankets. It may have a mattress and sheets but be attended only by auxiliary personnel; or doctors and nurses may be there, but a lack of equipment and materials may seriously limit the quality of service."[25] Without belaboring the point, the question must also be asked: What is a doctor? And the answer is not always encouraging.

These statistics also conceal something else: the differences between urban and rural settings. We said that the ratio of people to doctors in Thailand is about 8,500 to 1. In Bangkok it is about 900 to 1. In the rest of the country it is 16,000 to 1. But this, too, is misleading, for most of the doctors in the rest of the country cluster in the provincial capitals. For the truly rural areas, the ratio is more like 200,000 to 1.

Consider the money available for health. In the United States, total per capita expenditure per person 10 years ago was about

25 Ibid., p. 49.

$200, and it has since increased substantially. Government expenditure in the United States—and in the developing countries government expenditure is about all there is—was about $50 (in the United Kingdom, with its "socialized" medicine, it was $56). But look at the contrast. In Indonesia it was $0.20; in Thailand it was $0.60. Turning to Africa, in Nigeria it was $0.50; in Malawi it was $0.64; in Sudan, $1.02; in Senegal, $3.47. In Latin America, for some random samples, it was $2.36 in Guatemala; $3.50 in Colombia; and $9.60 in Jamaica.

For much of the underdeveloped world, the truth of the matter is that in rural areas 1 doctor, 1 nurse, and 2 or 3 helpers with much less training will care for from 50,000 to 100,000 people, usually with budgets of considerably less than $1.00 per person per year.[26]

Prospects for Improvement

What are the prospects for changing this depressing and dismal picture? Here again, we can give only glimpses of the final answer.

Consider the problem of training doctors. In northern Nigeria, the ratio of doctors to population is 1 to 170,000. If the goals of the Tannarive Conference are achieved, new schools are opened, money is found, and all the rest, then this ratio by 1980 could be changed to 1 to 80,000![27]

Take another example: a successful pilot program in Nigeria. The highest death rate of all is the group of "under fives." In western Nigeria a village named Imesi and a town named Ilesha, with a combined population of 200,000, were picked for an experiment involving the establishment of two out-patient clinics for these "under fives." The objective was regular supervision of children up to the age of five to prevent malnutrition, malaria, pertussis, smallpox, tuberculosis, and measles, and simple treatment for diarrhea, pneumonia, and common skin conditions. Each clinic had a doctor, a nurse, and locally trained auxiliaries. Methods and techniques were the cheapest possible, usually ad-

26 Ibid., p. 92.
27 Ibid., pp. 262–63.

ministered by the auxiliaries. About 40,000 children were served. The results were dramatic. Infant mortality fell from 295 per 2,000 to 72, and for children from 1 to 4 years, from 69 to 28.

The trouble was that the cost was $8.00 per child per year. Bryant tells the story: "Here is an example, a gallant one, of an effort to develop a highly practical approach to the problems of childhood illness—tailored to local needs, using inexpensive materials, and suitable for locally trained personnel. The results are fantastic in terms of saving human lives. But the brutal fact is that it is too expensive. Eight dollars per child per year is too much for a country that has only fifty cents per capita to spend on all health."[28]

Here, then, is one horn of the dilemma: cost. The medical answers to some diseases, like malaria and typhoid—getting rid of mosquitoes and providing clean water—are well known. But for many countries, getting rid of mosquitoes and providing clean water would take up more than the entire health budget.

Consider tuberculosis in Thailand. It is estimated that there are 250,000 active cases. By using mobile X-ray units, all these cases could be identified and treated. But the cost would be almost $20 million dollars in a national health budget of $29 million. What can be done is to vaccinate all the children of Thailand with BCG, which would cost about $100,000, reducing future cases, but leaving most of the existing cases untreated. The choice is hard.

Of all the steps toward good health, clean water is probably the most important. But as Bryant points out, to provide clean water for Cali, Colombia, would cost $2.25 per person per year, while the total health budget for Colombia is $3.50 per person per year.

And none of this considers population growth and capital costs. Most of the underdeveloped countries could not meet the capital costs to provide for the health of their growing populations, and they could not possibly meet the recurrent costs.

One further enormity: Most of these estimates are based on the assumption that per capita demand will remain about where it is. But current per capita demand is small indeed. In most under-

28 Ibid., p. 118.

developed countries the people are superstitious—they do not believe in modern medicine or, worse, they are afraid of it. But attitudes might change. In some places in Africa, for example, attitudes *have* changed toward obstetrical care. As Bryant points out, in colonial times in Africa obstetrical services were only for Europeans. The colonial governments were then forced to provide services for women in prison, for rather obvious reasons. Next, care came for another kind of outcast: the leper. But word got around. The reaction at first was extremely cautious and testing. A few then began to come in the later stages of "obstetrical disaster"—obstructed labor, ruptured uterus, postpartum hemorrhage, etc. Next, women came in for examination prior to birth—wanting assurances of a normal birth before returning to their village for traditional care. But confidence in obstetrical care gradually increases, and the result is a flood—"antenatal examinations, delivery, postpartum visits, child care—the desire is high for every service offered." Contemplate, for a moment, the social and political consequences if attitudes toward medical services in an underdeveloped country change all across the board fairly rapidly.

But even if the money could be found for vastly improved health services, which is the other horn of the dilemma, it is not at all certain that the end could be achieved by health services alone. Myrdal points out that in South Asia, and particularly in the bigger and poorer countries like India and Pakistan, the major cause of bad health is undernutrition and malnutrition. "The majority of South Asians spend much more than half their income on food, and still they are undernourished. Nor do they have access to the clothing, housing, and sanitary facilities they need to keep them reasonably fit."[29]

Grisly forces are at work. "Look at the grim facts: the leading causes of death in children are malnutrition, diarrhea, and pneumonia; in young women the leading causes are abortion and suicide; in young men it is homicide. There could be no more tragic illustration of Myrdal's thesis that health cannot be isolated from the other socio-economic facts in the development process."[30]

[29] *Asian Drama*, p. 1,549.
[30] Bryant, op. cit., p. 103.

Take only the most heart-rending of the tragedy of health in the developing world: children. "The great weapons of modern medicine are aimed at the patho-physiology and its susceptibility to pharmaceutical, immunological, or surgical attack. . . ." Bryant writes, "The dismal fact is that these great killers of children —diarrhea, pneumonia, malnutrition—are beyond the reach of these weapons.

"If children sick with these diseases reach the physician," he goes on, "there are sharp limits to what he can do. Diarrhea and pneumonia are often not affected by antibiotics, and the frequent presence of malnutrition makes even supportive therapy difficult or futile. And even these interventions by the physician, whether or not they are therapeutically effective, are only sporadic ripples in a running tide of disease. We are speaking of societies in which, at any given time, a third of the children may have diarrhea and more than that may be malnourished. Their lives are saturated with the causes—poverty, crowding, ignorance, poor ventilation, filth, flies. . . .

"What happens when the child does reach the physician earlier in the course of the disease? The long wait, the quick evaluation, a bottle of medicine, perhaps some words of advice, the slow walk back to the same home. What will be different now in the child, or in the way the mother takes care of him or of the other children?"[31]

Population

Given the facts on health in the underdeveloped countries, it is almost incredible that an explosive increase in population is also an obstacle to development. But it is. The fact of the matter is that in most underdeveloped countries the population increases come very close to canceling out entirely the gains of economic development and unquestionably are steadily widening the gap between the developed and underdeveloped countries. In the less developed world, average population growth generally projected is 2.4 per cent per year. If total income rises by 4 per cent, which is a rather optimistic projection, then per capita in-

[31] Ibid., p. 39.

come is lifted by only 1.6 per cent, and it takes 43 years for per capita income to double. "In the time it takes per capita income to rise from, say, the $200 to the $4,000 level, the population increases almost threefold."[32]

Recently, for the world as a whole, the birth rate has been 34 per thousand and the death rate has been 14 per thousand. Thus the population increase has been 20 per thousand—2 per cent. This means that the population doubles every 35 years. For the underdeveloped world it is much, much higher. India grows at the rate of 14 to 18 million people a year. For China it is about the same. For some of the countries of Africa it is astronomically greater.

Population Growth in the Western World

The pattern for the Western world was rather uniform. In traditional, agricultural societies in the West, the birth rate was very high and very steady. The death rate fluctuated with diseases, with war, with the food supply, and so on. In Ireland, for example, in the eighteenth and early nineteenth centuries, there was a drastic decline in the death rate and an increase of population three- or fourfold. The causes were multiple: an absence of devastating war and epidemic; the introduction of the potato, which flourished without diseases for three or four generations and, combined with buttermilk, was a perfectly adequate diet; and customs and traditions making for early marriage and large families. Conditions were ripe for a population explosion. But as the potato blight of the 1840s also showed, population can also decline precipitously if food supply, war, disease, or something similar increases the death rate sharply. And, as in Ireland, subsequent attitudes may also be affected that will lower the birth rate. The general pattern in the Western world, to repeat, was a high birth rate and a fluctuating death rate, and population went up and down dramatically. Over a long period of time, it increased, but slowly.

In the Western world this pattern changed with the beginnings of industrialization, the scientific revolution, and the

[32] Frank W. Notestein, "Population Growth and its Control," *Overcoming World Hunger,* ed. Clifford M. Hardin, for the American Assembly (New York, 1969).

introduction of a specialized, market-dominated economy. The death rate began to decline as a result not only of sanitation and better health care, but also better economic and political organization and the more efficient distribution of food, specialization, and more efficient production. After a lag, the birth rate also began to fall as a result of changed attitudes: a lower death rate among children, which enabled a couple to count on having the number of children they wanted actually to survive; other means than children for providing for security in old age; and the structure of the economy, in which children became not an asset but a liability. Finally, birth rates approached death rates, and the rate of population growth was reduced. The pattern became one of small families, a low and stabilized death rate, and a low but often fluctuating birth rate.

Growth Patterns in the Underdeveloped World

However, the underdeveloped countries may not follow this pattern, which was typical of the Western world. In the Western world, the decline in the death rate was gradual, mainly due to the slow development of scientific knowledge, and the population growth was large but not really an explosion. Today, the introduction of scientific techniques can bring a fabulous decline in death rates and with dramatic suddenness. As one authority puts it, "Many low-income areas of the world today—for example, Ceylon [now Sri Lanka], Malaya, some of the Caribbean islands, and much of Latin America—have, without abandoning their present agrarian structure, so reduced their death rates while birth rates have remained essentially unchanged that their rate of natural increase exceeds any recorded in the course of the demographic transition in the areas inhabited by northern and western Europeans and their descendants."[33] The result is a burst in population.

The same motivations that kept the birth rate high in the Western countries still applies. Custom and tradition encourage early marriage and large families. Children are frequently the

[33] Ansley J. Coale and Edgar M. Hoover, *Population Growth and Economic Development in Low-Income Countries: A Case Study of India's Prospects* (Princeton, 1958).

only existing old-age insurance. The expectation, continuing in spite of changed conditions, is that one must have many children if enough are to survive to adulthood to provide for that insurance. Children are little additional expense: Housing is no serious problem, and the costs of education are minor, since so little education is provided. On the other hand, in an agrarian economy children make a real economic contribution at a very early age. It takes time for attitudes toward these motivations to change.

Even if through some miracle the underdeveloped countries should reduce their birth rate to 2 per couple, the growth rate would not be zero. The population would still increase since the upcoming generation is so much larger than the preceding one. But any reduction in growth rate is highly unlikely. A conservative estimate, as mentioned above, is for population to increase at the rate of 2.4 per cent per year, which means that the underdeveloped countries will be doubling their population every 20 to 30 years. Consider what this means. Merely to maintain their present position, they must double everything—food production, jobs, housing, transportation, hospital and medical facilities, doctors, schools and schoolteachers, judges, prisons, water facilities, sanitation facilities—everything must be doubled. As one pessimistic pair of observers says, "It is problematical whether the United States could accomplish a doubling of its facilities in 20 years, yet the United States has abundant capital, the world's finest industrial base, rich natural resources, excellent communications, and a population virtually 100 per cent literate. . . . [The underdeveloped countries] have none of these things. They are not even going to be able to maintain their present low standards of living."[34]

[34] Paul R. Ehrlich and Anne H. Ehrlich, *Population, Resources, Environment: Issues in Human Ecology* (San Francisco, California: W. H. Freeman, 1970), p. 2.

CHAPTER 14

Consequences

IN THE VAST majority of the underdeveloped countries, then, one or another leadership group will sooner or later attempt to launch the country on a course of modernization and industrialization. If nationalism has not already seized their imaginations, they will find that of all the possible instruments in mobilizing the people for modernization and for consolidating the power they need at the center, nationalism is the most potent. Inevitably, they will take steps to encourage and foster it.

But self-sustaining growth is a myth. Modernization and development will not occur automatically because of a fortuitous input by some benevolent outside force. Development will come only because a leadership sets it as a goal, works unceasingly to achieve it, mobilizes the populace in its pursuit, and pushes them to massive efforts to change all aspects of life all across the board, simultaneously.

It is both interesting and instructive to ask what happened, if

self-sustaining growth is a myth, in the *first* countries to modernize. What did they do that was right?

It seems unlikely that change would occur simultaneously all
across the board by pure accident. Walt W. Rostow names Britain
as the first to modernize and predictably says that modernization
occurred first in Britain because the necessary conditions just
happened to be fulfilled. "This combination of necessary and sufficient conditions for take-off in Britain was the result of a convergence of a number of quite independent circumstances, a kind of
statistical accident of history which, once having occurred, was
irreversible, like the loss of innocence."[1]

Gunnar Myrdal, of course, would cite circular causation and
posit an input large enough to overcome the threshold of inertia.
Only C. E. Black, in his book *The Dynamics of Modernization:
A Study in Comparative History*, agrees with our view that the
key is leadership. Black points out that Britain and France were
the first. In both countries, he argues, a political revolution transferred power to a leadership group dedicated "to a critique of
traditional authority and a search for new values that are modern
in their essence." Both the commitment to a critique and a search
for new values and the determination to make a bid for power
stemmed from their social background. "There are significant common elements among Puritans, Jacobins, and Bolsheviks, for instance, in the social origins of their leaders, in their emphasis on
order and discipline, and in their efforts at a rational reappraisal
of the old order."[2]

In addition, it should also be remembered that in both Britain
and France development and modernization were both uneven
and erratic and that when the process was proceeding well it was
because of nothing either automatic or mysterious, but because
the leadership were deliberately inducing change pretty much
across the board.

Leadership, to repeat, is the key. Much will depend not only
on their abilities, but on their outlook and strategy. A modern,
industrialized nation-state built by a middle class pursuing a lib-

[1] *The Stages of Economic Growth: A Non-Communist Manifesto* (Cambridge,
1962), p. 31.
[2] New York, 1966, p. 107.

eral strategy will be different from a modern, industrialized nation-state built by a Communist party pursuing a Marxist strategy.

In the Western world, among the first countries to modernize, the struggle was generally led by the middle classes. But, as we already suggested, other strata might lead the march today. In Japan it was a segment of the traditional aristocracy. In Iran it has been the Shah. The possible leaders of a march to modernization in the future seem to be: (1) a middle class; (2) an aristocratic elite; (3) a Communist party elite; (4) a charismatic leader; and (5) a state-bureaucratic elite.[3]

Middle-Class Leadership

In general, a modernizing middle class is a new, rising class, sensitive to the gains possible from new means of production. It is likely to be drawn from commercial or artisan groups, often composed of religious or ethnic minorities, who were not integrated with the aristocratic elite, but coexisting, and who are now in opposition. Modernizing states led by the middle class are not likely to be a common phenomenon among the developing countries of the world today. Few have anything but the beginnings of a middle class, and the competitors for leadership are strong. It is likely, however, that as modernization proceeds, a middle class will develop, and at some stage in certain countries it is at least conceivable that this new middle class could take over. It seems most likely to be successful against an aristocratic elite that has survived other threats long enough for a middle class to develop, but there are also other possibilities for a growing middle class to come to dominance. The Philippines is a possible example. There is no traditional aristocracy in the Philippines. The ruling elite is an old and well-established oligarchy with many middle-class characteristics, although many of its members are corrupt and self-serving. The defeat of the Communist Hukbalahap movement reduces the chances of either a takeover by the Communists or a

[3] Clark Kerr, John T. Dunlop, Frederick H. Harbison, and Charles A. Myers in their book *Industrialism and Industrial Man: The Problem of Labor and Management in Economic Growth* (Cambridge, 1960), propose the following leadership typology: (1) dynastic elite; (2) a middle class; (3) revolutionary intellectuals; (4) colonial administrators; and (5) nationalist leaders. Although I have adopted a different typology, theirs was the inspiration.

takeover by the Army in response to the threat of the Communists. Democratic forms were instituted when the Philippines attained independence and survived long enough for them to be given at least lip service even when President Marcos suspended the constitution and took a number of "emergency" measures concentrating power in his own hands. As time goes on, the old oligarchy may become more middle class under these conditions and join with newly emerging elements of a middle class to form a leadership stratum capable of assuming power in some future crisis. The pattern might be similar in certain Latin American countries.

In any case, if the middle class does take over, the system will then tend toward being more individualistic, toward greater tolerance for dissent and political conflict, and toward a more pluralistic policy-making process involving a larger number of power centers.

Aristocratic Elites

The term "aristocratic elites" is meant to include a single man, such as the Shah of Iran, and a much broader group, such as the samurai of Japan. In a modernizing state led by an aristocratic, traditionalist elite, a central feature will be the struggle within the elite—as Kerr and his associates say, between the "traditionalists" who seek to hold back modernization and the "realists" who recognize that industrialization will eventually come to dominate. "They seek to identify the essentials of the past and to preserve them in the face of the new form of production; but they will make whatever compromises are necessary to permit industrialization to proceed under their guidance."[4] If the realists do get control, they emphasize not only tradition, but stability—law, order, and firm administration. Both the political and the economic system will tend to be paternalistic. Since preserving old values is a central goal, industrialization and change will be slow—and never faster than the pressure on the elite, whether internal or external. The emphasis is on stability and a smooth transition.

For our purposes, the central question about an aristocratic

[4] *Industrialism and Industrial Man*, p. 52.

elite is its ability to survive. In the short run, a modernizing state run by an aristocratic elite is particularly vulnerable to attack from the left, led by the Communist party. If it survives long enough, a middle class will arise and will eventually take over. The aristocratic elite then tends to merge into a middle-class elite.

The Communist Party Elite

A Communist party elite intends not only to take power but to eliminate the old elites and the old culture. Their goal is revolution. A second characteristic is that they are armed with a theory of history that "specifies for them the place to act, the time to act, and the means to act." They are armed with a fully developed ideology. The final characteristic is that the main determinant of who is to belong to the new ruling group is faithfulness to this ideology. People are recruited on the basis of ability plus political reliability.

In general, as we say, the goal will be to eliminate the old elites and to destroy the old culture. But this goal will be modified on occasion, most often to resist being politically and culturally engulfed by a larger Communist neighbor. Some such motive, for example, was apparently behind the move of the Romanian leaders in the late 1960s when they began to stress not only Romania's independence in foreign policy, notably by declaring its neutrality in the Sino-Soviet dispute, but its cultural distinctiveness by reviving purely Romanian national heroes, customs, and traditions. A similar motive—independence from a larger Communist neighbor—also seems to have been behind Hanoi's decision to go to Paris to negotiate on Vietnam peace in 1968 despite China's advice against it. In both cases, nationalism seems to have been more central than ideology.

In the economic sphere, the tendency in the Communist-led countries has been to place greatest emphasis on the development of heavy industry at the expense of consumer goods, housing, and the rest, and this tendency seems likely to continue. In the past, too, Communist-led countries have had peculiar, persistent difficulties in the field of agriculture. The ideological bias toward communes and collectives has been reinforced by the greater ease with which the state can extract surpluses from the agricultural sector when it is organized collectively. The incentives that can be offered the peasant, on the other hand, cannot rival the pull of owning his own land and the incentive he then has for improving it as well as working it. Thus, this tendency for the Communist countries to have difficulties with agriculture is also likely to continue.

In the past, the ideology and the commitment to wiping out the old elites and culture have made vigilance a necessity and inevitably increased the power of the political police. Conformity inevitably assumes a high value, and almost all aspects of life and society tend to become politicized. Forced-draft industrialization, strengthening the state, and constructing a "socialist" society are the overarching goals, and everything—education, the labor unions, the peasant, art, and literature—all must make a contribution. Later on, after industrialization is well under way, the state bureaucracy tends to take over more and more of the leadership in the march to modernization, and since the bureaucracy tends to be more pragmatic, the Communist state to some extent comes to resemble a country in which the modernizing elite is a state bureaucracy. The result is not "convergence"—in which Communist and non-Communist countries are supposed to converge on some common form—but only that the strategies of industrialization that the two follow come to be similar in certain respects, but only in certain respects.

The Charismatic Leader

A modernizing state led by a charismatic leader and his small group of intimates was very often the pattern in the period immediately following World War II, when so many colonies gained their independence. Indonesia under Sukarno, Cambodia under Sihanouk, Ghana under Nkrumah, and Egypt under Nasser all approximate the ideal type that is intended. But like the state led by a middle class, it is likely to be a rare phenomenon in the years immediately ahead. Partly this is because new states will appear less frequently. Charismatic leaders have fewer opportunities to rise to prominence in the long and dreary work of nation-building than they do in the heat of a struggle for independence.

Another reason that charismatic leaders are likely to be few in the immediate future is because those who have already achieved power are so peculiarly vulnerable. The individual human being is mortal, and the charismatic type is very nearly unique. When a charismatic leader dies, he is not likely to be replaced by another. Nasser is not replaced by another Nasser, but by Sadat. But even greater than the vulnerability of the charismatic leader as a mortal individual is his vulnerability to a *coup d'état*, especially a *coup* led by the military. The techniques of charisma by their very nature preclude building the solid, hierarchical organization that is the greatest protection against *coups*. The well-established organization provides ways of replacing a leader who fails to satisfy enough of the different power centers within the organization. The charismatic leader cultivates the mass, as we have said, and the measures required to cultivate the mass and those required to build a solid political organization tend to be mutually exclusive. The charismatic leader can manipulate and maneuver for a surprisingly long time—as Sukarno balanced the Communist party, the Army, the Air Force, and the various Muslim power centers off against each other. But the charismatic leader who dies a natural death at a ripe old age while still in power is a rarity.

Thus it was not just the passage of years that accounts for the fact that so few of the leaders of the independence movements still led their countries in the third decade after World War II. And it is no accident that those who did survive tended to be men, like Nyerere of Tanzania, who relied more on building a solid organization and state bureaucracy and less on charisma. In general, we can say that the charismatic leader has the lowest survival capability of any of the modernizing elites. He is less vulnerable to attack from the left, led by the Communists, than the aristocratic elites—that is true. It is also true that he is only slightly more vulnerable to an attack by the aristocratic elites, which is what happened in Cambodia. But the charismatic leader is very, very vulnerable to attack from the right, led by the military. Thus the charismatic leader's most likely successor in leading the march to modernization is a state bureaucracy under the direction of a government controlled by the military.

So long as the charismatic leader lasts, he is likely to concentrate on the mass of the people and make them chiliastic, feeding their expectations for instant improvement. He tends to sponsor spectacular projects—the Aswan Dam in the case of Nasser, the Volta River project, a useless steel mill, and a dual highway leading to nowhere in the case of Nkrumah, and the port of Sihanoukville in the case of Sihanouk. The effort is overextended and out of balance. Industrialization is not a flow but a series of episodes.

In addition, the charismatic leader is likely not only to mortgage the economy but to substitute international adventuring for progress in development. His goal for the country is instant greatness, and at the same time he has a need to present the chiliastic mass with excitement and accomplishment. Foreign adventures offer tempting possibilities of fulfilling both needs. Again, it is no accident that Nasser found it useful to keep the feud with Israel hot and dreamed of a pan-Arab union; that Nkrumah was so active in the Congo crisis and dreamed of uniting black Africa; and that Sukarno made so much of confrontation, first with the Netherlands over West New Guinea and then with the British over Malaysia.

The State-Bureaucratic Elite

The state-bureaucratic elite, as the name suggests, arises when the state and its bureaucracy constitute the instrument for modernization. The second characteristic is a corollary of the first, that the modernizing elite is not based on any particular class. The third characteristic is that it is not committed to a particular ideology. This does not mean that ideology does not influence, but only that there is sufficient flexibility for the modernizing leadership to change if some particular doctrine has failed. Most of the leadership of developing countries, for example, have a variety of socialist dogmas that they cherish. The point is not that these do not influence their behavior, but that these leaders are not so ideologically committed that they cannot rather easily abandon something, like, say, a commune program, that has failed. The fourth characteristic is that the leadership has organizational con-

tinuity, that it is based on something more lasting than the charisma of a single individual. Whether this organizational continuity is provided by political parties or by an army that has taken
over the government is not the important point here. The important point is that an organization provides two mechanisms that
are absent if the top leader bases himself solely on charisma. The
first is that an organization, by bringing a larger number of people into the policy-making process, provides a mechanism for
testing policy proposals, which lessens the probability of gran-
diose, cure-all schemes like the Aswan Dam or wild swings in policy. The second mechanism is a way of providing for changes in
the top leaders that will usually avoid wholesale purges of officials down the line and the kind of instability that such purges
engender.

Thus our definition of a "state-bureaucratic" elite would not
include the Communist countries—for even though the various
Communist countries differ on ideology, they are more committed
ideologically than our definition contemplates. Our definition
would also rule out countries like Indonesia under Sukarno, Cambodia under Sihanouk, and Ghana under Nkrumah on the
grounds that the leadership when these men ruled was based too
much on the "cult of the personality," too much on the charisma
of a single individual. Our definition would also rule out a country like Egypt under Nasser. Although it had the organization,
being a military regime, Nasser based his claim to legitimacy
too much on charisma to fit. On the other hand, our definition of
state-bureaucratic elite would fit India under Nehru, Korea under Park Chung Hee, and Indonesia under General Suharto.
Nehru had some of the personality traits characteristic of charismatic leaders, but he did not claim legitimacy through charisma.
What is more, the Congress party provided organizational continuity and the state bureaucracy was the instrument for modernization. Neither Suharto nor Park could be termed charismatic
leaders, and in both Indonesia and Korea the Army provided the
organizational continuity and the state bureaucracy the leadership in the struggle for modernization.

Countries whose modernization effort is led by a state-bureaucratic elite will clearly be the most common in the decades

that lie ahead and on into the twenty-first century. In most cases, the state bureaucracies will do their work under the control of a government dominated by the military. In others it will be under a government dominated by a single party, sometimes with genuine parliamentary forms, as in India, and sometimes without them. On some rare occasions, the state bureaucracy might do its work under a government controlled alternatively by rival parties in true democratic tradition. But in all these cases, the basic strategy is likely to be the same. The effort will be pragmatic and more or less expert, in the sense that technical expertise will have a large role and significant influence. An effort will be made to draw on outside capital and foreign aid, whether from the World Bank; from an international consortium whenever one is available; or from one or both of the superpowers, depending on the state of the Cold War, the geographic location of the country in question, and on the politics of its government. In addition, the tendency will be toward a planned economy; toward state-sponsored investment; toward state-controlled labor organizations, and workers who are dependent on the state for benefits; and toward calls by the state for hard work, sacrifice, and unity.

Political Implications

The questions now are: What consequences can be foreseen flowing from all this? What other predictions can be made about the underdeveloped world? In the political sphere, the result that seems most likely and most striking is internal turbulence—turbulence deriving not only from economic troubles but also from the forced rise of nationalism. The combination of a high propensity for failure in the attempts to develop with the efforts to foster nationalism seems bound to bring a high level of internal violence.[5] When an effort at modernizing and developing by one particular leadership group fails—or even if it is succeeding, but too slowly for the unrealistic expectations that are likely to abound—other groups will be encouraged to make their bid for power. *Coups d'état* and attempted *coups* are likely to be plentiful.

[5] Myron Wiener goes even farther and argues that growth itself is "politically unstabilizing." See his *The Politics of Scarcity* (Chicago, 1962), pp. 237–40.

Probability of Secession and Rival Nationalisms

Failures in development or uneven development in different parts of the country will stir up regional animosities. When the attempt to foster nationalism runs into tribal, religious, cultural, ethnic, or regional differences, resistance is very probable. If failure in development or uneven development for different parts of the country coincide with regional resistance to the state-fostered nationalism, the result will often be that the region attempts to secede and develop its own, rival nationalism. This pattern has been frequent in the history of developing countries. It is what we saw in the American Civil War, in the Irish struggle for independence, in the more recent attempts to secede by Katanga Province in the Congo in the early 1960s, by Biafra in Nigeria in the later 1960s, and by the Bengali in East Pakistan in the early 1970s. India is obviously vulnerable to this kind of development, so is Indonesia, and so are a number of states in Africa.[6]

There may also be in these crises of secession another similarity to the American Civil War. Tocqueville, as we saw, predicted that the South should secede, but concluded that the North would let it go without fighting. Once the North did decide to fight, the tendency for power to flow away from the central government and to the states was reversed. The very decision became a historical "turning point." So it may also be in the case of a secession like that of Biafra from Nigeria. The fact that a war has been fought over the issue of whether Nigeria should remain one state may well be a decisive boost in the development of a nationalism that is essentially *Nigerian*.

Of the recent attempts at secession, the only success has been that of Bangladesh. In the Congo case, the central government requested the UN to send in troops to restore order, and these troops eventually put down the rebellion of Katanga and prevented its secession. It does not seem likely, however, that the UN will intervene in attempts at secession again in the immediate

[6] Even rather highly developed states can be troubled by the same pattern. The Quebec separatist movement derives not only from the fact of ethnic, cultural, and language differences but also from the fact that Quebec has lagged so far behind the rest of Canada and its development.

future. For almost everyone concerned, the Congo crisis was an unpleasant experience. The Soviet Union became convinced that the Secretary General and his representatives in the field worked against Congolese parties sympathetic to communism and is not likely to vote for such an intervention again. The United States, for its part, came to feel that bringing the UN into such struggles runs undue risks of turning them into great power confrontations. Many of the smaller members and the Secretariat were alarmed at the constitutional crisis the intervention provoked and the possibility that the struggle might end up destroying the UN itself. And everyone agreed that the cost of such operations was prohibitive. Thus at the time of Biafra's attempted secession and East Pakistan's, there was little sentiment for having the UN intervene.

There is real doubt that the central government of the Congo could have prevented the secession of Katanga without outside help. Katanga had some troops native to the province, and with the help of mercenaries from South Africa and elsewhere and with outside arms aid, it was able to build an army equal to that loyal to the central government. Since most of the mining and industry of the whole of the Congo was situated in Katanga, it would probably have been able to outstrip the central government in size and equipment very quickly.

In Nigeria, there was no overt intervention, but both sides received considerable amounts of arms and other aid. France and Portugal sent supplies to Biafra; Britain and the Soviet Union sent them to the central government. Eventually the central government put down the rebellion, but it was not easy. The Biafra struggle was a bloody, destructive civil war that lasted 2½ years.

The successful secession of East Pakistan to form the state of Bangladesh is also instructive. As mentioned previously, the differences between East and West Pakistan were profound. The Bengali in East Pakistan and the Punjabi in West Pakistan shared only their Muslim religion. In ethnic background, in language, and in culture, they differed, and they were separated by a thousand miles of another country, India. The Bengali believed that the fact that East Pakistan lagged so far behind West Pakistan in economic development resulted from a deliberate decision of the central government. They believed that these suspicions about the attitude of the central government were confirmed by the indifference it showed during the great cyclone and tidal wave. When the rebellion came, the Pakistani Army, who were mainly Punjabi, went on a rampage of killing, rape, and destruction. If the Bengali population had not previously been unanimous in their support of secession, they were now. Yet it is clear that the secession achieved the quick success it did only because the Indian Army intervened in massive force and defeated the Pakistani Army decisively. Unlike Katanga, East Pakistan had no army of its own and no time to build one. Eventually the Bengali may have won their independence through guerrilla warfare, sabotage, terrorism, and acts of civil disobedience. But it would have taken at least a generation.

Presumably central governments will heed the obvious lessons in these several attempts at secession and will be sensitive to the possibility that neglect of regions that differ from the rest of the country in terms of ethnic background, culture, language, or religion might lead to secession. If so, examples in the future will not be too frequent. Even then, the odds favor the central government, largely because of the power of modern weapons—tanks, artillery, and jet aircraft—and the difficulty the seceding region has in acquiring them.

Possibilities of Coups d'état

Neither is true of the *coup d'état—coups* are likely to be frequent and successful, especially by the military. Aristocratic and charismatic leaders will be particularly vulnerable for the reasons already given, and the difficulties of modernization will, as we have suggested, give other types of leadership at least a certain vulnerability. Squabbling between political parties and factions about development policy will provide still another provocation for a *coup*, especially for the military. And *coups* attempted by the military are more likely to succeed, precisely because of their superior weapons and organization. It is no great feat of prediction to say that governments controlled by the military will be a familiar phenomenon in the underdeveloped world over the decades that lie ahead. At the opening of the 1970s, as mentioned earlier, eight of the seventeen non-Communist, underdeveloped states of Asia were governed by the military; in the Middle East, it was five of sixteen that were military; in Africa, twelve of thirty-eight were military; and in Latin America, five of thirty-one were military.

Prospects for Communism

What is the outlook for the Communists in all this? Will they be able to use the turbulence to take over, either by a *coup* or by leading a guerrilla movement, as they did in Vietnam? Through-out the 1950s, American policy in Southeast Asia, at least, was motivated by the so-called "domino theory" enunciated by President Eisenhower at a news conference on April 7, 1954—that the countries of Southeast Asia were like a row of dominoes: If the first one fell to communism (he was speaking of Indochina), then all the rest would also fall, like dominoes. In 1965, too, both President Johnson and his Secretary of State, Dean Rusk, in their public statements justified their decision to bomb North Vietnam and make Vietnam an American war by sending ground forces in terms of this same danger of "dominoes."[7] If turbulence, *coups,* and internal struggle will be the hallmark of the future in the underdeveloped countries, there is at least a *prima facie* case that it is the Communists who will benefit.

However, on both theoretical grounds and in terms of historical experience, I would argue just the opposite—that it is doubtful that there were any dominoes in Southeast Asia at the time President Eisenhower was speaking, almost certain that there were none in 1965, and highly unlikely that there will be any in the future.

In the wake of World War II, in the late 1940s, of course, there were obviously "dominoes" in Southeast Asia. Many of the countries were devastated by the war and newly emerged from colonial status. Their governments were weak and the new leader-

[7] Looking back on those decisions in 1971, the Assistant Secretary of State for East Asian Affairs at the time argued not only that they were made on that basis but that they succeeded in preventing not only a Communist takeover in countries like Indonesia but "a wave of Chinese expansion into the rest of Southeast Asia." See William P. Bundy, "New Tides in Southeast Asia," *Foreign Affairs* (January 1971).

ship was inexperienced. These countries were, in a word, fragile—vulnerable to any group of organized and determined men. But by 1954, most of these countries and their governments had made great strides. In Indonesia, the government had put down an attempted Communist coup in 1948, and although the Communist party was large and dangerous, the countervailing forces, especially the Army, were also powerful. In Malaya by 1954, the British had defeated the Communist insurgency begun in 1948 and granted Malaya independence—only mopping-up operations remained. Also in 1954, the Philippines put down the Communist Hukbalahap rebellion, which had begun with independence in 1946. In Thailand, no Communist threat of any proportions ever developed. Outside of Indochina itself, Burma was the only Southeast Asian state that was menaced by a Communist insurgency, and even Burma seemed to have the insurgents contained.

By 1965, the trend was even more markedly away from anything resembling dominoes. The Burmese Communist insurgency had been stamped out and its leaders killed. In Indonesia in 1965 the Communists attempted a *coup*—from the evidence available, with the connivance of Sukarno, who wished to destroy the political power of the Army. The *coup* failed, and in the ensuing months the Muslim peasants and the Army between them slaughtered at least three hundred thousand members of the Communist party and perhaps many more than that. Even in parts of the former Indochina, the trend was in the other direction from dominoes. Sihanouk in Cambodia could not prevent the Vietnamese Communists from making use of his territory in their war in South Vietnam, and with typical cunning he made no attempt to do so. But he had succeeded in winning the support of the vast majority of the Cambodian peasants and thereby reduced the membership in the Cambodian Communist party to no more than a few hundred, most of whom were in exile.[8] In Laos, the most fragile and vulnerable of all, the neutralization negotiated in 1962 still held. The Communists remained in con-

---

[8] Sihanouk's only enemies were members of the aristocratic elite, of which he was himself a member. A *coup* by these aristocrats unseated him in 1970, and this was followed by an invasion by American and South Vietnamese forces. The South Vietnamese remained; Sihanouk fled to Peking, and called on the Cambodian peasants to join with the Viet Cong and North Vietnamese Communists to resist. Thus a domino was created in 1970 where none had existed before.

trol of the territories they had held at the time of the negotiations, and the neutralist government of Souvanna Phouma effectively controlled and commanded the political support of all the rest.

It seems clear that the reason the Communists have been so successful in China and Vietnam and so unsuccessful in the other countries of Southeast Asia is that in China and Vietnam the Communists captured the leadership of nationalism and elsewhere they did not. In China, Chiang Kai-shek and the Kuomintang failed even to make a beginning in development and modernization, while the Communists at least had their Marxist ideology and its verbiage of development. This may have had little impact on the masses, but it did constitute an effective appeal to young, able intellectuals who had a potential for leadership. More important, however, was the fact that the Communists did mount a meaningful resistance to the Japanese, the foreign invader, becoming a rallying point for both anti-foreign and nationalist forces, while the Kuomintang never really rose above its warlord factionalism and corruption. In Vietnam, the fact that the only organized Vietnamese resistance to the Japanese was Communist-led probably had some effect, even though minor. But the important fact was the monumental stupidity of the French in attempting to reimpose colonialism in Vietnam at a time when colonialism was clearly dead all over the world. In the circumstances of the time, a politically conscious Vietnamese who decided to resist the French and looked around for an organized, determined, disciplined party dedicated to ousting the French found only the Communists and Ho Chi Minh. As a consequence, from every segment of Vietnamese society, with the possible exception of the most devout Catholic community, such individuals—politically active, ambitious for themselves and their country, and determined—joined the Communists. But the point to remember is that their motives were nationalist. In both China and Vietnam the leaders accepted the Marxist ideology, but the forces that motivated them and their supporters in the wider population was nationalism.

But elsewhere in Southeast Asia, it went the other way. The Philippines was given independence promptly after World War

II, and the Communist Hukbalahaps were left with economic injustice as their only issue, rather than the more potent one of nationalism. Potential Filipino leaders fired with nationalism turned to the task of unifying the country, running it, and developing it rather than struggling for independence. In Thailand, much the same thing happened, since Thailand had never lost its independence. In Malaya, the British defeated the Communist insurgency militarily, but coupled their military efforts with rapid progress toward independence—indeed, the military efforts would probably not have been successful if they had not been coupled with independence. In Indonesia, unlike Vietnam, there was a party other than the Communists dedicated to the ouster of the colonial master, and it was this nationalist party that got most of the credit for achieving independence. The Communist party, however, was large and powerful, and Sukarno actually encouraged it, at least in part because he saw in the Communists a force that he could use to balance off the Army. But as time went on, the Communists became increasingly identified with a foreign power—China—and came more to alienate the force of nationalism than to capture it. The bloodbath that followed their attempted *coup* in 1965 was no surprise.

The situation in Burma by 1965 was similar to that in Indonesia. A nationalist party got the credit for independence. One of the two Communist parties became identified with the foreigner to the north—the much-feared Chinese—and the other was impotent. The regime clearly captured nationalism—ousting not only the British colonialists, but the Indian commercial and money-lending "exploiters." In addition, the government, although a military dictatorship, talked in socialist as well as nationalist terms, and thus pre-empted even the economic issue from the Communists.

In India, again, an organized party dedicated to ousting the British, the Congress party, was available. Eventually the British agreed to leave, and it was the Congress party that got the credit.

In Ceylon, now renamed Sri Lanka, things were more complicated. The United Nationalist party, whose leaders were the wealthy, English-educated elite, including both Tamils and Sinhalese, negotiated independence and took over the job of running the country. But the forces of Sinhalese nationalism, centered in the Buddhist priesthood, resented the prominence of the Tamils, and S. W. R. D. Bandaranaike, a plantation owner, formed the Sri Lanka Freedom party and came to power—with the help of both the Trotskyite and Moscow-oriented Communist parties—on a platform of making Sinhalese the sole official language. Thus for the time being, at least, one cannot say that anyone has captured the banner of nationalism. Neither has anyone permanently lost it either, if one excepts the Tamil parties. It might be said that the Communist parties at the moment share the leadership of nationalism with the Bandaranaike party. However, this may change. In early 1971, several extreme left groups, calling themselves "Guevarists" and "Maoists," staged an uprising. The government charged that the uprising was sponsored by North Korea, declared some of the North Korean diplomatic representatives *persona non grata*, and hinted at a role by Communist China. If the government can make these charges stick on these particular parties and factions and extend suspicion to the others, then all the Communist parties and factions in Sri Lanka might find themselves in a situation similar to that of the Indonesian party.

The analysis here, to repeat, is that the Communists in Southeast Asia succeeded or failed depending upon whether or not they captured the leadership of nationalism or alienated it—that nationalism is the key to understanding events. If this analysis is correct, then on theoretical grounds I would argue that Vietnam —whether or not the Americans intervened—would have turned out to be unique, unique in the sense that it would have been the last Asian nation in which communism captured the leadership of nationalism. By the same token, on theoretical grounds, I would argue that Communist-led insurgencies, *coups*, or efforts to get elected are not likely to be successful in Southeast Asia in the future—that there are no dominoes.

The principal reason, of course, is nationalism. In most countries of Southeast Asia nationalism has already begun to take hold. At the end of World War II in some of the countries of Southeast Asia it is true that many in the mass of the population identified more with their village, region, religious group, caste, or tribe than with the nation. But the intervening 25 years—a whole generation—has seen at least the beginnings of a nationalist awakening in almost every single country. If our judgment is correct that the leadership in all these countries will discover the potency of nationalism as an instrument in consolidating power at the center and in mobilizing the people for development, then nationalism will become stronger and stronger, sweeping all before it.

With nationalism rampant, it is clear beyond any doubt that if the Communist party of a particular country becomes identified with a foreign power, whether China or the Soviet Union, it can have no hope of ever achieving power. Even in the countries where communism has captured nationalism, like Vietnam, nationalism has also captured communism. Hanoi is clearly determined to remain independent of both Peking and Moscow. The Communist world, in a word, has long since ceased to be monolithic, and the reason is nationalism.

Even when the Communist party is not identified with a foreign power, nationalism will be suspicious of it. Any worldwide ideology, such as communism, is in some sense inconsistent with nationalism, which puts its own uniqueness at the center, and is suspect. There was a time when the ideology of communism offered itself as a sure-fire blueprint for rapid economic development. But any country that has made a beginning at development or has among its leaders people with some training who have looked at other countries' efforts at development is likely to be highly skeptical of those claims and turn more to pragmatism than to communism in planning its particular development. Sékou Touré, for example, after visiting China, emphatically rejected the idea of taking it as a model for the development of Guinea: "I have just been over China. It is a very different country from ours. I found nothing in China's experience that interests us."[9] In countries where the nationalist leadership is less sophisticated, the Communists are still unlikely to be able to ride the issue to power. If it is not sophisticated, the nationalist

[9] Brian Crozier, "Six Africans in Search of a Personality," *Encounter* (May 1960), p. 40.

leadership is usually eclectic and simply adopts as much of Marxism and its slogans as suits their own needs, whether economic or political. In Burma, for example, the economy in the late 1960s and early 1970s was in a mess, but since it got that way under slogans borrowed from socialism, the Communist program had little appeal.

In these circumstances—where communism has not captured nationalism but not alienated it either—the only effective issue open to the Communist party is not a Communist program for development but a Communist protest against economic injustice. If there is an entrenched conservative oligarchy using its power more or less deliberately to hold back development and thus retain its privileged status, a protest might well be the vehicle to power. In a sense this was Castro's vehicle, although he also had a nationalist issue in the dominating American economic presence in Cuba. In Asia, it could be argued that the Philippines runs this kind of risk. But even if there is merit in the argument, the antagonism between nationalism and communism deriving from the Huk rebellion and from the fear of China would seem to nullify it. In Asia, in sum, there are few if any dominoes.

The Middle East, Africa, and Latin America

This judgment that communism has little future in the underdeveloped countries of Asia can also be extended to the rest of the underdeveloped world—the Middle East, Africa, and Latin America—but only with certain qualifications. The argument that communism is unlikely to have much appeal as a sure-fire blueprint for rapid economic development seems to be valid everywhere—Africa, the Middle East, and Latin America as well as Asia. Most leaders and potential leaders would echo Sékou Touré —the countries are just too different. To the extent that Marxism has any applicability to their problems of development, it seems likely that nationalist leadership groups will, again, simply adopt as much of Marxism and its slogans as seems politic. What happened in Burma is also happening in Guinea, Ghana, Tanzania, Algeria, Libya, Syria, Bolivia, and Peru, among others.

It also seems doubtful that Communist-led guerrilla movements are likely to meet with much success elsewhere in the underdeveloped world, either. In the Middle East, as in Asia, nationalist parties are already well established, and whatever their failures, it is unlikely that they can be effectively challenged on the issue of nationalism, which would seem to be essential for a guerrilla movement to be successful. In Africa, nationalism has not yet taken hold among the masses to the degree that it has in both Asia and the Middle East. In most countries of Africa, indeed the issue is whether nationalism can transcend tribalism or must merely coincide with it. But in almost every country the Communist parties face formidable contenders for the leadership of nationalism. In such circumstances and in the absence of a long-standing issue of economic injustice in which one segment of society has kept another down, the chances of a Communist-led guerrilla movement succeeding are small. In Latin America, however, the issue of economic injustice is very much in the forefront. What is more, in those Latin American countries in which the old-line oligarchs are allied with American business interests, the issue of nationalism might also come to the fore. It may be that these two issues will combine in one, two, or even three Latin American countries so as to permit a Communist-led guerrilla movement to overcome the apathy of the masses, but even then the chances of success seem small. Building up the necessary organizational cadre for guerrilla warfare is much more difficult in these circumstances than when the revolutionaries are dealing with a colonial regime. Then, too, from the beginning a guerrilla effort in Latin America is likely to be faced with massive police and military forces—backed and supported by the United States.[10] The example, of course, is Che Guevara's attempt to start a guerrilla war in Bolivia. He had no organizational cadre among the people to build political support, and the Bolivian peasant was either indifferent to him or served against him as a voluntary intelligence agent for the government. The police and military, with powerful support from the United

[10] This over-all judgment is shared by Gunnar Myrdal, who also addressed himself to the question of whether revolutionary movements would be successful in Latin America. See his *The Challenge of World Poverty* (New York, 1970), p. 484.

States, launched a massive effort to run his little band to earth—and it did not take them long.

On the other hand, in Africa and Latin America, unlike Asia and to some extent the Middle East, communism is less likely to be identified with a foreign power or itself be regarded as foreign and therefore the natural enemy of nationalism. Thus the chances of the Communists coming to power in an African or Latin American country through an election are very much better than in Asia and at least slightly better than in the Middle East.[11] Here again, the Communists' chances are best of all where they can exploit the issue of economic and social injustice. Latin America, again, seems the most fertile field. An example is the election of a self-styled "Marxist," Salvador Allende, as President of Chile in 1970. But here again, too, the chances are that any Communist party that does achieve power through elections and unlike Allende succeeds in holding it against a military *coup* is likely to be itself nationalistic and thus to pursue its own policies quite independently of either Moscow or Peking.

In general, then, it can be said that communism is not the wave of the future in the underdeveloped countries. At the same time, it should also be said that neither is some kind of *Pax Americana* or development under American tutelage on a model of the American social and economic system a candidate for the role. Nationalism is the wave of the future in the underdeveloped world, quite clearly, and to the extent that the underdeveloped countries succeed in developing and modernizing, it will be on some model that is peculiarly their own.

Basic Pattern of Political Implications

In general, then, the basic pattern that seems most likely in the underdeveloped world is along the following lines. Sooner or later

11 Parenthetically, it should be noted that just because communism seems unlikely to make much headway among the peoples of the underdeveloped world does not mean that the Soviet Union may not be able to enlarge its influence in those same countries. The example, of course, is the Soviet effort in the Middle East in the 1960s and 1970s. The Soviet Union supplied Egypt with enormous quantities of arms, sent advisers, and exercised significant influence over Egypt's policy in spite of the fact that members of the Egyptian Communist party were by and large either in jail or exiled. Such questions as these, however, we have dealt with elsewhere.

one or another leadership group with power or that is successful in seizing power launches the country on a development effort, including deliberate and extensive efforts to create and arouse nationalism. Failure or too slow a pace creates turbulence. Occasionally there are attempts at secession by regions that are antagonized or left behind. *Coups* are frequent. Aristocratic and charismatic leaders are very vulnerable. Systems in which one party dominates a parliamentary government, such as we have seen in Mexico and India, are considerably less so, and a few of these will dot the landscape. Parliamentary governments in which power changes hands in an orderly fashion between two or more parties will be rare. Communist governments in addition to those already established will also be rare. The most frequent type of government will be that resulting from a military *coup*.

Thus, increasingly, the development and modernization effort will be managed by state bureaucracies, operating very rarely under a parliamentary government in which power alternates between or among two or more parties, occasionally under a parliamentary government dominated by one party, and most frequently by a government of the military. What we can expect, to repeat, is a pragmatic and more or less expert effort, a willingness to draw on outside help, through international organizations, but also from the great powers, if the state of the Cold War and geographic location permit. The tendency will be toward a planned economy, toward state-sponsored investment, controlled labor organization, state calls for hard work and unity, and above all state efforts to mobilize the people through nationalism.

A number of countries in Asia, Africa, the Middle East, and Latin America will undoubtedly succeed—achieving and maintaining a high rate of growth and at the same time keeping down the increase in population. A few others may fail spectacularly, with a small elite arrogating any gains to themselves and the mass of the population sunk in apathy untouched even by nationalism. There is some possibility also for the emergence of our "curious creature"—supranational organization combined with continuing nation-states—*simultaneously* with the further development of nationalism in Latin America and the Middle East, but little such possibility in Africa. However, one other possibility might also be conceivable: a regional organization and a common market *without* the presence of nationalism or its use as an instrumentality for mobilizing the populace. If something like this were to happen, it would seem most likely to occur in Africa among some of the countries where nationalism has not yet begun to take hold and tribalism is strong. But the possibility seems remote. As Rostow argues, "In Africa, it would be utopian to try to by-pass the nation-state, to seek the social integration required for modernity on a continental, Pan-Africa basis."[12]

But the result for most of the underdeveloped countries of the world seems likely to be none of these. In most countries, the economy will undoubtedly move to higher grounds of production, but with neither sustained growth nor growth across the board and with much of the gains absorbed by an increase in population. The country may even have steel mills and some heavy industry, yet the mass may continue to live at extremely low levels, with any surplus over subsistence going into any number of things, from luxuries for the elite to armaments. Thus the most common result seems likely to be the combination—the possibly explosive combination—of a highly aroused nationalism but neither a high, sustained rate of growth nor a slowed-down, contained population increase.

Implications

Just what the implications of all this are for humanity, other nations, and the people of the underdeveloped countries themselves may be beyond the powers of analysis. Of course, some of the consequences are obvious. One is sheer human misery. The plight of the millions who will be caught in the vicious circle of population pressure and poverty is appalling. Another consequence is still more turbulence—more *coups*, more attempts at secession, more civil war, more rebellion, more riots, more senseless violence out of frustration that is driven to mindless desperation. Beyond this our judgments will be more speculative, but some useful things can probably be said. We will attempt to deal first with possible changes in values and attitudes, and then,

[12] *A World of Nations* (Washington, D.C., 1967), p. 280.

later, with possible implications for international politics and the rest of the world.

Looking first at the countries that do succeed in reaching a stage of development comparable to the United States of the 1970s, one is tempted to assume that their values and attitudes will change in a pattern similar to what happened in the Western countries during their period of development and that the world of the future is one in which everyone pretty much shares the same basic values and attitudes. Surely we can be confident that certain kinds of attitudes, ones that are dysfunctional to development or at odds with scientific knowledge of health, will change into something more like those in the West. The practice in certain parts of India of using cow dung as a poultice on an infant after the umbilical cord is cut is an example, and so is the superstition that leads some northeastern Thais to put their privies where they contaminate the water supply. Still another example of a dysfunctional attitude is that toward time. Factories cannot run efficiently, as mentioned earlier, if the workers are not regular in appearing for work.

Effects on the Extended Family

We can also be sure that certain other kinds of changes will take place. An extended family system, for example, performs essential social functions in an agricultural, pre-industrial society. It is a substitute for unemployment compensation, for retirement, and a whole range of similar benefits. It also serves very complicated functions of the dissemination of information and the aggregation of values. But in an industrial society, the functions are either unnecessary or performed elsewhere. What the government doesn't assume is performed by other kinds of organizations, such as trade unions and interest groups, which play an important role in the aggregation of values, and a great variety of other institutions and associations. In the West, the final result of the changes wrought by the creation of an industrial society was the nuclear family.

In some of the underdeveloped countries, it may well be the same. There is some evidence that it is happening in Communist

China, for example.[13] Recent visitors report that the man-wife-children group is much, much more frequent than before. But it must also be said that it has been the Communist government's policy to break up the old Chinese family system, and it may be the policy that is having the effect rather than industrialization. It must also be said that the government may be exaggerating the success of its policy.

On the other hand, an extended family system may survive a long period of industrialization, although becoming modified in the process and performing different functions. Japan could be cited as an example.

However, in general, we would expect rather substantial changes in something like an extended family system under the impact of industrialization and modernization, even though it did survive and the final result was different than in the West.

A Completely Different Value Structure?

In general, in fact, beyond attitudes and values that are directly dysfunctional to development or directly affected by it, our expectation would be that the values and attitudes in developing countries would *not* follow the same pattern as in the West. If our analysis of the way values and attitudes change given above in connection with Myrdal's "circular causation" is correct—that is, that values and attitudes tend to *adapt* to other changes, and therefore to change as little as possible—our hypothesis would be that rather than everyone sharing the same basic values and attitudes in the future, national and cultural differences will persist.

Not very much systematic research has been done on this question as yet, but the evidence available is convincing. In a study of Mexican entrepreneurs and leading businessmen, Raymond Vernon found a value and attitude syndrome that "smacks a little of England's industrial class of 1810, Pittsburgh's moguls of 1890, and some of the Texas millionaires of the past decade or two." Yet all these characteristics were modified in peculiarly Mexican ways and set in a peculiarly Mexican context. In general this same conclusion applied to all segments of Mexican society.

[13] Tillman Durdin, "China's Changing Society Seems to Cut Birth Rate," New York *Times* (April 21, 1971), pp. 1, 8.

"According to seasoned observers of Mexican culture," Vernon writes, "many of the characteristics of the Mexico of the nineteenth century have apparently survived into the middle of the twentieth, though somewhat altered in form and emphasis."[14] For what it is worth, the conclusions of formal and systematic studies, such as Vernon's, are also supported by our more casual, commonsense observations. Industrialized, modernized Japan is not the same as the Japan of the period before the Meiji restoration, but it is not the same as industrialized, modernized America either.

Among those countries who fail to reach full development of their entire society, the contrasts and incongruities in values and attitudes will probably be amazing. Examples abound, but legislation against cow slaughter in India will suffice to illustrate. Over the past few years legislation prohibiting not only the slaughter of cows but the sale of beef products of any kind has been introduced in a number of the larger Indian states. Statutory support is thus being sought for attitudes—Hindu veneration of the cow—that already cause an enormous waste of grazing resources and an obstacle to agricultural development as well as preventing the use of a food that would go far toward relieving the mass of the people from malnutrition. India supports one quarter of the cattle population of the entire world, yet the great majority of the human population are deficient in protein.

Finally, it may be worth repeating our most fundamental conclusion about the central dynamic, the future crouching in the present, for all the underdeveloped countries. If our analysis is correct, both the countries that do achieve a level of development comparable with that of the United States and those that fail will share one set of attitudes that is likely to be even more significant than all the rest: a vibrant, thoroughly aroused nationalism.

Implications for the Rest of the World

When one turns to the implications of all these forces for the rest of the world and for international politics, the first thought that comes to mind is that the combination of aroused nationalism and failure in development might tempt many leaders into inter-

[14] *The Dilemma of Mexico's Development: The Roles of Private and Public Sectors* (Cambridge, 1963), p. 159.

national adventures. Sukarno and his policy of confrontation is an example. The great powers, with their nuclear arsenals, have the power to prevent such adventuring in theory, at least, but the mere existence of nuclear weapons may actually make nationalist leaders of underdeveloped countries freer to adventure than they have been in the past. The great powers will be very cautious about getting into situations that might lead to confrontations with other nuclear powers, and they may be even less inclined to become involved than in the past.

Whether or not the combination of aroused nationalism and only partially successful development leads to international adventuring, it does seem probable that many of the ancient hatreds, fears, and rivalries will be hard to lay to rest in such an environment. The tension between India and Pakistan or between Thailand and Cambodia is not likely to be lessened in an atmosphere of aroused nationalism.

Aroused nationalism might also transform itself into violent attempts to achieve even wider national identification: Pan-Arab, Pan-Malay, and Pan-African movements.

It could also be argued that the turbulence of the underdeveloped world will tempt great powers to adventure as much as it would the frustrated leaders of the underdeveloped world. Although the evidence offered in the chapters on the developed nations leads to the conclusion that they will be deterred from adventuring and that values and attitudes in a superindustrial society are likely to be opposed or indifferent to power and prestige values, still it must be recognized that the temptation is there.

One final consequence seems very likely indeed: an increasing bitterness and resentment of the developed countries, especially of the predominantly white countries, and most especially of the United States, which is the richest, most powerful, and most ubiquitous of them all. Although the poor countries do not actually grow poorer (even though some segments of the population in some countries may), the rich countries will be getting richer so much faster that the gap will continue to widen. If anyone doubts the degree of resentment that this combination of frustration, sense of oppression, and inability to do anything to achieve equality generates, he need only go to Latin America and gauge the depth of anti-American feeling there.

What we see then is tension between the developed world and the underdeveloped world. Lin Piao, Mao Tse-tung's designated successor before Lin's disgrace and downfall, in a major policy statement for Communist China on September 3, 1965, contained an analysis that may be more relevant than most people in the West realized at the time. He said that the main battlefield of the future was the "vast area of Asia, Africa, and Latin America" and that it was an "urgent necessity" for the people of these countries "to master and use people's war" as a weapon. "The contradiction between the revolutionary peoples of Asia, Africa, and Latin American and the imperialists headed by the United States," he wrote, "is the principal contradiction in the contemporary world." He painted a struggle not so much between communism and capitalism as between the underdeveloped world and the developed world: "Taking the entire globe, if North America and Western Europe can be called the 'cities of the world,' then Asia, Africa, and Latin America constitute the 'rural areas of the world.' . . . In a sense, the contemporary world revolution also presents a picture of the encirclement of the cities by the rural areas." In the framework of our analysis here, the possibility this seems to suggest is that even though communism as an ideology may have little future in the underdeveloped world, Communist and non-Communist underdeveloped countries may join in alliance against the developed countries of the world, both non-Communist and Communist.

In the end, it seems we cannot say with any confidence just where the growing tension between the developed and the underdeveloped worlds may lead, but only that it is clearly there and growing. And to be able to say this is probably enough—for no matter which particular form it takes, the outcome of tensions so acute and dangerous is bound to be bad.

Part V

CHINA: A ROAD APART

CHAPTER 15

The Rise of Communist China

IN 1831 Alexis de Tocqueville predicted that the United States and Russia would dominate the twentieth century. He based his reasoning on the fact that both had extensive territory and natural resources, that both had large, hard-working populations, and that both had the promise, visible beyond their immediate internal discord, of the kind of national unity and political organization necessary to direct their populations and resources to the achievement of national goals. It was presumably for lack of this third ingredient—effective political organization and direction— that Tocqueville left China off his list.

Today, the question of whether China has political unity and direction is still pertinent, and to it have been added several other questions. One concerns the forces of radicalism in China, of which Mao himself is only a part, although an important part. Will these radical forces succeed in forging a new kind of society and a new kind of human being? Another question concerns whether China will succeed in making itself a great power. If China does forge a new society and also becomes a great power, the repercussions will resound in both space and time. The fact that what happens to China will determine what happens to the "underdeveloped Communist world" may mean little, since the "underdeveloped Communist world" consists, in addition to China itself, only of North Korea, North Vietnam, Albania, and Cuba. But if China does succeed in becoming a great power, all the underdeveloped world will be affected. And if China succeeds in creating a new society and a new man, no part of the world will ever be the same.

To answer these questions we need to look briefly at the history of the Chinese Communists' rise to power, at Mao's personal history, at the ideology of radicalism in China, and, in somewhat more detail, at the product of all these factors: the Great Proletarian Cultural Revolution.

Early History

The Communist party of China was founded in 1921. Beginning in 1924, through the urging of Stalin, they co-operated for a time with Sun Yat-sen's party, the Kuomintang. But in 1927 came the break, hastened by Chiang Kai-shek's massacre of the Shanghai workers, whose insurrection had delivered him the city. The Communists attempted uprisings in the provinces of Hupei, Kiangsi, Kwangtung, and Hunan, which Mao headed, but all ended in disaster.

The Communists spent the next several years licking their wounds in several widely separated base areas. It was a time for questioning and for theorizing, and out of the debate, to which Mao contributed, came some of the Chinese Communist notions on guerrilla warfare and the strategic concept that the Chinese must turn orthodox Communist doctrine upside down and base their bid for power on the peasants and the countryside rather than on the proletariat and the cities.

In their periodic clashes with the Kuomintang, the Communists suffered successive defeats, and in October of 1934, they started on their famed Long March—an 8,000-mile trek to Shensi and eventually Yenan, an incredible distance over incredible terrain, fighting as they went. Over 125,000 began the march, but only 25,000 survived.

But in Yenan, the Communists had the base they needed. From it, they sallied out on guerrilla forays against the Kuomintang and the Japanese forces of occupation, and they also began to build a regular army. By 1945, they were ready to resume the battle for control of China. Japanese equipment they had either captured or acquired from the Soviets was an important ingredient in their new strength. But vastly more important was the fact that their willingness actually to fight the Japanese invaders had won for them in the minds of many Chinese the place and status of being *the* party of nationalism.

The Chinese Communist dictum was "talk/fight, talk/fight." In dealing with the Kuomintang, the Communists talked when negotiations promised to further their cause politically or when negotiations might forestall outside intervention; they fought whenever fighting could extend their control. In the fighting that continued between the talking, the Kuomintang won most of the battles at first. Then there was a trickle of defeats. Suddenly the trickle turned into a flood: Whole battalions, regiments, and even divisions started going over to the Communist side with all their American-supplied arms and equipment. In 1945, the Chinese Communists controlled a section in the north of China containing perhaps ninety million people and commanded an army of a million men, while the Kuomintang controlled a population at least five times as large and had an army of three million. By 1948, the balance was even, and by 1949, the struggle was all over: The Chinese Communists controlled the mainland and Chiang Kai-shek and what was left of the Kuomintang had escaped to Taiwan.

Mao Tse-tung

In the West, the tendency to simplify and symbolize what has happened in China makes it appear that the whole Communist revolution was wrought by one man, Mao Tse-tung. The Communists themselves have contributed to this impression by their use of Mao and the "thought of Mao" as rallying cries and symbols, the "cult of the personality." The truth of the matter is that the top leadership of the Communist party of China has always been more an uneasy coalition of different power factions than the dictatorship of one man. Mao's power to rule has always been limited. Still and all, Mao has held the formal title of top leader for many years, and there is no doubt that his personal input into the evolving Chinese Communist ideology and its operational strategy has been great. It is not only that we in the West have more information on Mao's personal role, but it was in fact a large one!

The bare facts of Mao's life are as follows.[1] He was born to a peasant family in Hunan. His father was harsh, and forced Mao to quit school, books, and learning, which Mao adored, to work on the land. The society was traditional—with all the social pressure for conformity that the term *traditional* suggests—whose central ethic was filial piety. Thus it seems significant, as we shall see, that at the age of sixteen Mao found the strength to confront his father and break with him. Mao left home and never saw his father again.

Mao joined one of Sun Yat-sen's revolutionary army units, but seems to have seen no fighting. Afterward, he went back to school, the First Normal School in Changsha, from which he graduated in 1918. He became active in the so-called May 4 Movement, formed by nationalists to protest the Japanese twenty-one demands. Following the lead of some of his former teachers, Mao became interested in Marxism. When the Communist party was launched in 1921, there were six Marxist study groups in all of China. Each sent two delegates to the Congress, and Mao was one of the two from Changsha.

In June 1923, Mao was elected to the Central Committee of the party, and moved to Shanghai, where the headquarters was maintained. When Moscow persuaded the Chinese Communists to collaborate with the Kuomintang, Mao threw himself into the

[1] For the following account of the life of Mao, I have drawn most heavily on Stuart Schram, *Mao Tse-tung* (London: Penguin Books, 1967). Others of particular value are Edgar Snow, *Red Star Over China* (New York, 1938); and Jerome Ch'ên, *Mao and the Chinese Revolution* (New York, 1965).

work. Then came the break, the attempted uprisings, the Long March, the years in Yenan, and ultimate victory.

It was a life of hardship and great danger. From 1927 to 1949—twenty-two years—the Communist forces were continuously at war. The toll of comrades and friends killed in combat or captured and executed was enormous. What happened to Mao's immediate family is illustrative. His first wife, whom he clearly loved deeply, and his sister were captured by the Kuomintang in 1930 and executed. His brother, Mao Tse-t'an, was killed in action on the Long March. His one remaining brother, Mao Tse-min, was executed by the Kuomintang in 1943. A son, Mao An-ying, was killed in the Korean War. Years later, in an interview with Edgar Snow, Mao himself spoke in wonderment that, of so many of his family and those closest to him, only he should survive.

It was also a life of unremitting struggle—for power, and once power was achieved, to bring about the revolution in Chinese society to which he was committed. What drives a man to such efforts? What motivates him to attempt the remaking of his society, which in this case was also the most ancient of civilizations?

Sources of Mao's Philosophy

Mao has been called a "poet without pity." His ideas and writings, certainly, are idealistic, even romantic. His acts, on the other hand, have shown a harder side, an impatience and a capacity for utter ruthlessness. An example is the Fut'ien incident in 1930, when Mao put down a revolt by a rival faction in the Twentieth Red Army in a repression that took the lives of some two thousand to three thousand officers and men. Those who have known him also describe a two-sided personality. Edgar Snow, for example, speaks of Mao's "deep sense of personal dignity," on the one hand, and his "power of ruthless decision," on the other.

Paradoxically, some instructive similarities can be seen between Mao, a Communist and thus an avowed atheist, and Martin Luther, a man of God who was also a revolutionary of historic proportions. Like Luther, Mao was an avid reader when young—Mao said of himself that he read "greedily, like an ox that has rushed into a vegetable garden. . . ." Also like Luther, Mao is an effective pamphleteer. He writes with an earthiness that any peasant can understand. Luther, for example, often used the sow as an image in vulgar, peasant ways: "Thou shalt not write a book unless you have listened to the fart of an old sow, to which you should open your mouth wide and say, 'Thanks to you, pretty nightingale; do I hear a text which is for me?'" Mao, for his part, once described the party's economic program as being "like the footbandages of a slut, long as well as smelly." On another occasion, while lecturing his soldiers, he explained that a base area was to an army what the buttocks were to a person—without the buttocks to sit on, a person would have to run about until exhausted; without a base, so would an army. Mao hated his father, and so did Luther. Luther's father hatred took the form of a profound doubt of divine righteousness, of the goodness of the Heavenly Father. Since the thought was unbearable, Luther's doubt turned against the earthly manifestion, and he used his gifts of language and leadership to bring about a massive revolution against the Church of Rome.[2] Mao's father hatred may have been no less far-reaching, for it may well have been a factor in arming him for the monumental task of destroying the Chinese family system—a system whose central ethic, as we have said, was the Confucian ideal of filial piety.

But even though father hatred may have given Mao emotional strength for some aspects of his work, his motivations also had other sources. The books that Mao read with the most oxlike greed of all in his childhood and youth were the popular novels that had been put together a few centuries earlier from oral traditions—especially the *Romance of the Three Kingdoms* and *Water Margin*.[3] The *Romance of the Three Kingdoms* is, in the words of one authority, "utterly impregnated with Confucian principles," and *Water Margin*, the most famous of the great traditional novels of peasant revolt, has the bandit heroes defending the true Confucian way when the Emperor is not fulfilling his proper role. Both influenced Mao "profoundly."[4]

[2] Erik Erikson, *Young Man Luther: A Study in Psychoanalysis and History* (New York, 1962).
[3] *Water Margin* was translated by Pearl Buck under the title *All Men Are Brothers*.
[4] Schram, op. cit., p. 21.

In addition to this early infusion of Confucian principles, Mao also had a romantic pride in China and a burning desire to see China great again. What all this suggests is a receptivity to the new notions of nationalism that were beginning to spread at the time. Certainly a form of nationalism seems to have been the first manifestation of political interest and the prime motive in Mao's early political activities. Many, many years later, talking to Edgar Snow, Mao dated the beginning of his political awareness to the age of sixteen and a "pamphlet deploring the loss to China of Korea, Taiwan, Indochina, Burma and other territories and tributary states," and Mao vividly remembered the opening sentence, "Alas, China will be subjugated." At eighteen, Mao joined Sun Yat-sen's army against the "foreign," Manchu dynasty. It was the nationalist, anti-Japanese May 4 Movement that got him into student politics and political organizing. And it seems likely that it was nationalist motives that led him toward Marxism.

Beyond father hatred and nationalism, it was probably Mao's five years at the First Normal School in Changsha and the teaching of the man who became his father-in-law, Yang Ch'ang-chi, that most influenced him. Yang Ch'ang-chi was professor of ethics, and he introduced Mao to the ferment bubbling among intellectuals throughout China at the time. Its source was the impact of the West on traditional China, and the debate was how China should respond, how it should avoid subjugation, what it should borrow from the West, and what it should preserve of its own. It was out of this ferment that arose the new nationalism. The mainstream of the radical intellectual life in China at the time were those who wanted to Westernize as rapidly and completely as possible, represented by what came to be known, from the incident already described, as the May 4 Movement. Before 1911, hardly anyone dared advocate anything more than adapting certain Western innovations to China's particular needs. But afterward, there came a change. The most vivid example was the review established at Peking university under the editorship of Ch'en Tu-hsiu (later the first secretary general of the Communist party) that advocated total and radical Westernization. Ch'en maintained that the salvation of China "lay in the hands of 'Mr.

Democracy' and 'Mr. Science,' who would sweep away the ignorance, superstition, and barbarism of the past and lay the foundations for a new, modern, secular state on Western lines.[5]

Yang Ch'ang-chi was an enthusiastic supporter of the new review and urged Mao and his other students to read it. But in his courses, Yang taught Chinese ideas as well as Western. Yang had spent ten years studying abroad in Japan, England, and Germany, but he had had a solid classical Chinese education before that. "Each country," he seems to have drummed into his students, "has its own national spirit, just as each person has his own personality. The culture of one country cannot be transplanted in its entirety to another country." Thus Yang also introduced Mao and the other students to another group that was seeking the inspiration for a rebirth of China in its own heritage, principally in the writings of Wang Fu-chih, who had refused to serve the new masters at the time of the Manchu conquest. Mao attended their meetings and "absorbed their point of view."

Thus Mao's personal input to the Communist party program came out of these diverse motivations and influences: father hatred in a society devoted to filial piety; a new nationalism reacting to the impact of the West; the contrary pulls of pride in one's heritage and the need for modernization; and, finally, the searing experiences of almost twenty-five years of war and revolution.

The Ideology of Chinese Communism

Except for father hatred, most of the other members of the party leadership were subject to similar influences: nationalism, the contrary pulls of pride in China and the obvious need to destroy much of the old to build the new, and the twenty-five years of war. Judging from their actions, all undoubtedly understood that the first task, after victory, was to consolidate their power. The Army was the instrument in the first phase of this, and it was used ruthlessly, brutally crushing any show of armed opposition wherever it appeared. The next task was to break the power of the old order. The landlord class had to be eliminated,

[5] Ibid., p. 38.

eventually including the Chinese equivalent of the Kulak, the rich peasant on his way to becoming a landlord. In the cities, it meant breaking the power of the middle class engaged in industry, business, and commerce. On the other hand, the contrary pull of modernization required preserving individuals whose skills would be needed in running the enterprises taken over by the state. For Mao, and others who read the history of other revolutionary movements, it also meant constant vigilance to prevent the Communist party and the state bureaucracy from falling back into the traditional ways and corruption, as had happened to the Kuomintang. And ever present was the thought, unquestionably disturbing to men who were clearly nationalists above all else, that much of the ancient value system of China might also have to be destroyed, including the Chinese family system itself.

The positive side of the evolving Communist goals was the vision of a new society and a new man. In Mao's case, it seems fairly clear that the vision drew on Mao's romanticism, especially of things Chinese, his idealization of the peasant, his intense nationalism—to all of which we have already referred. It drew also on his experiences through the long years spent in attaining power. For example, it was this pragmatism that made him receptive to the idea of turning Communist doctrine upside down, as mentioned above, basing the bid for power on the peasants and the countryside rather than on the proletariat and the cities. But this is not the only difference between the vision and the orthodox Marxist-Leninist view. Perhaps the most central belief of Chinese communism as expressed in the "thought of Mao Tse-tung" is also the most un-Marxist: the extreme voluntarism, the conviction that ideas are more important than material conditions, that human will and determined men can and will prevail no matter how awesome the obstacles. Although Mao gives lip service to Marxist materialism, voluntarism is his true belief: "While we recognize that in the general development of history, the material determines the mental and social being determines social consciousness," he writes, "we also—and indeed must—recognize the reaction of mental on material things, of social consciousness on social being and of the superstructure on the economic base."[6] On occasion, he even omits the bow to Marxist tradition: "It is man's social being that determines his thinking. Once the correct ideas characteristic of the advanced class are grasped by the masses, these ideas turn into a material force which changes society and changes the world."[7] An official volume to guide one in the study of Mao's thought applied the principle not just to social affairs but to nature: "Many living examples show that there is only unproductive thought, there are no unproductive regions. There are only poor methods for cultivating the land, there is no such thing as poor land. Provided only that people manifest in full measure their subjective capacities for action, it is possible to modify natural conditions."[8]

Will and determination are also the keys to military success. With them, the inferior power can overcome the superior. The imperialist enemy must be respected tactically, but strategically he must be despised. In the final outcome, "the imperialists and all reactionaries are paper tigers." As Lin Piao says in describing the official Chinese party line on the subject, it is "objective law" both that imperialism will rely on armed force and that there will be "peoples' wars" of resistance. "The people subjected to its aggression . . . are fighting for independence and freedom on their own soil. Once they are mobilized on a broad scale, they will have inexhaustible strength. This superiority will belong not to the United States but to the people subjected to its aggression. The latter, though apparently weak and small, are really more powerful than U.S. imperialism."[9]

Against will and determination, even nuclear weapons are paper tigers. "However highly developed modern weapons and technical equipment may be and however complicated the methods of modern warfare, in the final analysis the outcome of a war will be decided by the sustained fighting of the ground forces, by the

---

[6] "On Contradiction," *Selected Works*, Foreign Languages Press: Vol. I (Peking, 1960), p. 336.
[7] "Where Do Correct Ideas Come From?" (Peking, 1963), p. 1.
[8] Hsüe-hsi Mao Tse-tung ti szu-hsiang fang-fa ho kung-tso fang fa, Peking, Chung-kuo Ch'ing-nien Ch'u-pan-she (1958), p. 73, as quoted and translated by Schram, op. cit., p. 295.
[9] "Long Live the Victory of People's War!," *Peking Review* (September 3, 1965).

fighting at close quarters on battlefields, by the political consciousness of the men, by their courage and spirit of sacrifice. Here the
weak points of U.S. imperialism will be completely laid bare,
while the superiority of the revolutionary people will be brought
into full play. The reactionary troops of U.S. imperialism cannot
possibly be endowed with the courage and the spirit of sacrifice
possessed by the revolutionary people. The spiritual atom bomb
which the revolutionary people possess is a far more powerful
and useful weapon than the physical atom bomb."[10]

"Thought Rectification"

This belief in voluntarism, in the dominating power of human
will, led Mao and his colleagues in the leadership to put the
"revolution for men's minds" central. Each individual in the whole
nation must undergo an intellectual and psychic rebirth if the
revolution is really to succeed. Success depends more on changing men's attitudes than it does on social forces, which would be
the more orthodox Communist view. It is only this emphasis on
a revolution in individual thought patterns—on mass "thought
reform"—that can explain the enormous emphasis on the many
re-education campaigns the Communists later launched, the necessity for everyone in China to carry the "little red book" of the
thoughts of Chairman Mao, and to explain every success from
increasing fertilizer production to inventing a nuclear bomb as
the result of applying the thought of Chairman Mao. When Stalin
lost confidence in the party organization, he loosed the secret police in a massive purge that left thousands dead or in prison
camps; when Mao lost confidence in the party organization, he
unleased the Red Guards in a mass campaign of "thought rectification."

Salvation in Collectivity

But the stress on the central importance of re-educating each
and every individual in society is not to be understood as a form
of individualism. On the contrary, the Chinese Communists
tended to see man's salvation in collectivity, in such arrangements

10 Ibid.

as the true commune, rather than simply the Marxist notion of abolishing private property. In part, this notion that man's salvation lies in collectivity was Mao's romanticizing of the people, which many of the other leaders seem to have shared. Over and over again, they saw true goodness, true wisdom, true virtue in the simple peasant masses, and official party propaganda continually urged the high and mighty to turn to the peasant mass for their instruction. It was not always rhetoric, either. An example is the "down sending" campaign, in which officials of all kinds, professors, students, and other experts and specialists, were "sent down" to the villages for periods of manual labor.

It should also be said that the source of this notion that man's salvation lies in collectivity stems not only from the romanticism of Mao and the other leaders but from deep within Chinese culture. One authority, for example, has argued that their culture has conditioned the Chinese to abhor individual freedom and to seek security in organization, hierarchy, and ideological uniformity. "Whenever groups of Chinese are brought together they seem quickly to form themselves into structural organizations. In their overseas communities the Chinese have tended to sort themselves into their various associations, their *huis* and *tongs*. It is entirely consistent with their culture that the Chinese prisoners of war in Korea did not become the apathetic mass of demoralized individuals that prisoners usually are, but they quickly and almost spontaneously became intensely organized political groups; leaders emerged overnight and the vast majority soon formed themselves into solid hierarchical structures."[11]

Another source of the attitude that man's salvation lies in collectivity may be the idealization of the military life by the Chinese Communist leadership. They spent most of their lives within a military organization, and it was those years that they tended to look back on as the golden age of the revolution. It is no accident that one of the campaigns of indoctrination was titled the "Learn from the Army" campaign. In the words of one of his biographers, Mao himself "regards the army as the natural reposi-

[11] Lucian W. Pye, *The Spirit of Chinese Politics: A Psychocultural Study of the Authority Crisis in Political Development* (Cambridge, Massachusetts, 1968), pp. 172–73.

tory of the ethos of struggle and sacrifice which is for him the hallmark of every true revolutionary movement. The army also tends naturally toward the combination of discipline and initiative which is Mao Tse-tung's constant preoccupation. It is thus not surprising that the heroes recommended as models to Chinese youth in the last few years have been soldiers."[12] But whatever its source, an important part of the Chinese Communist vision is a social organization in which mankind lives together in communal groups with the discipline and purpose of a military organization.

Social Forces

But for all the emphasis on voluntarism and the central importance of "correct thinking" and remolding the individual mind, the Chinese Communists still attribute considerable importance to social forces. Mao himself sees the social process in terms of "contradictions"—of struggle and conflict. "Changes in society," he writes, "are due chiefly to the development of the internal contradictions in society, that is, the contradiction between classes and the contradiction between the old and the new; it is the development of these contradictions that pushes society forward and gives the impetus for the supersession of the society by the new."[13] In Mao's view, class struggle does not cease just because the Communist party has taken over, even though it may have successfully created a socialist state and started the transition to communism. "The class struggle between the proletariat and the bourgeoisie, the class struggle between the different political forces, and the class struggle in the ideological field between the proletariat and the bourgeoisie will continue to be long and tortuous and at times will even become very acute. The proletariat seeks to transform the world according to its own world outlook, and so does the bourgeoisie. In this respect, the question of which will win out, socialism or capitalism, is still not really settled."[14]

If the party ever neglects the class struggle or relaxes in any

12 Schram, op. cit., p. 325.
13 "On Contradiction," p. 314.
14 "On the Correct Handling of Contradictions Among the People," selected works, Lawrence Urshort, Vol. 2 (London, 1950), pp. 51–52.

way, "then it would not be long, perhaps only several years or a decade, or several decades at most, before a counter-revolutionary restoration on a national scale would inevitably occur, the Marxist-Leninist party would undoubtedly become a revisionist party or a fascist party, and the whole of China would change its colour."[15] It is for this reason that Mao felt not only that the revolution was not assured but that the only possibility of success for the revolution is for it to be *continuous*. The revolution must be waged unceasingly, everywhere, at all times, against manifestations of the bourgeoisie in all segments of society, even within the party itself—or, more accurately, *especially* within the party itself. Thus the concept of permanent revolution.

To sum up, the Chinese Communist vision for the future is a new society and a new human being. Man will find the meaning of his existence in an ideal collectivity with the discipline and organization of the military life. The means to the goal are voluntarism, the power of the human will, and the means to achieving the necessary will and dedication are through an intellectual and psychic rebirth, through mass indoctrination and the mass cultivation of "correct thinking." The enemies of the revolution, also, are everywhere, powerful, and persistent, and the only possibility of final success is unremitting, unrelenting, unceasing struggle—the permanent revolution. Yet side by side with this harsh and militant side is the softer, more pragmatic side. This is the side that accepts the coalition nature of the Chinese leadership and the corollary need for compromise among divergent views. It is the side that accepts the talk side of "talk/fight, talk/fight." It is the side that accepts the "Bandung spirit" of coexistence in foreign policy. Indeed, it is the side that accepts the need for inviting President Nixon to Peking and a normalization in relations with the United States.

Consolidating Power

The effort to consolidate power and the attack on the old order began in earnest on February 21, 1951, with the so-called "Regu-

[15] Mao Tse-tung in May 1963, as quoted by Lin Piao in his "Report to the Ninth National Congress of the Communist Party of China," *Peking Review*, No. 18 (April 30, 1969).

tions for the Punishment of Counter-revolutionaries" and the land reform program that was carried out at the same time. Mass trials were held in every village, the peasants were encouraged to denounce landlords and former officials and their families for past crimes and "exploitations," and the crowds themselves were urged to judge and condemn. Shouts of *"Sha! Sha!"* ("Kill! Kill!") were followed by execution on the spot. Apart from the fact that in the eyes of the Communist party, landlords deserved the death penalty for past crimes, there was purpose in the method chosen; for it was only when the peasants had personally denounced the crimes of their former exploiters and seen them put to death that they would come to understand that the world had really changed.[16]

The official Chinese estimate is that the people's courts dealt with eight hundred thousand people in this way in the first half of 1951, but the evidence available indicates that the actual figure was much higher. A "reasonable" estimate puts the figure at about two million.[17] The purge continued throughout 1952 and was again renewed in 1955. No one knows the grand total, but its effect was to eliminate from Chinese rural life both the landlord and the rich peasant.

The next step in establishing control over the countryside was to set up collective farms on the Soviet model, and this was completed in one spectacular rush in the winter of 1955–56. In those few months five hundred million people were grouped together into collective farming units.

In the cities, the program against the middle class centered around the "three anti" and the "five anti" campaigns against evils that were charged to the business community, such as tax evasion and bribery. In addition, factories and businesses were nationalized.

By the end of 1956, all possible focal points for opposition within the Chinese population had been eliminated. By a combination of organization and positive direction, the Communist party, in the judgment of some Western authorities, had "politicized" the entire Chinese population, and had created the "abil-

[16] Schram, op. cit., p. 259.
[17] Ibid., p. 267.

ity to mobilize the mass of the people for purposes which it chooses."[18]

The "Hundred Flowers" Campaign

A test of this judgment came in 1956, with the so-called "Hundred Flowers" Campaign, in which the regime relaxed its controls and deliberately tried to provoke discussion. In May, Mao proclaimed the slogan, "Let a Hundred Flowers Bloom Together; Let Diverse Schools of Thought Contend." Cautiously, a few intellectuals spoke of minor things. Then, after the Hungarian rebellion and the Soviet intervention to put it down—events that had been followed with wonder by both the people and the party in China —the Communist leadership decided in May 1957 to go even farther and take the lid off entirely, inviting criticism as well as "discussion." The motive behind this decision was probably complex. It may be that the then-dominant faction of the leadership thought that the measures taken to destroy the old order had gone far to produce the dream of a new society and a new man, and that they wanted a test of just how much had been accomplished. It may also be that the top leadership thought a loosening of controls for a time would head off the kind of discontent that had led to the rebellion in Hungary and stimulate co-operation. In any case, the results were astounding. Some of China's most respected intellectuals spoke out bluntly, and there followed a flood of public criticism—of communism, of police-state methods, of economic policies, of relations with the Soviet Union, and of almost every other aspect of the regime and its policies. To those who were present at the time, it was almost unbelievable. As a Chinese intellectual and diplomat who later sought asylum abroad said, "I think the Hundred Flowers Campaign was the most amazing campaign during the past fifteen years of Chinese Communist history. The people really pour [sic] their heart out and the criticism and the condemnation against the Communists were just incredible. People like me in Communist China were amazed to see that the people had so much grievance against the Communist regime. I did believe Mao Tse-tung was sincere in launch-

[18] A. Doak Barnett, *Communist China and Asia: Challenge to American Policy* (New York, 1960), p. 18.

ing that Hundred Flowers Campaign. Obviously, he was quite confident that his regime gained the support of the Chinese people, so the Chinese Communists can afford to be a little lenient and liberalize a little bit of their regime. . . ."

The outpouring of criticism was indeed an amazing display of how much disaffection the Communist regime had created. But in a peculiar twist it also revealed a certain amount of support for the regime in an unexpected place—among intellectuals. For most of the criticism from intellectuals was of means and specific policies; over-all goals and purposes were accepted, either explicitly or implicitly. As one authority put it, "despite the disaffection which came into the open in 1957, it is clear that many intellectuals in China, for reasons of nationalism and ideology, continue to give the regime strong backing in its basic aims."[19]

For exactly one month, the outpouring continued. Then, brutally and effectively, the Communist leadership reversed the "Hundred Flowers" policy and launched on a "rectification" program to root out opposition, leading eventually to a purge in the party itself and the transfer of over a million government and party bureaucrats from the cities to the villages.

The "Great Leap Forward" and the Commune Program

The effort to create a new society and a new man had clearly not made the headway for which Mao and the others had hoped. Neither had much headway been made on the nationalist goal of making China strong economically and militarily. The seriousness of the economic problems China faced—population growth, as well as some of the results of collectivization—became more apparent to the top leadership. Mao's proposal was to combine the two—characteristically, to opt for boldness, to create the new society and make China strong in one fell swoop. "Throughout the country," Mao wrote in 1958, "the Communist spirit is surging forward. The political consciousness of the masses is rising rapidly. . . . In view of this, our country may not need as much time as was previously envisaged to catch up with the big capitalist countries in industrial and agricultural production. . . . Apart from

[19] Ibid., p. 32.

their other characteristics, China's six hundred million people are, first of all, poor, and secondly, 'blank.' That may seem like a bad thing, but it is really a good thing. Poor people want change, want to do things, want revolution. A clean sheet of paper has no blotches, and so the newest and most beautiful words can be written on it, the newest and most beautiful pictures can be painted on it."[20] Apparently there was an internal debate of considerable intensity, but Mao and the advocates of boldness won. Early in 1958, the government announced the "Great Leap Forward" program—a plan to mobilize the entire population in a vast development scheme to build small and medium-size factories all over China (including the highly publicized "backyard steel furnaces") and to increase the rate of economic growth at a fantastic pace. Coupled with this was an attempt to realize the dream of salvation through a collectivity along the lines of an idealized military organization—the program to turn the agricultural collectives, which were essentially administrative units that permitted large-scale rather than small-plot farming, into true communes in which the tasks of cooking and caring for the children would be done in mess halls and nursery schools, and men and women would work as equals side by side in the fields.

If nothing else, the Great Leap Forward demonstrated the propaganda capabilities of the regime—newspapers, radio, wall posters, and mass rallies whipped the masses up to frenetic activity. The result was a release of human energy unlike anything seen in the world since the burst of religious fervor that brought the hundred-year spurt of cathedral building in the Middle Ages. And it was nearly matched in the commune program, for in one year some 700,000 collectives were supposedly turned into 26,-000 communes.

By the end of 1958, it was clear to everyone that both the Great Leap Forward and the commune program were spectacular failures, although the public admission was delayed. Even so, as early as August 1959 an official communiqué issued by the plenum of the Central Committee admitted that the grain harvest had actually been only 250 million tons rather than the 375 million previously claimed. As it turned out, things got even worse

[20] "Introducing a Cooperative," *Peking Review*, No. 15 (June 10, 1958), p. 6.

the next year. The harvest of 1959 was lower still—partly because of the weather, but partly due to the disorganization of the economy brought about by the Great Leap Forward and the resistance of the peasants to the communes.

Mao on the Shelf

The public admission came later, as we say; but the policy was changed in December 1958, when the plenum of the Central Committee took the first step in calling off the Great Leap Forward and in muting and camouflaging the communes. Mao had earlier announced his intention to resign from the post of Chairman of the Chinese People's Republic (the "government"), which he held along with the post of Chairman of the party, but it was probably no accident that no effort was made to "persuade" him to change his mind. Mao did not stand as a candidate, and the plenum elected Liu Shao-ch'i to the post of chief of state. Chou En-lai became Premier, and Mao retained the post of Chairman of the Central Committee. Whether Mao's colleagues forced him to take this step or he did it on his own initiative is not known, but it does seem clear that the final result was a compromise between Mao and his critics, led by Liu Shao-ch'i. Mao seems to have given up his predominant role in domestic affairs. At the same time, he apparently was allowed to retain the role of all-seeing leader—the so-called "cult of the personality" continued to reign supreme—and, perhaps, a still-large role in foreign affairs, over which there was no serious disagreement.

Foreign Affairs

In foreign affairs, the consensus among the top leadership included both goals and tactics. As in domestic affairs, the goals were a mix of dreams and practicality. The dream was to restore China to a position of greatness, of national power and prestige. "Our nation," Mao said in September of 1949, "will never again be an insulted nation. We have stood up." It was clear that the top leadership dreamed of China taking her rightful place in the world as a great power with a large voice in world affairs. But tactically they certainly did not intend to take undue risks in achieving such goals, to embark on provocative action or rely on military force as the primary instrument in achieving their goals. In terms of the immediate situation, in fact, they saw themselves as threatened, dangerously threatened, by both the West and by their Communist fellow, the Soviet Union. And when they felt the threat was immediate or aimed at vital interests of national security, they did not shrink from using military force and accepted both the risk and the sacrifice that using force entailed.

The Korean War

There is no reason to believe that the Chinese had anything to do with initiating the Korean War. Khrushchev in his memoirs says that Kim Il-sung, the Premier of North Korea, came to Stalin for permission and support for an attack on the South, and that Stalin granted it only if Peking also approved, which they did. The other evidence available is at least consistent with that account. But the Chinese decision to intervene in the war when the American and South Korean forces crossed the thirty-eighth parallel and neared the Yalu River border with China was most likely an independent decision, taken from a sense of threat.[21] At the outset of the Korean War, President Truman ordered the Seventh Fleet to "neutralize" the "Formosa Strait" and declared that the legal status of Taiwan was an open question, subject to determination by a peace treaty with Japan or by the UN. The Chinese Communists reacted violently to these actions, which they regarded as intervention and "armed aggression against the territory of China." Over the first few months of the war, in fact, they seemed to be more preoccupied with Taiwan than with what was happening in Korea.

Following the successful counterattack by the UN forces at Inchon and especially as they approached the thirty-eighth parallel, the Chinese became more agitated. Chou En-lai, the Chinese Foreign Minister at the time, said on September 30, 1950, that "the Chinese people will not tolerate foreign aggression, nor will they supinely tolerate seeing their neighbors being savagely invaded by the imperialists." Even stronger reactions and warnings were expressed to K. M. Panikkar, the Indian ambassador to

[21] The authoritative account is Allen S. Whiting, *China Crosses the Yalu: The Decision to Enter the Korean War* (New York: Macmillan, 1960).

Peking, culminating in a specific and formal warning in a dramatic midnight meeting on the night of October 2–3, that if the American forces crossed the thirty-eighth parallel, the Chinese would intervene in the war.

The UN General Assembly had been debating the issue of crossing the parallel and unifying Korea by force of arms in one form or another since the Inchon landings on September 15. Soviet attempts to obtain Chinese Communist participation in the debate failed, and so did Indian efforts at a compromise. On October 7, the General Assembly passed a resolution endorsing "all appropriate steps to ensure conditions of stability throughout Korea," and the United States 1st Cavalry Division crossed the thirty-eighth parallel that same day. On October 16, a few Chinese Communist "volunteers" entered Korea secretly, followed in late October and early November by forces that totaled over three hundred thousand.

The Chinese Communists also took the opportunity to seize Tibet. On October 24, 1950, they announced that their troops had been ordered to "liberate" the country. The Tibetans were quickly defeated, and when the Chinese offered a treaty—the so-called "Agreement on Peaceful Measures with China"—that seemed to permit Tibet some degree of autonomy under Chinese sovereignty, they accepted.

But if the Korean War demonstrated Chinese Communist determination, it also demonstrated that they could make a realistic assessment of the situation and respond flexibly to it. By June of 1951, it had become clear that neither side could win in Korea without risking a world war. The pattern of limited war in which the Communists had a sanctuary in Manchuria and the UN forces had a sanctuary in Japan had also become well established. It was at this time that the Soviets arranged for negotiations on a cease-fire—clearly with the approval of the Chinese and probably on their initiative.[22] As the cease-fire talks dragged on, the Chinese were also negotiating with the Soviet Union for economic aid, and the fact that it was not until after Stalin's death in early 1953 that the Soviet aid agreement was announced and that the Chinese brought the cease-fire negotiations to a con-

[22] Barnett, op. cit., p. 95.

clusion may be indicative of a divergence in Chinese and Soviet interests at the time.

Still another sign of the realism and flexibility in Communist China's foreign policies came at an "Asian and Pacific Peace Conference" held in Peking in October 1952. The Chinese had made enormous efforts to see that the conference was well attended, and they then used it to launch a policy of "peaceful coexistence," calling on the United Nations both to end the fighting in Vietnam and Malaya and to "bring about just and reasonable settlements through negotiations." It was a dramatic departure from their usual dogmatic preachments of violence, revolution, and irreconcilable hostility between East and West.

The Indochina War

Clearly, the Chinese Communists were about to embark on a new course in foreign policy, but one untidiness still remained. Immediately following World War II, the Communist parties of Southeast Asia—in Burma, Thailand, Malaya, the Philippines, and French Indochina—had launched campaigns of terror, using weapons left over from the war. In most places, these insurrections were crude and unsophisticated campaigns of indiscriminate killing, and they alienated more people from communism than they enlisted. Only one of these was making any real headway, the guerrilla war against the French in Indochina. The Chinese had given the Communist-led Vietminh some arms and equipment, and throughout the rest of 1953, they increased their shipments. By the spring of 1954 the French had agreed to the Geneva conference. When it convened, the Chinese came to Geneva as equals with the great powers, a symbol of status and prestige that was itself a Chinese Communist goal. When the French were defeated shortly afterward at Dienbienphu, the Communist North Vietnamese apparently wanted to keep on fighting until they controlled all of Vietnam, but they were persuaded to settle for less by both the Soviets and the Chinese. The Soviet national interest would not be served by further fighting in Asia, and there may also have been a link between Soviet pressure on Hanoi to end the war and the French decision to reject the proposed European Defense Community. But it was the Chinese whose influence was undoubtedly the greatest in engineering the compromise that created two Vietnams and permitted the separate settlements for Laos and Cambodia. Whether it was because they wanted a pause in the fighting on their border areas so they could concentrate their resources on internal development or because they feared that the United States would intervene when they saw all of Vietnam passing to Communist control in spite of their decision to stay out, the Chinese Communists decided to compromise. But the important fact is that it was the Chinese who made the decision, not the Vietnamese. At Geneva the representatives of the Vietnamese Communists complained bitterly of the Chinese pressure to all who would listen, including Western newsmen. But the power to make decisions for the region was also undoubtedly a Chinese goal.

The New Line

With the signing of the Geneva agreements in July 1954, the stage was set for the new Chinese Communist line. The theme was the *panch shila*—five principles of peaceful coexistence consisting of mutual respect for sovereignty and territorial integrity, for nonaggression, for noninterference in each other's domestic affairs, for mutual benefit and equality, and for peaceful coexistence. At first, most of the foreign offices in the West thought of the *panch shila* as a vague and rather simplistic propaganda gimmick. But they misunderstood the appeal in Asia. The shadow of China had always been long in Asia, and any sign of Chinese willingness to move toward accommodation was bound to be welcomed and encouraged. The "five principles" also reflected an essentially Asian attitude and approach—Asians are not only anticolonial, but they are suspicious of alliances and "foreign bases in the countries," and they are powerfully attracted by such ideas as neutrality and nonalignment.

Even as early as the fall of 1954, this diplomatic campaign to improve relations and seek friendships had made enough progress to permit the Chinese to take some risks. Reminding the world and especially its newfound friends that Taiwan and the offshore islands, which the Kuomintang still controlled, were part of China even in the Kuomintang's view, and making a distinction between the use of force for external aggression and the use of force to regain control in one's own territory, the Chinese Communists began the bombardment of Quemoy and Matsu, the largest of the offshore islands. In a carefully paced and politically disciplined program of bombardment and military probes, the Chinese tested the Kuomintang and American determination to support them—combining diplomatic and political pressures with bombardment and the threat of invasion, but stopping short of full-scale military assault. The crisis reached a peak in early 1955—but then began to subside, partly because the American response had been firm and partly because the Chinese Communists apparently felt that there was more to be gained politically by continuing their diplomatic peace offensive.

The Bandung Conference

The opportunity came with the Bandung Conference in 1955. The Conference had been called by the "Colombo" powers— India, Burma, Indonesia, Pakistan, and Ceylon—as a formal meeting of the governmental leaders of Asian and African countries only. For the first time, it brought together in one place, with no Western powers present, such Asian and African leaders as Nehru of India, Chou En-lai of China, U Nu of Burma, Mohammed Ali of Pakistan, Kotelawala of Ceylon, Sihanouk of Cambodia, Romulo of the Philippines, Nasser of Egypt, and Nkrumah of what became Ghana—leaders from a total of twenty-nine Asian and African countries.

Nehru and Chou dominated the conference, but it was clearly Chou who profited most. Repeating that "revolution is not for export," Chou adopted a stance of reasonableness and accommodation. At every opportunity, whether private dinner party or public occasion, he maintained that Communist China was devoted to peace and that it wished "to establish normal relations with all Asian and African countries, with all the countries of the world, and first of all with our neighboring countries."

In the next two years, the Chinese Communists exploited the theme of "Asian solidarity" to the full. The Chinese sent high-level, high-prestige visitors, including Madame Sun Yat-sen, wherever an invitation could be wangled, and in turn arranged for a whole string of visits to Peking: Prime Minister Suhrawardy of Pakistan, U Nu of Burma, Sukarno of Indonesia, Sihanouk of Cambodia, and Souvanna Phouma of Laos. And they also embarked on an aid program, modest in actual value but important in terms of impact. Prince Sihanouk, for example, was given a radio station—with one of the most powerful transmitters in all of Southeast Asia.

East Wind over West Wind

But those among Asian leaders who hoped that "peaceful co-existence" and "Asian solidarity" were something more than just tactics in Chinese Communist policy were doomed to disappointment. Just why the Chinese shifted to a harder line is not yet known, but the hard-line faction in Peking was undoubtedly strengthened by the failure of the Bandung policies to gain China any significant benefit—indeed, the United States response had been to *increase* its buildup in the western Pacific. The event that triggered the new, harder line was the Soviet launching of the first Sputnik, in the autumn of 1957. This feat gave the Communist world enormous prestige, not only as the leader in space science, but also in military and strategic terms, as the first nation to achieve a workable intercontinental ballistic missile. The Communist leaders were undoubtedly encouraged to believe they could risk a new direction in policy, but it may also be that tensions internal to the Communist countries themselves had created a need for external hostility, especially in the case of Communist China, which had just experienced the "Hundred Flowers" outpouring of criticism. In any case, Mao Tse-tung declared a shift back to a harsher, more hostile policy in a dramatic speech on November 18, 1957, at the celebrations in Moscow of the fortieth anniversary of the Bolshevik Revolution. "I consider," Mao said, "that the present world situation has reached a new turning point." Re-emphasizing the Cold War between the Communist and non-Communist worlds, he went on to say that there were "now two winds in the world: the east wind and the west wind. . . . I think the characteristic of the current situation is that the east wind prevails over the west wind; that is, the strength of socialism exceeds the strength of imperialism."

The first serious and risky manifestation of the new policy came in the late summer, when the Chinese Communists moved large numbers of troops into position opposite the offshore islands and, as in 1954–55, threatened to invade. The threat was combined with subtleties—publicly and privately, through agents in Hong Kong, the Communists appealed to the Kuomintang leaders to make a deal. But it also ran a high level of risk— Communist China and the United States, in the words of Secretary of State John Foster Dulles, came to the "brink of war" before the Chinese decided to let the crisis taper off.

Secondary Effects

One of the ironies of the new Chinese policy was that it produced a growing hostility toward India, which had long pursued policies of friendship and accommodation with China, and even toward Nehru himself, who had sponsored Chou En-lai's introduction to Asian and African leaders at the Bandung Conference. The immediate cause was Tibet. Following their occupation of Tibet in 1950–51, the Chinese had begun to build a network of roads permitting truck traffic between the different segments of Tibet and three main highways linking the central Tibetan plateau with Sinkiang and China proper. These roads in some cases crossed Indian territory or territory in dispute, but the real trouble was political. The roads permitted the Chinese to consolidate their hold on Tibet, and they began to use this control to eliminate the Buddhist religion and remake Tibetan society. The methods included every instrument that conquerors have used on an alien population, including torture and degradation of the Buddhist monks and the mass removal of children to China for re-education and to break the influence of parents. In 1959, the Tibetans revolted. The Dalai Lama, traditional leader of the Tibetan people, fled—with the help of the American CIA. The fact that the CIA had the capability to help the Dalai Lama to escape may have led the Chinese to believe it had also inspired the revolt. In any case, the Chinese not only put down the revolt, but did so with savage brutality. When the Dalai Lama reached the border, the Indians gave him sanctuary. Their motive may have been simple humanitarianism, for they were sensitive enough to the policy implications for their relations with China to keep him in one of the most inaccessible places in all India and to refuse permission for journalists and others to see him. But the Chinese nevertheless reacted with vehement hatred and promptly precipitated the first of the Sino-Indian border crises.

The Vietnam War

Another consequence of the new Chinese policy—of which the Chinese must have been fully aware—was that the North Vietnamese and the Viet Cong in South Vietnam understood that the Chinese no longer had any objections to their making an attempt to reunify Vietnam by force through guerrilla warfare. It seems probable that the Vietnamese sought approval from both Peking and Moscow, and obtained it, but in any case not long after Mao's "East Wind" speech, guerrilla cadres began to come down the old Ho Chi Minh Trail through Laos from North to South Vietnam.

As we said, the Chinese undoubtedly understood that the North Vietnamese would interpret the "East Wind" speech as a green light. And Lin Piao's article of September 3, 1965, made it clear that central to the Chinese Communist strategy was the doctrine of "revolutionary warfare"—guerrilla tactics plus political action. But it is important to note that the Chinese contemplated only a very limited role for themselves in such wars. China and their own revolution, which was based on the peasants, was to provide the example. Mao's many writings on guerrilla warfare and the article by Lin Piao were to provide the doctrine. China, too, could provide some training for local leaders in certain circumstances and perhaps some supplies and military equipment. It could certainly provide moral and political support. But people's war, in the Chinese view, is very definitely do-it-yourself war. The fighting must necessarily be done by members of the national liberation movements themselves.

The Sino-Indian War of 1962

Both the Eisenhower and Kennedy administrations responded to the guerrilla threat to Vietnam by sending military aid and American advisers, which the Chinese undoubtedly saw as a threat to themselves. Beginning in 1960, Chiang Kai-shek and the Kuomintang on Taiwan also began to make threatening noises. The Chinese Communists, they said, were growing weaker, and 1962 was the "year of the tiger" in the ancient Chinese calendar, which was a very good omen. They argued that an invasion in 1962 would be followed by an uprising of the Chinese people, and tried very hard indeed to persuade the United States to back them in their plans. To most American officials it seemed absurd that the Kuomintang could make a successful landing on the mainland, and the United States patiently but firmly resisted. But the Chinese Communists were either genuinely frightened or in no mood to take chances. They massed almost the entire People's Liberation Army on the "invasion coast" opposite Taiwan and the Quemoy-Matsu area.

In the meantime, both China and India were behaving toward each other in ways that could not help but be mutually frightening and mutually provocative. Following the border skirmishes of 1959, China had continued to build a road across the uninhabited, eighteen-thousand-foot-high plateau, the Aksai Chin, that was in fact Indian territory. They had also occupied a number of border posts in what was generally accepted as Indian territory. On the other hand, the Chinese had some historical claims in the Northeast Frontier Agency, which the British had long ago annexed. A long string of vituperative notes went back and forth about the border incidents, and China attempted to seduce Nepal away from India's tutelage. In the heady political atmosphere following India's successful seizure of the Portuguese enclave of Goa in December of 1961, V. K. Krishna Menon, the controversial, caustic Defense Minister, said publicly that India would reclaim her border areas "one way or another"— a gratuitous insult to the Chinese. The Sino-Soviet dispute was worsening by this time, and, to the annoyance of the Chinese,

Indian diplomacy was designed to enlist Soviet support. What was worse, it was having some success, for the Soviets announced that they hoped the Chinese and the Indians would come to a "peaceful accommodation," implying that the Soviets were at least neutral. The Indians also attempted some crude pressure tactics. They notified China that the 1954 trade agreements between the two countries would be allowed to lapse unless the Chinese evacuated the disputed territories. At the same time, the Indians unwisely provided the Chinese ample provocation by adopting a "forward strategy"—establishing isolated outposts *behind* the Chinese outposts that India felt had encroached on what they considered their rightful territory—and Prime Minister Nehru, in the early fall of 1962, announced that the Indian Army had been ordered to clear India's territory of the Chinese "aggressors." The Indian position, in sum, seemed a clear provocation.[23]

The Chinese attacked. Within a week, Indian resistance was effectively destroyed. The Chinese armies had penetrated to within thirty miles of the plain of Assam, and there was no effective Indian fighting force standing between them and the Indian capital of New Delhi.

The motivations behind the Chinese Communist decision to let themselves be provoked by the Indian actions were probably complex, but a look at them is instructive. One motivation—and probably the least important—was simply geographic—i.e., ease of communications. The Chinese were determined to consolidate their hold on Tibet, and, to do so, they had carried out an impressive program of road-building through some of the most difficult terrain in the world. They had a genuine need for the Aksai Chin, while its value to India seemed to be mainly symbolic of national prestige and sentiment—part of the "sacred soil" of Kashmir. The very least gain the Chinese could hope for probably was that their claims in the Northeast Frontier Agency could be traded for the Aksai Chin.

A second motivation, also probably secondary, was probably related to Chinese relations with the Soviet Union and the grow-

[23] This same conclusion was also reached by Neville Maxwell. See his *India's China War* (New York, 1970).

ing Sino-Soviet dispute. The quarrel between the two Communist giants had several facets, as we shall see below, but one of the arguments was over how the Communist bloc should deal with the in-between powers. The Soviet Union had encouraged India's neutralism and poured huge amounts of economic aid into the country and much political and diplomatic effort. India, which aspired to leadership of the Asian and African neutrals, had become a symbol of the Soviet policy of "peaceful coexistence" to which the Chinese had come to object. Thus the Chinese attack was a slap not only in the face of India, but in the face of the Soviet Union as well.

Still another secondary motivation may have been ambition for China to take her place as a great power. A clash with India could be tightly controlled and carefully limited, so the risks could be held to manageable proportions. At the same time, inflicting a defeat on India would undermine India's bid for leadership in the Third World and boost China's. It would project Chinese power into the subcontinent and demonstrate that China was a force to be reckoned with in the councils of the world.

But all these, as we say, were probably secondary. The primary motivation for the attack on India was probably, again, a sense of threat. The guerrilla war in Vietnam had been instigated by the North Vietnamese, but the United States response of military aid and advisers might well end up by creating a base for American "imperialism." Chiang Kai-shek in full public view was calling for an invasion of the mainland and openly appealing to the Americans to aid and participate in the invasion. The American CIA had helped the Dalai Lama escape and may well have been the prime mover in the Tibetan revolt. In any case, the Khamba tribesmen inside Tibet had since been armed by the CIA, and they might become the spearhead for yet another revolt. The Indians must not only have known of these activities but connived in them with the CIA. And the Soviet Union had stationed troops all along the Chinese border, clashed with Chinese troops, and were doing what they could to stir up minorities on the Chinese side of the border.

All this illustrates something of the nature of the Chinese

Communist leadership. But the short, sharp Sino-Indian war of 1962 also illustrated other, very fundamental facets of the character of the Chinese leadership: caution, a respect for the realities of power, and a capacity for self-discipline and control. In the midst of the battle in the Northeast Frontier Agency, when it was becoming apparent that India was about to suffer a crushing defeat, Nehru had called on the United States, Britain, and the Soviet Union for help. Each country did send aid of some kind, and both the United States and Great Britain also dispatched high-level missions to assess what more could be done. But even before the two teams departed from their home countries, the Chinese Communists announced a *unilateral* ceasefire and stopped short of a line in the Northeast Frontier Agency to which they had some vague historical claim. Later, again unilaterally, they withdrew 12½ miles.

The Chinese, quite clearly, understood their own doctrines of guerrilla warfare and the difficulty of invading and occupying a country even though its armies had been defeated. They understood that going so far as to occupy India would run an unacceptably high risk not only that Britain and the United States might feel compelled to intervene, but that the Soviet Union might. And they also understood the importance for all their other political goals of preserving their reputation in the Third World. The Indian provocation made the Chinese attack justifiable in the eyes of the Third World so long as it was confined to a short, sharp engagement that could be regarded as a proper and appropriate punishment. But if the attack turned into something so serious as an occupation and some new form of Asian colonialism, then the Third World's sympathy for China would vanish.

Perhaps an even more portentous lesson of the 1962 attack was what it demonstrated of the Chinese leadership's skill and sophistication in international politics. The whole affair had been a masterpiece of orchestrating military, political, and psychological instrumentalities as a single, limited, disciplined, and controlled operation directed toward and subordinated to a political end. In their propaganda and political moves, they had made skillful use of the provocation the Indians supplied, and succeeded in taking much of the sting out of the charge of aggression. They had launched a military attack over what had always been considered the world's most difficult terrain barrier, accomplishing feats of logistics and road-building as they went; and they inflicted a convincing defeat on the Indian Army, humiliating a principal rival for Asian leadership and projecting Chinese power into the subcontinent for the first time in history. Throughout the whole affair, they had also retained the political initiative, calling for cease-fires and negotiations at every politically sensitive turn and succeeding in putting the onus for rejection on India. And they enhanced their posture of "peaceful intent" still further by going ahead with the 12½-mile withdrawal in spite of the fact that the Indians rejected their proposal. The fact that political considerations so consistently overrode military considerations in their policy decisions was most impressive. It was particularly so to Kennedy's White House, which had been having trouble with the Pentagon. "There is no doubt who is in control over there," one Kennedy aide remarking in grudging admiration. "Can you imagine the difficulty we would have with the Pentagon in pulling back and giving up territory that had cost so many casualties, no matter how great the political end it served?"

The Sino-Soviet Dispute

The place of Communist China in the world has also been forged by one final series of particularly momentous events, so momentous in fact that future historians may well regard them as among the most significant international political facts of our day: the Sino-Soviet dispute.

The dispute between China and the Soviet Union, certainly, has been fundamental in every connotation of the term. It has been concerned, first of all, with ideology, with the true meaning of the sacred texts of the Communist world and the Communist vision of the future. It also has been concerned with power, with who should lead and who should follow. In a very real sense, communism is a doctrine for getting and holding power, and in their bid for leadership of the Communist world, the

Chinese were just following their ideology. The dispute has also been concerned with the oganization of decision-making within the Communist world and the nature of the relationship among the different parties. The key words in this aspect of the debate have been "centrism" and "polycentrism"—the tags for whether the Soviet Union's *national* interests should be synonymous with the interests of the *whole* of the Communist world or whether the national interests of the other parties would also be considered in determining policy. The differences have also extended to policy toward the in-between world, as mentioned earlier, whether the friendship of the Communist world should be extended to "national-bourgeois" regimes, as in India, or only to the radical nationalists and "national liberation movements." The Soviets, as we mentioned, chose friendship with such states as India and encouraged them in a policy of "neutralism," while China came to advocate support only for the militant. And the dispute has also been concerned with grand strategy, with the question of how assertive the Communist world should be in its dealings with the West and how much risk should be run of nuclear war. This difference was symbolized by the exchange between Mao and Khrushchev following the Cuban missile crisis, with Mao saying that the West was only a "paper tiger" and Khrushchev replying that this particular paper tiger had "nuclear teeth."

All of these different aspects and themes appeared and reappeared as the dispute unfolded. It apparently began in 1956 at the twentieth congress of the Communist party of the Soviet Union—the congress at which Khrushchev attacked the memory of Stalin and began the process of "de-Stalinization."[24] In a published statement in April 1956, the Chinese offer a "balanced"— i.e., rival—analysis of Stalin's "serious mistakes" and his merits, concluding that his contribution outweighed his errors.

The Chinese carried their bid for a larger voice in policy one step farther later in 1956, during the Polish and Hungarian crises. The Polish Communist leadership had demanded greater auton-

[24] See Harry Gelman, "The Sino-Soviet Conflict: A Survey," *Problems of Communism* Vol. XIII (March–April 1964), and Donald S. Zagoria, *The Sino-Soviet Conflict, 1956–1961* (Princeton, 1962), on both of which I have drawn heavily.

omy, and the Soviets met the demand, in the words of the Chinese accusation, by moving up "troops in an attempt to subdue the Polish comrades by armed force"—an act of "great power chauvinism." The situation was reversed in the Hungarian crisis. This was not a bid for greater autonomy by a Communist leadership, but a mass revolt that both the Soviets and the Chinese regarded as "counterrevolutionary." But the Soviets were slow to intervene, the Chinese charged, and did so only after the Chinese had insisted on "the taking of all necessary measures to smash the counterrevolutionary rebellion. . . ."

Both sides recognized the dangers to the Communist world of a split, and they intermittently made efforts to heal it. The Soviet government, for example, issued a declaration on October 30, 1956, recognizing the need for "mutual respect" in the relations between "fraternal countries," and Peking responded with a statement supporting the Soviet declaration—although it also expressed approval for the Polish position and warned against "great power chauvinism." Also, we now know that sometime in 1957 the Soviets signed an agreement to assist China in the area of the "new technology for national defense"—nuclear weapons.

It was undoubtedly the signing of this agreement that led the Chinese to make two important concessions. The first was a public declaration by Mao that the "socialist camp must have a head; and this head is the U.S.S.R." The second was that the Chinese dropped Gomulka—the reality that the phrase about the U.S.S.R. being the head of the Socialist camp reflects. The Chinese got a nuclear commitment, in other words, in exchange for helping Moscow restore discipline in Eastern Europe.

But the dispute continued to grow. During the 1958 Quemoy-Matsu crisis, the Soviets were extremely cautious and no more than lukewarm in their support of the Chinese. In its exposé of September 1963, Peking said that the Soviets had withheld a commitment of support the Chinese needed to face down the United States until Moscow was sure no risk remained. And from the Chinese point of view, Soviet behavior was even worse in the political sphere. The Chinese implied that in his talks with Mao, when he visited Peking in October 1959, Khrushchev sought to end the civil war with the Kuomintang and to institute a policy of "two Chinas."

On top of all this, there were disagreements and misunderstandings about just how much the Soviets had promised to do in helping Communist China develop nuclear weapons. In their later statements, the Chinese suggest that it was no misunderstanding but a Soviet decision to renege on what had been a commitment to help them build a nuclear capability. Some Western observers suspect that the Chinese asked for the weapons themselves and Khrushchev countered with conditions that the Chinese found unacceptable—for the Chinese alleged that the Soviets "put forward unreasonable demands designed to bring China under Soviet military control." In any event, it was immediately after this episode that the Chinese publicly reasserted that the atomic bomb was a "paper tiger."

In June, according to the Chinese, the Soviet Union finally rejected Peking's request for a "sample" atomic bomb. Moscow, furthermore, apparently dabbled in subversion by encouraging Marshal P'eng Teh-huai, the Defense Minister, to push the Communist leadership even farther from Mao's policies. Unfortunately for P'eng, his move threatened to upset the delicate compromise between Mao and his critics, and both factions of the leadership united in a prompt purge. Khrushchev's visit to the United States in September of 1959 and the "Camp David spirit" that came out of his meeting with President Eisenhower apparently brought all these developments into crisis, for Khrushchev found it necessary to make a sudden trip to Peking immediately following his visit to the United States. But it seems only to have made matters worse. Not only did the ebullient Khrushchev use the occasion to push the "two Chinas" policy, as mentioned earlier, but he also warned the Chinese in a public speech against "testing by force the stability of the capitalist system."

Throughout 1960, the exchanges of propaganda between the two were more and more virulent. Much of the Soviet output was aimed at Albania, but everyone in the world knew that the real target was Albania's mentor, Communist China. Then, in July of 1960, Moscow, in Peking's words, "suddenly took a unilateral decision recalling all Soviet experts in China within one month"—a most serious blow to the developing Chinese economy.

In 1961, Khrushchev forced the Albanian issue to a crisis, breaking diplomatic relations, withdrawing Soviet naval units from the base at Vlorë, and ending all Soviet aid. The Chinese stepped in with aid to replace what the Soviets had stopped, and at the twenty-second party congress, Chou En-lai made a speech attacking Khrushchev for his Albanian policy. Then he left the Congress early—ostentatiously laying a wreath on Stalin's tomb as he departed.

Actual fighting broke out on the border between China and the Soviet Union in 1962, and the Soviets attempted what was apparently a large-scale subversion in the Chinese province of Sinkiang. In retaliation, the Chinese closed Soviet consulates throughout the country.

A fierce competition then began for the allegiance of the Communist parties of every country in the world. And the debate grew hotter still—with each side publishing more and more of their formerly secret correspondence in an effort to bolster its own case. By early 1963, Peking was denouncing the Soviet Communist party leaders as betrayers of the revolution, arguing that the underdeveloped areas of the world were the real focus of the "struggle against imperialism" and that the real leader of the struggle was the Chinese party. Moscow, in turn, was attempting to show that the Chinese were indifferent to the risks of nuclear war and bent on dividing the Communist world along "racist" lines. In the summer of 1963, the Chinese distributed, first in Moscow and then throughout the world, a letter, dated June 14, 1963, declaring that they intended to split every Communist party whose leaders sided with the Soviet Union.

Thus by 1965 it was clear to both sides—and to the outside world—that the dispute was, as we have said, fundamental. It was also clear that the dispute would continue as a dispute for some time—that it would not proceed rapidly either to a complete and final break or to a complete and final healing. Finally, it was also clear that even if a way could be found to end the dispute in the more distant future, relations in the Communist world would never again be the same. If the Communist world

ever had been monolithic, it was no longer and never would be
again.

Conclusion

By 1965, it seemed possible to answer the first of our two questions about China: It seemed clear that the Communist party
had united China and that it was in firm control. As for the second question—the direction that a unified China would take in
the world—it seemed less clear. At times China seemed to pursue
goals of national power and prestige, although with caution and
restraint. At other times its only motive seemed to be a sense of
threat from outside forces. The continued emphasis by Mao and
the radical faction on creating a new society and a new man often clashed with the goal of national power and prestige, and
even with security and survival. What was not clear was whether
Mao and the radicals would regain power in time to try to carry
out the vision or whether they would be successful in remaking
man and society even if they did gain the power to try to carry
out the vision. But beginning in 1966, both new doubt and new
light were shed on both of these questions by the remarkable—
even astounding—events of what was called the Great Proletarian
Cultural Revolution.

CHAPTER 16

The Great Proletarian Cultural Revolution

ON THE SURFACE, the situation in Communist China in 1965 seemed calm. The arrangement between Mao Tse-tung and Liu Shao-ch'i continued as far as the world knew, with Liu officially designated as Mao's successor. Mao continued to be the object of fulsome public homage, with Liu occasionally sharing in it. The ubiquitous phrase, "Under the leadership of Chairman Mao," was occasionally altered to read, "Under the leadership of Chairman Mao and Chairman Liu." In general, Mao seemed detached from everyday affairs. He spent long periods away from Peking, in the Yangtse Valley and other places. During the winter of 1965–66, in fact, Mao disappeared completely from public view, causing worldwide speculation that he might be dead or dying.

The economy was doing well, continuing the recovery that began in 1963 following the three terrible years caused both by the dislocation of the Great Leap Forward and three consecutive years of impossibly bad weather. In domestic affairs, a "rectification" program under Liu Shao-ch'i was under way in 1964–65—the so-called "four cleanups" movement (politics, ideology, organization, and economy)—designed to strengthen the rural party apparatus by replacing commune men with others completely loyal to the central party apparatus. In foreign affairs, the year opened with what many Chinese Communist officials, especially military men like the chief of staff of the Army, Lo Jui-ch'ing, regarded as a frightening development—the decision by President Lyndon B. Johnson to bomb North Vietnam and to send American ground troops to South Vietnam. Toward the end of the year, the Chinese suffered a grave disappointment in Indonesia with the failure of the *coup* plotted by the Communists with the encouragement of Sukarno and the subsequent destruction of the pro-Chinese Indonesian Communist party. Finally, the Sino-Soviet dispute continued at the new height of vituperation reached in 1964 in an article on Khrushchev's "phoney communism," in which the Chinese Communists charged that Khrushchev's "revisionist clique" were the "political representatives of the Soviet bourgeoisie" and that as a result of Khrushchev's revisionism "the first socialist country in the world built by the great Soviet people with their blood and sweat is now facing an unprecedented danger of capitalist restoration." To these adverse developments, the Chinese reaction at the level of words was strong. But at the level of action, their reaction was cautious. They continued to criticize the Soviet Union and its "revisionism" but made no move to break relations. They condemned events in Indonesia, but went no farther. They sent aid to North Vietnam, they stationed troops along the border, they even sent engineer troops into North Vietnam to build airports and roads and to help repair the damage caused by the American bombing. But they stopped short of matching the direct American intervention with direct intervention of their own.

Mao's Mood

But underneath this façade of calm, an upheaval of Chinese society was in the making—sparked by the return of Mao and the radicals to power—an upheaval that was more dramatic and mystifying to the outside world than anything else in Chinese Communist history. Thanks to a remarkable interview that Mao granted to his old American newspaper friend, Edgar Snow, in January 1965, we know something of Mao's mood at the time. It was, in Snow's words, that of a person "reflecting on man's rendezvous with death."[1] Mao said once in the interview, and then repeated, that he was "getting ready to see God very soon" (although he acknowledged to Snow's question that as a Communist he did not believe in God). He recalled that his brothers, his wife, and his son had all been killed, as well as his bodyguard and many others around him. He remarked that he felt that "it was odd that death had so far passed him by." Mao went on to say that he had begun life as a primary school teacher and had no thought of fighting wars or of becoming a Communist. He said that he sometimes wondered by what chance combination of reasons he had become interested in founding the Chinese Communist party. And then, in a curious reversal of his lifelong commitment to voluntarism and the power of human will, he said that "Anyway, events did not move in accordance with the individual human will. What mattered was that China had been oppressed by imperialism, feudalism, and bureaucratic capitalism."

"Man makes his own history, but he makes it in accordance with his environment," Snow then quoted, remarking that Mao had changed the environment of China fundamentally and that many now wondered what the younger generation would do. Mao said that he could not know, that he doubted that anyone could be sure. One possibility was continued development of the revolution toward communism. The other was "that youth could negate the revolution, and give a poor performance; make peace with imperialism, bring the remnants of the Chiang Kai-shek clique back to the mainland, and take a stand beside the small percentage of counterrevolutionaries still in the country." Then, in what was the most interesting and revealing passage of all, Mao said that "future events would be decided by future generations,

[1] "Interview with Mao," *The New Republic* (February 27, 1965). Snow's interview lasted four hours. His summary of the interview was approved by an official who was also present, but Snow was not permitted to quote Mao directly. The quotations given here are from Snow's article.

and in accordance with conditions we could not foresee. From the long-range view, future generations ought to be more knowledgeable than we are, just as men of the bourgeois-democratic era were more knowledgeable than those of the feudal ages. Their judgment would prevail, not ours. The youth of today and those to come after them would assess the work of the revolution in accordance with values of their own."

Snow reports that Mao's voice dropped away, that Mao half closed his eyes, and then Mao remarked that man's condition on this earth was changing with ever-increasing rapidity. "A thousand years from now all of them," he concluded, "even Marx, Engels and Lenin, would possibly appear rather ridiculous."

We now know that at this time Mao was engaged in a struggle over both power and policy with two or more factions within the Communist party. In the period between December 1958, when Mao gave up the post of Chairman of the government apparatus, and 1965, he issued a number of pronouncements that expressed his own worries and warnings over the direction of events. In 1962, he issued his call never to forget the class struggle, for example. Almost every year he issued a statement about one field or another—rural work, education, propaganda, and in 1964 on the training of the young to become worthy successors of the revolution—although many of Mao's actual statements were not made public until 1967–69. Looking back over that period now, we can see that the propaganda media dutifully took up the line Mao laid down even when they did not identify Mao as the author. This, in turn, suggests an explanation of a puzzle noted in the West at the time—the fact that the public rhetoric and the actual policies pursued often differed noticeably.[2] We suspect that Mao retained enough power over the propaganda media to ensure that his line was publicized, but not enough over the party and government to see that it was carried out. We also suspect that those among the top leadership who did have power over the party and government still needed Mao as a symbol, and that the "cult of Mao's personality" may have been as useful to them in

[2] On this point see Michel Oksenberg, *China: The Convulsive Society*, The Foreign Policy Association Headline Series No. 203 (December 1970), pp. 36–37.

combating dissatisfaction among the masses as it was flattering to Mao's ego. At the time that Mao was talking so somberly with Edgar Snow, we now know that he had already embarked upon what he probably thought was the most fateful of all the many struggles of his life—a struggle to regain power and to impose again a radicalist direction to the revolution by launching still another revolution, this time against the Communist party itself.

The Debate over Strategy

We also now know some, although not all, of the details of how it came about. We know that Mao had taken a personal hand in the attack on Khrushchev's "revisionism." The 1964 article on Khrushchev's "phoney communism" mentioned earlier was attributed to the joint efforts of the editorial boards of both *People's Daily* and *Red Flag*, but it bears the unmistakable marks of Mao himself—it is, in the words of one authority, "the closest thing we have, at present, to a personal testament of Mao's."[3] We know that the professional military faction suffered a setback when ranks and insignia were abolished. Just how this came about is not yet known, but the connection with the Sino-Soviet dispute seems clear, since it was during the period of collaboration between the Chinese and Soviet armies that rank and insignia were established. We also have reason to believe that following the United States bombing of North Vietnam early in 1965 and the introduction of American ground troops into South Vietnam, one faction of the Chinese military led by the chief of staff, Lo Jui-ch'ing, were arguing that the threat from the United States required greater defense measures by China. They also argued that since China had to rely on Soviet nuclear strength to balance American nuclear strength, it was also essential to ease the tension with the Soviet Union. The issue was grand strategy. Was Soviet "revisionism" or American "imperialism" the greater threat? In either case, how should the threat be met if it came to fighting? The debate over this issue marked the first and apparently crucial battle between Mao's faction and the others.[4]

[3] A. Doak Barnett, *China After Mao* (Princeton, New Jersey, 1967), p. 47.
[4] On the strategic debate of 1965 and the purge of Lo Jui-ch'ing, see the following: Harry Harding and Melvin Gurtov, "The Purge of Lo Jui-ch'ing: The

Both Lo Jui-ch'ing and the factions opposing him agreed that China's policy toward the American escalation of the Vietnam War should be cautious, and official announcements did not mention actually going to war unless the United States "imposed" war on China. The difference of opinion was that Lo saw a high probability that the United States would initiate hostilities against China. To deter the United States, he argued, China would have to change her domestic priorities, take the Army off the political tasks it then performed to concentrate on military training, change the domestic priorities to concentrate on rearmament, and ease tensions with the Soviet Union so no doubts would arise about the Soviet nuclear deterrent extending to China. Lo was opposed by the Maoist radicals, who had a different strategic assessment, and their allies, principally Lin Piao and a "political" faction of the military. It is not known whether Lin and the "political" military actually shared the Maoist strategic view or merely went along with it as a necessary tactic in pursuing their own power goals, but Lin did become a public spokesman for the view, principally in the famous September 3, 1965, article mentioned earlier. This rival strategic view assessed the probabilities of a United States attack as being much lower. The Korean War had shown that the United States would not attack China unless it was directly provoked. "People's wars," like Vietnam, were also a diversion that kept the United States busy. Even if a serious clash were to occur, China's growing nuclear arsenal and the prospect of having to face as many as a hundred million Chinese soldiers, even though they were not well equipped, were powerful deterrents. There was therefore no need to make concessions to Moscow. On the contrary, the Soviet Union was the more immediate as well as the closer enemy. The United States was an *external* enemy, whereas the Soviet Union was not only taking hostile actions along China's border but was also using subversive methods to interfere in China's *internal* affairs. The Maoists and their allies of the Lin Piao faction there-

Politics of Chinese Strategic Planning," A Report Prepared for United States Air Force Project RAND (February 1971); Uri Ra'anan, "Chinese Factionalism and Sino-Soviet Relations," *Current History* (September 1970); and Donald Zagoria, *Vietnam Triangle: Moscow, Peking, Hanoi* (New York, 1967).

fore argued not only that confrontation with the United States should be postponed until after the Soviet "revisionists" had been overcome, but that it might also be necessary to reach a temporary understanding with the United States.[5]

On the question of how to fight a war if it came, both sides apparently agreed that if the Americans did attack, the first stage would be the nuclear bombing of China's major centers.[6] The disagreement came on the issue of how to meet the second stage, an American ground invasion. Lo Jui-ch'ing and the professional military faction he represented wanted to fight a traditional war, as they had done in Korea, with battle lines and resistance each step of the way. They wanted Soviet help with nuclear weapons if necessary, and in the meantime they wanted Soviet aid in getting ready to fight that kind of war. The Maoists and Lin Piao, on the other hand, advocated a defense based on guerrilla tactics and "people's war." The Army would retreat, giving up the damaged cities, and base themselves in the countryside. The enemy would be "lured deep" into rural areas, as the Japanese had been lured in World War II, and guerrillas of the people would cut them up.

There was a genuine strategic issue here and an honest difference of opinion on the issue. But power considerations were also present. Mao's strength lay with his popularity with the mass of the people. A strategy that relied on the people, strengthening the militia and village-level organizations while downgrading the professional Army and the institutions of party and government, enhanced Mao's power and weakened that of his enemies whose power was based on these institutions.

The Liu Shao-ch'i Faction

Another faction, led by Liu Shao-ch'i and representing principally the party hierarchs, was sympathetic with the notion of easing tensions with the Soviet Union, but for different reasons,

[5] On this point see Ra'anan, ibid., p. 136.
[6] See Morton Halperin and John Lewis, "New Tensions in Army-Party Relations in China, 1965–1966," *China Quarterly* (April–June 1966) and Zagoria, *Vietnam Triangle,* op. cit., p. 94.

related to the economy and the need for Soviet industrial and technical aid. On the other hand, this same faction was opposed to other aspects of Lo's position. Their goal was to ease *all* international tensions and concentrate on domestic development, and a crash rearmament program of the kind envisioned by Lo went dead against those aims. It was probably the opposition of this third faction that was decisive.

The Lin Piao Article

Although we do not know the details, the Maoist radicals won the battle. The September 3, 1965, article by Lin Piao outlining the Maoist strategy confirmed the victory. Lo Jui-ch'ing was last seen in public in November, and some time later it was learned that he had been purged.

The Lin Piao article was an analysis of the forces shaping the world and a prescription for dealing with them. But it had a message for several audiences. To the underdeveloped countries it carried Mao's word that the "imperialist" powers should be respected strategically but despised tactically. It offered fairly detailed methods by which a weak country could defeat a strong one and a small army conquer a large one. It told the "national liberation movements" that they should expect no outside help beyond political support and some aid. Indeed, it argued that the essential task of winning the support of the mass of the people could be done no other way. To the West and the "imperialist" powers it said much the same thing, that they need not fear the *direct* involvement of Chinese troops, and hence had no cause to retaliate against China. To the Soviet Union it said that China had no real need of her help—the atomic bomb was a paper tiger—and that the Soviet Union should expect no lessening of the Sino-Soviet dispute because China feared the "imperialists" and their nuclear arsenal. To the Chinese professional military faction it said that they could expect no reconciliation with the Soviet Union and no great alteration in domestic priorities to enhance the position of the professional military or institute a crash program of rearmament.

Reasons for Mao's Victory

Thus the Lin statement marked a victory on a number of policy issues that cut across both domestic and foreign affairs. It was also a victory in terms of political power. Several factions had in the end supported this analysis of the foreign and strategic situation for a variety of reasons. In all probability, some of these factions were concerned more with the consequences for their own policy preferences on the whole range of related issues than for their power position. It is doubtful if the Mao faction would have won if the struggle had been perceived by everyone only in power terms. But now that the policy battle had been won, even though it had been won with the help of rival factions, it did enhance the power position of Mao and his supporters. The most subtle way that Mao's power was enhanced was the fact that China's strategy was to be based on the people, where Mao's strength was greatest. The most direct was that Lo Jui-ch'ing and a number of high officers in the military were replaced by men more sympathetic to Mao. In effect, one of the several centers of opposition to Mao and his faction had been eliminated.

Beginnings of the Cultural Revolution

Apparently seeking to take advantage of the opportunity presented by the victory on the strategic issue, Mao went before the Central Committee later in September and proposed a "cultural revolution" against the intellectuals.[7] The opposition succeeded in watering down the proposal substantially, apparently on the grounds that the Vietnam situation was too dangerous to permit disruption at home. P'eng Chen, the mayor of Peking, was put in charge of the program, but the reason is not known. The opposition may have appointed him to thwart Mao, or he may have been appointed by Mao, either to test his reliability or as a way of entrapping him in an impossible job. In any case, Mao himself

[7] An authoritative account of the revolution is given in Edward E. Rice, *Mao's Way* (Berkeley, California: University of California Press, 1972). Rice was consul general in Hong Kong, and hence the United States Government's chief China watcher, throughout the Cultural Revolution.

withdrew to the Yangtze Valley and Shanghai, where he spent the next six months apparently laying his plans for the next series of moves and making arrangements for the formation of the Red Guards.

The most powerful faction that Mao saw against him was probably that centering on the party hierarchs and headed by Liu Shao-ch'i and Teng Hsiao-p'ing, general secretary of the party. In policy terms, as mentioned above, this group stood for a reconciliation with the Soviet Union to obtain aid in developing the Chinese economy. They wanted a relaxation of international tensions so China could concentrate on domestic concerns—"construction before destruction" was one of their slogans. And they also apparently wanted a relaxation of various controls on the economy, including making profitability the measure of efficiency for small enterprises, a free market to provide incentives, and larger private plots in the collective farms.

Another smaller, but allied faction was apparently headed by P'eng Chen, mentioned above. The only major difference in policy between this faction and Liu's group was that P'eng shared the Maoist view on foreign affairs and most particularly the view that no compromise at all should be made with the Soviet "revisionists."

Still another faction seems to have been that headed by Chou En-lai and centering in the governmental bureaucracy. Here the policy differences with the Maoists were much less acute, the hallmark of the Chou group being mainly a more pragmatic and less ideological posture on each of the particular issues.

Using the Shanghai party and its apparatus as his spokesmen, Mao launched an attack on Wu Han, former deputy mayor of Peking, for his historical play, *Hai Jui Dismissed from Office.* That play and writings of other of P'eng Chen's aides, it was charged, were really veiled attacks on the Lushan meeting of 1959 that had purged P'eng Teh-huai. P'eng Chen himself was then attacked for covering up for his subordinates. His dismissal was announced in June, amid questions of whether he was in fact the puppet of someone still higher up in the hierarchy of the party.

Mao had appeared only once in public for many months—at a

picture-taking ceremony with a visiting delegation from Albania. But word came from his retreat at Hangchow that Liu Shao-ch'i had been appointed to head the Cultural Revolution, which was described at the time as a nationwide effort to instill in the people, and especially the youth, the revolutionary values of the "Yenan spirit" and included encouragement for the formation of "Red Guards" of youth. On July 16, Mao went for his famous swim in the Yangtze, and pictures were circulated worldwide to scotch the rumors that he was too sick or old to rule.

Mao returned to Peking shortly after his swim and charged that the leadership of the Cultural Revolution was stifling revolutionary spontaneity and creativity rather than encouraging it. He openly broke with Liu, blaming him for the failure. The Eleventh Plenum of the Central Committee, which was packed with pro-Mao Army men and Red Guards, met from August 1 to August 12. It replaced Liu Shao-ch'i as Mao's designated successor with Lin Piao, and it adopted a new statement on the aims of the Cultural Revolution.

On August 11, Mao appeared before a mass meeting of a million people at T'ien An Men Square, of whom the most prominent were the newly appeared Red Guards, each waving a copy of the little red book, *Quotations from Chairman Mao*. The Great Helmsman, as Mao was thenceforth styled, stepped forward and a girl student placed a Red Guard armband on his arm. The Great Proletarian Cultural Revolution had begun in earnest.

The Red Guards

The guidelines for the Red Guards were contained in two documents adopted by the Eleventh Plenum: "Decision of the Chinese Communist Party Central Committee Concerning the Great Cultural Revolution" and "Communiqué of the Eleventh Plenary Session of the Eighth Central Committee of the Communist Party of China."[8] The documents called upon young people to form Red Guard units and become the vanguard of the Cultural Revolution. Their main slogan was to be to "Dare to Rebel"—to have the courage to attack "power holders who have sneaked into the

[8] *Survey of the China Mainland Press*, Nos. 3761 and 3762 (August 16 and 17, 1966).

party and who take the capitalist road." The Red Guards must stamp out the "old ideas, old culture, old customs, and old habits of the exploiting classes (the 'four olds')." They must go into the schools, factories, and villages and help the masses to re-educate themselves. "Full use must be made of such means as big-character posters and large-scale debates so that views and opinions may be aired and the masses helped to elucidate the correct viewpoints, criticize the erroneous opinions, and uncover all demons and monsters. Only in this way will it be possible to make the broad masses heighten their consciousness in the midst of the struggle, increase their capacity for work, and distinguish between the right and wrong and the enemies and ourselves."[9] The ultimate and overriding goal was to "hold high the great red banner of Mao Tse-tung's thought"—as embodied in his writings and summarized in the little red book of quotations. The specific points were some nine policies that Mao had enunciated over the preceding four years, on such matters as the training of successors in the revolutionary cause, on strengthening political and ideological work, on breaking down foreign conventions and following the Chinese road of industrial development, on his call for the whole party to grasp military affairs, and for everybody to be a soldier. At the same time, the documents urged caution in three matters. First, the Red Guards were cautioned not to criticize officials by name in print without first obtaining approval of higher party committees. Second, they were warned that except for a small number of anti-party counterrevolutionaries, the purpose was not to purge cadres from schools, industry, collectives, government, and party institutions but to reform their thought. Finally, the Red Guards were admonished that in "the course of the debates, people may argue with one another but must not use their fists."

In the months that followed many millions of young people—no one knows just how many millions—converged on the major cities. Official Chinese Communist documents mention over eleven million in Peking alone. Even before August, the Red Guards had attacked the officials heading the major universities

[9] "Decision . . . Concerning the Great Cultural Revolution," ibid.

with "big character" posters detailing charges against them and with mass meetings of criticism. These tactics and the accompanying disruption forced out the president of Peking University in June, and heads of other major universities soon followed. Professors and other officials deemed "bourgeois" or old-fashioned were forced to wear dunce caps, to endure mass criticism sessions, to humble themselves by such menial work as cleaning student latrines, and to make public "confessions" as the price of being left alone. Admissions policies were attacked as favoring bourgeois elements of society, and the curriculum was attacked as furthering bourgeois ideas. In midsummer 1966, the government canceled all new admissions for the fall semester so that new enrollment policies could be worked out. Later, universities and secondary schools were closed until new curricula could be developed.

The Red Guard attack then broadened to the whole of society. In the cities, former owners who still drew fixed interest as payment for their enterprises were paraded through the streets with dunce caps on their heads. Shopkeepers who sold "revisionist, capitalist, or counterrevolutionary" articles were denounced. Books and music stores were stripped of "feudal, bourgeois, and revisionist" works, which were burned. Street names, business names, or place names judged to show feudal or bourgeois influences were changed. In Shanghai, for example, the Red Guards put up posters on one of the biggest department stores proposing that the name be changed from "Eternal Peace" to some suitably Maoist name, such as "Red Forever" or "Struggle Forever." The boss of the store in the old society had named it, according to the posters, because "he wanted to be left in peace forever to exploit the working people."[10]

Foreigners were only rarely molested—although at one stage a number of embassies in Peking were physically attacked, to the acute embarrassment of the foreign office, and the Soviet Embassy was actually under a state of siege for a number of days. But foreign "influences" were attacked everywhere. The burning of books and music included Shakespeare, Bach, and Beethoven. Names of streets and businesses to be changed included any with

[10] *People's Daily* (October 22, 1966).

foreign connotations as well as those that showed feudal or bourgeois influence. Girls with long hair—deemed foreign—had to submit to having it cut by Red Guards armed with scissors. Anyone appearing in a Western business suit was likely to have it ripped to pieces. At times the attack on foreign influences reached extremes that became nothing less than absurd. One of the few comic notes was a Red Guard proposal to change the meaning of traffic lights, which had been laid down in foreign lands. In China, red should mean go, since red symbolizes the revolution, and "it is possible to move forward only at the red light signal."

Attack on the "Four Olds"

The slogan to destroy the "four olds" led the Red Guards to attack historical and cultural monuments and art and cultural objects on the grounds that they represented feudal and bourgeois ways and that respect for them impeded true revolutionary thinking. A number of museums were attacked and much of their contents destroyed, including the Central Institute of Arts in Peking. It was also reported that a number of shrines and temples were destroyed, including the twenty-five-hundred-year-old Temple of Confucius at Chu Fo in Shantung Province. Private homes of those known to have art and historical collections were broken into and the objects destroyed. All across the country museums and shrines were closed to prevent their destruction, including the Forbidden City in Peking.

In factories, collective farms, and government bureaucracies administrators and officials who were judged to be guilty of "bourgeois" behavior, like university officials, were subject to attack in the "big character" posters and to mass criticism. At a certain stage, in a particular organization the management would institute its own Cultural Revolution thought-reform program, advised and assisted by representatives of the workers and the Red Guard contingent. This happened in government as well as in factories. At one stage, for example, diplomatic personnel were recalled from Chinese embassies all over the world to be re-educated along the lines of the Cultural Revolution.

The final target of the Cultural Revolution, of course, was the

Communist party itself. The propaganda streaming out of the headquarters of the Cultural Revolution in Peking harped continually on the "handful of persons within the party who are in authority and taking the capitalist road" and on "China's Khrushchov" or the "No. 1 Party Person taking the capitalist road."[11] Although never named, everyone understood that the "No. 1 person," "China's Khrushchov," was Liu Shao-ch'i and that the "handful of persons . . . taking the capitalist road" were his appointees, allies, and friends in the provincial and local party organizations and government. It was these people in the party structure whom the Red Guards were encouraged to attack.

Throughout the fall of 1966, many millions of the young surged back and forth across China, concentrating in the cities, but visiting villages on their way. Mass meetings, wall posters, dunce caps, the burning of books and art treasures—a nation of eight hundred million people in a state of mass agitation. The world had never seen its like. Understanding it seemed impossible, but yet imperative. Such a prodigious upheaval must have its effect on China's future, and such a giant nation must also have its effect on the rest of us.

Revolutions are supposed to come from the bottom. This one came from the top—conceived and directed by Mao himself. What was his purpose?

Sources and Aims of the "Cultural Revolution"

One interpretation is that the Cultural Revolution was a power struggle, crude, simple, and naked. Mao had been maneuvered out of power in 1958 and into a largely honorific position by Liu and others, as we know. The theory is that Mao used the Cultural Revolution to go to the masses and make a comeback.

Another interpretation is that the Cultural Revolution was a power struggle, all right, but an extraordinarily complex and Byzantine power struggle. The decision of the party leadership in 1958 to encourage Mao's "cult of the personality" for their own purposes even though his power had been limited meant that by 1965 Mao's name was the only source of legitimacy.

[11] The Chinese anglicize Russian proper names in ways different from Western usage (hence "Khrushchov" rather than "Khrushchev").

Different political cliques were attempting to manipulate him to attain power. One of these, according to this theory, was an ultraleft group composed of Mao's wife, Chiang Ch'ing; his speechwriter and former political secretary, Ch'en Po-ta; his security organizer, K'ang Sheng; Yao Wen-yüan, whom Soviet sources have identified, apparently incorrectly, as Mao's son-in-law; and his former bodyguard, Wang Tung-hsiang. It is important to note that four of this group became key members of the Peking headquarters of the Cultural Revolution following the dismissal of P'eng Chen and Liu Shao-ch'i—Ch'en Po-ta, chief; Chiang Ch'ing, first deputy; K'ang Sheng, and Yao Wen-yüan.

According to this theory, Chiang Ch'ing and her associates planted the suspicion of Liu in Mao's mind. They then manipulated Mao into "testing" Liu by appointing him to head the Cultural Revolution—knowing full well that Mao's programs were so vague and ambitious that it would subsequently be easy to convince Mao that Liu was not only a failure but a saboteur.

The evidence available suggests that both of these theories may be at least partly true. We know that Mao gave up or was deprived of his post as Chairman of the People's Republic. We also know that he voiced resentment of this in a meeting with some Red Guards. Posters put up during the Cultural Revolution charged that during the years between 1958 and 1965, the top party leaders—Liu Shao-ch'i, Teng Hsiao-p'ing, P'eng Chen, and others—no longer consulted Mao, treating him, as Mao himself is quoted as saying, "like a dead father." Mao undoubtedly wanted to reassume a more central and powerful role, and he may well have seen his opportunity in the debate over defense policy following the American escalation of the Vietnam War in 1965. If so, it is logical that he would forge such instruments as the Cultural Revolution and the Red Guards.

At the same time, we know that Chiang Ch'ing was ambitious to play a political role, which the party had denied her as a condition for approving her marriage to Mao in 1936. We also know that she envied and hated Liu Shao-ch'i's wife. Chiang Ch'ing, Ch'en Po-ta, and the others may well have used their access to Mao to plant suspicion of Liu and to manipulate Mao in order to enhance their own position and policies.

But it would be a mistake to think that power was the only consideration or, in the case of Mao at least, to think that power was even the central consideration. We have seen that Mao was romantic, deeply committed to an idealistic vision of a new society and a new human being. We have also seen that in 1965 his mood was somber and pensive, with a note almost of melancholy. What all this suggests is that Mao's primary motivation was disappointment in what the revolution had accomplished, doubt about how deeply the party and his probable successors were committed to his vision, and the growing conviction that he had only one more chance to set off a truer revolution and create the society of his dream.

In 1964, Mao retained some authority in foreign affairs, particularly concerning the dispute with the Soviet Union. We know that he spent much time studying the problem and developing the analysis on which Communist China based its policy toward the Soviet Union and the dispute. The most complete and detailed, and at the same time, the most vivid statement of this analysis and the policy flowing from it is contained in the article, already mentioned, on Khruschchev's "phoney communism," which Western observers are convinced was largely written by Mao himself.

Mao's Analysis of Soviet "Revisionism"

This remarkable document begins with an analysis of the worldwide, historical struggle between socialist revolution and the forces of reaction. The picture it paints is of persistent and powerful reactionary forces working long after a socialist state is established to corrupt and bring it down—so persistent and powerful, indeed, that the "complete victory of socialism cannot be brought about in one or two generations" but will require "five or ten generations or even longer." The "overthrown bourgeoisie and other reactionary classes" are not reconciled to their defeat and "stubbornly continue to engage in trials of strength with the proletariat. . . . They sneak into government organs, public organizations, economic departments and cultural and educational institutions so as to resist or usurp the leadership of the proletariat." They attempt to sabotage the economy, the ideology, culture, and education.

In their efforts to penetrate and subvert, the bourgeoisie are aided by "spontaneous capitalist tendencies" that spring up in every segment of society. The peasants, for example, inevitably retain some of the inherent characteristics of small producers. So do certain urban elements.

"The activities of the bourgeoisie as described above, . . ." the article continues, "constantly breed political degenerates in the ranks of the working class and Party and government organizations, new bourgeois elements and embezzlers and grafters in state enterprises owned by the whole people and new bourgeois intellectuals in the cultural and education institutions and intellectual circles." All of these attack socialism together. "The political degenerates entrenched in leading organs are particularly dangerous," the article concludes, "for they support and shield the bourgeois elements in organs at lower levels."

All this is at home. Abroad, "international imperialism" will seize every opportunity "to undertake armed intervention against the socialist countries or to bring about their peaceful disintegration." The reactionary forces at home are encouraged by those abroad.

Having painted the over-all threat, the article then shows how it has actually worked inside the Soviet Union. The "revisionist Khrushchov clique," the article says, claims that "antagonistic classes have been eliminated and that class struggle no longer exists." But the true situation, the article goes on to say, is quite different. In fact, "the old bourgeoisie and other exploiting classes which had been overthrown in the Soviet Union were not eradicated and survived after industry was nationalized and agriculture collectivized. The political and ideological influence of the bourgeoisie remained. Spontaneous capitalist tendencies continued to exist both in the city and in the countryside. New bourgeois elements and kulaks were still incessantly generated."

Scanning reports in the Soviet newspapers, the article continues, one sees the results. "Leading functionaries of some state-owned factories and their gangs abuse their positions and amass

large fortunes by using the equipment and materials of the
factories to set up 'underground workshops' for private production, selling the products illicitly and dividing the spoils.
. . . Such people do not operate all by themselves. They invariably work hand in glove with functionaries in the state departments in charge of supplies and in the commercial and other
departments. They have their own men in the police and judicial
departments who protect them and act as their agents. Even
high-ranking officials in the state organs support and shield them.
. . . These examples show that the factories which have fallen
into the clutches of such degenerates are socialist enterprises
only in name, that in fact they have become capitalist enterprises by which these persons enrich themselves. . . . Their
activities against socialism are definitely class struggle with the
bourgeoisie attacking the proletariat."

It is to be expected, the article continues, that bourgeois elements exist in a socialist country and attack socialism. What
makes the situation in the Soviet Union so grave is "the fact
that the revisionist Khrushchov clique have usurped the leadership of the Soviet Party and state and that a privileged bourgeois
stratum has emerged in Soviet society." In the Soviet Union,
according to the article, not only have new bourgeois elements
increased, but their social status has fundamentally changed.
"Before Khrushchov came to power, they did not occupy the ruling
position in Soviet society. Their activities were restricted in
many ways and they were subject to attack. But since Khrushchov took over, usurping the leadership of the Party and the
state step by step, the new bourgeois elements have gradually
risen to the ruling position in the Party and government and in
the economic, cultural and other departments and formed a
privileged stratum in Soviet society."

The diatribe in this article is directed at the Soviet Union
and its "revisionists," but the analysis applies to *all* socialist
states. The fundamental philosophical notion underlying the analysis is, of course, Mao's familiar notion of permanent revolution.
But it is much more fully developed, more precisely reasoned—
and the threat implied in the notion of permanent revolution is
much more immediate and urgent. What is suggested is that

as Mao made this analysis of developments in the Soviet Union and the applicability of his concept of permanent revolution, he became increasingly convinced that the Chinese revolution was succumbing to the same forces, the forces that had corrupted the Soviet Union and all previous revolutions in the world's history. Specifically, what is suggested is that Mao became increasingly convinced that routine, bureaucracy, narrow self-interest, and the corruption of power was creating a new class of "exploiters" in China, that this new class of "exploiters" was in fact the Communist party, and that the leaders of the new class of "exploiters" were in fact among his closest associates.

It seems probable, then, that each of these explanations for the Cultural Revolution contains some truth—that Chiang Ch'ing, Ch'en Po-ta, and their clique did attempt to manipulate Mao to enhance their own power position and to further their particular policy views; that Mao, too, was making a bid to regain his former power position, but that he also saw the Cultural Revolution as one more chance to create the new society and new man of the radical vision. The question now is: What does the evidence available permit us to say about the outcome? Who *really* holds power in China today? How *has* the Cultural Revolution affected Chinese society?

Climax of the Cultural Revolution

By January 1967, as we said, millions of young Red Guards were surging back and forth across China. Schools and universities were closed. Production in both the factories and on the farms was seriously disrupted, in spite of Mao's injunction to combine making revolution with increasing production. Violence, too, was rising. Mao had charged the Red Guards to use words, not fists. In the beginning, although there were some beatings, this charge seems to have been honored. But a number of officials committed suicide rather than face humiliation and ouster, and even more intellectuals and artists seem to have done so, perhaps in despair over the wanton destruction of China's cultural and artistic treasures. At some stage, among some of the Red Guards, the practice seems to have grown to encourage these "suicides."

Also, in some factories, collective farms, government offices, or local party headquarters, people were bound to resist the Red Guards' attack. At times, the fighting was bloody.

Violence also came about in another way. Mao was assaulting the established institutions of Chinese Communist society—the party and governmental structure—and he had to go outside the established structure to find a weapon for his assault. He called forth the Red Guards to be that instrument, capitalizing on his mass appeal and on the idealism and energy of youth and their freedom from ties to wives and children or career. But such a disorganized mass is difficult to control. Others can appeal to the idealism of youth, too, including natural leaders among the youth themselves. Rival factions developed in the Red Guards. Some factions wanted to carry Maoism to extremes that even Mao himself had never contemplated. Others formed Red Guard units with aims that were actually rightist. And some of the old institutions under attack formed their own so-called Red Guards as well. Pitched battles among these many different factions were taking place with greater and greater frequency.

The "January Storm"

In the latter part of January 1967, events seemed to be reaching a climax. A "January storm" took place in Shanghai, in which workers and peasants were to reinforce the Red Guards in an attempt to seize power from the "powerholders following the capitalist road." The members of the party committee, however, did not give in. In a wave of what the Maoists called "economism," the peasants took the opportunity to demand an end to the communes, and workers in turn tried to better their economic lot. "Economism" swept over Shanghai with "crushing success," spread to the rural areas, and became a "nationwide phenomenon." As Edward E. Rice wrote, "It was a manifestation of the revisionism against which Mao fought, and if not checked it would defeat his Cultural Revolution."[12]

These events in Shanghai made it finally clear to Mao, the

[12] *Mao's Way*, op. cit., p. 289.

radical faction, and their allies that the Red Guards not only were impossible to control but that they were not equal to the task of taking over from "powerholders following the capitalist road." These events also showed that the workers and peasants were too "hoodwinked," to use Mao's own phrase, by "economism" to be used as reinforcements for the Red Guards. The only other potential ally was the People's Liberation Army, and after purging some of its leaders suspected of disloyalty, it was to the Army that Mao and the radicals turned.

Calling in the Army

The decision to involve the Army in conducting the Cultural Revolution in local areas violated long-standing understandings, reflected in Army directives. It may be for this reason that the decision was not made explicit until after the Army had begun to move in several important provinces. The effort succeeded in Heilungkiang and a few other places, but mainly failed. Reports from Anhwei seem to have annoyed Mao particularly, and he ordered Lin Piao to see that the Army helped the left-wing revolutionary masses and quit playing a nonpartisan role. An editorial promptly appeared in the *People's Liberation Army Daily* attacking the idea that the Army should stand on one side in the Cultural Revolution, as it had been doing, and arguing that nonintervention was a "pretext for suppressing the masses."

An unanticipated result of the directive for the Army to intervene was that all over the country Army headquarters were inundated by requests for help by rival contenders seeking the might of the Army to put down their opponents. The Army commanders were in a quandary trying to decide which among the multitude of opposing organizations was really the "true left" blessed by Mao and the leaders in Peking.[13] In other areas, Army headquarters actually came under physical assault.

The "Three in One" Committees

To solve this dilemma and to aid in putting the Red Guard jinni back in the bottle, Mao, the radicals, and their allies

13 Ibid., p. 310.

were forced to make some sort of compromise both with Army leaders, who were interested less in politics than in making the Army strong, and with the old cadres of party government. They hoped that the Army could be made sufficiently "revolutionary" to be an *instrument* of the Cultural Revolution and also that ways could be found to keep in power only members of the old cadres that had come over to the Maoist view and that were considered truly revolutionary. The compromise was embodied in the so-called "three in one" committees.

On January 30, 1967, the Central Committee broadcast a call for a nationwide seizure of power from the "top party persons in authority who are taking the capitalist road." On the face of it, this would seem to be a call for the Red Guards and the Army to seize control of the local party organizations and government. But the broadcast then went on to warn "revolutionary mass organizations," which is the party jargon for the Red Guards and their allies, to pay "adequate attention" to the "revolutionary leading cadres" and the People's Liberation Army. The vast majority of the "revolutionary leading cadres," the jargon expression for the party hierarchs and government officials who had previously held office, had also, in the words of the broadcast, "waged struggles within the party against the handful of people in authority taking the capitalist road." They had adhered firmly to Mao's "proletarian revolutionary line," and they and their knowledge and long experience were the "treasure of the party." Those who had taken the capitalist road were, after all, only a "handful." "A clear distinction must be drawn," the broadcast continued, "between those in authority who belong to the proletariat and those who belong to the bourgeoisie, between those who support and carry out the proletarian revolutionary line and those who support and carry out the bourgeois reactionary line. To regard all persons in authority as untrustworthy is wrong. To oppose, exclude and overthrow all indiscriminately runs counter to the class viewpoint of Marxism-Leninism, Mao Tse-tung's thought."[14] The message of the broadcast, then, was not only that power should be seized, but that it should be seized jointly by the Army, the Red Guards and their allies, and the old party

[14] "On the Proletarian Revolutionaries' Struggle to Seize Power," broadcast by the Central Committee on January 30, 1967, *Red Flag*, No. 3 (1967).

cadres. Some days later an editorial in *Red Flag* spelled out the details. Revolutionary committees were to be set up in each province, town, and city composed of these three elements: "revolutionary mass organizations," local commanders of the People's Liberation Army, and "revolutionary leading cadres." The slogan was power should go to this "three in one alliance."[15]

In Shanghai, the response seemed to reflect a misunderstanding. On February 5, power was finally seized from the party committee, and it was announced that a "Paris commune" had been formed. At the very beginning of the Cultural Revolution, on March 24, 1966, an article celebrating the one hundredth anniversary of the Paris commune had been published that described the Paris commune as a society in which people governed themselves through *elected* leaders who could be recalled at any time. It was also described as a society in which the people were armed. It might be questioned how accurate a description this is of the situation in Paris in 1871, but it certainly bore little resemblance to what was intended by the compromise reflected in the calls for "three in one" committees. No notice was taken of the event in broadcasts and editorials from Peking. It is clear that Mao and the radicals felt that a system of general elections would result in revisionist rather than revolutionary government. Mao called the leaders from Shanghai to discuss the matter, and on February 24, the "Shanghai Municipal Revolutionary Committee" was established and no further mention was made of "Paris communes."

The "February Adverse Current"

The compromise struck with the Army and the old cadre, the power relations that were behind it, and the need for the services of the experienced old cadre to keep the government running altered the atmosphere in China. The old leaders of the center took the opportunity, and in the words of Ch'en Yi, the Foreign Minister, "tried to save each other and formed a group." The radicals called the effort the "February Adverse Current."

[15] "On the Revolutionary 'Three in One' Combination," *Red Flag*, No. 5 (1967).

The Spring of 1967

The entire spring of 1967 was a period of doubt—doubt whether the Maoist-Army-old cadre coalition would hold together and doubt whether the people in the provinces would accept the direction of Peking whatever faction they belonged to. Of the 29 special municipalities and provinces, the top level of local government, only seven formed revolutionary committees fitting the "three in one" description between January 31, 1967, and October 31, 1967, and the proportion of towns, villages, collectives, and factories forming revolutionary committees was similar. Peking frequently complained about the way that local commanders of the Army were conducting their "intervention." Of the three factions forming the coalition, the "law and order" group of "old cadres" identified with Chou En-lai seemed to speak out most strongly. On May 22, 1967, for example, Chou warned the rebels in the provinces that "beating, destroying, robbing, confiscating, kidnaping . . . the destruction of state property . . . are strictly prohibited."

However, the coalition seemed to hold together, at least in Peking. Liu Shao-ch'i and his allies continued to be the universal enemy and whipping boy, and Chiang Ch'ing and her allies were clearly very powerful. In her speeches, she supported the compromise line, but she was prominent, and other incidents indicate she had her way on a number of matters. In April 1967, for example, a Red Guard group in Peking lured Chiang Ch'ing's old enemy Madame Liu Shao-ch'i to a place where they could seize her (by a story that her daughter had suffered an accident) and subjected her to a mass criticism session of abuse and villification at Tsinghua University, stronghold of the ultraleft and Chiang Ch'ing. It is difficult to believe that this could have been done without Chiang Ch'ing's consent.[16]

A climax of some sort came in a summer of disorder in 1967. The ultraleft and the more radical of the Red Guards continued to invoke Mao's name and thought, although they were clearly

[16] For support for the view that Chiang Ch'ing's consent must have been necessary, see Klaus Mehnert, *Peking and the New Left* (Stuttgart, Deutsche Verlags-Anstalt, 1969), p. 58.

unhappy that he opposed the Shanghai commune and supported the "three in one" revolutionary committees, which they pointed out were tantamount to helping the reinstatement of the bureaucrats already toppled in the "January storm."[17] These acts were, in the words of an ultraleft manifesto, "something which the revolutionary people find hard to understand." They justified Mao's action on tactical grounds, that only "immature revolutionaries" believed that communes could be established immediately. But they then went on to attack the "three in one" committees and to advocate the full range of the ultraleft line. Mao, for his part, seemed equally disappointed in the Red Guards and the young intellectuals of the ultraleft. On August 31, 1967, at the turning point of the turbulent, climactic summer, he spoke of the Red Guards in sorrow and bitterness. "It was desired to bring up some successors among the intellectuals," he said, "but now it seems to be a hopeless task. As I see it, the intellectuals, including young intellectuals still in school, still have a basically bourgeois world outlook, whether they are in the party or outside of it."[18] To say that the task of bringing up young intellectuals as successors was "hopeless" and to say that their outlook was "basically bourgeois" was for Mao the ultimate condemnation.

The Wuhan Rebellion

The radicals of the Cultural Revolution group in Peking continued their efforts to encourage seizures of power. They came to feel that the Army was not so much helping the leftist revolutionary groups as blocking them. This view seemed to be confirmed by the rebellion of an Army unit and a conservative local "Red Guard" unit associated with them in Wuhan in

17 Resolutions of the Sheng-wu-lein, *Survey of the China Mainland Press,* American Consulate General, Hong Kong, No. 4,190, pp. 1–18. The Sheng-wu-lien was one of the better-known ultraleft youth organizations. This particular one was based in Hunan. Several of its key documents were published in ultraleft newspapers on the mainland, copies of which found their way out of China. These documents are also the source of the two quotations immediately following.

18 Speech for visiting foreign military delegation, August 31, 1967, published by "Proletarian Revolutionaries of PLA Factory No. 7,215," *Survey of the China Mainland Press,* No. 4,200 (September 1967), pp. 1–5.

July. Two representatives of the Cultural Revolution group in Peking, Hsieh Fu-chih and Wang Li, had been on a tour to centers where the Army had been suppressing leftists. In Wuhan they conducted a meeting with officers of the rank of divisional commander and above and laid down the law, charging them with errors and supporting conservative rather than true left groups. The commander of People's Liberation Army Unit 8201 rose to his feet, but Wang Li refused to let him speak. Both the commander and his political commissar stalked out. That night Unit 8201 occupied key points in the city and led an uprising by their local "Red Guard." Wang Li and Hsieh Fu-chih were seized, beaten, and crowned with dunce caps. Peking ordered an airborne division to Wuhan to disarm the rebels and appointed a new commander. The events were a blow to the Cultural Revolution group mainly because they dramatized the Army resistance to the order to help the leftist organizations. The Cultural Revolution group had already planned a purge of Army Leaders opposed to their views, and the Wuhan rebellion served to confirm their worst suspicions.

The Ultraleft and the "Arms Grabbing" Campaign

In any case, the ultraleft continued to quote Mao and to act in his name, but to do so in violent ways directly counter to the instructions coming from Peking and the coalition of which he was clearly a part. However, it must also be said that the Cultural Revolution group undoubtedly encouraged many of the actions of the ultras among the Red Guards.

It was during this period that Chou En-lai was most threatened, and the action against him was probably one of those encouraged by the Cultural Revolution group. In August 1967, at a time when both Mao Tse-tung and Lin Piao were absent from Peking, Chou was besieged for two days and nights in his office by five hundred thousand ultraleft Red Guards who were attempting to seize both the files of the Central Committee and Chou himself. Chou's great skill as a negotiator and his charm with young people saved him. By talking to small groups day and night, he gradually persuaded the Red Guards to disperse. The toll of such confrontations and the sheer overwork of con-

tinued crises on a man of Chou's age, even though he was
possessed of extraordinary energy and stamina, were immense.
A foreign visitor in March, some months before the events described above, who had an appointment with Chou reports that
a substantive discussion was impossible. Chou's hands were shak-
ing so badly that the visitor had to open a cigarette box for him,
and Chou was so exhausted he could not speak in coherent
sentences.

Some parts of the action campaign of the ultraleft seem bizarre,
but the campaign apparently came close enough to success to be
very dangerous indeed. One of the tests of a "Paris commune"
was that the masses be armed, and following this criterion in
July and August the ultraleft Red Guards embarked on the so-
called "arms grabbing" campaign. For legitimacy they seized on
what was apparently a chance remark by Chiang Ch'ing and
turned it into a slogan. Chiang Ch'ing was adhering closely to
the compromise line at this time, but in July she said something
to the effect that the Cultural Revolution should be defended
by arms if necessary, and the ultraleft took up the statement as
their authority. Quite literally, bands of Red Guards would wrestle
weapons out of the hands of soldiers, who were still under the
order never to use firearms in the Cultural Revolution, but the
Red Guards also seem to have mounted raids on arsenals, and
even taken over trainloads of weapons and ammunition destined
for Vietnam.[19] It seems that the soldiers were more restrained
than one might have expected, both as individuals and as units,
and the Red Guards succeeded in acquiring rather large quantities of weapons. But there was considerable fighting and more
as time went on. Some Army units suppressed local Red Guards.
Also, the different Red Guard factions clashed, Red Guards fought
with workers and collective farm groups, and disruption and
bloodshed spread. An example of just how serious matters had
become was the fact that in Canton the international trade fair

[19] Our authority for this is Chiang Ch'ing herself. See "Important Talk Given
by Comrade Chiang Ch'ing on Sept. 5 at a Conference for Representatives of
Anhwei Who Have Come to Peking," *Great Preparatory Committee of People's
Automobiles, Red Flag, Municipal Communications and Transportation Department* (September 18, 1967).

had to be canceled, in spite of its importance to China's foreign-exchange earnings.

Appeals and orders to stop the factional fighting and end the "arms grabbing" campaign and attacks on the Army went out from all levels in Peking. And action followed. On August 28, 1967, the first of a series of public trials of leaders of militant factions was held in Shanghai, followed by execution. Both the trial and the execution were televised. Other trials and executions followed in Peking, Shantung, Heilungkiang, and elsewhere. On September 5, a directive was issued to return the weapons and ammunition to the Army, which the ultraleft met with a "nation-wide, mass 'arms concealment' movement." Over the following months, however, the Army took control.

Unity Behind the "Law and Order" Policy

Quite clearly, the coalition in Peking closed ranks behind a "law and order" policy that summer and autumn of 1967. Chiang Ch'ing, the symbol of the radicals in Peking, gave speeches on September 1, September 5, and September 17 attacking various ultraleft groups as reactionaries flying under the colors of the left. What is more, she appeared on the same platform with Chou En-lai, whom the ultraleft had nominated to replace Liu Shao-ch'i as the "No. 1 party person following the capitalist road." And she seconded Chou's very blunt threats. The September 17 occasion illustrates both Chou's posture and Chiang Ch'ing's. "This group [the May 16 Corps, a leading ultraleft group being castigated at the meeting] vulgarly attacked our comrades in the Party Center. . . ." Chou said from the platform, "As one of the responsible persons in the headquarters of the proletariat, I do not allow anyone to aggravate the relations between the Central Cultural Revolution Group [the organization of which Chiang Ch'ing was deputy and Chen Po-ta chief] and myself. They intended to alienate me from the Central Cultural Revolution Group." Chou went on to remark that young students "who have not had much experience are easily led to believe things. . . . Now let me inform you that all students should go back to school in a month, or they will be dismissed."

Chiang Ch'ing at this point interjected still another threat: "The government will not offer them jobs either."[20]

The evidence is that the situation in Peking could be described as a continuation of the coalition of Maoists, professional Army leaders, and party and government cadres looking to Chou as their representative, but with Chou and his "law and order" faction at least temporarily ascendant, in the sense that it was their line that all followed. In the country, the professional military seemed to gain more prominence and also to be more independent. At any rate, broadcasts and editorials emanating from Peking complained less of the actions of the local military commanders, and the implication seems strong that they acquired more autonomy.

Curbing the Red Guards

From September 1967, both Peking and the local commanders seemed to concentrate on the task of getting the youth back under control. Two basic methods were used. One was to assign them to work in the villages, denying them residence permits and the equivalent of ration cards if they stayed in the city. Mao had long extolled the virtues of working alongside the peasant, and at various times, programs—termed *hsia-fang* or "down-sending"—were instituted to send people from the cities "down" to the countryside to do manual work in the villages. The ideological and idealistic purpose was to teach the dignity of manual labor and humility and to combat bureaucratism. In 1958–59, the program aimed at party cadres, and some 1.3 million are supposed to have been sent down. In the period following the "hundred flowers" episode, it was intellectuals and students. Now it was the Red Guards. On October 8, 1967, an "urgent notice" was issued jointly by the Central Committee of the party, the State Council, the Central Military Commission, and the Central Cultural Revolution Group. It directed that "educated youth be sent down to the countryside and up to the hills to grasp revolution and stimulate production in the rural areas."

[20] *Chinese Communist Affairs: Facts and Features,* Vol. I, No. 4 (Taipei, December 13, 1967), pp. 23–26.

The second method was by means of the so-called "workers' propaganda teams." In July of 1968, the Chinese press was flooded with articles extolling the virtues of the workers and ridiculing intellectuals. Stories were reported in which a lecture by a worker made everything clear after one by an intellectual had only confused. What the worker had was practical knowledge, which is vastly superior to the theoretical knowledge of the intellectual. "Those who teach science and engineering do not know how to operate or repair machines; those who teach literature do not know how to write essays; those who teach agricultural chemistry do not know how to use fertilizer."[21] Then on July 27, 1968, a "workers' propaganda team" took over Tsinghua University in Peking—famous, as mentioned earlier, as a stronghold of the ultraleft and of support for Chiang Ch'ing. A few days later, on August 5, Mao Tse-tung sent the workers a basket of mangoes that he had received as a gift from a foreign delegation, and on August 9 a breathless account of what happened next was published. "As the joyous news spread, the Tsinghua campus was a scene of jubilation. Cheers of 'A long, long life to Chairman Mao' rang out to the skies."[22] People gathered around the mangoes jubilantly singing and cheering. A mango was sent to each of the factories from which the "workers' propaganda team" had been drawn, and in one factory they succeeded in preserving it for display in a glass case.

Shortly thereafter, on August 23 and August 25, two of Mao's "latest directives" were published. One stated that the working class is the leading class and as such it should take the "leading role" in the Cultural Revolution. The other stated that it was essential to have worker leadership in education and that the "workers' propaganda teams" should remain permanently in the schools and universities. The message was clear, and all over the country "workers' propaganda teams" moved into the universities and schools to take over.

[21] The quote is from a major article by Yao Wen-yüan, reportedly Mao's son-in-law, as mentioned previously, and a close associate of Chiang Ch'ing. Although actually dated later than the period referred to, the quote is typical. *Peking Review*, No. 35 (August 30, 1968), pp. 3–6.

[22] *Peking Review*, No. 31 (August 9, 1968), pp. 5–6.

End of the Cultural Revolution

In January 1967, as we have already noted, only seven of the twenty-nine provinces and special municipalities had "three in one" revolutionary committees—the ultraleft resistance to the old cadres was simply too great. But with the ascendancy of the "law and order" policies, matters began to change. The twenty-eighth and twenty-ninth Revolutionary Committees were formed just a year after the decisive policy shift of 1967, in September 1968.

The Communist party of China has held only three Congresses since 1928, when the Sixth Congress took place. The Seventh Congress was held seventeen years later, in 1945, after Mao had consolidated his position at the head of the party and World War II was drawing to a close. The Eighth Congress was held eleven years later, in 1956, after the party had consolidated its hold on the mainland. When the Ninth Congress was convened in Peking in the spring of 1969, it was clear that Mao and the others had decided that the Cultural Revolution was over.

What had it all accomplished? Who had won? Had a new society been created? A new human being? What did it all mean for the rest of humanity? The next chapter will attempt to answer the question of who now holds power in China, and the one following the question of a new society.

CHAPTER 17

Who Is to Rule?

WHO WON POWER in the Cultural Revolution? Who rules China, and who is likely to rule in the future?

Look first at the composition of the Revolutionary Committees in the provinces. The dictum from Peking was that power was to be equally divided among the military, the old cadres, and the "mass organizations"—the Red Guards and their allies. In fact, the largest contingent in the period immediately following the Cultural Revolution consisted of military men. The second-largest were people from the old cadres, and the smallest were from the "mass organizations."

The composition of the new Central Committee elected by the Ninth Party Congress, held in 1969, is also revealing.[1] With 279 members, the Central Committee cannot be a policy-making body, although it is supposed to ratify major decisions taken

[1] The study on which I have relied most heavily is that by Donald W. Klein and Lois B. Hager, "The Ninth Central Committee," *China Quarterly*, No. 45 (January/March 1971).

between plenums. The significance of being a member of the Central Committee is the recognition it implies. A member of the Central Committee generally holds an important position in the party structure, in the armed services, or in the governmental structure. Almost all the chairmen of provincial Revolutionary Committees, for example, are full members of the Central Committee, and no provincial-level committee is without one member who is also a full or alternate member of the Central Committee. What happened to the leadership in China during the Cultural Revolution can thus be seen by comparing the membership of this new, Ninth Central Committee with those that preceded it.

The Seventh Central Committee, elected in 1945, consisted principally of men who made the Long March, with a few positions occupied by "Northerners"—natives of Shensi and neighboring provinces who received Mao and the Long Marchers at the Yenan base. A few positions were also occupied by "fallen leaders," men whom Mao regarded as dissidents; for unlike Stalin, Mao not only did not physically eliminate his party opponents, but provided at least token representation for them. In examining the composition of the Eighth Committee, elected in 1956 and enlarged in 1958, one is struck by the continuity demonstrated. Almost all the members of the Seventh Committee were carried over, including the token dissidents, and most of the alternates were promoted to full membership. At the same time, the number of "Northerners" was increased. The Ninth Central Committee, however, retained only 53 of the 173 surviving members and alternates of the Eighth Committee. Some 120 were purged. In brief, what happened was that Mao's inner core remained largely intact, whereas the "northern" element was systematically eliminated.[2]

What about the new members? As with the Revolutionary Committees, the major new beneficiaries immediately following the Cultural Revolution were the military. Thirty-five per cent of the 1,512 delegates to the Party Congress had military affiliations, and 100 of the 279 members of the new Central Committee were military men. The majority, furthermore, worked in

2 Ibid.

the provinces mainly at the military region level, rather than in Peking.

Another striking fact about the new membership was that there was no "new generation." After all the emphasis on the Red Guards in the Cultural Revolution, it is surprising that the average age of full members for whom data are available was 59, and for alternates, 53. Yao Wen-yüan, Chiang Ch'ing's collaborator, who was about 40, appears to be one of the youngest if not *the* youngest of the members.

The Liu Shao-ch'i Faction

It is clear, then, from the historical record and from data such as these on the background of members of the Central Committee, that certain factions of the party were quite thoroughly eliminated—those headed by Liu Shao-ch'i and Teng Hsiao-p'ing and rooted to some extent in the government hierarchy but mainly in the structure of the party. A rival for power was eliminated, Liu, along with the structure that constituted his power base. In addition, a rival set of policies had also been discredited, at least for the time being.[3] In foreign policy, Liu Shao-ch'i and his allies differed from the Maoists mainly in that they were not willing to write off the Soviets completely and that they still entertained notions of a reconciliation. What they wanted was the assurance of Soviet protection from the Western "imperialists" so they could concentrate on the domestic tasks of development, and they may also have hoped for a restoration of economic aid to assist that development. Even this difference between those associated with Liu and the Maoists was not entirely clear-cut. P'eng Chen, for example, who was mayor of Peking and the first to be purged, was even more violently anti-Soviet than the Maoists. The major differences are concerned with domestic issues—policy toward the economy and development, education, and agriculture—and with ideology. Liu Shao-

[3] For an analysis of the policy differences of the different factions, see Donald Zagoria, *Vietnam Triangle: Moscow, Peking, Hanoi* (New York, 1967) and Uri Ra'anan, "Chinese Factionalism and Sino-Soviet Relations," *Current History* (September 1970) and his "Peking's Foreign Policy 'Debate,'" *China in Crisis* (Chicago, University of Chicago Press, 1968), ed. Tang Tsou.

ch'i and his group stood for a conservative approach in domestic matters, an almost Western orthodox view of economic development, including larger private plots for members of agricultural collectives, and economic incentives for industrial workers. It has happened before in a Communist country that the victor adopted the policy of the loser, but for the time being at least this more conservative set of domestic policies was set to one side.

The Lo Jui-ch'ing Faction

It is also clear that one faction within the professional military had at least been decapitated, and that their particular policy preferences had also been set aside. The policy differences on strategic questions, to repeat, stemmed from the fact that the chief of staff, Lo Jui-ch'ing, the spokesman for a professional military faction, put the risks of an American invasion high and advocated a strategy of defense along orthodox lines. He argued that if war came, China should fight the kind of conventional warfare the People's Liberation Army had fought in the Korean War. It flowed from this that a reconciliation with the Soviet Union would be necessary not only to ensure a nuclear deterrent to the United States, but also to acquire Soviet aid in modern armaments. The Maoists, on the other hand, and their allies among the "political" military—the commissars and their followers whose spokesman was Lin Piao—put the threat of an American invasion low, and advocated a guerrilla strategy based on luring the Americans deep into Chinese territory if the invasion did come. This defense strategy would be based on the militia rather than the regular Army, and it would require no help from the Soviet Union. That this professional military faction suffered in the Cultural Revolution is beyond question. It is very significant that the rate of survival among military members of the Eighth Central Committee was no better than their civilian colleagues. Although the Ninth Central Committee ended up with a much higher percentage of military members, it was a different group of the military. What seems to have happened is that not only was Lo Jui-ch'ing purged, but so were his supporters and those who took his more orthodox approach to questions of strategy. Lin Piao and his group came out on top, and Lin was named as No. 2 after Mao, as Mao's successor and heir, and as his "closest comrade in arms."

The Red Guard Leaders

The absence of a "new generation" suggests that a third set of leaders, or at least potential leaders, who lost out in the Cultural Revolution were ironically those on whom Mao had relied as his main instrument in carrying out the Revolution. Not only was the near-anarchy of the height of the Red Guard power ended and the Red Guard jinni of millions of rampaging youth put back into the bottle, but the group of natural leaders who came to the fore during the upheaval does not seem to have appropriate representation at the top levels of the party or to have survived as a group or faction of its own. But this impression may be true only in the short run. Radicals who emerged during the Cultural Revolution can be found on almost every one of the local party committees, and in many cases they have significant political clout. For the moment, however, the policies associated with the radicals have also been set aside—the idealistic vision of a "Paris commune" of elected officials subject to criticism and recall by the masses who are armed.

An Uneasy Coalition

Thus in 1969, immediately following the Cultural Revolution, Mao remained at the top, although he seemed somewhat divorced from the direction of day-to-day affairs. Below Mao himself was an uneasy coalition of at least three factions. One was the extreme Maoists—represented by Mao's wife, Chiang Ch'ing, Ch'en Po-ta, Yao Wen-yüan, and K'ang Sheng. The power base of this group had been the Red Guards and the administrative cadre of the Cultural Revolution. Little of either remained, and their power apparently derived mainly from the fact that they constituted Mao's "court." However, being Mao's "court" probably remained a position of some power in spite of the fact that the policy this group advocated was probably too extremist even for Mao much of the time. An illustration is the effort Peking made on several occasions to prevent provincial and other local leadership groups from veering too far to the right and ignoring the claims of the left for representation. In October 1968, for example, Radio Honan warned against any tendency to have the new Revolutionary Committees in the provinces composed *entirely* of old party cadres, since that would mean "restoring the old." More specifically and from the very top were a series of pronouncements from the Central Committee praising the "smashing of the February Adverse Current" a year and a half earlier—a clear warning to the "law and order" factions not to go too far. Such warnings against too heavy representation for the old cadres in the Revolutionary Committees and too little for the left-wing groups were repeated in the last part of 1968 and early 1969. The extremists seemed quite clearly to be the weakest of the factions making up the coalition at the top, but they obviously retained some power.

The Lin Piao Military Faction

The second faction was the military group looking to Lin Piao as their leader. If the military in China had been monolithic and hierarchical, centering in one place, Peking, and in one man, Lin Piao, this faction would undoubtedly have dominated the coalition completely. In fact, however, the military in China tend to be regionally based, with loyalties to one or another of the five field armies, which compete with their loyalties to the high command, and this alters the situation.[4]

The Apparatchiki

The third faction was the group of party and government *apparatchiki* who looked to Chou En-lai. In ideological and party terms, the Chou En-lai group was not in obvious opposition to Mao, as was Liu Shao-ch'i and his faction. The evidence is that the Chou group accepted Mao's goals and his policies, but urged a more pragmatic and moderate application of the principles to specific problems. Chou, for example, seemed to be in complete agreement with Mao's view of Soviet "revisionism" and the policy

[4] William Whitson, "The Field Army in Chinese Military Politics," *China Quarterly*, No. 37 (January/March 1969).

of continued tensions with the Soviets. But it seemed to be Chou who urged a lessening of tension with the United States, precisely to compensate for the need to maintain tension with the Soviets. However, it is most important to add at this point that this kind of balancing policy is also very typical of Mao and his closest associates as well. "Talk/fight, talk/fight" is a slogan that Mao himself espoused, and a speech he made in 1949 defending negotiations with the enemy is republished whenever such a change in the tactical line is indicated—as, for example, in November 1968, when China made its offer to resume the Warsaw talks with the United States. Lin Piao made the most explicit statement of all on this point in May 1965, during the debate on strategy. "Providing the basic interests of the people are not violated, it is perfectly permissible and even necessary," he wrote, "to conduct negotiations with the imperialists and to reach certain agreements with them on certain occasions." Thus the Chou faction was not so much in opposition to Maoist ideology and policy as representing an approach that stood for moderation and pragmatism in applying Maoism to specific problems and issues.

A Second Wave of Struggle

A second wave of struggle and purges came only a few months after the Ninth Party Congress. Several members of the ultra-Maoist group were purged even earlier, in the latter stages of the Cultural Revolution. Then, in the summer of 1971, Ch'en Po-ta himself was implicitly denounced in the Peking press as a "sham Marxist" and a "big careerist." The significance for the balance between the three coalitions is clear when it is recalled that Ch'en was not only speechwriter for Mao and head of the Cultural Revolution high command, with Chiang Ch'ing as his deputy, but that he was officially listed in party rankings as No. 4, after Mao, Lin Piao, and Chou En-lai. Western researchers established that he had not been seen in public for a year—since August 1970—and speculated that his disappearance might be linked to the subsequent overtures to the United States.[5] When the Tenth Party Congress was held in August 1973, it was noticed that Chiang Ch'ing and Yao Wen-yüan were not listed

[5] New York *Times* (August 8, 1971), p. 3.

among the top party officials, although they had not actually been purged.

The most dramatic developments, however, concerned Lin Piao and his allies among the military: the chief of staff, Huang Yung-sheng; the commander of the Air Force, Wu Fa-hsien; the commissar of the Navy, Li Tso-peng; the director of the Logistics Department of the People's Liberation Army, Chiu Hui-tso; and a host of others farther down the line. On the night of September 12–13, 1971, a Chinese military aircraft, apparently fleeing to the Soviet Union, crashed in Mongolia. Nine badly charred bodies were found in the wreckage, none of which were identifiable, according to the Mongolians. On September 13, 14, and 15, no members of the Politburo were seen in public, and it seems likely that the rump of the Politburo was meeting in continuous emergency session to consider how to deal with the crisis. Also on September 13, 14, and 15 *all* flights of both military and civilian aircraft were banned throughout China. It was then announced that the Peking celebrations of National Day—October 1—were being canceled as an "economy measure," although it was obvious to everyone that the preparations were so far along that most of the expense had already been incurred. Both measures strongly suggest fear of a military *coup*. Western observers recalled that Lin Piao had not been seen in public since June 1971, at a reception for the President of Romania, and their suspicions were confirmed when articles began appearing in the press obliquely attacking Lin for a variety of crimes—distorting Mao's thought, estranging Mao from the masses, splitting the allegiance of the army, establishing illicit relations with the Soviet Union, punishing cadres who made mistakes rather than educating them, and sabotaging agricultural policy. In Moscow, the speculation was that Lin Piao and his wife were among the nine bodies found in the plane wreckage. Spokesmen in Peking, however, denied that Lin was dead.

Gradually in 1972 and 1973, Peking changed its line. Lower officials and then Chou En-lai himself said that Lin Piao had attempted a *coup d'état*, that Lin had three times attempted to assassinate Mao himself, and that he had attempted to escape to the Soviet Union on the fleeing aircraft and was killed in the crash.

Some skeptics in the West doubt that Lin Piao actually attempted a *coup*, much less that he tried to assassinate Mao. One theory is that Lin was purged not for having betrayed Mao, but for having served him too well.[6] We know that the commanders of the Nanking, Canton, Shenyang, and Tsinan military regions took a strong stand against the Red Guards during the Cultural Revolution and that they clearly won a powerful voice in the Politburo at the Ninth Party Congress. The theory is that Lin Piao alienated these regional military authorities while attempting to reassert Peking's control, as he was ordered to do by Mao and the rest of the leadership. This left Mao and the central authorities a choice between purging Lin and a confrontation with these local military authorities, which risked a military *coup* or even civil war.

The evidence to make a definitive judgment on exactly what happened is simply not available in the West. It seems likely, however, that Lin Piao was engaged in some sort of power struggle with other factions even if he did not actually attempt to assassinate Mao or launch a *coup*, and that the allegations that he was attempting to seize power are at least to that extent justified.

Interestingly enough, it may also be that the question of an invitation to President Nixon to visit China became an element in the struggle. Although other issues were prominent and probably more important, it seems clear that Chou and the pragmatists argued for an easing of tension with the United States to be brought about by Nixon's visit, while other factions argued *against* it, and that this policy debate came to be involved in the power struggle.

In any case, by the time of the Nixon visit it was clear that Lin Piao and the "political" military who had been the top layer of the military faction had been purged and that they had been replaced by "professional" military leaders. Throughout the Nixon visit, for example, Chou En-lai was most frequently accompanied

[6] Simon Leys, "Downfall of a Trusting Zealot," *Far Eastern Economic Review* (February 26, 1972).

by Marshal Yeh Chien-ying, the most senior of the professional military.

The New Axis of Power

By the time of the Nixon visit, then, and at least partly as a result of it, the situation was changed. Again, Mao symbolically and probably to a large extent in fact was at the top as leader. Below him power was shared by an axis coalition between the party and government hierarchs, headed by Chou En-lai, on the one hand, and, on the other, by the professional military, who at least looked to Yeh Chien-ying, even if he was not so clearly their head. The ultra-Maoists survived in the form of Chiang Ch'ing and a few of her henchmen, but it was clear that their power was limited.

Mao's Power Position

Just exactly how much power Mao actually exercised in this period may be subject for debate. He seemed divorced from day-to-day affairs, and his position may have been to some extent honorific. Even so, he clearly had power to some degree. In a showdown struggle Mao would probably have won. In a policy battle, he might also have won if he chose to push all-out and if he was willing to sacrifice other of his policy preferences. But it is doubtful that at this time Mao was all-powerful. Although he may well have felt that the Cultural Revolution had accomplished many of the goals he had intended, events did get out of hand, and Mao had been forced to call a retreat. Retreat meant —at the very minimum—making concessions to the various factions in the military, party, and government in terms of policy and in terms of power. In 1971 and 1972, Chou En-lai was clearly running the country in terms of day-to-day decisions. The evidence is not clear, but it may also be that his power was even greater than this implies—much greater, with Mao as only a figurehead. More likely, however, there was some sort of balance between the two. Mao, to give a purely hypothetical but rather plausible example, might have succeeded in insisting on continuing the high level of tension with the Soviet Union, while Chou might have been successful in arguing that if a high level of tension was continued with the Soviet Union, then China must balance the risk by reducing tension with the United States. Thus Chou may have insisted on an invitation to President Nixon as the price Mao had to pay. In any case, Mao remained the symbol of the Chinese Communist revolution. The "cult of the personality" had put him so central in the consciousness of the masses that removing him would require a re-education beyond the strength of any faction or combination of factions then on the scene. As a result, any policy—even one in opposition to Mao and Maoism—had to be garbed as the "thought of Mao Tse-tung." This fact alone gave Mao impressive power.

So long as Mao lives, some more or less uneasy coalition of potentially rival factions under at least the nominal leadership of Mao himself seems likely. There is evidence that Mao has not given up his ideas of permanent revolution and dreams of launching still another "Cultural Revolution." He has been quoted as saying that the "situation changes from a great upheaval to a great peace once every seven or eight years," and 1974 was the eighth anniversary of the start of the Cultural Revolution. Also, in 1973 and 1974 Confucius was attacked repeatedly in the party organs as a tool of the "slave-holding aristocracy" with "blood ties" to recent villains like Liu Shao-ch'i and Lin Piao. Confucius was something of a hero in academic circles in the early 1960s, but in 1974 public meetings were held on the campuses to denounce him. The Communist party tradition is to "use the past to attack the present," and the question that puzzled China watchers in the West was: Who is the present-day Confucius? What individual, or more likely, faction, too powerful to be attacked openly, is the target of this indirect assault? These signs may portend still another upheaval, but another "Cultural Revolution" is not likely to be any more successful than the last one in eliminating either the military faction or the faction of the party *apparatchiki*. Similarly, the two factions may chip away at individuals in the ultra-Maoist faction, but it would be difficult for them to eliminate the entire faction without seeming to threaten Mao himself. It also seems unlikely that the factions contending for power would find it in their interest to agree among themselves to depose Mao until the issue between them is settled. And it seems even more unlikely that any one faction can gain sufficient ascendancy over the others to depose Mao while Mao is still alive.

When Mao Dies

When Mao dies, however, a renewed power struggle seems inevitable. Who the contenders might be, and who the possible victor, is of no small moment to the rest of us. Of course, speculation on the kind of evidence available is perilous, but a few worthwhile conclusions do seem possible.

The most obvious point to be made is that the only possible contenders for power in China are different factions of the Communist party. Chiang Kai-shek and the Kuomintang were thoroughly discredited by the events of 1949, and the many years of exile since 1949 have erased even their name and existence from the consciousness of the mass of Chinese. No other possible contender exists.

From among the different factions within the Communist party, several possible contenders seem possible. It is even conceivable that Liu Shao-ch'i and his faction could stage a comeback, in spite of their resounding defeat in the Cultural Revolution. Those who are more familiar with Stalin and his methods than with the Chinese find it surprising that few of those purged in China are known to have been physically eliminated. Kao Kang was the only high official known to have died in the period, and he reportedly committed suicide. Most of the others were kept in house arrest or sent to work in obscurity in some remote place. Because of what Stalin would have considered an inconceivably meticulous attention to the legalities, some of those purged, such as P'eng Teh-huai, continued to be listed as members of the Politburo long after they were ousted and relegated to minor posts. In the case of Liu Shao-ch'i, this concern for the legalities led to an almost bizarre anomaly. A National Congress of the Party expelled Liu from the *party*, but he remained Chairman of the government. According to the legalities, only a National Congress of the *government* could remove him from that post, and normally only the Standing Committee can convene a National Congress. Liu Shao-ch'i was Chairman of the Standing Committee, and he apparently refused to convene a meeting. Thus attention to the legalities meant that matters remained at an impasse for what any other country would regard as an intolerably long period. The Chinese do not seem to be bothered by the ambiguity or inconsistency, but it does require even the Chinese to do some wriggling. The invitation to Mr. Nixon, for example, according to international protocol should have come from the chief of state—since Mr. Nixon was chief of state as well as chief executive officer of the United States. Thus the invitation should properly have come to Mr. Nixon not from Mao, who was chairman of the party but held no government position or title at all, but from Liu Shao-ch'i. The Chinese got around the problem by having the invitation come from the Chinese chief executive officer, Chou En-lai, in his capacity as Chairman of the State Council, or Premier. Presumably Mr. Nixon was to accept in his capacity as chief executive officer, rather than in his capacity as chief of state, or perhaps he was merely supposed to overlook the gap in protocol. In any case, the Chinese later appointed an "acting" chief of state as a way around the problem.

Even though Liu Shao-ch'i, P'eng Teh-huai, and the others who were purged are still alive, and even though many who were not purged may still view them with some sympathy and regard, it seems most unlikely that they could return to power as a group. They have been scattered as well as discredited, and too many others, like the military, would lose too much of what they have gained by Liu's and P'eng's downfall. The conservative policies that Liu advocated on economic and domestic matters and that P'eng advocated in military and strategic matters may be revived someday, but it is doubtful that the advocates themselves will reappear on the scene.

The Secret Police

If we were concerned with the Soviet Union, we would at this point also have to consider whether the secret police would provide an effective base for a bid for power. But in China the secret police has never developed the position that it did in the Soviet Union. In China the secret police can be ruled out as a potential contender.

The Principal Candidates for Power

Thus the principal candidates for power after Mao's death are the members of the coalition that emerged after the Cultural Revolution: the ultra-Maoists, the military, and the *apparatchiki* in the party and governmental structure who looked to Chou En-lai for leadership in the period following the Revolution.

The ultra-Maoists have steadily weakened. What is more, the principal source of what strength they have is Mao himself. The other, more powerful members of the coalition are not really against Maoism, and it would be a mistake to underestimate the strength of radicalism in China, which will undoubtedly continue as a major force. But among these other factions, the memories of the chaos and excesses of the Cultural Revolution are too vivid to permit them to let the ultras succeed in a bid for supreme power.

The military's chances are much better, whether the "political" military or the "professional" military. Although Lin Piao himself is probably dead, some other "political" general might well succeed in using the military as his base for a bid for supreme power. The "political" men—men who are political commissars, career party men whose work is with the military, rather than being competent as soldiers—have sometimes been in tension with the professional military in the past. They have also on occasion been extremely popular with the military. But even if a "political" general achieves supreme power by using the military as a base, it does not necessarily mean that the military will henceforth rule China.

One reason to doubt that power will permanently shift to a military faction is the evidence showing localism and regionalism in military loyalties—that the ties are more to each of the five regionally based field armies than to the military as an entity. Generally speaking, military men in China have long-standing ties to one or the other of these five field armies, usually the one located in the area in which they serve. This is not meant to suggest that something resembling the old warlordism may emerge in China. On the contrary, the military themselves take pride in the national unity achieved under the Communists and seem determined to avoid any new fragmentation. But the loyalties developed over the twenty to thirty years of association within each of the field armies do seem to have significant consequences in the governance of China. An extensive study of military elite biographies strongly suggests that "Party-military personal relations coalesced into five major sub-elites [the five regional field armies] whose continuing informal bonds have remained a significant factor, first, in deciding key Party as well as military personnel assignments and, second, in reaching compromises on national policy and regional policy implementation. This is not to deny the importance of formal institutional arrangements whereby policies have been executed. It only argues that a Party member's actual power, since 1950, may well have been primarily a function of the collective status of his Field Army associates, whether in or out of uniform."[7]

A second reason to doubt that power will permanently shift to a military faction is the pressure, already mentioned, toward professionalism. In a small, underdeveloped country whose army's main function is internal security, the military not only can but frequently do serve as the training grounds for politics and for administering all kinds of large-scale tasks—transportation, communications, flood control, and many others. This also happened in China during the Cultural Revolution. But in a large country that has a real problem of defense around long borders and that aspires to great power status, including a credible nuclear deterrent of both warheads and missiles, the military tasks are not only full-time, but formidable in their complexity and requirements for technical expertise. If the military in China do take over the government, they will very quickly lose their military competence and themselves be faced with a new military—younger officers who retain their competence and whose top value preferences are most likely to be military professionalism. The combination of these two forces—regional loyalties of the military and the pres-

[7] Whitson, op. cit., pp. 25–26.

sures toward professionalism—make it unlikely that the military will themselves and as a group have the thrust and unity to take power on Mao's death. Even if the head man should turn out to be a general, it seems likely that he will be, like Lin Piao, more a party man who has specialized in military affairs than a professional soldier. And even if a professional soldier does make the bid, it seems more likely that he will become a "political" man than that the military as a group would take over the government.

At the same time, the military as a group will still have enormous power. It seems doubtful that any individual or group can win the struggle for power against the concerted opposition of the military. Thus the military will have a veto over who does achieve power and will have a very large voice in the policy decisions that are subsequently made—on the allocation of resources and the determination of how much to spend on arms, on the level of risk and hostility that is permitted in China's relations with the Soviet Union and the United States, and on China's posture toward the other nations of Asia—Japan and India and the rest.

Of the groups we know to exist that could serve as an adequate base for attaining power, this leaves Chou En-lai and the *apparatchiki* who look to him as their principal representative. These people occupy key positions in both party and government. As a group they represent wider experience than the military, and they do not have the pressure toward specialization and narrow professionalism that inevitably operates on the military. Thus a likely series of events is that on Mao's death Chou En-lai, if he is still alive, will take over as the head of a party-military coalition. Chou would undoubtedly take steps to weaken potential rivals, but he, too, is in his seventies and still another problem of succession will soon occur. Chou, certainly, will attempt to designate who his successor will be, and whoever is designated will have an opportunity, although fleeting, to consolidate his power.

Conclusion

But to make this kind of detailed prediction about the events following Mao's death is clearly foolhardy. Men die, power shifts, and entirely new factions may appear either before Mao dies or after. The truth is that given the limited amount of information available, we should not be surprised if some faction of which we are totally ignorant is already in a position powerful enough to be unassailable. But what we *can* say—and it may be of crucial importance—is that in China after these years of upheaval, only the Communist party provides the kind of essentially political experience that makes an adequate training ground for the kind of manipulative skills that the effective exercise of power requires. What is more, only the party has the right and duty to place personnel within other bureaucratic structures, to ensure ideological and political orthodoxy. And only the party occupies the central position and has the responsibility for overseeing and coordinating the activities of the other bureaucratic structures. It is conceivable that in time the government civil service might provide a rival training ground and power position, but for the time being the governmental bureaucracy lacks the authority to penetrate the other bureaucracies or the power to oversee and coordinate.

We have already concluded that the struggle for power in Communist China is not over, but will be renewed on Mao's death and probably continue for some time thereafter. We have also already concluded that the only effective contenders for power in that struggle are the different factions of the Communist party. No base for a bid for power exists outside it, although all factions have connections with outside power centers. Now, finally, we also conclude that eventually the victory seems most likely to go to the faction that is most solidly based in the party's bureaucratic structure.

CHAPTER 18

Mao's New Society

IN THE IMMEDIATE aftermath of World War II, when the Communist world was united and still dutiful in taking direction from Moscow, to say that China would be ruled by the Communist party, or even to say that it would be ruled by a faction of the Communist party, would be to say something both meaningful and significant. But today, when communism has so long ago ceased to be monolithic, it is not to say nearly so much. Which communism is it to be? Stalin's communism? Khrushchev's? The communism of Brezhnev and Kosygin? Will it be the liberal communism and national independence of Tito of Yugoslavia? The less liberal but equally independent communism of Ceaucescu of Romania? The still greater heresy of Dubcek of Czechoslovakia? Will the Chinese be faithful to Maoism—which includes not only independence of the Soviet Union and the pursuit of national greatness but also an idealistic revolutionary drive to remake man and society? Is it conceivable that the winning faction, solidly based on the bureaucratic structure of the party, as we expect, could also be even more militantly revolutionary in their ideology and attitude toward the rest of the world than Maoism ever was? Alternatively, is it conceivable that the winning faction could be militantly nationalistic and power-oriented, pursuing high-risk policies to make Asia a Chinese sphere of influence and achieve worldwide status as a great power? Obviously, what we can say in answer to these questions is limited: To all the normal risks of attempting to divine the future are added the risks of inadequate information. But we can still say a number of things about the policies Mao's successors are likely to pursue that may be quite useful.

Visible Change in China

What has almost a quarter of a century of Communist rule accomplished in China? Has Maoism and the Great Proletarian Cultural Revolution wrought a new society and a new man? What first strikes the eye of the visitor who knew China before is the change in the countryside—in what Edgar Snow called "the worn face of the rural landscape." Looking out the windows of the train—although airlines connect the major cities, most travel is by train—one sees the results of the twenty-year program of tree planting. Irrigation projects have also had their effects. Most of the plows in the fields are still pulled by water buffalo, but a few tractors are seen in the fields, and trucks on the country roads. At construction sites—where a new road or dam is being built—the visitor still sees a thousand or more blue-clad men and women with picks and shovels moving the earth in hand-carried baskets, but some heavy equipment can now also be seen.

In the cities four things smite the foreigner's eye: the propaganda posters, the uniformity of dress, the total absence of private automobiles, and how clean and neat the streets are. Fading pictures of Mao, quotations from Mao's thought, political exhortations and slogans that were put up during the Cultural Revolution are still everywhere. Few new ones are to be seen. The clothes people wear are all the same—both men and women wear plain gray or blue trousers and jackets. The traditional *cheong sam*—a sheath dress with a slit at the side to the knee or higher—is nowhere to be seen, and neither is any sign of lipstick or rouge. The only ornamentation is the ubiquitous button with the picture of Chairman Mao. Automobiles are rarely seen, since cars are used only for official purposes. Instead, the streets are filled with bicycles, hordes of bicycles. Bus transportation, too, is good and very cheap. The streets are clean not so much because of the efforts of street cleaners, but because the people are disciplined and do not litter. All this represents some change in China, but what is most remarkable to people who knew China before 1949 when the Communists took over and have recently returned for visits is how little it has changed compared to cities like Tokyo, Seoul, Manila, or Djakarta in countries that have begun the process of development under auspices less committed either to planning or revolution. "Visually," a foremost authority on China and recent visitor, A. Doak Barnett, writes, "the countryside and cities seemed at first glance to have changed much less than I had expected—certainly much less than Tokyo, Hong Kong, or Singapore. Despite obvious signs of economic progress, I was forcefully impressed by the fact that China is still a poor and developing nation in the early stages of modernization."[1]

Changes in Attitude

The visitor who has known China before may find that other than what he can see has changed more radically. In the campaign against the "four olds" during the Cultural Revolution, Red Guards not only destroyed symbols of religion and the past in public places but they also invaded homes to smash family altars to ancestors and to destroy books and other old things. The damage may not have been extensive, but there is evidence that attitudes may still have been affected. It is not surprising that the streets and public places contain so little manifestations of the past, but visitors who have been invited to private homes report seeing no family altars, tablets to ancestors, or religious representation of any kind. On the other hand, many Chinese behavior

[1] "China in Transition," *The Brookings Bulletin*, Vol. 10, No. 2 (Spring 1973). See also his "There Are Warts There, Too," New York *Times Magazine* (April 8, 1973).

patterns apparently continue unchanged. "The majority of Chinese one meets today," Barnett writes, "still show the same civility, politeness and preoccupation with personal relationships, as well as the matter-of-fact practicality, which have long been admired by foreigners, including me. The Chinese still impress one as able, proud and hard-working, as they always have. They also still show deep-rooted traditional predispositions to think in terms of status and hierarchy, stress protocol, submit to authority, conform to orthodoxy and fit into the social roles required of them—despite the efforts that China's revolutionary leaders have made over the years to change many of these patterns."[2]

The public holidays and festivals of the Old China, too, are no more. May Day and National Day on October 1 are celebrated and so is New Year's Day—but on January 1 rather than on the traditional, shifting date. There is a celebration at the traditional time, but it is called the festival of spring. Even weddings and funerals are no longer the grand and colorful displays they once were, but ceremonies as plain and simple as those of the Pennsylvania Amish.

Second-quality examples of traditional Chinese art objects are for sale to foreigners in special shops, but the ordinary Chinese never sees them. Little of the old literature is for sale in the bookstores, which offer political tracts, such as the works of Mao, and books and periodicals on such practical matters as engineering and medicine. No traditional operas or plays are offered, although traditional music is played. Drama, what there is of it, is contemporary and conveys a political message or exhortation to harder work, to greater economic production, and to national vigilance against foreign enemies.

Standard of Life

The standard of life has also changed. Full employment is the rule, although spotty problems of unemployment do exist in particular regions. The fact of full employment, of course, is due in substantial measure to the "sending down" program that transfers bureaucrats, excess factory workers, recent secondary school

2 "There Are Warts There, Too," ibid., p. 101.

graduates, and other city dwellers to work in the communes in the countryside. It has reduced the pressure in the cities not only for jobs, but for housing and all the rest. But to some extent unemployment in the cities has been replaced by underemployment in the countryside.

The great extremes of wealth and poverty have been eliminated. No one who has visited China reports the flocks of beggars, the shantytowns, the utter misery of the very poorest stratum of society that one saw in the cities of old China and occasionally, although less frequently, in the rural areas. This minimum subsistence standard that has been established is austere and Spartan, but accomplishing even this much has been no mean achievement.

But even though the great extremes of poverty and wealth have been eliminated and in spite of the constant harping on egalitarianism, surprising differences in income levels persist. Apprentice factory workers may make as little as 18 or 19 yuan a month—roughly $10. "Average" factory workers receive in the neighborhood of 60 yuan, or about $30. A factory manager makes 300 yuan or $150 a month or even more—five times as much as the ordinary worker. State and party cadres at the higher levels reach 400 yuan, or $200, and at the very top even higher. Primary school teachers earn about 40 yuan, $20, secondary school teachers, 50 yuan, or $25; and higher-education teachers, 75 yuan, or $37.50. University professors' salaries range from 150 yuan, $75, to 300 yuan, $150. A highly paid actress apparently makes as much as 400 yuan, or $200, a month.

The peasants, of course, see very little cash, and their standard of living is well below the factory worker's. But the extreme hardship of bad years has apparently been alleviated considerably by the commune system. In the communes, wages are based on work points, which entitle the peasant to a share in the earnings of his production team. If a man is sick or his family is too large or for some other reason he cannot feed them from his wages and the output of his private plot, he is entitled to a subsidy from the commune's welfare fund, built up by a tax on the commune's total earnings. In addition, all peasants and their families are supposed to receive medical care for a minimal annual fee.

With wages as low as they are, the woman of a family frequently has a job as well as the man, with the children cared for in a day nursery or by grandparents. Housing is bad and very crowded. Still, for the peasants and the workers, housing is better than it was before, and the rents are very cheap. A factory worker, his wife, who also works, and 2 children, to cite a specific example, are cramped in their apartment of 2 tiny bedrooms, a kitchenette, and a lavatory, but the rent takes only 7 yuan a month out of their combined income of 90 yuan (about $45). Utilities, electricity for light, and gas for cooking are also cheap.

Vegetables in season are plentiful and cheap. Factory workers, at least, are apparently able to have meat once a day. Grain and cotton are still rationed. The prices of consumers goods are high. A bicycle—which is very near to being a necessity for a city worker—costs about $45. A pair of shoes costs $8.00, almost half a month's pay for many workers.

The work week is 6 days. Time must also be spent at the factory or commune in studying Mao's thought in groups under the supervision of the Army propaganda team. Since there is little in the way of public entertainment, games, such as Ping-Pong, are popular.

As mentioned above, the commune has a welfare system to ensure a minimum income. So do the factories. Both communes and factories also have retirement plans.

Great strides have apparently been made in primary and secondary education. Enrollments in primary schools were reported to be 127 million in 1972, and in secondary schools, 36 million. It is claimed that 80 per cent of children of primary school age attend school, even in the rural areas. Higher education, on the other hand, suffered fantastic setbacks during the Cultural Revolution. The universities were closed down, and most did not reopen until as late as 1971 or 1972. China seems to have been deprived of university graduates for a total of some 6 years.

Health care is supposed to be virtually free for every peasant family by means of medical collectives, with dues of 1 to 2 yuan a year. The factory worker is entitled to medical service for a minimal fee, but his dependents are entitled only to 50 per cent of their medical costs through the worker's factory. Just how well this ideal of cheap and complete medical care is achieved is difficult to find out. Edgar Snow asserts that the Peking district, with a population of about 6 million, is served by 8,600 medical college graduates and about 2,000 practitioners of traditional medicine, 17 municipal hospitals, and 30 district hospitals with a total of 29,000 beds. He believes that the whole country may have about 150,000 medical college graduates and perhaps 400,000 medical technicians with 2 to 4 years' training. Although Snow is regarded as excessively pro-Chinese, it is at least possible that China has achieved the level of medical care suggested by these figures, which would compare very favorably with other underdeveloped countries.

First priority has been given to prevention and public health measures. On this aspect, Snow's report is ecstatic: "By 1960 most epidemic and contagious diseases had been exterminated or brought under control. Venereal disease disappeared, with mass cooperation following complete suppression of prostitution. Polio, measles, typhoid, etc., are prevented by vaccines and hygienic measures. (Flies and mosquitoes are nearly extinct.) All this I know to be true."[3]

Although Snow's rather breathless account seems much too good to be true, remarkable progress does seem to have been made, especially with such diseases as cholera, typhoid, and typhus. On the other hand, schistosomiasis, the parasitic disease borne by snails, continues to be the scourge of the population of the Yangtse Valley and its tributaries despite some success in combating it. In 1971, Mao personally both acknowledged the difficulty and urged renewed effort by writing and publishing a poem on the subject: *Farewell to the God of the Plague.*

A great effort has been made to bring health care to the rural areas, spurred on by a very typical Maoist propaganda campaign. "The Ministry of Health," Mao declared in a 1965 slogan, "is an urban overlord. In medical and health work put the stress

[3] "Report From China III: Population Care and Control," *The New Republic* (May 1, 1971), p. 22.

on the rural areas." Teams of doctors, nurses, and technicians from the cities tour the countryside, treating patients and training technicians. Again, Snow reports that the Peking district has organized 6,000 medical and health workers into 430 teams that share this work in rotation. A certain number of doctors and medical workers were also "sent down" to live and work permanently in the countryside. In addition, the "barefoot doctor" program trains commune workers to serve as first-aid men. They apparently receive two training periods of 3 months' each to qualify them to treat minor ailments and to identify those who should be sent to hospitals.

Acupuncture

What has intrigued the West most about medicine in China is the revival of the ancient traditional medicine, and most especially, acupuncture. Herbs were vital in traditional Chinese medicine, but all kinds of illnesses were also treated by inserting long, thin needles in various parts of the body, often anatomically unrelated to the area affected by the disease. A needle inserted just below the knee on the right leg, for example, is used to cure appendicitis.[4] The ancient theory was that two life forces, *yin* and *yang*, flowed through the body in channels, and the needles affected this flow. Sickness came when the *yin* and *yang* were out of balance, and the needles, properly placed, restored it. The modern practitioners of acupuncture say that they do not know how the method works, but that it does work, and they argue that many Western medical successes also lack adequate explanation. In any case, in Communist China over the past few years, the press has reported that efforts to explore the uses of acupuncture have had remarkable success in curing blindness, deafness, and, especially, as an anesthetic. Western, or at least American, interest in acupuncture was given a lift in 1971 when James Reston of the New York *Times* submitted to it following an appendectomy performed in Peking. The operation itself was performed with orthodox Western techniques, preceded by a spinal injection as an anesthetic. The operation went smoothly, but during the second night after the operation, Reston suffered

[4] "Seminar Is Held on Acupuncture," New York *Times* (July 23, 1972).

considerable discomfiture from the pressure of gas in his stomach and intestines. With Reston's permission, the hospital's doctor of acupuncture inserted sterilized needles into the outer part of Reston's right elbow and below each knee. Two pieces of an herb were lit and held close to Reston's abdomen while the needles were manipulated—which started, in Reston's words, "ripples of pain racing through my limbs." Reston says that within an hour there was noticeable relaxation of the pressure and distension and no recurrence of the problem thereafter.

Edgar Snow reports seeing acupuncture—needles inserted in the lobes of the ears—used as anesthesia for the abortion technique that uses a vacuum pump. Since this technique is relatively painless, the benefit in this case may be mainly psychological. But Dr. Samuel Rosen, clinical emeritus professor of otology at the Mount Sinai School of Medicine in New York City, describes in detail an operation for the removal of a lung, a piece of major surgery, in which the only anesthesia was acupuncture by means of a needle inserted two centimeters into the patient's forearm midway between the wrist and elbow. What is more, Dr. Rosen claims to have witnessed a total of fifteen operations in which the only anesthesia was acupuncture—"in brain operations, thyroid adenomas, gastrectomies, laryngectomies and tonsilectomies performed in Canton, Peking and Shanghai. Each time, the standby Western-style anesthetist's skills were not needed, because this relatively new application of an ancient form of medical practice has not only replaced anesthetics but has permitted the patients, in every case, to leave the operating room or the dentist's chair alert, smiling, either walking in some cases or on a stretcher in others—and waving his 'Quotations from Chairman Mao Tse-tung.'"[5]

Some of the successes of acupuncture are explainable, and some are at least conceivable. In the case of Reston's gas, the professor of surgery at the hospital told Reston that he had put barium in a patient's stomach and observed by fluoroscope that the manipulation of needles did in fact stimulate movement in the intestines and thus relief—presumably through the effects of the "ripples of pain." Some of the success of acupuncture as

[5] "I Have Seen the Past and It Works," New York Times (November 1, 1971).

an anesthesia is probably psychological, but it is conceivable that a needle might anesthetize if it is inserted to touch an appropriate nerve. The effect of acupuncture used as an anesthesia is described as a general feeling of numbness over the whole body, and it is also conceivable that the stimulation of a particular nerve or set of nerves might deaden the entire nervous system to some extent in certain circumstances. This effect combined with the power of psychological suggestion might account for certain successes even in major operations. It is also conceivable that certain maladies involving the nervous system, such as blindness or deafness, might be cured by stimulating appropriate nerves. But many of the examples of acupuncture, such as curing appendicitis by inserting a needle in the right leg below the knee, are beyond the possibility of Western imagination.

However, it is not difficult to understand why traditional medicine is stressed by the government in China today, and it is not necessary to assume that the officials and doctors who praise and encourage it believe in the more extravagant claims. The goal of medical care for all is obviously sincere. But the doctors available and the capability for training more are so severely limited that compromise is unavoidable. "Barefoot doctors" can fill part of the gap. But only part. The practitioners of traditional medicine must be used. Quite apart from the issue of acupuncture, the herbs and other remedies of traditional medicine are undoubtedly effective against some ailments, and the practitioners can be equipped with a number of specifics from modern drugs and persuaded to refer more complicated cases to hospitals. In any case, faith in traditional medicine remains high among the masses, and at the very least a patient has the psychological benefit of receiving some kind of treatment. Mark Twain, speaking of Christian Science, once said that three quarters of people's sickness is in their mind anyway, and everyone knows that faith is a sure cure for that kind of illness. A three quarters cure rate, Twain went on to say, is a lot better than scientific medicine can claim!

Indoctrination of New Goals and Attitudes

A central theme of Maoism is indoctrination and continuing, long-term education through struggle and criticism. Certainly this notion has a sound psychological base, in that it is a process by which a person first learns and then internalizes both values and patterns of behavior. In any case, this continuous process of indoctrination is reflected in both the organization of work life in China and its psychological atmosphere. The description by a New York *Times* reporter of a typical factory in the spring of 1971 will illustrate.[6] The factory was ruled by a revolutionary committee, headed by a chairman, an "old cadre" who had been director of the plant before the Cultural Revolution, and including an Army officer, head of the Army propaganda team stationed at the factory, and a young woman worker, the representative of the "mass organization." In spite of the presence of foreign reporters, the young woman worker criticized the chairman vigorously, although she did praise him for having changed greatly since the Cultural Revolution. The chairman, for his part, admitted that he and his staff had been "divorced from production and the masses" and that they formerly "did not take part in manual labor and had bureaucratic airs." Under the revisionist influence of Liu Shao-ch'i, he said, material influences had ruled in the factory and the development of technology had been emphasized rather than production. With the help of the Army propaganda team, however, the factory had passed through a period of struggle and criticism and was now being run according to Maoist principles. Work, production, selflessness, rejection of material incentives and rewards, and the dignity of manual labor (managers and intellectuals must spend a proportion of their time at manual labor) are held up as ideals. Everyone must attend study meetings conducted by the Army propaganda unit to ensure that the lessons are well learned. So it also is in the communes.

A. Doak Barnett, on the other hand, although impressed by the "overwhelming emphasis" placed on "Maoist objectives and goals, including extreme egalitarianism, far-reaching decentralization, and Mao's emphasis on ideology rather than material incentives," concluded that despite this enormous effort put on Mao's "revolution within a revolution," the changes at the grass-

[6] Seymour Topping, "'Revolutionary Committees' Insure Discipline in China," New York *Times* (June 2, 1971), p. 2.

roots level had in many respects been quite limited. "With regard to the impact of the Cultural Revolution, I was surprised
to find how similar the organizational system still is—economically, politically, and socially—to that of the pre-Cultural Revolution period, particularly at the lower levels in the enterprise,
the commune, and the urban neighborhood. . . . we probed in
place after place and in institution after institution, asking how
it compares with what existed before the Cultural Revolution.
Time and again, our judgment was that at the bottom level of
society, things are organized and working today very much as
they were before."[7]

A major goal in both the factories and the communes is self-
sufficiency. Factories are encouraged to make the tools and
machines they need rather than wait for state-supplied equipment, which may also have to be imported. Much publicity is
given to any especially ingenious device that the workers in
some particular factory have devised. In the communes the same
emphasis is also given to making their own tools and machinery
—trucks from scrap metal and cast-off motors are favorites. The
communes are also urged to supply their own food of all kinds,
even in adverse conditions. Communes whose main crops are
vegetables, for example, or some specialized crop like tea, are
urged to find ways of growing at least the grain they themselves
consume, to ease pressure on the central reserves for the cities.

The over-all goal is not only to encourage the individual factories and communes to take care of themselves as much as
possible, but to develop regional self-sufficiency for the entire
country. People are urged to visualize the country as a chess
board, with each square "self-sufficient but related." The industrial center of Mukden, for example, being far in the North, has
a short growing season and has been dependent on imported
grains. New seeds and new techniques of intensive cultivation
have now brought them close to self-sufficiency.

The rationale behind the drive for self-sufficiency and decentralization is mainly to save foreign exchange, to ease the burden
on the inadequate transportation system, and to broaden the
development effort. But it is interesting that it is sometimes also

[7] "China in Transition," op. cit., pp. 7–8.

pointed out that decentralization and regional self-sufficiency also give China the capacity to absorb a nuclear blow and still function.

The constant drumming of propaganda extolling the virtues of work, production, selflessness, the dignity of manual labor, and condemning the sin of "bureaucratic airs" and the rest is only one aspect of education and Maoist indoctrination. During the Cultural Revolution, cadres suspected of "following the capitalist road" were sent to May 7 schools in the countryside for a year or two to be rehabilitated through manual labor and supervised study, self-criticism, and indoctrination. Today, the May 7 schools continue to operate but apparently for "refresher" courses —officials, scientists, intellectuals, and others go to a May 7 school every year for a month or two.

The "Sending Down" Program

The "sending down" program, already mentioned, also continues. In effect, the program permanently transfers both young people and older people with particular skills from the city to the countryside. Some of the young serve as pioneers in opening new lands, building canals, dams, and irrigation projects, and similar tasks. Others serve as primary school teachers or perform clerical and other white-collar functions on the commune as well as doing manual labor. For the older people, the program is a way of transferring skills that are "surplus" in the cities to places where they are more needed, or at least to spread the skills as fairly as possible. Doctors are an example. Although the total number is probably too small to serve even the cities satisfactorily, the "sending down" program ensures that the 80 per cent of the population that lives in the countryside will get at least a proportion of the services of the more highly skilled physicians.

When the universities reopened after the Cultural Revolution, it became policy to give preference in admission (and readmission) to those who had on their record a year or two of work in the countryside. Thus for many of the youth the "sending down" program was probably similar to a year in the Peace Corps or VISTA program for an American. Some of those who do not make it back to the city, however, clearly harbor some bitterness and resentment. Of the several hundred or so people who managed to escape to Hong Kong each month in the years immediately following the Cultural Revolution, most were young people who had been "sent down" from the city to the countryside.

As for the others, scientists, intellectuals, and bureaucrats who were required to spend one or two months a year in the communes, perhaps the most persuasive testimony came from Dr. Yang Chen-ning, Albert Einstein professor of physics at the State University of New York at Stony Brook and winner of the Nobel Prize. Dr. Yang, who was studying in the United States in 1949 when the Communists took over and who became an American, went back in 1971 to visit his ailing father, a retired professor of mathematics at the University of Shanghai. Yang comes from a family with long-time academic roots in China, and these connections plus the fact of his being a Nobel Prize winner enabled him to see and talk to many of China's scientists. He said that the scientists have adapted well to the policy of alternating laboratory and classroom work with manual labor in the factories and on the farms. They build houses in the communes and farm the land, as well as train technicians. "Since everyone is required to do it," Dr. Yang said, "it is no longer regarded as a form of punishment. The scientists take it in stride. Some of them get so interested in the farms that they even go back on Sundays to check on the crops."[8] A number of American professors at universities in New York City who have weekend places in Connecticut or Vermont would completely understand!

A New Society?

Against this background, what can we say to the question of how successful the Communist party and Mao have been in creating a new society and a new man? In terms of Mao's vision, the answer would clearly have to be that very little success has been achieved. Mao himself indicated to Edgar Snow that he was far from satisfied.[9] There are also stories of Mao emotionally upbraiding a group of Red Guard leaders, charging that the youth had failed him in the one last chance.

[8] New York *Times* (September 23, 1971), p. 21.
[9] Snow, "Aftermath of the Cultural Revolution," *The New Republic* (April 10, 1971), p. 18.

The accounts of Western reporters also support the view that the changes wrought in both society and the individual fall far short of Mao's vision. In Edgar Snow's words, "The man in the street has grown neither horns nor a halo."[10]

Even more convincing is the testimony of the official organs and representatives of the Chinese regime. The official propaganda continuously harps on the point that "capitalist tendencies" remain strong among both peasants and workers and that any relaxation will be fateful for the whole of the Chinese Communist revolution. The peasants continue to find ways of enlarging their private plots, of neglecting commune work in favor of work on their plots, and of responding more to profit and other private incentives than to communal incentives. Workers, too, are continuously accused of "capitalist tendencies," and not just in the propaganda media. Leaders of Army propaganda teams in the factories, for example, have volunteered to outsiders that they must continue to "grapple with resentments and dislocations caused by a decision taken in the Cultural Revolution to eliminate such material incentives as bonuses, payments for piecework and overtime pay."[11] Officials are accused of "bureaucratic airs."

To some extent, of course, outsiders may only be confused by the rhetoric. The exhortation is couched in chiliastic terms—remaking mankind—but the content of the exhortation is more often than not eminently practical. The virtues of traditional medicine and acupuncture are spoken of in terms of miracles, but, as suggested above, behind the kowtowing is the very practical reason that there is a long-term shortage of doctors and the fact that the practitioners of traditional medicine, still having the confidence of the peasants, can help to fill the shortage temporarily. Behind the public downgrading of scientist-engineers and scientist-agronomists and the exaggerated glorification of the knowledge of the ordinary worker and peasant is a similar shortage of experts and an absolute need to accept the level of expertise that is available—in this case, the practical knowledge of the mechanic and peasant. At the same time, a blow can be struck against the traditional Chinese attitude that no educated person

[10] Ibid., p. 20.
[11] Seymour Topping, "China: Economic Policy Stresses Local Self-Help," New York *Times* (June 27, 1971), p. 20.

should let himself be soiled by manual labor. The "sending down" program, as we have seen, is couched in terms that glorify the humble peasant, the dignity of manual labor, the cleansing of "bureaucratic airs," but it also has the extremely practical effect of holding down the population in the cities—a perennial and particularly vicious problem afflicting all countries in the early stages of development. Similarly, the emphasis on egalitarianism and simplicity in the government's insistence on uniformity in dress, narrow differentials in salaries (to the extent that it is actually achieved), and in the use of bicycles rather than private automobiles also have very practical consequences for a country attempting to channel production into the infrastructure for development and away from consumption and luxury goods.

A Pre-Industrial Society

But if the Chinese have not really succeeded in creating a new society and a new man in terms of Mao's vision, they have certainly gone a long way toward effecting change in both society and individual attitudes as profound and far-reaching as that brought about by the Industrial Revolution in the West. If Maoism and the effort of the Chinese Communists are judged not by how close they have come to achieving a new, ideal man and society but how effectively they are eliminating the old, traditional, essentially feudal society of China and replacing it with modern attitudes, values, and institutions, the conclusion has to be quite different. By this standard of judgment, Maoism and the Chinese Communist effort seem to be achieving considerable success, at least in the cities and those rural areas where they have had time to work. Although the results are uneven, as one would expect, attitudes clearly *are* being changed. What is probably most impressive, however, is not so much the fact of change as what might be called the economy of the effort. In almost all developing countries, development has been hampered by a tendency to develop an enormously bloated governmental bureaucracy; by a tendency toward production and import of luxury goods either because of corruption or the need to provide incentives; and by excessive lag in changing key institutions, such as land tenure. A bloated bureaucracy comes in the first instance from nepotism and the effort of officials to build a structure of loyal supporters, both natural in the circumstances. To this is added the tendency to give too many people as much education as possible, which is inevitably only partial. The half-educated are not satisfied with manual labor, yet they have too little education for anything but clerical chores in an inefficient bureaucracy, which they demand and too often get as a result of empire building and Parkinson's law. All developing countries have been afflicted with bloated bureaucracies, the Communist countries particularly so. The Soviets and others have on occasion made strenuous efforts to stem the bureaucratic tide, but nothing quite so heroic as the Chinese. In many developing countries, corruption is a serious drain on the resources needed for development. But in these and many more an even more serious drain is probably the perfectly legitimate and beneficial diversion to the production and import of luxury items that serve as incentives for entrepreneurs, managers, and, indeed, workers. The evidence suggests that China has not completely escaped corruption, but that it has been held as low as in the best of the other developing countries, Communist or non-Communist. On the other hand, the evidence also suggests that China has probably kept the production and import of luxury items as incentives to a much lower level than any other country. To the extent that they have been able to maintain motivation through other appeals, they are clearly ahead.

Of all the obstacles to development, of course, it is the persistence of old attitudes and institutions that is most formidable. In China, the constant, drumming propaganda, the May 7 schools, the indoctrination sessions conducted by the Army propaganda teams, the glorification of Mao and "Mao's thought"—all of these may seem not only breathless but terribly naïve. As a Soviet official said to a Westerner, "I shudder to think that we may have looked so childish during the days of Stalin's 'cult of the personality.'" There is also evidence that educated Chinese take it all with a certain cynicism, implying that at worst the propaganda may serve as a relatively harmless way to gratify the ego of leaders and at best that the peasants are too ignorant and superstitious to be reached by anything but hyperbole and claims to omniscience. Even Mao himself, musing aloud to Edgar Snow, seemed to imply that the Chinese people had such feelings or a need for such feelings, and asked straight out if it was not possible that Khrushchev's fall was due to the fact that he had had no cult of the personality at all.

But even though a modernized man—whether Chinese or Western—might feel that the domestic propaganda in China is somewhat childish, saccharine, and even silly, it is still based on sound psychological principles, as mentioned before. Lacking any more specific data, our conclusion here must rely on a "common sense" reaction. All the forces working in other developing countries, both Communist and non-Communist, to erode traditional attitudes and values and replace them with attitudes more appropriate to a modern, industrial society are also at work in China. The conscious and deliberate propaganda effort made by the government in China is an additional force. The Cultural Revolution undoubtedly set back the drive toward development. The higher schools were closed for several years, factory production was clearly affected by the Red Guard turmoil, and there must have been practical consequences stemming from the psychological effects of the upheaval. But all these, certainly, did not hinder attitudinal change, and may well have facilitated it. Thus if we are right in assigning particular importance to attitudinal change, the long-run effects of the Chinese domestic propaganda effort, including the turmoil of the Cultural Revolution, may in the end result in more gain than loss. In any case, our conclusion is that China will do no worse than the others in bringing about changes in traditional attitudes and values, and may do considerably better.

The Question of Population Growth

Speaking of the non-Communist underdeveloped countries, we said, to repeat once more, that far from being automatic or inevitable, modernization and industrialization would require unremitting, determined effort to *force* change. So far, it would seem that the Chinese leadership fits that prescription rather well, and that if one had to bet on which of the larger underdeveloped countries would be first to develop a more modern, industrialized society, one would be inclined to bet on the Chinese before some of the others. Thus China may well become a rather formidable military power in only a few decades. We will explore that possibility in a moment, but at this point it is important to understand that it is possible for China to develop the industry to become a military power while the bulk of its people remain at a very low level in terms of standards of living, of education, and even of modernization and industrialization. Whether the Chinese people can be brought into an industrial age along with its military capability depends on how effectively the Chinese control the growth of population. If the Chinese population continues to grow at the rate it has in the past, for most Chinese truly spectacular achievements in raising the gross national product will simply disappear. And the effect is magnified when the base for growth is so large—some 750 to 850 million. The UN, whose estimates are regarded as low, assumes a 10 million increase each year since the 1953 census, yielding a population of 750 million in 1970. The U. S. Census Bureau concluded that the growth rate from 1953 to 1970 was 2.25 per cent adjusted for a loss of 20 million during the 1959–62 famine, which yields a 1970 population of 843 million. The State Department concludes that the 1970 population was 813 million and that the increases for the preceding 5 years were 20 million, 23 million, 19 million, 15 million, and 14 million. This means that each year 10 to 20 million more people were added to the population of China, which is roughly like adding the whole population of Texas to the total each year, if the lower figure is taken, or the whole population of California, if the higher figure is taken. Each year, year after year, jobs for 10 to 20 million people have to be created, clothing for 10 to 20 million more people has to be provided, housing for 10 to 20 million more people has to be built, and all other facilities, goods, and services have to be increased accordingly—medical facilities, hospital beds, transportation facilities, and all the rest.

Even if China is not able to stem this tide of population growth, it may still, as we have said, become a formidable military power. On the other hand, if the evidence indicates that China has succeeded in lowering its birth rate, we will have in that fact a powerful indicator that modernization and industrialization will come faster than we could otherwise suppose. Birth control measures, perhaps more than any other policy, excite the antagonisms of traditional attitudes in China, and if birth control measures have made significant progress we can be confident that traditional attitudes toward other aspects of life are also undergoing rapid change. Thus if we are right in placing central importance on attitudes and values as obstacles to modernization, evidence that these are changing suggests that the steps so far taken toward modernization have been more effective than expected.

The official policy of the Chinese Communist Government is to encourage birth control and limit the growth of population. To accomplish this goal, the regime relies on several methods. The first is a propaganda campaign encouraging late marriage and small families. The recommended marriage age is twenty-five for women and twenty-eight for men, and the recommended number of children is two. Social pressures of various kinds are used to supplement the propaganda appeals. Second, contraceptive pills and devices, with the emphasis on the twenty-two-day pill, are distributed free of charge through every conceivable channel: hospitals, clinics, doctors, "barefoot doctors," factories, communes, and other organizations. Abortions are free on demand of the woman alone, and the vacuum procedure is apparently safe, painless, free of after-effects, and sufficiently simple so that it can be used down to the level of commune clinics. Male sterilization is also free. Neither abortion nor male sterilization seems to be popular in China, but the evidence is that a substantial number of women do use the pill—it is said, in fact, that demand for the pill has exceeded supply.

Few statistics are available on the Chinese birth rate, and those that are available are not very reliable. Edgar Snow reports that Chou En-lai and others in authority told him that the birth rate actually dropped below 2 per cent in 1966, but that it shot up again during the Cultural Revolution when male and female Red Guards roamed so freely over the land. It is claimed that in Peking recently the rate has dropped below 2 per cent, but in Sian the estimate was 3 per cent. Members of the revolutionary committees of individual communes, on the other hand, have sometimes claimed a rate as low as 1 per cent for their particular commune. When pressed by outside observers, however, commune officials frequently back off from this claim.

With such spotty, unreliable, and speculative statistics, a judgment is difficult. A very careful study done by the United States Government, based on reasonable, prudent assumptions, and taking an optimistic but only slightly optimistic view of the success of the Chinese Government's efforts in population control, sees the birth rate declining slowly but steadily. The study starts with a 1965 population of 755 million and assumes that China will succeed in achieving an average birth rate of 1.8 per cent for the decade 1965–75, 1.5 per cent for the decade 1975–85, and 1.3 per cent for the remaining 15 years of the century. Thus the population projected for 1975 is 903 million; for 1985, 1.052 billion; and for the year 2000, 1.271 billion.[12] Herman Kahn and Anthony J. Wiener in their projections take this State Department estimate as the medium. Their low estimate gives 992 million for the year 2000, and their high estimate gives 1.6 billion.[13] A low estimate for China's GNP in the year 2000—a 1965 base of $60 billion (in 1965 U.S. dollars) and a growth rate of 3 per cent—is $169 billion dollars. A medium estimate—a starting base of $74 billion and a growth rate of 5 per cent—is $408 billion. A high estimate —a starting base of $90 billion and a growth rate of 7 per cent— is $961 billion. Thus assuming that for countries like China and India large populations impede economic growth, and that high population goes with low GNP and low population goes with high GNP, Kahn and Wiener get a low estimate of per capita GNP for China in the year 2000 of $106 (in 1965 U.S. dollars), a medium estimate of $321, and a high estimate of $969. This compares with a 1965 per capita GNP in the United States of $3,557 and in Japan of $857.

Taking into account everything that we have examined, I am personally inclined to take the higher estimate as the most likely outcome. This is not to suggest that the difficulties in development are not just as great for the Chinese as for any other under-

[12] U. S. State Department, Bureau of Intelligence and Research, Research Memorandum REV-69, *Indicators of East-West Economic Strength* (October 11, 1966).

[13] *The Year 2000: A Framework for Speculation on the Next Thirty-three Years* (New York, 1967), p. 157.

developed country or that the Chinese have not made very serious mistakes that have impeded economic growth, such as the Great Leap Forward. Nor is it to suggest that the Chinese are any less likely to make serious mistakes in the future. But if we are right in our analysis of both the obstacles to development and the requirements for it, China seems to be in a rather good position. First, it seems to have most of the necessary requirements— not just resources but internal discipline in the leadership cadres through the Communist party, capacity to direct and control the general population, and the necessary determination among the leaders. On the other hand, the only obstacles peculiar to the Chinese are either not particularly serious or are overbalanced by assets. The mistakes that have been made are partly natural mistakes—that is, adopting mistaken policies in circumstances in which human knowledge was inadequate and reasonable men could honestly differ about the wisest course. Those mistakes that could have been avoided stemmed from the naïve idealism of Maoism, like the Great Leap, or from the doctrinaire rigidities of more traditional Marxism, such as collectivization in agriculture. All Marxist countries have striven for a collectivized agriculture on ideological grounds, and all have had enormous troubles because of the difficulties in providing incentives for the peasants in a collective. For the Chinese leadership, however, most of these tendencies to create their own obstacles to development are compensated for in some measure at least by their demonstrated pragmatism. Often they learn from their mistakes and manage to avoid repeating the worst of them. Certainly this has often been the case with their "natural" mistakes. Of those stemming from ideology, on the other hand, one has more doubts. Giving up the Marxist commitment to agriculture would probably be too heroic a heresy. But they may well be able to put aside some of the grosser excesses of Maoism now, even if they have not been able to in the past. The fact that radicalism is deeply rooted in China and Communist thought and will survive to some extent even after Mao is gone is the major point to be made on the other side. The case for optimism rests on what may admittedly turn out to be a rather shaky premise: that the chaos of the Cultural Revolution shook the real power centers of China—the party hierarchs, the government bureaucrats, the industrial managers, and the professional military—just as fundamentally as the Stalinist "arbitrariness" shook the Soviet power centers, and that they want no more of it. Added to this is the fact that "permanent revolution" goes against other very deep ambitions—to modernize and develop, to be strong in military terms and otherwise as a nation, to be able to plan and work toward goals in cultural, artistic, medical, educational, and professional fields that give richness and dignity to life for all segments of society, and to be able to plan individual careers. The Soviet Union did not develop because of Stalinism and its excesses, but in spite of them. The same thing seems likely to happen in China. On balance, in sum, I personally would bet on a Chinese population in the year 2000 of no more than 1 billion, a national income of about $1 trillion, and a per capita income of about $1,000. This would put the ordinary Chinese citizen of the year 2000 higher than the Japanese citizen of 1965, i.e., somewhere between 1965's citizen of Japan and 1965's citizen of Italy.

China's Developing Military Capability

It is the fact that the Chinese effort at population control, modernization, and industrialization will achieve such modest results even if it conforms to this optimistic estimate that leads so many people who have tried to look far ahead to downgrade China's place in the future world.[14] The conclusion here is the opposite, for a variety of reasons. The first is the likelihood that China will develop what might be called a dual economy and the power potential of such a development. By dual economy, I mean the likelihood that even though the fastest conceivable pace of industrialization will still leave the vast majority of the Chinese people living at standards comparable to the middle and lower industrial countries of today, there will also develop side by side with that economy a highly sophisticated industrial plant and the scientific and technical personnel to operate it. This rather sophisticated industrial plant will probably be devoted to a large

[14] E.g., ibid., pp. 230–32. Kahn and Wiener feel that China's population is a liability, not an asset, and that Japan will soon begin to overshadow China as the dominant force in Asia.

extent to national security and the means to make China a military power of stature. After all, the per capita income of the Soviet Union today is just a little over one third of that of the United States, but in military and power terms the Soviet Union is its equal. China is not likely to achieve anything so dramatic. But even though it cannot expect to reach the status of a superpower by the year 2000, it seems very likely to reach the status of a great power.

A recent study by Manfredo Macioti aimed at determining China's capacity to develop the military-industrial side of a dual economy compared China with the major powers in terms of two general indicators: the level of higher education and the investments made for scientific research, and then went on to examine in detail China's capacities in four key technologies: nuclear, missiles, jet planes, and computers.[15]

Some idea of how higher education in China compares with that of other countries can be derived from such statistics as the number of research libraries, the number of students in higher education, and the total number of scientists and technicians. As of 1969, China had 6 libraries of over 1 million books, exactly the same as Japan. West Germany had 9, Britain 13, the U.S.S.R. 66, and the United States 87. As of 1960, China had 800,000 students in higher education, which was 100,000 more than Japan. Germany, on the other hand, had only 290,000, and Britain had only 285,000. Only the U.S.S.R., with 2.3 million, and the United States, with 3.6 million, had more students in higher education than China. Also as of 1960, China had a total of 200,000 scientists and technicians, compared to 200,000 for Japan. West Germany had 370,000, Britain 250,000, the United States 1.1 million, and the U.S.S.R. 1.2 million. As of 1970, it was estimated that China has 65,000 qualified researchers working full time on research and development and spent $1.5 billion on the effort per year. As of 1965, for comparison, Japan had 115,000 researchers and a budget of $1.1 billion; West Germany had 33,000 researchers and a budget of $1.8 billion; Britain had 60,000 and a budget of $2.2

---

[15] "Scientists Go Barefoot," *Successo* (January 1971), as reprinted in *Survival* (London: The Institute for Strategic Studies, July 1971).

billion; the Soviet Union had 550,000 and a budget of $8 billion; and the United States had 500,000 and a budget of $20 billion.

In nuclear technology the basic facts about the Chinese achievements are well known. China's program began in 1953. The first chain reaction was achieved in 1956, and the first large-scale reactor, built with Soviet help, went into operation in 1958. In 1959, as the Sino-Soviet rift worsened, the Soviets rejected the Chinese request for a sample atomic bomb, and in 1960 all the Soviet experts were withdrawn. Four years later, the Chinese exploded their first atomic bomb, and in 1967 their first hydrogen bomb.

It is perhaps instructive to note that China took only 3 years to develop the H bomb after it had successfully exploded an atomic weapon. For the United States, which of course was pioneering, the period was 7 years. For the Soviets, which is probably a fairer comparison, it was 4 years. For Britain it was 5 years, and for France, 8.

What impresses experts like Macioti even more, however, is the ambition of the Chinese program and its quality. All of the nuclear powers except the United States based their programs on plutonium, the simplest fissionable material to produce. But even though the Chinese did not have the resources for a gaseous diffusion plant so soon, they succeeded in developing a new technique for separating the U-235 isotope from the natural U-238, probably by a series of high-speed centrifuges. Thus the first Chinese atomic bomb was much more sophisticated than the first Soviet, British, or French bombs. Again, not only did it take only 3 years for the Chinese to develop a hydrogen bomb, but they launched it from an airplane rather than firing it in place. This indicates that their first H-bomb was a fully miniaturized, operational weapon—which had taken the United States 4 additional years to do after they exploded their first H-bomb device.

Taking all this into account, Macioti estimates that China has a production capacity of a few hundred kilos of plutonium and a few hundred kilos of U-235 each year. We know that China has been working on a gaseous diffusion plant and on an atomic-powered submarine for launching missiles.

In missiles, the Chinese effort was probably helped by the return in 1956 of Dr. Chien Hsueh-sen, one of the cofounders of the Jet Propulsion Laboratory in California, but it was undoubtedly already well begun. In any case, China launched a 1,500-kilometer medium-range missile equipped with a nuclear warhead in 1966. By 1970, it had developed even longer-range missiles, as indicated by the fact that they were able to put an artificial satellite into orbit. It is well known that the Chinese have had a plant for producing solid fuels in operation for several years, and it seems likely that as they did in the nuclear field, China will attempt to leapfrog some of the intermediate steps that the other missile powers went through. China will probably have an 8,000-kilometer ICBM in the mid-1970s, and even if it relies on liquid fuel, as the first Soviet and American ICBMs did, it seems likely that China will not be very long in developing solid-fuel ICBMs very similar to the most sophisticated weapons in the American and Soviet arsenals. It is possible, in sum, that China could have a force of 10 to 25 liquid-fueled ICBMs capable of carrying 3-megaton warheads a distance of 6,000 miles by 1975, although it seems more likely that this capability will not be achieved until somewhat later in the decade.[16] The significance of this possibility was pointed out by Melvin Laird when he was Secretary of Defense under President Nixon. Because of differences in urbanization and population distribution, Laird pointed out, the Chinese "can do proportionately as much damage to us with a relatively few missiles as we can do to them with a relatively large number of missiles."

Jet airplanes are less important in the development of a strategic nuclear capability than missiles, but the progress that China has made is still instructive. By 1958, China was producing its own version of the MiG-17, including engines. By 1965, it was producing MiG-21s, with a speed twice that of sound. In 1970, it was producing jet engines of 8,000-kilogram thrust. With this engine, Macioti points out, it is only a short step to extremely modern Mach 2.5 fighters comparable to the French Mirage and the American Phantom. That China intends to leapfrog in the jet

[16] Charles H. Murphy, "China's Evolving Nuclear Deterrent," *Bulletin of the Atomic Scientists* (January 1972).

field as well is indicated by the fact that they have built a super-sonic wind tunnel of Mach 5 capacity.

The Chinese computer program began with the establishment of a special institute in 1956. Two university faculties of computer sciences were opened two years later, in 1958. That same year the first computers were produced. A transistorized, large-capac-ity, digital computer was developed in 1967. In 1969, China produced its first integrated circuits. By comparison, Britain pro-duced its first integrated circuits in 1957, the United States in 1958, Japan in 1960, and the U.S.S.R. in 1968.

Thus there is no question that China has the scientific and engineering talent in all of these fields to rival any nation in the world. It is also probable that the Chinese leadership recognizes the importance of research and development and has the power and determination to see that the Chinese research and develop-ment effort is given the resources that it needs. At the very begin-ning of the Cultural Revolution, for example, in August of 1966, a directive of the Central Committee ensured that everyone en-gaged in the national research and development effort was iso-lated from the turmoil, and it is clear that the directive was reasonably effective. This is amply illustrated by the fact that the first H-bomb was exploded during the year of the very greatest turmoil, 1967.

Thus in spite of the fact that China's per capita gross national product cannot hope to rival those of the great powers by the year 2000, it seems very likely indeed that China will develop a dual economy, and that long before the year 2000 the more sophisticated, power-oriented side of that duality will create for China a military potential that will give the leaders of any other nations pause. In the meantime, of course, both the Soviet Union and the United States will also continue their research and de-velop even more sophisticated weapons. Thus parity between the United States and the Soviet Union, on the one hand, and China, on the other, may be considerably delayed. But certainly the experience of the past, including the most recent experience of the Soviet Union and the United States, is that no nation can maintain a lead in weapons technology forever.

Within five years after the end of World War II China's renewed unity, her manpower, and her small industrial capacity inherited from the past made her a power to be reckoned with in Asia. But though she could exert effective power in the vicinity of her borders, the heartlands of the great powers—and the sources of their power—remained beyond her reach, while China's own heartland and the sources of her power remained terribly vulnerable. But within a decade, or at the most, two, China will develop long-range power of its own. Soviet and American power will still reach to China's heartland, but Chinese power will then reach to the Soviet and American heartlands as well. Although Soviet and American capacity will remain vastly more sophisticated than the Chinese for some time after that, the Chinese capacity to strike at the sources of Soviet and American power will mark a shift in the world balance. And even though it takes several more decades, sooner or later parity will inevitably follow. If Tocqueville could say in 1830 that in the twentieth century Russia and the United States would tower over all other nations of the world, we can surely add that in the twenty-first, China will take its place by their side.

China's International Political Goals

One last question remains: For what purposes are the Chinese likely to use the formidable power that they will soon possess? Toward the end of the Johnson administration, Secretary of State Dean Rusk, in an address that seemed so alarming to the press that they labeled it the "Yellow Peril" speech, warned that in a few decades there would be "a billion Chinese armed with nuclear weapons." The label was unfair, but the speech did contain the clear implication that the Chinese intentions toward their neighbors were aggressive. The evidence, however, does not really support this dire foreboding. At the same time, neither does the evidence support the opposite contention, that the Chinese are without ambition and can be safely trusted to cause no trouble in the world at all. The truth seems to lie somewhere in between.

Winston Churchill, as mentioned earlier, called World War II "the unnecessary war." By this he meant, first, that the essence and dynamism of the Nazi ideology and the logic of the policies it pursued, as well as the psychology of Hitler, glorified war, made it central to their purposes, and therefore made a world war inevitable. This was the obvious and unavoidable conclusion that even the most superficial examination of Nazism had to reach. Faced with such an enemy, it was inexcusable that the Allies failed to nip Hitler and the Nazis in the bud, to intervene and destroy Nazism before it could mobilize German power for war. Preventive measures were fully justified by Hitler's actions soon after taking power, and failing to take such measures by the time of the German occupation of the Rhineland in violation of the Treaty of Versailles bordered, in Churchill's view, on the criminal.

Maoism, as we have seen, is radical. But there is nothing in either the Communist ideology or the Maoist additions to it that contain anything similar to the inevitability of Nazism's thrust to war. Nazism stressed a master race that was destined for imperial sway over others, thus focusing attention on international affairs. Maoism, as we have seen, stresses class struggle, the making of a new society and a new man, thus focusing on affairs internal to China. There is of course no doubt of the threat of Maoism to established order. But the threat is of internal revolution, a war of "national liberation" rather than international war. In Mao's definition a war of "national liberation" is revolutionary war, guerrilla tactics plus political action, and it is "do it yourself" war. It is axiomatic to the Maoist concept that a war of "national liberation" must be fought by locals of the country being liberated and not by outsiders, such as the Chinese. The Maoist vision sees China as the leader of an Asia of sympathetic, even subordinate, Communist Asian states. It sees China as the vanguard and mentor of Third World revolutionary states in Africa, the Middle East, and Latin America. It sees China as replacing the Soviet Union as the true leader of communism all over the world. It sees China as having a large voice in world affairs. On the other hand, the Maoist vision denies any ambition for superpower status. This may be regarded with appropriate skepticism, but there is nothing in Maoist ideology that sees China as an imperial power in the sense that Nazism saw Germany, that sees China as invading and occupying and then annexing or administering neighboring countries.

If there is nothing in Maoist ideology that thrusts toward international adventuring and war, neither is there anything in the Chinese past action, as opposed to their rhetoric, in international affairs that indicates such a thrust. As we have seen, Chinese actions in foreign affairs from 1949 when they took control on the mainland, on to the present reveal a leadership that is undoubtedly both ambitious and hostile to the outside world, but also realistic in its assessment of China's power position and exceptionally cautious in its actions. The Chinese intervention in the Korean War was both costly and risky, but it must be conceded that the Chinese saw the move as essential to the defense of the Chinese homeland. Intervention came only after the UN forces had crossed the thirty-eighth parallel and threatened China's borders. Even so, as we saw, they were realistic in facing the stalemate that resulted and flexible in adjusting to it in the negotiations at Panmunjom. Similarly, even though the fighting between Soviet and Chinese troops along their common border that has occurred on different occasions was undeniably risky, the Chinese must have regarded it as an unavoidable defensive action. All the other examples of the Chinese use of force are remarkable mainly for the caution exhibited. On many occasions that might have called for the use of force, they did not use force. One example is Vietnam before 1954. Indeed, at the time of Dienbienphu, it was the Chinese who put the severest pressure on Ho Chi Minh to accept the compromise that divided the country, which seems excessive caution in view of the fact that France had announced its intention to withdraw and the United States had announced its intention not to intervene. When the United States combat forces entered the Vietnam War in 1965, bombing North Vietnam and introducing American troops, the Chinese railed against the moves in public pronouncements, but their action was confined to giving North Vietnam a certain amount of military aid, sending road and engineer units, and supplying them with anti-aircraft personnel. On occasions when they did use force, the risk was always very low. An example is the invasion of Tibet, the one time that China has used force to expand its territory, although even this charge is complicated by the fact that China's claims to suzerainty over Tibet were not seriously questioned by the outside world. But the risk in invad-

498   *China: A Road Apart*

ing and annexing Tibet was minimal. India at the time certainly could be counted on not to intervene, however much they might complain. Neither was any other power likely to send armed forces to aid Tibet given the facts of the terrain and Tibet's landlocked position behind India and Pakistan. Always, the Chinese use of force has been very tightly controlled and limited. In the series of Quemoy-Matsu crises, for example, the Chinese Communists shelled the islands and threatened to invade them, but never made any serious attempt to do so, much less to launch an attack directly against Taiwan.

But perhaps the best illustration of all, both of Chinese caution and of the kind of circumstances in which they are willing to use force, was the Sino-Indian conflict of 1962. As we saw, India created a favorable political setting for the Chinese by being sufficiently provocative to permit the Chinese to justify their attack to the Third World. In the fighting, the Chinese virtually destroyed the Indian Army as an effective fighting force—yet they stopped short of a line to which they had some historical claim, and then drew back unilaterally. It was, as we said, a masterpiece of orchestrating military, political, and psychological instrumentalities as a single, limited, disciplined, and controlled operation directed toward and subordinated to a political end.

Both the ideological and historical evidence, in sum, indicate that the leadership of Communist China has no inherent drive toward war or toward grand adventures of simple territorial expansion. The only circumstances in which it seems likely that it will attempt to invade and occupy a neighbor is if it becomes convinced that an enemy power, principally the United States or the Soviet Union, seems to be taking steps to make that neighbor an anti-Chinese bastion and a military base against China itself. The rather high risks that the Chinese took during the 1969 border conflict with the U.S.S.R. is suggestive on this point. To the extent that the Chinese do use military force to achieve their goals—and on occasion they will—it will probably be done only in political circumstances, as in the 1962 conflict with India, that are highly favorable and that entail only manageable risk. Even then force will probably be used only in severely limited ways designed to accomplish very concrete and specific political goals.

Fear of China as the instigator of wars of national liberation is better founded, in at least two senses. The first is that Mao and the Chinese leadership have indeed analyzed and thought through both the political and the military elements of the doctrine of revolutionary warfare, developed it into sound programs, and attempted to spread the doctrine by every available means. The second is that the Chinese will undoubtedly give moral support to any future attempts at wars of national liberation and most likely training facilities to potential liberation fighters and a certain amount of arms aid.

On the other hand, if we are right in our analysis of the future of the developing countries, it seems doubtful that efforts of this kind will enjoy any significant success. In Communist terms, there is not likely to be much revolutionary potential, and the reason, to repeat, is the rise of the new nationalisms. For the first time in two or three millennia, as we said, the teeming millions of Asia, Africa, and the rest are awakening, breaking out of the essentially village culture that turned them inward on themselves, isolating them economically, politically, and psychologically. The motive forces and aspirations are deep and powerful: a search for identity, a deep demand for national independence and expression, a yearning for modernization, and a determination to control their own destinies and to have a voice in the affairs of the world. Anything foreign is the enemy of this nationalism, whether it is a foreign invader or local ideologues who seem to be dominated by foreigners or even to have borrowed a foreign ideology. The implication is that the new nationalisms are indigestible, that once nationalism is aroused in a people no power, however mighty, can hope to subjugate them. If there once were dominoes in Asia and elsewhere in the world there will be none in the future. Vietnam, indeed, is likely to be unique—unique in the sense that it will probably be the last nation in which communism captures the leadership of nationalism. If so, the pragmatism of the Chinese leadership seems likely to lead them as time goes on to place less and less emphasis on the doctrine of revolutionary warfare in both word and deed.

None of this means that China will not continue to be ambitious to take a place as one of the great powers of the world and the dominant power in Asia. What it does mean is that China is likely to continue to pursue its ambitious with the instruments that are at hand and that avoid unduly high risk, which implies not military measures or even the techniques of subversion, but a drive toward industrialization and development at home and the more traditional and orthodox instrumentalities of international politics and diplomacy abroad.

Part VI

RESOURCES AND THE ENVIRONMENT

CHAPTER 19

Population and Resources

WE HAVE identified a long-term trend toward industrialization in both the developed world and the underdeveloped world. In the case of the developed world, this will take the form of increased affluence, with profound implications, as we have seen, for values and every other aspect of life. In the underdeveloped world, the struggle will be toward development—an attempt to reach the industrialized stage now enjoyed by the developed world. These conclusions pose two questions in the starkest terms. The first is: Does the planet earth have the resources to support the industrialization of all mankind to the levels toward which the trends seem to point? As the oil crisis of 1973–74 showed, the problem may be upon us sooner than we think. The second is: What will such widespread industrialization do to the environment and ecology of "spaceship earth"?

Population Trends

If the number of people on the earth continues to grow at the explosive rate that it has since the beginnings of the modern era, the answer to the first question is clearly and emphatically, "No!" Consider the projections of present population trends collected by Dr. Paul R. Ehrlich and Anne H. Ehrlich.[1] Around 8000 B.C., the human population of the earth was about 5 million. It took 1,500 years to double to 10 million. By A.D. 1650, the population had reached about 500 million, and it was taking about 200 years to double. By A.D. 1850, the population was 1 billion, and it was taking about 80 years to double. By 1930, the population was 2 billion, and the doubling time was 45 years. By the 1970s, it was something over 3.5 billion, and the doubling time was 35 years.

If this rate of 35 years' doubling time stayed constant—*stayed constant and did not increase at all*—in 900 years the population of the earth would be 60 million billion people. Dr. Paul Ehrlich quotes a physicist who has calculated that such a population could be housed in a continuous 2,000-story building covering the entire planet. Air conditioning and other equipment would occupy the top 1,000 stories, and people would occupy the bottom 1,000, leaving 3 to 4 square yards of floor space per person. When the population reached about 1 billion billion, the temperature of the world roof would be at the melting point of iron merely to radiate away the heat so many humans would generate. The ultimate fantasy is that at the current growth rate it would be only a few thousand years before the visible universe would be filled with people, and the mass of humans would be expanding at the speed of light.

Dr. Ehrlich believes that people will overcrowd the earth and that this will happen very, very soon. He offers convincing arguments that we will run out of food, that we will run out of space, that we will run out of resources, that we will run out of places to dump our wastes, that our wastes will so pollute the atmosphere, the water, the ocean, and the earth that the planet will soon become unlivable for all forms of life. "The explosive

[1] *Population, Resources, Environment: Issues in Human Ecology* (San Francisco, 1970). Also, Paul R. Ehrlich, *The Population Bomb* (New York, 1968).

growth of the human population is the most significant terrestrial event of the past million millennia," he writes. "Three and one half billion people now inhabit the Earth, and every year this number increases by 70 million. Armed with weapons as diverse as thermonuclear bombs and DDT," he goes on to say, "this mass of humanity now threatens to destroy most of the life on the planet. Mankind itself may stand on the brink of extinction; in its death throes it could take with it most of the other passengers of Spaceship Earth. No geological event in a billion years," Ehrlich concludes, "—not the emergence of mighty mountain ranges, nor the submergence of entire subcontinents, nor the occurrence of periodic glacial ages—has posed a threat to terrestrial life comparable to that of human overpopulation."[2]

An Alternative View

My own view is somewhat more optimistic, even though still alarmed. I believe that mankind will *eventually* solve his problem of population growth. He has done it before in certain isolated places. The Polynesians, for example, were faced with limited resources and space on their islands, and they restricted population growth by means of infanticide and other practices that were drastic and inhumane, but nevertheless effective.

Even under the most optimistic assumptions, however, the population of the planet will undergo an enormous growth. For example, if the Americans, whose birth rate has been falling at an impressive rate, beginning today restricted their families to no more than two children each, the population of the United States would still increase significantly over the next generation. The reason is that the current generation has more females of child-bearing age than the preceding one. It will take a generation, *at least,* to stabilize the population of the United States barring only a disaster that kills people at truly monumental rates. For the underdeveloped countries, again under the most optimistic of circumstances, overcoming the cultural obstacles so that families could be limited to two children each will take several generations. We must therefore assume a world population of about 7 billion in the year 2000 as compared to 3.5 billion today,

[2] *Population, Resources, Environment*, p. 1.

and perhaps as many as 14 billion by the year 2035, although one hopes that the rate of growth can be lowered enough to keep it below that figure. In any case, we must assume that the best that mankind can realistically do is to find a solution to the problem of population growth somewhere between those 2 figures—7 billion and 14 billion. The question is: Will the planet support such a population in terms of food, resources, and energy at the high levels of industrialization we have concluded that mankind will strive for?

Food

Many experts wonder whether we can even feed 7 to 14 billion people. The Food and Agricultural Organization of the United Nations estimates that the minimum number of calories needed by a person doing active work is 2,200 a day. Before World War II, slightly less than half the people of the world ate that many. By 1955, the number of people receiving less than 2,200 calories a day had *risen* to 66 per cent. There is simply no question that today as many as 10 to 20 million people are slowly starving.[3] Many, many more are dangerously undernourished—living on diets that are deficient in essential nutrients, lacking proper vitamins, or some such. According to a foremost authority, Georg Borgstrom, there may be as many as three fourths of the world's people who suffer from undernourishment or malnourishment.[4] "Over most of the world," writes another authority, "there is an agricultural and food crisis."[5]

Paradoxically, however, in this same period some of the developed countries enormously increased their food supplies. We have already mentioned that in the United States about 4 per cent of the population remain on the farms—feeding the whole population and still having surpluses to be sent abroad. The techniques used to achieve such high production were multifaceted. The farms were mechanized; new hybrids were developed; the use of chemical fertilizers was vastly increased, and so was the use of pesticides. All this permitted marginal land to be

[3] Ibid., p. 72.
[4] *Too Many* (New York, 1967).
[5] Raymond F. Dasmann, *Environmental Conservation* (New York, 1972), p. 155.

abandoned. Small, inefficient farms gave way to very large farms —to agro-industry.

Progress was also made in the underdeveloped countries. In the 1960s and early 1970s came the "Green Revolution," and with it the hope that the underdeveloped countries could end their food shortage once and for all. The Rockefeller Foundation financed experiments in Mexico with new varieties of wheat and corn that produced fabulous yields. Mexico produced only 50 per cent of her wheat at the beginning of the 1940s, but by 1960 it was self-sufficient. Encouraged, Rockefeller and others put money into the International Rice Research Institute in the Philippines and produced a rice with a potential yield several times the normal, and almost always three times the normal. The Philippines, too, became self-sufficient in rice production.

Hope ran high, but many experts remained skeptical. Dr. Ehrlich, for example, points out that the "Green Revolution" depends on enormous quantities of fertilizer, on efficient distribution systems, and on an educated farming population.[6] Take fertilizer alone. The Netherlands uses 100 times the fertilizer used by India. If India were to use fertilizer at a comparable rate, it would require half the world's total production. Such use of fertilizer worldwide is not only almost incredibly unlikely, but, as we shall see, would bring staggering problems of pollution.

The pessimists—for the time being at least—seem to be right. Although there has been some improvement in world food supplies, the shortage has not been solved by the miracle grains. To work, they need knowledgeable, literate farmers, agricultural extension services, fertilizer in huge quantities, pesticides, favorable weather or dependable irrigation, the co-operation of governments, and receptive attitudes on the part of the peasantry. The miracle grains are steps in the right direction, but nowhere near a final solution.

What of new lands? Cutting forests? Putting grasslands into crop cultivation? Watering deserts?

Most of the forests and grasslands not now under cultivation are in the tropics, and utilizing them for agriculture presents problems. When the forest is cut in the tropics, the torrential rainfalls

[6] *Population, Resources, Environment*, pp. 96–97.

wash away the topsoil and leach out the nutrients. What is often left are iron oxides, which form a hard layer called laterite. Laterite is so much like stone that the ancient Khmer used it as the principal material for building the temple of Angkor Wat. Food cannot be grown on laterite. "Most of the soils of the tropical foreign country [Africa, the Amazon, etc.]," Dasmann writes, "cannot produce sustained yields of crops even with the best of treatment, since they do not hold or respond well to fertilizer. At best, they are adapted to the shifting cultivation that allows them decades to recover fertility under covers of natural vegetation."[7]

Some experts believe that most of the potentially arable land, under today's economic and technological conditions, is already under cultivation.[8] The more hopeful believe that between 2½ and 3 billion acres are currently under cultivation and that another 1½ billion acres that are *more or less* suitable for agriculture remain unused.[9] This land will help in the short run, but it offers little hope for the longer future.

As for watering deserts, there is already a water shortage in many parts of the world. The main trouble is that much of the fresh water we have is in the wrong places for agriculture, and there is no way to get it to the right places. Fresh water constitutes only about 3 per cent of the world's water, and of this, 98 per cent is tied up in the icecaps of the Arctic and Antarctic. Underground water reserves are part of the available water supply, but they are being depleted all over the world, as the drop in water tables shows. Most of the water we use is supplied by the recycling process of rain and snow. About 875 cubic kilometers are evaporated from the sea each day. Of this, 775 cubic kilometers return to the sea through precipitation, while 100 cubic kilometers are blown over the land and precipitated there. About 100 cubic kilometers of water are evaporated from the land each day, and these are also precipitated mainly over the land. Half of the total water precipitated over the land, whether its source is land or sea, runs off into the sea through rivers and streams. Thus the

[7] *Environmental Conservation*, p. 135.
[8] *Population, Resources, Environment*, p. 91.
[9] *Environmental Conservation*, p. 131.

maximum available if the runoff could be fully utilized would be 200 cubic kilometers a day. This sounds immense, but vast quantities of water are needed. Producing a pound of dry wheat requires 60 gallons of water; a quart of milk, some 1,000 gallons; a pound of meat, between 2,500 and 6,000 gallons; and an automobile, some 100,000 gallons. Each American, directly or indirectly, uses up almost 2,000 gallons each day! A measure of the problem is the falling water tables, as we said. In the developed countries they are falling at rates that are truly alarming. It has been estimated that the people of Europe have been taking out 3 times as much water from the underground reserves as is returned by the water cycle and that Americans are taking out twice as much.[10] Desalinization of sea water is a possibility, but limited. Ehrlich's studies have convinced him that desalinization of sea water will help in a few isolated places, but not enough to make even a dent in the total problem.[11]

Another hope has been food from the sea, but this, too, seems overly optimistic. The present production of food from the world's oceans is about 60 million tons. John H. Ryther of the Woods Hole Oceanographic Institute says that the maximum that can be hoped for is about 100 million tons.[12] Others, however, believe that the total can be raised to 150 million tons. Unfortunately, neither figure offers much hope when the long-term needs are considered.

Another idea has come from British Petroleum experiments that indicate that yeast can be grown on petroleum in the ratio of 2 tons of petroleum producing 1 ton of pure protein.[13] A total of 160 million tons of petroleum would supply 9 billion people with 50 grams of protein a day. The trouble is that petroleum is simply not sufficiently plentiful—something that anyone living through the energy crisis of 1973–74 already suspected.

All of this, of course, is in the long run. In the immediate future the problems of starvation and malnourishment apparently could be solved. "Indeed," writes Raymond F. Dasmann, "in the 1970s

[10] *Population, Resources, and Environment*, p. 65.
[11] Ibid., p. 94.
[12] "Photosynthesis and Fish Production in the Sea," *Science*, Vol. 166 (1969).
[13] Nigel Calder, *Eden Was No Garden* (New York, 1967), p. 147.

there is little doubt that we have the soils, the science, and the technology to produce enough food for all the present population of the earth, and to support some increase in numbers. It is also quite apparent that we are not doing so. The reasons are, for the most part, not scientific nor technological. They lie in the political resistance of governments to cooperate for the common benefit of man; in economic systems that do not permit food to go to those who require it; and in social attitudes and behavior that resist those changes that would favor human survival."[14]

For the long run, however, there seem to be only two hopes that can now be foreseen. One is a revolution in developing new plants as dramatically different from the present ones as the H bomb is from dynamite. Mankind has recently solved the genetic code.[15] We now know the mechanism by which information is transmitted whereby forms of life reproduce themselves. This means that eventually man should be able to create entirely new forms of life as well as altered forms of existing life. The most likely first step in this direction will be in plants, and of these the most likely advance of practical use to mankind will probably be in grains.

The second hope, of course, is the one to which we must always return: the control of population. Stephen Enke has estimated that channeling resources into population control might be 100 times more effective in raising per capita incomes than putting them into attempts to increase production.[16]

Raw Materials for Industrialization

What about the raw materials for industrialization: the iron, aluminum, manganese, and other metals; the nonmetallic minerals, like sulphur; and the whole range of other raw materials on which industrialization is dependent?[17] A pessimistic view is

[14] *Environmental Conservation*, p. 159.
[15] For a fascinating account of the discovery as well as a description of the process, see James D. Watson, *Double Helix: Being a Personal Account of the Discovery of the Structure of DNA* (New York, 1968).
[16] "The Economic Aspects of Slowing Population Growth," *The Economic Journal* (March 1966) and "Birth Control for Economic Development," *Science* (1969).
[17] For the following section, I have drawn mainly on the research of Raymond F. Dasmann, *Environmental Conservation*, Preston Cloud, "Resources, Popula-

presented by Preston Cloud. Assuming a world population of 7 billion people living at the *current* level of the United States, he calculates that more than 60 million tons of lead, 700 million tons of zinc, and more than 50 million tons of tin would have to be kept in circulation. This would be somewhere between 200 and 400 times present world annual production. "As it is not possible to increase metal production by anywhere near the suggested amounts by the end of the century, if ever," he writes, "rising expectations among the deprived peoples of the earth that they too may share the affluent life are doomed to bitter disappointment without population control and eventually reduction in population to its present or lower levels."[18]

At the other end of the scale, we can also find unqualified optimists. "From time immemorial," writes J. H. Westerbrook, a metallurgist, "pundits and alarmists of one sort or another have predicted the impending shortage of this or that critical material. Yet none of these dire forebodings has come to pass. . . . Instead, intensified exploration, improved prospecting techniques, more efficient means of production, and intersubstitution of materials have in concert effected in every case a vast increase in supply and reserves with concomitant reductions in price."[19]

When the experts disagree, what conclusion can a mere layman hope to reach? Estimates about the need are themselves hard to come by. Estimates about the supply are even more difficult. Not all potential reserves are known. Billions of tons of high-grade iron and nickel have recently been discovered in the state of Western Australia. Vast quantities of manganese have been found on the ocean floor in the form of nodules. New ways of extracting minerals from air and ocean water are frequently being found. The nitrates of Chile, for example, became insignificant when

---

tion, and Quality of Life," *Proceedings*, AAAS (1969); J. H. Westerbrook, "Materials for Tomorrow," *Science and Technology in the World of the Future*, ed. Arthur B. Bronwell (New York: Wiley-Interscience, 1970), pp. 329–65; Ehrlich and Ehrlich, *Population, Resources, and Environment*; Georg Borgstrom, *Too Many*; Ali Bulent Cambel, "Energy for a Restless World," *Science and Technology in the World of the Future*; and William C. Gough and Bernard J. Eastlund, "The Prospects of Fusion Power," *Scientific American* (February 1971).
[18] Cloud, ibid.
[19] "Materials for Tomorrow," op. cit.

a way was found for the fixation of nitrogen from air. Reserves, too, are always in terms of the technology of extracting minerals from ores and the cost. It is not economical to extract oil from shale at the present cost of crude, but if the cost goes up as supplies of high-grade sources dwindle, it will become feasible. As Dasmann says, "New processes have made possible the extraction of iron from the relatively abundant, but low-grade deposits of taconite rock, and, as a result, have confounded the predictions of an iron shortage in the United States."[20] Shifts also occur in the use of metals. Copper was once used for tools, until iron became available. Recycling will undoubtedly ease the problem with many metals and other materials. For those that it does not, substitutes might be found. Nylon replaces silk; plastics replaces a thousand other materials. Thus the fact of the matter seems to be that the layman can reach no conclusion. Indeed, one suspects that the expert can't either. It is obvious that mankind is going to have a problem of shortages. A moment's thought makes that clear, and for anyone incapable of thought, the practical experience of the energy shortage of 1973–74 should accomplish the same result. What eludes both expert and layman is whether the problem is solvable.

Energy

But even though we can reach no firm decision about the adequacy of resources, there is one area that may give us at least a clue: energy. With sufficient energy, ways can probably be found around the other shortages; without it, nothing at all can be done.

On the question of energy, the experts are also divided. Ali Bulent Cambel, the dean of engineering at Wayne State University, is an optimist. He points out that the energy consumption of the entire world at the present time is .1 Q—a Q being 1 quintillion British thermal units, which is the equivalent of 40,000 million tons of coal. Known recoverable fossil fuel reserves are 22 Q, and it is estimated that the potential reserves amount to 12,500 Q. He goes on to say that the potential reserves of uranium and thorium will last 3 billion years even if the annual consumption

[20] Dasmann, ibid.

rises to 15 Q. If controlled thermonuclear fusion becomes a reality, as he believes it will, another 1½ billion years' worth of fuel will become available through the use of deuterium in sea water. "There are other energy resources," he concludes, "that are nondepletable or renewable such as solar, tidal, geothermal, areo, and hydro energy. Clearly, man need not fear a shortage for billions of years!"[21]

Harrison Brown is more pessimistic. Assuming a world of 7 billion people living at the standards of the United States in 1950, he foresees the need for an energy equivalent of 70 billion tons of coal per year. Petroleum would be exhausted long, long before consumption reached that level, and coal not long afterward. The only possible solution would be nuclear fuel, with some supplemental supplies coming from using direct solar power obtained by covering 30 million acres of desert with machines designed to capture sunlight and turn it into heat.

A more thoroughgoing and persuasive estimate was prepared by William C. Gough and Bernard J. Eastlund.[22] They begin with an estimate of .17 Q as the current consumption level, which is higher than Cambel's assumption. They then assume a population of 7 billion consuming energy at a rate 20 per cent higher than the current U.S. rate, giving a total in the future of 2.8 Q per year.

Most "renewable" sources of energy—water power, tidal power, geothermal power, wind power, and solar radiation—are simply insufficient for the needs. The one possible exception is solar radiation. Although the investment would be huge, it is conceivable that mankind could follow Harrison Brown's suggestion and cover the deserts with giant machines for converting sunlight to heat and pipe it all over the world in the form of electrical energy.

Known reserves of fossil fuels—coal, oil, and gas—will be exhausted at current rates of consumption in 132 years, and at 2.8 Q in 8 years. Estimated reserves might last as long as 2,832 years at current consumption and 173 years at 2.8 Q.

[21] "Energy for a Restless World," op. cit.
[22] "The Prospects of Fusion Power," op. cit.

Known reserves of uranium available at a cost of from $5 to $30 per pound will last 4 years at 2.8 Q, and estimated total reserves would stretch the time to 8 years. If the price is raised to from $30 to $500 per pound, the picture looks better—2,600 years for known reserves at 2.8 Q and 10,400 years at 2.8 Q for estimated reserves.

If breeder reactors become a practical economic reality (creating plutonium 239 from uranium 238 by neutron bombardment, and uranium 233 from thorium 232), things become happier still —536,000 years at 2.8 Q for known reserves and 1.8 million years for estimated reserves.

If fusion power is ever successfully harnessed, energy will no longer be a problem. Deuterium from the ocean would give fuel for 2.7 billion years at 2.8 Q, and tritium from lithium would give 7.6 million additional years.

Conclusions

If Gough and Eastlund are correct, things may not be quite so dismal as they first seemed. Nuclear power utilized with present scientific knowledge and supplemented with solar radiation machines might supply the needs of a population of 7 billion for a time, and if future research made breeder reactors and fusion power practical, an even larger population could enjoy a high level of affluence for an even longer time.

Notice, however, that these happy conclusions depend not just on the success of future research. The thrust toward the super-industrial society among the developed countries is strong. The thrust toward development among the underdeveloped countries will soon be overwhelming. The obstacles posed by shortages, formidable though they are, are not going to lessen the momentum of these thrusts toward further development, and the encouraging conclusion that the potential exists for the necessary energy does not change the fact that the shortages pose momentous problems. And the least of these is the need for a concentrated, massive effort of research of every kind. The fact is that the *kind* of technology on which the developed societies rest will have to be fundamentally changed. It is not a question of a technology that will permit recycling, the use of substitutes, and similar palliatives. An entirely different technology, different in its essential nature, is needed. What is more, it is needed not only for the long-term future, but as we shall see in the next chapter, it is needed now, and urgently.

CHAPTER 20

Ecology and Technology

But can the planet earth survive the kind of industrialization we foresee? Will not the air, water, and soils be polluted beyond their capacity to support life of any kind?

To start, we need a few definitions. All life on earth exists in the biosphere—that thin layer at the surface of the earth made up of the seas and oceans, the top crust of the land, and a few thousand feet of air. Within the biosphere are innumerable ecosystems by which energy is passed through extremely complicated food chains. In a very simple example, cows eat grass, and humans drink cows' milk and eat beef. In a more complicated chain, like that of a pond, say, plankton eat organic debris, such as the bodies of larger fish that die, and each other. Small fish, insects, and shellfish eat the plankton. Larger fish eat the smaller fish, and birds, man, and other animals eat the larger fish. When the birds and larger fish die, their bodies form food for the life at the bottom of the scale. The whole system is intimately interconnected, and a change in any one element will bring changes in all the others.

The basic energy through which all these processes operate comes from the sun, but other substances are also needed for life —carbon, nitrogen, phosphorus, and others. Each of these is recycled by plants and animals to make the continuation of life possible. Consider the carbon cycle. Carbon dioxide is a major component of the air and also exists in solution in water. Plants take in the carbon dioxide and by photosynthesis turn it into carbohydrates and other organic compounds, releasing oxygen in the process and so replenishing the oxygen in the atmosphere. Herbivores eat the plants, carnivores eat the herbivores, and the carbon moves along the food chain. By a complex biological process, animals combine the oxygen they breathe with carbon, turning it into energy and respiring carbon dioxide. The whole cycle is then repeated.

The nitrogen cycle is quite different. Plants need nitrogen, but cannot use it directly from the air, which contains about 80 per cent nitrogen. However, certain blue-green algae have the capacity to fix nitrogen—that is, convert it to more complex compounds that can be used by plants. Lightning and volcanic action also have this effect. Some bacteria, acting on the roots of certain plants, like peas, can also fix nitrogen. The excretia of animals contain nitrogen compounds, so do the animals' decaying bodies. And there are many other similar processes, of which man's activity in fixing nitrogen from the air by industrial processes is not inconsiderable.

Phosphorus, which is also essential to life, comes originally from sediments uplifted by geological processes. It is weathered out of phosphate rock (and mined by man). It is partially recirculated by the waste and decaying bodies of animals, by fish and guano used as fertilizer, and by upwelling in the sea. A significant proportion is eventually lost at least semipermanently by returning as sediment to the bottom of the sea.

As we have said, if any one element of these complicated ecosystems is disturbed, the balance is destroyed. Eventually, a new balance is achieved, but inevitably the world has become a different place. The English sparrow is introduced to America. Its natural endowment makes it better adapted than some of the native birds to certain niches in the American environment, and it drives out those birds from their habitat. Some may become extinct. Eventually, however, a new balance is struck, and the natural enemies of the sparrow put a limit on their numbers. The gypsy moth arrives in America, spreads with frightening rapidity, and thousands upon thousands of acres of trees are denuded of vegetation. Those that were stripped for several years' running may die, and the nature of whole forests may change. Sooner or later, however, insects and other predators develop a taste for the gypsy moth or mutate in ways to take advantage of this new and prevalent source of food. Again, a new balance is struck.

It is because of the complicated nature of these ecosystems that so many of man's attempts to eradicate pests have turned out badly. An example is Azodrin, a broad-spectrum insecticide. Since predatory insects are inevitably smaller in number than the insects on which they feed, the predators suffer even more than the pests when Azodrin is applied to a field. "Therefore, when the field is reinvaded by pests, or when pest survivors make a comeback, their natural enemies are often absent, and overwhelming population booms of the pest may occur. Experiments by University of California entomologists clearly indicated that, rather than controlling bollworms, Azodrin applications, through their effect on the bollworms' natural enemies, actually *increased* bollworm populations in treated fields."[1]

To put matters into perspective at the start, it is important to remember that the ecology of the earth never stands still. Climatic changes brought an end to the age of the dinosaurs. The ice ages eliminated other species and permanently altered the landscape. Predators, man among them, have eliminated still others. The introduction of a foreign species, like the sparrow or the gypsy moth, works its changes. The land is constantly being changed. Species die off and new ones arise. The fact of the matter is that of

[1] Dr. Paul R. Ehrlich and Anne H. Ehrlich, *Population, Resources, Environment: Issues in Human Ecology* (San Francisco, 1970), p. 175. Authors' emphasis.

perhaps billions of species of animals, insects, and plants that have lived on the earth, only a few million have survived.

Primitive Man and Ecology

And modern man is far from being the only guilty one of his particular species, even though he may be the most efficient in his destructiveness. Primitive man was responsible for the elimination of many different kinds of animals and major changes in ecology. Man certainly had a significant role in eliminating the mammoth. He also helped to eliminate other large animals both directly and especially indirectly in the case of predators by competing for their game. The snakes of Ireland were apparently eradicated by man, as well as those of Hawaii when man imported the mongoose for that very purpose. Wolves in England have long since disappeared. The carrier pigeons of America, now extinct, were once so numerous as to blacken the skies for days during their annual migration. The moa of New Zealand, a flightless bird larger than an ostrich, was destroyed by the Maori very quickly sometime after the Maoris' arrival in about the fifteenth century.

Primitive man also altered the landscape. The slash-and-burn technique of agriculture still practiced by the mountain tribes of Southeast Asia and elsewhere created the giant Thar Desert in India, which was a jungle only two thousand years ago. A similar desert was created in Burma. The slash-and-burn system worked so long as the population was small enough to permit a cycle of sufficient duration for the forest to replace itself. What is incredible is that improper land management is today enlarging the Thar Desert at its perimeters by a reported five miles a year. Much land has been lost in Java by overcutting the forests in an attempt to make new rice paddies. Korea and China are other examples. Europe and America were once largely forests. The cedars of Lebanon are no more. Superficially, it is puzzling that the ancient cities of Mesopotamia are situated in deserts that can now support no more than a few nomads. Some of this may have been caused by climatic changes, but much of it came from cutting the forests at the headwaters of the rivers. Egypt escaped this, because the flooding of the Nile replenished the layer of topsoil each year, and so for six thousand years the Nile Valley has supported a high level of civilization. But man has now interfered with the cycle of the Nile. The Aswan Dam was built for irrigation and electric power. But it is also encouraging the multiplication of the snail that carries the crippling disease bilharzia. The reduced flow of the Nile will prevent the deposit of silt that has kept the delta fertile. Salinization of the soil is becoming a problem.

Some of these changes are not regretted. Few of us would want to live in an age of dinosaurs. Few Irishmen or Hawaiians regret the passing of snakes or Englishmen the extinction of the wolf. Some ecological changes of the future will also not be mourned. Others may be mourned, but judged worth bearing when the cost of preserving them is taken into consideration. The ecological changes that worry most of us are those that make life unbearable or unpleasant for mankind or needlessly destroy the beauty of nature. The principal threats are overcrowding, pollution of the air, pollution of rivers and lakes, pollution of the ocean, the action of pesticides, the destruction of topsoil, noise pollution, the accumulation of solid trash, and the possibility of certain very extreme effects that might result in such drastic consequences as the melting of the polar icecaps.

Overcrowding

Overcrowding is a phenomenon of the cities. But the cities are where the jobs are, and the cities are where the people are. In the United States the percentage of the population living in urban areas in 1910 was 46 per cent. By the census of 1970, it was 73.5 per cent. What has developed in the United States are huge urban complexes—the Boston-New York-Washington complex, the San Francisco-Los Angeles-San Diego complex, and the complex centering around Chicago. In these huge areas one city and town merges into another in one vast urban sprawl. It is here that the problems of transportation are most severe, as are water shortages, power shortages, noise pollution, filth, and the hundred other annoyances that go with overcrowding, not to mention crime in the streets, drug abuse, and other such phenomena.

But it is not just in the developed countries that cities are burgeoning. According to the Secretary General of the United Nations, 40 per cent of the world's peoples live in urban areas, and the percentage is growing fast. Between 1950 and 1960 the urban population of the developing countries increased by 55 per cent. There has been little or no planning for this tremendous expansion, and the result is the growth of shantytowns on every available space, with inadequate water and sewerage, breeding places for disease and misery. But this is nothing new in the world. In all developing countries throughout history people have flocked to cities in hopes of jobs and a better life in greater numbers than were planned for or could be provided for. One only has to look at mid-nineteenth-century pictures of what is now Central Park in New York City to dispel any doubt. It, too, was an unspeakably filthy shantytown.

Air Pollution

Air pollution, as well as trash and filth in the streets, is particularly a problem of the cities, although by no means confined to them. Yet this, too, is not a new phenomenon, only a different one. One thinks of the filth of seventeenth-century London described by Samuel Pepys in his diaries and the grime of nineteenth-century London due mainly to the use of soft coal for heating. But my very favorite story of pollution is of New York City in the heyday of the horse as the principal motive power for transportation.[2] The horse, it is calculated, produces 22 pounds of manure and one-half gallon of urine each day. In 1900 New York City had 120,000 horses, which therefore littered the streets of New York each day with 2.5 million pounds of manure and 60,000 gallons of urine. On a busy street corner like Broadway and Pine, as many as 8,000 horse-drawn vehicles would pass each day, many of them two-horse vehicles. Crossing that intersection on foot was hazardous on dry days. On rainy days it was a cesspool! After a dry spell when the manure turned to dust, the air was full of it. One health officer of the time, Harold Bolce, was convinced that many of New York's health problems came from horse pollution. In an article written in 1908, "The Horse versus Health," he estimated that as many as 20,000 deaths a year came from this cause alone. Undoubtedly he exaggerated, but horse manure did

[2] "The Urban Dung Problem in Historical Perspective," *The Public Interest* (Fall 1971), p. 122 (as adapted from a forthcoming article, Joel A. Tarr, "The Horse—Polluter of the American City," *American Heritage*).

provide the breeding ground for a plague of flies that carried disease and contributed heavily to the irritation of respiratory organs. The irony is that the coming of the automobile was viewed as the end of New York's problem of pollution.

Today, of course, the automobile *is* the problem. One cause of pollution is dust and other solid particles from smokestacks and incinerators. Following Barry Commoner, our example will be Los Angeles, the city that has suffered most from air pollution due to the fact that it lies in a bowl surrounded on three sides by mountains and is frequently subjected to temperature inversions that trap the air in the bowl for days at a time.[3] Before World War II some 100 tons of dust and other such particles fell on Los Angeles each day. By 1946 the total had increased to 400 tons. Legislation was passed and enforcement procedures instituted, and soon the dust was back to its prewar levels.

The second cause was true smog—a mixture of smoke and fog. London in 1952 suffered the worst such disaster on record. A temperature inversion trapped the smoke and fog over London for five horrifying days, and some four thousand people died. The culprit was sulphur dioxide, produced by burning coal and oil with high sulphur content. London, Los Angeles, and many other cities passed legislation and enforcement procedures that gradually cut the sulphur dioxide emissions to safe levels.

But in Los Angeles and other cities, a new pollutant began to appear. Haze would cover the bowl in which Los Angeles is situated. People's eyes would smart, the people would cough, and deaths among those with respiratory troubles mounted. Paradoxically, London suffered from the same type of smog only rarely.

The cause was nitrogen oxide. In high-temperature power plants and high-powered gasoline engines, nitrogen and oxygen interact to form nitrogen oxide. When activated by sunlight, these nitrogen oxides combine with organic compounds, given off by waste gasoline, for example, to form a noxious chemical, peroxyacetylnitrate—resulting in a sort of photochemical smog. The

[3] In the following section I have drawn most particularly on Commoner, *The Closing Circle: Nature, Man, and Technology* (New York, 1971); Raymond F. Dasmann, *Environmental Conservation* (New York, 1972); and Ehrlich and Ehrlich, *Population, Resources, Environment*.

reason London did not suffer as much as other cities was simply because it has so little sunlight!

Again, Los Angeles passed stringent laws on the activities of oil fields, refineries, and other parts of the petroleum industry. The level of hydrocarbons emitted by the petroleum industry was reduced from 2,100 tons per day to 250 tons.

Nevertheless, conditions got steadily worse. According to Commoner, "In 1959 eye irritation was reported in Los Angeles County on 187 days of the year; in 1960 there were 198 such days; in 1961, 186 days; in 1962, 212 days."[4]

The culprit was the automobile. Whereas in 1957 the petroleum industry was emitting 250 tons of hydrocarbons a day, automobiles, trucks, and buses were emitting 2,500 tons a day—80 per cent of the total.

The problem became more complicated when it was discovered that devices designed to reduce the hydrocarbons in the exhaust fumes of automobiles actually *increased* the amount of nitrogen oxides, and, most ominously, nitrogen *dioxides*. And nitrogen dioxide is a notorious poison and industrial hazard.

The automobile is also guilty of another form of pollution: lead. The modern automobile engine operates on high-octane fuels, which are usually created by the addition of tetraethyl lead. Traffic policemen and others regularly exposed to automobile exhaust fumes have shown alarmingly high levels of lead in their systems. Industry is also a source of lead in the atmosphere. We know that people who smoke cigarettes run a high risk of lung cancer, but it is worth pondering that the death rate of smokers in smoggy St. Louis is four times what they are in smog-free Winnipeg, Canada.[5]

Air pollution is concentrated in the cities, as we said, but all of our air is affected. Some figures from the United States Public Health Service in the late 1960s are instructive. Heating houses and office buildings contributed 2 million tons of carbon monoxide, 3 million tons of sulphur oxides, 1 million tons of hydrocarbons, and 1 million tons of particulate matter to the atmosphere of the United States. Trash burning alone contributed 1 million

4 *The Closing Circle*, p. 69.
5 Ibid., p. 122.

tons of carbon monoxide, almost 1 million tons of sulphur oxides and nitrogen oxides, 1 million tons of hydrocarbons, and 1 million tons of particulate matter.

Industrial sources, such as paper and pulp mills, iron and steel mills, petroleum refineries, smelters, and chemical plants, contributed 2 million tons of carbon monoxide, 9 million tons of sulphur oxides, 3 million tons of nitrogen oxides, about 1 million tons of hydrocarbons, and 3 million tons of particulate matter.

The 90 million automobiles and trucks of the late 1960s contributed 66 million tons of carbon monoxide, 1 million tons of sulphur oxides, 6 million tons of nitrogen oxides, 12 million tons of hydrocarbons, 1 million tons of particulate matter, and a variety of other harmful substances.

And there are many other pollutants of the air than we have named that are dangerous to life. We know that asbestos fibers from the brake linings of automobiles and the fireproof spraying of asbestos on steel girders of buildings are serious causes of lung cancer. A study of city air by the United States Public Health Service showed thirty-nine substances not found in natural air. Many of these may be hazards to health as bad as those we have listed, and many might combine with others to form hazards to health.

Nuclear Radiation

The dangers from the use of nuclear power to generate electricity are of two types: radioisotopes released into the atmosphere, and thermal pollution. Utilizing today's technology, a nuclear power plant generates heat by fission, which is used to turn water into steam, which then is used to drive turbines that generate electricity. Huge amounts of heat are generated, and vast quantities of water are needed as coolants. The plant releases small quantities of radioisotopes in the water and through its smokestacks. There is also some danger of accidents—not explosions, but other kinds that might release a certain amount of radioactive substances into the atmosphere.

Most experts think that the amounts of radioisotopes released by nuclear power plants are trivial. A few experts, however, are worried about the potentialities of concentrations in certain forms of life. Swallows, for example, exposed to smokestack effluents can concentrate radioactive materials 75,000 times higher than in the atmosphere. Certain algae can concentrate radioactive materials 850,000 times higher than in the water in which they grow. However, the danger from radioactive isotopes from the peaceful uses of atomic energy appears to be very slight. Raymond F. Dasmann, after careful study, says that there appear to be no very good reasons why there should be general opposition to nuclear plants on these grounds. "Insofar as the radiation hazards are concerned, it is worth noting that no other potential pollutant has been so carefully monitored and controlled as the nonmilitary use of radioisotopes. If our control over other pollutants came close to equalling our control over radioactive pollutants, we would have a remarkably clean planet today."[6]

The same comfort cannot be derived from the thermal effects of present-day plants. Nuclear power plants use far more water than fossil fuel, because they must be kept cooler. The discharge of heated water into rivers and bays can drastically affect their ecology. One example will suffice. A nuclear power plant was proposed for Calvert Cliffs in Maryland of 2 units, each generating 800,000 kilowatts of electricity. A group of Johns Hopkins University scientists who opposed the plant calculated that cooling water from Chesapeake Bay would be required at about 2,500 cubic feet per second, "equivalent to a lake one foot deep and 7.7 miles square each day." They estimated that there would be a 10 degree Fahrenheit rise of temperature when the cooling water flow is 1,200,000 gallons per minute. As they say, the volume would make the discharge Maryland's fourth-largest "river," and the discharge of so much heated water into Chesapeake Bay is bound to have major—and bad—effects on the biotic communities of the bay.

All of this could be avoided, of course, by holding the effluent waters in cooling ponds, running it through cooling towers, or in other ways. The companies had not provided for these in an attempt to hold down the cost.

[6] *Environmental Conservation*, p. 398.

Noise Pollution

Another problem associated particularly with urban complexes is noise pollution. The noise level of a room in which people are conversing quietly is about 50 decibels. At 80 decibels noise becomes annoying. An automobile creates about 70 decibels. Heavy automobile traffic creates about 100. The noise that people often are subjected to in cities—riveting machines or discotheques—is frequently 110 decibels or more.

There is no question that noise pollution can do more harm than merely annoy. It has been discovered that some teen-agers have suffered some permanent loss of hearing after listening for long periods to amplified rock music. Noise levels as low as 50 decibels may disturb sleep. Ninety-decibel noise levels may also damage the nervous system and be a factor in diseases related to stress, such as ulcers and hypertension.

In the face of this evidence, the fear of the sonic booms caused by supersonic aircraft seems well-founded. It was mainly for this reason that plans to develop an American supersonic aircraft, the SST, were abandoned.

Solid Wastes

Still another form of pollution particularly associated with urban environments is the problem of solid wastes, although it is also affecting small towns as well. Solid wastes in the United States have increased enormously since World War II. Many people think this is mainly the result of our greater affluence, but affluence is not a really significant cause. Some solid wastes are due to greater affluence—more automobile bodies must now be disposed of than before, more worn-out refrigerators, more worn-out TV sets. The increase in population is also partly responsible. If there are more people there are more old clothes thrown away, more empty food containers to be thrown away, and so on. But the major responsibility for the stupendous increase in solid wastes lies with the new technologies. Beer now comes in cans rather than in returnable bottles. Soda bottles are no longer re-

turnable—the production of nonreturnable soda bottles since
World War II has increased 53,000 per cent![7]

One authority estimates that each year the United States "must
dispose of some 55 billion cans, 26 billion bottles and jars, 65 billion metal and plastic bottle caps, and more than half a billion
dollars worth of other packaging materials. Seven million automobiles are junked each year, and the amount of urban solid wastes
(trash and garbage) collected annually is approximately 150
million tons."[8]

What is to be done with all this solid waste? If burned, it
greatly contributes to air pollution. Flashlight batteries, for example, contain mercury. Burning trash puts this mercury into the
air as vapor; the vapor is transformed into methyl mercury, and
one more poison has been added to the atmosphere. If the waste
is dumped at sea it pollutes the ocean and creates "dead seas." If
the trash is put into open dumps, the result is not only unsightly,
but it is a breeding ground for rats, flies, and other such disease-
carrying pests. Water percolating through the dump also contributes to the pollution of streams and rivers. Using it for fill in
the wetlands destroys the nurseries for marine life.

There are things, of course, that can be done. A tax can be put
on goods that create solid trash to provide money to pay for dis-
posing of it in satisfactory ways. Some cities, after suitable treatment of wastes, for example, have used it to build hills. The hills
are covered with topsoil to create attractive parks. The solid waste
that presents the most serious problem is that of radioactive materials, and here the best solution seems to be to sink it deep into
abandoned mines and seal them over.

Water

From the start of the industrial age, streams, rivers, and lakes
have been used as dumping grounds for industrial waste. Raw
sewerage, of course, is a source of disease and makes the water un-
drinkable downstream. It also uses up oxygen to break down the
organic compounds, leaving insufficient oxygen for fish and other

[7] *The Closing Circle*, p. 143.
[8] *Population, Resources, Environment*, p. 128.

life. The same is true for certain industrial wastes that have high organic content. Industrial wastes also put poisons into the water. Mercury is only one example. Over the years much mercury has found its way into the sea and through the food chain has made its way into the bodies of such predator fish as swordfish. Many are now no longer fit to eat.

But this still does not end the problem. One of the greatest disasters hitting streams, rivers, and lakes is the destruction of aquatic life and the "dying"—eutrophication—of lakes. Enormous algae blooms have been appearing more and more frequently. They, too, consume huge quantities of oxygen, leaving too little for other forms of marine life.

Algae require three main nutrients: carbon dioxide, phosphates, and nitrates. Carbon dioxide, of course, is plentiful in nature. *Treated* sewerage also supplies both phosphates and nitrates, but the vast increase in these two algae nutrients have sources in the new technology.

Phosphates in great quantity are coming from the new detergents that have driven soap from the markets. Soap is made by treating fat, such as palm oil, with alkali. Soap is biodegradable. Bacterial enzymes break it down in a sewage plant, and what is left is only carbon dioxide and water. Thus there is only a trivial impact on the environment. The new detergents, however, produce a violent environmental impact. In the first place, detergent is manufactured from petroleum and other substances, including chlorine, in a process that pollutes the air, including the release of the mercury involved in the production of chlorine. The energy used in the process is three times that used in the production of soap.

But this is only the beginning. The first detergents caused water coming from the tap to foam. This effect was finally corrected. The newer detergents, however, had a benzene unit that can be converted to phenol in aquatic systems, and phenol is toxic to fish.

Then we come back to phosphate—one of the nutrients, as we said, that stimulate the growth of algae, depleting the oxygen supply, killing the fish, and contributing heavily to the eutrophication of lakes. Detergents deposit huge quantities of phosphates in sewerage systems and into rivers and streams.

What makes it all so ridiculous is that the new detergents are really no better than soap, except in hard water. And in areas with hard water, the water could be treated by household water softeners. Citing the results of a number of studies, Barry Commoner reaches the conclusion that the substitution of detergents for soap has nothing to do with their relative merits. "It would appear," he writes, "that advertising, rather than the detergent's virtues, is the most important determinant of sales."[9]

Nitrates, the third stimulant to algae blooms, are coming mainly from the new agriculture. Barry Commoner describes what happens. In Illinois before 1948, when very little nitrogen fertilizer was used—about 10,000 tons—the corn yield was about 50 bushels an acre. In 1965, 500,000 tons of nitrogen fertilizer were used and the yield was 90 bushels an acre. "Obviously," Commoner writes, "the law of diminishing returns is at work here; increasing amounts of fertilizer nitrogen must be used to obtain the same increment in yield as cultivation becomes increasingly intense."[10] To make a profit, the farmers must get more than 80 bushels an acre, and to do this they must use vast quantities of fertilizer, not all of which can be taken up by the corn. This, however, doesn't matter to the farmer because the cost of fertilizer is so low.

The trouble is that the unused nitrogen must go somewhere. Where it goes is into the rivers, streams, and lakes. All over America the phenomenon of algae blooms is occurring, with a resulting oxygen depletion and thus fish kills and permanent damage to the ecology. Lake Erie has suffered most of all the lakes in North America, and in the opinion of Barry Commoner no one knows how Lake Erie can ever be restored to its former pristine state. "For it should be clear," he writes, "that even if overnight all of the pollutants now pouring into Lake Erie were stopped, there would still remain the problem of the accumulated mass of pollutants in the lake bottom. To my knowledge," he goes on to say, "no one has proposed a means of solving that problem which is even remotely feasible. It is entirely likely, I believe, that practically speaking Lake Erie will *never* be returned to anything ap-

9 *The Closing Circle*, p. 157.
10 Ibid., p. 95.

proximating the condition it was in, say, twenty-five to fifty years ago."[11]

But this is not the only harmful effect of the excess of nitrates. Nitrate itself is not toxic, but it can be converted into *nitrite* by certain intestinal bacteria that are usually more active in infants than adults. Nitrite *is* toxic. In a complicated biological process it prevents the blood from absorbing oxygen. The victim turns blue and may well die.

Of the other kinds of water pollution, we have already spoken of thermal pollution from nuclear power plants. We might add the growing use of feedlots for beef cattle. When cattle were fattened on the farm, the manure was returned to the soil as fertilizer. But in feedlots it accumulates in enormous quantities. Eventually, it is washed into streams and rivers by rain—contributing still more organic material that uses up precious oxygen to break it down.

Not exactly concerned with pollution, but with another aspect of the water problem, Dasmann cites the practice of confining rivers, such as the Mississippi, by dikes. Since the river does not overflow in normal years to deposit its silt on the delta lands, the silt is deposited in the riverbed itself. The dikes must be raised higher and higher until the river is actually flowing above the land around it. In extraordinary flood years, the result is a disaster.

Barry Commoner has two other fears. One is that he feels that it is not yet absolutely certain that chlorination of water does not have harmful effects. The other is that high organic contents in water, even when chlorinated, might protect certain viruses from the chlorine. Infectious hepatitis, he points out, has been spreading at an alarming rate.

Finally, although we have used examples principally from the United States, these problems are common to all industrial states. Even Lake Baikal in the remote Siberian regions of the Soviet Union is threatened by the effluent from paper mills. Pointing to the Hudson River from my apartment window to some Soviet visitors, I once remarked that that once-beautiful river was now little

[11] Ibid., pp. 110–11.

more than a sewer. "And what," one of my Soviet visitors asked, "do you think has happened to our rivers?"

Pollution of the Ocean

The pollution of the ocean that has attracted most attention is oil spills. The death toll in sea birds, fish, and crustaceans from oil spills is appalling. The damage to beaches and the loss of revenue from tourism are also regrettable. But potentially much more serious pollution of the ocean is also taking place.

Mercury has already been mentioned. It is used for a variety of industrial purposes: the production of chlorine, mildew-resistant paints, and so on. In the process, some mercury escapes in waste materials and is converted by bacteria into methyl mercury. It is this form that poisons fish and humans who eat those fish.

Another form of pollution is the dumping of waste materials at sea. New York City is one guilty party. Bargefuls of solid waste are dumped at sea outside New York and have created an area that oceanologists have already described as a "dead sea."

Still another form of pollution is plastics. Plastics—toys, utensils, wrappings, packages, and all the myriad of plastic goods produced by contemporary society—are not biodegradable. They litter our landscape and highways. But more recently and most alarmingly it has been found that they also litter the ocean. Broken and torn into tiny particles, plastics have been found over enormous stretches of the ocean. Just what the consequences of this pollution may be cannot yet be determined.

Another form of pollution is the filling in of the wetlands along the shores of the oceans to make new land. The trouble is that the wetlands are the nursery of many of the world's fish. At present, food from the sea provides almost one fifth of the world's animal protein, and two fifths of it if milk and eggs are excluded. What is more, there is hope that the ocean can supply at least a fraction of the additional food that will be needed—but only if the wetlands are preserved.

Finally, one authority also believes that DDT accumulating in the ocean, in addition to all its other harmful effects, is also reducing photosynthesis by phytoplankton—the basic food of all marine life.

What is even more disturbing is the possibility that the combined impact of all these different kinds of pollution—oils, plastics, mercury, DDT, and so on—will be a collapse of oxygen-producing plankton. The main contribution of oxygen in the carbon-oxygen cycle is apparently the ocean. Some contend that an industrial country like the United States, for example, already or soon will use more oxygen than its vegetation returns to the atmosphere. If something really serious happened to the oxygen-producing plankton of the oceans, all life would be endangered.

Pesticides

The story of DDT is too well known to bear more than a brief review here. But it suffices nicely as an example of the danger of a whole range of pesticides, such as those containing lead and mercury. DDT is a very effective insecticide and has been widely used by farmers and others. Indeed, the more it was used, the more it was needed, for it killed off the natural predators of insects as well as the insect pests. The trouble is that DDT is not biodegradable, but persistent. Water carries it off the land into the streams, rivers, lakes, and oceans. Micro-organisms incorporate it into their bodies. So do plants and grasses. On the land, herbivores ingest DDT with the plants they eat, and carnivores do the same when they eat the herbivores. In aquatic environments, micro-organisms incorporate DDT into their bodies. Small fishes eat these and concentrate the DDT still further. Larger predators concentrate even higher doses, since DDT tends to accumulate in fatty tissues. Worse off still are predator birds who live almost exclusively on predator fish. DDT inhibits the formation of egg shells, which then break under the pressure of the brooding hen. As a result, for example, in some parts of the Eastern seaboard of the United States, the osprey has almost disappeared. Other pesticides undoubtedly have similar effects, many of them as yet unknown. That man himself is affected by DDT and is a victim of the concentration of DDT there is no doubt. Breast-fed babies in Sweden get 70 per cent more DDT than what is considered the maximum acceptable amount. In America, most mother's milk contains so much DDT that it would be declared illegal in interstate commerce if it were packaged in any other way.

But there is another side to the DDT story. Abandoning the use of DDT in the United States increases the price of certain foods and other crops by a few cents. But abandoning its use in underdeveloped countries, where it is used against the mosquito, is something else again. Malaria, carried by the mosquito, is the greatest single killer in much of Asia and Africa, and abandoning the use of DDT might mean the death of perhaps several million people who would otherwise live. In Sri Lanka (then Ceylon), for example, a malaria epidemic in 1934–35 may have been responsible for the deaths of seventeen people out of every thousand (the total death rate that year was thirty-four per thousand). In 1945, the death rate was twenty-two per thousand, and again as many as half that number may have been directly or indirectly attributable to malaria. A large-scale DDT spraying program was begun, and by 1969 the death rate in Ceylon had dropped to eight per thousand. Until some equally effective but less persistent and dangerous pesticide is developed, the tension over the use of DDT between the developed and the underdeveloped worlds is bound to continue.

Topsoil

Man's life depends on a very thin layer of topsoil that covers only a small proportion of the earth's surface. It must be preserved. We have mentioned how mankind created deserts in India, Burma, in the Middle East, and at least contributed to the creation of the Sahara. A more recent example is the dust bowl created in the 1930s in the American Middle West.[12] The Great Plains of the Middle West have had recurrent droughts throughout history. But the short, sod-forming grasses that provided their natural cover were resistant, and little damage was done. From the 1880s, when the plains were first settled and the grasslands plowed, until 1931, periodic droughts occurred with sometimes severe, but not crippling damage. Then in 1931, in the

[12] For the following accounts of both the dust bowl and Mexico, I have drawn on Dasmann, *Environmental Conservation*, pp. 140–43 and 114–15.

midst of the Great Depression, came the most severe drought on record. In 1933, the dust storms began. "Dust blew across the continent, darkened the skies, reddened the sunsets, and made the plains region almost uninhabitable in spots for man or live-stock. Millions of acres of farms were damaged, with an esti-mated loss of topsoil ranging between 2 and 12 inches in places. Drifting dunes moved over farms, burying roads, fences, and even dwellings. A mass exodus of farmers, ruined by drought and un-able to find work, streamed from Oklahoma, Kansas, Texas, and adjoining areas and moved west to California or east into city bread lines. It was a period of misery and privation difficult to match in American history." Without careful conservation meth-ods, such disasters can easily occur again, especially in the un-derdeveloped countries, but by no means there alone.

We have already mentioned what happens to many tropical topsoils when the forests are cut and the torrential rains wash away the topsoil, leaving only the rocklike laterite. Another illus-tration is what happened to the foothill area north of Mexico City. Visiting the area in 1803, Alexander von Humboldt described it as a beautiful place covered with a tall open forest of pine and oak. Only the lower slopes were cleared and farmed. As the population grew, the land was cleared farther and farther up the slopes, first by lumberers and charcoal makers and then for farming. Corn and wheat were the first crops, but they provide poor cover, and the topsoil was steadily washed away and vital minerals leached out. The barren subsoil would still grow maguey, a cactuslike plant grown for its fibers, but it, too, offers little cover. Finally, only a bare and impervious hardpan re-mained that could support the grazing of a few goats and don-keys. Then the soil became even too poor to support them, and today nothing remains but wasteland.

Irrigation frequently brings another kind of problem. When the water table rises or when water is drawn up by capillary action through evaporation, it brings with it various salts. If the water used for irrigation is plentiful and the drainage good, these salts are washed away and no damage occurs. But when water is not plentiful or drainage is poor, the salts are left on the surface and eventually make the land unsuitable for any plants except those few that are tolerant to high salt levels.

One of the most abhorrent practices that destroys topsoil is strip mining for coal. The topsoil and subsoil are bulldozed off and the coal taken, leaving only bare rock and debris. Conditions are created that cause landslides that devastate areas downhill from the sites. Streams are dammed with debris, and sooner or later the accumulated water breaks through and causes floods. The oxidation of sulphur compounds creates acid runoff from the strip-mining wastes that pollutes the streams and rivers.

Happily in the case of topsoil, like the problem of solid waste, a solution to the problem is possible if mankind will only adopt it. Contour plowing, windbreaks, and most especially keeping unsuitable land in grass can prevent the creation of dust bowls. By using standard practices of crop cultivation and rotation with due care, European forest and similar soils cannot only be preserved but actually improved. We need to know much more about how to handle tropical soils, but there is clearly reason for hope. Even strip mining can be done without destroying the land. In Germany a tax is levied on strip mining that is used for rehabilitation, and the techniques are now highly developed. "Some areas mined in the not-too-distant past are now among the more attractive landscapes of the region."[13]

"Far Out" Possibilities

At least two rather fantastic, "far out" possibilities of man affecting the environment have also been suggested. One is the so-called "greenhouse effect." The mantle of atmosphere around the earth acts the same way as the glass in a greenhouse. It keeps the temperature higher on the inside than the outside by trapping and reradiating heat back into the greenhouse. Water vapor, water droplets, and carbon dioxide are the constituents involved. When fossil fuel is burned, carbon dioxide is added to the atmosphere, and it has been estimated that since 1880 the carbon dioxide in the atmosphere has increased by about 12 per cent. Until the 1940s, the average temperature also rose, and many

[13] Gerhardt Olschowy, as described in Dasmann, *Environmental Conservation*, p. 400.

people believed that it would continue to rise until the polar icecaps began to melt and much of the inhabited portions of the earth would be flooded. However, since the 1940s, in spite of a continued rise in the carbon dioxide content of the atmosphere, the average temperature has gone down. The hypothesis is that the greenhouse effect is being countered by the shielding effect of an increase in the dust in the air and other particulate pollution and by increased cloud cover triggered by the contrails of jet aircraft.[14]

Another "far out" possibility has been advanced by Lamont C. Cole, a Cornell ecologist.[15] Cole has calculated the recent rate of increase in man's use of energy at 7 per cent a year, which means a doubling time of 10 years. At this rate, the average temperature of the earth would be raised 1 degree Centigrade in 91 years. A 3-degree Centigrade warming of the earth would take 780 years if these trends continued, and that would also melt the polar caps, putting most of the coastal lands under water. In 980 years the earth would be uninhabitable.

The fallacy in this reasoning, as Dasmann has pointed out, is the assumption that the present trends would continue for so long a period. As we saw above, the maximum energy consumption for mankind so far foreseen (by Dr. Cambel) is only 15 Q, and this would be achieved at a 7 per cent rate of increase in less than 90 years.

Causes of the Crisis

What conclusion can be reached from all the above? What has caused the environmental crisis, the alarming rise in pollution, what can be done about it, and what are the implications for our central question about the future of mankind and international politics? There was little change in pollution levels before World War II, but since then the rise is somewhere between 200 and 2,000 per cent. One of the most frequently offered explanations is the population explosion. More people pollute more. The second is the rise in affluence. People with more material possessions pollute more. No doubt both increased popula-

[14] *Population, Resources, Environment,* p. 146.
[15] *Thermal Pollution: Man's Impact on Environment* (New York, 1971).

536   *Resources and the Environment*

tion and increased affluence have contributed to the rise in pollution and the environmental crisis. But the evidence seems overwhelmingly persuasive that neither of these is the true explanation—that the true explanation is that offered by Barry Commoner, author of *The Closing Circle*.

Population, Commoner points out, has increased in the United States 42 per cent since World War II. More than that, productivity has also increased, which means that *less* industrial activity produces the same amount of goods. Pollution should not have risen the same amount as population, much less by 200 to 2,000 per cent more. The one factor connected with population that has contributed most to pollution is the changed distribution of population. Suburbanites who work in the city but don't want to live there commute, while ghetto dwellers who work in outlying industries but can't afford to live in the suburbs also commute. Thus automobile "vehicle miles" traveled in metropolitan areas has increased from 1,050 miles in 1946 to 1,790 miles in 1966. In this way, the growth in population has undoubtedly increased pollution perceptibly, but not nearly enough to account for the true increase.

The affluence argument is that since we are all so much more prosperous, at least in the United States, we have much more with which to pollute. Commoner begins by pointing out that the per capita GNP simply has not changed that much. A 1946 per capita GNP of $2,222 and a 1966 per capita GNP of $3,354 is a 50 per cent rise, not a 200 to 2,000 per cent rise. He then looks at more detailed statistics. Food consumption has changed in composition, but not in total calories or in quantity. The same for clothing. More variety is offered and styles have changed, but the over-all per capita production of clothing has remained about the same. Shelter is also about the same—an increase in quality but no significant increase in per capita quantity, although many rich city people do have second homes in the country. "There has been an increase in the per capita utilization of electric power, fuels, and paper products, but these changes cannot fully account for the striking rise in pollution levels. If affluence is measured in terms of certain household amenities, such as television sets, radios, and electric can-openers and corn-poppers and in leisure items such as snowmobiles and boats, then there have been certain striking increases. But again," Commoner concludes, "these items are simply too small a part of the nation's over-all production to account for the observed increase in pollution level."[16]

The villain, Commoner argues, is neither population nor affluence. Neither is it technology per se. It is the *kind* of technology we have developed.

Commoner looked at the growth rate of different products, and the results were astounding. The production of nonreturnable bottles, mentioned before, has increased by 53,000 per cent since World War II. Synthetic fibers are up 5,980 per cent. Mercury used for chlorine production is up 3,930 per cent; mercury for mildew-resistant paint up 3,120 per cent; air conditioner compressor units are up 2,850 per cent; plastics, up 1,960 per cent; fertilizer nitrogen, up 1,050 per cent; electric housewares, up 1,040 per cent; synthetic organic chemicals, up 950 per cent; chlorine gas, up 600 per cent; electric power, up 530 per cent; pesticides, up 390 per cent; wood pulp, up 313 per cent; truck freight, up 222 per cent; consumer electronics, such as TV sets and hi-fi equipment, up 217 per cent; motor fuel consumption, up 190 per cent; and cement, up 150 per cent.

Another group of products grew at about the same rate as the population, 42 per cent—food, textiles and clothes, household utilities, steel, copper, and other basic metals.

What increased less than population or went down was railroad freight, lumber, cotton fiber, returnable beer bottles, wool, and work animal horsepower.

Look at particular industries. Agriculture has changed the most. Formerly, farming was an ecological cycle in basic balance. Plants withdrew nutrients from the soil, nutrients that were derived by bacterial action from organic matter. Organic matter was in turn maintained by the return to the soil of plant debris and animal manure and the fixation of nitrogen from the air into a usable organic form.

In the new agro-industry, cattle are fattened in feedlots. Their waste products are not returned to the soil, but contribute heavily

[16] *The Closing Circle*, p. 139.

to water pollution. Denied manure, the soil is depleted of its humus content. The farmer turns to nitrogen fertilizer in quantities that cause the runoff of nitrogen in unbelievable amounts—contributing further to pollution. Pesticides are similar. They kill insect predators as well as pests, and so increasingly large applications are needed.

Detergents we have already discussed. Soap is just as good, but advertising has succeeded in virtually replacing it. Phosphates from detergents contribute more pollution.

Textile production is next. Natural fibers, such as wool and cotton, have been replaced by synthetics. The process of producing wool and cotton is part of the cycle of life (under the traditional farming methods), but the process of producing synthetic fibers emits heavy doses of pollutants in both air and water. Further, the synthetic fibers are generally not biodegradable. This means that they must either be destroyed by burning, which contributes to pollution, or accumulate as solid trash. Plastics are the same, as we have already discussed.

Now take the automobile. The sheer numbers of automobiles now on the road have clearly increased pollution. But Commoner argues that the *kind* of automobile we are driving today contributes more than the increase in numbers. The total number of vehicles in the United States increased by 166 per cent from 1947 to 1968, and the total vehicle miles by 174 per cent. But lead and photochemical smog attributable to the automobile have gone up much, much faster. Commoner estimates that the entry of lead in the environment has increased by 400 per cent in the past 25 years, and the increase in photochemical smog levels by 1,000 per cent. He blames the increase on the new, high-compression engines. They burn more gasoline. They cause engine "knock," which makes it necessary to add tetraethyl lead to the gasoline and thus to the atmosphere. And, finally, the high temperatures required in the new engines increase the nitrogen oxides emitted. A 1946 passenger car emitted 500 parts per million of nitrogen oxides; a 1968 automobile emitted 1,200.

Examples of how the *kind* of technology we have developed in these past 25 years brought about the environmental crisis can be expanded almost indefinitely. Briefly, what has happened is really due to the revolution in science. Mankind has learned more about the nature of matter in the past 50 years than in all his previous experience. Nuclear energy has given him vast new power sources. Solid-state theory has led to the transistor and the technological base for the computer. But chemistry has been the most fateful of all, at least in terms of the environmental crisis. Man has learned to make materials that never appear in nature. For a time, new substances were made, but no one knew what to do with them, and they were put on the shelf until some use was found, usually by accident. DDT was synthesized in 1908, but it was not until 1931 that man learned that it had the power to kill insects.

Knowledge kept on growing until it became possible for chemists deliberately to set out to *create* a molecule for a specific purpose. The tragedy of DDT—and many other substances such as thalidomide, which cripples unborn children when ingested by pregnant women—is that they have been put to use without thorough study of how they might affect the ecosystems into which they were introduced—how they might affect the totality of life on our planet.

Commoner estimates that the increase in population accounts for from 12 to 20 per cent of the various increases in pollution since 1946. He attributes 1 to 5 per cent to affluence. To the new kind of technology, he attributes 40 per cent in the case of passenger travel, but for all the rest of pollution, *he attributes to technology 95 per cent!*[17]

Conclusions

An examination of pollution reinforces the conclusions we reached in regard to resources. Mankind is entering a period of crisis—in shortage of resources, of energy, of food, and in the pollution of air, water, soil, and the ocean. To meet the crisis man must learn more about nature, but also to control his numbers, to recycle, to live as a compatible part of ecosystems, not their destroyer. Doing this will require redirection to a new *kind* of technology. Mankind will obviously not abandon tech-

[17] *The Closing Circle*, p. 176.

nology and return to the life of our ancestors. Our only alternative is to use our scientific knowledge to develop a different technology that is compatible with continued life on the planet. More than this, the organization of economic, social, and political life must be recast. The content of our relations with each other has already inevitably begun to change. If we are to avoid being overwhelmed by the new problems and tensions, we must find new ways of organizing ourselves to deal with them.

Part VII

THE FUTURE OF WAR

CHAPTER 21

Thermonuclear War and Beyond

Is WAR PART of the future? War has been so integral a part of the past of mankind and so frequent an occurrence in the present that it would seem wishful dreaming even to raise the question. What makes it possible to ask seriously whether war is part of the future arises from the overwhelming power of nuclear weapons and the awesome speed, range, and accuracy of missile delivery systems—plus the additional fact that we live on what is a rather small planet.

Wars in the past have sometimes been enormously destructive. In the Thirty Years' War, for example, the population of what is now Germany was reduced by three fourths, the countryside laid waste, the farms burned, and the fields untended. In World War I, the total killed in battle was 8,020,780, and another 6,642,-633 million died of disease and other causes. In World War II, some 15,000,000 were killed and 26,000,000 to 34,000,000 died of indirect causes.[1] In World War I, the physical destruction was not great, mainly because most of the fighting was confined geographically to the stalemated trench warfare in France. In World War II, however, the fighting ranged more widely, and the bomber spread destruction farther still. What was devastated was not the countryside, as in the Thirty Years' War, but the cities. Moscow, Leningrad, Stalingrad, Kiev, Warsaw, Berlin, Hamburg, Köln, Frankfurt, Dresden, Rotterdam, London, Manila, Chungking, Tokyo, Hiroshima, and Nagasaki all felt the hammer blows of the bomber. But neither the Thirty Years' War nor World War II had levels of destruction that is likely in an entire war fought with nuclear weapons.

Nuclear weapons are of three types: fission, fusion, and fission-fusion-fission. The fission bomb, which was the type used on Hiroshima and Nagasaki, utilizes a natural isotope of uranium, U-235, or plutonium 239. The latter, plutonium, is an essential by-product of nuclear reactors, produced when U-238, the more plentiful natural isotope, absorbs neutrons. U-235 and plutonium are unstable, spontaneously breaking down and releasing neutrons in the process. If one of these neutrons strikes the nucleus of another atom of U-235 or plutonium, that, too, will split, releasing still more neutrons. If a certain amount of U-235 or plutonium is assembled in one mass—the so-called critical mass—a chain reaction will occur, resulting in the release of enormous amounts of energy. A bomb is simply a device to bring together this critical mass very quickly—usually by means of chemical explosives.

The fusion bomb works on an entirely different principle. Fission occurs when a very *heavy* atom splits, releasing energy. Fusion occurs when the nuclei of two very *light* atoms are brought together and they fuse—making a heavier element and releasing even more enormous quantities of energy. In the fusion bombs so far tested, the light element used has been hydrogen. To accomplish fusion, very high temperatures are required—hence the term thermonuclear—and these are so far obtainable only by exploding a U-235 or plutonium bomb as the first step of a two-step process.

[1] R. Ernest Dupuy and Trevor Dupuy, *The Encyclopedia of Military History* (New York: Harper and Row, 1970), pp. 990, 1,198.

Hydrogen is cheaper than U-235 or plutonium. But of even greater practical consequence is that there is no theoretical limit to the size of a fusion bomb, while there are very definite limits to the size of a fission bomb. In a fission bomb, once a critical mass of U-235 or plutonium is brought together, explosion occurs. Practical engineering difficulties set a top limit on the amount of material that can be safely and effectively brought together that is not much larger than the critical mass itself. The rest is simply blown away unexploded. There is no such limit to the amount of hydrogen that can be brought together.

The third type of nuclear bomb presently available is the fission-fusion-fission device. The U-238 present in a U-235 bomb does not split. But in the environment of an H-bomb, with its higher temperatures and faster-moving neutrons, it does—releasing still more energy. Thus the very cheap U-238 can be used as a jacket for the H bomb. A tamper is needed in any case, and the U-238 first does the job of tamping and then contributes itself to the total energy released. Quite apart from the fact that the fission-fusion-fission bomb is economical, it is also compact, which is an important military consideration.

Fisson bombs and shells for atomic cannon have been made as small as 1 kiloton—that is, having the energy equivalent of 1,000 tons of TNT. The Hiroshima bomb was 20 kilotons. Fusion and fission-fusion-fission bombs and warheads have been tested that range from about one third of a megaton (i.e. one third of 1 million tons of TNT equivalent) up to 57 megatons, which was the size of a test bomb fired by the Soviet Union in 1961. Present-day arsenals include a wide variety of the so-called tactical or battle-field atomic weapons in the kiloton range. Submarines of the Polaris type carried missiles with warheads of about 1 megaton. The American land-based missiles throughout the 1960s carried 1 warhead of about 3 megatons, while some Soviet missiles carried somewhat larger ones. The American B-52 bomber and Soviet manned bombers generally carried bombs in the 10-to-20-megaton range, although much larger ones are possible.

The effects of nuclear weapons when exploded on or near the surface of the earth are achieved through blast, heat, and nuclear radiation.

The blast at Nagasaki knocked down buildings, which requires

5 psi (pounds per square inch of overpressure), at a distance of 7,500 feet or 1.4 miles from ground zero (the bomb was exploded at an altitude of 1,850 feet). A 3-megaton warhead exploded on the surface will topple brick structures at a radius of 4 miles from ground zero, giving a total area of such destruction of 50 square miles. For a 10-megaton bomb, the radius is 6.5 miles, and the area is 133 square miles.

The urban area of Greater Moscow is 1,035 square miles; the urban area of Greater New York City[2] is 2,136 square miles. Thus Greater Moscow could be destroyed by 21 missiles with 3-megaton warheads, if they were perfectly targeted, and Greater New York City by 43. Bombers carrying 10-megaton bombs could wreak the same damage on Greater Moscow with 9 bombs and on Greater New York City with 16 bombs.

These figures are for blast alone. The thermal effects of nuclear weapons can be even more destructive. Nuclear explosions will start fires at considerable distances, depending on the weather. As a rule of thumb, however, the distance can be assumed to be 3 times that of the blast effect and 9 times the area. With a large number of fires starting simultaneously at many different points in a city under attack, "fire storms" will develop. The large amount of heat rising from many fires draws strong winds in from the surrounding areas, which fan the flames even higher into one great conflagration. The casualties from burning and suffocation in the areas subject to fire will be as great as the casualties in the blast zone. Because of fire storms, only 3 3-megaton missiles or 1 10-megaton bomb would probably be all that was needed to destroy Greater Moscow, and 5 missiles or 2 bombs for Greater New York City.

Nuclear radiation can vary widely, depending on how a bomb is made and whether it is exploded at the surface or high in the air. A fission bomb exploded high in the air deposits only the radioactive products of the splitting. The area covered and the level of dangerous radioactivity will depend on wind and weather conditions at the particular altitude. A fission bomb exploded at the surface sucks up other material and makes it radioactive—depositing both fission products and radioactive surface material downwind in a cigar-shaped pattern.

[2] This includes Nassau, Rockland, Suffolk, and Westchester counties.

Although an H bomb exploded high in the air produces tritium, carbon 14, and certain other radioactive products, it is no more "dirty" with dangerous radioactivity than its fission trigger. An H bomb exploded at the surface, however, will like an ordinary fission bomb suck up surface material and make it radioactive. The H bomb that was tested by the United States on March 1, 1954, that apparently had a yield of between 10 and 20 megatons deposited radioactive fallout that covered 7,000 square miles in which "survival might have depended upon prompt evacuation of the area or upon taking shelter and other protective measures."[3]

The "dirtiest" bomb of all, however, is the fission-fusion-fission type. Many fission products have more intense radioactivity than surface materials made radioactive. Also, surface materials lose their radioactivity much more rapidly than some of the more dangerous fission products. Many surface materials will lose their radioactivity in a matter of hours, while strontium 90, one of the products of fission that enters the food chain, has a half-life of 27.7 years.

Areas dusted with radioactive fallout will be highly dangerous to all forms of life. Many people in such areas will die within a matter of several days. Others will develop cancers that kill them later. Still others will survive, but with genetic damage that will affect future generations.

Nuclear War—1970

To help us comprehend the consequences of weapons like these for the future, let us see what would have happened had the United States and the Soviet Union fought a nuclear war in the year 1970.

The nuclear arsenals of the United States and the Soviet Union totalled well over a million megatons in 1968, according to David Inglis, a senior physicist at the Argonne National Laboratory writing at the time, and soon thereafter may have been "approaching a hundred million megatons."[4] The limiting factors,

[3] "The Effects of High-Yield Nuclear Explosions," Atomic Energy Commission release (February 15, 1955).
[4] "The Outlook for Nuclear Explosives," *Unless Peace Comes*, ed. Nigel Calder (New York: Viking Press, 1968).

then, are delivery vehicles—land-based strategic missiles, submarine-based missiles, and manned bombers—both in terms of the numbers on each side and in terms of how many are likely to be successful in penetrating the other side's defenses and in delivering their warheads on target.

Both the Soviet and American ICBMs available in 1970 had a range of well over 5,000 miles, which they could travel in about 30 minutes. Warning time at best would be 15 minutes. The Americans had no missile defense of any kind. Although the Soviets had installed a number of antiballistic missile launchers around Moscow, there is reason to believe that the weapon was primitive and ineffective. It must therefore be assumed that if one side or the other had struck first, in a co-ordinated surprise attack, *all* of its ICBMs would have been successfully delivered on target. Although the accuracy of both the Soviet and the American weapons was excellent, it was not good enough to guarantee 100 per cent success against enemy missile sites that had been hardened. It must therefore be assumed that even if the side attacking first succeeded in achieving surprise, half of the enemy's missiles would have survived to strike back. As of 1970, the United States had 1,074, land-based ICBMs; the Soviet Union had 1,300.[5]

Both sides in 1970 also had submarine-based missiles. Submarines have the great advantage of mobility over the vast areas of the ocean. They also have the advantage of being able to maintain a high level of secrecy in their movements. Radar is not effective underwater, and the only method of detection under present technology is by sonar. Submarines, however, can operate at great depths, and this permits them to hide under temperature inversion layers that reflect sonar waves or under schools of fish. For all these reasons, it must be assumed that both sides would have been able to fire all of their submarine-based missiles no matter who attacked first. American submarines in 1970 carried a total of 656 missiles; the Soviets, 280.

Both sides in 1970 also had strategic bombers capable of reaching the other side's homeland. The side receiving a surprise

[5] *The Military Balance, 1970–71* (London: Institute for Strategic Studies, 1972). Same source for figures given below.

blow would probably have lost all of its bombers. The side launching a surprise blow—if it were very lucky—might have succeeded in penetrating the other side's air defenses with half of its bombers, of which as many as 75 per cent might have then succeeded in actually delivering its bombs on target. In 1970, the United States strategic bombers carried a total of 1,835 bombs; Soviet bombers carried a total of 450.

Under these assumptions, a nuclear war fought between the United States and the Soviet Union in 1970 would have had the following results:

Nuclear War I

If the Soviet Union attacked first and achieved surprise:
The United States would have been hit by as many as:
1,300 land-based missile warheads
  280 submarine-based missile warheads
  169 bombs (three fourths of one half of 450)
  ___
1,749 *total*

The Soviet Union would have been hit by as many as:
  537 land-based missile warheads
  656 submarine-based missile warheads
    0 bombs
  ___
1,193 *total*

Nuclear War II

If the United States attacked first and achieved surprise:
The Soviet Union would have been hit by as many as:
1,074 land-based missile warheads
  656 submarine-based missile warheads
  688 bombs (three fourths of one half of 1,835)
  ___
2,418 *total*

The United States would have been hit by as many as:
  650 land-based missile warheads
  280 submarine-based missile warheads
    0 bombs
  ___
  930 *total*

The next question is how these weapons would have been distributed over each country and what level of casualties they would have caused. The side attempting a surprise first strike probably would have given top priority to the other side's missile emplacements, second priority to the other side's strategic bomber bases, and third priority to its air defense systems. As a practical strategic matter, the country striking first would probably have devoted *all* of its missiles, whether based on land or sea, to these three priorities, and used the slower-flying bombers for a follow-on attack on the cities.[6] Some of the missiles aimed at targets in the three top priorities would just incidentally wipe out a number of heavily populated areas, and the bombers could concentrate on the remaining ones.

Using such a strategy, the Soviet Union, if it struck first, would hit American cities and urban complexes with 169 nuclear bombs of from 10 to 20 megatons. If the United States struck first, they would be able to deliver 688 such bombs on Soviet cities.

Our estimate above was that New York could be destroyed by two well-placed 10-megaton bombs and Moscow with 1. Thus the Soviet Union's 169 would be ample to destroy the 67 metropolitan areas in the United States containing 500,000 people or more —a total of almost 113 million people, well over 50 per cent of the entire population. It can also be assumed that the strikes on military installations combined with fallout would kill 15 to 25 per cent of the remaining population, bringing the total casualties to a total of from 125 to 135 million.

The Soviet population is not so heavily concentrated as the American, but with 688 bombs, the United States could easily destroy the 199 most populous areas—which would mean casualties of about 67 million. Here again attacks on military installations would inevitably kill another increment, probably in the neighborhood of 10 to 15 per cent of the remaining population. Thus the grand total for the Soviet Union in a war beginning with an

[6] An alternative to this strategy would be to hold back the bombers, and use them to force surrender by threatening a follow-on attack on the cities. The argument against this variation is that the bombers would be very vulnerable to whatever second-strike capacity the enemy retained. The point would be made that given the uncertainties of nuclear war in any case, no such risk of losing forces should be taken, and that every ounce of strength should be used at the outset to make victory as likely as possible.

American first strike would be 84 to 93 million, or not quite half of the Soviet population.

If the United States attacks first, to sum up, the Soviet Union loses just under half of its people; and if the Soviet Union attacks first, the United States loses well over half of its people.

What about the casualties that the *attacker* is likely to sustain? This particular calculation depends on the strategy adopted by the victim of a successful surprise attack, and it is consequently more complicated. One option for the victim would be to hold back all of his remaining forces and, utilizing the hot line, attempt to turn back the follow-on bomber attack by threatening to use the whole lot against the enemy's cities only. If the victim adopts this strategy and it works, the attacker suffers no casualties at all. The victim suffers only those casualties that occur incidental to the attack on the three top-priority targets. Such an outcome for a war in which the United States attacked first would mean zero American casualties and Soviet casualties of about 20 per cent, or 48 million people. Such an outcome for a war initiated by the Soviets would mean zero Soviet casualties and American casualties of 25 to 30 per cent, or 51 to 62 million.

Now, this kind of outcome to a nuclear war—with the victim not only holding back his forces but successfully using the brief time available to him to negotiate for the follow-on attack to be called off—this kind of outcome is conceivable, but extremely unlikely. In the first place, it would require phenomenal command and control facilities, considering the probable level of destruction, to see that the order to hold back reaches all local missile commanders and phenomenal discipline on the part of local missile commanders if they do receive it. In the second place, it seems doubtful that negotiations could be effective in the kind of conditions that would exist and in the short period of time available.

At the other extreme, the victim could adopt a strategy of pure revenge—devoting his entire remaining strength to maximizing the other side's casualties. This strategy, too, is conceivable, but unlikely. The Soviet Union would have 930 warheads available for a second strike, and the United States, 1,193. Either country could inflict millions of casualties with half of their remaining

capability, and the argument to use at least the other half to reduce the attacker's capability to mount still more follow-on attacks would be overwhelming.

The most likely strategy that the victim of a first strike would
adopt, then, is probably some sort of mix. Two basic alternatives
present themselves, although the proportions could be varied:

Alternative A:
   one third to attack the other side's bases
   one third against the population centers
   one third in reserve for purposes of negotiation
Alternative B:
   one half to attack the other side's bases
   one half in reserve for purposes of negotiation

An Alternative A strategy would give the attacker casualties
not too different from those suffered by the victim of a first strike.
The United States would have 1,193 warheads in its second
strike, and half against bases and half against cities would inflict
casualties at least approaching the 67 million the Soviet Union
would suffer in a first strike. The Soviet Union would have 930
warheads in its second strike, and the results are really not all
that different. The United States would lose very close to half its
population.

An Alternative B strategy would be a little like the results of the
first option we considered—holding back the second strike and
successfully negotiating a calling-off of the follow-on attack. In
effect, the casualties suffered by *both* sides would be those incidental to an attack on bases—Soviet casualties of about 20 per
cent, or 48 million people, and American casualties of 25 to 30 per
cent, or 51 to 62 million people.

In a nuclear war fought in 1970—or any time in that decade—
the decision-makers on each side would therefore have to start
with two assumptions. The first is that in the best probable circumstances their country would suffer 20 to 30 per cent dead,
even if they struck first and achieved surprise. The second is that
the decision as to whether they would suffer more like 50 per cent
dead would be made by the *other* side, according to the strategy

they chose. And they would have to remind themselves that it would take a rather Christ-like set of decision-makers in the victim country *not* to choose the option (Alternative A) that would result in 50 per cent casualties for the attacker.

Such a situation, to underline the obvious, is unique in history. For although it has always been possible for war to result in losses this high or even higher and has on occasion happened, never before was it necessary to assume at the outset that such a level of casualties would be both likely and unpreventable—and for both sides.

Future Possibilities in Military Technology

But before we can assess the implications of this conclusion, two further questions must be asked: Are future technological developments likely to make the situation any worse? Are they likely to make the situation any better?

In the field of explosives, H bombs can be made much, much bigger, and fission-fusion-fission bombs can be made much, much dirtier. But there is no particular reason for anyone to want to. If a 20-megaton bomb will destroy New York City, why bother with making a 100-megaton bomb? The fact is that it is probably more efficient in military terms to attack populated areas with several smaller warheads rather than one even so large as 20 megatons. The only foreseeable incentive for larger weapons would be to crush blast shelters or hardened missile sites, but improving the accuracy of delivery systems would do the same job with greater effectiveness.

An extremely "dirty" bomb can be made by putting a cobalt jacket around an H bomb. Either the Northern or Southern hemispheres could be made uninhabitable with such a bomb. But until the world is organized politically into two blocs conterminous with the two hemispheres, no nation would have an incentive to make such a bomb. By using cobalt bombs in both hemispheres, it is also possible to make "doomsday" machines— weapons capable of making the whole planet uninhabitable. But the incentive is unimaginable.

Beyond fusion as a source for explosives lies only one process suspected by scientists: the mutual destruction of matter and antimatter. Various antimatter particles—antineutrons, antiprotons, and anti-electrons—have been made experimentally. But the difficulties and costs of making and storing sufficient quantities for practical weapons are so astronomically great that the possibility can be almost completely discounted. The explosive warheads of the future will be smaller, more compact, cheaper, and more plentiful. But for as long as it is useful to look ahead, the power of warheads will be in the ranges we know today.

Delivery Vehicles

For delivery vehicles, on the other hand, there are several possibilities. Two very significant developments are already well on the way. One is the increase in the accuracy of ICBMs. Improvements in inertial guidance systems and even such relatively mundane things as better maps as a result of satellite photography are steadily increasing missile accuracy. It seems very likely that the time will come when no amount of hardening will protect missile sites effectively. The consequences will be greater emphasis on submarine-based missiles, on antiballistic missile systems to knock down the incoming missiles, and on improvements in warning systems and reaction time so that a second strike can be launched before the incoming first-strike missiles arrive.

The second development already under way is MIRV—the acronym for multiple, independently targeted re-entry vehicle. Instead of one warhead on the tip of a missile, there will be two, three, or more, each of which can be directed at a different target. The consequence of this development is, first, of course, greatly to increase the number of warheads that can be delivered from a given number of launching pads. Perhaps more important, however, is that MIRV greatly complicates the problem of achieving an effective antiballistic missile defense. It also complicates the problem of achieving and carrying out a disarmament agreement. Before MIRV, each side could determine the number of warheads the other could deliver in a single salvo by simply counting the launching pads revealed in satellite photographs. Each pad could accommodate one missile, and each missile could carry one warhead. With MIRV, the missile on the pad might contain only one or as many as five or more warheads, and the only way to be sure would be through on-the-ground inspection.

Another weapon that is immediately possible with today's technology is the orbiting or satellite bomb. A bomb could be constructed as a satellite, and then "parked" in orbit for an indefinite period, to be brought down in case of war by radio command. The advantage to this weapon is simply that it requires less time to descend from orbit than an ICBM takes to come down from the apogee of its flight path, and it would cut down the warning time an antiballistic missile system would have in which to operate. The disadvantages, however, are impressive. The first is that a large number of bombs would have to be maintained in orbit to ensure that a bomb was over the target at all times. The second disadvantage is that safety precautions guarding against accidental explosions or re-entry, which would trigger retaliation, would be difficult and complicated. The only incentive for this particular weapon is to counter a successful antiballistic missile system, and for both these reasons other alternatives are more likely to be chosen.

The major developments that a future technology is likely to bring probably lie in computers and electronics. Sooner or later it should be possible to automate missiles and to co-ordinate a country's entire missile system—so that all the missiles in a system could be fired simultaneously and without warning to the other side. The second likely development is in electronic countermeasures to radar. Missiles will probably be developed that reflect back only a fraction of the radar waves that present-day missiles do and that also contain devices to confuse the other side's radar acquisition systems. All of these developments will greatly complicate the problem for antiballistic missile defense systems.

Submarines and Undersea Warfare

The most dramatic change in the effectiveness of delivery systems will probably be in reducing the effectiveness of submarine-based missiles—which are now virtually invulnerable. The nuclear submarine was as revolutionary as the missile. It can remain underwater indefinitely; it has an unlimited range; it can travel underwater as fast as surface vessels; and it is very quiet. All these characteristics, plus the fact, already mentioned, that the only detecting system that will work underwater is sonar—reflected sound waves—and that sonar is confused by temperature inversion layers, schools of fish, and so on, make the missile-carrying submarine a most formidable weapon. It is a nuclear missile with a mobile launching platform capable of a high degree of concealment anywhere in the vastness of the world's oceans. Submarines can, of course, be improved. They can already go very deep, for example, but future technology will undoubtedly permit them to go the bottom of the very deepest parts of the ocean, which will add even more to their potential for concealment.

But the possibilities for improvement in the techniques for hunting and killing submarines are much greater. And one further development will give these new techniques added effectiveness. William A. Nierenberg, director of the Scripps Institution of Oceanography, foresees a time in the not-too-distant future when mankind will not only have explored the resources of the ocean depths but will have developed the tools necessary to exploit them and built installations on the ocean bottom for deep-sea mining, with men working in them at all levels.[7] He visualizes a rather well-populated ocean with numerous installations distributed throughout it. Some of these will merely be a "cover" for military installations of various types, but principally for the detection and destruction of missile-carrying submarines.

Chemical and Biological Warfare

Chemical and biological warfare weapons will also undergo further development in the future. Both the Soviet Union and the United States have various chemical and biological warfare weapons in their present arsenals, but only one has any possibility of rivaling nuclear weapons—the so-called nerve gases.

[7] "Militarized Oceans," *Unless Peace Comes.*

Nerve gases are odorless and colorless and can be absorbed in a minute or two by breathing or through the skin. Since the gas causes no irritation of either skin or lungs, the victim is given no warning until it is too late. The effects occur rapidly in the following order: the nose runs; the chest feels tight; the vision dims and the pupils pinpoint; breathing becomes difficult; there is drooling, excessive sweating, nausea, vomiting, and cramps; the victim involuntarily defecates and urinates; he twitches, jerks, and staggers; he develops a headache, is confused, and drowsy; he goes into a coma, has convulsions, stops breathing, and dies. The whole sequence usually takes from 1 to 10 minutes, although it may sometimes be delayed for 1 or 2 hours.[8] It has been estimated that 250 tons of nerve gas, delivered by either plane or missile, would cover a city the size of Paris with a lethal dose.[9]

Future research will undoubtedly discover even more deadly gases and biological warfare agents than those now known. Stunning or incapacitating gases and diseases will also be developed. LSD is one drug with which there have been military experiments. One can imagine a "humane" war in which no one is killed, but merely put to sleep—awakening to find his country defeated and under military occupation.

Yet it seems doubtful that missiles tipped with nerve gas, germs, or somnifacient drugs will be substituted for the present ones with nuclear tips. If one side began to add such missiles to its arsenals, the other side would discover it sooner or later. Protective clothing, masks, and fifteen-minute warning systems could be developed that would be highly effective at very reasonable cost. But only very deep and very strong blast shelters give any protection at all from nuclear weapons, and such shelters would be fantastically expensive and only of very limited effectiveness.

The real danger from chemical and biological warfare agents in the future will not come from the great powers, but from the fact that with such weapons a very small number of people can do a great deal of damage. Some of these agents can be manu-

[8] U. S. Army Technical Manual *TM 3-315.*
[9] Marcel Fetizon and Michel Magat, "The Toxic Arsenal," *Unless Peace Comes.*

factured with relatively little equipment, and there will be more of these agents as time goes on. The members of a terrorist organization, for example, could secretly manufacture a nerve gas or biological agent and distribute it simultaneously over several cities from rented airplanes.

Weapons of the Future

The arsenals of tomorrow, to sum up the argument to this point, will contain nuclear weapons not much different from those we know today, except in being more compact, efficient, and cheaper. Missiles will be much, much more accurate. It will be possible to put an ICBM within a hundred feet or so of the target on inertial guidance alone, and, if terminal guidance is used to compensate for unpredictable atmospheric fluctuations, "down a smokestack from a range of 6,000 miles."[10] Submarines will be improved in a variety of ways, but most especially in their capacity to operate at greater depths. Other developments, principally the exploitation of the ocean, will increase the vulnerability of submarines. Chemical and biological weapons will be developed that can cause death even more effectively than present ones, and others will be developed that can induce sleep and even alter behavior. Every application of computers and electronics, finally, will be improved—all forms of communications, the ability to co-ordinate large numbers of weapons, to analyze data, to guide and control.

Beyond this, it now seems clear that the laser will have a prominent role. Lasers can be used to provide secure communications between spaceships, for example, or to burn holes in an enemy vehicle, whether spaceship or tank, and it may turn out that they will be suitable as part of an antiballistic missile weapon. It is also conceivable that lasers may form the basis for "disintegrator" or death-ray weapons.

Further development of known technology will clearly make robots of all types available, including those capable of making their way through all sorts of obstacles, taking evasive action, directing fire, and making certain kinds of repairs on themselves.

[10] D. G. Brennan, "Weaponry," *Toward the Year 2018*, ed. Foreign Policy Association (New York: Cowles Education Corporation, 1968).

These could include tanks that can walk, run, and swim while carrying nuclear weapons in armored shells that would be impervious to anything but another nuclear weapon. It will undoubtedly also be possible in the not-too-distant future to manipulate the weather, either in the long run to alter climate or in the short run to create man-made hurricanes. It will also be possible to cause tidal waves and possibly earthquakes—although it seems doubtful if any of these could achieve military results that could not be accomplished cheaper and quicker by existing weapons.

Future developments might also include a technique to do with magnetism what lasers are doing with light, and some way of manipulating gravity, either neutralizing it or directing it.

On balance, then, the answer to our queston as to whether things will get much worse is "No"—mainly because they are already so bad.

Nuclear Proliferation

This answer, however, applies only to technological developments. Things may get much worse in terms of nuclear proliferation. First of all, the scientific and engineering knowledge to make nuclear weapons and at least minimal delivery systems is well known. As for the raw materials, an H-bomb requires a fission trigger.[11] This means that to have an H-bomb, a country must have access to supplies of uranium on which there is no military restriction. (It must also have means of separating the U-235 isotope from the more common U-238. A much cheaper process by centrifuge may soon be developed, and the evidence is that the Chinese already have an operational centrifuge process. The gaseous diffusion method used in the past is very expensive.) A fission bomb, however, can be made of plutonium, and plutonium is a natural by-product of reactors used to generate power. By changing the fuel rods in its power reactors slightly more often (to prevent the plutonium 239 from being converted to the 240 isotope), a nation could accumulate a respectable stockpile of plutonium just incidentally to filling its power needs.

[11] Sir John Cockcroft, "The Perils of Nuclear Proliferation," *Unless Peace Comes*, p. 31.

According to the International Atomic Energy Agency, Canada, Czechoslovakia, West Germany, India, Israel, Italy, Japan, the Netherlands, Pakistan, Spain, Sweden, and Switzerland were all operating power reactors in 1970 that produced plutonium as a by-product in sufficient quantities to make at least 1 warhead a year and as many as 100. And if any one of these nations has a "breeder" pile deliberately designed to produce plutonium, the capacity would be much, much higher.

Building a bomb would still be expensive, however. And building even a minimal delivery system would be even more expensive—although most of the medium and smaller powers acquiring nuclear weapons would probably follow the example of the French and use manned bombers in spite of their vulnerability. A bargain-basement force of manned bombers and half a dozen plutonium bombs might be built for under $100 million dollars. A larger, more credible force of, say, the size of the British or French nuclear forces would be considerably more expensive. It has been estimated by experts working at the Institute for Strategic Studies in London that it would cost $200 million a year for a period of 5 years for India, for example, to build an acceptable strategic nuclear force.

Such a level of expenditure is within the capacity of quite a few nations, and it is obvious that it is possible for a very large number to be armed with nuclear weapons in the future. In 1970, it was generally assumed that all that stood between Israel and an operational bomb was a screwdriver—that it had built all the component parts for a nuclear weapon, and had merely to assemble the pieces and hook up the wires. India and Japan were assumed to be not very far behind, and India proved it by exploding a nuclear device in 1974. West Germany, Sweden, Switzerland, Australia, Canada, Argentina, and Italy all have the capability. And the number will grow. It has been estimated that by the 1990s, as many as 50 countries might have nuclear weapons.[12]

The second question—are technological developments likely to make the situation better?—is really to ask if technological developments are likely to produce a defense against missiles

[12] Herman Kahn and Anthony J. Wiener, *The Year 2000: A Framework for Speculation on the Next Thirty-three Years* (New York, 1967), p. 246.

effective enough to cast doubt on the conclusion reached earlier that statesmen must now assume that in a nuclear war 50 per cent casualties are both likely and unpreventable.

Missile Defense Systems

How effective would an antiballistic missile defense system be using present-day technology plus improvements that can reasonably be expected in the immediate future if a suitable research effort is made? Like the Safeguard/Sentinel system proposed for the United States, such a system would have two different kinds of radar, the largest and most complex computers ever built, and two kinds of interceptor missiles. The first radar would be very long-range, designed to pick up the incoming missile at maximum distance—several thousand miles from target and about ten minutes in time—and acquire enough information so that its trajectory could be calculated by the computers (in the Safeguard/Sentinel system this radar is called the Perimeter Acquisition Radar). The second radar (the Missile Site Radar in Safeguard/Sentinel) then takes over tracking the incoming missile, and, on command from the computer, guides the interceptor missile as well. This radar is designed to handle a large number of both missiles and interceptors at the same time. The first type of interceptor (Spartan in Safeguard/Sentinel) is long-range, with a very large warhead, designed to destroy the incoming missile several hundred miles from its target, while it is still in outer space. The second interceptor (Sprint in Safeguard/Sentinel) is a short-range back-up missile, with very fast acceleration and a small warhead designed to intercept and destroy the incoming missile 5 to 20 miles away from its target.

Both interceptors use nuclear warheads, but each depends on different effects to destroy the incoming missile. The shorter-range, lower-yield missile, which explodes in the atmosphere, could destroy the incoming missile by blast, depending on how strongly it was built, but a surer method is by neutron flux. The neutrons released by the interceptor warhead would penetrate the outer casing of the warhead and cause fission to take place in the U-235 of the incoming warhead, the temperature would rise, and the material would melt, destroying its shape and making it impossible to detonate. The kill radius of a weapon depending on neutron flux is small, but interception can be successfully accomplished with high-performance radar if interception takes place fairly close to the interceptor's launch site.

The longer-range interceptor, designed to destroy the incoming missile while it is still in outer space, utilizes a different principle, the so-called X-ray effect. Most of the energy in a megaton-size nuclear warhead is carried off by X-rays. A large quantity of these striking an incoming warhead will cause the surface layer of the heat shield to evaporate so rapidly at such high velocity that a shock wave is created that will destroy the heat shield and may also damage the underlying structure as well. In the absence of atmosphere, the X-rays can travel unimpeded and the kill radius can be many, many kilometers.

Technically, the most difficult parts of this entire weapons system are the computers—all the other components are clearly feasible. For the system to be effective, the computers would have to perform a number of complicated tasks simultaneously. They would have to compute the trajectory of the incoming missile, calculate the firing data for the interceptor, and continuously recalculate both to provide corrections for controlling the interceptor in flight. But they would also have to do the same thing—simultaneously—for a large number of both incoming missiles and interceptors. In addition, the computers will need to make the calculations necessary to pick out the real warheads from the decoys. They will also have to have a capacity to make corrections for a variety of possible countermeasures and to check on their own performance. Complicated as all this is, there is no reason to believe that the necessary computers could not be built, and hence the entire system.

Doubt about the effectiveness of an antiballistic missile system of this kind comes not from its ability to cope with present-day missiles, but from the countermeasures available to the attacker.[13] One measure open to the attacker is simply to add more

[13] For the following I have drawn on Hans A. Bethe, "Countermeasures to ABM Systems," *ABM*, eds. Abram Chayes and Jerome B. Wiesner (New York: Harper and Row, 1969).

missiles—some of which can be cheap decoys that imitate the
way a warhead looks to radar. No matter how many missiles an
antiballistic missile system is designed to handle simultaneously,
the attacker could always send in enough more to throw the
computers into confusion. The attacker can also do quite a bit to
shield his warheads from X-ray effects. Shielding again neutrons
is more difficult, since it requires so much weight. Another
countermeasure would be for the attacker to make his bombs
very "dirty" and program them to explode in the first instant of
an interceptor's explosion, or in any case just out of range of the
second interceptor—so as to attack the cities with fallout. Some
measures for evading the defenses are also possible. Submarines,
for example, can come in closer before launching their missiles,
shortening the warning time. Missiles can also be launched in
so-called "fractional orbits." A normal trajectory takes an incoming missile to an altitude of over 1,000 kilometers—which
makes it possible for the long-range radar to pick it up 10 minutes
before impact. The missile could also be programmed for a "fractional orbit," which takes it to an altitude of only 150 kilometers
and permits only 3 minutes of warning time.

The attacker can also take a number of steps to confuse the
defending radar. He could, for example, fit the missiles with
electronic jammers tuned to the defender's radar. Use of chaff
is another method for confusing the radar. If very fine metal wire
is cut to about half the wavelength of the defending radar, each
wire will act as a reflecting dipole. If the chaff wires are dispersed
over a large volume of space, the radar will see only the cloud
and could not tell where in the cloud the warhead was hiding.
Several interceptors would have to be used, and even then the
defense could not be certain of a hit. Still another method of
blinding or confusing the defending radar is through radar
"blackout" caused by a nuclear explosion. The fireball produces
ions through high temperature; the radioactive debris produce
them through beta rays. As a result of both effects, a cloud of
ionized gas is produced that both absorbs and bends electro-
magnetic rays—thus both blinding and confusing the radar. The
effects last for about ten minutes, which is the time it takes for
an incoming missile to travel from the point where it would

ordinarily be picked up by radar to the target. Although designed to minimize this effect, even the explosions of the defending interceptors will tend to blind its own radar to follow-on missiles.

Considering all the countermeasures available to an attacker, it seems obvious that an antiballistic missile defense system of the kind contemplated here does not change the earlier conclusion. A defense system, combined with a large-scale shelter program, might give enough protection to reduce the percentages for a few years, but then the other side would have taken sufficient additional measures to nullify the defense.

And the same situation is likely to prevail in the future. One or another technological development may give the defense a temporary advantage. But the time it will take to build and deploy the new weapon will usually give the offense time to develop something that will even the balance. And even when the advantage does actually last long enough to permit the defense to build and deploy a new weapon, no one could be certain that it would work exactly as planned or that the offense did not have some secret up its sleeve.

Barring the discovery of some entirely new scientific principle so far unimaginable—like an antigravity shield—a defense that achieves anything even close to 100 per cent effectiveness is highly unlikely. And the power of nuclear weapons is such that anything less than a perfect defense will result in very high casualty levels. No matter what technology brings, in sum, the world is simply a different place than it was before the discovery of nuclear weapons and missiles. Human beings are too frail and the planet is too small.

CHAPTER 22

Attempts to Abolish War

IF NUCLEAR wars are likely to bring 50 per cent casualties and if no future technological development is likely to change that probability, what are the prospects? Is there any hope in abolishing war or, if it cannot be abolished, in reducing its destructiveness? What about arms control, the United Nations' peace-keeping role, traditional devices of diplomacy such as the concert of powers, a world state?

Arms Control

The limited test ban treaty of 1963 prohibits all but underground testing of nuclear weapons, and within a decade it had been signed by all the major powers except China and France. The nonproliferation treaty limiting the further development of nuclear weapons came soon after, and at the end of the same period it had been signed by all the major powers except Argentina, Australia, Brazil, China, France, India, Indonesia, Israel,

Japan, Pakistan, South Africa, and Spain. The Strategic Arms Limitation Talks (SALT) between the Soviet Union and the United States also made encouraging progress in the same period. If current tensions can be eased, further agreements will also be worked out, including a complete ban on all nuclear tests, limiting the numbers of strategic arms, and perhaps even reducing their numbers. All this is good, but it seems doubtful just how far arms control can be pushed and especially doubtful if any sort of "general and complete" disarmament will be achieved, much less the even bolder step of entrusting the monopoly of nuclear weapons to an international body.

One problem is that some countries fear that arms control will turn out to be a trick to disarm them and not their enemies. Others fear that arms control will set forces in motion that will eventually destroy their society. This fear has been exacerbated by the invention of MIRV (multiple, independently targeted re-entry vehicle), as already suggested, and the fact that MIRV makes on-site inspection mandatory. Until the invention of MIRV, each side could check on the other side through satellite photography. But when any one missile can carry three, five or more warheads, the only way of finding out just how many missiles the other side has built is periodically to send a man with a screwdriver to look inside each and every missile. For the United States and other countries whose social systems are based on parliamentary democracy, on-site inspection poses political difficulties, since it arouses considerable opposition among military and technical people who fear the loss of national and industrial secrets. But in the Soviet Union and other countries with social systems based on one party or similar arrangements, on-site inspection would pose difficulties for the system itself, creating strains throughout the whole society.

No one doubts that arms control agreements will ease tension and contribute to maintaining peace. But the truth of the matter is that no one has successfully demonstrated that arms races by themselves inevitably lead to war or that arms control agreements by themselves are very effective even in lessening the probability of war.[1] Even if it were a lot easier than it is to

[1] The most thoroughgoing analysis of arms races is Samuel P. Huntington's. See his "Arms Races: Prerequisites and Results," *Public Policy*, eds. C. J. Friedrich and S. Harris, 1958, Harvard, 1959.

achieve arms control agreements, something much more fundamental would be needed to make any real progress toward
abolishing war.

The UN and Peace-keeping

When the UN was formed in the wake of World War II, many
saw it as the one best hope for peace. In its work in the fields
of health, food and agriculture, refugees, economic development, labor, children, and in the specialized organizations dealing with the postal union, aviation, and telecommunications, the
UN has been invaluable. It has served as a forum for debate
and as such has undoubtedly contributed to world peace. But
as an instrument for keeping the peace in any direct sense, its
record is not at all impressive.

When one of the great powers has been involved in a dispute,
the only action the UN has so far succeeded in taking has been
the condemnatory resolution. Almost all the great powers have
at one time or another been so condemned. The Soviet Union
was condemned for its actions in Hungary; Britain, for its attack on Egypt at the time of the Suez crisis of 1956; and Communist China was condemned for its intervention in Korea. So
far, the United States has escaped being condemned, but this
is probably more a function of voting blocs and a desire on the
part of some countries to avoid jeopardizing the American aid
they were receiving than of exceptional virtue in the eyes of
other countries. Certainly the American intervention in both
Vietnam and the Dominican Republic would otherwise have been
prime candidates for censure motions.

The effect of these resolutions has not been very impressive.
The resolutions served to focus public attention on the issue,
and in some cases this may have acted as a deterrent to the
government concerned—but little else.

With the exception of the resolution calling for member nations to fight in Korea, which was passed during the absence of
the Soviet Union at the time of its boycott of the Security Council,
the UN has gone beyond a mere censuring resolution only when
small powers were involved and when the great powers felt
that their interests were not at stake or when the action seemed

to serve their interests. The UN peace-keeping forces stationed between the Israeli and Egyptian forces served a useful function for a time, even though they were not able to prevent the war that came in 1967. Again, the UN forces stationed in Kashmir served a useful function even though they, too, were not able to prevent war from coming eventually. The intervention in Cyprus has also been judged useful. But the troubles that plagued even the most successful intervention of all, that in the Congo, illustrate the weakness of the UN in its peace-keeping role.

The most obvious weakness is that effective action by the UN depends on continuing unanimity among the great powers, and maintaining that unanimity is difficult. In the Congo intervention, the Soviet Union and the United States both voted for the original Security Council resolution authorizing the Secretary General to take steps to provide military forces for intervening in the Congo, but as events unfolded, the Soviet Union came to see the presence of UN forces and the actions of the Secretariat as against its interests. In attempting to keep the peace between warring factions, the Secretary General inevitably had to make decisions, and inevitably these favored one side or the other. At one point, the UN closed the airports. The action prevented much bloodshed, but it also ensured the defeat of the pro-Soviet contender for leadership, Patrice Lumumba. The Soviets were outraged and saw their interests sufficiently involved to provoke the UN's first constitutional crisis. The Soviets called for the post of Secretary General to be abolished and put forward the so-called *troika* scheme to reorganize the Secretariat into pro-Western, pro-Soviet, and neutralist factions. For the United States as well as the Soviet Union, the lesson of the UN intervention in the Congo was that even though one's interest might not be involved at the beginning of the crisis, events might change the situation dramatically.

And it was not only the great powers that lost some of their enthusiasm for the UN's peace-keeping role during the Congo crisis. As events forced the Secretariat to make more and more decisions with political consequences, the UN secretariat itself became as much a political contender as any of the great powers. By the time the controversy reached the proportions of a constitutional crisis, the Secretariat found itself not reaching out for more responsibility in peace-keeping, but fighting to preserve its minimum power and influence and to salvage as much as possible of its reputation as a nonpartisan and impartial international civil service.

A Concert of the Powers

Perhaps the most promising of the more familiar instruments for maintaining the peace lies in the traditional devices of diplomacy such as the so-called "concert of the powers." It was something along these lines that underlay the original concept of the United Nations. The experience with the League of Nations was that a world body in which every state, no matter how small, had equal power could never succeed in building an effective consensus or act decisively. To get around the difficulty of too many states with equal sovereignty, the notion of a concert of the great powers only was put forth during the deliberations on the structure of the UN. It was to be small enough in numbers to reach a consensus and yet powerful enough to impose its will on all the others. The instrument was the Security Council. The five great powers—the United States, the Soviet Union, Great Britain, France, and China—would be permanent members, with four other members serving temporary terms; custom came to dictate that these would be so chosen as to represent regions—Asia, Africa, the Middle East, and Latin America. A majority would be necessary to pass a binding resolution, but any one of the great powers had the right of a veto. As we said, the idea broke down partly because of the failure to develop machinery by which decisions of the Security Council could be enforced, but mainly because of the failure of the two superpowers to develop a consensus between themselves. What we want to know is whether there is still some promise in this notion of a concert of the powers.

Ranking the Powers

The first question is who the members of the concert are to be. For at least another century and probably longer, the Soviet Union and the United States will continue to rank not only as great powers but as superpowers. China, according to our analysis, will develop a dual economy, and will exercise considerable leverage in the world. It will have sufficient nuclear strength to give the superpowers pause, and its voice will be heard. But it will be a great power, not a superpower. India, whose population and territory rivals China's, would also be excluded from superpower status for many of the same reasons as China. In addition, India will continue to have problems of internal unity for at least two or three generations. Japan must also be excluded from superpower status, in spite of the fact that its population will rival that of the United States and the Soviet Union and the fact that its national income will not be far behind; we so rank Japan on the grounds of its small territory, its dense and concentrated population, and a set of attitudes and policies that have turned away from the goals of national power and prestige. No other countries have the combination of population, territory, and national income to make them contenders.

On the other hand, there is no doubt that China, India, and Japan will exercise considerable power and influence in the century that lies ahead. So will France, the United Kingdom, West Germany, Italy, and Canada. All will certainly enjoy the status of "great powers."

Herman Kahn and Anthony J. Wiener, who have done the most extensive work on this subject of the ranking of the powers, would agree.[2] They put the Soviet Union and the United States first, and head and shoulders above any potential rivals. Next they put the "large powers"—Japan, West Germany, France, China, and the United Kingdom, in that order. Then will come, also in order, India, Italy, and Canada, the "intermediate powers." After that come all the rest, the "small powers."

A Concert of the Two Superpowers

Consider first a concert of the two superpowers. Let us assume that the Soviet Union and the United States find a way past their current tensions and rivalries and that they cease to be disturbed

[2] *The Year 2000: A Framework for Speculation on the Next Thirty-three Years* (New York, 1967), p. 130.

by the differences in their systems, lose interest in proselyting their own systems, and lose the fear that the other will continue to proselyte theirs. Let us further assume that they also agree that any *international* quarrels that *run the risk of war*, even limited war, are threatening to world peace and their own security, and they therefore decide to co-operate closely in preventing these quarrels from escalating into actual war.

It is important to note that this particular "alternative future" does not require that the Soviet Union and the United States "converge" and become more like each other. The principal requirements are really only two: (1) that the leadership in the Soviet Union and the United States decide to live with each other—i.e., each accepts the other as a global power of essentially equal strength and voice and recognizes that any attempt to change that status will lead only to disaster; and (2) that certain kinds of third- and fourth-party actions and struggles are threatening to world peace and thus to their own survival.

The first step would be a simple declaration by the two superpowers that they would jointly go to war against any state that uses nuclear weapons. If the threat could be made believable, it would be at least a partial substitute for the umbrella of the state's "monopoly of legal violence" that does so much to make it possible to resolve disputes within a single state without resort to violence. Also, if the threat could be made believable, it would at least put a limit on any wars that were actually fought.

The two superpowers might also find it possible to extend the principle of using their own military power as a substitute for an individual state's "monopoly of legal violence" beyond the first use of nuclear weapons. They might say that they would intervene to stop *any* use of violence. They might couple this declaration with another declaration that any such dispute that required their intervention would then be placed before the International Court of Justice. The domestic analogy would be compulsory arbitration in labor disputes.

Notice that an international political system based on this kind of "concert of the powers" is not so much a substitute for war or the threat of war as a process in which war and the threat of war are the principal instruments for resolving quarrels and disagreements. In this system, as in the existing international system, the measurement of power is the capacity for physical violence. On the other hand, when the "monopoly of legal violence" lies elsewhere than with the contenders to a quarrel, as within a single state, then power is measured by other yardsticks.

But even the politics of war and the threat of war has its techniques that can be used to avoid or evade any *particular* war—the popular term is "crisis management." Between adversaries these techniques are the maneuverings between deterrence and threat on the one side and compromise and negotiation on the other. The Cuban missile crisis of 1962, the Berlin blockade in 1948, the maneuvering in 1946 to persuade the Soviet Union to remove its troops from Iran—all these provide examples of two major adversaries manipulating power in just this way, combining the threat of force with negotiations and compromise.

Among allies, the techniques are a more subtle mixture of pressure and bait, of trade-offs between one good and another. One good example is the United States trying to prevent Chiang Kai-shek from embroiling the United States more deeply in the Quemoy-Matsu crisis than it wanted to be. Another is the Soviet Union pressuring Castro to go more slowly in his attempts to stir up revolution in Latin America. The Laos crisis of 1962 is an example that combined all types of these techniques—what has been called, as we said, "crisis management"—in which the Soviet Union and the United States both confronted each other and negotiated with each other, while behind the scenes the Soviets pressed their allies toward agreement and the United States pressed theirs.

Notice that it is not really necessary that the two superpowers *act* in concert, but only that they are agreed on the result. At the time of the India-Pakistan war in 1965, for example, the Soviet Union at Tashkent served as midwife for the negotiations by itself. All that was required of the United States was that it do nothing to impede the Soviets in their role as mediator and that it do not envy them the credit.

The fundamental weakness of a concert of the two superpowers is that it works only so long as amity between them continues and that their basic interests continue to be shared interests. So long as these conditions hold, a concert of the two might provide a very high level of stability and peace—and once the arrangement was established, those conditions might hold for rather a long time.

Still and all, it takes real optimism to believe that the United States and the Soviet Union can reach such a high degree of amity by traditional means. A second weakness is that a number of other countries might not really like the idea very much, and this is a weakness that would also be an impediment to the two making use of their consensus to strengthen the UN or provide other international machinery. The trouble is that not all the other powers would relish having the world run by the big two, and some might actively resent it.

The third weakness is merely a different facet of the first: There is nothing in this arrangement that facilitates the resolution of disagreements and quarrels between the big two—nothing, that is, except the bait of being one of a duumvirate that runs the world! If a consensus is to be developed between the two, it must be brought about by the age-old techniques of traditional diplomacy, negotiation, compromise, bargaining, and threat and counterthreat.

A Concert of Great Powers

What about a modification of this concert of the superpowers that may help to get around the objection that many states would not relish a world run by the big two? It could be a kind of renewed and revitalized Security Council, a concert not of the two superpowers, but of all ten of the major powers plus rotating representation for the smaller powers of Asia, Africa, the Middle East, and Latin America.

This larger concert of the powers could come about in one of two ways. The top ten and a number of the smaller powers could develop a consensus and shared interests that pointed them in this direction, or such a concert could grow out of the concert of the two superpowers, as more and more states began to share the consensus and assumed their share of the responsibilities.

But one can hardly be hopeful. It is obviously going to be so frustratingly difficult to get a consensus between the United States and the Soviet Union that one might be very pessimistic about the possibilities of a consensus among so many more.

On the other hand, even if a concert of the two superpowers is going to achieve any notable success, they must make the attempt to build a concert among the larger group; for if their efforts are to have any degree of acceptance at all rather than united opposition, the Soviet Union and the United States must not only be willing but also be anxious to share their responsibilities with other states. Most especially, these two must themselves be capable of accepting change, and the prerequisites of their attitude toward each other—that of accepting the realities of each other's power and each other's right to a share of the responsibility—must be extended to the rising powers, like China and Japan, as they rise.

Out of the original concert of the Soviet Union and the United States might grow, in other words, something like a concert of all the great powers and many of the smaller, as other like-minded states assume their share of the responsibility.

It seems all too obvious, however, that even this more optimistic future would not be successful in avoiding a substantial number of less-than-nuclear wars and very doubtful that it could entirely avoid nuclear war, although it might succeed in limiting any that did occur. The fact of the matter is that there are just too many conditions that are just too difficult to maintain—not only continued consensus between the Soviet Union and the United States, but the even more idealistic conditions of generosity toward rising powers. It would take a very high degree of optimism indeed for the observer in the 1970s to have much confidence in complete peace. Perhaps the best that could be hoped for is that if wars do come, and perhaps even if a *nuclear* war comes, that those wars could be contained and ended in circumstances that did not constitute a "turning point" toward some more horrendous future, but simply a setback on the path of this more optimistic one.

In other words, it is conceivable that if the Soviet Union and the United States were agreed on the over-all goal of preserving the peace, as they were in the Cuban missile crisis, they could manage crises so as to avoid war without placing very much reliance on the machinery of the UN or other formal international organization. In a word, it is conceivable that a reasonably satisfactory world could be created without altering the basic structure of the present system of international politics, but merely by using the traditional methods of diplomacy, bargaining, balancing of power, military force, and the threat of military force with more consistent skill and effectiveness.

But even though these traditional techniques might enable the powers to avoid any particular war through the wise use of techniques of crisis management or even to avoid a long series of wars over time, no real and lasting progress would necessarily be made toward a permanent solution to the problem of war itself. The threat of war will continue to hang over mankind's head, and—sooner or later—war itself will come.

A World State

The truth of the matter is that the only proposal for abolishing war that is logically persuasive is the creation of a world state. Since war has been effectively abolished over whole continents that are controlled by stable, well-established states, it seems logical that war could be effectively abolished throughout the entire planet by establishing a stable, well-established state governing the whole world. But like the proposal for ending the Nazi submarine menace in World War II by boiling the oceans, the policy is easy to lay down, but implementing it is something else again.

In the first place, there is no sign or scintilla of evidence that mankind will move very soon or very rapidly toward the establishment of a world state. On the contrary, as we have seen, the direction with only one exception is toward nationalism and even more and stronger nation-states.

In the second place, even though a world state would be a promising means of eliminating war in the long run, the attempt to establish it might have just the opposite effect in the short run. Before a world state could be effectively established, men's loyalties would have to shift away from the nation and toward a larger political concept, really the organization of all mankind. As we have said, similar shifts of loyalties from smaller to larger political units have occurred in history. Athenians and Spartans at some stage began to think of themselves as Greeks. Alsatians and Provençals came to think of themselves as Frenchmen. Bavarians and Prussians came to think of themselves as Germans. But nationalism remains the most powerful political force that has yet activated the human animal, and such fundamental attitudes do not change very quickly or easily. And what will make the process even more difficult is the additional fact that most nationalisms already have the territorial and economic bases to develop the means to make war—in many cases sufficient means to oppose domination by even the combined strength of all the rest of mankind. The point is that it might well take one or more wars of frightening proportions to establish a world state, and once established, mankind might well be destined to go through a series of violent civil wars as well.

Nuclear War

It has been suggested that one sure way to establish permanent world peace would be to have a nuclear war, that the very horror of nuclear war would force mankind to take the drastic social and political measures needed to eliminate war forever and entirely.

It seems fairly certain that one consequence of nuclear war would be, as we have seen, that the two contenders would be removed from the chessboard of international politics. The surviving citizens of the two belligerents would be few, and the devastation would be overwhelming. But it is also clear that the rest of mankind would suffer relatively few casualties, although some countries would have to take countermeasures against fallout. Certainly it is difficult to conceive of circumstances bringing a war so large and widespread as to destroy the whole of mankind as envisioned by books like Neville Shute's *On the Beach* or even the whole of a hemisphere or a continent.

The question is whether the shock of seeing two hundred mil-

lion or more dead and cities and industries of two major countries
incinerated all in a matter of hours would bring the rest of mankind to make the fundamental political changes that would eliminate entirely the possibility of any repetition of the holocaust.
Would a nuclear war, to use the terminology developed in the
Preface, become a "turning point"?

If historical experience with past disasters is any guide to such
a quantitatively greater cataclysm, the answer is—probably not.
The horrors that mankind has seen in the past may not have
been quite so bad as those of nuclear war, but they have been
bad. And mankind failed to make any really significant changes
in direct response. A total of forty million to forty-five million
people died as a result of World War II, and the potential of nuclear weapons to multiply that figure was adequately demonstrated by Hiroshima and Nagasaki. Yet the UN was the most that
the sovereign states would agree to, and they did that only after
monumental bickering. It might be argued that a nuclear war
would be different, that the suddenness of it all, the fact that so
many deaths and so much destruction came in so short a time,
the fact that it really happened and did not have to be imagined
—all these, it is argued, would have a dramatic effect that forty
million to forty-five million deaths over six years did not have.
But the case is not persuasive. Hiroshima and Nagasaki, to repeat, were there as examples. Then, too, before World War II, air
power enthusiasts argued that heavy bombing raids on the enemy capital and civilian populations would have decisive trau-
matic effects, leading to the country's collapse and surrender.
Strategic bombing was more effective than some of its critics realize, especially at Hamburg and Tokyo, where fire storms occurred, but still it fell short of a level of destruction that would
break a victim's will.[3] It seems more likely that different people in
the surviving countries would draw differing conclusions. Some
would undoubtedly argue for a world state. But others would
probably argue that the real lesson for their country of someone
else's nuclear war is that it should have a bigger deterrent, or an
ABM system, or a better shelter program. Some might argue for an
alliance system, and some for a strategy of pre-emptive strikes!

[3] On this point see Bernard Brodie, *Strategy in the Missile Age* (Princeton, 1959).

Conclusions

Two conclusions seem inescapable. The first is that none of the instrumentalities so far proposed are likely to abolish war entirely. Arms control, the UN, the traditional devices of diplomacy such as the "concert of the powers" all can help avoid any particular war, but not war itself. War is part of the future.

The second conclusion concerns the probability of nuclear war. Nuclear war carries with it levels of death and destruction so high that no political leader could assume in advance that it was a rational instrument for achieving national goals. But political leaders can and do assume that limited, conventional wars continue to be rational instruments for achieving national goals. The world continues to run the risk that conventional war between small- and medium-size powers will suck the great powers into its vortex and escalate into nuclear war or that the great powers will themselves take what they believe to be limited actions, only to find that events spiral out of hand and into Armageddon. It seems the better part of wisdom, in other words, for mankind also to assume that nuclear war, too, is part of the future.

Part VIII

CONCLUSIONS AND IMPLICATIONS

CHAPTER 23

Implications for Foreign Policy Today

IF ALL THE trends, forces, implications, and conclusions we have so far reached are more or less on the mark, what are the implications for United States foreign policy today? How do these long-term trends affect the issues we so strenuously debate today?

The Cold War and Relations with the Soviet Union

We see the Soviet Union, like the United States, moving into a superindustrial stage with similar implications of a change in values, including a change away from national power and prestige values, and less emphasis on ideology. We see an interest-group structure arising in the Soviet Union, in which the Communist party serves as political broker but must win support for major policies from a significant number of power centers. We also believe that the Soviet leaders fully understand the dangers of nuclear war. A hard-line faction continues to exist among the top echelons of the Soviet Union, but they are increasingly balanced by highly sophisticated and pragmatic men in a number of the various Soviet power centers. If these conclusions and related ones we have reached about the world are soundly based, at the very least we can say that the Cold War has been transformed, that what rivalry remains between the Soviet Union and the United States is becoming less and less dangerous in military terms. This does not mean that the United States can relax, junk its nuclear deterrent forces, and spend the money improving the quality of life. The long-term trend in the Soviet Union is away from power and prestige values, but short-run decisions can still bring formidable risks. The Soviet decision in 1962 to deploy offensive missiles to Cuba is one illustration of the point, and their policy in the Middle East may well turn out to be another. Because of this, the United States must maintain a certain military defense posture, the nature of which will be discussed later. In the meantime, however, moves toward further détente with the Soviets can and should be pushed with both more imagination and vigor than they have in the past. Our stand on arms control, on trade and other economic matters, and on a variety of other sore points in East-West relations can be softened with only minimum risk and with the potentiality of considerable gain. As Senator Mansfield has argued for several years, the United States should reduce the troops it has stationed in West Germany and other parts of Europe by half and perhaps more. If our analysis is correct, in the long run a very minimal American conventional ground and tactical air force in Europe will be more than adequate. The argument that any reductions should be made only as a result of negotiations in which the Warsaw Pact forces are reduced simultaneously misses the point that the trends and forces we have identified justify the United States in taking the offensive in a movement toward peace and the normalization of relations. The circumstances give us latitude to test the proposition that our own actions can reinforce and strengthen these trends inside and outside the U.S.S.R.

China

As for China, we concluded that the Communist party was in firm control, and that China was determined to take its rightful place among the world's powers. We also concluded that Mao failed to create a new man and a new society, except in the sense that he and the Communist party have brought China from an agricultural society to a pre-industrial society, which is no mean feat. We concluded that China by the year 2000 would create a dual economy—an economy of 900 million or so people with relatively low but improving standards of living containing within it an economy of about 100 million with the technological capabilities of any other developed country of comparable size, including a nuclear deterrent of about the same order as that of France and Great Britain. We expect that Mao's death will precipitate a struggle over the succession but that power will eventually go to the leader of the faction that has the deepest roots in the structure of the party, rather than the government or the Army. We expect that Mao's successors will be ambitious, but at the same time realistic and cautious. In view of these trends and forces acting upon China and its leaders, President Nixon's trip to China and the efforts of his Administration toward normalizing relations with China should be applauded. However, if our analysis is correct, these efforts, too, could be pushed even more vigorously. Trade and all aspects of economic relations are worth a particular effort. Also, as with the Soviet Union, we should take steps toward establishing a lower American military posture. Our troops stationed in Korea should be reduced to a token force. We should re-examine our military base structure in Okinawa, the Philippines, Japan, and Guam, and reduce it appropriately. Here, again, a very minimal deterrent will be adequate.

The knottiest issue, of course, is the ultimate nature of the relations between China and Taiwan. But this can be put at the very bottom of the agenda. China has neither the intention to attempt to occupy Taiwan by force nor the capability in terms of landing craft, airplanes, and all the rest. It is an issue that can be put to one side indefinitely or until the whole situation in Asia has changed sufficiently that the parties directly concerned can work out a mutually satisfactory arrangement entirely on their own.

The Communist World in General

There is no longer a Communist bloc taking its orders from Moscow, if there ever was, and we would do well to rid our thinking of this anachronism. We concluded that the Sino-Soviet dispute was fundamental in every sense—concerned with ideology, power, the organization of decision-making, strategy toward the in-between world, and grand strategy toward the West. Even if China and the Soviet Union re-establish friendly relations, they will never be the same as they once were. This is also true of Moscow's relations with the other Communist powers to a greater or less degree. Moscow's Eastern European allies have been demonstrating increasing independence in all spheres, although they have the example of the Soviet move into Czechoslovakia as an illustration of just how far that independence will be allowed to go. Nevertheless, the Eastern European Communist states can no longer be called "satellites." In any case, it would be the height of foolishness for the United States to attempt to play on the differences in the Communist world—either the Sino-Soviet dispute or the relations between the Warsaw Pact countries. In the latter case, indeed, considering the lingering trauma of the devastation Germany wreaked on the Soviet Union in World War II, it probably serves our national interest that the Soviets feel that the Eastern European countries are trustworthy allies in the face of a threat from Germany. But no real threat can now be seen anywhere on the horizon. The Eastern European countries desperately want access to Western and American technology, research, and trade as a boost to their own development, and they want, therefore, an improvement in relations. We can welcome and encourage this, but only so long as we refrain from any policy or action that could make Moscow suspicious that our real intentions were to break down the tier of buffer states that stand between the Soviet Union and Western Europe.

Western Europe

Our major conclusion about Western Europe was that there, as in Eastern Europe, nationalism is no longer a force for changing the status quo but is itself the status quo. Especially as a referent for the integration of personality, nationalism seems destined to remain a fundamental part of the political landscape. But in the European Economic Community, we did see arising something entirely new in the world—a "curious creature" that was a more or

less integrated regional association performing some of the functions of a superstate while the constituent nation-states continue
to operate in certain spheres. No harm seems to lurk in this development for the interests of the United States, but considerable possible benefit. Further integration enhances European security, for one thing, and the fact that a truly united Europe has
the potential of being a third superpower of this peculiar nature
should be no cause for alarm. If anything, a strong, united Europe is most likely to be a force for peace and stability. A united
Europe also permits steps to be taken to ensure economic prosperity not just for Europe, but for us all. It can be especially important in reforming the antiquated international monetary system. For all these reasons, encouragement of the integration of
Europe should be the keystone of United States policy.

The issue of the division of Germany and Berlin into Eastern
and Western halves was once regarded as an obstacle so formidable that until it was solved no progress could be made toward
normalizing East-West relations. In fact, the opposite is true. The
more steps are taken toward normalizing East-West relations,
the easier the problem of a divided Germany and Berlin becomes. Like Taiwan, this issue should be put at the bottom of the
agenda, not the top. West Germany's *Ostpolitik* has gone far to
ease the situation, and as other tensions ease around the world,
it becomes increasingly likely that the parties most directly concerned can work out a mutually satisfactory arrangement almost
entirely on their own.

The Developed Pacific—Japan, Australia, and New Zealand

We concluded that for reasons of geography, distribution and
density of population, and dependence on markets and overseas raw materials, Japan would be reluctant to become involved in the nuclear power game, but would prefer to exercise
the influence appropriate to her great power position more
through political and economic means. It is presumably for these
reasons, among others, that Japan has chosen alliance with the
United States. Australia and New Zealand also feel the need of
close ties to the United States for security reasons. For our part,

considering these factors and the other trends and forces we have analyzed—especially those concerning China—the United States, in prudence, needs Japan, Australia, and New Zealand as much as they need us—as a hedge, if nothing else, in case our policy of normalizing relations with China and the Soviet Union is less successful than we would like. Economic relations, especially with Japan, are likely to be troublesome. But they are solvable, and however troublesome economic relations may be, close security ties are essential. Remembering the strength of nationalism, what we must particularly guard against in maintaining good relations with these countries is the kind of gratuitous insult that Mr. Nixon indulged in when he failed to consult with Japan prior to his China trip. In their alliance with the United States, the Japanese had put their fate to some extent in American hands, in that it was American hands that held the nuclear umbrella. Yet on a matter so central to their concern as China policy, the Japanese were not even consulted.

The Underdeveloped World in General

In the underdeveloped world, we found that the "future crouching in the present" was nationalism, modernization, and industrialization. But we also concluded that self-sustained growth was a myth and that attaining their goals would be extraordinarily difficult for most of the underdeveloped countries. In general, their endowment of natural resources is poor, the structure of their economies inappropriate, their population lacking in education or even literacy; the underdeveloped world is poor, sick, underfed, and malnourished, but at the same time its population is mushrooming and so magnifying the problem. We concluded that in many countries whose boundaries included diverse ethnic and cultural groups the question of *which* nationalism combined with all the other problems would lead to fantastic turmoil—to civil wars, attempts at secession, struggles between regions, *coups d'état*. Noting that it was this kind of instability that led President Johnson and Secretary of State Dean Rusk to make Vietnam an American war, we asked whether the Communists, Moscow, or Peking might be the benefactors of all this turbulence. We concluded that they would not, that again nationalism was the key, that the only countries in which the Communists had been successful in the past were those in which they had captured the leadership of nationalism, and that the time for this sort of opportunity had long passed. The wave of the future in the underdeveloped world, we decided, was neither communism nor some kind of Pax Americana, but a nationalist eclecticism that was peculiarly their own.

Although the trend toward ever-increasing affluence in the developed world coupled with the drive toward industrialization and modernization in the underdeveloped world threaten to exhaust the resources of the earth and gravely damage its ecology, the problems posed are not unsolvable, and we do not believe that either threat will reverse either the trend toward increasing affluence in the developed world or the drive toward industrialization and modernization in the underdeveloped world.

But one of the first things that leaps to the eye when these trends are considered together is the gap between the developed and underdeveloped countries, what has been called the "North-South" problem. Lenin's prediction that the rich countries would get richer and the poor countries would get poorer has come to pass only in rare cases. Most of the poor countries have in fact been getting richer. But the poor countries have been getting richer at a much slower rate than the rich countries, and the gap between them has tended to widen. As we saw, this widening gap became the central thesis of Chinese Communist strategy in the 1960s, as enunciated in Lin Piao's article described earlier that pictured the underdeveloped world encircling the developed world as the rural areas of China encircled the cities during the Communist revolution. The article was, in effect, a declaration of war in the name of the underdeveloped world against the developed world.

Certainly it cannot be said that the developed world has been unaware of the problem. Excluding military items, the United States has pursued an economic aid program since World War II that has totaled in the billions of dollars. Other countries have also had economic and developmental aid programs. Also, the United Nations called for the decade of the 1960s to be the "de-

velopmental decade" and urged each of the developed countries
to devote 1 per cent per year of its gross national product to foreign aid. Only Sweden responded with that degree of generosity, and the decade fell hopelessly short of the goals, although
some gains were made. But the mere fact that they agreed to the
calling of a development decade illustrates that the developed
countries were at least aware of the problem, aware that something had to be done.

This is not to say, however, that Lin Piao was right. In the first
place, modern international wars are not fought by the "have
not" nations, but by the "haves." War is a very expensive business, outrageously expensive. Guerrilla warfare is the only possible exception, and then only in terms of money rather than lives.
If the task is persuading a colonial or other occupying power that
continued occupation is simply not worth the cost, guerrilla warfare is frequently an effective instrument. But it is hardly appropriate to an international war of aggression.

Where Lin was unquestionably right was on the political level.
Unless the underdeveloped countries feel, first, that the developed world is playing fair in economic matters that affect the development of the underdeveloped world and, second, that some
progress is being made in development, then envy, tension, bitterness, and even hatred will mount. Even though the underdeveloped countries will be unable to use major warfare as the instrument of expressing their feelings, they will find ways of
making life difficult for the developed world politically, economically, diplomatically, and in other, ingenious if not diabolical
ways.

Finally, the most potent of the weapons at the disposal of the
underdeveloped world is probably none of these rather tangible
instruments of power but the guilt the developed world will inevitably feel about the width of the gap, about the human misery
and suffering in the underdeveloped countries, and about their
own sense of obligation to their fellow man.

The cynical may argue that however badly the developed
countries may feel, they will stop short of giving away capital to
the extent of 1 per cent of their GNP. The argument will be that
altruism goes only so far and that the major historical example of

a country giving aid at appropriately high levels was the American aid program at the height of the Cold War, when the inspiration came as much from fear of communism as from altruism.

There is, however, another side to the argument. The liberals in the American Congress, the most stalwart supporters of aid, have in recent years become increasingly disenchanted with the *form* of the aid program. Their reasons are three. The first is that liberal congressmen began to realize that capital input was only one part of successful economic development, and not necessarily the most important part. They began to understand what we spelled out above—that without good government, competent administration, adequate communications, adequate health programs, appropriate social attitudes, and all the rest, capital would be wasted at best and, at worst, go merely to line the pockets of corrupt politicians. The proponents of aid in Congress began to sense, without always realizing it in any articulated way, the truth in our conclusion that self-sustaining growth is a myth.

Second, the liberal congressmen increasingly came to agree with Senator J. William Fulbright, chairman of the Senate Foreign Relations Committee, that unilateral aid inevitably brought with it other, undesirable policies and that all aid should therefore be multilateral. They increasingly believed that unilateral aid could never escape being tied with political and military strings. The temptation was simply too great. No matter how good the intentions, unilateral aid became an instrument of foreign policy and in some ways actually helped to perpetuate the Cold War.

Finally, multilateral aid—aid given through international agencies—would ensure that *all* the developed countries would at least feel pressure to carry their share of the burden.

Parenthetically, it might be noted that our judgment about the relative importance of capital input is also supported by estimates that have been made about the capacity of the underdeveloped countries to *absorb* capital. A group of economists at the Center for International Studies at MIT, for example, estimated that the most capital the underdeveloped world could use effectively was 5.7 billion dollars per year.[1] The estimate of

[1] Max F. Millikan and Donald L. M. Blackmer, eds., *The Emerging Nations: Their Growth and United States Policy* (Boston, 1961), pp. 122, 156.

experts at the UN was $5.7 billion per year for the period 1962–71 and $4.7 billion per year for the period 1972–76.[2] As a measure of comparison, it might be noted that 1 per cent of the United States GNP is in the neighborhood of 10 billion dollars.

Beyond capital, the developed world can supply or co-operate in supplying a few other ingredients, some of which are important but none decisive to development. First, the developed and underdeveloped countries can combine to set up an organization to administer the aid program in a way that would minimize not only political strings but also local corruption. The groundwork for this has been laid in existing organizations— the World Health Organization, the Food and Agricultural Organization, the World Bank, and so on—but there is urgent need for an over-all co-ordinating and planning agency. Such an international organization will find itself in the very cockpit of international politics, much as the UN Secretariat found itself in the Congo crisis during the Katanga secession. But the need is crucial and can only be filled through machinery that is international. Presumably the organization can also be shielded from at least some of the political heat.

The developed and underdeveloped worlds could also combine to set up international research units or strengthen those that already exist on agriculture for the development of hybrids, fertilizers, pesticides, and all the rest; on health problems; on population controls; and on the myriad of other problems that stand in the way of development. It borders on criminal negligence that mankind left the most important work on development of the new rice and wheat hybrids to private philanthropic organizations; it simply cannot do so on the problems that face us now. An international research organization must also be created to concentrate on the problem of scarce resources, such as oil, and on the ecological consequences not only of all the new products, techniques, and methods that will come out of these new research efforts, but of existing practices as well.

The developed world can also supply certain kinds of expertise

[2] United Nations Department of Economic and Social Affairs, *The Capital Development Needs of Less Developed Countries: Report of the Secretary General* (United Nations, New York, 1962), pp. 12, 14.

for educational institutions and other activities similar to what the United States Peace Corps has attempted. Here again, however, it is essential that the corps of advisers and helpers should be *international*, not national, as the Peace Corps is. Proud though the Peace Corps is of its achievements and diligent though it has been in staying out of politics and the Cold War, it still has remained not just an object of genuine suspicion but a convenient target even when the government accusing it of misbehavior knew in its heart that the Peace Corps was innocent.

Finally, there is one other possibility, although as yet it remains only a possibility. Norman Macrae, deputy editor of the London *Economist*, argues that the technological revolution in computers is only just beginning and that its implications are staggering. One implication is for urbanization. In the not-too-distant future people with nonmanual jobs can live anywhere they want to and communicate with each other and central data banks by television phone rather than having to commute to a central city. Far more profound, in Macrae's opinion, will be the effect of the computer on education.[3] Computers could record and analyze feedback from the student and then use this information to tailor teaching to the individual child's learning patterns, turning the whole process of education into something quite different from anything ever imagined before. Norman Macrae is fascinated by the implications for the underdeveloped countries. "There have been two main difficulties here," he writes. "The first has been the inelasticity of supply even of ordinary education in poorer countries: especially while we have all laboured under the belief that we can instil the learning process even for literacy only over long years at school for small children taught in a labour-intensive way by scarce supplies of very skilled people . . . Secondly, it has become apparent that there is a special difficulty of communicating in these countries the more multi-layered sort of knowledge which is generally called knowhow, and which requires two-way involvement in a teaching process of trial and error and retrial."[4] Macrae believes that

[3] This view is elaborated in John Diebold, *Education, Technology and Business: A Case Study of Business in the Future—Problems and Opportunities* (New York: Praeger, 1971).
[4] "The Future of International Business," *The Economist* (January 22, 1972), pp. xii–xiii.

this computer-based revolution in education will make it possible in the next forty years for the rich one third of the world to concentrate more on the knowledge-creating and knowledge-processing industries, while more and more of the old manufacturing industries—*through the instrumentality of the multi-national corporation*—move to any parts of the poorer two thirds of the world that are politically stable. In a word, Macrae believes the computer may put industrialization of the underdeveloped world not only within reach but within easy reach.

There is extraordinary hopefulness in the notion that computers will revolutionize education in the underdeveloped world, as Macrae visualizes, and that multinational corporations will be able to make use of this development to transfer huge segments of the more ordinary and familiar manufacturing industries from the developed to the underdeveloped countries. There can be no doubt that technological developments will arise and that some of them will make the problem of development easier than it now appears to be. It may also well turn out that the bulk of this technological advance will lie in the field of computers. But one may be permitted considerable skepticism that even such marvelous inventions as these will greatly alter the conclusions we have reached above. Too many of the more formidable obstacles to development lie in the areas of social attitudes, the structure of societies, and the institutions of government and social life on which computers can have only an indirect effect.

Other Implications

What other implications are there here for U.S. foreign policy in the immediate future? First and foremost, Vietnam should have taught us to stay out of the civil wars, insurgencies, turmoil, and turbulence that will plague so much of the underdeveloped world in the decades that lie immediately ahead. There is still a role for the great powers in deterring international war, as we shall discuss later. But these essentially internal struggles, which are at bottom struggles over who shall have the power to determine the content of the local nationalisms—just what it means to be Vietnamese, or Nigerian, or Congolese, or Pakistani—these are none of our business. And the notion that Moscow or Peking can take control of these countries by fomenting trouble is nonsense. Even if they do succeed in taking advantage of the situation in one or another country, it will inevitably be an isolated incident, and we will still be better off by keeping out of such struggles. In the underdeveloped world the United States should maintain a low posture. American governmental agencies should be as inconspicuous as possible, and it would be well if American business would follow that example. We should do our utmost to understand and respect the new nationalism and be exquisitely sensitive to the pride and justified suspiciousness that accompany these new nationalisms. At the same time, we should do all in our power to help them develop, to have a true voice in world affairs, and to maintain their independence. Nationalism is the future in the underdeveloped lands of the world, and the United States should be unequivocally on the side of the future, not the past.

Africa

Africa south of the Sahara will probably be the last area of the world to which nationalism will come in full force, since tribalism remains so strong and since the boundaries of states follow the power balances established by European colonial conquests rather than tribal, ethnic, or other lines that might have helped to facilitate nationalism. The dream of a pan-African, all-black superstate will continue to occur to charismatic leaders, as it did to Kwame Nkrumah of Ghana, but it seems doomed, not only by tribalism and growing nationalism, but also by the different languages and the cultural and administrative legacies of colonialism.

The other problem specific to Africa south of the Sahara is, of course, the racism of white South Africa and Rhodesia, and their determination both to maintain segregation between whites and blacks and at the same time to make use of black labor as the foundation of their economies. Now that the *coup* in Portugal has brought a change in that country's policy toward Angola and Mozambique, South Africa and Rhodesia are the major vestiges of colonialism in Africa. Since we are skeptical of the rise of a pan-African nationalism, we must be equally skeptical of the possibility that the black African states will join in some grand coalition to wage a war of liberation against South Africa and Rhodesia on behalf of their oppressed fellow blacks. What the black, independent neighboring countries will undoubtedly do, as they have done in the past, is give sanctuary to guerrillas, and help them with equipment and supplies. The whites in Rhodesia and South Africa are badly outnumbered. What they have is the education, the training, the skills, the technology, the equipment—all of the elements of power to keep the blacks in subjugation except numbers. But sooner or later, the blacks will acquire what they now lack, and sooner or later there will come a reckoning. We can surely say of segregation and oppression of the blacks in these countries what Tocqueville said of slavery in the United States: "By the act of the master, or by the will of the slave, it will cease; and in either case great calamities may be expected to ensue." At the same time, we will take care to avoid the mistake that Tocqueville made in thinking that the final dénouement will come sooner rather than later. The forces of oppression are strong, stronger than some may think, and it may be several generations before the blacks in these countries achieve anything like substantial equality.

What is perhaps even more discouraging than this last pessimistic note is that there is not very much that the United States can do about it. We can take a stand against it; we can vote on the side of racial justice in the UN; we can legislate against investment by American firms in South Africa and trade with South Africa; we could join an economic boycott. But the history of such measures offers little hope that they will accomplish much of significance in changing such deeply ingrained attitudes as racism in South Africa.

The Middle East and North Africa

The countries of the Middle East and North Africa share most of the problems of the other underdeveloped countries of the world, but they have some peculiar problems—and one asset— of their own. The asset, of course, is oil. The problems are the genuine pull of pan-Arabism, the antagonism to Israel, and the fact that the Middle East has become an arena in the rivalry between the Soviet Union and the United States. United States policy over the years has generally been to support anti-Communist regimes—blowing not so much from hot to cold in this as from hot to warm. The second consistent thread has been a policy of trying to maintain friendly relations with both the Arab states and Israel in order to bring a settlement that would guarantee Israel's survival even if it were someday to find itself facing one gigantic Arab state rather than a bevy of smaller ones. The third consistent element of U.S. policy has been to try to maintain a rough military balance by selling arms to Israel whenever the Arab states obtained enough arms from the Soviet Union to threaten that balance seriously. Is there anything in the trends we have analyzed in this book that would indicate a change in this long-term policy?

Any judgment about pan-Arab nationalism is difficult. Egyptian nationalism is likely to succumb to the pull of pan-Arab nationalism only if Egypt could be the acknowledged leader. In Lebanon, a Lebanese nationalism; a "Little Syria" nationalism; a "Greater Syria" nationalism to include Iraq; and a pan-Arab nationalism seem to coexist with each other and a rather high degree of cosmopolitanism. Except for the cosmopolitanism, the situation in Syria itself is similar. In Iraq, a "fertile crescent" if not a "Greater Syrian" nationalism competes with the Iraqi and pan-Arab nationalisms. In Jordan, Saudi Arabia, Yemen, and Southern Yemen, the pull of pan-Arab nationalism is very strong; and in both Algeria and Libya, it has also been strong. Only in Morocco and Tunisia does the evidence of local nationalism—that is, of Moroccan and Tunisian nationalisms—seem at all persuasive. Throughout the Arab world, in sum, loyalties seem to be still rather fluid, the pull of pan-Arab nationalism is always present, but the inertia of statehood is also always there, and the incentives of the leadership strata are mixed. On balance, the best judgment seems to be that although Egypt, Tunisia, Morocco, and Lebanon are close to being proximate nation-states, the situation today is that all the Arab states should be regarded as ones in which there is a potential for the development of rival nationalism. Of course, the Arab countries may act in concert against Israel even though they do not coalesce into a pan-Arab superstate. They may also again act in concert in an oil boycott against countries sympathetic to Israel, as they did in 1973. The oil boycott hurt the Western world, especially Japan and Western Europe, and many countries will undoubtedly trim their policies accordingly. But the crucial support for Israel is American, and the United States can find ways to lessen the impact of a boycott both through developing alternative sources and through shifting to a technology less dependent on oil, which is desirable for a host of other reasons as well. The Arab success in the 1973 war marks the end of the easy assumption that Israel cannot be defeated militarily, but defeat is a long way from total destruction. That could happen only if the United States abandoned Israel entirely, which would require an extraordinary set of circumstances indeed. On balance, it is difficult to visualize events inside the Middle East that would put the continued existence of Israel in jeopardy.

But it is not difficult to visualize developments *outside* the Middle East that could put the existence of Israel in jeopardy —mainly, a decision in Moscow to intervene with Soviet troops. In our analysis of the Soviets, we concluded that they were turning away from power and prestige values, the implication being that direct intervention in the Middle East is not a very likely policy for them to adopt. So far in the Middle East, Soviet motives seem to have been more "Russian" than "Communist." A Czar could easily have played the same game in the Middle East that the Soviets have been playing. They have supported the Arab states politically and with an impressive program of arms aid. Yet they have been sensitive to the possibility of the situation getting out of hand and have attempted to keep events under control with a commendable sense of responsibility. If their goal has been to attain a permanent place of influence in the Middle East, they have clearly succeeded. In the circumstances, there seems to be much wisdom in the past United States policy of trying to maintain friendly relations with both sides to help in bringing about a permanent solution that would guarantee the survival of Israel coupled with maintaining the military balance, grudgingly and parsimoniously, perhaps, but doing it nevertheless.

It has been argued that neither side is above criticism in the Middle East, that the Israeli position has not always been as flexible as it might have been, and that the United States ought to use whatever influence it has with Israel somewhat more vigorously. There is undoubtedly some truth to this argument. What is also true is that the 1973 war created the best opportunity for a permanent Middle East settlement yet seen. The Arabs achieved enough success to restore their pride, yet not enough to lead their more sober leaders to believe that it is realistic to hope for the kind of victory that would eliminate the Jewish state. This is the stuff of which permanent peace can be made. For the United States, the most promising strategy is to link the Middle East more closely with the over-all effort to achieve détente with the Soviet Union and a peace that is truly worldwide.

Latin America

Latin America is in general terms farthest along toward development of all the areas that we think of as underdeveloped. This means that it has all of the problems of the underdeveloped world plaguing one or another part of Latin America. Second, it means that the "demonstration factor" is hard at work. The "demonstration factor" was a phrase coined to describe the historical fact that political and social upheaval is more likely to occur when a "have not" country or region of a country is close enough to a "have" country or region for the "have nots" to see what they are really missing. The same notion is contained in the phrase, "the revolution of rising expectations." The people of northeastern Brazil can see how much worse off they are than others in Brazil, and their resentment grows. The people of Bolivia can see how much worse off they are than the people of Argentina, and their resentment grows. The people of *all* of Latin America can see how much worse off they are than the Americans, and their resentment not only grows but balloons. This last resentment, anti-Americanism, has been infinitely exasperated by U.S. interventions in Latin American affairs in the past, by the economic exploitation of Latin America by U.S. business interests, and by the just plain awesome power of the "colossus of the North." A few statistics will illustrate the dominant position that American-owned business occupies in Latin America. The sales of U.S.-controlled oil and minerals in Latin America, for example, during the 1960s were $5 billion a year and constituted more than 5 per cent of the gross domestic product of the area and obviously a very much larger percentage of the total oil and mineral output. In manufacturing, American-controlled businesses in Latin America were responsible for one sixth of the total, concentrated in automobiles, chemicals, and machinery. "Even where the concentration is not very great in relation to local industry, as in food products," one observer writes, "the most prominent trademarks and brands tend to be those of the U.S.-controlled enterprise."[5] If all this did not create resentment enough, by 1968 *exports* of manufactured goods by U.S.-controlled enterprises had come to represent more than 40 per cent of all Latin American exports.

Throughout its history, much of Latin America has been ruled by a European-descended oligarchy that kept the Indian, the black, and the mestizo populations down and oppressed. For political, strategic, and economic reasons, the major U.S. interest in Latin America has been in stability—especially political stability—and its natural allies have more often than not been these same elitist oligarchs. There have been times, of course, when the United States has made an effort to change this general theme in its policy. President Roosevelt's "good neighbor" policy was a shift away from doctrines of open intervention by force. President Kennedy's "Alliance for Progress" was an attempt to force social revolution in Latin America by denying aid to any country that did not come forth with economic plans for development that would break the pattern of oligarchic control. Neither policy, however, was pursued consistently and vigorously enough by succeeding administrations to overcome the accumulated resentment. If our analysis of the forces shaping the future

[5] The quotation and figures both come from Raymond Vernon, *Sovereignty at Bay* (New York: Basic Books, 1971), pp. 24 and 102.

in the underdeveloped countries has any validity at all, the need for drastic change in the Latin American policy of the United States is as obvious as it is urgent.

Southeast Asia and Vietnam

Vietnam, former French Indochina (including Laos and Cambodia), and Southeast Asia in general constitute a perfect illustration of the profound differences in policy that can result from understanding the basic forces we have been examining in this book, misunderstanding them completely, or understanding them only partially. What is more, how the problem of Vietnam, Laos, Cambodia, and the rest of Southeast Asia is finally settled will also have a determining influence on events throughout Asia for at least the rest of this century.

We have said repeatedly that the fundamental driving force behind political events in Asia, including Southeast Asia, these past few years and into the future is nationalism and a desire for modernization and industrialization. We have also said that President Johnson and Secretary Rusk thought of Vietnam as a simple Communist aggression, when in fact it was an anticolonialist, nationalist movement, feeding on social discontent in the South, such as the need for land reform, whose leaders just happened to be members of the Communist party. We have said that making Vietnam an American war was not only a mistake, but a failure, that the American military effort was efficient but inappropriate to the political goal it was assigned, that of destroying communism as a political force in South Vietnam, especially since communism had become identified with nationalism. American policy in Vietnam and former French Indochina changed as the American leaders' understanding of these basic forces changed—but unfortunately understanding did not always improve but sometimes became worse.

President Roosevelt was convinced that colonialism should be eliminated from the world, and he understood something of the potency of the new nationalisms. As World War II drew to a close, the United States supported Vietnamese demands for independence.

Tragically, however, Vietnam got caught up in the Cold War between the two superpowers. Although the United States under President Truman continued to support the idea of independence for Vietnam, the United States gradually turned away from the notion of a compromise that would permit Communist participation in an independent government and eventually came to find itself carrying the principal financial burden of the French military effort.

Under the Eisenhower administration, the French suffered their final defeat at Dienbienphu. The 1954 accords negotiated at Geneva split Vietnam in half, provided for elections two years later, and also provided for the United States to furnish a military aid mission to South Vietnam to train its Army. With American support, President Ngo Dinh Diem subsequently announced that he would not co-operate in holding elections, giving as his reason the fact that the Communist side would not permit free speech and campaigning in the North, which were essentials for a free and fair election.

The Eisenhower policy was to give the South Vietnamese aid and to provide them with American advisers, who numbered about a thousand at the end of the Eisenhower administration.

Following Mao's "East Wind Prevails Over West Wind" speech in November 1957, guerrilla warfare in South Vietnam began in earnest. In the fall of 1961, when President Kennedy was in office, Diem called for help. Kennedy sent a mission to Vietnam, and even though he refused their recommendation for American combat forces, he increased both American aid and the number of American advisers. By 1963, when he was killed, the advisers numbered 16,500.

President Kennedy's policy toward Southeast Asia and Vietnam actually went through three stages, as his understanding of the forces operating there increased and as the situation changed. The first stage concerned Laos, rather than Vietnam, and Kennedy was something of a hawk. President Eisenhower in briefing his successor had said that Kennedy might well find it necessary to send American troops to Laos to fight, and that he, Eisenhower, would support him in that decision. Only two months later, Kennedy appeared before the TV cameras in a press conference and issued a solemn warning calling for a neutralized Laos and hinting at harsh reprisals if the Communist side did not co-operate. This was Phase I of Kennedy's policy.

Shortly thereafter, Kennedy suffered the setback of the Bay of Pigs fiasco in Cuba. He said that he learned two lessons from that debacle. The first was not to trust experts, whether they be generals or CIA officials. The second was, as he said, that the American people did not want a military solution to such problems. "The American people do not want me to use troops to remove a Communist regime only ninety miles from our coast," he remarked. "How can I ask them to do the same thing nine thousand miles away?"

Phase II of Kennedy's policy was in two parts. The first concerned Laos, which was in a crisis situation. His solution was to negotiate a neutralized Laos under a coalition government. The second concerned Vietnam. There was no neutralist faction on which to rest a negotiated settlement, as in Laos. But President Kennedy, too, was coming to appreciate the potency of nationalism. If nationalism was the root force behind the struggle in Vietnam, it followed that Americans, with their foreign faces, should never be sent there. It also followed that bombing and other purely military measures would inevitably fail. Killing would only turn the population against the government. President Kennedy and his advisers therefore devised a three-part strategy, which they recommended to the South Vietnamese:

1. Protect the people—don't chase Viet Cong; the struggle is political, not military.
2. Win the people—by means of land reform and other measures correct social injustice and remove the resentment on which the Viet Cong so successfully played.
3. Arm the people—once the people's loyalty has been won and their faith in the government's determination to protect them established, the people can be trusted to deal with the guerrillas themselves.

The fundamental point to the policy advice offered by the Kennedy administration was that the Americans could do no more than advise. "It is their war—the South Vietnamese," President Kennedy said. "We can give them aid; we can even send advisers. But they must win it or lose it."

The South Vietnamese, under President Ngo Dinh Diem, never accepted the advice. They took some of the slogans—like "winning the people" and "local reforms"—but none of the real substance.

Then came the Buddhist crisis that pitted the Catholic President Diem and a largely Catholic elite against a largely Buddhist peasantry, and President Kennedy became increasingly skeptical that Diem's government had the wisdom or capacity to cope with the insurgency. President Kennedy felt that if this skepticism turned out to be correct, he could not and would not escalate the struggle. Rather than bomb North Vietnam or send American ground troops, he was determined to negotiate a neutralized Vietnam as he had negotiated a neutralized Laos.

Within weeks of President Kennedy's assassination, it became clear that President Johnson did *not* understand the potency of nationalism in Southeast Asia, that he was not willing to accept a negotiated settlement in Vietnam, and that rather than do so he would escalate the war and turn it into an American affair. This he did in the spring of 1965.

When Mr. Nixon became President, he recognized that almost all Americans—both hawks and doves—wanted to see an end to American involvement in the Vietnam war. Thus Mr. Nixon was inspired more by his understanding of the mood of the American people than by his understanding of nationalism and the other forces operating in Southeast Asia. Mr. Nixon's policy response to this desire was "Vietnamization."

Vietnamization was a plan not so much to end the war as to turn it over to the Vietnamese. The Vietnamese Army was greatly enlarged and modernized. Eventually, an agreement was reached with the Communist side in Paris for a cease-fire, for the withdrawal of American troops, for an end to American bombing, and for a return of American POWs. Unlike the Laos agreements of 1962, however, the Paris agreements of 1973 did not provide for a coalition government or for any procedure or method by which a *political* settlement could be reached. What is worse, it provided that both sides could be resupplied with any equipment or supplies that were used up, worn out, or destroyed. Thus the most likely prospect was for fighting to continue in all of the countries of former French Indochina, although perhaps intermittently rather than steadily and on a reduced scale. Nothing was really settled, and the period was prolonged when events might get out of hand, tempting still another intervention by a great power, non-Communist or Communist.

On the other hand, if our analysis here of the more basic forces is correct, an alternative to Nixon's plan should have been available. We have decided that nationalism is more important in the underdeveloped countries—and that would include North Vietnam—than any other political force, including ideology. We have also concluded that the Communist world has long since ceased to be monolithic, with the implication that North Vietnam will pursue independent, *nationalist* policies rather than submit to the domination of either the Soviet Union or China. One would therefore expect them to be interested in a different kind of agreement, one that would be more likely to exclude the great powers, both Communist and non-Communist, rather than prolong the period in which further intervention might occur.

What is interesting is that the evidence available indicates that the Communist side did in fact have some such solution in mind. From 1968 through 1972, in various public and private statements, the Communist side suggested a six-point settlement: (1) a negotiated settlement providing for the neutralization of Vietnam based on a coalition government; (2) a cease-fire followed by a phased withdrawal of American troops; (3) the return of American and Vietnamese POWs; (4) postponement of the reunification of Vietnam for a period of from five to ten years; (5) international guarantees of the territorial integrity of Laos and Cambodia; and (6) some sort of international inspection machinery. In other words, the Vietnamese Communist side seemed to be offering a settlement very much like that agreed to in Laos in 1962 (which was aborted by the continued fighting in Vietnam) with the additional suggestion or at least implication of the neutralization of all of Southeast Asia.

The only explanation of why the Communist side seemed to be interested in this package during those years that fits the facts of what they did and said is that they were motivated by a desire to maintain their independence of all the great powers, including their own awesome neighbor China, more than by any ideological affinities.

Mr. Nixon's policy, which permitted the withdrawal of American troops and the return of the POWs, was clearly more closely attuned to the forces we have identified in the underdeveloped world than Mr. Johnson's policy of making Vietnam not only a war but an American war. But if our analysis of the forces operating in these countries is accurate, Mr. Nixon's policy still fell short of fully adapting to those forces or of taking advantage of the opportunities they presented. What Mr. Nixon let slip was an opportunity for an old-fashioned political deal based on the interests of the countries concerned and the deeper forces operating on them—a deal that depended not on "trusting" the Communist side but on the imperatives of their own self-interest. The Soviet Union indicated that it preferred a neutralized Southeast Asia to one dominated by Communist China. Hanoi indicated that it, too, preferred a neutralized Southeast Asia to one dominated by China. Certainly the United States should also have agreed that its interest would be better served by a neutralized Southeast Asia than either one dominated by China or one continuing to be dangerously unstable by protracted war, even if the war was at a lowered intensity. Paradoxically, there is reason to believe that China itself might have—in this period following the Cultural Revolution—also preferred a neutralized Southeast Asia to what they got, a Southeast Asia in which fighting continued. Mr. Nixon turned his back on the notion of a coalition government and a neutralized Vietnam for fear that the Communists might in the end win the political struggle for control that would then ensue. Yet if our analysis is correct, even if the Communist side did eventually come to control South Vietnam, it would still maintain its independence from either Moscow or Peking. The question is: In any cost-effectiveness analysis conducted in 1968, when the suggestion was first discussed by W. Averell Harriman in Paris, would not American interests have been better served by this kind of deal, which promised to neutralize Southeast Asia, than by four more years of war? Or, to put the question to more recent events, would not this kind of deal, which promised to neutralize Southeast Asia, have better served American interests than the Kissinger agreements, which seemed to promise continued warfare, even if it was warfare from which American ground forces had been withdrawn?

Economic and Financial Policy

The analysis here has focused more on the political than economic, fiscal, and international financial problems facing the world. Still, a few implications suggest themselves. It is clear from our examination of the growing shortage of resources, such as oil, and the impact of technology on the environment, for example, that the problem is global. The use of persistent pesticides, such as DDT, has worldwide consequences. Maintaining the balance of oxygen in the atmosphere, dust and other particulates from industry, the presence of mercury and lead in waste that finds its way into the oceans—all have global implications. The North-South problem, too, illustrates the interconnections between the economies of all the countries of the world. As we concluded, the trend is toward more specialization, in any case, and it seems most likely that in some of the underdeveloped countries industrialization will necessarily be through even more specialization. All this will mean even greater interconnections among the economies of the world.

If the economies are to be more closely interconnected, then new international monetary machinery must be invented. The economic history of the period following World War II is filled with economic troubles that can be directly attributable to the inadequacies of the international monetary system. The unhappy experiences the American dollar underwent in the early 1970s is only one of the more recent examples.

A solution to both the North-South problem, in sum, and to some of the economic troubles of the developed countries—fiscal instabilities and cycles of business ups and downs—both seem to depend on a worldwide approach to economic planning.

Military and Defense Policy

In our study of war, we concluded that war is part of the future, that it is endemic to state systems, and that there is no evidence that the state system will soon be replaced by something like a world state. As for nuclear war, we concluded that the leaders of the great powers must assume that any nuclear war will result in 50 per cent casualties, no matter who initiates the war, and that nuclear war could not be a rational instrument of policy. Yet we also concluded that conventional wars would occur, which carry with them an intrinsic risk of escalation, and that the great powers would undoubtedly on occasion take actions that run the risk of escalating into something greater than was intended. From this we concluded that mankind must assume that nuclear war, too, is part of the future. If these conclusions are correct, what are their implications for military and defense policy, especially when they are placed alongside our other conclusions about developments in the Soviet Union, the underdeveloped world, and all the rest?

What kind of army will be prudent for the different countries to maintain in the world we foresee? For small- or medium-size powers with big neighbors, the implication seems to be that there is little point in having armed services any larger than those needed to maintain internal order. There was a time when a Switzerland, a Belgium, a Netherlands, a Denmark, or a Sweden might hope to maintain armed forces sufficiently large and powerful at least to give a great power enough trouble to deter it from attacking except when the country's territory was absolutely vital to the great power's strategic plans. That time is past. The only feasible deterrent for such a small- or medium-size power lies not in armaments but in politics and diplomacy.

For a small power surrounded by small powers, as for example many of the countries of Africa, somewhat larger conventional forces might seem desirable in certain circumstances. But here again, the deterrents of politics and diplomacy still seem to make more sense.

For an Israel, of course, the circumstances are very special indeed. Israel is not just a small country, but it is surrounded completely by a coalition of very hostile small- and medium-size powers. In these circumstances, a powerful argument can be made for as large a conventional army as Israel can field backed up by keeping alive at least the possibility that in an emergency it could produce a nuclear weapon on short notice.

For the great powers that are less than superpowers—countries like France, Great Britain, Germany, Japan, and China—the problem becomes considerably more complicated. In truth, there are probably only three options.

One is the option argued by De Gaulle and France: Maintain a conventional army large enough to compel an aggressor to be forced to use nuclear weapons; and build a nuclear deterrent which, although small, is enough to "tear an arm off" any aggressor and hence give him pause. France has chosen this option, as we said, and so has China—although China may regard her action more as a first step toward true superpower status than as a permanent defense posture. The argument against this option is that it is very expensive for a country of such size and, second, that in time of extraordinarily great crisis—which is the only time anyone would think of using nuclear weapons—a modest nuclear capability might be more of a provocation than a deterrent.

The second option is to ally oneself with a superpower on the assumption that *his* nuclear umbrella is large enough to cover you both and that he will use it if it becomes necessary. Both West Germany and Japan have for the moment found this the preferable arrangement. The argument against this option is that putting yourself under the protection of one of the superpowers places at least some limitations on your own freedom of action; and second, the doubt always lingers as to whether if the crunch comes a United States, for example, will risk trading a New York for a Hamburg or a Detroit for a Yokohama.

The third option is a modification of the policy of a small- or medium-size power—to rely on politics and diplomacy as the deterrent to an enemy's use of nuclear weapons but to introduce a modification by maintaining a rather sizable conventional force. In a sense, this is the course that India followed until 1974, although the size of her conventional force was probably determined more by her fear of Pakistan than by her fear of either the Soviet Union or China.

Which option is best for a particular country, of course, depends on its own peculiar circumstances. It also depends upon the climate of international politics at the time. In any case, however, the first option—that of maintaining both conventional forces and a modest nuclear capability—seems to make the least sense of all. In the height of a Cold War, a France can be confident that an American nuclear force would be used if France were attacked. It would be too risky for the United States to do otherwise. In a climate of détente, on the other hand, France can be equally sure that no one will want to attack her. Of the other two options, the first has all the advantages of economy and most of those of security and seems the wisest course of all if geography and the political climate will permit it. It is the course which good fortune in both have made possible so far for Japan.

What are the options of a superpower? Most particularly, what are the options of a superpower when there are just two of them?

On the conventional level, it seems less and less likely that the superpowers will be called upon to play any very major role. Our conclusions are that most violence will be internal—attempts at secession, civil wars, struggles between rival nationalisms within a single state, *coups*, and such like, with an occasional conventional war between smaller or medium-size powers that is likely to be limited, short, sharp, and very susceptible to mediation and limitation by the superpowers. For the foreseeable occasions on which the superpowers might find use for conventional forces, in other words, rather small, light-to-medium airborne ground forces, the air and sea lift to transport them rapidly, and the tactical air forces to support them would seem to be more than adequate.

On the nuclear level, the option of the small power—maintaining an army for internal security only and relying on politics and diplomacy for the rest—seems hopelessly Utopian for either superpower in the light of our conclusions about the unlikelihood of world government or effective arms control. If this is correct, then two options remain.

One option is to arm against every foreseeable contingency— on the nuclear level to maintain fixed, hardened, land-based ICBMs; mobile intermediate-range submarine-based missiles; and a sophisticated manned bomber force, combined with an ABM system if it can be developed and civil defense measures to include fallout protection. This has been the goal of both of the superpowers throughout the Cold War, although neither has fully attained it.

The second option is to maintain a minimum nuclear deterrent. This minimum deterrent would rely primarily on submarine-based missiles. They are mobile, they have an incredible capacity for keeping concealed, and in case of war they tend to draw enemy fire *away* from the homeland and the centers of population.

In the light of our conclusions about the trends within the superpowers themselves, the change in values away from national power and prestige goals, and all the rest, on balance the weight of the argument seems to lie on the side of a minimum deterrent rather than a maximum one. If madmen, like Hitler and his gangsters, come to control one of the two superpowers, all bets are off. But if sane men continue to rule, a submarine-based deterrent, efficient and formidable as it is, should be more than sufficient.

A United States Policy for the Far Future

All this concerns the problems of today. United States foreign policy must also concern itself with the changing content of international politics. Beyond that, foreign policy must aim toward something more vital still: There must be some vision of the kind of world toward which both the United States and mankind might work—a goal that contains the promise of peace and dignity and happiness for all men, but that is not so Utopian as to be beyond the reach of practicalities. The changing content of international politics is the subject of the chapter that follows. The final chapter will then turn to the question of a possible goal.

The Changing Content of International Politics

WE HAVE concluded that affluence, growing egalitarianism, the development of subcultures, and other forces in the developed world would bring about fundamental changes in values. In terms of international politics, one of the most significant of these is our conviction that values associated with national power and prestige will become less prominent—that, in fact, it will be difficult for the leaders of the developed nations to justify such goals to their peoples. Paradoxically, we also decided that nationalism would continue to thrive in the developed countries, especially as referents in the integration of personality, and that it would be a central driving force behind a substantial proportion of the events occurring in the underdeveloped world. How can these seeming contradictions be reconciled, and what further implications do they hold?

One is that the lessening interest in power and prestige values in the developed countries juxtaposed to the overwhelming power of the nuclear weapons and the incredible speed and accuracy of intercontinental rockets means that the great powers will abjure wars of any kind as deliberate acts of policy directed against another great power or in circumstances that seem likely to affect the interests of another great power. In a nuclear age, to quote a popular witticism of the Cuban missile crisis, nations make war like porcupines make love—carefully. If nuclear war comes between the great powers, it will come by accident or through essentially irrational mutual fears and a series of escalatory steps, each one of which seems harmless and reasonable to reasonable men. But nuclear war between the great powers will not come by design.

These probabilities combined with the growing power of nationalism in the world have still another implication. This is that new empires seem clearly to be impossible. Some existing empires may hang on for a time, like Portugal's African empire did, although doomed eventually. A very few might actually hold together indefinitely, especially those "empires" that are made up of a group of geographically contiguous nationalities, such as Yugoslavia, the Soviet Union, and India. But the forces of nationalism will resist any attempt at the creation of a new empire, and the risks in attempting to create one of frightening the rest of the world into a coalition, resistance, enlarged war, and an escalation into nuclear war are simply too great.

It also seems likely that spheres of influence will also become a thing of the past. Most countries of the underdeveloped world, ruled by nationalism, are fiercely determined to be masters of their own fate. This will make them want to have relations with whomever they choose, and the vastly improved technology of communications will make it possible. The only sphere of influence, as distinguished from alliance, that seems likely to survive for a time is probably in Eastern Europe. The fear in both the Soviet Union and the Eastern European countries of a revival of German militarism left over from World War II seems likely to preserve their political and strategic ties for perhaps several more decades.

Another time-honored concept of international politics that seems likely to become increasingly anachronistic is the traditional balance of power. Although the idea may hang on for a time, the balance of power seems likely to be increasingly outmoded as a description of international politics, as an analytical tool, and as a strategy of foreign policy. The balance of power is already irrelevant to small- and medium-size powers, as we have seen. Eventually, it will also become irrelevant for the superpowers as well.

Rivalries sparked by empire, by spheres of influence, and by shifts in the balance of power have all been among the causes of war in the past. Other issues that have led to war also seem to be disappearing. Religion has become increasingly depoliticized, beginning with the sixteenth century, although it lingers on in Northern Ireland, the Indian subcontinent, and a few other places. In our analysis of the developed world, both non-Communist and Communist (which as a practical matter here means the Soviet Union) we also concluded that ideology is becoming less important and that the likelihood of a major power embarking on an ideological crusade is also remote. Communist China, too, seems to be placing internal development higher on its list of priorities than proselyting its particular ideological convictions, and in any case China will be in no position to launch on a major aggressive war even if it wanted to, although China would be formidable indeed in a defensive war.

Marx to the contrary notwithstanding, few modern wars have their first causes in economic considerations; and, given their probable destructiveness, future wars are even less likely to be brought about by economic drives. Most of the traditional causes of war, in sum, and hence much of the traditional content of international politics, seem likely to be much less significant in the future than they have in the past.

But this conclusion that the older rivalries are unlikely to lead to war does not mean that the world will lack for the fuel of disagreement and dispute, or even that some of the older issues will not make their contribution to the tensions. Economic considerations in particular seem likely to loom large among the issues of international politics in the future, even if they seem unlikely to be a cause of war. In the highly developed technologies, sub-stitutes can be found for almost everything, but access to certain raw materials is still important. We have seen a hint of what would happen to Western Europe and Japan if they were denied access to the oil of the Middle East, in the boycott of 1973–74. Both the Soviet Union and the United States must inevitably consider the strategic importance of oil as they calculate their policy moves in the Middle East. Though none are quite so dramatic as Middle Eastern oil, other raw materials are not unimportant—tungsten, tin, aluminum ore, soy beans, and all the rest. Markets for their own surplus goods enter the policy-making calculations of states at least to some degree, and so do monetary and fiscal policies and the complex interconnec-tions of international finance.

The Multinational Corporation

A new phenomenon, the multinational corporation, suggests that some of the economic issues that will form a significant pro-portion of the content of international politics in the future will be entirely new.[1] A multinational corporation is one that is thought of as not just selling its product in more than one country, but one that manufactures in more than one country as well as obtaining raw materials, labor, and capital in more than one country. Perhaps even more important, it is thought of as be-ing *managed* as a worldwide business.

An idea of the rise of the multinational corporation can be gained from a few figures. Of the $3 trillion estimated world pro-duction, multinational firms account for $450 billion—15 per cent. It is estimated that by 1985 about 300 multinational cor-porations will produce over half of the world's goods and serv-ices.[2] A majority of the multinationals at present are American, but many are not, and the proportion of foreign multinationals is increasing. Unilever, Phillip (electrical equipment), British

[1] For the following I have drawn especially on Raymond Vernon, *Sovereignty at Bay: The Multinational Spread of U.S. Enterprises* (New York, 1971) and Harvey D. Shapiro, "The Multinationals: Giants Beyond Flag and Country," New York *Times Magazine* (March 18, 1973).
[2] Howard V. Permutter of the Wharton School as quoted by Shapiro, ibid., p. 20.

Petroleum, and Nestlé Alimentana are among the better known, but over 500 foreign companies have plants in the United States.

For a large company, going international makes good economic sense. When they have conquered the home market, foreign markets naturally beckon. Cheaper labor, nearness to raw materials, cheaper transportation costs from plant to market, and political considerations—foreign governments are more likely to welcome products made in their own country rather than imports—often lead companies to build their factories in the country where the goods will be sold.

In the case of Europeans investing in the United States, the attraction is the large market, and the successive devaluations of the dollar have made such investments even more attractive.

Nationalism, however, is affecting the multinational corporations as it is everything else. Traditionally, foreign investment in the underdeveloped countries has been in the extractive industries and other raw materials—oil, various minerals, tea, coffee, cotton, sugar, and similar products. Recently, investment has been in the more sophisticated industries—synthetic fibers, chemicals, and electronics. The future, however, looks different still. Many of the underdeveloped countries will no longer permit 100 per cent foreign ownership, and quite a few demand that majority ownership be in the hands of their own nationals. Capital, of course, is still important, but becoming increasingly important to the underdeveloped countries are technologies, the benefits of advanced research, management skills, and worldwide sales organizations. The most likely form of relationship between a multinational corporation and an underdeveloped country is likely to be the "management contract." The companies invest patents, know-how, technology, and management skills more than money. TWA, for example, had managed Ethiopian Airlines for many years, and in the early 1920s Goodyear agreed to operate two state-owned tire factories in Indonesia for a fee based on sales and profits.

Many observers see the multinational corporation as the wave of the future. Worldwide markets permit the economies of scale; financing is easier for a giant; and only a giant can command the kind of money that is needed for many kinds of modern research. IBM, for example, is reported to have spent $5 billion developing its "360" series of computers.

The multinational company has a number of what also might be called social contributions that it can make. Increasingly, multinational firms are multinational in personnel—management personnel included—as well as in operations. It was suggested by Carl A. Gerstacker, chairman of Dow Chemical, for example, that they would be better called "*a*national" companies—companies with no nationality at all. Another social contribution is that the multinational companies undoubtedly do speed up the process of development in many of the less developed countries by bringing in advanced technology and management techniques. It has also been argued that the final result is egalitarianism. Multinational companies will tend to move to places where land and labor are cheap. This will raise standards of living in those places, and the economies of all parts of the world will tend more and more to be tied together.[3] Of one thing, however, there can be no doubt. The multinationals will have an impact on all the world's economies. For example, it seems very likely that normal, precautionary operations in shifting funds from less favorable currencies to more favorable currencies by the multinational companies exacerbated the position of the dollar in the three crises it went through beginning in 1971.

Raymond Vernon has pointed out that the "asymmetry" between the imperatives of the state and those of the multinational company are inherently in tension. The imperatives of the multinational corporation are a free flow of goods, capital, and even labor. The imperatives of the state, on the other hand, are those inherent in sovereignty—to have the power to control everything that takes place within its borders, and to the extent that its power will permit, all things abroad that affect it. If the state blocks the multinational corporation—or any foreign enterprise, for that matter—it magnifies its problems of keeping up with the world in research, in marketing, in management techniques, and all the rest. The multinational corporation today is subject to regulation

[3] There will also be a tendency for them to move to places where antipollution laws are less stringent, too, bringing egalitarianism in the curses of industrialization as well as the blessings.

by both its home government and the host government, but as Shapiro points out, the multinational corporations are tending to outgrow the traditional sources of countervailing pressure within a state—trade unions, consumer groups, and local and state governments. At the very least it can be said that many host governments fear the loss of technology, research, marketing, and other benefits that the multinational corporations bring and that this fear gives the companies a bargaining power that is sometimes most impressive. It seems clear, in sum, that at least a part of the new content of the international politics of the future will be regulating the multinationals.

"The basic asymmetry between multinational enterprises and national governments may be tolerable up to a point," writes Raymond Vernon, "but beyond that point there is a need to re-establish balance. When this occurs, the response is bound to have some of the elements of the world corporation concept: accountability to some body, charged with weighing the activities of the multinational enterprise against a set of social yardsticks that are multinational in scope."[4]

Affluence and Industrialization vs. Pollution

We have concluded that the trend toward increasing affluence in the developed countries and the drive toward industrialization in the underdeveloped countries are both likely to continue. We have also reached two other, conflicting conclusions. The first is that mankind is entering a period of crisis—in shortage of resources, of energy, of food, and in the pollution of air, water, soil, and ocean. The second is that solving these problems will require population control, recycling of materials, new agricultural techniques, and, most important, a complete redirection of the *kind* of technology on which we rely. What are the implications when these conflicting trends and forces interact?

In the case of population control, most governments of most countries will most probably come to see that it is in their own interest and in the interest of their people to curb population growth. Still, as we say, the world's population will probably

[4] *Sovereignty at Bay*, p. 284.

not stabilize until it has reached at least 7 billion and perhaps not until it reaches 14 billion. Each country, furthermore, will undoubtedly experiment with various methods, incentives, and inducements to limit family size. It also seems clear, finally, that some countries, for one reason or another, will be laggard in controlling their population or merely ineffective. In these cases, the problem of population growth may well become an issue in *international* politics as well as domestic.

As our study of pollution and ecology shows, another sore point between different countries is inevitably going to be the individual countries' policies on matters of environment that affect other countries and the world as a whole. We have used the example of DDT. Sri Lanka (formerly Ceylon) uses DDT against malarial mosquitoes, and for it to stop using it before some substitute can be found that is harmless to humans and other life will mean thousands of human deaths in Sri Lanka a year. Yet the DDT used in Sri Lanka makes its way into the fish that Americans, Japanese, Russians, and many others eat and that some people depend upon for the protein to sustain their very lives. The same is true for many other materials and practices. Mercury is another example we have mentioned. Oxygen is another. It is said that the United States uses up more of the oxygen in the atmosphere of the earth than the plants and vegetation within its borders return. Plastics polluting the oceans, oil spills, and an unknown number of other substances and practices by one country are hurting other countries in similar ways.

Recycling and a change in the kind of technology will cause painful readjustments. Sulphur, for example, is a prize candidate for recycling, but one of the costs will clearly be a drastic reduction in the existing sulphur industry. A change in the kind of technology on which we rely will also be painful. Many existing businesses will have to cease operations—although many new businesses will also undoubtedly be created. Such a shifting of industry will also clearly have political repercussions, both in domestic and international politics.

Barry Commoner has attempted to estimate the cost of converting the American economy to ecologically sound industry.[5] He estimates, first, that the total capital equipment of the United States in 1958 dollars is $2.4 trillion, and second, that one fourth—$600 billion—would have to be replaced as damaging to the ecology. He argues that this is feasible on the grounds that private investors spent $1 trillion for capital equipment in the period from 1946 to 1968.

In addition, the over-all result is probably that the rates of growth for the developed countries will end up being considerably slower than those we projected, and the time of such changes as the establishment of a birthright income will be postponed. What we have foreseen for the developed world will probably still come to pass, but if the ecological problems are taken as seriously as they should be taken, the changes will come later rather than sooner.

However, we see no great harm in that postponement. Political repercussions come when economies go downhill, not when they go uphill more slowly than they might have done. Paradoxically, a slowdown in the rate of growth of the developed countries may actually have some positive benefits, for it will give the underdeveloped countries an opportunity to make progress at closing the gap and thus lessen the tension between the developed and underdeveloped worlds.

What hurts, of course, is that the underdeveloped countries will also have to pay a price for a clean planet in terms of their own goals of industrialization and modernization. To the extent that nonpolluting technologies are more costly, their industrialization will also be slowed. However, the effect may sometimes be beneficial. The bombing in World War II so damaged Japan's textile industry that it had to start virtually from scratch after the war. Naturally, they put in the very latest types of equipment, which gave them a cost and trade advantage that was one of the major bases of their truly fantastic postwar prosperity.

One other effect of the trends toward affluence and industrialization and the need for nonpolluting technologies may also be a much higher degree of economic specialization throughout

[5] *The Closing Circle: Nature, Man, and Technology* (New York, 1971), pp. 284–85.

the world. If we turn from producing synthetic rubber automobile tires, which pollute, for example, to producing nonpolluting natural rubber tires, it might be better for Malaysia not only to grow the rubber, but to build tire-making factories, rather than something like a steel industry, and trade in the finished product. If we drop polluting detergents and go back to soap, countries producing palm oil ought to build the soap-making factories as well.

The interaction of growing affluence and industrialization on the one hand and a crisis in resources and pollution on the other has at least one other implication. We have said that the interaction is likely to bring about a higher level of specialization. Specialization will also mean a higher level of economic interdependence. Much interdependence already exists, although the really giant economies like those of the United States and the Soviet Union are less dependent on foreign goods than many suppose. The point, however, is that avoiding pollution of the planet will have something like the same effect, that of increasing economic—and other—interdependence. Mercury dumped into an American river finds its way into fish eaten by Japanese and Russians—and the other way around. In this way, too, what each country does or does not do about pollution and the destruction of the environment can become an international as well as a domestic issue.

Reason and persuasion between governments combined with domestic pressures from within the country engaged in harmful practices may bring about some of the necessary changes. The international treaty governing the taking of the northern fur seal that breeds on the Pribilof Islands off Alaska is a model of regulating the "harvesting" of wildlife in ways that preserve and even enhance a species' chances for survival. At the turn of the century, hunting by Russians, Americans, and Japanese pushed the species very close to extinction until the three, along with Canada, signed a treaty in 1911 providing for an annual take of seals at a rate that would permit a sustainable yield. Since then the fur seal has increased from near extinction to a population of over one million animals. There is no reason, as Raymond F. Dasmann says, that fur seals cannot go on forever to yield skins and other by-products for the use of man without any threat at all to the species itself.

But look at the case of whaling. Amazing though it may seem, the romanticized whale-hunting of the nineteenth century brought some species close to extinction. But it was the highly developed technology of contemporary times that put the whale in real jeopardy. Harpoon guns with exploding warheads replaced hand-thrown weapons. Modern, motor-powered factory ships replaced sailing vessels. Hunter-killer speedboats replaced hand-rowed dories. And within hours the factory ship could reduce a giant whale to its commercially valuable components. The catch of the blue whale, the world's largest mammal, exceeded the sustainable yield from 1930–31 until well into the 1960s. Finally, the few blue whales left in the oceans were given complete protection by an international agreement in 1964, and since then the blue whales have recovered slightly.

The fin whale was next, and by the late 1960s the total population was down to three thousand—nearing extinction. The humpback was small in numbers to begin with, and it, too, soon was threatened. Sei whales were next, and now they, too, are in some danger. Speculation in the whaling industry now centers on the possibility of concentrating on porpoises and dolphins.

In an attempt to save the whale, an international whaling commission was formed to regulate the activities of the various whaling nations and assign quotas that would permit the different whale populations to recover and maintain a sustainable yield. Political considerations, however, overruled scientific and biological factors, and the whaling industry continued to take more than sustainable yields. The United States and certain other countries passed their own laws prohibiting their own nationals from engaging in whale hunting and prohibiting the importation of whale products in an effort to dry up the market. But Japan and the Soviet Union, the two major whaling nations, have so far been adamant in refusing to close down the whaling industry.

The shortsightedness of the Japanese and Soviet whaling industries has been pointed out by Georg Borgstrom. The great whales eat plankton and convert it to their own oil and meat. This is a much more efficient way of producing protein and fat for human use than most fishing. Consider the more usual food chain. Five hundred pounds of phytoplankton goes into producing 100 pounds of zooplankton. This yields 10 pounds of herring, which yields 1 pound of mackerel. If tuna eat the mackerel, the end result is that 500 pounds of phytoplankton have produced 1½ ounces of tuna. As Raymond F. Dasmann says, "We could be cultivating blue whales and their relatives as marine livestock equivalent to cattle on the land, and taking from them an annual sustainable crop. Instead we have treated them as we once did the American bison, and talk glibly about building plankton-harvesting devices that at their best would be less efficient than whales."[6]

What we have in the shortsightedness of the whaling industry is Garrett Hardin's "tragedy of the commons." If pasture land is a commons without regulation, then each individual has an incentive to increase his herd, for if he doesn't, someone else will. The result is that the pasture is overgrazed, and ruined for all.[7] The paradox is that even though the individual herdsman contributes to his own ruin through the ruin of the commons—just as the whaling industries of the Soviet Union and Japan are bringing about their own demise—it may be profitable to do so. Referring to the whaling industry specifically, Daniel Fife has pointed out that it still makes economic sense for the individual entrepreneur if he derives enough extra profit from his action, which is essentially irresponsible as far as society as a whole is concerned, to yield a return on investment elsewhere *for him* that outweighs the ultimate effect of killing off the whaling industry. Fife's argument is that it is profitable for an individual to kill the goose that lays the golden eggs so long as the goose lives long enough to pay for the purchase of a substitute money-maker.[8]

The Means and Instrumentalities of International Politics

The contents of international politics, to sum up the argument so far, will change. The traditional causes of disagreement will increasingly fade, but others will come forward to take their place,

[6] *Environmental Conservation* (New York, 1972), p. 321.
[7] "The Tragedy of the Commons," *Science*, Vol. 162 (December 13, 1961).
[8] "Killing the Goose," *Environment* (April 1971).

if not as causes of *war* at least as causes of *disagreement*. At the same time, war and military force, as we have said, are no longer rational instruments for achieving national goals. One implication of this is that the *means and instrumentalities* of international politics will undergo a change.

We have suggested that the awesome power of nuclear weapons and the incredible speed and accuracy of missiles were largely responsible for this change in the utility of military force, but in at least one part of the spectrum of political change, nationalism probably deserves a large share of the credit. Consider the Vietnam War. Most Americans—whether hawk or dove—now seem to regard the decisions in 1965 to make the struggle an American war by bombing North Vietnam and introducing American ground forces as a mistake. But what is particularly pertinent to our thesis here is that making Vietnam an American war was also a *failure*. It was not a failure in military terms. The American troops fought well, they were well led, and the logistics effort was superb, perhaps the most impressive in history. The Americans succeeded in destroying the main-force units of both the North Vietnamese and the Viet Cong. This is military success. But the purpose of military force is to accomplish political goals, and it is here that the American effort was a failure. Apologists of the Vietnam War point out that the goal set for the American military was modest and sharply limited. It was not the reunification of North and South Vietnam. It was to destroy communism as a political force in *South* Vietnam. The goal was political—as is all use of military force—and the failure was political.

Any analysis of why Vietnam was a failure must start with the nature of the struggle. President Johnson and Secretary of State Dean Rusk thought that Vietnam was a simple Communist aggression. But it was actually much more complicated than that. Fundamentally, it was an anticolonialist, *nationalist* movement, feeding on social discontent in the South, such as the need for land reform, whose leaders just happened to be—through a historical accident—members of the Communist party.

Hence the American failure. Against nationalism, outside military force is ineffective. Bombing merely unites a nationalistic people, as World War II illustrated. Furthermore, bombing can hardly be decisive against an underdeveloped country. Little is produced in North Vietnam that was used in the war in the South, except reinforced bicycles for transporting supplies, and the bicycle factories were in caves. The relevant supplies came from Eastern Europe, the Soviet Union, and China. They numbered no more than a thousand tons a day, and that much can be brought into South Vietnam by porters, reinforced bicycles, and trucks, and into North Vietnam by rail and road through China no matter how heavily the routes are bombed or how effectively the ports are blockaded.

On the ground, American troops, with their foreign faces, merely convinced the peasants that the Communist propaganda was right—that French colonialism was being repeated. The American troops fought well, but inevitably their presence recruited more Viet Cong than they could ever kill. Americans certainly should not find this difficult to understand. We have had trouble in Watts, in Newark, in Detroit, in Chicago, on innumerable campuses, and elsewhere. But what would the American people do if a President of the United States called in five hundred thousand *foreign* troops to put down riots in our cities? Most Americans—conservative or liberal, Republican or Democrat—would do what the Vietnamese peasant did. Most Americans would take up arms against the foreigner, no matter how they felt about the issue of the riots themselves.

Vietnam was not a nuclear war, but the use of military force was a failure. It was a failure because its use was inappropriate to the political goals being sought. "Military force can be used to kill an enemy and thus to stop him from hostile action," General Matthew B. Ridgway once remarked, "but the one thing it can never do is change his political convictions."[9] Nationalism is a political conviction—a very deeply held political conviction, much too deeply held to be changed by mere force.

Moral Suasion and Example

If military force will become less important as one of the means in international politics, what will become more important?

[9] Oral communication to the author.

One might hope that the role of moral suasion would be one of the means enhanced, and one might be rather confident that at least the role of example will be. Even the most cynical can think of examples when moral suasion has worked in the past. Adherence to the provisions against using poison gas in World War II might be an example, although true cynics might argue that the motive was fear of retaliation more than moral compunctions. On the other hand, even the most idealistic can think of examples where moral suasion had no effect at all—Hitler's attempted annihilation of the Jews, for example. To close the gap between the cynics and the idealists, one might alter the argument to say that *persuasion through the interconnection of interests* will be the means that has a larger role. All of the great powers and many of the intermediate and smaller powers have a variety of interests in different parts of the world. Truly outrageous policies on their part may sufficiently arouse the ire of other states to affect those interests and thus make the culprits more vulnerable to persuasion.

In the long run, and in a much more subtle fashion, the role of example may play an even greater role than persuasion in the function of bringing about social and political change. It is no accident that in the late 1930s and in the immediate postwar period, among the first things that visitors to the United States from the underdeveloped countries wanted to see was the Tennessee Valley Authority. The Tennessee Valley had suffered greatly from the shortsighted and ignorant methods of the early settlers and the farmers of the nineteenth century. The forests had been cut down, and with nothing to hold the topsoil, it washed away. Dust storms similar to those of the dust bowl were frequent. So were disastrous floods. The entire region was a blighted area.

Probably the most important innovation that TVA represented was putting a whole region under a single authority with responsibility for advancement in all fields of conservation and the development of resources. TVA built 20 dams, and when these were added to those already built, they made the Tennessee and its many tributaries one of the most completely controlled river systems in the world. On the main river are long dams creating a continuous chain of lakes; on the tributaries are high dams, creating great water reservoirs.

Thus the purposes that TVA serves are highly varied. It produces a fantastic amount of electrical power at low cost. This power provides for over 90 per cent of the farms in the area and some 148 municipalities. It is the source of power for some of the largest of America's chemical and fertilizer factories, of aluminum plants, and of the atomic energy facilities at Oak Ridge, Tennessee. By deepening the waterways and providing locks in the dams, TVA provides for river shipping that regularly exceeds 1 billion ton-miles per year. It controls floods and provides irrigation for farms. TVA has provided 250 million seedlings to reforest over 211,000 acres. The forests, lakes, and streams provide recreational and vacation facilities for thousands of people every year. The control of water levels and other techniques have also controlled malaria-carrying mosquitoes, and malaria has almost disappeared in the area. As we say, it was no accident that TVA was among the first things that visitors from underdeveloped countries wanted to see—providing as it did industrial development, electrical power, water, and doing so in ways that enhanced rather than damaged the environment. There is no way of measuring the effect that TVA has had throughout the world, but it seems safe to say that it has influenced the thinking of economic and development planners in every country of the entire world.

The United States is in the forefront of the countries moving into a superindustrial society. It is the first to experience the high material standards of superindustrialization, but it is also the first to experience both the trauma of rapidly changing value structures and the seamy side of superindustrialization—pollution of air, water, and land; overcrowding and decay in the cities; transportation and traffic jams; and all the rest. If the United States wishes to influence the course of mankind, the most efficacious means available would be to solve these two problems in ways that arouse the admiration of the world and the desire to imitate. It is not just simple idealism to say that the world is watching our confrontation with the problems of changing values and the problems of industrialization while providing a clean environment, along with the related problems of race, minorities, civil rights, and civil liberties. If we solve these problems in fairness to all concerned and in ways that will minimize the use of violence, others will be influenced to follow. If we turn our energies and resources to the problems of pollution, ecological damage, urban decay, and mass transportation and solve them in ways that preserve the beauty and dignity of life, our influence will be vastly greater than it was when we put so much effort and resources into military means. The loss of life is the real tragedy of Vietnam, but losing the opportunity to use the billions spent on the war to solve these other problems makes it greater still.

Implications

Beyond all this, the trends toward further development in both the developed and the underdeveloped countries present mankind with a problem of awesome dimensions. Merely bringing the present population of the world up to today's standards of the developed world in terms of food alone is staggering. When one considers the trends in population growth, the difficulty of bringing that growth under control, and then of bringing the total resulting population up to the still higher standards that the developed world will undoubtedly reach, the mind simply boggles. Even so, it is only when we go back to consider the strength of the push toward further development that the full measure of the dilemma makes its impact. It becomes increasingly obvious that the present organization of the world is no longer appropriate to the task that mankind faces. The energy crisis of 1973–74 is minor compared to the problems that lie ahead. But it does illustrate the dilemma. The developed countries, even the wealthy United States, cannot really become self-sufficient in petroleum. Yet neither can the industrialized countries leave the power to control their economies, employment levels, and standard of life in the hands of the countries that just happen to produce the oil on which their economies are dependent. It seems inescapable that mankind will find itself again and again confronted in brutal and crude ways— as a dog is trained by having its muzzle forced into its own excrement—with the fact that the only possible solution is a fundamental recasting of the organization of every aspect of mankind's economic, social, and political life.

The explosive growth of population, shortages in food, in

arable land, in water, in petroleum, in the other fossil fuels, and in the whole range of resources on which industrial society depends have brought mankind to a crisis—not a crisis of tomorrow but a crisis of today. The implications are portentous. In the past international politics has been concerned with the power and prestige of states, their rivalries, and their fears of hostile states rather than with the welfare of individual human beings. In the future, international tensions are more likely to come from the interaction of these new forces—the thrust toward development, population pressure, the cruel and inhumane fact of starvation itself, and the impact that the combination of them all will have on the lives of individuals. As we say, the essential nature of the technology on which modern society rests will have to be changed. The very essence of the organization of man's economic, social, and political life will have to be recast. The consequences will be that the substance, the very content, of international politics will be different from what we have always known.

CHAPTER 25

An Alternative to War

BUT WAR still is part of the future. Although the changes in the content and instrumentalities of international politics are far-reaching, war and the threat of war continue to be the central dynamism of international politics. Even more frightening, if mankind accepts war as an inevitable fact of existence, as a part of life no more manipulable than gravity, then nuclear war, too, will be part of the future.

Admittedly, the efforts that man has so far made to mitigate, control, or abolish war are not encouraging. As we saw, arms control, peace-keeping by the United Nations, and such devices of traditional diplomacy as the concert of the powers are helpful and may regularly succeed in avoiding particular wars. But they do not pretend to attack the root causes of war and make no claim to have even the promise of eliminating war entirely. At the other end of the spectrum, a world state does promise to eliminate war entirely, but none of the proposals so far put forward have gotten anywhere. Realistically, we must say that there is no evidence that mankind is moving in the direction of a world state and much evidence that he would resist efforts to create a world state so strenuously that the result might be world civil wars even bloodier than international wars.

But surely man is not so completely helpless. Surely there is something that can be done. Surely ways can be found to re-arrange the structure in which man's affairs are organized that will begin to get at the root causes, ways that are drastic enough to lessen the probability of war sharply and significantly without going so far as to arouse the kind of hostility engendered by proposals for world government. One means of getting at the problem may be to ask why wars have been so prevalent in the past. Is it possible that war has served a purpose that man could find no other way of accomplishing? The role of war has been so prominent and pervasive in the affairs of men that it is neither morbid nor ghoulish to suspect that war has performed some necessary social functions. If so, and if they can be identified, other instruments than war might be found to serve the functions.

The Social Functions of War

The most thoroughgoing attempt to identify the functions that war has served in history was undoubtedly that of Quincy Wright and his associates in their monumental work, *A Study of War*.[1] On this subject of the possible functions of war, Wright makes a distinction between the psychological and instinctual drives that lead to fighting and the functions that fighting serves. With this distinction in mind, he then examines differents kinds of fighting: animal fighting, primitive warfare, historic warfare, and modern warfare.

Animal Fighting

The drives behind animal fighting are food, sex, home territory, activity, self-preservation, dominance, independence, and the in-stinct to preserve a society. Individual animals are motivated to violence toward members of other species mainly by the drive for food. They are motivated to violence against members of the same species by drives of sex, territory, dominance, and activity. The

[1] Second ed. (Chicago, 1965).

instinct to preserve a society operates only among species with highly organized societies, like bees and ants as well as man. Most of the other drives toward fighting function mainly to preserve the individual, and through his survival, or his instinct to reproduce, the genus and the species. Whether or not there is any grand design to protect the species in it, the fact is that among the same species in the animal world, fighting is seldom lethal. Man is the principal exception.

Primitive Warfare

All the drives seen in animal fighting can also be observed in primitive warfare. According to Wright, however, the function in primitive warfare is generally to maintain the solidarity of the political group, defined as the group that sanctions the use of force, internally and externally. The secondary function is to satisfy "certain psychic needs of human personality." Citing particular anthropological studies in support of each point, Wright lists the following ways that primitive warfare assists in preserving social solidarity: "by keeping alive the realization of a common enemy who will destroy the group if it is not prepared to resist; by strikingly symbolizing the group as a unit in a common enterprise; by creating a certain discipline and surbordination to leadership; by providing an outlet for anger in activities not hostile to the harmony of the group by preventing the amalgamation of neighboring groups into units too large and heterogeneous to function unitedly with the available means of communication and civic education; by sanctioning the tribal mores; and sometimes by limiting population, particularly the male population, to a figure adapted to the economy and mores of the group."[2]

Historic Warfare

By historic warfare Wright means warfare within or between literate civilizations, as identified by Arnold J. Toynbee in his *A Study of History*, from Egypt and Mesopotamia down to the age of discovery in the fifteenth century. Although all the same drives observed in primitive warfare exist in civilized warfare, according to Wright, a study of drives provides a far from satisfactory

[2] Ibid., pp. 71–72.

explanation of the existence of war. A number of recent books—
Robert Ardrey's *African Genesis* and his *The Territorial Imperative*, Konrad Lorenz's *On Aggression*, and Desmond Morris's *The
Naked Ape*, to cite only four—have attempted to analyze the origins of man and his drives in ways that imply that aggression and
warfare are basic to human nature, with the implication that war
is natural and inevitable. But these books grossly oversimplify
both the motivations of the human animal and the causes of war.[3]
In the first place, among civilized man, drives are combined with
the individual's personal experience to form complex behavior patterns. In the second place, while "animal war is a function of
instinct and primitive war of the mores, civilized war is primarily
a function of state politics." As a result, "there is seldom an immediate causal relationship between any one drive and a war. The
drives do not account for the war; they originate the behavior
patterns of the people, which in turn provide the materials out of
which war may be made."[4]

Wright's discussion of the functions of historic warfare is less
useful than that of primitive warfare because of his reliance on
Toynbee's concept of civilization and their stages of being young,
middle-aged, and old, a concept that has been discredited. It is
clear from the evidence Wright offers, however, that warfare has
served two main, but somewhat contradictory functions. Like
primitive warfare, historic warfare served the function of preserving social solidarity. War also served to spread cultures—although
travel, trade, and education have at times been just as important.
It has also served to spread religion and ideologies—a function
unknown to primitive warfare, since "the beliefs and practices of
the group are considered its peculiar heritage incapable of extension to others."[5] The major function of war, however, has been
to be the midwife of political change—adding to the size of states,
reducing them, creating new states, and destroying old states.

Modern Warfare

In modern warfare, like historic warfare, drives are not an immediate cause of war, but provide the material for enlisting popu-

---

[3] See Alexander Alland, Jr., *The Human Imperative* (New York, 1972).
[4] Wright, op. cit., p. 132.
[5] Ibid., p. 79.

lar support—although the personality traits of high officials undoubtedly play a role.

Again in modern warfare as in historic warfare, the principal function has been in being the midwife of political change. "War," says Wright, "has been the method actually used for achieving the major political changes in the modern world, the building of nation-states, the expansion of modern civilization throughout the world, and the changing of the dominant interests of that civilization."[6] Wars and rebellions amalgamated the feudal principalities of Europe into nations and broke up empires. Imperialistic wars spread the culture and institutions of modern civilization. And war has played a large role in the "historic transitions of human interest and ideas during the modern period," although more by facilitating a synthesis of conflicting opinions rather than the victory of one. "The Thirty Years' War resulted in victory for neither Protestant nor Catholic but for the sovereign state and the family of nations. The Napoleonic Wars resulted in victory for neither hereditary absolutism nor revolutionary democracy but for constitutional nationalism."[7]

In the modern era, war has also played a role "in maintaining the established status of nations and the established international order." As with primitive and historic warfare, it contributed to social solidarity by "recalling to the population the necessity of political loyalty as the price of immunity from invasion."[8] At the same time, war and the threat of war have been means for "maintaining the balance of power upon which the political and legal organization of the world community has in large measure rested."[9] The balance of power system, with its intricate minuet of alliances and coalitions and threat of war whenever the balance was disturbed, "prevented any one of the modern states from getting sufficiently powerful to swallow or dominate all the others, as Rome swallowed the states of its time."[10]

By way of summary, then, we can say, first, that although the personality traits of top leaders can be decisive influences for war or peace, the process by which states decide on war is too com-

[6] Ibid., p. 250.
[7] Ibid., pp. 252–53.
[8] Ibid., p. 253.
[9] Ibid., p. 254.
[10] Ibid.

plex and the number of participants too many for there to be any direct link between particular psychological or emotional drives and war. War has served as an outlet for various emotions, and emotions have been used to build popular mass support for war, but we can reject any notion that human pugnacity and aggressiveness make war inevitable.

As to functions, war in modern times has served a number of secondary functions. It has reinforced the dominance of the nation-state, for example, both by emphasizing patriotism and by inhibiting, through the operation of the balance of power system, the growth of empires. It undoubtedly provided a means for discharging a whole gamut of emotional frustrations and aggressions, even though none could be said to be proximate causes of war.

But the major function of modern warfare like historic warfare, has been to be the instrument of political and social change—either to bring about such change or to prevent it. War had a major part in creating nation-states out of feudal principalities or through the breakup of dynastic empires. It was the major instrument for extending the dominance of Western civilization, its values, and mode of life. It has been the means for adding to the power of one state at the expense of another. Most recently, Hitler and the Japanese militarists used war to accomplish several such purposes—to create a new kind of empire, a new political and ideological dominance, and a new distribution of power. The Allies used war to prevent them.

International War vs. Civil War and Revolution

Parenthetically, it might be worth noting that in recent times, *international* wars seem to have been the instrument for more social and political change that was not intended than for change that was the *goal* of those who decided on war. As we said, Hitler and the Japanese militarists set about to create new empires, establish a new political and ideological dominance, and alter the distribution of power in the world. The Allies prevented them from achieving these goals, but that was not the end of the matter. In the catalyst of war, and more or less incidentally, the colonial empires were broken up and colonialism was destroyed. War had performed what Wright would have called a secondary function.

In fact, it is probably no accident that other than stopping Hitler and the Japanese militarists, one of the more far-reaching consequences of World War II, the destruction of colonialism, was something that neither side set out to do. Not only has international war brought more *unintended* than intended change, it has not been very successful in achieving very much of the change it was intended to accomplish. Indeed, since the rise of nationalism, civil wars, revolutions, rebellions, insurrections, insurgencies, and wars of secession seem to have been responsible for a greater proportion of social and political change than international wars. There was a time when a victorious state would annex the territory of its enemy and so increase its power, but nationalism is likely to make an annexed territory more of a liability than an asset. Although Hitler and the Japanese militarists tried to use war to increase their power, war has not been very successful in increasing the power of any state in recent times. The two states whose power has increased most dramatically, the Soviet Union and the United States, owe their power not to victory in World War I and World War II but to their large populations, the skills of those populations, their natural resources, and their industrial capacity. Neither war even added significantly to the territorial base of their power. The major effect on power relations of the two wars was to make people the world over recognize and accept that the power of these two states had vastly increased relative to all the rest.

Also, nationalism is isolationist. Nationalism incites revolution to bring about social and political change within its own nation, but it discourages concern with social and political conditions in other countries.

Nuclear War as the Midwife of Change

We said that war and the threat of war were the central dynamics of international politics. We also said that the social and political functions of war are to be the instruments of social and political change. If so, we can also say that nuclear war, at least, is an anachronism. Any instrument that carried with it such high levels of both casualties and destruction could work vast changes in the world. It could reduce major powers to minor ones.

In its "secondary" functions, to use Wright's term and to speak brutally, it could eliminate the problems of overpopulation. But to speak of nuclear war as serving a social function is only to be macabre.

Of course, the fact that nuclear war is too costly to serve the social functions that war has served in the past settles nothing. The threat of nuclear war remains. What the costliness of nuclear war does eliminate are the rational motives for war. It is difficult to imagine a rational decision-maker risking 50 per cent casualties and the accompanying destruction for a possible gain in territory, economic advantage, and national prestige to proselyte religion or ideology, or for an increase of power. The only possible rational motive for war that remains is fear. Circumstances are at least conceivable in which the leaders of a state could come to see the choice before them as either accepting 50 per cent casualties or total annihilation, and reluctantly deciding to choose 50 per cent casualties.

Barring only the rise to power in a major state of a madman like Hitler, even fear seems an inadequate motive for a decision to *initiate* a war with nuclear weapons. If nuclear war comes, it seems most likely to come through miscalculation, in the midst of a lesser war as the result of a series of incremental decisions, each one of which seemed reasonable at the time to reasonable though anxious men.

And there's the rub: the likelihood that nuclear war will come in the midst of lesser wars; for nonnuclear, limited, conventional war still can serve as the instrument for social and political change, and the leaders of states, great and small, still can and do believe that nonnuclear war can be used to accomplish all the social and political goals for which it has been used in the past. Their only concern is that the risks of nonnuclear war escalating into nuclear war be manageable, a judgment that cannot always be calculated with complete precision.

War and the State System

However, if the social and political functions of war are that they serve as the instruments of social and political change, we do have a clue not so much as to why war has been more frequent in one period of history than in another but as to why war has persisted as a social institution. The existence of war as an institution is related to the way the world is organized politically. In any political system composed of sovereign states, war is endemic. This is true whether the states are cities, empires, or nations. If the world is organized as a system of states, then war and the threat of war are inevitable.

In the past, wars have been fought, as we said, for territory, for economic advantage, for prestige, to proselyte for both religion and ideology, for power, and out of fear. And in the course of making decisions to go to war, every conceivable human emotion has undoubtedly contributed: hate, revenge, greed, envy, pride, fear (and through fear, love), and, in all likelihood, deep primordial aggressiveness and a sadistic fascination with violence. But neither the motives for war nor man's instincts toward violence have much to do with the fact that war is endemic to state systems. Most of the motives for war and all of the emotions also work on men acting as individuals or as members of a vast variety of different groups and organizations—fraternal organizations, mutual protective societies, business firms, trade unions, political parties, special-interest groups like the National Rifle Association, neighborhood and community organizations, and even Boy Scout troops. As a result, violence also occurs—between individuals and between groups and organizations. On occasion, the violence is organized and sustained. And sometimes it takes place on so large a scale that it is indistinguishable from war. Examples are revolution, rebellion, civil war, and perhaps even some other kinds of phenomena, such as the strike-breaking violence that marked the rise of the trade union movement. But even though large-scale, organized violence sometimes occurs between groups of men organized in other ways than as sovereign states, war is not endemic to those relations.

War in this sense of large-scale, organized violence is endemic to state systems for two fundamental reasons. One concerns the absurdly elementary but intensely practical problem of acquiring and maintaining the means for large-scale, organized violence. In any dispute between men, of course, violence is the ultimate arbiter. But what makes the state unique among mankind's infinitely varied organizations is that it alone possesses, in Max

Weber's phrase, the *monopoly* of *legal* violence. The state is consequently the legal and political authority for developing the means, both the material means and the manpower means, through compulsory military service, necessary for the large-scale, organized violence that is war. As a practical matter, it is most difficult for an insurgent movement to manufacture, buy, or steal hand weapons and ammunition within the borders of its own state for large-scale, sustained combat, and it is only in extraordinary circumstances that it could manage to acquire machine guns, artillery, tanks, military aircraft, missiles, or nuclear weapons.[11] To do so, the insurgents would have to subvert a substantial portion of the armed forces already possessing the weapons or seize a territorial base large enough to provide the necessary resources, and to hold the territorial base long enough to develop a rival arsenal of its own.

If the first reason that war is not endemic within a state is the practical difficulty of acquiring the means for waging it, the second is that within all states the incentive to wage war is reduced by the fact that for most disagreements or grievances other arbiters exist that are more or less satisfactory alternatives to the risk inherent in an attempt at large-scale violence. Principally, these alternatives are law and politics.

All states have legal systems that provide an opportunity to redress certain kinds of grievances and to settle certain kinds of disputes. The law may cover a wider range of disputes in one country than in another, and it may be more just and impartially enforced in one country than in another. But in even the most

[11] If the insurgents acquire the weapons not from within the borders of their own state, but from an outside power, the situation will increasingly resemble interstate war rather than intrastate or civil war. International law holds that if a state permits its territory to be used so as to harm another state, the aggrieved state may take such action to protect itself as is necessary. For example, it is of course arguable that South Vietnam was a sovereign state after the Geneva Agreements of 1954. But if it is accepted that it was, then the fact that North Vietnam permitted its territory to be used for training bases for the Viet Cong and supplied them with weapons and equipment gave South Vietnam the legal right to ask the United States to bomb North Vietnam, even if North Vietnam did not attack South Vietnam with its own troops. And, given the premise, the United States was within its legal rights to accede to the request, however unwise the action was politically or questionable in moral terms. The same argument could have been used by Cuba against the United States at the time of the Bay of Pigs incident. The fact that the United States trained and supplied the Cubans who landed at the Bay of Pigs gave Cuba the legal right to retaliate or to try to persuade others to retaliate on its behalf.

authoritarian of states, law provides an alternative arbiter to the use of force for certain kinds of disputes, depending on the particular state.

All states also have political systems, and no matter whether it is authoritarian or democratic, a political system serves as an alternative arbiter to war for most groups in the society possessing the potential for organized violence. The point is that a political system provides the means by which one group or the other can acquire the power to impose its will in a disagreement without the use of large-scale, organized violence. In one state the political system may involve elections and in another behind-the-scenes maneuvering for allies with the secret police and the army in preparation for a *coup d'état*, but the social function is the same. In both the election and the *coup* there may also be violence —whether campus riots, street fighting, or the murder of a king in the palace corridor—but it is not the large-scale, organized violence of war.

Law and politics, of course, also are present in the relations between states. A wide variety of disputes are settled by appeals to international law, and certainly there is politics between states, in the sense that states maneuver for support from other states, bargain, make deals, whether for support as allies or for votes in the United Nations, and even attempt to affect public opinion in other states and so go over the heads of the governments. But there is a difference. Only minor matters have so far been settled by the International Court of Justice, and politics among nations has not been so much the politics of persuasion as the politics of force and violence. Although war itself, the actual use of force, is infrequent, the threat of force is present behind every political maneuver and every negotiation. The difference goes back to the fact that the state has the monopoly of legal violence. Law can be a successful arbiter on weighty questions within a state in those cases when force, held by the state, stands behind the law and above the disputants. In international politics, the force that is present stands not behind the law and above the disputants, but is held by the disputants themselves. And politics can be a successful arbiter within a state when the struggle is among groups that do not have a legal right to maintain and use force in and for themselves, even though the purpose of their struggle is to determine who shall control the state, including its monopoly of legal violence, and for what end. In international politics, on the other hand, the struggle is never between unarmed contestants, but always between groups that have not only the right to maintain armed forces, but the duty to do so.

If both the legal and the political system of a state fail to provide satisfaction to very important, deeply held aspirations of a significant group within the population over a sufficiently long time, violence will eventually ensue. The form it takes may be individual acts of terrorism, assassination, arson, bombings, strikes, and riots. But, as suggested above, for an insurgent movement to transform its actions into full-scale revolution and civil war, it will need the weapons of war rather than those of terror: machine guns, tanks, artillery, and military aircraft. If these are acquired from an outside power, the situation will begin to resemble interstate war rather than civil war or revolution. Otherwise, to turn mere violence into something resembling war, the insurgents would have to subvert a substantial portion of the armed forces already possessing the weapons or seize a territorial base large enough and hold it long enough to develop a rival arsenal of its own. The difficulties are obvious.

It is no accident, in sum, either that the large-scale, organized violence that is war is endemic to state systems or that the similar large-scale, organized violence of civil war and revolution is exceptional within a single state. Within a single state, no matter how turbulent and aggressive its people, it is reasonable and plausible to hope that levels of organized violence resembling war can be effectively abolished; within a state *system*, it is not. A conspiracy of events can on occasion bring violence at the level of war within a single state; within a state system it takes a conspiracy of fortunate events to avoid it.

Law and Politics

The possibility of virtually abolishing large-scale, organized violence within a single state lies in the fact that law and politics provide an alternative way of accomplishing social and political change. Even though a world state seems out of the question in the immediate future, the possibility arises that legal and political processes might be developed that do not require the structure of a state in which to operate and that they might then provide a similar alternative to the large-scale, organized violence that is war. What we visualize is the development of a global political process similar to what exists in individual states today but in which certain features are much more prominent and certain other features are considerably less prominent.

Presumably law and legal processes would be among the less prominent. Law comes about as the result of formal legislation and through precedent set by the courts. Since the global political process we visualize would lack the structure of a state and hence the state's monopoly of legal violence, it would presumably also lack not only the formal legislative institutions but also the more formal enforcement powers by which a state implements its laws. But this is not necessarily a fatal lack. In its essence, law is the outcome of the kind of political process that exists in the individual state, not a rival to it or a substitute for it. Similarly, if all the laws, rules, regulations, and agreements by which the individual state is governed had to be enforced by the formal institutions of police and other regulatory agencies, no state would be effectively governed. The point is that some considerable portion of both a political process and a legal process that is the alternative to violence within a single state can be visualized in an interstate system as well as within a single superstate.

Politics Defined

The question now is: What do we mean by the word *"politics"*? How one defines politics depends very much on what analytical purpose one has in mind. Politics has been defined as the struggle to determine "who gets what, when, how" for one analytical purpose.[12] It has been defined as a struggle for power, pure and simple for other purposes, and there are many other definitions.[13]

[12] Harold Lasswell, *Politics: Who Gets What, When, How* (New York: McGraw Hill, 1936).
[13] Charles E. Merriam, *Political Power: Its Composition and Incidence* (New York: McGraw Hill, 1934) and Hans J. Morgenthau, *Politics Among Nations*, 4th ed. (New York, 1970). Although they by no means exhaust the list, three others might be noted here. The first is V. O. Key's definition of politics as the "human relationship of superordination and subordination, of dominance and submission, of the governors and the governed." (*Politics, Parties and Pressure Groups*, 4th ed.

Most of them are reasonably valid and useful for particular purposes, and most of them are not completely satisfactory for all purposes. It is probably not necessary to strain for the perfect definition—most people have a common-sense definition that is good enough. People speak of "office politics," for example, and everyone knows what they mean. As a general rule, it is assumed that politics is concerned with power, that it is more likely than not concerned with matters of government (although there are many exceptions), and that political decisions of the largest moment are concerned with the ordering and regulating of society itself. In its broadest meaning, politics concerns the activities and relationship of groups of people as groups.

For our purposes here, it seems most useful to look at a political process with the latter emphasis—as a device for making group decisions, a procedure by which a group of people can decide what they should do as a group, the goals they should seek and the means for achieving them, how they should divide among themselves those benefits already available, how the necessary sacrifices should be alloted, the rules governing competition of various kinds, and how disputes between different groups should be resolved. Politics is concerned both with the making of such decisions and the maneuvering to acquire the power and influence to affect them.

Other devices can also be used to make group decisions. Judicial and administrative procedures constitute one: Decisions are made by the interpretation, guided by precedent, of sets of laws, policies, rules, and regulations, or perhaps by tribal custom. Conceivably, group decisions could also be made in a purely hierarchical way, in which only the head man has a voice. At the other extreme, a pure type of democratic decision-making is also conceivable, in which there was no leader at all and decisions were

---

(New York: Crowell, 1964). The second is David Easton's definition of politics as the making and executing of the "authoritative," i.e., legally binding decisions in a society (The Political System and "An Approach to the Analysis of Political Systems," *World Politics* [April 1957]). The third is Gabriel A. Almond's: "that system of interactions to be found in all independent societies which performs the functions of integration and adaption [both internally and *vis-à-vis* other societies] by means of the employment, or threat of employment, of more or less legitimate physical violence" (*The Politics of Developing Areas* [Princeton, 1960]).

made unanimously or by the majority, with each man having only one vote and no influence other than his vote. But the real world is more complex. It differs from the pure hierarchical model of decision-making in that more than one person has power or influence on decisions and from the pure democratic model in that the participants have differing amounts of power and influence. The active co-operation of some people may be required for a decision, while only the acquiescence of others may be necessary. Some participants might have to give formal approval before some decisions could be made; on other decisions these same people might be safely ignored.

And in the real world nothing is very clear-cut—several different kinds of group decision-making will undoubtedly exist at the same time. Within a single department of the United States Government, to use that as an example, some decisions are made by hierarchical procedures, some by judicial, and some by political, and perhaps some by a bewildering combination.[14]

Characteristics of a Political Process

A political process of decision-making can be distinguished from other ways of making group decisions by three characteristics. In the first place, politics implies a diversity of goals and values that must be reconciled before a decision can be reached. It is not just a question of whether this or that value should be pursued, but what mixture of values should be pursued. It also implies alternative means for achieving values whose precise effects may be in dispute. Political debates, for example, never take place over the question of what tensile strength is required for the truss members of a bridge, which can be determined scientifically, but political debates frequently do take place over where to locate the bridge. Sometimes this is because the social and economic consequences of locating the bridge in one place rather than another cannot be predicted with sufficient exactitude. A proposal to build a bridge from Long Island to Connecticut has divided opinion in Connecticut into those who think the Connecticut

[14] On the overlapping of different forms of decision-making and the pyschological problems posed for the individual, see Robert A. Dahl, "Hierarchy, Democracy, and Bargaining in Politics and Economics," *Research Frontiers in Politics and Government* (Washington, D.C.: The Brookings Institution, 1955).

economy will benefit more from having the bridge go to Bridge-
port from the middle of Long Island and those who think it will
benefit more if it goes from near the end, to Old Saybrook at the
mouth of the Connecticut River. Economic and social theory at
the present time is not sufficient to give a decisive, completely
"scientific" prediction about the consequences of either alternative, and the result is political debate. Sometimes, however, the
question of where to locate a bridge causes political debate *because* a prediction can be made with exactitude. The people of
Old Saybrook are against the bridge because they know beyond
any doubt that it will destroy the essentially rural atmosphere of
that small, peaceful, rather remote New England town, an atmosphere they ardently want to preserve. Politics also arises, in other
words, when a decision is uneven in its effects or call to sacrifice,
when it brings either untoward benefit to one segment of society
or untoward hurt.

Frequently a political struggle over the probable effects of alternative means is really a mask for an unspoken disagreement
about goals. But it is noteworthy how often the struggle is truly
over means and rival predictions about what a particular means
will or will not accomplish. On the question of Vietnam, to go
back to our earlier example, both the doves and the hawks
wanted a stable and lasting peace. The trouble was that the doves
thought a stable peace could be achieved by withdrawal and
negotiations, and the hawks thought it could only be achieved by
defeating the Communist side and thereby deterring them from
future actions. Ending both the recession and inflation have been
the goals of all sides to the economic argument during the Nixon
administration; it was the effectiveness of the various means and
whether the cost would fall most severely on workers or business
that has brought forth the political battle.

Politics, in other words, begins to come to the fore when there
is disagreement. The disagreement can take any one of several
forms: (1) It could be about the goals the group should seek as
a group. Should the United States try to go to the moon? Should it
make Vietnam an American war? (2) It could be about the effects
of alternative means for achieving the goal. Will bombing North
Vietnam cause the Communist side to give up, or will they fight
even harder? Will a tax cut stimulate business enough to end

the recession, or will a federal deficit be needed? (3) The disagreement can be about the rules governing competition between individuals and subgroups. The antimonopoly laws, the regulation of interstate commerce, and the laws regulating the stock market are all examples. So is civil rights legislation and equal-rights legislation for women. (4) It could be about the allocation of benefits held or distributed by the group as a whole. Welfare payments, unemployment compensation, medical care, and farm subsidies are examples. (5) Finally, the disagreement can be about the sacrifices required by different segments of the group as a whole. Will the recession be ended by means that make for high unemployment so that workers bear the brunt of the sacrifice? Will college students, whose ranks contain a disproportionate number from the upper middle classes, be deferred from the draft? The point is that it is not competition as such that produces politics. If there is substantial agreement, for example, that unrestrained economic enterprise should govern the distribution of material benefits, the competition will take place in other than political terms. It is when there is *disagreement* about the rules for economic competition that politics begins.

The Second Characteristic of Politics

The second characteristic flows from the first—the presence of competing groups of people who are identified with each of these alternative goals and policies. One thinks most readily of the traditional political parties and the formal interest groups—farmers, workers, right down to very special interests like the National Rifle Association fighting against gun control laws. In this approach, the emphasis is on formal, organized interest groups. Yet much of policy making in the United States, at least—and one suspects in most other countries as well—is made in the struggle between highly informal coalitions and alliances. In the American policy-making arena, to continue to use the United States as an example, there are subgroups of many kinds within the Executive branch and even within a single department or the White House itself. More often than not, these are not only informal but temporary alliances that cut across departmental or institutional lines, including the line between the Executive and Congress. Throughout the struggle over policy toward Vietnam, to continue with that example, the group within the State Department that took a "hawk" view had friends and allies in the Pentagon, in the CIA, in Congress, in the press, and in the attentive public; while the rival group that took a "dove" view had an entirely different set of allies in the same institutions.[15] This pattern of subgroups and informal alliances runs through most of the major policy disputes in Washington, whether foreign or domestic, sometimes more and sometimes less prominently.

The Third Characteristic: Power

In a political process, finally, the relative power of the different groups of people involved is as relevant to the final decision as the appeal of the goals they seek or the cogency and wisdom of their arguments. If the blacks could have organized and used the ballot sooner, to use another example from the United States, civil rights legislation might have not had to wait until the 1960s for passage. Another example is transportation. Since World War II, the United States has built a multibillion-dollar highway system with federal funds, which has contributed heavily to urban sprawl, automobile traffic congestion, the decline of the inner cities, and to air pollution, while the railways and other mass-transit systems have been allowed to deteriorate to a state that makes them almost useless. But it was not the wisdom of this policy that won the day. City planners and others warned of the consequences. It was the power of the highway lobby—the informal coalition of state officials; construction companies; unions; oil and gasoline producers and local distributors; and the automotive industry, from manufacturers to local dealers and repairmen. Who advocates a particular policy is as important as what he advocates.

Political Processes in Practice

In our examination of the United States and the Soviet Union, we have already seen how a political process operates in practice.

[15] On the struggle over Vietnam policy, see my *To Move a Nation* (New York, 1967), Chaps. 28 to 34; Townsend Hoopes, *The Limits of Intervention: An Inside Account of How the Johnson Policy of Escalation in Vietnam Was Reversed* (New York, 1969), passim; and David Halberstam, *The Best and the Brightest* (New York, 1972).

We saw that in spite of the fact that more power is concentrated in the office of the presidency than in any other single place in American society, Presidents can very rarely command. As a consequence, we found that Presidents must persuade, maneuver, and pressure, using all the levers, powers, and influences that they can muster in the conflict and consensus-building process to get the people concerned to come around. With so much leverage at their disposal, they often succeed, but sometimes they do not. Then they must either pay the political costs of public disunity or make some concession to achieve the unity of compromise.

We found that in the making of decisions in the United States there are a multiplicity of participants. The President, his personal staff, the secretaries, undersecretaries, and assistant secretaries and their aides who make up an administration are only the beginning. There are a host of subagencies, bureaus, and offices within the various departments that may have interests of their own at variance with the interests of the departments to which they belong. Congress has its stake, with rival committees and committee staffs. The whole court system plays its part, unmaking the "decisions" of the Executive and Congress, and making decisions of its own. And there are a lot more people involved than just those who hold official positions. It is no accident that the press is called the "fourth branch of government." It plays a role in the process of governance and performs necessary functions. There are lobbies and formal interest groups. The academic world plays a role, and there are the quasigovernmental research groups like RAND and the Hudson Institute, both contributing to policy and possessing the power to influence it. There are the political parties, which play a role in policy-making as well as getting people nominated and elected. There are the "attentive publics"—audiences who are not formally organized, but who are knowledgeable on particular issues, who follow them closely, and whose opinions influence the outcomes. And there is the vast electorate, which on occasion makes its weight felt in a most decisive way.

Between this mass electorate and the more proximate centers of power is also the "intermediate structure"—the array of not just interest and pressure groups, but organizations of all kinds, corporations, universities, banks, trade unions, manufacturers and business associations, churches, professional societies, the major media of mass communication, the local political parties, the state and local governments.

The mechanics of the process can be seen as a set of inputs and a set of outputs. In terms of our interests here, the most significant input is a function of this intermediate structure. The intermediate structure articulates interests. It is in this way that people define their interests and work out the implication of various policy proposals, laws, and so on for the interests identified. The intermediate structure articulates interests, identifies their interests to the individuals concerned, and identifies people sharing an interest to each other and to those with the authority to do something about satisfying the interest. The structure also facilitates movement in the opposite direction: the transmission downward to the membership of information, interpretation, and potential conflict with other values and interests and with other, rival, or opposition interest groups.

At the output side of policy making—in this example, the Washington end—there is struggle and conflict. At the same time, there is a "strain toward agreement," an effort to build a consensus, a push for accommodation, for compromise, for some sort of agreement on the policy decision. There are independent participants in the process who may be able to block a policy, or sabotage it, or at least to snipe away at it from the sidelines. There may be other men whose active, imaginative support and dedicated efforts are required if the policy is to succeed, and it may take concessions aimed directly at them and their interests to enlist this kind of willing co-operation. Finally, there is among all participants an intuitive realization that prolonged intransigence, stalemate, and indecision on urgent or fundamental issues might become so intolerable as to threaten the very form and structure of the system of governance.

A description of the political process in the Soviet Union in these terms requires several modifications. The Soviet system clearly has an intermediate structure, which articulates interests and transmits information downward about potential opposition and costs that may lead to a scaling-down of aspirations or even a change of interests. But since the masses lack the ultimate sanction of the ballot as a means of expressing their interests and since such institutions as the secret police have greater power, the downward function of the intermediate structure in shaping interests and manipulating mass attitudes and demands obviously gets greater emphasis in the Soviet Union than in the United States.

The number of power centers in the Soviet Union is also likely to be smaller and often different in nature. Among them the armed forces, the managers of industry and agriculture, the police, and the party are clearly foremost, but there are others.

The penalties for being on the losing side of a policy battle have also been greater in the Soviet Union, at least until recently. Loss of influence and power are the first penalties in both countries. At times, as in the McCarthy witch-hunts, being on the losing side in the United States could carry other, more severe penalties as well, although nothing to compare with what happened to Stalin's opponents at the height of his power.

But we can still describe the political process in the Soviet Union in the same terms as we do the political process in the United States. At the top levels in the Soviet society, to repeat the conclusions of our analysis of the Soviet Union, we see a number of organized power centers with particular, parochial interests: the police; the armed forces; the managers and executives of industry and agriculture; the scientific and academic community; the cultural and literary community; and various regional interests, such as the Ukraine or the Leningrad area. We see particular segments of the top leadership of the Communist party and the Soviet state as representing these particular power centers and drawing their own individual power from them. We see the party as providing the arena for a process of conflict and consensus-building by which these various interests are reconciled and policies are adopted, with the top leadership serving as the political brokers as well as power centers with particular interests themselves. Between this top structure and the mass of the people, we see an intermediate structure, which serves the function of transmitting policy and interpretation to the masses, molding opinion, and mobilizing the masses but also passing upward information on attitudes, values, and interests among the masses. Thus the masses of the population, although denied the kind of ballot that could change leadership as an expression of discontent with policy, do in fact have influence on policy through the expression of attitudes, values, and interests through the intermediate structure. Partly this is because the co-operation of the masses required on so many policies, and partly it is because the intermediate structure, which is tied in with the power centers at the top, derives its power and influence from its role as spokesman of the masses. The top levels of any particular power center have a stake in representing and serving the interests of the intermediate structure associated with them. The intermediate structure, in turn, has a stake in representing and serving the interests of the masses with whom they are connected. Thus people at all levels have some stake in seeing that particular interests are served, at least sufficiently to blunt discontent and to enlist loyalty.

Political Process on the International Level

We have said that a rudimentary form of political process already exists in international affairs, that international politics, too, is a process of conflict and consensus-building. In international affairs, the principal mode of conflict is war, and people thus tend to assume that conflict between states is fundamentally different from the conflict within a single country or in private lives. Yet even in the "total" wars of recent times, the use of force has always been limited. Mankind uses force against some natural enemies with the full intention of exterminating them; as we saw, the wolves in England were exterminated deliberately, and so were the snakes in Ireland and Hawaii. But except for Hitler's maniacal policy toward the Jews, no modern state has deliberately set about to destroy another people. Physical violence, in fact, is not really a very common state of affairs between states. In the history of most countries the years of peace far outnumber the years of war. Even when conflict is the dominating theme in a set of relationships, statecraft is not really concerned as much with actual physical violence as it is with *threats* of physical violence.

It is on the conflict in international affairs that a pure-power theory of world politics focuses. Yet for all its utility in explaining the maneuvering of states, a pure-power theory has limitations. Without a sizable list of inelegant qualifications, it cannot account for the long periods of peace in interstate relations, for the stability of certain friendships, and for the not uncommon occasions when states knowingly relinquish positions of power. For the practical purposes of estimating the consequences of different policies and so of choosing among them, at least, a pure-power theory of politics is a cumbersome and uneconomic tool.

The difficulty comes from the multiplicity of values shared by people on both sides of state boundaries; peace, security, prosperity, self-determination, and the sanctity and freedom of the individual. Thus one state's gain is not always another's loss, and accommodation and concerted action occur almost as frequently in interstate affairs as conflict.

The obvious example of states acting in concert are alliances for security against a common enemy, but states also act in concert for a variety of lesser purposes: to regulate trade, to counter economic depressions, to conserve such natural resources as fisheries, to combat crime, and to provide international postal and other services.

There is also accommodation between adversaries. Rival states often agree, formally or tacitly, to respect spheres of exclusive influence, to act together in neutralizing a third country, or to refrain from bringing certain matters into the arena of competition. The bitterest rivals have a stake in restricting their competition to means that are appropriate to the goals at issue and in avoiding measures that will bring about the sacrifice of things more cherished than those to be won. Even states at war have reached agreements. Use of poison gas was outlawed in World War II, although not all the participants had signed the convention on the rules of war. In the Korean War there was a tacit agreement to respect sanctuaries. The United Nations forces refrained from bombing north of the Yalu River and the Communist forces conformed by avoiding Pusan and our bases in Japan. In Vietnam there was until 1965 a tacit agreement that the United States would refrain from bombing North Vietnam and the North Vietnamese would refrain from infiltrating their regular battalions into the South.

Thus interstate politics has a mixture of conflict and accommodation similar in many ways to that in domestic politics. As a consequence, the business between states, like the business of reaching decisions within a single state, requires techniques for persuasion, negotiation, and bargaining, as well as for manipulating power.

The practitioners of statecraft, the operators in foreign offices and embassies, do not make a practice of generalizing about the "political process in international affairs" or about the "interstate decision-making system." Yet faced with the problem of *doing* something in international affairs—whether it is trying to bring about a Geneva conference for peace or implementing a decision to blockade Cuba—any practitioner, from desk officer to secretary, would unerringly tick off the steps to be taken. *This* great power would have to be consulted in advance; *those* lesser powers need only be informed; *this* line of argument should be taken in the UN; *that* line of argument, with the press. Moscow should be told *this* at *that* stage; Paris should be handled in a different way. Practitioners may not generalize about the "international political process," but they know it exists, and they know how to operate it.

All this, to repeat, adds up to what is only a rudimentary political process. Of the several functions we listed that a political process serves, the present-day international political system provides an arena and techniques for resolving certain kinds of disputes, for allocating certain kinds of benefits, and for establishing rules for certain kinds of competition—but little else, and certainly not enough to be as effective an alternative to war as the political process within a stable, well-established state.

In present-day international affairs, the actors are states. If we are to move toward a global political process that is something more than what we have just described, it must be possible for both groups of individuals and individuals to act in ways other than through the state. If the present structure is inadequate and providing the structure of a world state is unrealistic, still it is essential to have some kind of structure through which groups and individuals can act. And both groups and individuals must be able to develop power and influence independent of the state.

Power

It would be a mistake to try to be too specific about either how groups and individuals might develop power independent of the state or the precise structure through which power might be exercised. We are working toward something entirely new in the world, and as we go along surprising possibilities might open up for new sources of power, for innovations in the structure through which power might be exercised, and in other aspects of this new kind of global political process. But even though we cannot be too specific about it, at least the outlines can be discerned.

Power, as we said before, is an elusive concept. Everyone recognizes the obvious fact that in every society some people have more power than others, and all the great social thinkers of every age and in every culture have noted it. As Dahl says, the mere existence of so much comment arouses the suspicion not only that some thing that can be called power exists, but that it may be many things. Mao said that "power grows out of the barrel of a gun." No one would deny it. But in our analysis of the domestic political process in the United States we also identified other sources of power.

We found that power could be the legal and constitutional right to decide in a formal sense. The President, Congress, and the courts all draw power from this source. Power can come through holding day-to-day responsibility for certain matters. This is the power of the bureaucrat in the Executive, and it can be very large indeed, as J. Edgar Hoover demonstrated. Power can be influence, in the sense of having the ear of the President or the respect of the leaders of Congress, without holding any office at all. It can be the ability to have one's views taken into account simply because one has convinced the world that one speaks for a wider public and that there will be political consequences if one is ignored. The example we gave earlier is Ralph Nader, who picked up the issue of automobile safety and raised enough hell to make some of the giant corporations tremble. Power can also be the ability to have one's views taken into account because of one's personal expertise. Power can also come simply because one has a "platform" that gives him the opportunity of enlisting a particular constituency. Chester Bowles and Adlai Stevenson as private citizens could command a hearing before "liberals," and this carried at least the implied threat that they might swing the whole constituency if their views were not considered. In some circumstances, power can be a position from which simply to *interpret* events—which is the real power of the press. Power also comes from organizations—from a position in a trade union, grange, corporation, bank, business association, church, voluntary organization, interest group, professional society, local government, and all the rest. It comes from every part of the intermediate structure, even those parts that have no official standing in government, for they perform functions without which a modern government could not successfully operate. Indeed, power is not only elusive, it is so varied and subtle in its source that we began to wonder whether "power" was the most useful word to describe the phenomenon we were observing.

On the international scene, the principal sources of power are the states, which are the main actors in present-day international politics. Groups and individuals derive power out of their position in a state and their ability to influence the behavior of the state. They also affect international affairs through the states, again by influencing the behavior of their own state. But even though rudimentary, as we say, there are sources of power in present-day international affairs independent of the state. "How many divisions does the Pope have?" Stalin asked Roosevelt and Churchill in denigrating the power the Pope might exercise. But the Pope does have power. And there are others who derive power from sources other than the state. The chairman of the board of Chase Manhattan Bank, which operates in twenty-eight countries, has power. International constituencies already exist for the preservation of wildlife and for ecological and environmental goals that strive to influence the behavior of states both in their own legislation and in their joint efforts with other states through international agreements. It is a similar kind of international constituency that has given both Aleksandr I. Solzhenitsyn and Andrei D. Sakharov the power to criticize the Soviet regime on the issue of civil liberties. Solzhenitsyn's novels and the fact that he won the Nobel Prize has given him great prestige in literary circles in the Soviet Union and around the world. Sakharov is a physicist who is known in academic circles in the Soviet Union and around the world as the "father of the Soviet H bomb." Their high prestige in their own fields and the admiration they have won for their stands on civil liberties have given them such great prestige that they have been able to make public criticisms of Soviet policy that would have long ago landed an ordinary citizen in prison. With the increased interdependence of modern life and the vastly greater ease of communications, we visualize similar constituencies to all the above developing that will serve as sources of power independent of the state, although those who hold power may frequently exercise it through the state by affecting its behavior.

We also visualize power generated from whatever new structure of international affairs that can be developed. The present structure has provided sources of power for the Secretary General and Secretariat of the United Nations and for the heads and influential members of such present-day international organizations as the World Bank, the International Monetary Fund, the Food and Agricultural Organization, the World Health Organization, and so on. A new structure will provide similar sources of power, although whether there will be enough and whether the power generated will be sufficient to operate a global political process of the kind we visualize depend upon the nature of the structure that is developed.

Again, the structure of an effective global political process, like the sources of power, will have to be something more than what is provided in the present-day international political system, but something less than the kind of structure to be found in a world state. It would have to be something that does not supplant the nation-state, since nationalism is so much a part of the future, but something that can exist with it side by side. What comes to mind, of course, is the "curious creature" we saw developing in Western Europe: a new kind of structure that combines regional organizations with authority over some aspects of life with the nation-state, which retains authority over others.

The evidence we have seen certainly indicates that when nationalism has accomplished the functions of achieving and legitimizing statehood, and when it has substantially accomplished the function of modernization, it may under certain circumstances no longer impede certain kinds of international integration. What we seem to be headed toward in Western Europe, we concluded, is neither a superstate nor a no-war community, but this curious combination of both: a pluralistic, no-war community in which the nation-states continue as individual entities for certain purposes, especially those related to culture and personality integration, but transfer decision-making in a wide number of specified fields to international organizations.

It does seem obvious that a "curious creature" of this kind could deal effectively with many of the problems that press so insistently on mankind. Problems in the economic sphere, problems of scarce resources, of pollution, of population problems, and many of those concerning the tension between the developing and the developed worlds would all seem less formidable and intractable if there were some such structure through which they could be approached. And there is at least the hope that some such structure could eventually develop into an effective alternative to war itself.

But again, it would be a mistake to try to push our speculations too far. It is not within the potentialities of forecasting to see more than the general outlines of something so entirely new in the world. What we see now is weak and rudimentary and could hardly provide either the power or the structure for an effective global political process. But what we see today *is* suggestive. It does not constitute a trend, and what it foreshadows is far from being inevitable. But it does provide the outlines of a goal toward which mankind might work.

The need for some such goal that is realistic and yet holds the promise of serving the social function that war has served in the past is as urgent as it is obvious. By his rivalries, envies, ambitions, and fears, man is driven toward collision with himself. In his weapons and his technology, man has instruments that can spiral events beyond his control. It may seem ironic that politics, so often despised, offers the only hope that is also realistic. But perhaps it is not so strange. Politics, Max Weber once remarked, is the striving for power and the using of power in the service of a cause. Some kind of faith, he insisted, must always exist. And politics does not always fail. In these crisis years since World War II, someone else remarked, the only thing that has stood between the world and disaster is a thin red line of men practicing politics. What was true of politics in the past may also be true in the future.

Acknowledgments

THIS BOOK HAD its beginnings in a year of interviewing in Europe, Asia, and Africa made possible by the Ford Foundation rotating research professorship at Columbia, for which I am most sincerely grateful. For his academic entrepreneurship in this and in helping to find the financing for a sabbatical in which I did the major part of the writing, I am grateful to W. T. R. Fox, Director of the Institute of War and Peace Studies, School of International Affairs, Columbia University. I am also grateful for his counsel on many points in the book itself.

The summer of my year abroad I spent at the East-West Center of the University of Hawaii as a senior fellow. I am deeply grateful to the center and to its then director, Howard P. Jones, for their support and for the stimulating discussions with the other fellows in our seminar. I am also grateful to Werner Levi of the university for his special encouragement.

During my year abroad, I was assisted by innumerable officials, journalists, academics, and many others in several dozen countries who gave me their time in interviews. I offer them my thanks even though it is neither possible nor politic to name them. I am also grateful to American officials in the State Department and in our embassies who helped me along my way.

My thanks go to Walter I. Bradbury for his counsel and for guiding the manuscript through the labyrinthine processes of publication. I am also grateful to Kenneth McCormick of Doubleday and to Lawrence Freundlich for their encouragement.

Donald S. Zagoria, Michel Oksenberg, Warner R. Schilling, Eleanor H. Hilsman, and Amy K. Hilsman read portions of the manuscript and gave valuable advice.

For research assistance, various administrative tasks, and secretarial chores, I am grateful to Pamela Greenberg, Eleanor H. Hilsman, Amy K. Hilsman, Norman L. Eule, Michael Krasner, Roger Cohen, Peter Schoettle, Anna Hohri, Larry W. Fuchser, Josephine Cuneo, and Yvette Hebert.

Finally, the quotation at the very end of the book is from Warner R. Schilling. My thanks go to him not only for letting me use it, but for letting me tamper with it slightly. What he originally said was that all that has stood between the world and disaster is a thin red line of *politicians*.

ROGER HILSMAN

65742